C528009

CHANGING BRITAIN

Families and Households in the 1990s

Edited by

SUSAN McRAE

OXFORD
UNIVERSITY PRESS

Great Clarendon Street, Oxford OX2 6DP

Oxford University Press is a department of the University of Oxford.
It furthers the University's objective of excellence in research, scholarship,
and education by publishing worldwide in

Oxford New York

Athens Auckland Bangkok Bogotá Buenos Aires Calcutta
Cape Town Chennai Dar es Salaam Delhi Florence Hong Kong Istanbul
Karachi Kuala Lumpur Madrid Melbourne Mexico City Mumbai
Nairobi Paris São Paulo Singapore Taipei Tokyo Toronto Warsaw

and associated companies in Berlin Ibadan

Oxford is a registered trade mark of Oxford University Press
in the UK and certain other countries

Published in the United States
by Oxford University Press Inc., New York

First published 1999

British Library Cataloguing in Publication Data

Data available

Library of Congress Cataloging in Publication Data

Changing Britain: families and households in the 1900s/edited by Susan McRae.
Includes bibliographical references.
1. Family–Great Britain. 2. Single-parent family–Great Britain.
3. Stepfamilies–Great Britain. 4. Unmarried couples–Great
Britain. 5. Living alone–Great Britain. 6. Kinship–Great Britain. I. McRae, Susan.
HQ614.C45 1999 306.85′0941–dc21 99-24527
ISBN 0-19-829636-3
ISBN 0-19-829637-1 (pbk.)

1 3 5 7 9 10 8 6 4 2

Typeset by Best-set Typesetter Ltd., Hong Kong
Printed in Great Britain
on acid-free paper by
Bookcraft Ltd
Midsomer Norton, Somerset

PREFACE

Over the past twenty-five years, major changes have occurred across the Western developed world in areas which lie at the intersection of demography and prevailing forms of living arrangements. Marriage rates have fallen; divorce and cohabitation rates have risen. Women are having fewer children, later in life, and there has been a marked rise in childbearing outside marriage at almost all ages. Migration is now a more important source of differences in regional populations than are variations in either births or deaths.

These changes have significance for economic and social behaviour and policy that goes beyond individual families or households. New patterns of partnership formation and dissolution, and the associated growth in both one-person households and lone-parent families, have implications for housing demand and income support services. They may also have longer-term consequences for labour force participation rates and for the provision of care for the elderly. Ageing populations and shifts in patterns of childbearing and household mobility all influence the availability of help from relatives and friends, the need for supporting health and social services, and the possibilities for rejuvenation of inner-city areas.

In order to markedly improve our understanding of this set of complex, interrelated issues, the Economic and Social Research Council (ESRC) established the Population and Household Change Programme in 1994. The aim of the Programme was to stimulate new research on the interrelationships between household living arrangements and broader demographic change in the United Kingdom, and in particular to examine the causes and consequences of change at three overlapping levels: the demographic context; the structure of family, household, and living arrangements; and wider kinship networks. Seventeen individual research projects were supported by the Programme. These projects investigated most major issues associated with understanding, and informing policy about, household and demographic change, including partnership formation and dissolution, one-person households, stepfamilies, ageing, non-heterosexual relationships, lone parents, teenage mothers, absent fathers, migration, changing attitudes, and kinship.

This book is one outcome of the Programme. It includes seventeen contributions from sixteen of the research projects plus an introductory chapter by the Programme Director. These contributions reflect the multidisciplinary nature of the Programme and the wide variety of research approaches adopted by the project teams. There are chapters by demographers, sociologists, gerontologists, and geographers, who variously employed secondary analysis of large data sets, statistical modelling, life stories, comparative analysis, survey research, and in-depth interviewing to carry out their research. This book is one result of their work and provides a comprehensive portrait of British families and households at the end of the twentieth century.

S. M.
Oxford
May 1999

CONTENTS

LIST OF FIGURES

LIST OF TABLES

ABBREVIATIONS

BHPS	British Household Panel Survey
DENI	Department of Education, Northern Ireland
ESRC	Economic and Social Research Council
FRS	Family Resources Survey
GHS	General Household Survey
INSEE	Institut national de la statistique et des études économiques
ISSP	International Social Survey Programme
IUSSP	International Union for the Scientific Study of Population
JISC	Joint Information Systems Committee
LFS	Labour Force Survey
NCDS	National Child Development Survey
ONS	Office for National Statistics
OPCS	Office of Population and Census Surveys
SARs	Sample of Anonymised Records
SPCR	Social and Community Planning Research
TFR	Total Fertility Rate

NOTES ON CONTRIBUTORS

ALAA AL-HAMAD is a Research Associate in the Centre for Applied Statistics at Lancaster University. He is co-author of several papers on migration and population, including 'Residential Change: Differences in the Movements and Living Arrangements of Divorced Men and Women' (with R. Flowerdew and L. Hayes) in P. Boyle and K. Halfacree (eds.), *Migration and Gender in the Developed World* (1998) and two papers in *Environment and Planning A* (1997).

ISOBEL ALLEN is Professor of Health and Social Policy of the University of Westminster at the Policy Studies Institute. She is the author of many books on health and social care, including *Family Planning and Pregnancy Counselling Projects for Young People* (1991), *Doctors and their Careers: A New Generation* (1994), and *Education in Sex and Personal Relationships* (1987).

MIRIAM BERNARD is Head of Department and Reader in the Department of Applied Social Studies at Keele University. Her publications include *Women Come of Age* (co-edited with K. Meade, 1993) and, most recently, *The Social Policy of Ageing* (co-edited with Judith Phillips, 1998).

RICHARD BERTHOUD is a Professor at the University of Essex Institute for Social and Economic Research, where his work includes studies of the interactions between family forms and economic activity. He was previously at the Policy Studies Institute, where he was at different times responsible for its programmes of research on family finances, social security, and ethnic minorities.

JOANNA BORNAT is Senior Lecturer in the School of Health and Social Welfare at the Open University. She has been joint editor of *Oral History* for twenty years and writes and researches on ageing, remembering, and oral history. She is co-editor of *Community Care: A Reader* (1993, fully revised 2nd edn. 1997) and editor of *Reminiscence Reviewed: Perspectives, Evaluations, Achievements* (1994).

SHIRLEY BOURKE DOWLING was a Research Fellow at the Policy Studies Institute. She is co-author with Isobel Allen of *A Leading Role for Midwives?* (1997), and is currently conducting a review of the literature on the health and care of mentally disordered offenders.

JONATHAN BRADSHAW is Professor of Social Policy at the University of York, Director of the Institute for Research in the Social Sciences, and Associate Director of the Social Policy Research Unit. His previous research in family policy includes *Lone Parent Families in the UK* (with Jane Millar, 1991) and *The Employment of Lone Parents: A Comparison in 20 Countries* (with Steven Kennedy and others, 1996). Between 1994 and 1998, he was Co-director of the European Observatory on National Family Policies.

TARANI CHANDOLA is a Research Assistant in the Department of Applied Social Studies and Social Research at the University of Oxford. He is the author of 'Social Inequality of Coronary Heart Disease: A Comparison of Occupational Classifications', *Social Science and Medicine* (1998).

DAVID COLEMAN is the Reader in Demography at the University of Oxford. He is the author (with John Salt) of *The British Population* (1992) and about sixty papers on demography, and the editor of *Europe's Population in the 1990s* (1996). He was elected to the Council of the International Union for the Scientific Study of Population in 1997 and has been the joint editor of the *European Journal of Population* since 1992.

BRIAN DIMMOCK is Lecturer in Health and Social Welfare at the Open University and Chair of the National Stepfamily Association. He is co-author of *Understanding Stepfamilies* (with Jane Batchelor and Donna Smith, 1994) and Director of the National Open Learning Diploma in Social Work Programme at the Open University.

CATHERINE DONOVAN is a Lecturer in Sociology at Sunderland University. She has researched in the area of HIV and sexual behaviour and reproductive technologies. She is currently working on self-insemination and the role of the donor. She is also working on a co-authored book with Jeffrey Weeks and Brian Heaphy on families of choice.

ROBIN FLOWERDEW is Senior Lecturer in Geography and Director of the North West Regional Research Laboratory at Lancaster University. He is interested in, and has published papers on, many aspects of internal migration and statistical modelling of social data, and has recently co-edited *Methods in Human Geography* (1997).

HARRY GOULBOURNE is Professor of Sociology at South Bank University. He has published extensively on politics and society in East Africa, the Commonwealth, the Caribbean, and Britain. Some of his major publications include *Race Relations in Britain since 1945* (1998), *Ethnicity and Nationalism in Post-imperial Britain* (1991), and *Teachers, Politics and Education in Jamaica 1892–1972* (1988).

EMILY GRUNDY is Reader in Social Gerontology at the University of London and works in the Centre for Population Studies, London School of Hygiene and Tropical Medicine. She has written close to one hundred papers and book chapters, including 'The Health of Older Adults 1841–1994', in J. Charlton and M. Murphy (eds.), *The Health of Adult*

Britain, Vol. II (1997), 'Population Dynamics and Health', in the *Oxford Textbook of Public Health 1997*, 'Population Ageing in Europe', in D. Coleman (ed.), *Europe's Population in the 1990s* (1996), and *The Dynamics of Retirement* (with R. Disney and P. Johnson, 1998).

RAY HALL is Senior Lecturer in Geography at Queen Mary and Westfield College, University of London. Her current research focuses on changing households in Britain and elsewhere in Europe, looking particularly at people living alone. She has written about both world and European population issues and her publications include *World Population Trends* (1990) and *Europe's Population: Towards the Next Century* (with Paul White, 1995).

LYNN HAYES was a Research Associate at Lancaster University. She is co-author, with Janet Finch and others, of *Wills, Inheritance and Families* (1996) and is now working with the Ombudsman in the Department of Health.

BRIAN HEAPHY is a Research Fellow in Sociology at South Bank University. He has carried out research in the areas of intimate relationships, sexuality, and AIDS/HIV and is currently working (with Jeffrey Weeks and Catherine Donovan) on a book which is based on the 'Families of Choice' research project.

CATHERINE HILL is a medical demographer who worked as a Research Fellow on the Population and Household Change Research Programme between 1995 and 1997. She is now a Research Officer in the Social and Regional Reporting Branch of the Office for National Statistics.

DAVID JONES is Lecturer in Psychology at Buckinghamshire Chilterns University College. He has a long-standing interest in qualitative methods, particularly in the context of family relationships and in connection with mental illness. Publications include 'Distressing Histories and Unhappy Interviewing', *The Oral History Journal* (1998) and 'Families' Experiences of Mental Distress', in T. Heller *et al.* (eds.), *Mental Health Matters* (1996).

KATHLEEN KIERNAN is Reader in Social Policy and Demography and Co-director of the ESRC Centre for Analysis of Social Exclusion (CASE) at the London School of Economics and Political Science. Publications include *Lone Motherhood in the Twentieth Century: From Footnote to Front Page* (with H. Land and J. Lewis, 1998), 'The Legacy of Parental Divorce', CASE Paper No. 1 (1997), *Cohabitation, Extra-marital Childbearing and Social Policy* (with V. Estaugh, 1993) and *Family Change and Future Policy* (with M. Wicks, 1991).

JENNIFER MASON is a Senior Lecturer in Sociology and Deputy Director of the Centre for Research on Family, Kinship and Childhood at the University of Leeds. Her publications include *Negotiating Family Responsibil-*

ities (with Janet Finch, 1993), *Wills, Inheritance and Families* (with J. Finch, L. Hayes, L. Wallis, and J. Masson, 1995), and *Qualitative Researching* (1996).

FRANCIS MCGLONE is a Senior Research Officer at the Family Policy Studies Centre. He is author and joint author of a number of articles and reports, including *Disability and Dependency in Old Age* (1992), *A Crisis in Care* (1994), and *Families and Kinship* (1998).

STEPHEN MCKAY is a Research Fellow at the Centre for Research in Social Policy at Loughborough University. He conducts research on social security and family dynamics, currently including a longitudinal evaluation of the Jobseeker's Allowance and a study of pension rights. He was previously a member of the social security team at the Policy Studies Institute.

SUSAN MCRAE is Director of the ESRC Programme on Population and Household Change, and Professor and Head of the School of Social Sciences and Law at Oxford Brookes University. Formerly a Senior Fellow of the Policy Studies Institute, her publications include *Maternity Rights: The Experience of Women and Employers* (1991), *Cohabiting Mothers: Changing Marriage and Motherhood?* (1993), and *Women's Employment during Family Formation* (1996), as well as articles on women's employment, cohabitation, and inequality.

GANKA MUELLER was a Research Assistant at the London School of Economics.

MIKE MURPHY is Professor of Demography at the London School of Economics. His research interests include technical models for demographic analysis; household, family, and kinship demography; and the explanation of family formation and dissolution in developed societies. Recent publications include 'The Contraceptive Pill and Women's Employment as Factors in Fertility Change in Britain 1963–1980: A Challenge to the Conventional View', *Population Studies* (1993) and 'The Dynamic Household as a Logical Concept and its Use in Demography', *European Journal of Population* (1996).

PHILIP E. OGDEN is Professor of Geography and Vice-Principal of Queen Mary and Westfield College, University of London. His main research interests are in the population geography of France, Britain, and the Caribbean. He is author of *Migration and Geographical Change* (1986) and editor of *Migrants in Modern France* (1989) and *London Docklands: The Challenge of Development* (1992).

JIM OGG is a Visiting Researcher at the Caisse Nationale d'Assurance Viellesse, Paris. He is also a Visiting Fellow to the Centre for Social Gerontology, University of Keele. Previously he was Research Fellow to the ESRC-funded project Kinship and Family Change in the Urban

Environment, based at the Department of Applied Social Studies, University of Keele. He is the author of a number of articles examining research issues in the field of elder abuse.

ALISON PARK is a Research Director at Social and Community Planning Research (SCPR). She is Co-director of SCPR's British Social Attitudes survey series and a member of the Centre for Research into Elections and Social Trends, an ESRC Research Centre.

SHEILA PEACE is a Senior Lecturer in the School of Health and Social Welfare at the Open University. She has written widely in the field of social gerontology and residential care. Key publications include *Private Lives in Public Places* (1987) and *Re-evaluating Residential Care* (1997), both with D. Willcocks and L. Kellaher, and *Researching Social Gerontology* (1990). She is currently Sub-dean of Research in the School.

JUDITH PHILLIPS is Senior Lecturer in Social Work and Gerontology and Programme Director for the MA/Diploma in Social Work Programme at Keele University. She is author of *Private Residential Care* (1992) and editor of *Working Carers* (1995). She recently co-edited *The Social Policy of Old Age* (1998) with Miriam Bernard.

CHRIS PHILLIPSON is Professor of Applied Social Studies and Social Gerontology and Director of the Centre for Social Gerontology at Keele University. His most recent book is *Reconstructing Old Age: New Agendas for Social Theory and Practice* (1998).

CERIDWEN ROBERTS is Director of the Family Policy Studies Centre and UK expert at the EC's Observatory on National Family Policies. Originally a labour market sociologist, she previously worked in academia and the Department of Employment. Publications include *Women and Employment: A Lifetime Perspective* (with J. Martin, 1984), *Parenting Problems* (1995), and *Policies for Families: Work, Poverty and Resources* (1995).

KAREN ROWLINGSON is a Senior Lecturer in Sociology at the University of Derby. She was formerly a member of the Family Finances Group at the Policy Studies Institute, and is continuing her series of studies of the relationship between income, wealth, and family life.

JACQUELINE SCOTT is in the Faculty of Social and Political Sciences at the University of Cambridge and a Fellow of Queens' College. She was formerly Director of Research at the ESRC Interdisciplinary Research Centre on Micro-social change at Essex. She is currently working on a project, as part of the ESRC Programme on Youth and Social Change, using BHPS data to examine how young people overcome family disadvantage.

CHRISTINE SKINNER is a Doctoral Student in the Department of Social Policy and Social Work at the University of York. Her interests are family policy, Child Support policy, theories on family obligations and the social meanings of money in family relationships. Previously Christine was a Nursing Sister in the private health sector and for a time was also involved in the field of medical research.

CAROL STIMSON was a Research Fellow in the Social Policy Research Unit at the University of York and previously at the Institute of Psychiatry at the Maudsley Hospital. Her previous research on family policy includes *Using Child Benefit in the Family Budget* (with Jonathan Bradshaw, 1997). Carol Stimson was killed in a car crash in May 1997.

JANE WADSWORTH was a Senior Lecturer in Medical Statistics in the Academic Department of Public Health at St Mary's Hospital Medical School. She was a principal investigator on the National Survey of Sexual Attitudes and Lifestyles and published widely in the fields of child health and education and sexual health. Jane Wadsworth died in July 1997.

DUOLAO WANG is a Senior Statistician at the Charterhouse Clinical Research Unit, Royal Masonic Hospital. He has published a number of articles in demographic studies and applied statistics, including 'Family and Socio-demographic Influences on Patterns of Leaving Home', *Demography* (with Mike Murphy, 1998) and 'The Use of the Mixture Model for the Analysis of Contraceptive Use Duration with Long-term Users', *Journal of Applied Statistics* (with Mike Murphy, 1998).

JEFFREY WEEKS is Professor of Sociology and Dean of Humanities and Social Science at South Bank University. He is the author of numerous articles and books on the history and social regulation of sexuality and personal life, including *Sex, Politics and Society* (1981; 2nd edn. 1989), *Sexuality and its Discontents* (1985), *Invented Moralities* (1995), and *Sexual Cultures* (with Janet Holland, 1996).

KAYE WELLINGS is Senior Lecturer at the London School of Hygiene and Tropical Medicine and Head of the Sexual Health Programme in the Department of Public Health and Policy. She is co-author of *Sexual Behaviour in Britain* (1994) and *Sexual Attitudes and Lifestyles* (1994).

JULIE WILLIAMS has been a Research Fellow in the Social Policy Research Unit at the University of York since 1990. Her main interest is data analysis, in particular survey analysis and the secondary analysis of surveys such as the Family Resources Survey and the British Household Panel Survey.

1

Introduction: family and household change in Britain

Susan McRae

> Much about modern family life is changing, but one thing that never seems to change is the notion that family is not what it used to be.
>
> (Gillis 1997: 1)

This book describes and analyses change in British families and households at the end of the twentieth century. That there has been such change is without doubt. Britain today is a much more complex society than in past times, with great diversity in the types of household within which people live: one-person; cohabiting; families with children and families without; stepfamilies; lone parents—whether divorced or never-married; gay and lesbian couples; pensioners. Much of this diversity has been gained at the expense of tradition and there has been a downward trend in the prevalence of certain types of family—most particularly, the traditional two parents plus dependent children. For some, change means decline; or more strongly, the 'death of the family'. But household diversity does not by itself entail family decline. While there has been a reduction in the number of traditional family households, there has also been a growth in opportunities—to live alone or to cohabit, for example, or to avoid a shotgun wedding or to develop an openly gay or lesbian household. It is true that some changes have had devastating consequences for individuals and their families, perhaps across generations. Some household diversity has been built upon, or brought about, by a concomitant decline in employment opportunities, in people's chances to earn wages on which families can be established, much less survive and prosper. Despite some improvement in recent years in the incomes of the poorest, overall income inequality was greater in mid-1990s Britain than at any time in the post-war period, and among the persistently poor are lone mothers, single pensioners, and couples with children but without jobs.

However, it is also the case that not all that has changed in families and households is harmful—nor is it necessarily new. Instead, much of what we are seeing in Britain today is the continuation of trends briefly interrupted by the 'ideal family' of the 1950s and 1960s. The first two columns of Table 1.1 indicate the extent of change from the mid-sixties to the mid-nineties in a range of family and demographic indicators including, for women, age at first marriage and first birth, total fertility rate, and proportion remaining childless, as well as showing the rising incidence of divorce, births outside marriage, cohabitation, and lone-parent families. Table 1.1 paints a familiar picture of the changing British family over the post-war period: as age at marriage and first motherhood has risen, family size has fallen and childlessness has increased. Cohabitation has become common, both before marriage and between marriages. With rising cohabitation has come a sharp increase in births outside marriage; rising divorce rates, in their turn, have been accompanied by a near-trebling in the number of lone-parent families. These changes are frequently cited to demonstrate the decline of traditional family life.

The third column of Table 1.1 steps back from women born just after the Second World War to focus on those born before the first war, and presents a rather different picture of contemporary family change—one that signals the existence of long-term trends in demographic behaviour and reminds us that, in many respects, it is the sixties family that stands out, not the nineties one. Precise historical data on the incidence of divorce, cohabitation, births outside marriage, and lone-parent families are not presented in Table 1.1, although indications of their frequency may be gleaned from many sources. For example, prior to 1850, which marked the beginning of the long period of divorce reform, there were at least five ways to end a legal marriage: Parliamentary divorce for the rich; judicial separation for the middle classes; wife sales or desertion for the working classes; and private separation for everyone. And these avenues were used: as his-

TABLE 1.1. *Family change in Britain: mid-thirties to mid-nineties*

	Mid-1960s	Mid-1990s	Mid-1930s
Mean age at first marriage	22	26	26
Mean age at first birth	23.9	26.5	26.7
Fertility rate (TFR)	2.93	1.8	1.8
Childlessness (%)	10	20	23
Divorces per 1,000 marriages	2	13	
Births outside marriage (%)	5	35	
Cohabitation before marriage (%)	5	70	
Lone-parent families	570,000	1,500,000	

torian Lawrence Stone notes; 'the number of private separations continued to grow by leaps and bounds' (Stone 1995: 158). Moreover, death ended marriage: it has been calculated that prior to the nineteenth century, 17 per cent of children in England were fatherless by age 10, and 27 per cent by age 15 (Gillis 1997: 9). For women born in the 1930s, almost one in ten experienced the death of a parent before age 16, and it was not until the cohorts born in the 1950s that children under 16 were more likely to live in one-parent families because of divorce than the death of a parent (Lewis and Kiernan 1996: 382, table 6).

Nor were unmarried pregnancies, illegitimacy, or living together outside marriage uncommon in earlier periods (cf. McRae 1993). It has been estimated that between the mid-eighteenth and mid-nineteenth centuries, as much as one-fifth of the population in England and Wales may have cohabited unlawfully for some period, either as a prelude to legal marriage or as a substitute for it (Gillis 1985: 219). Moreover, the men and women who defied both church and state in this manner were not, as in earlier centuries, vagabonds, ne'er-do-wells, or the disinherited. Rather, common-law marriage practices were found throughout Britain, in whole communities, rural and urban, and often where small farming mixed with new manufacturing. Furthermore, a fixed certainty of the righteousness of such practices typified the views of many a marital non-conformist: 'The folk of Framlingham say that none but Whores and Blackguards Marry; Honest Folk take each other's word for it' (quoted in Gillis 1985: 209).

These comments are not made to suggest that nothing has changed. Families and households have altered substantially since the early nineteenth century and, indeed, the early twentieth century, when divorce, for example, could be described as 'expensive, demeaning and often sordid' and divorce legislation as 'encouraging adultery and perjury' (McKibbin 1997: 302). Childlessness in the last century existed for different reasons than it does today. The consequences of a parent's death for children are different to those following divorce. What was once the behaviour of the marginal or the eccentric has become normal—as the large majority cohabit before marriage; as one in three babies are born outside legal marriage; as it becomes increasingly common for children to have more than one set of parents or two sets of grandparents. Nonetheless, in order to explain the changes captured in Table 1.1, it is prudent to look backwards in time to beyond the immediate post-war period. Taking a long view suggests that the usual explanation for the changes in family life since the 1950s and 1960s—women's rising labour force participation—is at best incomplete. It is, in fact, implausible to attribute causality to women's rising labour force participation in the 1970s and 1980s for long-run trends and changes in behaviour that were evident well before that period. But as Oppenheimer and Lew have pointed out (1995: 133),

> The notion that women's rising employment is the major reason for recent demographic changes has become such an article of faith that it is hampering our ability to recognise negative empirical findings or to appreciate some of the inadequacies of a purely female-oriented theory.

There has been an almost continuous increase in the proportion of women in paid work since the mid-1960s, based largely on the entry of middle-class married mothers and on decreasing gaps in women's participation due to childbearing and childrearing (Martin and Roberts 1984; Joshi 1985; McRae 1991). In the post-war period, the economic activity rate of British women roughly doubled, until recently almost exclusively through part-time employment. But rather than being the cause of family change—high rates of cohabitation, marital dissolution, childbearing outside marriage, and low rates of marriage—women's increased economic participation is more reasonably seen as a necessary but not sufficient factor, which acts in tandem with, or as a conduit for, other equally necessary (yet insufficient) influences. Of primary importance among the latter is the widespread acceptance of 'post-materialist' values, namely a belief in individual autonomy and in individuals' right to choose (Inglehart 1977, 1990; Lesthaeghe 1991, 1995). Less well understood, perhaps, is the influence of structural economic change, particularly the role of men's deteriorating economic circumstances—an issue discussed in more detail below (cf. Irwin 1995; Oppenheimer and Lew 1995: 134; McRae 1997).

Of course, more than families and households have changed—throughout the 1980s and early 1990s, Britain experienced substantial economic turbulence, with high inflation and high unemployment, periods of growth and of recession, and a continuing restructuring of employment opportunities. A growth in labour market flexibility typified the 1980s and engendered heightened competition between individuals and families throughout the labour and employment markets, whose consequences for household and family formation are barely understood. One outcome of economic change is fully understood, however: over two decades, Britain became a more unequal place in which to live. In the late 1990s, both unemployment and inflation fell sharply; nonetheless, inequality between families remained. Given the importance of employment change and of growing inequality to families and households, and in order to provide a context for the chapters which follow, the next section reviews changes over recent decades in individuals' and families' economic opportunities.

EMPLOYMENT CHANGE AND THE GROWTH OF INEQUALITY

While the extent and permanence of changes in work and employment remain contested, and the implications of such changes largely unknown, it is undisputed that the structure of employment has changed. A far from exhaustive list of changes in post-war Britain would include alterations in the relative balance between manual and non-manual occupations, and between service sector and manufacturing employment; the virtual disappearance of traditional industries; the widespread introduction of new technology; an influx of women into the labour market, well matched in number by a continuing exit of men; and not unrelated to women's entry into the labour market, a near-continuous growth in part-time work, as both the demand and supply of labour have changed. During the 1980s and 1990s, increased instability of employment was added to these trends, which themselves intensified.

Changes in the distribution and nature of work cut across households and families and differentially affect their ability and propensity to offer themselves for work. Thus, income distribution has widened markedly in Britain over the past twenty years (Goodman and Webb 1994; Jenkins 1994), as have disparities in health and in death rates (Wilkinson 1994). One of the most important reasons underlying the growth of inequality has been the shift from an economy based on manufacturing to one based on services, a process which began long before 1979 and its acceleration by the Thatcher government. By 1979, the service sector provided 60 per cent of employment or 14 million jobs. Eighteen years later, 75 per cent of the working population held some 17 million service industry jobs, largely in retailing, health care, and social work. Manufacturing employment has risen in recent years but provides only about 4 million jobs compared with almost 7 million in 1979 (*Economist* 1997: 33–4).

One highly visible outcome of the switch to services has been a shift in the gender composition of the workforce. In the twenty years from 1975, while the aggregate employment rate remained largely stable, men's employment fell and women's employment grew. Throughout most of the 1970s, fewer than one in ten men of working age, but about 40 per cent of married women (and 30 per cent of non-married women), were economically inactive—not in work nor seeking work (Ramprakash 1981). Between 1979 and 1997, the number of economically inactive men doubled from 1.4 to 2.8 million, while the number of economically inactive women fell by one million to 4.6 million (ONS 1992–3, 1998*a*). Women's employment grew almost continuously throughout the turbulence of the 1980s and 1990s: in 1997, there were one-fifth more women working full-time, and one-quarter more working part-time, than was the case in 1984. For men, fluctuating employment opportunities resulted in the same number being employed full-time in 1997 as in 1984 (despite population growth), with increases in employment coming through part-time work, which more than doubled among men in this period to over one million jobs (Pullinger 1998). By 1997, working-age men's economic activity was below 85 per cent, while that of women had risen to over 70 per cent and women accounted for nearly one in every two people in the labour force (ONS 1998*a*).

Economic participation, however, neither grew nor fell equally across all groups of women and men. The shift towards services entailed a loss of stable low-skilled employment, forcing mainly poorly educated men into either unemployment or economic inactivity. Older male workers were particularly affected by the decline of manufacturing and concomitant rise of unemployment. Although jobless rates are highest among young workers, men and women over age 50 find it harder to leave unemployment and are significantly more likely than young workers to experience long-term unemployment. This is particularly the case among men: in 1997, almost 60 per cent of unemployed men aged 50 and older had been out of work for more than one year, compared with one-third of similarly aged women. The position of young men also worsened as the structure of labour markets and employment changed. There has been a tightening of the link between wages and education, and young men leaving school at the minimum age today are more heavily penalized than their predecessors. Low wages for young workers are substantially lower now, relative to average earnings, than in the late 1970s and there is little evidence that young men's wages improve over time through the acquisition of job-specific skills that allow them to move to better jobs (Gosling, Machin, and Meghir 1994).

Benefiting most from the new structure of opportunities which arose as the economy moved further away from its previous base in manufacturing were highly educated women, who experienced the largest rise in women's employment during the 1980s and early 1990s. By 1997, one-third of employed women worked in managerial, professional, and associate professional occupations, a rise from one in five in 1980 (Martin and Roberts 1984; Pullinger 1998). Many of these women have remained childless or delayed childbearing until after establishing their careers. Each of these demographic trends is concentrated among middle-class, highly educated women; adoption of such career strategies has led to 40 per cent of births being to women aged 30 and older and projections of 25 per cent childlessness by the year 2010 (ONS 1997*d*). It has also led to slow but discernible inroads being made by women into the top jobs in Britain (McRae 1996).

Moreover, the bulk of the increase in women's employment occurred among married women in households where the man was already in work. In 1975, just over half of women with employed husbands were themselves in paid work; by the mid-1990s, it was heading towards 90 per cent. At the same time, the fall in male employment was substantially less severe among men with working wives (Gregg and Wadsworth 1995: 347).

The outcome of these changed economic opportunities has been a growing polarization between two-earner and no-earner households and a substantial widening of income inequality. Households with no earners now account for about one-fifth of all non-pensioner households, up from one-twentieth fifteen years ago (Meadows 1996: 2). Among working-age families with dependent children, the proportion with no earners remained stable over this same period at just over one in ten, while the proportion with two earners rose from about half in the early 1980s to over 60 per cent in 1998 (Pullinger 1998). At the same time, income inequality grew more rapidly in Britain than in any other industrialized nation (Atkinson *et al.* 1995; Joseph Rowntree Foundation 1995). Between 1979 and 1995, average incomes grew by 40 per cent—but the incomes of the richest tenth grew by over 60 per cent, while that of the poorest tenth grew by 10 per cent, or fell by 8 per cent if housing costs are taken into account. In 1977, 6 per cent of the population had incomes below half the contemporary average: three times that proportion did in 1995 (Hills 1998: 5). Furthermore, both permanent inequality—lifetime differences in the positions individuals occupy in the income distribution—and short-term income risk have grown, particularly for younger generations, who face markedly greater inequality compared with that experienced by older generations at the same age (Blundell and Preston 1995: 46–52). Economic disadvantage appears, moreover, to be transmitted from fathers to sons: having an unemployed father roughly doubles a son's chances of unemployment, while being raised in a poor household is associated with both unemployment and poverty (Johnson and Reed 1996: 14–17).

Inequalities such as these underpin some but not all of the observable decline and/or diversity in families and households, and do so as both cause and consequence. Family change, in other words, often is not neutral, either in origin or in outcome. Rather, just as cleavages exist between families and individuals in terms of their economic participation and rewards, so too there are wide differences between social classes in their demographic and family formation behaviour. Indeed, an argument could be made for using Britain as a 'worst-case example' of change and its consequences. Britain leads Western Europe in at least three family outcomes associated with economic disadvantage: teenage births, divorce, and lone-parent families. As Coleman and Chandola point out in the next chapter, Britain's distinctiveness in European demography, which once mirrored a leading position in Europe's society and economy, now instead reflects Britain's disadvantage.

FAMILY CHANGE AND DISADVANTAGE

Teenage motherhood

Teenage motherhood is one of the most distinctive features of British demography: without teenage pregnancies, Britain's total fertility rate (TFR) would fall from 1.8 to 1.68 (Coleman and Chandola, Chapter 2; also Coleman 1997). Teenagers throughout Europe—both East and West—now engage in sexual intercourse at earlier ages than their parents or grandparents and for longer periods before they become either partners or parents. In large measure, this is a reflection of normative change that encompasses not only teenage sex but also cohabitation and births outside marriage. Far fewer of us now disapprove of pre-marital sex; and once the tie between sex and waiting for marriage was broken, little remained to prevent young people who are physically ready to have sex from doing so. Figure 1.1 draws on Scott's analysis of European social attitudes data (Chapter 3; also Scott, Alwin, and Braun 1996) and provides information about attitudes to pre-marital sex in various countries in 1994. Figure 1.1 reflects a real change in both attitudes and behaviour in the post-war period. Not only can those of us who were teenagers in the late fifties or early sixties testify to that change, but a survey carried out in England in the early 1950s found that:

> half of the married population claimed to have had no sexual experience with anyone other than their spouses; 52 per cent were opposed to men, and 63 per cent opposed to women, having any pre-marital sex; only a small number believed that pre-marital sex was 'natural' . . . (McKibbin 1998: 296)

The author of that survey, Geoffrey Gorer, wrote: 'I very much doubt whether the study of any other urban population would produce comparable figures of chastity and fidelity' (McKibbin 1998: 296). Of course, not everyone acted on their views, and about one in seven first marriages produced a baby within eight months (OPCS 1987).

For teenage men and women in Britain today, the average age at first intercourse is 17. But whereas in most of Western Europe, rates of teenage motherhood have fallen as teenage sexual activity has risen, this has not happened in Britain. Demographically, Britain more closely resembles Eastern Europe, where a tradition of early, and near-universal, marriage has long meant high teenage fertility rates (Coleman and Chandola, Chapter 2; also Coleman 1996*b*: 23). Almost all of the East European births

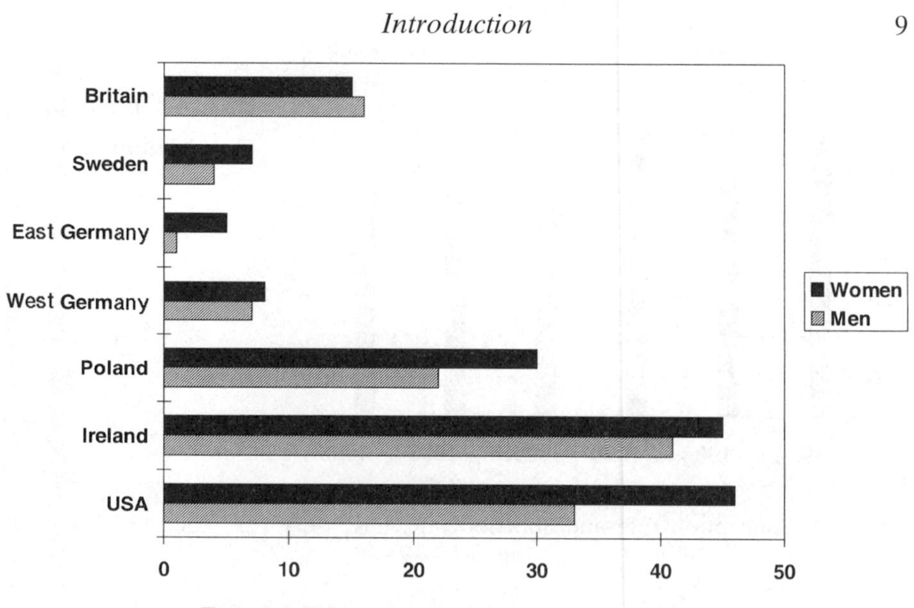

FIG. 1.1 Disapproval of pre-marital sex, 1994

are inside marriage, however, while virtually all of the Western ones are outside marriage, with a large number being outside partnership as well. In Britain, teenage births account for just over one-fifth of all non-marital births (21 per cent), while 80–90 per cent of teenage births are outside legal marriage (ONS 1997).

In 1996, there were 44,700 babies born to women aged 15–19. Although this represents a rise over the previous year, it is substantially fewer births to teenagers than during the 1970s and early 1980s. However, it is also the case that the number of teenage girls in the population was falling from the early 1980s onwards, and that the rate at which 15–19 year olds become pregnant and remain pregnant—the conception rate and the abortion rate, in other words—was either stable or rising throughout the period and into the late 1990s (ONS 1997*d*: 62). Figure 1.2 shows changes in the conception and abortion rates for selected years since 1974: there was a large drop from 1974–84, when teenage births fell steadily. From 1984 onwards, however, conceptions have fluctuated around 60, and abortions around 35, per 1000 women aged 15–19. The stability of both the conception and abortion rates gives few grounds for thinking that in the short term at least (or in the absence of any effective intervention by government) British teenagers will behave any differently than they have in the past. And as their numbers in the population are set to rise over the next decade or so, following a peak in the birth rate in 1990, we can expect to see a rise in the number of babies born to teenagers (Craig 1997).

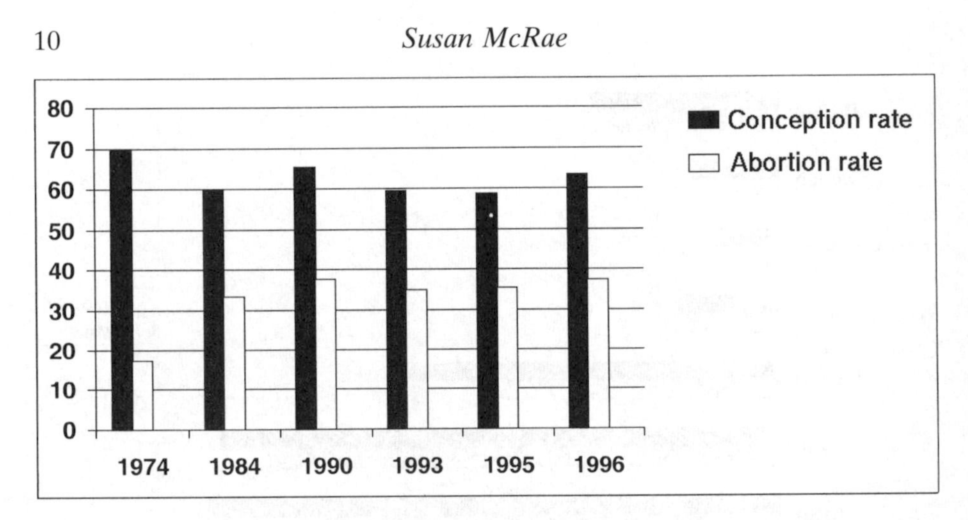

FIG. 1.2 Conception rate and abortion rate, UK, 1974–1996 (per 1,000 women aged 15–19)

Teenage mothers are feeding the rise of a 'new' family form—the single lone-parent family, which from 1986 increased at a faster rate than any other family form. They are not 'trailblazers', however, creating new lifestyles in the face of tradition. Qualitative studies of single lone mothers and teenage mothers reported in this volume (Berthoud, McKay, and Rowlingson, Chapter 15; also Rowlingson and McKay 1998; Allen and Bourke Dowling, Chapter 14; also Allen and Bourke Dowling 1998) indicate clearly that, given a choice, most of these women would have married before having their children; but the option was either not open to them or the young man in question was not worth marrying, often because of poor employment prospects or personal irresponsibility. Their pregnancies were, for the most part, something that just happened to them, about which they felt that they had little control. Of those who did form cohabiting relationships with the father of their child, half were living on their own within one year of the birth (Allen and Bourke Dowling, Chapter 14).

The rise in births to unwed, unpartnered women has been claimed to be the best predictor of an underclass in the making (Murray 1990: 4). Certainly, entry into teenage motherhood is not neutral: in both the United States and Britain, teenage motherhood is transmitted across generations; even after controlling for family status and education, the daughters of teenage mothers are more likely to have a birth in their teens than the daughters of older mothers (Kahn and Anderson 1992; Hobcraft and Kiernan 1995; Kiernan 1997; Manlove 1997; Wellings *et al.* 1997). There is also a more general link between teenage pregnancy and growing up with a disadvantaged family background, which appears to act through educational context and performance. This link is demonstrated in Figure 1.3, which draws upon Wellings and her colleagues' re-analysis of the 1991 Sexual Attitudes and Lifestyles Survey.

The relationship between education and having a teenage birth is circular—lack of progress in school can lead to an early pregnancy; having an early pregnancy impairs progress at school (Wellings and Wadsworth, Chapter 13; also Wellings *et al.* 1997). Having an early birth damages life chances: there is evidence that women who have teenage births are more likely to leave home early, to live in social or subsidized housing, to be in a manual job or unemployed, and to be welfare-dependent (Furstenburg *et al.* 1987; Phoenix 1991; Wellings *et al.* 1997; Allen and Bourke Dowling, Chapter 14). And although recent research on the long-term effects of teenage motherhood suggests that many young mothers have been able to escape from poverty, the experiences of their children reflect the obstacles arising from growing up in families with few economic and educational resources (Manlove 1997: 263).

However, the link between teenage pregnancy and economic disadvantage is not limited to the consequences of such pregnancies. As reported earlier in this chapter, young men's employment opportunities and wage rates have deteriorated markedly over the past twenty years. Consequently, their abilities to support young families have been impaired (Burges, Clarke, and Cronin 1997). Furthermore, having a baby seemingly provides working-class teenagers more opportunities for self-fulfilment than staying in school, a dead-end job, or unemployment. Social norms

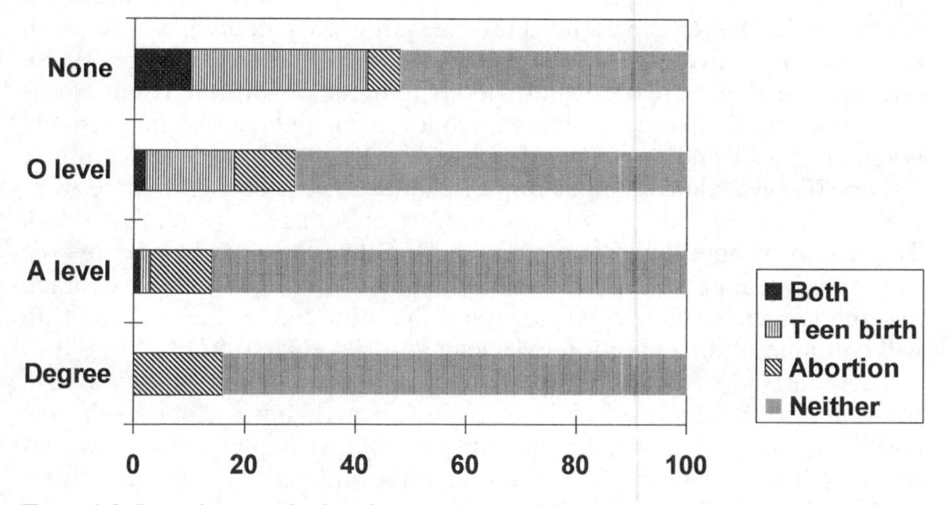

FIG. 1.3 Prevalence of abortion and teen birth by education, women aged 20–24 (%)

constrain the effective use of contraceptives by teenage girls and so they become pregnant; economic circumstances constrain competing opportunities and so they become mothers.

Divorce

Britain is also distinctive for its high divorce rate. Thirty years ago, there were two divorces for every 1,000 marriages. Liberalization of the divorce laws in the 1970s led to a sharp rise in divorce and by the mid-1980s, about 13 in every 1,000 marriages ended in divorce, a rate which has persisted throughout the 1990s (Pullinger 1998). The rate of increase is slower now than in the 1970s and early 1980s, largely because the married population contains fewer of those at high risk (Murphy and Wang, Chapter 4). Nonetheless, over 40 per cent of marriages will end in divorce—a tally which, on simple measures of divorce (per 1,000 marriages or per 1,000 population), puts Britain at the head of the European league table. As Coleman and Chandola show in the next chapter, however, even more subtle measures (such as crude divorce rate) keep Britain at the top, although in competition for first place with Sweden and Denmark.

Moreover, people are divorcing after shorter periods of marriage. One in ten marriages which took place in 1981 ended in divorce within 4.5 years, compared with one in ten divorcing within 6 years in 1971 and after 25 years in 1951 (Roberts 1996: 2). Early marriage and early parenthood have long been understood to be strongly associated with marital breakdown: the younger the age at marriage, the greater the likelihood of that marriage ending (Kiernan and Mueller, Chapter 16). Between 1971 and 1996, people under age 25 experienced the greatest growth in divorce rates, with rates increasing fivefold for men and fourfold for women (Pullinger 1998). Teenage marriages are particularly likely to break down. One result of this rise of youthful divorce is that the children of divorce are increasingly younger as well, and consequently more at risk of losing contact with their fathers. In 1995, almost 30 per cent of children experiencing divorce were under 5 years old and over 70 per cent were under age 10 (Pullinger 1998). The length of time that fathers and children live together before divorce or separation appears to be crucial to their chances of maintaining contact, and the longer the time spent together, the more likely their relationship will continue after separation (Maclean and Eekelaar 1997).

There are clear links between divorce and economic disadvantage: not only are the deprived more at risk of divorce, but divorce itself may compound deprivation. Kiernan and Mueller (Chapter 16) show that unemployment, reliance on benefits, and disability are key characteristics of the currently divorced population and, further, that the economically disadvantaged, particularly the unemployed and those in receipt of benefits, have higher probabilities of divorce. Unemployment and divorce seem particularly linked. Kiernan and Mueller report that both divorced men and divorced women are less likely to be in employment than their married counterparts. While Lampard (1994) suggests that some marriages appear to break down as a direct consequence of spells of unemployment, and that some spells of unemployment appear to be a direct consequence of marriage breakdown. Unemployed divorced men have difficulty making (or maintaining) formal or informal payments for child support, which Bradshaw *et al.* (Chapter 17) suggest may lead to an estrangement between father and child and to economic hardship for the child. Unemployed divorced women, particularly those with children, seldom avoid poverty, or at least considerable financial hardship (Bryson, Ford, and White 1997).

But even if unemployment is avoided, other deprivations may follow divorce. Housing quality, for example, declines markedly for both men and women after divorce. Flowerdew, Hamad, and Hayes (Chapter 18) show that divorced men and women move more frequently than both single and married people, with men continuing to move for several years following divorce. Moreover, divorce carries a high risk of losing owner occupation, with men particularly likely to move into their parents' home or to rented accommodation, and women to local authority housing. Manually employed men, especially at younger ages, frequently lose their place in the housing market and return to their parents' home at separation (see also Mason, Chapter 6). Women with children who retain the family home at separation or divorce are often unable financially to maintain their continued residence and are forced instead into local authority or housing association accommodation. Couples married for fewer than five years before divorce are especially likely to end up in social housing (McCarthy and Simpson 1991).

About one in every 65 children will experience the divorce of their parents before they reach age 16—twice the proportion in 1971 (Pullinger 1998). The economic consequences of divorce for children can be profound. Lone-parent families have repeatedly been shown to be more disadvantaged than the poorest two-parent families (Millar and Bradshaw 1991; Bryson, Ford, and White 1997; see also Layard, Piachaud, and Stewart 1978; Townsend 1979). In 1992, more than three-quarters of children in lone-parent families were living in poverty (Family Policy Studies Centre 1997). A recent review of over 200 research reports shows, moreover, that although long-term adverse consequences typically affect only a minority of children whose parents separate, such children have about twice the chance of experiencing poor outcomes as children who grow up in intact families. Thus, not only are the children of separated and divorced parents more likely to live in poverty and poor housing, they are also at greater risk of doing less well in school, leaving school and home when still young, becoming a teenage parent, and being poor when they become adults (Rodgers and Pryor 1998). They are also at higher risk of eventual marital breakdown themselves. Kiernan and Mueller (Chapter 16) identify only two factors from childhood and adolescence that are directly associated with higher probabilities of partnership breakdown in adulthood: parental divorce and poor emotional well-being. For some men and women, it seems, vicious circles of deprivation and divorce are handed down through generations.

Lone parents

The number of lone-parent families has more than trebled since the 1970s, bringing Britain to the forefront of the European Union in both the proportion of lone-parent families and the proportion of children raised in such families (Coleman and Chandola, Chapter 2). In the late 1990s, 1.6 million—or just over one in five—families in Britain with dependent children were headed by a lone parent, almost invariably a lone mother, encompassing some 15 per cent of dependent children (Haskey 1998*a*; Pullinger 1998). The dramatic growth in lone parenthood is due to a number of factors. During the 1960s, divorce overtook death as the primary source of lone-parent families, while throughout the 1970s and into the 1980s, sharply rising divorce rates and falling remarriage rates furthered their growth (Kiernan, Land, and Lewis 1998; Murphy and Wang, Chapter 4). From the mid-1980s, however, most of the growth in lone-parent families has come from never-married mothers, as changing attitudes towards pre-marital sex, shotgun weddings, and living together outside marriage have led to a sharp increase in births outside marriage. Official statistics suggest that never-married lone-mother families grew faster than other family types, and more than doubled in the space of eight years to become one in twelve of all families with dependent children. Never-married-mother families account for over 80 per cent of lone-parent families in which the parent is teenaged or in their early twenties (Haskey 1996*a*). About half of these 'officially single' women, however, would have entered lone parenthood following the breakdown of a cohabiting relationship. Thus, official figures overstate the growth of genuinely single motherhood; nonetheless, there has been a substantial increase in the number of single women who become mothers while not living with a partner, as well as in the length of time that they remain lone mothers (Berthoud, McKay, and Rowlingson, Chapter 15). Since the early 1990s, women who had never married before becoming mothers have outnumbered divorced lone mothers, and in 1997 accounted for nearly one in six lone mothers (Pullinger 1998).

The problem of lone motherhood is poverty. Research suggests that, as a group, lone mothers have few chances of obtaining other than low-paid work, often because they enter the labour market disadvantaged by their low level of qualifications (Bryson, Ford, and White 1998). The majority, however, have young children to care for and thus need jobs which provide enough income to meet the costs of child care. Consequently, lone mothers in Britain are less likely to be employed than in most other countries and since the 1970s, their employment rate has declined. The difference in economic activity between married and lone mothers is particularly sharp among women with children under age 5. In the 1970s, lone mothers with pre-school children were more likely to be in work or seeking work than married mothers with similarly aged children. This changed during the 1980s, and during the 1990s married mothers with young children have been twice as likely as lone mothers to be economically active. During the 1990s one in two married mothers with pre-school children have been in employment compared with fewer than one in four comparable lone mothers (Kiernan, Land, and Lewis 1998: 128). Most of the fall in employment among lone mothers has come in full-time work—while the full-time employment of married women has risen—with part-time work remaining stable. About six in ten employed lone mothers work part-time (Pullinger 1998).

The majority of lone mothers, therefore, gain little income from employment. Nor do the majority receive support payments from the fathers of their children. Before the introduction of the Child Support Agency in 1993, about 30 per cent of lone mothers received maintenance (Bradshaw and Millar 1991), a proportion that appears to have remained stable throughout the 1990s (Ford, Marsh, and McKay 1995; Ford, Marsh, and Findlayson 1998). The research of Bradshaw *et al.* (Chapter 17) among current non-resident fathers suggests, in contrast, that just over half were making maintenance payments, paying an average of 14 per cent of their net incomes (or £25 per week). Of the non-resident fathers who did not pay support, two-thirds provided informal support in the form of presents, clothes, shoes, pocket money, or holiday expenses. Sometimes, however, formal demands for child support mean that fathers are unable to continue informal support, and lead to difficult relations with former wives or partners and estrangement from children. All too often the ability of divorced fathers to make support payments, whether formal or informal, is constrained by unemployment, economic inactivity, or low wages—as was the situation of almost two-thirds of non-resident fathers found not to be paying maintenance by Bradshaw and his colleagues.

In the absence of paid work or adequate support from former partners, the majority of lone mothers in Britain rely on state benefits.[1] Research in the early 1990s suggested that more than two-thirds of lone parents at any one time receive Income Support, while many more have claimed it in the past. Even among employed lone parents reliance on benefits is not uncommon, with one-third in receipt of Family Credit, compared with fewer than one in twenty working couples (McKay and Marsh 1994).

The receipt of benefits describes a 'fault line' between lone-parent families which has marked consequences for their material well-being. McKay and Marsh (1994: 73) describe the gulf between benefit recipients and non-recipients: the former 'overwhelmingly were social tenants, manual workers, poorly qualified, had more children, were single or separated'; while the latter were 'owner occupiers, non-manual workers, better qualified, had fewer children, were divorced or widowed, or lone fathers'. Single or separated lone parents who live alone with their children in social housing are particularly vulnerable to the hardships that accompany dependence on benefits. Often young, and accounting for nearly one-third of all lone parents, single or separated lone mothers routinely experience difficulties with debt and essential expenditures. They, or their children, may also experience health problems. Indeed, lone parents appear increasingly likely to have health problems of their own or other family members that prevent economic activity (Ford, Marsh, and McKay 1995: 89). Moreover, the deprivation these single or separated mothers experienced as adults will for many be a reflection of childhood deprivation, as more than one in four young, never-married lone parents were themselves raised in lone-parent households (Ford, Marsh, and McKay 1995: 89). Research reported here (Allen and Bourke Dowling, Chapter 14; Berthoud, McKay, and Rowlingson, Chapter 15) suggests that few women plan to become single lone mothers. As, however, social norms have changed in ways that allow independent living, setting up a home with a man without a job or in low-paid work with few prospects seems a poor alternative to lone motherhood.

Cohabitation

The continuing growth of cohabitation in Britain—before marriage, between marriages, and instead of marriage—encapsulates the depth and breadth of changes in people's behaviour and attitudes towards sexual morality and living arrangements.[2] In the mid-sixties, fewer than 5 per cent of never-married women cohabited before marriage; in the early 1990s, 70 per cent did so. For remarrying women, the rise was from 30 per cent in the mid-sixties to 90 per cent in the early 1990s (Haskey 1996*a*). As cohabitation has increased, the number of marriages has plummeted: in 1995, there were fewer than 200,000 first marriages in Britain, less than half the number that took place in 1970, and the overall number of marriages

(322,000) was the lowest recorded since 1926 (Pullinger 1998). As cohabitation has increased, the number of births outside marriage has soared: well over a third of births in 1996 were outside marriage—more than twice the proportion in 1971. The rise in births outside marriage was particularly steep during the 1980s, as childbearing within cohabiting relationships became more common. By the end of the 1980s, 14 per cent of births outside marriage were jointly registered by parents living at the same address; by 1996, this had risen to 20 per cent (Murphy 1997). In one in five of all families with dependent children, the parents are cohabiting; one in sixteen dependent children live with cohabiting parents (Haskey 1996*a*). Indeed, most of the recent growth in cohabiting-couple families has come among those with dependent children, particularly among the under-thirties (Haskey 1995). Consequently, the proportion of young children in cohabiting families has grown and in 1994 about half of the children in such families were under age 5, compared with only one-quarter in married-couple families (Haskey 1996*a*).

Britain does not lead Europe in the growth of cohabitation, but it may do so in terms of the concentration of long-term cohabitation—particularly with dependent children—among the economically disadvantaged. Some economic theory links the growth of cohabitation directly to male relative deprivation in employment and career opportunities, implying that the strongest tendency towards cohabitation will be found among working-class men (Easterlin *et al.* 1990).[3] Support for this position can be found in Britain, where cohabiting couples with dependent children have substantially lower incomes and are more likely to receive Income Support or Housing Benefit and to live in council housing than is the case among married-couple families. They are also more likely to live in Inner London, the Metropolitan counties, and other urban areas. And when there is someone in work in such households—unemployment is common—their job is more likely to be semi-skilled or unskilled (Kiernan and Estaugh 1993; McRae 1993; Haskey 1996*a*). Previous research suggests that not only are those with the least material assets the least likely to marry (either before or after having children) (McRae 1993) but that men's inability to fulfil the traditional breadwinner role remains a key deterrent to marriage (Smock and Manning 1997).

In its appearance and (for some) its ideology, cohabitation may be viewed as no more than the modern equivalent of marriage. It is possible, further, to question whether there are any real differences between the two types of union, apart from ones imposed by state and church. Indeed, it seems probable that there is more variation *within* different cohabiting unions than *between* cohabitation and marriage. If this depiction of cohabitation is correct, then any implications arising from the concentration of cohabiting families among the economically disadvantaged, while important, are no more important than those pertaining to low-income families generally.

There is, however, a substantial body of research which suggests both that cohabitation is inherently more unstable than marriage and that couples who cohabit prior to marriage are more prone to marital dissolution (see Berrington and Diamond 1996 for a review of this literature; also Buck and Ermisch 1995; McRae 1997). Buck and Ermisch, for example, found that cohabiting couples were between three and four times more likely to separate than married couples, even after controlling for age and the presence of children. Buck and Ermisch were surprised at the relatively high instability of cohabiting unions with children present, and suggest that further research is needed. They go on to argue, however, that the higher rates of cohabitation breakdown should not be considered surprising per se. If cohabitation is being used by couples to test their relationship, then higher rates of dissolution might be expected as partners decide that they have not chosen well after all. Nonetheless, the apparently greater instability of cohabitation remains important, because cohabitation breakdown often throws women and children into poverty (Kiernan, Land, and Lewis 1998). In addition, formerly cohabiting fathers have been found to be substantially less likely than formerly married fathers to maintain a relationship with their children after separation (Maclean and Eekelaar 1997*a*).

Kiernan and Mueller (Chapter 16) use NCDS data to examine the stability of pre-marital cohabitation. In contrast to previous research, they find no differences in the risk of marital dissolution between people who do not cohabit before marriage and those whose first relationship was cohabitation followed by marriage. Kiernan and Mueller suggest that it is the experience of multiple spells of cohabitation prior to marriage that leads to enhanced risks of partnership breakdown, lending support to earlier research which attributes the association between pre-marital cohabitation and dissolution to differential selection into cohabitation. That is, men and women who cohabit before marriage have certain demographic and socio-economic characteristics which are themselves significantly associated with marital dissolution (Booth and Johnson 1988; Axinn and Thornton 1992; Hall and Zhao 1995; Berrington and Diamond 1997).

FAMILY CHANGE AND CONTINUITY

The previous sections concentrated on areas of British demography which demonstrate most clearly the links between family change and economic disadvantage. It seems likely that some, though not all, of the changes in family behaviour and household composition discussed above are related to the economic restructuring Britain has experienced throughout the second half of this century. However, not all family or household change arises from, or results in, disadvantage, nor is it necessarily linked to economic change. Within patterns of family change, moreover, continuity in both attitudes and behaviour can be observed. Research arising from the ESRC Population and Household Change Programme clearly suggests that despite diversity in households, most people still have strong family ties—that families still matter. Mason (Chapter 6), for example, demonstrates how living at a distance from kin can have little or no effect on the significance of family relationships, particularly if the reasons for living away are accepted as legitimate by all concerned. Similarly, Roberts and McGlone (1996) found that most people maintain regular contact with close relatives outside their household, and that family is seen as overwhelmingly more important than friends, by a margin of around eleven to one, while Scott (1997*a*) reports that 'family events were by far and away regarded as the most important aspect of people's lives . . . almost twice as many mentioned family events as mentioned employment' when asked what was the most important thing that had happened to them or to their family in the previous year. In accounting for such continuity in the face of remarkable change, Scott and Brook (1996; also Scott, Chapter 3) suggest that, for most people, individualist values are held simultaneously with a commitment to family values, and together result in complex attitudinal and behavioural choices.

Insights into the intertwining of change and continuity may be gained from the work of Bornat and her colleagues (Chapter 10), whose study of the impact of change on the family lives of older people found a commitment to the notion of family as a set of flexible, interconnecting, and supportive relationships. To accommodate change while preserving the continuity of family life, families and family relationships come to be seen as permeable and adjustable, allowing the acceptance of step-grandchildren, new in-laws, and new step-parents, as old relationships end and new ones begin. Nonetheless, this notion of the family co-exists with an enduring commitment to blood ties, particularly in the face of specific demands for care and support or in relation to inheritance (cf. Finch *et al.* 1996).

One of the more remarkable changes in the post-war period, which would seem to imply a break with traditional family values, has been the growth of one-person households among both pensioners and younger people. In 1950, only about 3 per cent of the population in Europe and North America lived alone (Hall *et al.* 1997). Since then, there has been an increase in one-person households in every West European country:

Sweden is at the top of the table with 40 per cent of households now one-person and Greece at the bottom with only 17 per cent. In Britain, 29 per cent of households (or about 10 per cent of the population) in 1997 were one-person, a figure set to rise to 36 per cent by 2016, accounting for some 8.6 million people (Bramley, Munro, and Lancaster 1997: 13).

The continuing increase in one-person households is being built upon gradual decreases in the proportion of traditional family households, both with and without children. Consequently, such households are sometimes seen to herald the demise of family life and the rise of 'non-families'. From another perspective, however, living alone at younger ages can show how lifestyles can be manipulated in order to enhance one's life chances, while among pensioners, in particular, the experience of living alone can demonstrate the strength of family ties in the context of change, and suggests that change is not necessarily for the worse.

Younger one-person households

People live alone for a variety of reasons. For some, living alone may be a deliberate and permanent choice; for others, it may be a temporary arrangement in response to particular circumstances; for others still, it may be a matter in which they have no choice. While there are more people living alone at all ages, the largest increases since 1971 have come among men and women under retirement age, particularly among those aged under 40 (Hall and Ogden 1997). The increase in solo living among people under pension age reflects the way in which household change is sometimes linked to economic change. There is evidence of a link between lifestyle choices and economic opportunity, particularly in major world cities such as Paris and London. As Hall, Ogden, and Hill report (Chapter 11) both cities experienced rapid growth in the number of younger one-person households during the 1980s, as economic and employment restructuring led to an increase in professional/managerial and intermediate occupations. Migrants living alone in Inner London in 1991 were more likely to have moved for employment reasons and to have experienced upward social mobility since 1981, compared with migrants living alone elsewhere in Britain. Partnership change—divorce and separation—lay behind the moves of people living alone outside Inner London, but this was a less important reason for men and women moving to London (Hall, Ogden, and Hill 1996). Consequently, men and women living alone in Inner London and in Paris are increasingly distinctive. Recent research by Hall, Ogden, and Hill (1996; Chapter 11) supports Lafancheur's (1989: 226) description of the distinctiveness of Paris: 'a young population living alone, more often in work than those in the provinces, more often in high status jobs, and more mobile', while in Inner London, men and women—but particularly women—who live alone are more likely to be found in managerial and professional jobs than either people living alone in England and Wales or the population generally. In addition, both men and women living alone today are more likely to be property owners than renters, which was the traditional pattern.

The rise of one-person households has been cited as evidence of 'the declining importance of the family and a consequence of changes leading modern societies not to "new families" but to "non families"' (Goldscheider and Waite 1991: 199). Claims such as this need to be viewed with caution, however, as there is evidence that living alone is not synonymous with no family ties or with social isolation (cf. Scott 1997*a*; Chapter 3). One French study suggested that one-quarter of men and one-third of women aged 21–44 living alone were in 'stable, loving relationships' (Leridan and Villeneuve-Gokalp 1988: 227), while Hall, Ogden, and Hill (Chapter 11), when interviewing men and women living alone in London's Docklands, found no one who 'found it lonely to live alone'. Many of their respondents had important relationships and spent part of their time with a partner, although they still considered themselves to be living alone. Families or couples who 'live alone together' (LATs) are, like younger one-person households, an increasing feature of middle-class urban life. Recent research among dual-career 'work-rich' households in which both partners were employed in managerial, professional, or associate professional occupations found that the majority had lived apart for at least one period of up to six months on at least one occasion—one couple 'had married in 1988 but had only been living together since 1991' (Green 1997: 650).

The family relationships of younger people who live alone or who live alone together remain relatively unexplored: are they 'non-families', as is sometimes suggested? Or do they offer evidence of the continuing importance of intimate ties in the face of changed economic opportunities, for women as well as for men? Whatever the balance of truth between these two explanations—and there evidently is truth in both—men and women in one-person households are without question developing lifestyles all but unknown in previous decades.

The family lives of older people

Since the beginning of the century, the proportion of people in the UK aged over 64 has trebled. In 1996, almost 16 per cent of the UK population was over pension age; over the next thirty years, this figure is projected to rise to almost 25 per cent. Some of the classic works of sociology and social policy involve the study of the family and social lives of older people: by Sheldon in Wolverhampton in 1948, Peter Townsend in Bethnal Green in 1957, and Young and Willmott in both East London (1957) and

Woodford (1960). These studies, and others, demonstrated the importance of kinship and family life to older people. Indeed, Sheldon questioned whether the phrase 'living alone' was of any value in Wolverhampton, given the degree of residential proximity between older people and their kin. To quote Ron Frankenburg (1966), old people in Britain in the 1940s and 1950s lived in an 'environment of kin'.

Without doubt, there has been growth in the proportion of older people living alone or with just their spouses, among both 'young' pensioners and the elderly. This was already observable in the 1970s when about a fifth of men and 40 per cent of women aged 75 and over lived alone. Between 1971 and 1981, there was a marked drop in the extent of intergenerational co-residence and by 1991, over half of women and about a third of men in this age group lived alone (Grundy and Murphy 1997; also Grundy, Chapter 8). There has also been a recent decline in contact with older kin—mothers and fathers—in part because of increasing geographical distances between relations (McGlone, Park, and Smith 1998: 19). Phillipson *et al.* (Chapter 9) went back to the three communities studied in the 1940s and 1950s and carried out a network analysis of 200 older people in each area, buttressed by qualitative interviews with a smaller number in each location. They, too, found evidence of increased living alone or with a spouse only.

But although living *near* is not the same as living *with*, most older people still live in relatively close proximity to at least one of their children. Among those interviewed by Phillipson *et al.* in Wolverhampton, half had at least one child within four miles, while in Bethnal Green and Woodford the proportions having a child within four miles were 33 per cent and 44 per cent respectively. Co-residence may have declined, but proximity seemingly remains. Moreover, the analysis of kin contact carried out by McGlone, Park, and Roberts (Chapter 5) found that as many as two-thirds of parents with grown-up children live less than an hour's journey from at least one of their sons or daughters, and around half live less than fifteen minutes away. Three-quarters of older parents talk to their sons or daughters by telephone at least once a week; half of British adults with a living mother see her at least weekly.

Even in the face of increasing residential autonomy among older people, then, family and close kin remain important. Moreover, they retain particular significance as the givers and receivers of emotional, practical, and financial support. The networks of older people have changed, with couples and friends more prominent than they were fifty years ago, but close kin still count. As Phillipson *et al.* report (1997: 374; see also Chapter 9):

> Most older people are connected to kinship based networks, these both providing and receiving from the older person different types of support. In respect of

kinship there is a central core to the network which is crucial . . . Close kin are still available and significant in the lives and networks of older people. They are also a major source of support . . .

Roberts and McGlone (1997; also McGlone, Park, and Roberts, Chapter 5) also demonstrate the continuing importance of the family as a source of support. For the first time in survey research, respondents were asked about *actual* help given or received. Of those who had provided care in the previous five years, three-quarters had given that care to a family member; of those who had given or received a loan or gift of £100 or more, 60 per cent had received money from a parent or parent-in-law. Compared with the United States, Britons with living parents are substantially more likely to be living with those parents or providing regular help to them (Grundy and Murphy 1997). Moreover, the breaking up of families and forming of new relationships does not necessarily affect the capacity of families to care for their older members. Instead, the expectation that support will be given, when the need for it arises, continues to underpin family relationships (Bornat *et al.*, Chapter 10).

Older people in Britain traditionally have shown a strong preference for independent living, for what has been called (by Rosenmayr and Kockies 1963) 'intimacy at a distance', a preference that substantial numbers have acted upon. The following words said by a widow living alone could come from a study carried out in the 1990s, but are instead from Peter Townsend's 1957 study (quoted in Phillipson *et al.* 1997: 365):

This is my idea. A mother's a mother no matter how old she is. She's got something she doesn't want her children to know, and they've got something they don't want her to know. There's that little something about your life you want to keep on your own. When I'm feeling I'm in the way, I just go.

What we are seeing in Britain today are increased opportunities for older people to realize their wish to live independently: they are healthier and live longer, so there are more close friends with whom to socialize; there is better state support and more facilities (both state and private) to support independent living; and there is a significantly larger housing stock, so older people have somewhere to live. Had these conditions existed fifty or sixty years ago, it seems likely that many more older people would have chosen to live apart from their adult children.

This is not to suggest that the social and family lives of older people have not changed. Phillipson *et al.* (1997: 382; also Chapter 9) suggest that over the past fifty years, we have moved from an old age experienced largely in family groups to one that is lived within 'personal communities':

there is now a more 'voluntaristic' element in social relationships in old age . . . whether or not kin are nearby there are now alternatives to kin . . . friends . . .

emerge clearly in a number of supportive roles, notably among those without children . . . and especially among those who are single.

In addition, the increase in divorce, cohabitation, and re-partnering has had an impact on the family lives of older people. While it is likely that these changes have led in some cases to poverty, solo living, and isolation (particularly among men) the evidence suggests that family breakdown can alternatively lead to stronger intergenerational ties and increased co-residence (Grundy and Murphy 1997; Bornat *et al.*, Chapter 10). Bornat *et al.* also find that following family breakdown and reconstitution, older people's conceptions of family can be highly elastic and can stretch to include a new crop of step-grandchildren, in-laws, and step-parents. Some of these findings are replicated in Chamberlain's and Goulbourne's study of Caribbean kin networks in Britain and overseas (1997; also Goulbourne, Chapter 7), including the potential isolation of elderly men following divorce. Neither study found a significant weakening or absence of commitment to family ties or obligations, however, whatever the changes in family life older people may have witnessed.

FUTURE FAMILIES

Both change and continuity characterize British families and households in the 1990s, much of which flows from, or is built upon, profound changes in people's economic opportunities and outcomes, and upon equally profound ideational change—called by some the 'second demographic transition' (Lestaeghe 1991) and by others a changed *viewpoint* (Oppenheim, Mason, and Jensen 1995: 6). Is the family not what it used to be? Certainly, the traditional family has lost its commanding position, as it has decreased in numbers and the acceptability of alternative living arrangements has grown. Moreover, it is not likely to recapture its pre-eminence in future years. As Murphy and Wang show in Chapter 4, if current trends in family formation and dissolution continue, by 2016 the number of adults living in families and the number married will both have fallen substantially, while cohabitation will have continued to grow. By 2016, children will be equally likely to be born outside marriage as within, and there will be over one million cohabiting couples with children. There are, moreover, indications that young people today are particularly disposed towards non-traditional living arrangements. The decline in the proportion married and the increase in the proportion cohabiting or raising children alone are much steeper among men and women under age 30 than at older ages (Haskey 1995, 1996: 11). A study of ten European countries including Britain found that most family change—plurality of living arrangements—is concentrated among younger generations of women, especially those in the early parental or pre-parental phase (Strohmeier and Kuijsten 1997: 414). McGlone, Park, and Roberts suggest, further, that the relatively reduced sense of 'family-centredness' found among young British men and women is not due simply to life cycle effects, and that consequently young people today are likely to remain less oriented towards traditional family life as they age (Chapter 5).

However, as Scott (1997*a*) reminds us, it is important to distinguish between family *decline* and family *diversity*. Complex and changing household structures do not mean that individuals have no permanent family relationships or ties. In order to understand families, it is necessary to look beyond changes in household composition to the relationships within which families live. Chamberlain and Goulbourne (1998; also Goulbourne, Chapter 7), for example, find that the tendency to focus on family *structures* has generally distorted our understanding of how Caribbean families provide care, affection, and spiritual and material support to their members. Consistent with Caribbean social and family patterns, mixed parentage, serial parenting, step-siblings, lone-mother families, and an apparently low participation of men in family and household matters are characteristic of the living arrangements of Caribbeans in Britain. Nonetheless, such families maintain strong kinship networks across generations and countries, through which family obligations and responsibilities are met, and family and communal values, customs, and traditions are reproduced. Looking only at household composition obscures the continuing importance of kin relationships and gives rise to a misperception that Caribbean families in Britain are somehow 'dysfunctional'.

What may be said about Caribbean families in Britain may also be said about other groups—older men and women who experience the breakup of their children's marriages, young men and women living solo in London, lone mothers and their children. There seems to be something enduring in the idea of family which underpins not only the 'flexible, interconnecting' relationships described by Bornat *et al.* (Chapter 10) but also the 'families of choice' established by non-heterosexual men and women as they seek values commonly associated with the traditional ideal of the family—a sense of involvement, security, and continuity (Weeks, Heaphy, and Donovan, Chapter 12). Many different living arrangements are now accepted as valid alternatives to the traditional family; individual choice is consequently easier (some would say *mandatory*: Giddens 1996) and diversity the inevitable outcome. This is not to deny the obvious deterioration of the personal and family lives of some people nor the damaging effects of change where they exist. But there never was a golden age of the family (cf. Gillis 1998) and it seems likely that given adequate economic opportunities, most men and women would fashion adequate family lives. It is equally important to remember that not everything has changed in families and households, and not all that has changed is harmful.

PLAN OF THE BOOK

The rest of the book is divided into six parts. The first part places Britain in context: in Europe, in attitudes towards family change, and in relation to future family changes. Coleman and Chandola (Chapter 2) begin by locating Britain in its European demographic space. Coleman's aim was to assemble demographic and related socio-economic data on Europe and other industrial countries from the Second World War to the present day, and to use these data to analyse the trends and patterns observed and test hypotheses about them. UK patterns and trends are compared with European averages and distributions at several points in time, with particular emphasis on those features of British demography where marked deviations from European norms are apparent. Coleman's and Chandola's analysis of the position of the UK in Europe reveals an increasingly deviant position with regard to fertility and marital dissolution, and a pattern which more closely resembles the trends found in the 'new Europes' overseas—Australia, New Zealand, Canada, and the United States—or a modified Scandinavian model within Europe itself. For Coleman and Chandola, Britain's distinctiveness in European demography, which once mirrored its leading position in Europe's society and economy, now instead reflects Britain's disadvantage.

In Chapter 3, Jacqueline Scott continues to place Britain in context through an examination of changing attitudes towards aspects of family and sexual behaviour. Scott's chapter seeks to answer the following questions: How much have attitudes changed in Britain over the past decade and to what extent are there gender and generational divides? How does the trajectory and pace of change in Britain compare with that of the United States? How do Anglo-American attitudes compare with those of Ireland, Germany, Sweden, and Poland? To answer these questions, Scott examines changing attitudes towards the morality of pre-marital sex, extra-marital sex, and homosexuality. She also examines change in attitudes towards abortion, which in turn reflects both the increasing separation of sexuality and reproduction and views on the importance of motherhood in women's lives. Finally, Scott examines changing attitudes towards gender roles and in particular, the perceived clash between women's labour force participation and their traditional role as mothers. Scott finds that while change has not been as revolutionary as is often claimed, neither is there any evidence of the backlash that has been predicted by some. Scott concludes that the demise of traditional values can be overstated, and that old proscriptions and prescriptions about sexual morality and gender roles are still influential in what people regard as acceptable family choices.

Murphy and Wang turn to the future in Chapter 4 and forecast the numbers of adults and children who would be living in single, married, cohabiting, divorced, or lone-parent families under alternative scenarios about trends in family formation and dissolution. In order to derive these scenarios, the evolving patterns of family and household arrangements are discussed, including the growth of cohabitation, marital breakdown, and lone parenthood. The ways in which forecasts of these groups may be made are considered, and a multi-state household projection model is used to make projections into the twenty-first century. Murphy and Wang discuss the implications of their forecasts, including the extent to which the likely numbers in different groups are already determined because of experiences of events such as divorce, and how much change in coming decades will depend on events that will occur in the future.

Part II begins an analysis of change and continuity in British kinship that is continued in Part III. In the light of much popular discussion on the extended family which assumes that it is either extinct or dying out, McGlone, Park, and Roberts (Chapter 5) report on their analysis of the 1986 and 1995 Kinship and Friendship modules of the British Social Attitudes Survey. They examine the extent of family and friendship networks in Britain: living with or near relatives, contact with relatives, the extent to which help is given and received, and if there has been any significant change in kin contact over the past decade. The chapter indicates that there has been some decline in contact with relatives (as well as with close friends), which the authors attribute to the changing nature of women's employment. Nonetheless, the chapter shows that for the majority, family still comes first: most people maintain regular contact with close relatives, although older people are more family-centred than younger age groups.

Jennifer Mason's analysis of the ways in which people make sense of, and negotiate, their kin relationships in the context of questions about place, location, and geographical mobility is reported in Chapter 6. Based upon case study interviews, often with members of the same kin group, the chapter shows how people who have lived away from kin reason about distance, proximity, and kinship, and that the significance of kin relationships exists independently of the distance between kin. Through the use of concepts such as *distance thinker* (reluctant or otherwise) and *local thinker*, Mason demonstrates the complexity of people's experience of migration, as she exposes the interrelatedness of negotiating power, gender, the need for care or practical support, access to resources, and social class in the decision to live near or away.

In Chapter 7, Harry Goulbourne utilizes detailed histories of three families (one each from Barbados, Jamaica, and Trinidad and Tobago) to analyse family and kinship ties across the Caribbean, the Atlantic, and elsewhere. Goulbourne suggests that through the frequency of visits by family members of different generations, the exchange of gifts, provision of mutual assistance, production of cultural artefacts, and 'talking to back home', families with Caribbean backgrounds maintain traditions and patriotic feelings about their islands that do not conflict with living in Britain. Functioning within strong, transnational kinship systems, Caribbean families in Britain are highly adaptive while maintaining openness, inclusivity, and pride in the customs, culture, and values they transmit across distance and generations. Far from being 'dysfunctional' or weak, the Caribbean family draws upon transnational kinship to provide the emotional and material support needed to equip individual members for life in a competitive and generally hostile society.

Part III turns to an examination of the family and kin relationships of older people, which Emily Grundy begins (Chapter 8) with an analysis of recent changes in the household patterns of people over 50, focusing particularly on intergenerational relationships. Grundy provides evidence of the marked decline in intergenerational co-residence among those currently in later old age, which in the 1980s reflected the growing use of institutional care. The risk of moving to an institution in old age has increased substantially over time, while the proportion of older people moving to live with relatives has declined. Differences in age, housing tenure, marital status, and household type all affect the chances of moving into an institution. Grundy also examines the co-residence of women in midlife and shows, contrary to popular belief, that passage to the 'empty nest' phase of family life depends more on the age at which women become mothers than on the age of young people when they leave home.

In Chapter 9, Chris Phillipson and his colleagues return to three communities first studied in the 1940s and 1950s to examine changes in the family and community relationships of older people. The original studies demonstrated the existence of an 'environment of kin' which was reinforced by the geographical proximity of elderly people to both immediate and extended kin. Phillipson, Bernard, and Phillips show that although kinship ties have stood up well to the large-scale changes in urban society over the past fifty years, old age has changed—from a time spent mostly living with others to one when it is increasingly the norm to live alone or with only a marriage partner. Nonetheless, few older people appear to be isolated, in the sense of lacking close relationships, although all three areas had vulnerable groups of people. In addition, personal communities have also become more important for older people. Whether or not kin are nearby, there are more alternatives to kin and neighbours; friends in particular matter more, particularly for the single and the childless.

Bornat and her colleagues used a life history approach to explore the capacity of families that have experienced change to care for older family members, intergenerational transfers of property, and the nature of intergenerational ties. Their findings, reported in Chapter 10, demonstrate the emergence of a 'new extended family' characterized by both vertical and horizontal ties. Older people draw upon experiences of family change in their own early lives in order to make sense of change among younger family members. At the same time, they operate within a morality which enables them to justify and explain re-partnering by their children and grandchildren. The new extended family accommodates additional members while sustaining traditional practices, particularly in relation to inheritance. It also provides a context within which older people are able to construct identities for themselves which centre on being good parents regardless of age.

Part IV comprises two chapters on ways of living that represent sharp breaks with traditional family structures: one-person households and non-heterosexual 'families of choice'. In Chapter 11, Hall, Ogden, and Hill examine the growth of one-person households among people under pension age over the last two decades in England and Wales and France. They show that living alone among younger people in both countries is especially associated with Paris and London, although increasing numbers of younger people are living alone in other large cities and elsewhere in each country. Further, the social class of those living alone has become more concentrated among the professional and managerial classes, particularly among women. Younger people living alone are now more likely to own their homes rather than to rent as in the past. They also have distinctive mobility patterns, with many making a geographical move to live alone. Geographical mobility is also shown to be associated with upward occupational mobility into professional and managerial jobs.

Chapter 12 draws on in-depth interviews with about one hundred self-identified gay, lesbian, and bisexual people to explore the concept 'families of choice'. Jeffrey Weeks and his colleagues demonstrate how the term 'family' is used among non-heterosexuals to denote something broader than family of origin: an affinity circle which has cultural and symbolic meaning for those who participate or feel a sense of belonging. The most commonly used terms applied to these networks are 'chosen' or 'created' and such elective families may be seen as examples of 'everyday experiments in living'. These life experiments are best characterized as fluid and adaptable networks whose core is made up of selected friends, partners, and members of family or origin. Weeks, Heaphy, and Donovan also show that lesbians and gays wish for the same rights as heterosexuals to choose their ways of life. There is a strong belief that on grounds of equity and justice, same-sex marriages should be legalized, although only a minority would themselves marry. Others want full access to the same couple-rights as available to heterosexuals, without necessarily having to register a partnership formally.

Part V turns to the topic of teenage sexuality and young motherhood. Kaye Wellings' and Jane Wadsworth's re-analysis of the 1991 Sexual Lifestyles and Attitudes survey is reported in Chapter 13. They show that early sexual expression and teenage parenthood are generally more common among girls from less favoured social backgrounds, and are themselves linked with adverse consequences. Those who report lower educational achievement and family disruption are more likely to start sex early; teenagers who become mothers have poorer employment prospects, are materially less well off, and are more likely to live in subsidized housing. Talking about sex with one's parents helps protect young women from early pregnancies: young women from families in which there was no discussion about sexual matters were more than twice as likely to have become mothers in their teens than those from families who discussed sex easily.

Chapter 14 explores the experiences of 84 teenagers who decided to keep their babies after becoming pregnant. The in-depth interviews carried out by Isobel Allen and her colleagues confirm the statistical picture described by Wellings and Wadsworth. Teenage motherhood for these young women overwhelmingly resulted in negative short-term outcomes: financial hardship, dependence on benefits, lack of a social life, unplanned responsibilities, unsatisfactory housing, and difficulties in forming new relationships. Few of the young mothers had intended to end up as single lone parents but around half of them had done so, and well over half of these were living alone with their babies. Only just over half were still in relationships with the baby's father. Teenage fathers, however, do not appear to suffer the same negative outcomes, particularly if they do not stay in a relationship with the baby's mother. The authors recommend improvements in education for both men and women, to ensure that men share the responsibility for teenage pregnancy and parenthood, and that teenagers of both sexes understand the limitations that parenthood can place on their current and future lives.

The experiences of single lone mothers are explored further in Chapter 15, which also tracks the growth of lone parenthood over time. Berthoud, McKay, and Rowlingson combined quantitative and qualitative approaches in their study. They show that the rise in lone parenthood in recent years is due predominantly to increasing numbers of women *becoming* lone mothers, although there is also some sign of an increase in the length of time that women *remain* lone parents. Berthoud and his colleagues distinguish in their analyses between women who had never legally married but who had cohabited prior to becoming lone mothers, and women who had had a child while not living with a partner. They show, like Allen, that single women rarely plan to become lone mothers and are not encouraged to do so by the prospect of social security benefits or council housing. Single women are more likely to become lone mothers if they come from poor socio-economic backgrounds, and although single motherhood was not considered an ideal option, it was seen as an acceptable one given the alternatives available at the time.

The final part of the book considers divorce and its aftermath. In Chapter 16, Kiernan and Mueller provide a statistical profile of the divorced population of Britain (including men and women who experience cohabitation breakdown). Use of data from the British Household Panel Survey (BHPS) and the National Child Development Survey (NCDS) allow the authors to examine both the background of divorce and its consequences or outcomes in later life. From their wide-ranging analyses, Kiernan and Mueller identify a small number of factors directly associated with partnership breakdown, including marriage at a young age, experience of multiple spells of cohabitation and of parental divorce, and economic, somatic, and emotional disadvantage. Their analyses contribute particularly to our understanding of the relationship between cohabitation and partnership breakdown, and demonstrate that individuals who cohabit prior to a *first* marriage do not have a higher rate of marital dissolution. Kiernan and Mueller suggest that the strong association between premarital cohabitation and divorce is therefore likely to arise from the experiences of those who had more than one cohabiting relationship prior to marrying.

In Chapter 17 Jonathan Bradshaw and colleagues examine one of the consequences of partnership breakdown: the rise of non-resident fatherhood. Their research was based upon a representative sample of over 600 non-resident fathers in Britain, identified through a screening question in omnibus surveys. Subsequent survey research was complemented by two qualitative investigations with small sub-samples focusing on contact with children and child support, creating thereby a rich and unique data set. Bradshaw *et al.* found that the socio-economic circumstances of non-resident fathers were substantially poorer than those of resident fathers, with predictable consequences for their ability to contribute child support either formally or informally. A much higher level of contact between child and non-resident father is reported by Bradshaw and his colleagues than that suggested by previous research—almost half saw their child every week; only one in five had had no contact in the previous year. After considering some possible explanations for their results, the authors conclude, with hindsight, that their emphasis on 'seeing the child' was too imprecise and open to different interpretations by fathers and mothers. In any event, the majority of the fathers were content with the amount of contact they had, although many reported that the present level and quality of contact had been achieved only after protracted difficulties. The chapter also explores the links between child support payments and non-resident fathers' contact with their children.

In the final chapter, Flowerdew, Al-Hamad, and Hayes analyse the relationship between divorce and migration. They find that divorced people move more often than married or single people and are more likely to move to rented accommodation. Women, especially those with children, are at particular risk after divorce of moving into local authority or Housing Association accommodation. The use of census data allowed Flowerdew and his colleagues to provide new information about the relationship between divorce and migration in ways not previously possible. Linking household change and migration through a detailed analysis of household records, they established a typology of movers which distinguishes between those who moved alone, with others, to join others, and to meet others. Their analyses show important gender differences in migration outcomes. Women, not surprisingly, are more likely than men to move with children and this is particularly the case for younger women (under age 30). However, women who move alone or with children only are less likely than men to form new households by either meeting or joining a new partner. The presence of children appears to have a strong deterrent effect on moving to meet or join others, and over three-quarters of women moving with children did not meet or join anyone. At all ages, divorced women who move alone are more likely than divorced men to remain alone.

NOTES

1. From Oct. 1998 all lone parents on Income Support were eligible for the government New Deal programme, which is intended to help lone parents find work by providing support in finding and securing employment, training, and child care. Results up to the end of Feb. 1998 from the New Deal's introduction in pilot areas suggests that 6% of Income Support recipients among lone parents found work (Family Policy Studies Centre 1998).
2. The increase in cohabitation also raises issues that cross the boundaries between heterosexual and non-heterosexual families. For example, legal issues surrounding parenting and inheritance can apply equally to gay or lesbian families and to heterosexual families (see Weeks, Heaphy, and Donovan, Chap. 12). In addition, recent attempts by a lesbian to secure travel privileges for her

partner, following the granting of such to a cohabiting heterosexual couple, suggests that this may also be the case for work-related issues.

3. In contrast, Becker (1981) argues that alternative living arrangements are the result of increased female independence, implying that the strongest effects would be found among career women with high educational or occupational status. A third explanation links the growth in cohabitation to normative change (Goode 1984; Lestaeghe and Meekers 1986; Lestaeghe 1990). Of course, these three explanations need not be mutually exclusive but might be complementary, with varying degrees of salience depending on gender and social class.

PART I
Britain in Context

2

Britain's place in Europe's population

David Coleman and Tarani Chandola

INTRODUCTION

Most papers in this book are dedicated to new developments in population and households in Britain. This paper has a different focus—to put Britain's demography in the context of the rest of Europe. Throughout the 1990s, Europe has seldom been off the front pages. European integration is much discussed: some hope for a unified European state of the future, sharing common economic, social, and legal institutions as well as a common currency. Others, conscious of the exceptionalism of the oldest nation-state in Europe, fear the submergence of national autonomy and distinctiveness by Euro-federalism and alien bureaucracy (Black 1994). In view of continued debate about Britain's political and economic place in Europe, it seems pertinent to see how our population and its behaviour compares with those of our European neighbours and where Britain is located in the post-transitional European demographic scene. Is our country an ordinary participant in Europe's demographic development, or does it occupy a more idiosyncratic or special position, as perhaps we might like to think? That question inevitably leads us to more general issues of convergence and divergence in contemporary Europe, which demographic data should reflect. Some of these differences have practical importance. Disquiet has been expressed about some of Britain's population trends: the high level of teenage motherhood, divorce, lone-parent families, and immigration. Is the behaviour of the British population in these and other respects really unusual in the European context? Can we explain these

Sara Beale and David Thomas acted as research assistants at an earlier stage in the project. We would also like to thank Susan McRae for her constant encouragement and support throughout this research. The work behind this paper was supported by grant L315253006 from the Population and Household Change Programme of the UK's Economic and Social Research Council and by a grant from the World Society Foundation, Zurich.

differences in terms of our particular preferences and social, welfare, tax, or housing arrangements?

Former distinction

More generally, is it possible to discern a new post-transitional European demographic regime, which might restore the equilibrium which existed before the demographic transition and in which Britain might share? For Western Europe from the sixteenth to the mid-eighteenth century, a distinctive demographic regime has been identified (Coale and Watkins 1986; R. M. Smith 1986, 1989; Goody 1996). Its most characteristic elements included moderate birth and death rates, late and avoidable marriage, frequent lifelong celibacy, distinctive household composition and neo-local household formation, and in most places, low levels of cohabitation and illegitimacy (proportion of births outside marriage). Britain, or at least England, shared these characteristics and indeed exhibited some of them (for example, husbandry service) to a marked degree, enjoyed lower fertility and death rates than its neighbours, and displayed even then a marked preference for market mechanisms (Macfarlane 1978; Flinn 1981), distinctively nucleated household patterns (Wall 1983), and high levels of geographical mobility. England was (and remains) conspicuously demographically homogeneous (Wilson 1984) compared with the marked regional variations characteristic of less well-consolidated European states.

The 'demographic transition' which began in the eighteenth century ended much of that, and Malthus's key homoeostatic feedback loops between population growth, prices, and the birth and death rates that drove the old regime have gone, or at least have been neglected in recent years (Wilson and Airey 1997). At one time, Britain was regarded as the paradigm of that process, but it is now known to be more complex and by no means causally related to high levels of urbanization and industrialization, in which Britain was first in Europe and the world in the early nineteenth century. The British transition to low fertility was unique in some respects, however; inhibited attitudes towards sex evidently induced some couples to favour sexual abstinence over new methods of family planning. Possibly for similar reasons, the old pattern of late marriage remained common into the 1930s, longer than in many continental countries, and well after the role of late marriage in constraining family size was made logically redundant by contraception (Mason 1994; Szreter 1996).

The developed countries, pioneers in the demographic changes which demolished that old system, all now face an uncertain future (Coleman 1998). A number of questions apply to them all, for example: Will fertility increase to the level required to replace the population? Are high rates of lone parenthood inevitable or sustainable? Can western countries control or adapt to high levels of immigration? Are there limits in sight to the extension of life expectancy?

THE EXPECTATION OF CONVERGENCE

Convergence is an explicit assumption of demographic transition theory, although one seldom elaborated: a stabilization around low rates of birth and death with negligible rates of population growth. On this view, current patterns of diversity merely reflect the different rates at which various societies are moving (Roussel 1994) towards the demographic 'point omega'. If so, then the UK will become demographically indistinguishable from the rest of Europe and the end of demographic history may be in sight. In the publications of the European Union convergence is regarded as a desirable policy aim and a welcome indicator of the minimization of differences in Europe; accordingly, demographic convergence has received explicit attention (European Commission 1995).

The expectation of demographic convergence also follows from wider considerations: that demographic characteristics are primarily determined by economic pressures, and that economic pressures are becoming similar across the industrial world (Kerr 1983; Goldthorpe 1984; Dowrick and Nguyen 1989). If demographic patterns are primarily influenced and constrained by economic realities, then the demographic patterns too will become more uniform (Jones 1993; Ermisch 1996), especially fertility (Roussel 1994) and family type (Goode 1963). Indeed, it is true that populations in all developed countries now have controlled, small families (in some cases very small) and live long lives; and that all face the challenge of ageing.

However, the door is still open to demographic variety at several levels. Not all accept the inevitability of economic convergence. Since the 1980s, further economic convergence in Europe has been modest, although it is the aim of Economic and Monetary Union to speed up this process. Empirical data by no means support an inevitable demographic convergence; some authors assert the opposite in relation to family type (Kuijsten 1996) and fertility (Bosveld 1996). Nor is it accepted that economic forces are pre-eminent in shaping demographic responses in late twentieth-century societies. Instead, cultural or ideational models of demographic change have risen to prominence in response to the inability of economic models to account adequately for demographic heterogeneity (Coale and Watkins 1986; Lesthaeghe and Meekers 1986; Simons 1986; Watkins 1991).

In particular, a series of changes in demographic behaviour, collectively known as the 'second demographic transition', has become marked in some but not all European countries since the 1960s—in divorce, births outside marriage, cohabitation, and the rise of single-parent families. Here the interest resides in the ability of shifts in values to change demographic behaviour in a similar direction. These shifts are not regarded as being entirely random or autonomous. According to Maslow (1954), as developed economies satisfy basic needs and minimize risk through welfare states, secular 'post-material' values emphasizing self-realization and autonomy are expected to gain ground (Inglehart 1977, 1990) at the expense of more conservative values emphasizing duty, responsibility, and order. An emphasis upon personal 'rights and entitlements' prevails over duties, religion, and respect for traditional authority. These changes particularly affect women's attitudes to partnership and to children (van de Kaa 1994; Lesthaeghe 1995), and men's sense of responsibility for children as they become less important as breadwinners and as role differentiation diminishes. The underlying process, however, still depends upon economic change and the acquisition and maintenance of a position of high affluence (de Graaf and Evans 1996), which liberates individual concerns from the avoidance of risk and poverty. With basic comforts assured, at least for the time being, other preferences can unfold.

Put in those terms, the rise of 'post-materialism' and allied attitudes might be assumed to be a convergent process, as it follows from a general achievement of material security which most Europeans have shared. But in fact culture and preferences remain distinctive in different European countries (Inkeles 1997). These differences, when enshrined in law and welfare arrangements through the democratic process, may preserve social and demographic differences, although the triumph of the European Union project may correspondingly diminish them. Some analysts have interpreted the dissimilarities in European health care systems, for example, as a manifestation of differences in their national culture. In order to categorize such diversity, 'families' of nations are proposed, based on the empirical recognition of groups of countries which share similar political cultures and preferences, with distinctive levels of overall taxation and welfare spending (Castles 1993). Such groupings tend to be geographically proximate, and to share common languages or histories, sociopolitical characteristics (Schmidt 1993), and demographic features (Castles and Flood 1993).

Quite independently, empirical demographic and geographical enquiries have shown that countries, or regions of countries, can be clustered on the basis of their demographic characteristics only (Grasland 1990; Decroly and Grasland 1992) in ways that make sense geographically or linguistically. The special demographic characteristics of the Southern European countries have attracted particular attention: high levels of familial proximity and of multi-generation households, combined with low levels of divorce, cohabitation, and births outside marriage (Bettio and Villa 1996). These have been explained as the outcome of limited family welfare and unfavourable labour and housing markets (Tapinos 1996) combined with cultural resistance to childbearing outside marriage and enduring and strongly felt obligations to both family and older relatives. In the course of such work, it has become apparent among other things that the nation-state has become a more statistically powerful focus of demographic variation since the nineteenth century, while regional differences within countries have tended to fall (Coleman 1991; Decroly and Vanlaer 1991; Watkins 1991).

FIRST CATCH YOUR DATA

Let us now turn to the question of Britain's place in all this European demographic turmoil. We immediately encounter an obstacle—that the limitations of appropriate international data seriously restrict the kinds of statistical comparison which can be made. The form and quality of data collected by different countries reflect national social priorities and problems, not the needs of demographers. The UK itself, for example, has difficulty even presenting itself as a statistically unified country. We have three Registrars-General, one each for England and Wales, Scotland, and Northern Ireland, generating data of unequal detail, sophistication, and timeliness. Although the Office for Population Censuses and Surveys (OPCS)—since 1996, the Office for National Statistics (ONS)—produces good data for England and Wales, less is available for the rest of the UK, especially for Northern Ireland, and therefore for the UK as a whole. Some data masquerading as 'UK' data in international publications, for example from Eurostat, in fact refers only to England and Wales. As the country's components move further apart, following recent policy developments, this problem may be assumed to become worse in future.

Existing international data sets, from Eurostat, the Council of Europe (1977), and other sources, which might be a short-cut to instant comparisons, are imperfect. No single existing international database is complete, even for the industrial countries. The provenance and restrictions on some data are inadequately labelled or not annotated at all: for example, it may not be noted whether births refer to legitimate births only (Belgium) or all births (Denmark). Even elementary data on population size from national censuses is often not compatible with time series of intercensal mid-year estimates. Other data can be self-contradictory (for example, mean age at all births less than mean age at first birth). There are particular difficulties in getting comparable data where definitions and law differ internationally, or where data are collected only periodically from surveys or censuses rather than through national registration systems: for example, on households, cohabitation, family planning, and immigration. A few examples only are given in Table 2.1.

These deficiencies inevitably restrict the comparisons that can be made, and rule out some variables, or some countries, from time series analysis. Indeed, one of the surprising findings of this work was the extent to which international demographic data are incompatible, incomplete, or in some cases demographically impossible.

The data set compiled for this project includes 51 developed countries, mostly European, excluding micro-states. It has been relatively easy to obtain population distributions and vital events by five-year age group and sex for each calendar year since 1970. Data on marital status, parity of women, or birth order of children are less satisfactory. Before 1970, and especially before 1960, data become more sparse, available only for census years or not at all. International migration data are inevitably unsatisfactory. Cohort series include completed family size and childlessness. Indices of marriage and divorce are patchy; household data are even more restricted. Death and cause of death data (from WHO), on the other hand, are good, at least since the 1960s. Time series are available on economic data and workforce participation, from the OECD, Penn World Tables, and World Bank; and on married women's employment from Eurostat Labour Force Surveys, the latter only from the 1980s. Data on attitudes and values (Eurobarometer and the World Values Survey) have been acquired from the ESRC Data Archive, and aggregate and individual-level data from the Family and Fertility Surveys from the United Nations Economic Commission for Europe (UN ECE). The wealth of such data may, however, only highlight the problems of obtaining stable measures of behaviour and

TABLE 2.1. *Selected problems of demographic data*

Country	Problem
Albania	Impossible to compute total first marriage rates, divorce rates
Belgium	Data published 3–4 years later than most other countries
France	Data on foreign population only in census years (uneven intervals)
Greece	No divorce, illegitimacy data before 1953; no cohabitation data
Portugal	No data on births outside marriage before 1960; population totals irregular
Romania	No data on births outside marriage before 1975
Former Soviet Union	No household data at all collected before 1992; fertility indices etc. only for irregular years for Ukraine, Belarus
United Kingdom	Fertility data incomplete before 1960 (Northern Ireland); misleading immigration data; odd definition of 'foreign population'
Former Yugoslavia	Data for 'modern' Yugoslavia must be recalculated before 1992; no data on Bosnia after 1992

attitudes: estimates of ideal family size in the 1990s, for example, are often (Switzerland, Sweden), but not always (Norway, Spain), considerably higher in the World Values Survey than in the Family and Fertility Surveys. Table 2.2 provides information about some of the sources used to compile the study's data set.

Selected extracts are held on an SPSS flat file with 2,550 'cases' (51

TABLE 2.2. *Some sources of data*

Source	Type of data	Comment
National VR, Censuses	General	
Alan Guttmacher Institute	Abortion	Covers Eastern and Western Europe
Council of Europe	General	Demographic Yearbook and 'DSSD' database; much data at only 5-year intervals
Eurostat	General	Demographic Yearbook and 'CUB-X' database of member states. No data before 1960. Special computation basis (Calot method). REGIO regional database: simple NUTS statistics. European Household Panel Survey. European Labour Force Surveys
Eurobarometer	Attributes	Includes individual-level data on attitudes and demographic characteristics.
Informal Consultations on Asylum	Asylum statistics	Covers almost all developed countries
OECD	Migration, economy	SOPEMI annual reports; Economic statistics
UN ECE	Aggregate and individual-level	Family and Fertility Surveys (selected European countries)
US Bureau of the Census	General	International Database, comprehensive
World Bank	Economic	
World Health Organization	Mortality	Health for All dataset
World Values Survey	Attitudes; some demographic behaviour; aggregate and individual-level data	
Mannheim Centre	General	Available only by special request
Penn World Tables	Economic	

countries nominally for each calendar year 1945–95), each with potentially about 1,300 variables (but with many blank spaces). For convenience, some socio-economic and other data are held in a parallel data set with the same format. Some of these data have been used below to give a very preliminary comparison of Britain in Europe. Wherever possible UK data are used. Most comparisons are with Western Europe only, as the position in Eastern and Central Europe is so aberrant. European averages are the unweighted averages of country-level data, as the aim is to compare Britain with the average European country, not the average European person. Each figure below is from several sources: Eurostat, council of Europe, national data, except where indicated.

SOME RESULTS

Population size, age, and structure

The UK's population (58.5 million in 1996) has been one of the 'big four' in Europe throughout the twentieth century, now marginally ahead of France and Italy but a long way behind Germany (81.5 million) and slowly losing ground, although it will remain second in Europe for the foreseeable future (Figure 2.1). Only Spain (39.2 million in 1995), and Poland and Romania in Eastern Europe (38.6 and 22.7 million respectively), come close elsewhere in Europe outside the former Soviet Union. No other Western European country exceeds 16 million (Netherlands); several are 5 million or less (Denmark, Finland, Ireland). Although the UK's population growth rate (0.36 per cent per year in 1995) has increased in recent years, it is quite modest compared with some Western European countries. This may seem paradoxical. Despite over twenty years of below-replacement fertility, UK natural increase (the annual excess of births over deaths) is still positive, exceeded only by that of France in 1995. Thanks to very low birth rates, deaths now (1995) exceed births in Italy and Germany. This is also true in a number of East European countries for somewhat different reasons, following the increase of (already high) death rates and the collapse of birth rates after 1990. The reason for these apparent contradictions is that in Western Europe, remaining population growth is increasingly driven by immigration, exclusively so in Germany, which has for many years been Europe's biggest immigrant destination, regular, irregular (asylum claimants), and illegal, with effects which are apparent in Figure 2.1. The last cohort of Germans to replace themselves was born in 1936. Elsewhere in Western Europe, net immigration has also grown substantially since the 1980s and revived population growth, but nowhere on the same scale as Germany.

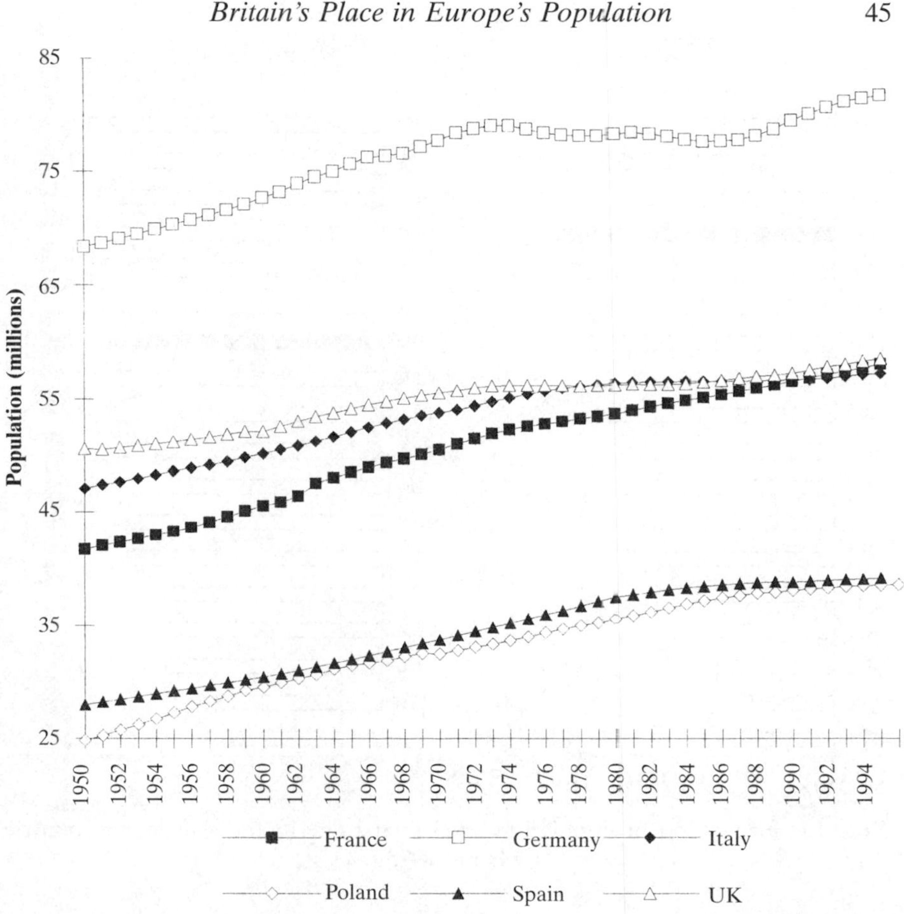

FIG. 2.1 Trends in population size, selected European countries, 1950–1995

The UK population structure was for many years, with Sweden's, the oldest in Europe. Thanks to that, much of the pain of population ageing in the UK is already over: the proportion of the UK population aged over 64 trebled from 1901 to 1996. In 1996 it was 15.7 per cent, not far below that proportion (22 per cent) generated by a stable population structure implied by the continuation of 1996 fertility and mortality rates. Because most European birth rates are now lower than ours, the UK's proportion of people aged 65 and over and its aged dependency ratio—(population 65 and over/population 15–64) * 100—has become more like the European average (15.3 per cent for 15 countries). The proportion of the UK population over age 64 in 1996 was exceeded not only by Sweden and Norway but also by Italy, Belgium, Spain, and Greece (Figure 2.2). In the 1970s, the two latter countries and Italy had relatively youthful age-structures, now

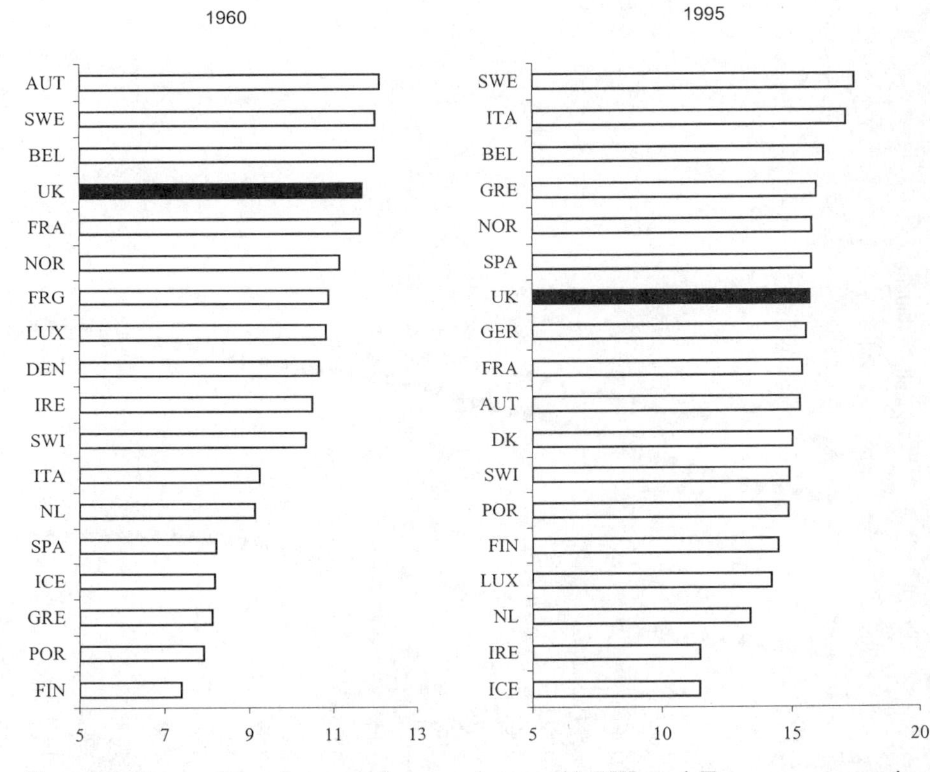

FIG. 2.2 Proportion of population aged over 64, UK and European countries, 1960 and 1995 (%)

dissipated by nearly two decades of very low fertility. Dependency ratios have moved in a somewhat different way. The youth dependency ratio—(population 0–14/population 15–65) * 100—has changed little in the UK in recent years and consequently has risen relative to the rest of Europe, where fertility has fallen further as noted below. The UK aged dependency ratio has changed little in relation to the rest of Europe since the 1960s, remaining almost one standard deviation above the European average.

There are many measures of population ageing; median age summarizes the balance between all parts of the age structure. On that basis, the UK is now merely average (Figure 2.3). Western European countries have now caught up with our median age (35 for males, 38 for females) and the UK stands tenth, behind Greece among others. As most of continental Europe's birth rates are lower than ours and have been for some time, their median age and relative numbers of elderly will continue to increase. In future, the UK population will be in the unusual position of being more

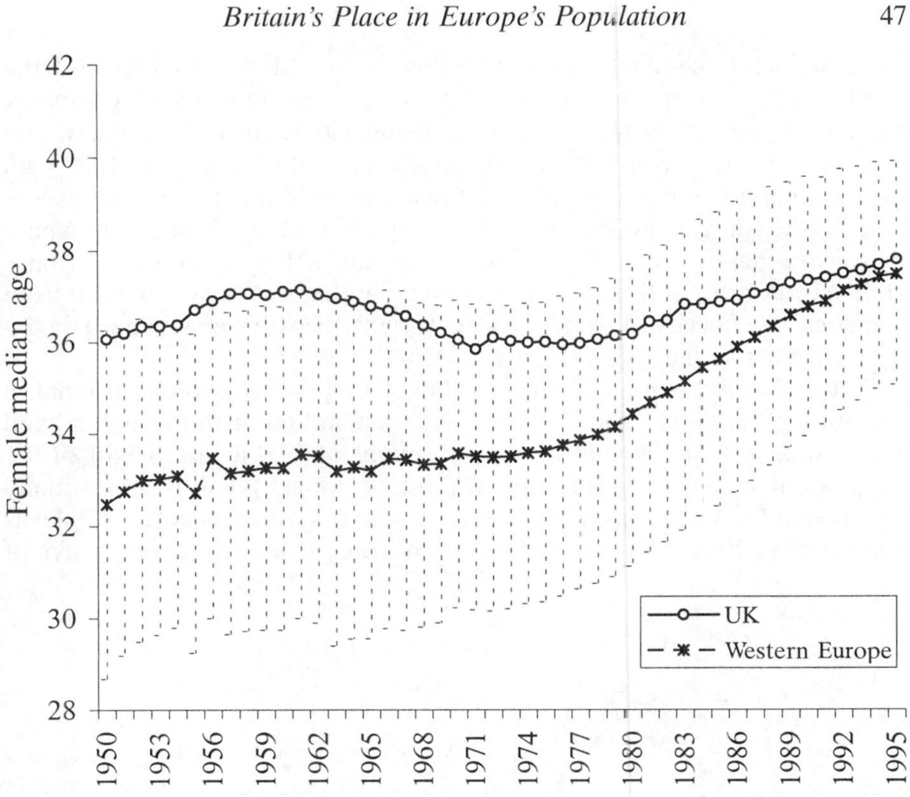

FIG. 2.3 Median age of female population, UK and West European average
Note: Dashed lines indicate one standard deviation each side of average

youthful than the European average. These ageing trends will exacerbate the well-known problem of paying for Europe's retirement pensions, which are sustained much less by funded schemes than is the case in the UK (Daykin 1997). The UK should be better protected by its demography than most other European countries although it is claimed that the UK's involvement in the EU may increasingly expose the UK taxpayer to paying for Europe's ageing (Stein 1997).

Fertility

The British birth rate, despite relatively high levels of childlessness, has been relatively and constantly high for over twenty years—equivalent to a family size of 1.8 children per woman—while birth rates have fallen in many other parts of Europe. Consequently, Britain now belongs to the European high-fertility club of mostly Scandinavian countries plus France and Ireland, sharply differentiated from the low-fertility area surrounding

Germany and the ultra-low birth rates of the Mediterranean and the Central and Eastern European states. In the Mediterranean countries, birth rates started to fall at the end of the 1970s. In many Eastern and Central European countries, birth rates fell precipitously from 1990 with the end of Communist certainties. Until about 1977, fertility in the UK was close to the (unweighted) European average. Since then, fertility elsewhere in Europe has fallen further, while in Britain it has remained constant. Hence birth rates in Britain, unexceptional in the past, have emerged from statistical mediocrity to become more deviant: by over one standard deviation for most of the 1980s (Figure 2.4).

British fertility is not only higher than average, it is also exceptional in Europe by its relative youthfulness. Mean age at first birth in England and Wales was 26.5 in 1994, up from a low point of 23.9 at the height of the baby boom in 1964 (Armitage and Babb 1996: table 2). This is substantially lower than the West European average age at first birth, which in 1994 was approaching 29 years. These data relate to true birth order (irrespective of

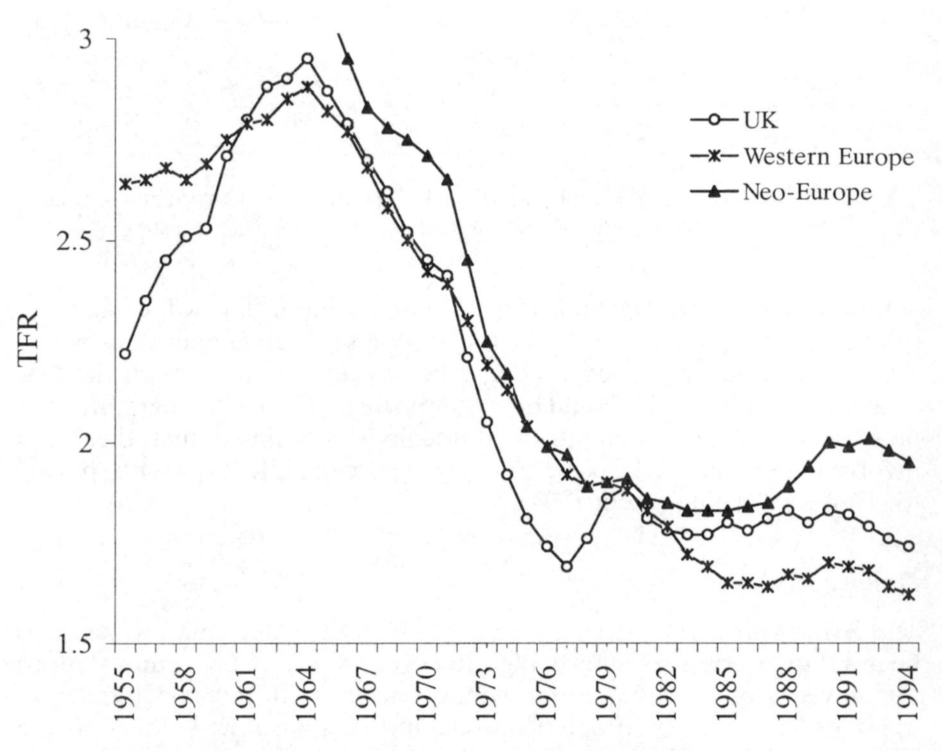

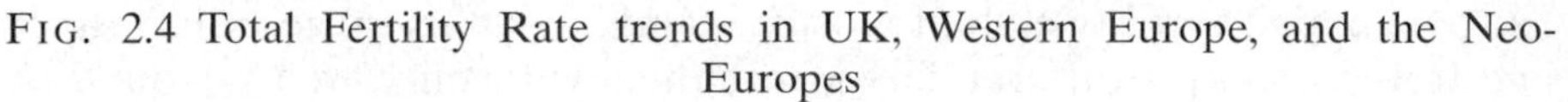
FIG. 2.4 Total Fertility Rate trends in UK, Western Europe, and the Neo-Europes

the marital status of the mother) unlike most routine birth-order data for England and Wales, which relates to legitimate births only.

Teenage motherhood is one of the most characteristic British demographic features. The rate of teenage births (mostly illegitimate) is about four times the West European average and is way outside the normal European variation (Figure 2.5). Teenage birth rates in Britain, about 30 per 1,000 since the mid-1970s, changed little in twenty years while the fertility rates of women in their twenties, here and abroad, have fallen substantially. That has caused the profile of British fertility rates to diverge further from the regular pattern characteristic of the 1960s and of some European countries today. It also inflates general fertility. Without this extra teenage fertility, most of which is unplanned, the UK's total fertility rate (TFR) would be below 1.7, somewhat closer to the European average.

Since the 1970s, the UK age-specific fertility rate profile has developed an asymmetrical bulge up to age 24 compared with most other European countries, a feature even more pronounced in the Republic of Ireland.

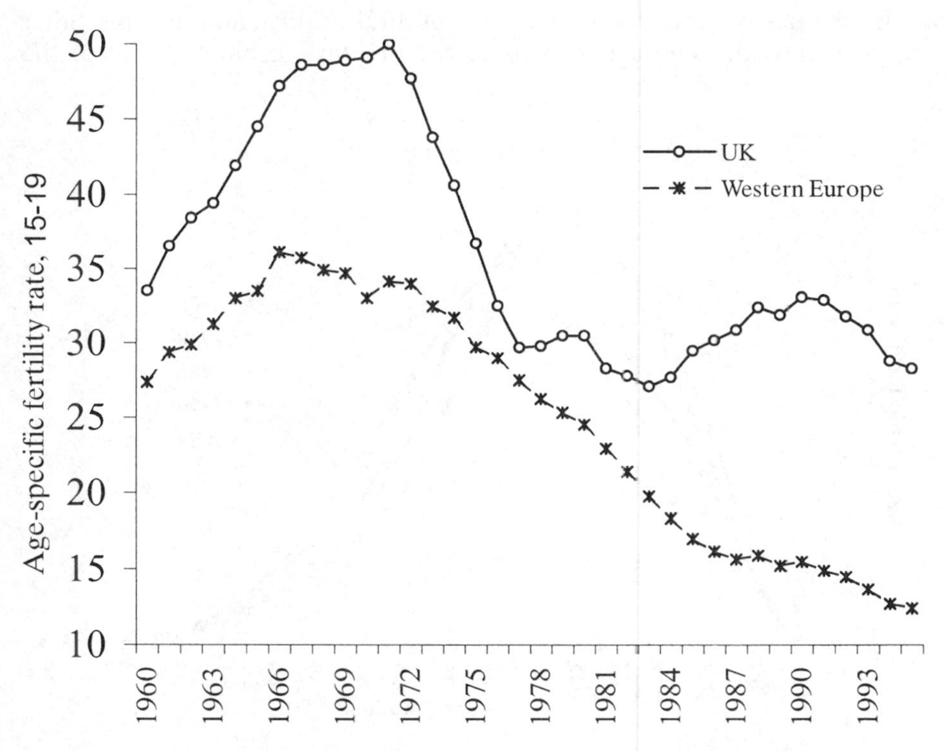

FIG. 2.5 Teenage fertility rates, UK and Western Europe

Note: Dashed lines indicated on standard deviation each side of W. Europe average.

Switzerland, France, Denmark, and Finland have a much more regular profile. By the 1990s, a number of European countries (for example, Switzerland, France, and Finland) had developed fairly symmetrical, smooth age distributions of fertility easily fitted by a three-parameter Hadwiger fertility function (Gilje 1972). However, higher fertility up to age 24 in some countries, notably the UK and Ireland, and to a lesser extent in Germany and elsewhere, generates a more complex curve representing a 'mixture' of two populations. In the UK, this more complex fertility distribution, best modelled as a combination of two populations with different age-schedules of childbearing, can be discerned from about 1975 (Figure 2.6). Before then the age-specific profile was a smooth curve resembling that of other countries. Now the distribution looks heterogeneous, as if the fertility of two populations co-existed: one retaining the precocious fertility of the 1960s, the other behaving similarly to the rest of Europe. Further work is in progress to see if the model parameters can be identified as real demographic variables and so identify the characteristics of the two 'populations' implied by the model (Chandola, Coleman, and Hiorns in press).

In its relatively high and relatively youthful fertility, and in some other respects, UK behaviour has in some recent years resembled that of the

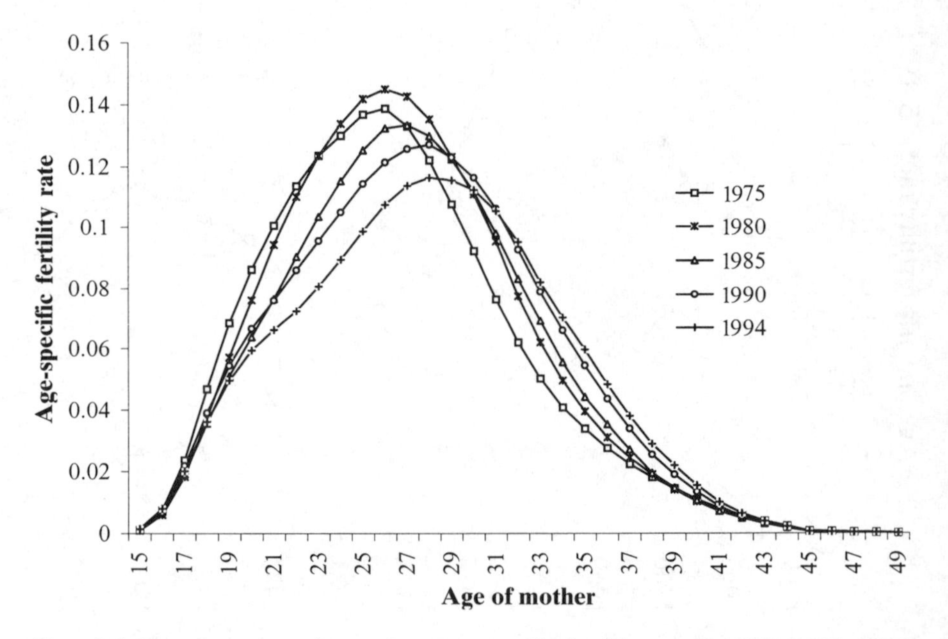

FIG. 2.6 Development of complex age-specific fertility profile, UK, 1975–1994
Source: Eurostat

Neo-Europes (the English-speaking countries overseas: the US, Canada, Australia, and New Zealand, particularly the last) more than it does many other European countries. Overall, fertility in Britain is intermediate between the European and Neo-European average, moving more towards the latter up to the end of the 1980s, and towards the former more recently (Figure 2.4). In respect of teenage fertility, however, Britain is much closer to the Neo-Europes. There, the age-specific fertility rate for females 15–19 is also high: 20.5 (per 1,000 births) in Australia (1995), 24.7 in Canada (1994), 34.0 in New Zealand (1995), and 56.8 (50 for whites) in the US (1995). The illegitimacy ratios of those countries are also of a similar order to the British 1995 level of 336: 277, 346, 407, and 322 respectively (the illegitimacy ratio is conventionally defined as the number of live births outside marriage per 1,000 live births per year).

In the 1990s, over 30 per cent of births in the UK have been outside marriage. The UK rate has risen well above the West European mean and, along with a few other countries such as France and Ireland, has been increasing faster than the rest of Europe since around 1978 (Figure 2.7).

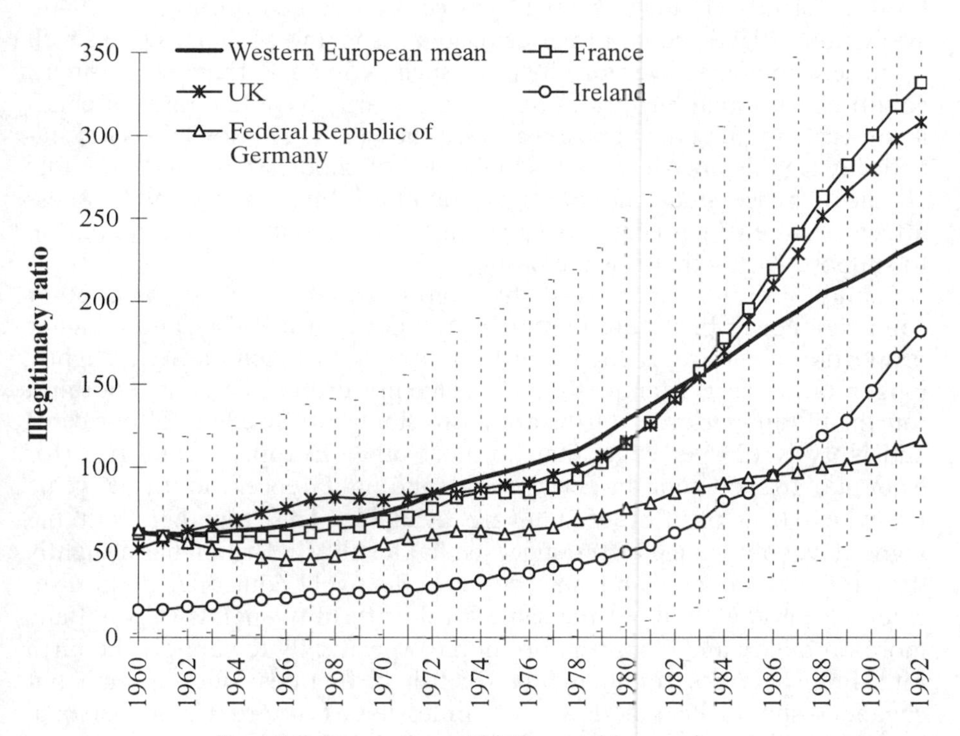

FIG. 2.7 Proportion of births outside marriage

Note: Dashed lines indicate one standard deviation each side of W. European mean.

The level in Britain is higher than the European average: less than Scandinavia, about the same as France, twice as high as in Germany or the Netherlands, over four times the level in Italy or Switzerland. Before the late 1970s, it was little different from the rest of Europe and hardly increased at all in the decade 1967–76. The increase is far from uniform in continental Europe: in the Mediterranean countries, especially Greece, the proportion of births outside marriage is increasing much less fast than the European average and in the last-named country still only accounts for about 3 per cent of births. In Britain as elsewhere, much of the increase has come from couples who are cohabiting (see McRae 1993). However, such 'stable informal unions', while certainly informal, are not particularly stable, dissolving at a much higher rate than equivalent marriages, and if followed by marriage being more prone to end in divorce.

Voluntary childlessness is a major issue facing all European countries (McAllister and Clarke 1998). Although birth rates in Britain may be higher than the European average, more women in Britain born in the 1940s have remained childless (over 15 per cent and rising in later cohorts) than in most other countries, including those with about the same average level of fertility (France, about 11 per cent of women born in the 1940s: Toulemon 1995; Sweden, 13 per cent: Johansson and Möller 1992) as well as those with much lower fertility rates, such as Spain. Perhaps surprisingly, countries with high birth rates do not necessarily have low rates of childlessness; if anything the opposite exists, although the relationship is not statistically significant. Most of this high level of childlessness, and probably all the increase since the 1950s, is voluntary. Involuntary childlessness affects between 5 per cent and 8 per cent of couples and there is no reason to suppose—yet—that it is increasing.

Family size in Britain is slightly more varied than in some other countries. Fewer births are first births (39 per cent in 1994), and a higher proportion are third or higher order (24 per cent), generating a slightly longer 'tail' of larger families than average in Europe. Percentage of third, fourth, and higher-order births are more similar to Sweden (24 per cent) and Norway (23 per cent) than to most other European countries (for example, 18 per cent in Switzerland and in Greece), in those years for which true birth-order data are available. This, together with the higher level of teenage births, suggests that fertility in Britain has a slightly 'free-range' character and may be less effectively controlled than elsewhere. France, with about the same level of fertility, spends substantially more on family and child support, in part specifically to support the birth rate. French critics complain that British birth rates—just as high but cheaper—should be put down to carelessness (Gérard Calot, personal communication).

Households, families, and their breakdown

European countries differ more strongly in their favoured living arrangements—marriage, cohabitation, separation—and in their consequences—births outside marriage and lone-parent families—than in any other demographic characteristic. Proportions cohabiting in Britain in the 1990s, although higher than in Germany and Austria, were barely half those in Scandinavian countries or in France (Kiernan 1996). Cohabitation delays or displaces marriage, as in many other Northern (but not Southern) European countries. But in Britain divorce is also extremely powerful. In terms of simple measures such as the crude divorce rate (divorces per 1,000 population) and divorces per 1,000 marriages each year, England and Wales is clearly first in Europe (Figure 2.8). The more subtle measure of total divorce rate (which estimates the cumulative number of divorces per person at current rates) shows England and Wales to have been jostling for first position with Sweden and Denmark over the last twenty years.

In consequence of these competitive rates of destruction of conventional family life, in recent years Britain has had the highest proportion in the European Union (15 per cent) of children living in lone-parent families—double the EU average and matched only by Denmark. In 1994, about a quarter of all families with dependent children (that is, those aged under 16) in the UK were headed by a lone parent, two to three times the level in countries such as the Netherlands and Germany (Figure 2.9). Otherwise British household structure is typical of the rest of North-western Europe, with small average size (2.5 persons) and few households (6 per cent) extending beyond the nuclear family to include other relatives, a pattern still relatively common in Southern Europe (20 per cent in Greece in 1994: Eurostat 1996). Thanks in part to a relatively elderly population, the proportion of households comprising just one person in Britain is at the high end of the European distribution—27 per cent in 1991—about the same as in France and Belgium but about double that in Greece (16 per cent) and Portugal (14 per cent).

Mortality

A century ago death rates in Britain were the lowest in Europe except for a few small rural countries (Ireland, Scandinavia). Now, as measured by expectation of life at birth, they are statistically relatively mediocre although they continue to fall in absolute terms for both sexes. For about twenty years now, male expectation of life at birth in Britain (now 73 years) has only just been keeping up with the European average. Women's mortality rates in the UK, exceptionally high from breast cancer, although improving in absolute terms, have in relative terms been deteriorating compared with those in the rest of Europe (Figure 2.10). UK rates of infant mortality continue to fall regularly in absolute terms but slipped from being lower than the European average in 1960 to higher by the end of the 1980s, although there has been some recovery of position since. Infant mortality rates are almost everywhere exceptionally low—under 6 per 1,000 births per year—and their further reduction through increasingly heroic measures may bring further problems in its wake.

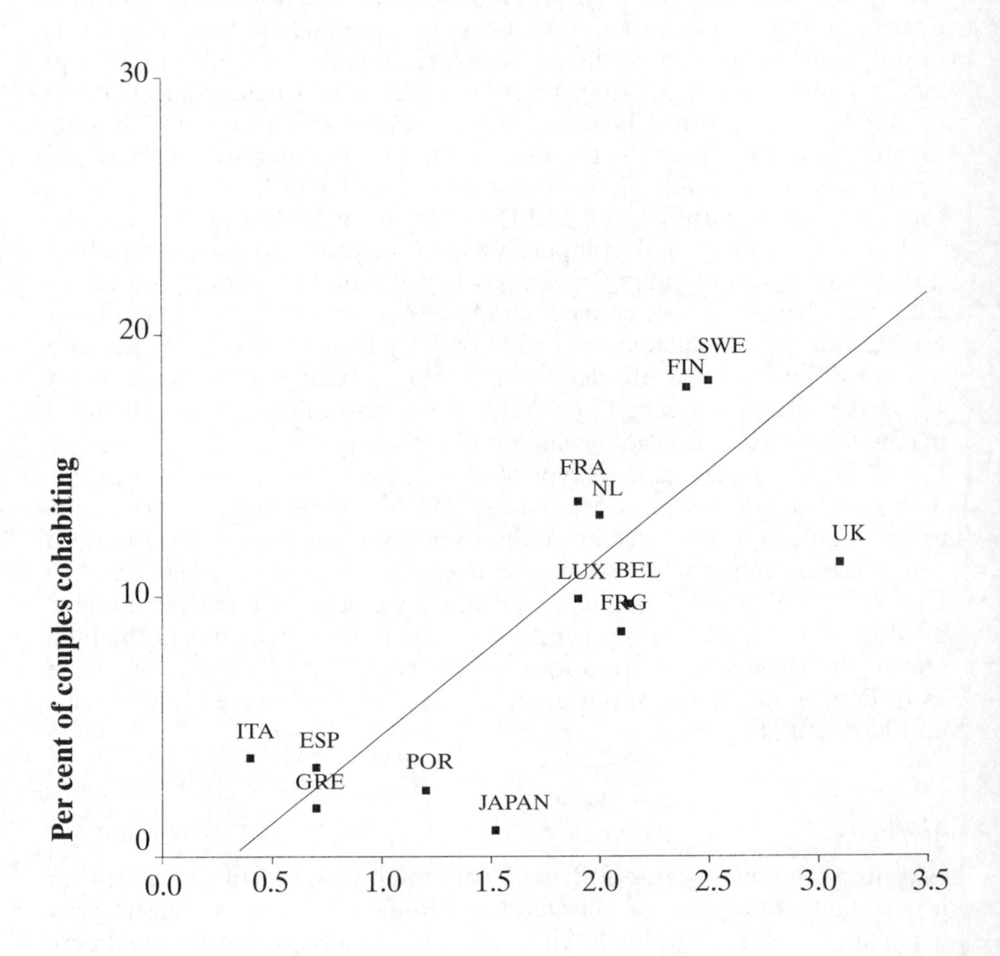

Note: $R^2 = 0.5640$.

FIG. 2.8 Scattergram of proportions cohabiting and crude divorce rate

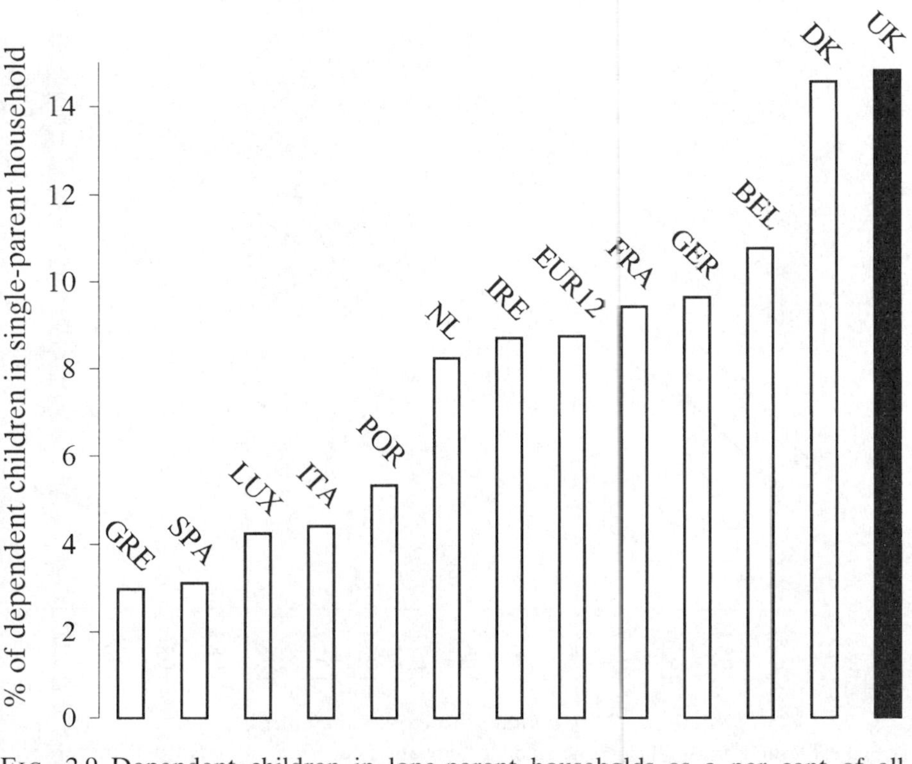

FIG. 2.9 Dependent children in lone-parent households as a per cent of all dependent children, 1994
Source: European Household Panel Survey

Men's mortality in Britain is characterized by a relatively high, although falling, level of deaths from heart disease and respiratory disease, especially in Scotland and Northern Ireland, where Western Europe's highest rates are found. The pattern of mortality in Britain is distinctive in other ways. For example, Britain leads the world in survival to age 50, a period of life when deaths by accident and violence are front-runners. UK driving habits, notably different from those in most of continental Europe, keep the road traffic accident death rate exceptionally low. Homicide is also relatively uncommon. Before age 50 in France for example, these two causes of death cancel out low death rates from other causes.

Immigration and ethnic minorities

Since the mid-1980s, all Western European countries have experienced renewed immigration pressure, partly from Eastern Europe but mostly

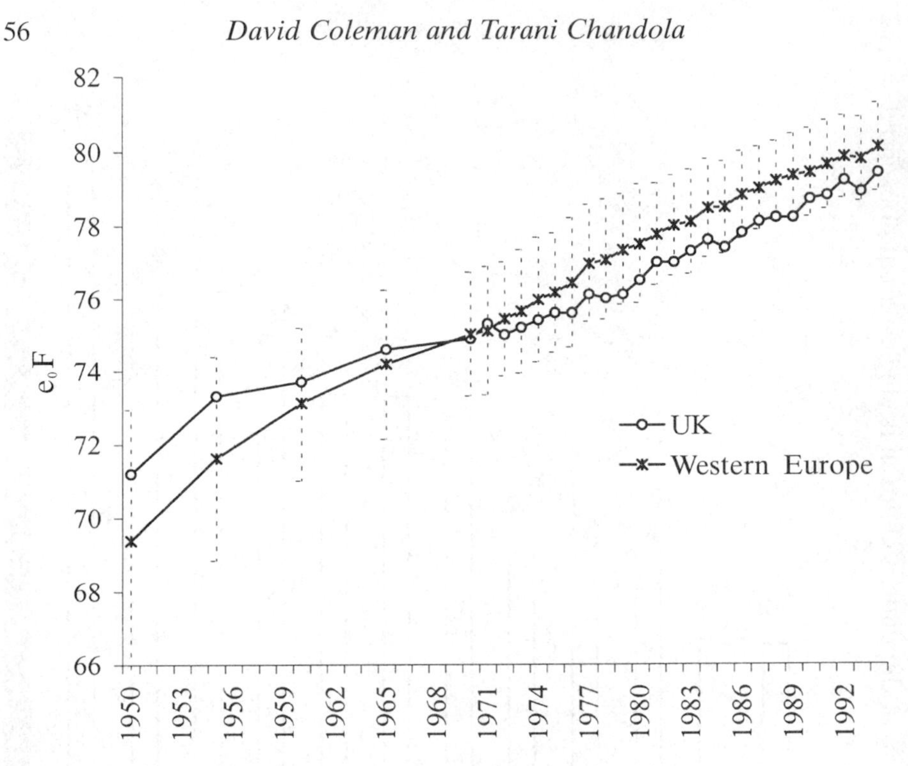

FIG. 2.10 Female life expectancy at birth
Note: Dashed lines indicate one standard deviation each side of W. European average

from the Third World. The UK was no exception. The claims from official and race relations sources that immigration to the UK has been declining, which seem to be widely accepted in the media and elsewhere, are without foundation. All components of international migration increased up to about 1992: legal (work permit, family re-unification, family formation), asylum claiming, and illegal immigration (asylum claimants are immigrants in the demographic sense as, in the UK as throughout Europe, most claimants intend to stay indefinitely and most succeed in staying even though most claims for asylum are rejected). Since about 1992, immigration and asylum claiming have peaked or been reversed elsewhere in Western Europe (OECD 1997), although illegal immigration may have increased in partial compensation. This is not so in the UK.

The UK is unusual in Europe in experiencing continued substantial increases in both legal immigration and asylum claims into the mid-1990s, although asylum claims declined temporarily in 1996 before increasing again in 1997 and 1998 (Figure 2.11). From being a relatively unfavoured destination up to 1988, since 1995 the UK has been Western Europe's

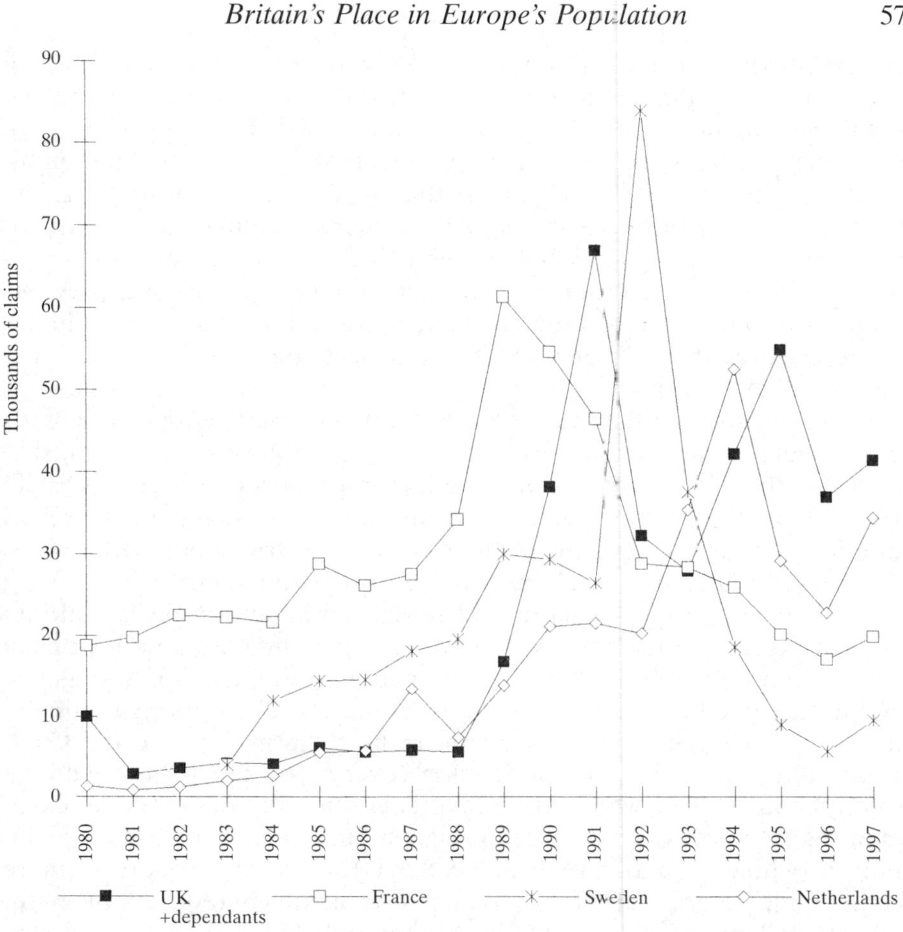

FIG. 2.11 Trends in asylum claims, UK and selected European countries
Sources: Inter-governmental Consultations, Geneva, and Home Office asylum statistics.

prime destination for asylum claimants after Germany, with 42,000 claims in 1997 including dependants (Home Office 1998). The cumulative total of about 400,000 claims represents at least 300,000 people, of whom most are believed still to be in the UK. In the first quarter of 1998, the number of claims was 18 per cent higher than in the same quarter in 1997. Despite some controversial amendments to asylum procedures, UK measures are clearly much less effective than those implemented recently in other European countries.

Annual net additions to the population from international migration have correspondingly increased, from an estimated 35,000 in 1992 to

109,000 in 1995—a net addition of 647,000 people in the decade. This is a substantial contribution to population growth and is partly behind the notable 4.4 million projected increase of households by 2017 (DoE 1995), which has caused so much political trouble. However, as actual net immigration in 1994 and 1995 was double that assumed in the projections, the next household projections should see a further substantial increase in projected population and household growth. The 1996-based population projections envisage an additional increase of 1.1 million people over previous projections, almost entirely due to the adoption of higher annual net immigration figures (65,000 per year) which at least partly reflect recent net inflows (Shaw 1998).

Recent figures put the UK second to Germany (but a long way behind) in absolute terms among European immigration-receiving countries, although the UK is closer to the average in proportional terms (OECD 1997). Migration figures are notoriously difficult to compare, however. Immigration has changed the composition of the British population since the Second World War, as in many other European countries, by creating large ethnic minority populations of recent immigrant origin (a majority of such persons in the UK in 1991 were, in fact, immigrants). European comparison is complicated by different national definitions of 'foreigners' and in the ease or difficulty of naturalization. The UK's 'foreign' population of 3.4 per cent in 1995 does not include the majority of the Commonwealth ethnic minority population (over 5 per cent of the national total), about half of whom are immigrants but most of whom, as Commonwealth citizens, were never 'foreigners' in a legal sense. Their inclusion, in whole or part, would make the UK 'foreign' proportion more comparable to that of France (6.3 per cent; much reduced by naturalization: Tribalat *et al.* 1991), the Netherlands (5.0 per cent), and even Germany (8.8 per cent).

A SUMMARY VIEW

Taking all this into account, where does the UK belong in Europe? Is the UK a European team player or semi-detached Anglo-Saxon or Scandinavian outlier? Is it at the 'heart of Europe', as former Prime Minister John Major used to claim, or distinguished more by its excessive level of myocardial infarction? Taking demographic characteristics in pairs, Britain's fertility and mortality, divorce rate and illegitimacy ratio place it in a distinct Scandinavian/Northern European cluster by 1990, although not far from France in Western Europe, as if Harold had lost at Stamford Bridge and not at Hastings (Figure 2.12). The first pair reflect 'first demographic transition' variables, the second pair are more of interest in the context of the

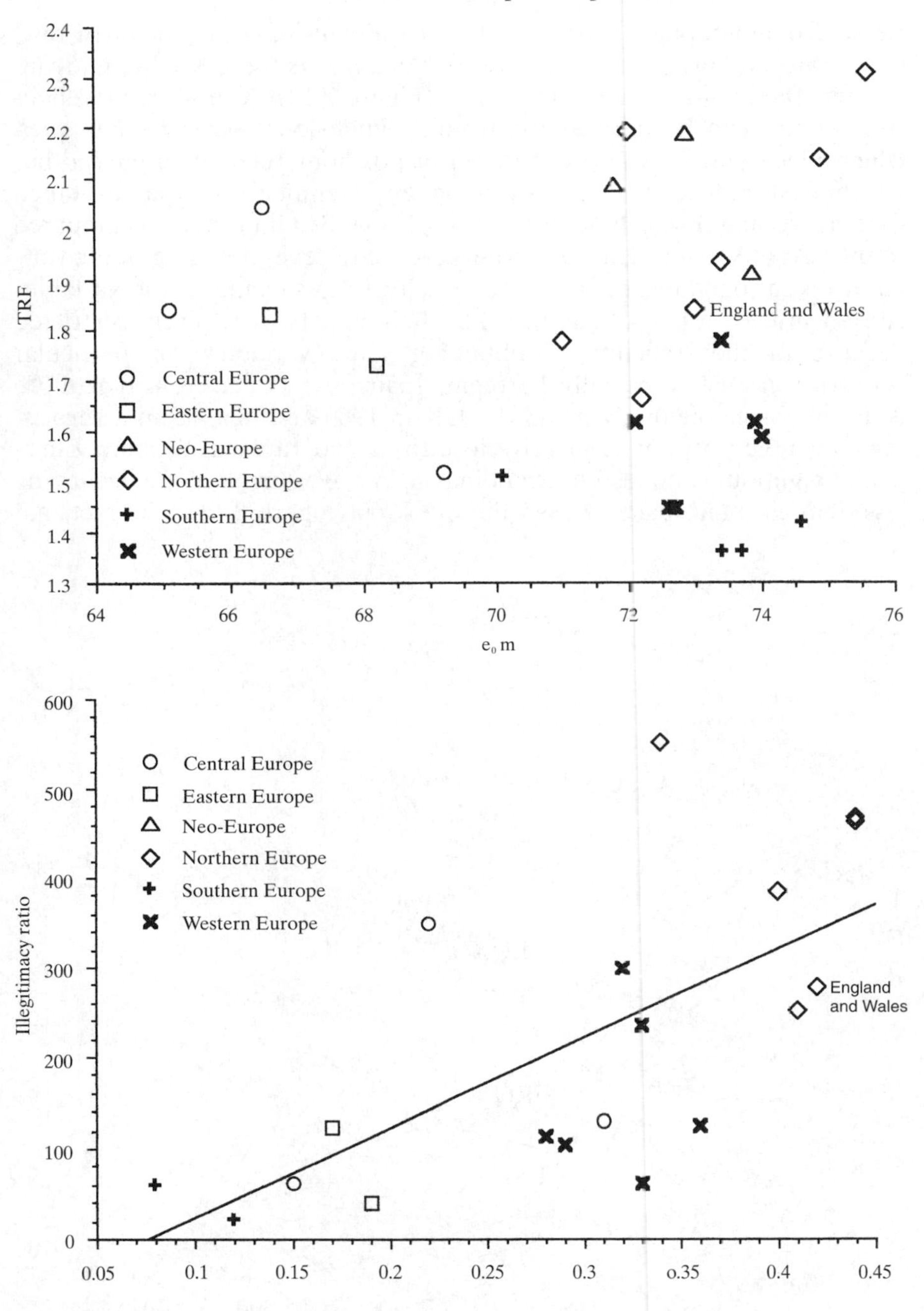

Note: Illegitimacy ratio = -74.365 + 990.881 .Total Divorce Rate; R^2 = 0.449.

FIG. 2.12 Bivariate plots of Britain's relative position on fertility and mortality, births outside marriage, and divorce.

'second demographic transition'. A three-dimensional plot of birth rate, death rate, and illegitimacy ratio in 1995 again puts the UK close to Scandinavia, the Neo-Europes, and France (Figure 2.13). A more comprehensive picture can be derived from multi-dimensional scaling techniques, which place entities (here countries) in positions relative to each other which best reflect their similarity on any number of variables taken together. Using this technique, we can see how Britain is placed compared to the rest of Western Europe with reference to several demographic variables taken together and weighted equally. In this example, the variables chosen are as noted in Figure 2.14. Their variety is severely restricted because of the difficulty of obtaining some variables for particular countries in 1960, especially Portugal, Spain, and Greece. On that more comprehensive picture, we find the UK in 1960 and in 1995 in a surprisingly average position, relatively close to its geographical Western European neighbours and also to Scandinavia, in a Western Europe occupying less demographic space in 1995 than in 1960 (Figure 2.14). The fact that

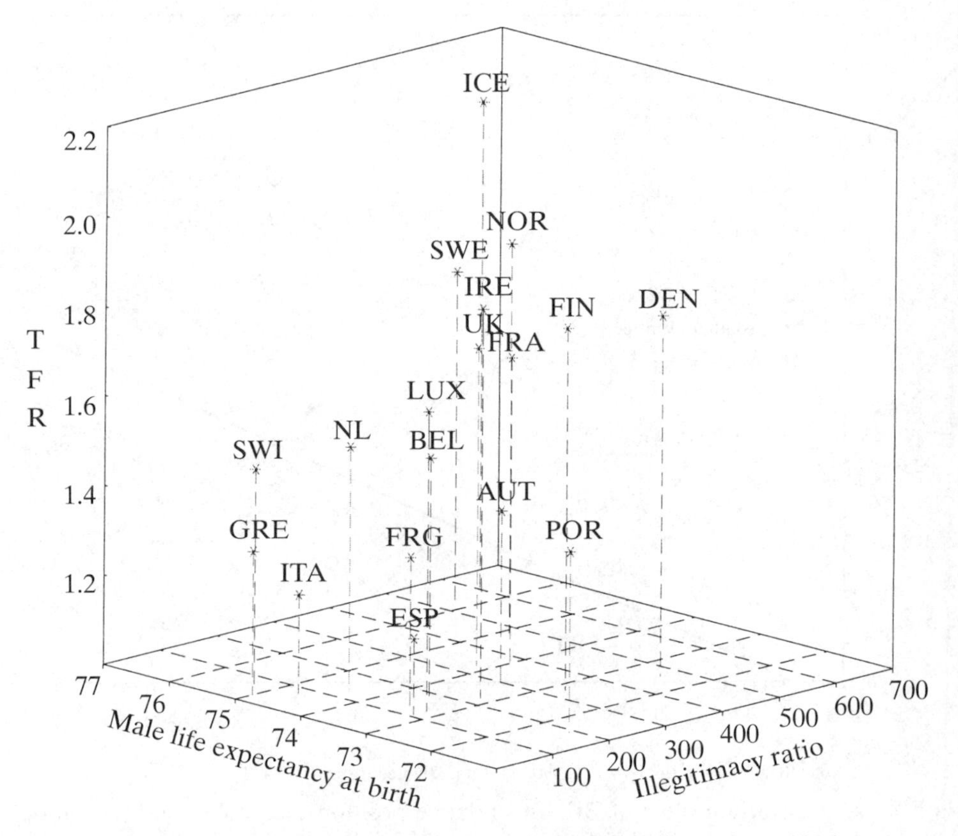

FIG. 2.13 Britain's position in Europe in three dimensions, 1995

the countries are in general closer together in 1995 than in 1960 on this plot reflects the fact that some convergence has occurred over thirty-five years, notably in mortality and age-structure.

That general tendency, however, conceals some simplification and a number of opposing trends. First, some of the variables which distinguish Britain from its neighbours, notably in household structure and age patterns of fertility, cannot be included in the analysis because they are not available for some of the eighteen countries in 1960. Also, some previously distinctive British demographic features have gone. We saw earlier that the rest of Europe is moving towards an older age-structure more like that of Britain. Some features which were favourably distinctive in the 1960s, such as infant mortality and expectation of life, have become either statistically average or, in the case of women, distinctively unfavourable. The British

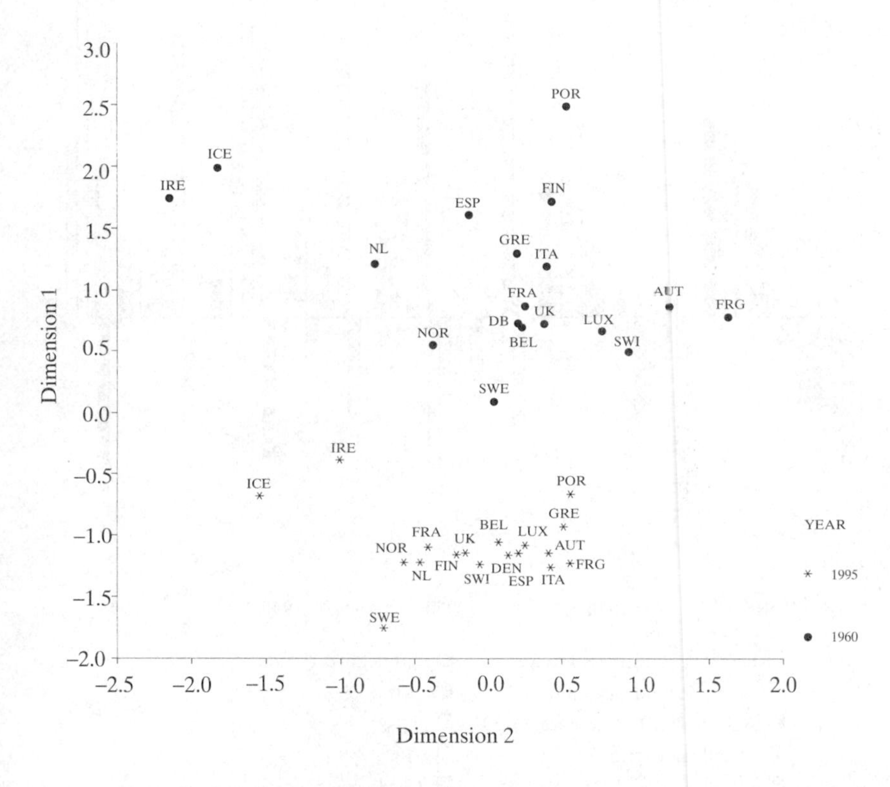

Note: Variables include: natural increase rate, net immigration rate, dependency ratio for aged and youth, per cent of population aged 15–64, median age difference between sexes, TFR, per cent of births to mothers under age 30, illegitimacy ratio, crude marriage and divorce rate, e_0f, e_0m, IMR.

FIG. 2.14 Multi-dimensional scaling plot of Britain's place in Europe, 1960 and 1995

position in the European demographic space has shared many recent trends. Where it is distinctive in recent years is in respect of unfavourable rather than favourable characteristics (Figure 2.15). Britain is now exceptional in Western Europe in respect of high teenage births, lone-parent

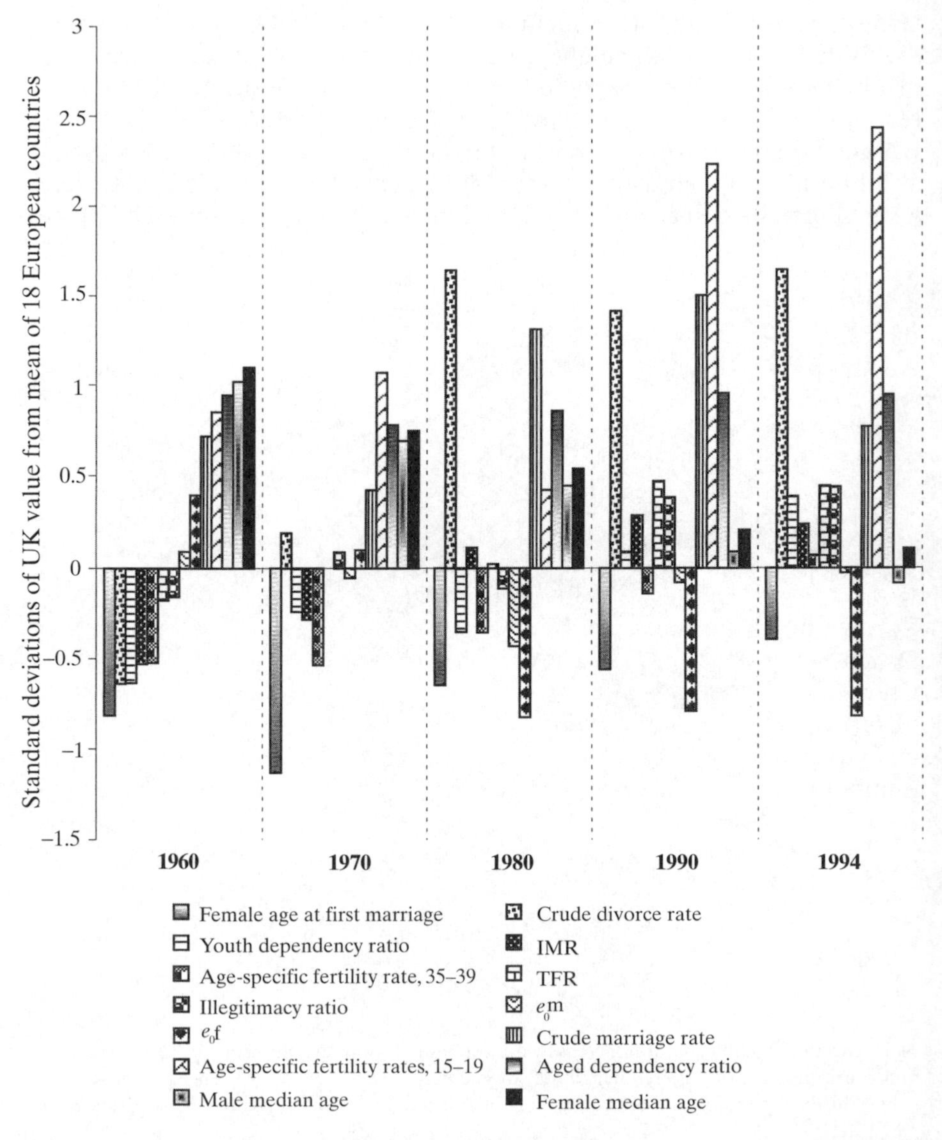

FIG. 2.15 UK differences from mean West European demographic indicators, 1960–1994 (in standard deviations)

families, and divorce and in its upward trends in immigration and asylum. Few of these changes are neutral. They reflect, over the last thirty or forty years, a failure to maintain previously higher relative standards of health and of family stability. The trends in teenage births suggest that important sections of Britain's population have experienced the sexual revolution in a less responsible or educated fashion than have the teenagers on the Continent—problems which we appear to share with the English-speaking counties overseas. These are all issues of public interest. To an extent which is (to these authors) rather alarming, Britain's distinctiveness in European demography, which once mirrored a leading position in Europe's society and economy, now instead reflects Britain's disadvantage.

There is some evidence for Western European countries becoming demographically somewhat more similar overall. They have, however, become much more internally homogeneous in their demographic characteristics and since the last war 'countries' have become statistically more important in accounting for demographic variability. With devolution in the air, it should be noted that the UK (even with the high fertility of Northern Ireland) is one of the most demographically homogeneous countries in Europe in respect of its birth rate; regional variation in England and Wales is by far the lowest of any major country for which data are available (Table 2.4).

THE SEARCH FOR EXPLANATION

Can we begin to make sense of these distinctive differences in terms of possible causal factors? At the moment the answer is probably no, and only a few general comments will be offered here. While socio-economic models of fertility (for example, models based on workforce participation (especially of women), employment, and GDP) can fit the fertility trends of a number of individual countries over time (Ermisch 1996), in recent years

TABLE 2.3. *Britain and the Neo-Europes compared: age-specific fertility and births outside marriage*

	Fertility rate, per thousand women aged 15–19	Illegitimacy ratio
Britain	30.0	336
Australia	20.5	277
Canada	24.7	346
New Zealand	34.0	407
USA	56.8	322

TABLE 2.4. *Variation of total fertility rate (TFR), UK and other selected countries, 1990s*

Country	Year	Population (millions)	Number of provinces	Mean population of provinces	Unweighted mean TFR	Coefficient of variation of TFR
Sweden	1993	8.692	8	1.087	2.01	4.24
UK	1994	58.293	11	5.299	1.75	4.73
Czechoslovakia	1991	15.661	2	7.831	1.96	6.72
Belgium	1992	10.022	9	1.114	1.62	6.86
Switzerland	1989	6.620	26	0.255	1.83	6.98
France	1990	56.577	22	2.572	1.75	7.65
Germany (Federal Republic)	1985	61.020	11	5.547	1.25	8.01
Netherlands	1991	15.010	12	1.251	1.65	8.63
USSR (Europe)	1990	218.107	7	31.158	2.02	8.70
Japan	1994	124.069	46	2.697	1.58	8.94
Canada	1994	29.251	9	3.250	1.70	9.77
Yugoslavia	1989	23.818	6	3.970	1.82	12.10
Spain	1987	38.667	17	2.275	1.45	16.20
Italy	1990	56.712	20	2.836	1.29	19.06
Median		33.959	11	2.766	1.73	8.32
Total		722.519	206			

Sources: national statistical yearbooks.

the cross-sectional relationship has disappeared when several countries are compared at one point in time. In other words, these variables can no longer account for international differences in fertility and therefore cannot account for the UK's special position. Modelling of the comparative international relationship between female workforce participation, GDP, and other variables and fertility rates in the UK and Ireland, Spain, and Sweden showed that in recent years, the (negative) relationship between GDP and TFR (total fertility rate) is still evident in Spain and Ireland (countries whose demographic transition was not completed until recently), but not in the UK or Sweden. That is not very surprising, in view of the trend towards a non-significant or even reversed cross-sectional international relationship between these two variables in recent years (Coleman 1993). In the UK and (even more) Sweden, little relationship can be discerned between female workforce participation and fertility in recent years, although the regression was strong earlier. However, a strong negative relationship is still evident in Ireland and Spain (Figure 2.16).

The kind of model appropriate for recent fertility change depends on the levels of economic development and female emancipation which a particular country has reached. We saw above that 'new home economics' concepts (for example, female workforce participation), which seemed to offer

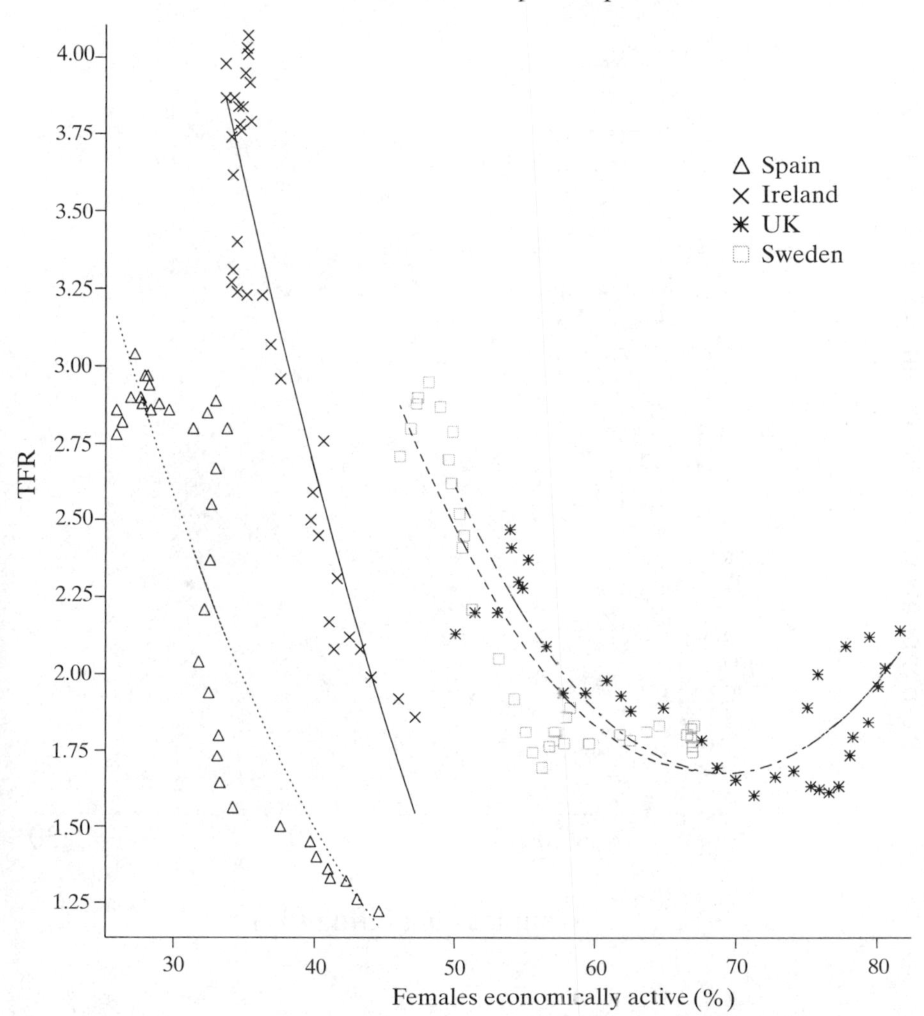

Note: Model includes country, per cent females economically active (linear and squared-term) and interaction term between country and per cent females economically active; lines are fitted regression lines for each country. Each data point is one calander year.

FIG. 2.16 Effect of workforce participation on fertility, selected countries, 1960–1995

good models of fertility change in the 1960s, now have less explanatory power in populations which have reached high levels of female workforce participation. Indeed, some critics deny that they ever had much explanatory power (Murphy 1992). It might be thought that the attitudinal changes discussed earlier might now account more effectively for international

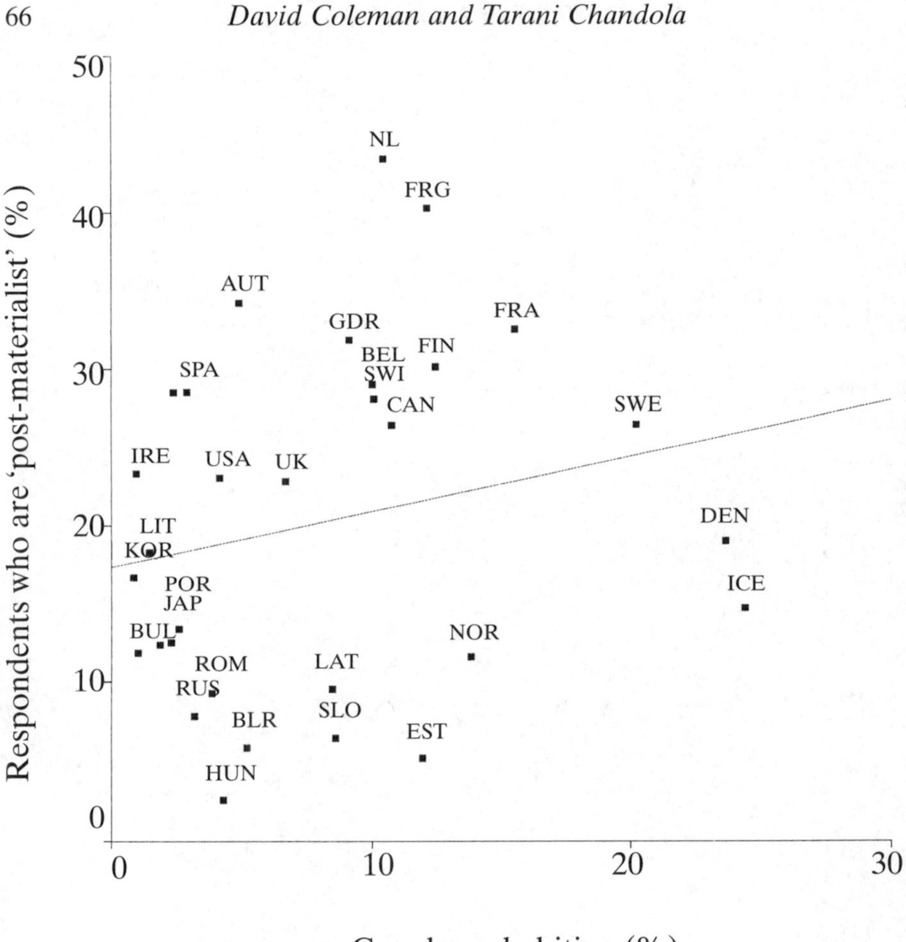

Note: $R^2 = 0.0445$

Source: World Values Survey 1991.

FIG. 2.17 Effect of average level of 'post-materialism' on proportions cohabiting

demographic differences in the 'post-material' and secular age (Lesthaeghe and Moors 1996). But countries differ considerably in the extent to which their populations have embraced new values. Furthermore, simple cross-sectional comparisons often show rather weak effects upon demographic differences of aggregate levels of national response to questions relating to values and attitudes when a broad variety of countries is compared. Individual responses to these questions are by no means always compatible with the behaviour of the same individuals. About the same proportion of Spaniards, Britons, Swedes, and Danes gave 'post-materialist' answers to a battery of questions on values in the World Values Survey of 1991, but those populations exhibit very different levels of cohabitation (Figure 2.17), divorce, and births outside marriage. Simple data of that kind throw little light on Britain's position with respect to the 'second demographic transition'. Compensation arrangements—welfare cushioning for divorce and lone motherhood or maternity leave arrangements—may have very powerful effects on demographic behaviour, as the recent ups and downs of Swedish fertility are claimed to have shown (Hoem and Hoem 1997). But these multiple welfare effects upon behaviour, both unintended and intended, are notoriously difficult to evaluate comprehensively (Gauthier 1996) although promising in theory. So it may take some time before the vexed issue of the possible perverse effects of UK tax and welfare systems on our high levels of divorce and lone motherhood can be answered definitively. Describing British demographic contrasts with continental Europe is undoubtedly easier than explaining them.

3

Family change: revolution or backlash in attitudes?

Jacqueline Scott

Most of the change we think we see in life
Is due to truths being in and out of favour . . .
(Robert Frost, 'The Black Cottage', 1914)

INTRODUCTION

On the eve of a new millennium, it is perhaps not surprising that so much stress is given to how much society has changed. Old certainties are fast disappearing in what has been referred to as post-traditional society. In the family sphere new choices abound. People have to decide whether to cohabit before marrying or to marry at all; whether and when to have children, and how many; whether to stay in an unhappy marriage or to separate or divorce. Although individual choices are constrained by gender, age, and socio-economic circumstances, the latitude of acceptable and feasible family options seems to have expanded enormously. The debate about sexual and family choices has shifted noticeably, with fewer options considered beyond the pale (Scott *et al.* 1993). With a bit of exaggeration, it has been claimed that 'anything goes' (Beck 1992: 116). Men and women have the task of planning their own life courses, and this includes finding ways of achieving both the economic and self-actualization goals associated with making a living, and satisfactory forms of personal relationships central to making a life.

In just one generation, there have been dramatic changes in family life.

The support of the ESRC is gratefully acknowledged. The project on which this chapter draws was done in collaboration with Lindsay Brooke, Kim Perren, Alison Park, and Daphne Ahrendt. I am also grateful to Duane Alwin and Michael Braun for their collaboration in earlier related research.

The numbers marrying have halved, the numbers divorcing have trebled, and the proportion of children born outside marriage has quadrupled (Pullinger and Summerfield 1997). People are marrying later and having fewer children than was the case in previous generations. Lone parents now head about a quarter of all families with dependent children. This reflects a threefold increase in the proportion in just two decades. The rapid increase in cohabitation among unmarried couples is one of the most spectacular ways in which traditional family life is changing in Britain (Kiernan and Estaugh 1993). Living together before marriage is now the norm. Among women, the proportion of those who cohabited with their future spouse prior to marriage has risen from less than 4 per cent of those whose first marriage was in 1966 to 68 per cent of those married in 1993 (Pullinger and Summerfield 1997). By the nineties, the vast majority of newly formed partnerships (over 70 per cent) were cohabiting rather than legally married, although many of those in such partnerships do go on to marry (Buck and Scott 1994).

These changes in partnership formation reflect and reinforce a fundamental shift in attitudes. Only a few decades ago, living together outside marriage was something shocking but times have clearly changed, and while older generations, who grew up in an era of stricter sexual morality, are far less likely to endorse cohabitation than the young, it is becoming increasingly acceptable as a prelude to marriage or as an alternative. Earlier analysis of the British Household Panel Study, for example, revealed that more than a third of both men and women born prior to 1930 thought that living together outside marriage was wrong, compared with only 7 per cent of those born since 1960 (Buck and Scott 1994).

Demographic Transitions, Feminism, and the Sexual Revolution

These trends in cohabitation, marriage, fertility, and marital disruption are widely shared across Western industrial nations. The pattern, as a whole, has been termed the 'second demographic transition', a term that contrasts the changes that have occurred since 1960 with those in the first half of the century. The second demographic transition can be characterized as having three phases (Lesthaeghe 1995). In the initial phase through to 1970, the trend in divorce accelerated considerably and the baby boom came to an end and was followed by a sharp decline in fertility, in part facilitated by the introduction of the contraceptive pill. During the second phase, roughly between 1970 and 1985, pre-marital cohabitation increased substantially and an increasing number of children were born outside of marriage. The third phase, from the mid-1980s onwards, has seen divorce stabilizing at a high plateau, with a marked increase in both pre- and post-marital cohabitation. One consequence of these developments is the rising number of single-parent households, the vast majority of which are headed by women. Another consequence is an increase in one-person households.

What has brought about these dramatic demographic transitions? In an article discussing the demographic transition in Europe, Lesthaeghe and Wilson (1986) make two points. The first is the importance of paying attention to the broader ideological development rather than focusing exclusively on the structural and economic conditions of modernity. Secondly, they point out that there may be reactions to changes in societal ethics, with the result that more fundamentalist views are juxtaposed with secular ones. In his discussion of the causes of the first demographic transition, Lesthaeghe (1995) points to the rising importance of individual autonomy, both in terms of individual freedom of choice and rejection of external authority. However, in the late nineteenth and early twentieth centuries, the 'act of dissent' occurred in private. By contrast, the second transition corresponds to a more pervasive manifestation of autonomy, with a very public reaction against authority expressed through social movements that challenged the foundations of traditional relations in the domestic and sexual sphere. These movements include the 'sexual revolution', with its creed of free love, and 'second-wave' feminism, which from the late 1960s through most of the 1970s asserted women's rights to be liberated from the straitjacket of traditional gender stereotypes and social arrangements (Oakley and Mitchell 1997).

Interestingly, just as second-wave feminism builds on the earlier feminist protest which came to an end shortly after women gained enfranchisement, so the 1960s sexual revolution also has an earlier counterpart. The term 'sexual revolution' was first coined to describe the changing sexual mores and behaviour of the 1920s (Martin 1996). The word 'revolution' is charged with meaning and implies a purposive overthrow of sexual morality. Yet, as Martin persuasively argues, the reasons that are evoked to explain the second sexual revolution are remarkably reminiscent of the first. In short, they involve changes in economic imperatives, the emancipation of women due to labour force participation, new sexual knowledge and contraception, the emancipation of youth due to technological change, and independence from adult authority. The various references change to meet the different period: it is women's entry into the workforce since the Second World War, rather than the first; it is the invention of the pill, not access to contraception; it is Woodstock, not the Jazz Age. Perhaps there has been one century-long revolution involving a constant set of causes (Seidman 1992: 21). Or perhaps, like reports of the death of Mark Twain, rumours of the sexual revolution have been grossly exaggerated (T. Smith 1990; Scott 1998*a*).

The 'revolutionary' impact of feminism has also been subject to question. Has feminism changed women's lives? As Oakley and Mitchell (1997) point out, there are really two questions here: one about the extent and direction of change and the other about its causes. It is too simplistic to attribute the changes in women's roles and the concomitant trends involving the family to the effects of the feminist movement. For one thing, many of the changes pre-date second wave feminism and have their origins in the increase in women's employment after World War II (Chafetz 1995). In most of the industrialized nations, technological, economic, and legal changes have occurred since 1945 that have had the net impact of substantially increasing the demand for labour, especially in service jobs where women have been traditionally concentrated. Although it is difficult to measure expansion in the demand for women's labour directly, a comparison of the total labour force growth and increases in the rate of employment for women is highly suggestive of expanding demand. For instance, between 1960 and 1970, the total labour force growth and the female labour force increased respectively by 18.6 and 37.5 per cent in the United States and by 4.5 and 17.8 per cent in Britain (Chafetz 1995). It can be assumed that most men and a substantial proportion of unmarried women were already employed by the 1960s. However, in the more highly industrial nations, the pool of such traditional labour force participants soon became insufficient to meet the rising demand for labour, especially in the growing service sector. Married women, including those with dependent children, were drawn into the labour market. Thus, in Britain, by 1970 over half of women of employment age were in the labour force.

Married women's employment patterns have several effects on family structure and functions that are independent of any impact that might be due to the emergence of a feminist consciousness, including delays in marriage and childbearing. Moreover, changes in labour force participation are likely to have ramifications for women's sexual freedom. For as Reiss (1990: 88) states: 'Economic autonomy reduces the dependence on others and makes sexual assertiveness a much less risky procedure.' Similarly, once women have paid employment, they are more likely to press for an equitable division of domestic labour and they may be less likely to defer to their husband's authority (Chafetz 1995).

Nevertheless, even if the feminist movement was not the origin of the wide-ranging changes in women's familial roles, it has clearly contributed to and accelerated changes in women's and men's roles as well as in other aspects of sexual equality and family organization. According to Chafetz, the feminist message that a large segment of the non-activist public took on board in the 1970s and 1980s was interpreted as encouraging women to avoid economic dependence on men by becoming or remaining employed. Feminism was popularly viewed as urging women to define autonomy and self-actualization as the major goals of their lives and to cease devoting all of their energies selflessly to others (especially to men) who only exploited them (Barrett and McIntosh 1982). At that time, it was often claimed that the two sexes were essentially the same and therefore that a gender-based division of labour at home or in the labour force was unnecessary and unfair. In addition, in every nation where a feminist movement emerged, women's right to reproductive control, including their right to abortion, was asserted as a means by which women could take control of their own bodies and their own lives.

Lack of Change and Backlash

Have the inequalities between men and women actually begun to change in Western countries over the past decade or two? As Beck (1992) asserts, there are two different answers. Clearly, epochal changes have occurred, especially in the area of sexuality. Contraception and the (conditional) right to abortion have radically changed women's situation. In other domains, however, these changes exist more in consciousness than in actuality. Certainly, when it comes to the conditions of men and women in the labour market or the domestic division of labour, although there exists a rhetoric of equality, conditions and behaviour have changed remarkably little (Gershuny 1997; Scott 1997*b*).

Lack of change is a theme echoed by Oakley and Mitchell (1997) in their assessment of the extent to which feminism has changed women's lives. They attack two myths: the first, that women are working on the same terms as men; the second, that of the domesticated man. Although women's employment activity has changed dramatically in recent decades, there is evidence to suggest that the change is somewhat cosmetic. In Britain, women's participation in *full-time* paid employment has risen quite slowly over the past few decades. In 1951, 30 per cent of women aged 20–64 were in full-time employment (Joshi 1989); forty years later, in 1991, this figure had risen only slightly to 34 per cent of women aged 16–59 (Buck *et al.* 1994). In the same period, part-time work quintupled (from 5 per cent in 1951 to 26 per cent in 1991). Part-time work can be regarded as a means of avoiding more basic changes in the relations between men and women. It allows women to combine labour force participation and family responsibilities by maintaining primary responsibility for the home and children while contributing to the family income. Whether women choose to work part-time in order to juggle family and work roles, or whether lack of child-care alternatives and a traditional gender-role division of labour within the home leaves them no choice, is something that is far from clear (see Hakim 1996, 1997; Scott 1997*b*). What is plain, however, is that part-time work has disadvantages for women in terms of poor rates of pay and loss of promotion prospects (see Dex 1988). The prevalence of women in part-time work also exacerbates the ongoing gender segregation of the workforce that has been dubbed the central feature of gender inequality in the world of paid work (Scott 1994: 329).

Change has also been slow in the way domestic tasks in dual-earner households are divided. In Britain, in the minority of dual-earner households where men and women are employed for approximately the same number of hours, women do some nine hours per week more of the unpaid domestic tasks than men (Gershuny 1997). There is a clear divergence between the actual sharing of domestic tasks and the declared belief that they ought to be shared. This discrepancy between practice and ideology is paralleled by the consistent finding that men are more likely to say they do more in the home than women report that their menfolk do (British Household Panel Study, unpublished analysis by author).

There is considerable debate about the merits of combining motherhood and paid work, with some castigating the 'selfish woman' who attempts to have it all. It has been suggested that there is a backlash within feminism itself, as well as against it, with some concerned that feminist claims have gone too far (Oakley and Mitchell 1997). There is the further suggestion that, with high levels of male unemployment, there may be far greater support for a more traditional division of gender roles, with the man earning the money and the woman looking after the home (Beck 1992; Beck and Beck-Gernsheim 1995). The belief that women's employment takes away employment opportunities for men, whether or not it is true, is likely to result in a backlash against women's labour force participation. Beck (1992) argues that continuing mass unemployment and the limited and generally shrinking capacities of the labour market in general conserve and re-stabilize the traditional roles and responsibilities of men and women. In Britain, some have suggested that the neo-traditional family might be the solution to what is seen as men's increasing level of disinvolvement with family life and rejection of the responsibilities of fatherhood (Dench 1997).

The reputed backlash is not only against changing gender roles, but also concerns the new-found sexual freedom. Nostalgia for a past age of fixed (unequal) gender identities and moral certainties tends to prevail, and traditional values are defended in the name of the natural order. Oakley (1997) argues that women can be successfully returned to the home once gender differences are re-naturalized and women are re-burdened with their traditional role as carriers of the moral order. Similarly, the New Moral Right's achievement in condemning homosexuality in both men and women is accomplished by returning it to the world of 'unnatural' deviation in which it started (Ryan 1997). Another main target for backlash against women and feminism concerns legal abortion. Second-wave feminism fought for women's right to decouple sex and reproduction, and to exercise choice over when and whether to become mothers. The gaining of such rights has been subject to constant attack in both Britain and, more extremely, the United States (Oakley and Mitchell 1997; Scott 1998*b*).

Attitudinal Revolution or Backlash?

Thus, on the one hand, there is talk of revolutionary change, with the demise of traditional sexual constraints and the acceptance of family diversity; on the other, there is talk of backlash. Moreover, backlash, for at least some feminist writers, is seen as a response to too little change, not to too much. In this chapter, I investigate the extent to which there has been a revolution or backlash in attitudes on three issues that concern related but distinct aspects of family change. First, I examine changing attitudes to the morality of pre-marital sex, extra-marital sex, and homosexuality, and investigate how far the traditional marital and procreative imperative has been overturned. Secondly, I present trend data on attitudes to abortion. Thirdly, I examine changing attitudes to gender roles and, in particular, the perceived clash between women's labour force participation and the traditional role of the mother.

One aim is to examine how Britain compares with other nations in terms of how attitudes on these issues are structured and are changing over time. Cross-national research is essential to determine which attitudinal changes are common throughout the industrial world and what is distinctive about each nation. For example, in Britain there is considerable speculation and concern in recent years about how the family is changing, but we know little about British attitudes in a comparative perspective. Is Britain in the forefront of change, or is it dragging its heels compared with other European nations and the United States? Cross-national attitudes have to be interpreted in the context of the social, political, and institutional differences that affect many aspects of family choice. In addition, there are important within-country variations due to gender, birth cohort, ethnicity, marital status, education, religion, and the like.

It is often asked: 'Why study attitudes, why not just look at behaviour?' Attitudes are important because they give some indication of how people are predisposed to respond to the opportunities and constraints that life poses (Scott *et al.* 1996). Behaviour often reflects a complex mix of preference, opportunity, and constraint. Yet studying attitudes is not without its problems. Politicians are not the only people who say one thing and do another. Certainly, when it comes to sexual morality, there is likely to be a gulf between attitude and practice; and, even when the two are related, it is not clear which causes which (Laumann *et al.* 1994; Wellings *et al.* 1994). The primary reason why attitudes are important, however, is not because they are good indicators of behaviour, but rather because they help constitute the climate of opinion against which behaviour is judged. For example, acute strain can result if mothers work while holding attitudes (or being exposed to attitudes) that take the view that their action is harmful to children. Thus, shifts in public attitudes, whether regarding mothers' employment, legal abortion, homosexual relations, or whatever, are likely to inhibit or facilitate social change. Of course, there are also feedback loops, and social change, in turn, has an impact on public opinion.

Unravelling the mechanisms of social change is clearly beyond the scope of this chapter. My goal is a far simpler one. It is often claimed that individualism has overturned traditional family values. By examining changes in attitudes to sexual morality, legal abortion, and gender roles, we can see whether traditional constraints have indeed been overturned. Before presenting the findings, however, I briefly discuss the theoretical debate concerning individualism and the demise of traditional values that helped guide this research.

THEORETICAL EXPECTATIONS: INDIVIDUALISM AND THE DEMISE OF TRADITIONAL VALUES

Social theorists have highlighted how, in advanced modern societies, there is a 'new individualism', whereby, in the context of daily activities both inside and outside the family, people have to construct their lives more actively than ever before (Giddens 1996: 243). Today, choice has become obligatory. In all realms of social action, people have to exercise individual choice, whereas in pre-modern societies, tradition provided a relatively fixed horizon of action (Giddens 1996: 30). The theorem of individuation, as Beck (1992: 90) calls it, is a key feature of the risk society in which 'The individual himself or herself becomes the production unit of the social in the lifeworld.' We live in a world of multiple authorities and risk calculation has to include whose authority, if any, is to be taken as binding. While this might be liberating, it is also profoundly disturbing, as all the ethical precepts taken for granted in the past are quite literally thrown into doubt.

Of course, as Giddens acknowledges, traditions do not wholly disappear in modern societies. Rather, he claims (1996: 56), they persist in one of two guises: traditions may be articulated and defended as a valued option in a world of competing values; otherwise tradition becomes fundamentalism, a reassertion of formulaic truth. The problem with this depiction is that it takes the demise of tradition as given: we live in a post-traditional society which has for ever severed the 'natural' authority with which tradition was once imbued. Thus, tradition, in its modern guise, has to be renamed as reaction (Lesthaeghe and Wilson 1986), fundamentalism (Giddens 1996), or backlash (Oakley and Mitchell 1997).

The demise of traditional values is associated with the era of risk society, when if not quite 'anything goes', there is at least an almost limitless range of acceptable choice. According to Beck, as modernization proceeds, the decisions and constraints on decisions multiply in all fields of social action, but especially with regards to sexuality and family. He writes, 'With a bit of exaggeration one could say 'anything goes' . . . Marriage can be subtracted from sexuality and that in turn from parenthood; parenthood can be multiplied by divorce and the whole thing can be divided by living together or apart (Beck 1992: 116). New modernity, for Beck, is equated with the risk society, and risk society in turn is a society where the normal state of love is chaos (Beck 1992; Beck-Gernsheim 1995).

Weeks claims (1995: 28–9) that the loosening of the bonds of sexual authoritarianism associated with the 1960s has continued and accelerated in both Britain and the United States, despite haphazard attempts at moral rearmament. He notes the irony that President Reagan and Prime Minister Thatcher, both keen proponents of traditional families, presided over 'probably the greatest revolution in sexual mores in the twentieth century, despite their best endeavour'. His explanation for this apparent paradox is that there is a link between radical individualism in economics and in sexual and ethical values: 'Individual freedom cannot stop at the market. If you have an absolute freedom to buy and sell, there seems no logic in blocking a freedom to choose your sexual partners, your sexual lifestyle, your identity or your fantasies' (Weeks 1995: 29). This theme is echoed by Giddens (1996: 241): 'The present day conservative still wants to conserve—to protect the traditional family, traditional symbols of state legitimacy, religion and the identity of the nation. Yet these are being eroded, smashed open even, by the very market forces modern conservatism fosters.' Thus, it is claimed, the market ethic is a powerful corrosive factor that undermines the traditional equation of sex with procreation and its containment in marriage.

It has been claimed that the chief 'beneficiaries' of the 1960s sexual revolution were young people and women (Martin 1996). Rising affluence gave the young greater access to privacy and the pill made pre-marital intercourse less risky. The combined effect was to give young people sufficient freedom to reject the 'old-fashioned' values of their parents and grandparents. In addition, women were gaining increased economic autonomy through their participation in the labour force and could demand an end to a double standard concerning sexual expression. Certainly, the feminist movement of the 1970s embraced the ideal of sexual equality. Moreover, contraceptive technologies and legal abortion made such sexual expression possible, without undermining women's independence through the birth of unwanted children. Thus, we can expect a marked generational difference in approval of pre-marital sex but little difference between the attitudes of men and women.

Rising expectations about women's social and economic position have been accompanied by a marked increase in public approval of more egalitarian gender roles both in Britain and in the United States (Mason and Lu 1988; Scott *et al.* 1996). Arguably, men stand to gain more than women from the traditional division of labour, which gives priority to the role of women as wives and mothers, and not surprisingly, most earlier research on gender-role attitudes has shown that women are more likely to endorse egalitarian views than are men (Mason and Lu 1988; Alwin *et al.* 1992; Braun *et al.* 1994; Scott *et al.* 1996). We can expect this gender difference in attitudes to continue, with women more likely than men to endorse egalitarian gender roles.

It seems equally plausible, given the relative benefits men and women reap from traditional family roles, that women would be more favourably disposed than men to legal abortion. Surprisingly, little evidence of gender differences in support of legal abortion has been found in either Britain or the United States (Granberg and Granberg 1980; Finlay 1981; Barnartt and Harris 1982; Scott 1987; Harding 1988). However, there may be marked generational effects because earlier cohorts of women were brought up in an era that viewed abortion as the wages of sin, whereas the post-pill generations have grown up regarding reproductive control as essential. Such cohort differences are likely to be less evident among men than women, as unwanted pregnancies have never had particularly dire consequences for the moral standing or employment prospects of men. Thus, we can expect a more pronounced generational effect on attitudes towards abortion among women than among men.

In the following three sections, I examine generational changes over time in men's and women's attitudes to sexual morality, abortion, and gender roles. First, I use time-series data from Britain to track men's and women's changing attitudes over the past decade. In particular, I investigate whether change is due to the rather slow but usually fairly stable process of cohort replacement or to the more 'revolutionary' process of period effects, which results in attitudinal change among individuals of all ages. Secondly, I compare how the trajectory of change differs between Britain and the United States. Thirdly, I investigate how British and American attitudes compare with those found in nations with different social and political backgrounds—Ireland, Germany, Sweden, and Poland.

BRITISH ATTITUDINAL CHANGE

Sexual Morality

The British Social Attitudes Survey[1] has included the same three items about attitudes to pre-marital and extra-marital sex, and sexual relations between adults of the same sex, since 1983 (the exact wording of these survey questions is shown in the Appendix). As can be seen in Figures 3.1*a* and 3.1*b*, the public's level of disapproval has varied considerably depending on the sexual behaviour in question, with levels of condemnation

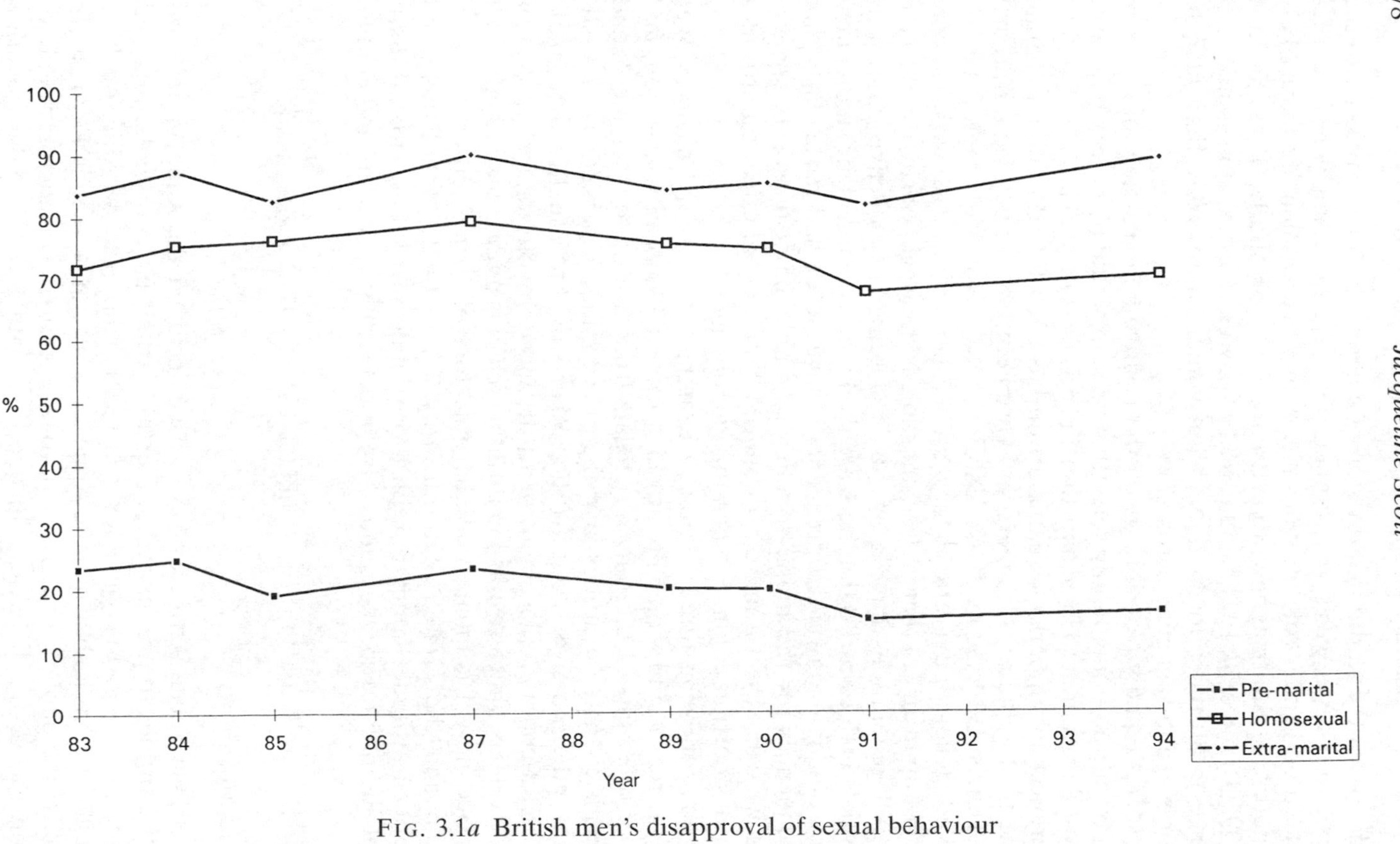

FIG. 3.1*a* British men's disapproval of sexual behaviour

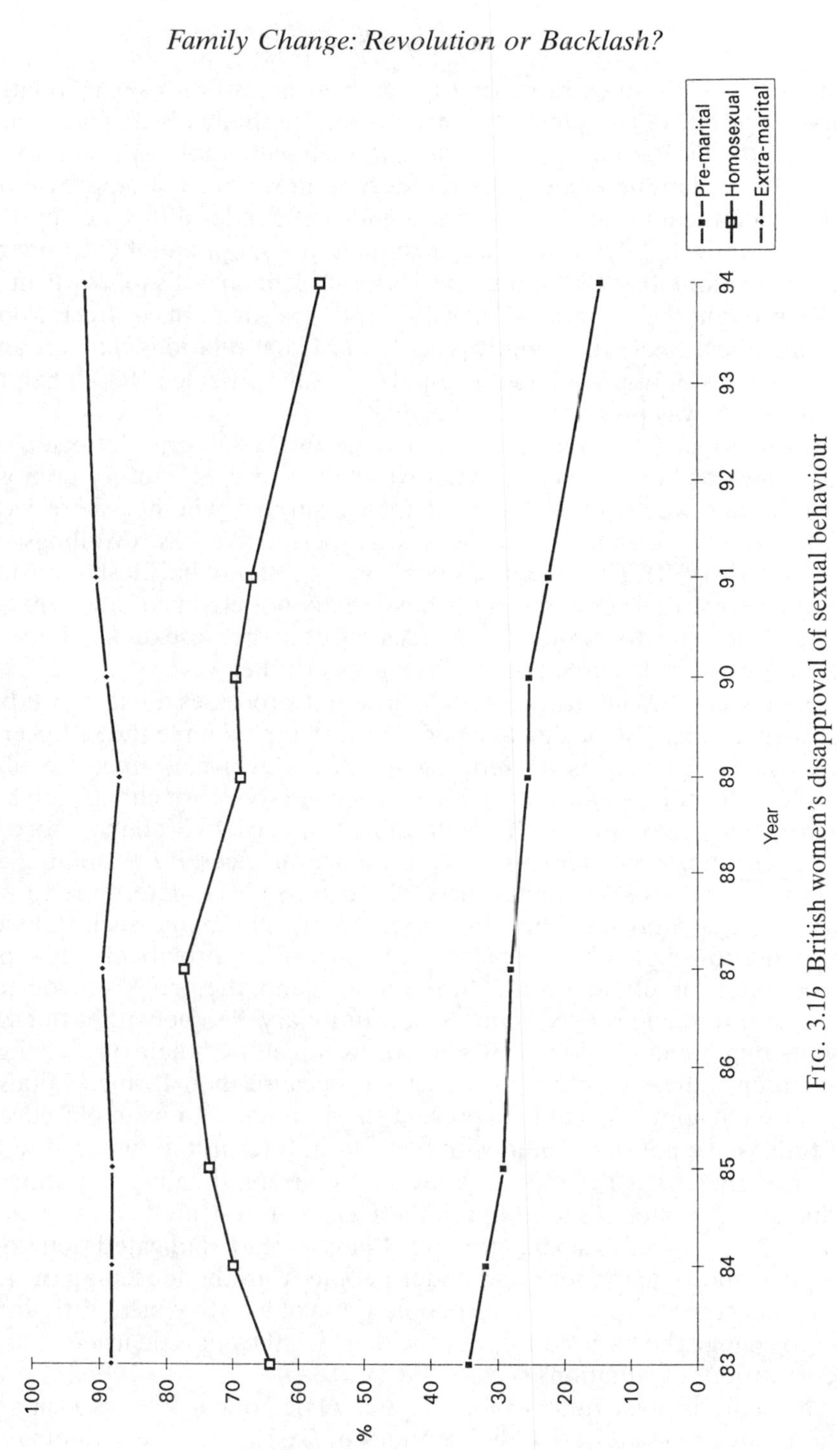

FIG. 3.1*b* British women's disapproval of sexual behaviour

consistently high for extra-marital sex, somewhat lower for sexual relations between adults of the same sex, and very substantially less for pre-marital sex. For the earlier part of the period, women were more opposed to pre-marital sex than men, but a marked decline in women's disapproval over the decade meant that there was no significant gender difference by 1994. Women were slightly more likely than men to disapprove of extra-marital sex throughout the 1980s, but the increase in men's disapproval in the 1990s brought their views in line with those of women. In contrast, women are much less likely to disapprove of homosexual relations than are men, and women's disapproval has declined quite sharply since 1987, when fear about AIDS was probably at its height.

It was no surprise that the unfolding of the AIDS crisis affected attitudes towards homosexuality. What was less clear was whether homosexual relations would be singled out for censure or whether there would be a broader backlash against sexual permissiveness (Wellings and Wadsworth 1990). The evidence does not suggest any backlash—for men, attitudes to sexual permissiveness have really not changed much through the decade; and for women, attitudes to both homosexuality and pre-marital sex have become less traditional over time.

Change can be due to two rather different processes. First, as we have just seen, change can be due to a period effect, for example the AIDS crisis. This can be viewed as an *intra-cohort* effect, which is likely to affect people's attitudes, whatever their age. A second source of change might be due to *cohort succession*—the replacement of earlier (probably more traditional) cohorts by later (probably more liberal) ones. By examining data from repeated cross-sectional surveys, it is possible to determine to what extent cohorts possess differing orientations. Normally, social changes occurring through cohort replacement proceed at a relatively slow pace and are not rapidly reversed. On the other hand, the process involved in intra-cohort changes may be more revolutionary. People within the same cohort might change their views, either as a result of their own changing life circumstances or life-cycle effects, or because their former values no longer seem appropriate in the present social climate: for example, because attitudes have got out of step with behaviour. Interpretations need to rely on prior theory, as there is no known way of empirically separating the influences of cohort, age, and period effects with repeated cross-sectional data.[2] With respect to sexual morality, I have already indicated that young people stand to gain more than older people from the loosening of traditional constraints. Moreover, as people grow older, they have little incentive to change the basic conceptions with which they have learned to assess the propriety of situations (Ryder 1965).

The analysis presented in Table 3.1 was carried out as follows. Using two time-points, 1984 and 1994, the attitudes of six 10-year age groupings are

TABLE 3.1. *British disapproval of pre-marital and homosexual relations, by cohort and gender (%)*

	Pre-marital sex				Homosexual relations			
	1984/5	1994	Δ1	Δ2	1984/5	1994	Δ1	Δ2
MEN								
Age								
18–27	6.3	3.7	−2.6	—	65.8	55.5	−10.3	—
28–37	4.3	11.3	7.0	5.0	59.8	60.6	0.8	−5.2
38–47	18.0	8.9	−9.1	4.6	74.0	59.8	−14.2	0.0
48–57	28.6	20.0	−8.6	2.0	87.0	74.5	−12.5	0.5
58–67	37.8	30.5	−7.3	1.9	86.5	90.4	3.9	3.4
68+	58.4	37.6	−20.8	−0.2	94.3	92.7	−1.6	6.2
Mean[a]	25.6	18.7	−6.9	2.7	77.9	72.2	−5.6	1.0
Minimum N	180	43			185	50		
Age (linear)[b]	216.0***	32.9***			95.6***	35.8***		
WOMEN								
Age								
18–27	8.4	0.6	−7.8	—	64.0	27.4	−36.6	—
28–37	11.4	5.9	−5.5	−2.5	54.5	44.6	−9.9	−19.4
38–47	23.1	4.8	−18.3	−6.6	64.2	47.7	−16.5	−6.8
48–57	40.2	15.2	−25.0	−7.9	77.0	73.9	−3.1	9.7
58–67	52.3	29.5	−22.8	−10.7	87.1	77.8	−9.3	0.8
68+	65.2	56.1	−9.1	3.8	93.2	90.7	−2.5	3.6
Mean[a]	33.4	18.7	−14.7	−4.8	73.3	60.3	−12.9	−2.4
Minimum N	222	49			210	51		
Age (linear)[b]	290.1***	222.9***			116.0***	60.9***		

Δ1 Net change for age groups (unweighted).
Δ2 Intra-cohort change (% difference).
[a] Means unweighted for different cohort size.
[b] Wald statistic (coefficient/standard error) squared.
*** $p < 0.001$.

shown: 18–27, 28–37, 38–47, 48–57, 58–67, and 68 and over.[3] The table indicates the percentage of the sample who disapprove of pre-marital sex and homosexuality (extra-marital sex is not included, as attitudes have changed so little), and shows attitudinal change broken down by cohort and gender. The figures for each age group at the two points in time can be read from the rows of the table. Thus, for example, among the youngest age group of men in the 1984 survey, 6 per cent disapproved of pre-marital sex, compared with 4 per cent of the same age group a decade later. The Δ1 column shows the results of comparing the same age group in 1984 and 1994. Thus, for the youngest age group of men the difference between the time-1 and time-2 surveys is –3 per cent.

For both pre-marital sex and homosexuality, as we saw in Figures 3.1*a* and 3.1*b*, women's attitudes have changed far more than have those of men. In Table 3.1, we can see that it is earlier cohorts of women who have shown the greatest change towards a more liberal position towards pre-marital sex; whereas for homosexuality, the reverse is true and the youngest age groups of women have changed most. By looking at the mean net change (Δ1), we can see that women's attitudes towards both pre-marital sex and homosexuality have changed twice as much as have men's.[4]

It is also possible to compare a given cohort category with itself across the two surveys. Thus, the time-2 figure for the 28–37 age group minus the time-1 figure for the 18–27 age group represents the intra-cohort change. In Table 3.1, the percentage of men opposed to pre-marital sex for this group moved from 6 per cent to 11 per cent over time and thus the intra-cohort shift (Δ2) is 5 per cent. As with the net change for age groups over time, it is the earlier cohorts of women who have changed most in terms of becoming more liberal towards pre-marital sex. This is more likely to reflect a period effect than the ageing process, as usually people become more conservative with age. If there was no change in attitudes within cohorts, that is, if overall attitude change occurred entirely because later cohorts differed in attitudes from earlier ones, then the mean change shown in Δ2 would be zero. Table 3.1 suggests that most of the change in attitudes towards sexual morality is due to the slow process of cohort replacement. Thus, there is little evidence of any revolutionary change over the decade.

Abortion

In order to assess changing British attitudes towards abortion, I examine a series of questions that have been posed in the British Social Attitudes Survey since 1983 concerning the circumstances in which people think that a woman should be allowed a legal abortion. There are six circumstances in all. Three reflect medical or 'hard' reasons for an abortion: if the mother's health is endangered by the pregnancy, if the woman became pregnant as a result of rape, or if there is a strong chance of a defect in the baby. The other three circumstances reflect social or 'soft' reasons for abortion, which make up the vast majority of cases for which women seek abortions: if the family is poor and cannot afford more children, if the woman is single and does not want to marry the man, or if a married woman does not want any more children. The exact wording of the questions can be seen in the Appendix. In addition to the separate items, Figures 3.2*a* and 3.2*b* show the change in consistent support for all six circumstances across time.[5]

The public's differentiation between approval of hard and soft circum-

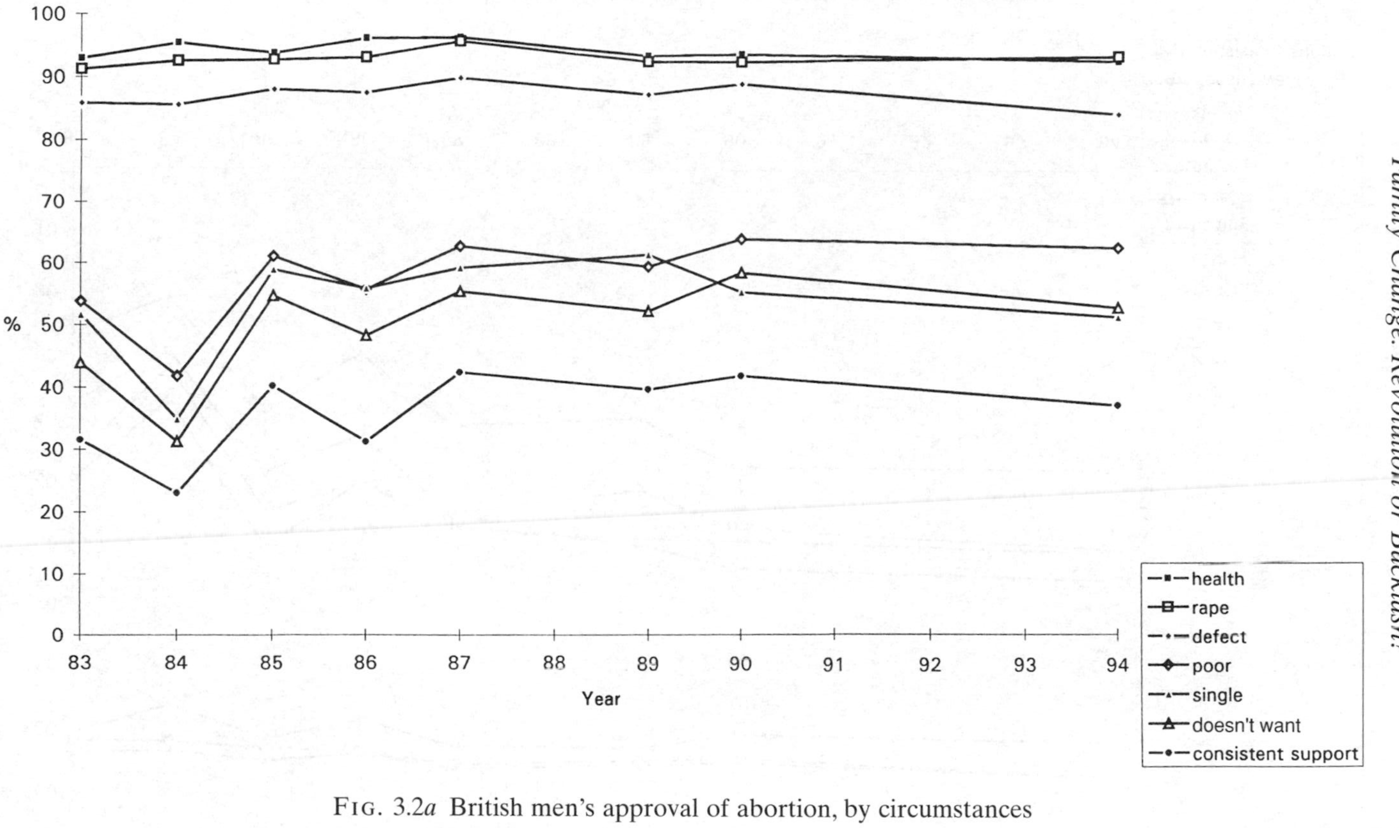

FIG. 3.2*a* British men's approval of abortion, by circumstances

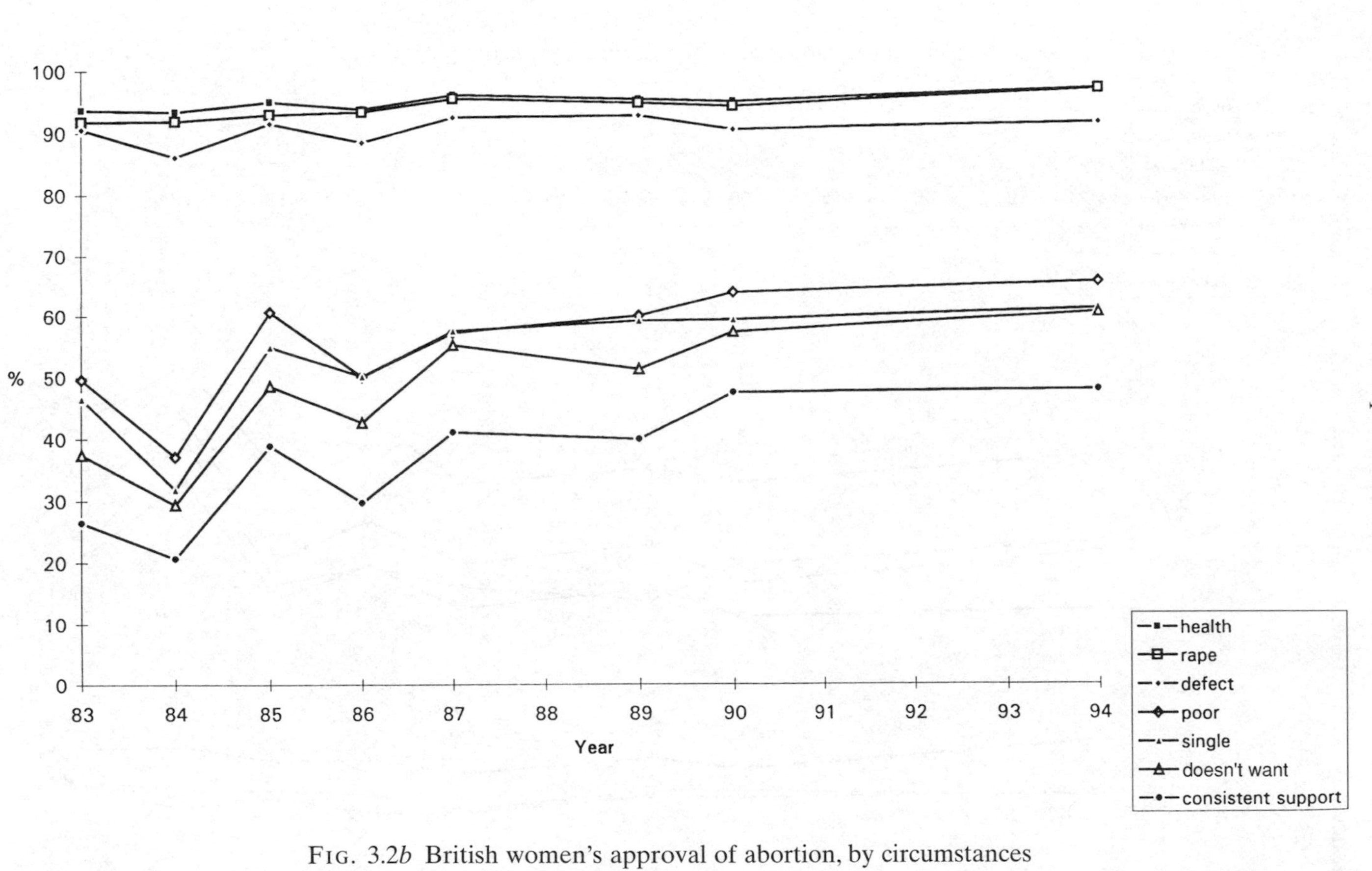

FIG. 3.2*b* British women's approval of abortion, by circumstances

stances is well known. Approval for medical reasons is high and has remained relatively unchanged over the decade. Approval for soft reasons has increased, but more among women than men. Figures 3.2*a* and 3.2*b* show an unexpected dip in support for elective abortions in 1984. Unfortunately, in that year, the item order was reversed so that the hard circumstances were placed first. The resulting drop in approval for the more social circumstances is likely to be due to a well-known context effect on abortion items (Scott 1987; Schuman 1992).[6]

For most of the period, gender differences in attitudes to abortion are negligible, although at the beginning of the decade men were slightly more favourable to abortion than were women. Approval of abortion has increased, however, especially among women, and by 1994, there is a significant gender difference, with women more likely than men to take a pro-abortion stance.

Again, as in the analysis of sexual morality, we can examine how far the liberalization of attitudes towards abortion is due to change within cohorts rather than change between cohorts. In Table 3.2, the analysis of abortion attitudes is based on respondents who favour abortion in all circumstances (the analysis of gender roles is discussed below).[7]

As in Table 3.1, figures for consistent abortion support over time for a particular cohort can be read going down the diagonals of the columns of the table. Among women, there has been a very high level of mean change over time both across the different cohorts ($\Delta 1 = 16$) and within cohorts ($\Delta 1 = 14$). All age groups of women have become more liberal.[8] The change among women, in just one decade, could be described as quite revolutionary. Moreover, in the main, these substantial intra-cohort shifts are far more likely to be due to period factors than to life-cycle or ageing effects, because attitudes tend to become more conservative with age. For men, the comparable changes are slight and abortion attitudes have remained remarkably stable over the past decade. This has resulted in the recent gender difference in abortion stance noted above, with men becoming significantly less supportive of abortion than women. One possible explanation for the marked period effect in Britain is that the heightened publicity given to the problems of lone motherhood has made women more sympathetic to the legal termination of unwanted pregnancies. Another explanation would be that as women become more supportive of premarital sex, they see abortion as a necessary backstop method for when contraception fails.

Gender Roles

If men are being outpaced by women in terms of changes in attitudes to sexual morality and abortion, then it might seem that the sex difference would be even more pronounced in attitudes towards gender roles. In Figures 3.3*a* and 3.3*b* we see that both men's and women's attitudes have become more liberal over the decade regarding the ideological stance that a husband's job is to earn money and a wife's job is to look after the home and family ('traditional roles'). By contrast, there has been little change over the decade in the belief that having a job is the best way for a woman to be an independent person ('job best'). For women, but not for men, the trends for these questions about traditional gender roles and the independence a job may bring can be traced back to 1980, because the same two items were included in the Women and Employment Survey (Martin and Roberts 1984).

Women are more likely than men to reject the traditional gendered division of labour, which is hardly surprising given the relative economic and psychological advantages men and women reap from traditional marriage. However, the most interesting differences between men and women occur in attitudes regarding the consequences of a woman working. In 1994, men were far more likely to reject the statement that family life suffers if the woman has a job (52 per cent) than they were to deny that the preschool child is likely to suffer (38 per cent). In contrast, women were fairly evenly split for both items. In an age of 'political correctness', men's opposition to gender egalitarianism is presumably more palatable if it is expressed in terms of children, rather than the needs of the family (which would include the husband). Thus, although men are changing in a more egalitarian direction overall, they remain considerably more traditional than women in endorsing the view that children may suffer if the mother works ($p < 0.01$).

The changes in Britain for the gender-role ideology item show quite large differences between cohorts (Table 3.2). The more recent cohorts—both men and women—are far more egalitarian than earlier cohorts in their stance towards the traditional gender division of labour. In Table 3.2, the analysis of gender roles presents respondents who reject the belief that it is the husband's job to earn the money and the wife's job to look after the home. Eighty-three per cent of women (78 per cent of men) aged 18–27 in 1994 disagreed with traditional gender roles, compared with only 27 per cent of women (21 per cent of men) over the age of 68. In each survey year, there is a monotonic decrease in the egalitarian position with age, although the age demarcation is clearer among women than men and far more marked in 1994 than in 1984.

Table 3.2 suggests that both cohort succession and within-cohort change in attitudes played a role in the overall change of gender-role attitudes between 1984 and 1994. Among women, the average intra-cohort change was 42 per cent of the change in the population as a whole (8.0/18.8). Thus,

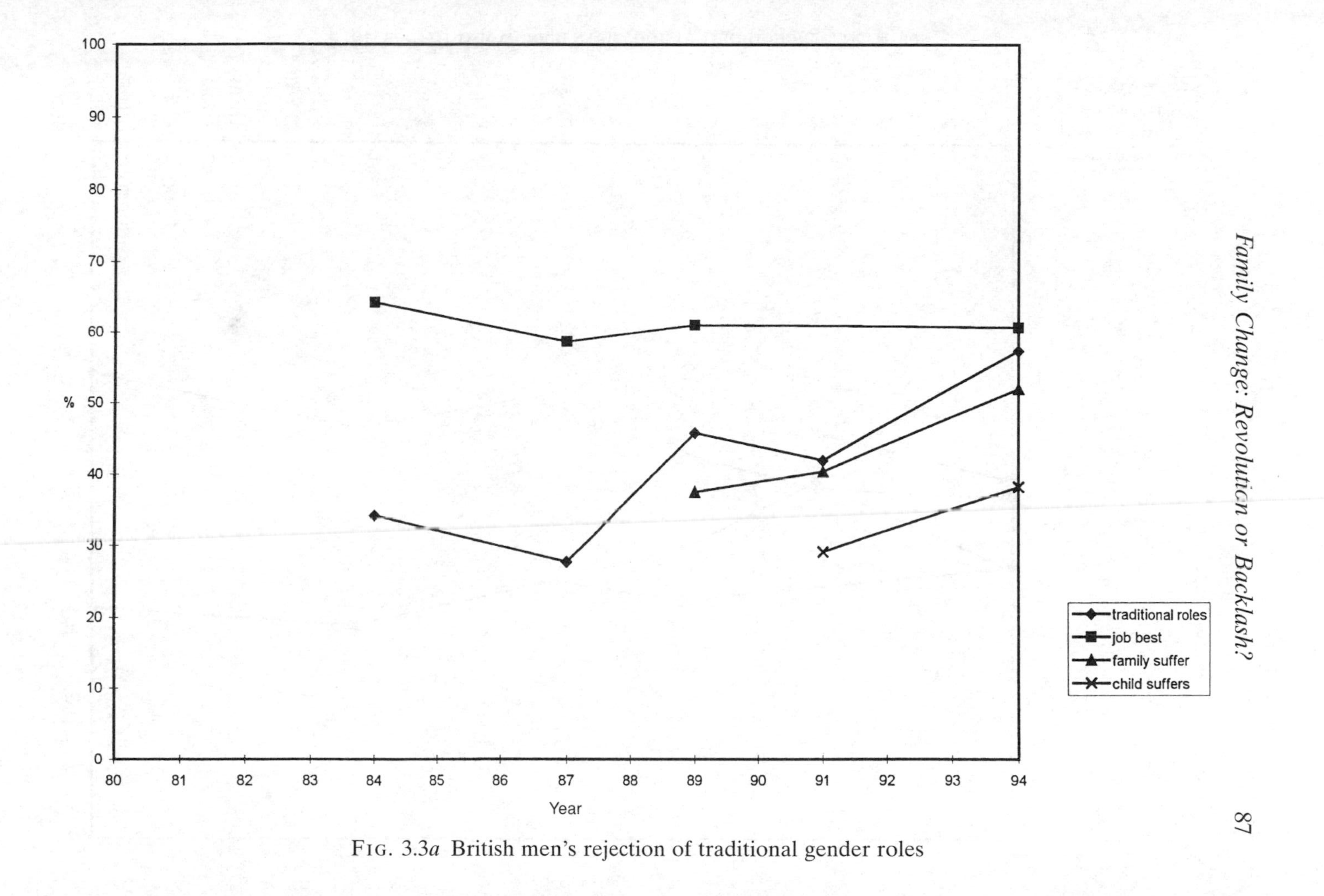

FIG. 3.3*a* British men's rejection of traditional gender roles

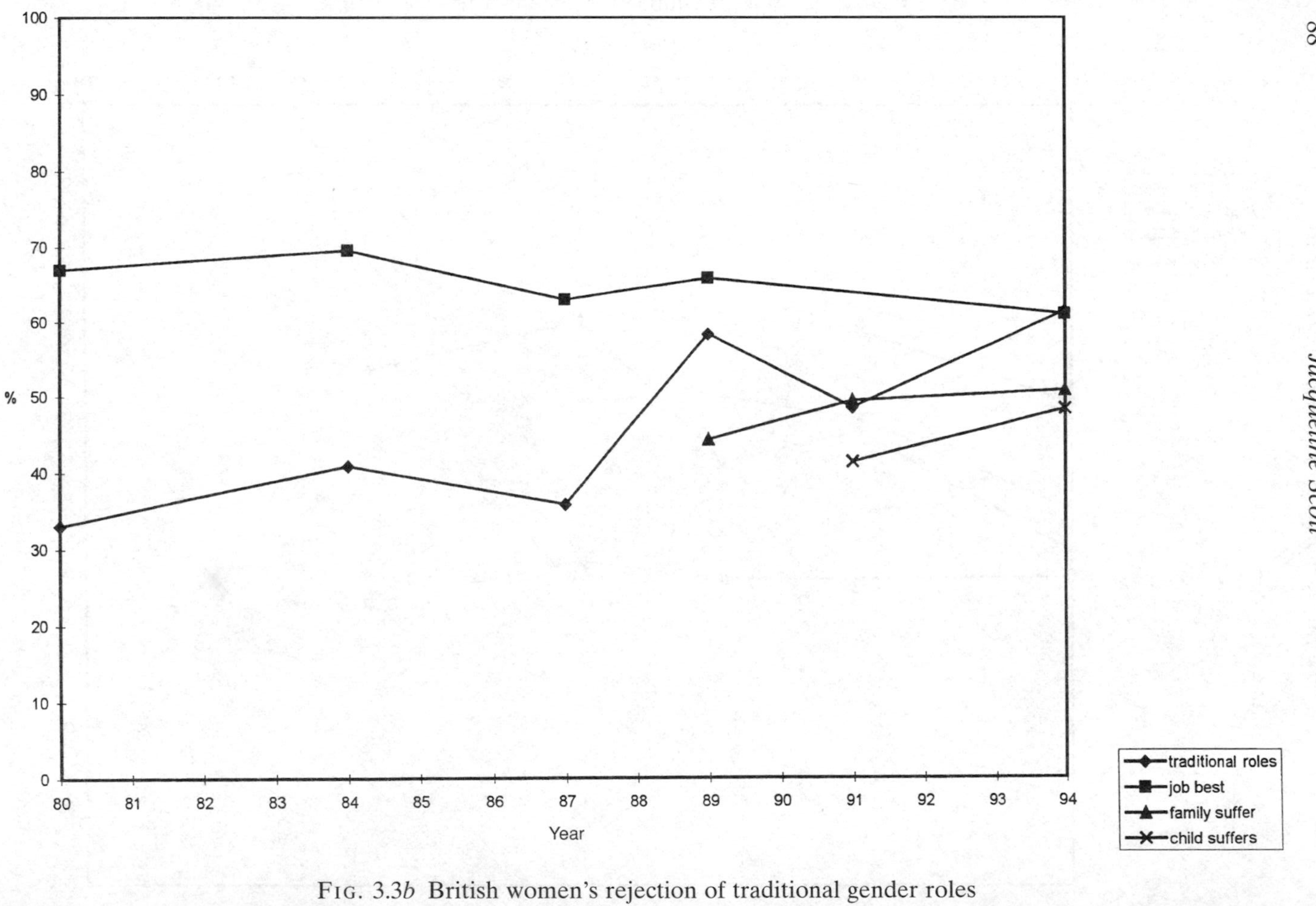

FIG. 3.3*b* British women's rejection of traditional gender roles

TABLE 3.2. *British approval of legal abortion and rejection of traditional gender role, by cohort and gender (%)*

	Approval of abortion				Rejection of traditional gender roles			
	1983/5[a]	1994	Δ1	Δ2	1984	1994	Δ1	Δ2
MEN								
Age								
18–27	38.0	32.6	−5.4	—	48.0	77.6	29.6	—
28–37	40.8	36.4	−4.4	−1.6	54.2	69.6	15.4	21.6
38–47	32.1	41.0	8.9	0.2	38.0	73.1	35.1	18.9
48–57	31.9	36.9	5.0	4.8	24.7	45.7	21.0	7.7
58–67	36.0	38.9	2.9	7.0	19.0	33.6	14.6	8.9
68+	33.6	35.8	2.2	−0.2	10.3	21.5	11.2	2.5
Mean[b]	35.4	36.9	1.5	2.0	32.4	53.5	21.1	11.9
Minimum N	137	53			89	55		
Age (linear)[c]	2.2[ns]	0.2[ns]			63.8***	65.3***		
WOMEN								
Age								
18–27	37.0	52.5	15.5	—	58.8	83.4	24.6	—
28–37	37.0	54.3	17.3	17.3	58.8	69.7	10.9	10.9
38–47	36.9	42.3	5.4	5.3	50.2	77.7	27.5	18.9
48–57	24.5	38.0	13.5	1.1	37.3	49.6	12.3	−0.6
58–67	32.3	50.7	18.4	26.2	17.4	38.4	21.0	1.1
68+	22.9	50.0	27.1	17.7	10.5	27.2	16.7	9.8
Mean[b]	31.8	48.0	16.2	13.5	38.8	57.7	18.8	8.0
Minimum N	192	54			104	59		
Age (linear)[c]	15.1***	0.5[ns]			99.2***	63.7***		

Δ1 Net change for age groups (unweighted).
Δ2 Intra-cohort change (% difference).
[a] The 1984 data are not used because of the change in question order.
[b] Means unweighted for different cohort size.
[c] Wald statistic (coefficient/standard error) squared.
[ns] Not significant.
*** $p < 0.001$.

in marked contrast to abortion, the bulk of change was due to cohort succession, a process that suggests that gender-role ideology will be relatively slow to change. Among men, however, the proportion of change due to within-cohort change was somewhat greater (56 per cent). Thus, at least on this issue, men seem slightly more open to change than women, although initially more traditional.

CROSS-CULTURAL COMPARISONS OF ATTITUDINAL CHANGE

Britain and the United States

Longer sweeps of comparable data exist for the United States than for Britain. The data come from the General Social Survey (GSS) of the National Opinion Research Center (Davis and Smith 1994), which has included the same sequence of abortion items and attitudes regarding sexual morality since 1972. In addition, the same items that are included in subsequent GSS surveys were first asked in a 1965 National Opinion Research Center survey. Thus, for sexual morality and abortion, we can trace attitudinal changes across three decades. The four items used for a gender-role index were first posed in 1977 (see Mason and Lu 1988). Because of slight differences in question wording and response categories, it is not possible to make any direct comparison of the absolute levels of attitudes in the two countries. What can be compared, however, is the trajectory and pace of change among men and women over the last decade. Further details of the American data can be found in Alwin *et al.* (1997) and Scott (1998*a*, *b*).

In the United States, as in Britain, disapproval of extra-marital sex has remained constantly high over the last decade. Disapproval of homosexuality has decreased substantially among Americans of both sexes, whereas in Britain the decline is only among women. However, Americans tend to view homosexuality and extra-marital sex as similarly culpable, whereas the British, especially British women, are far less condemnatory of homosexual relations. The decline in disapproval of pre-marital sex was marked in the United States between the mid-1960s and early 1970s, but since the 1980s, disapproval has steadied at just over 40 per cent for women and about 30 per cent for men. In Britain, disapproval has continued to decline into the 1990s, especially among women.

Regarding abortion, both American men and women have become more liberal, whereas in Britain men's attitudes have hardly changed although women have become far more approving of legal abortion. In both countries, changes in attitudes to abortion have been driven mainly by period effects, rather than by cohort replacement. Similarly, gender-role attitudes, in both America and Britain, have shifted in a more egalitarian direction, although in the US, the pace of change has been markedly slower since 1985 than it was in the earlier period. As in Britain, American women are, in general, more egalitarian than men regarding gender roles, but the gender difference is most marked concerning the belief that young children tend to suffer if the mother works.

In the United States, the rapid period of change was in the 1960s and early 1970s and the pace of change since the 1980s has slowed considerably. The only real exception is in attitudes to homosexuality, where attitudinal change since the 1990s is evident among both men and women. The political climate has changed quite markedly regarding homosexuality in the United States and the gay rights movements have had some notable successes. For example, gay rights activists have reached the Supreme Court with their claims that dismissal from the military on grounds of homosexuality violates the individual's First Amendment rights.

It seems surprising, however, that liberal attitudes to pre-marital sex and abortion have continued to gather pace among women in Britain but not in the United States. In part, these diverging attitudinal patterns may reflect the different trajectories of mothers' labour force participation in the two countries. Mothers' rates of labour force participation rose far more sharply in the United States through the 1960s and 1970s than was the case in Britain and by the mid-1980s had levelled off. In Britain, the labour force participation of mothers with dependent children, albeit mainly in part-time work, has continued to rise into the 1990s. Women's greater degree of economic autonomy (or the potential for greater autonomy) may have spillover effects in terms of increasing their tolerance of sexual freedoms and their demand for reproductive control, while reducing their tolerance of existing gender-role inequities.

Whatever factors underlie these attitudinal trends, it is clear that there is little evidence that 'anything goes' as far as sexual morality, control of reproduction, or gender-role choice are concerned. In both Britain and the United States, there is still considerable agreement about the relative culpability of different sexual behaviours. Only a minority endorse the right of a woman to have an abortion under any circumstance. Moreover, although most approve of women's employment, the majority are persuaded that children are likely to suffer if their mothers work. Taken as a whole, it would be hard to conclude from this investigation of Anglo-American attitudes that the departure from traditional values has been as radical as the literature often implies.

Britain, the USA, and selected European countries

The question I now examine is how Anglo-American attitudes compare with those of four European countries. The data come from the module on 'Family and Changing Sex Roles' appended to national social surveys in the United States, Britain, Ireland, Germany, Poland, and Sweden. (For general and technical descriptions of the International Social Survey Programme (ISSP) see Davis and Jowell 1989 and Jowell *et al.* 1993.) For the six-country survey of attitudes towards gender roles and sexual morality, we only have cross-sectional data collected at one point in time and cannot infer anything about social change within nations. Although these countries have been chosen, in part, for pragmatic reasons of data availability, they also present an interesting range of socio-political contexts within which to compare family and sexual attitudes.

Sweden is often represented as the liberal nation par excellence with respect to sexual enlightenment. Ireland, where abortion is still illegal and divorce has only recently been allowed, is at the other extreme (Dworkin 1993; Porter 1996). Poland makes an interesting contrast with Ireland, because although the Catholic Church wields considerable power, the country was until recently under Communist control. Similarly, the recent histories of the former two Germanies represent diverse political regimes, with very different social policies regarding gender and the family. This difference has been characterized as 'public progressiveness and private traditionalism in the East; and public traditionalism and private radicalism in the West' (Chamberlayne 1994).

Table 3.3 shows the percentage who adopt a traditional stance towards sexual morality across the six nations (columns (1)–(3)). In all six nations, extra-marital sex is widely condemned, pre-marital sex is widely approved, and homosexual relations are in between. Gender differences follow the pattern that was observed in the Anglo-American data, with women tending to be less approving of pre-marital sex and extra-marital sex, and more tolerant of homosexual relations than are men.

Regarding pre-marital sex, East Germany, Sweden, and West Germany are by far the most liberal, with the United States and Ireland at the other extreme. The range of disapproval across countries is substantial, but interestingly, Poland, despite its strong Catholicism, adopts a rather moderate stance relative to the other countries. The pattern is quite different with respect to homosexual relations and here the two Catholic countries are the most disapproving, with the Poles taking a particularly intolerant stance. West Germans are by far the most liberal towards sexual relations between adults of the same sex, and the British, on this issue like all others, are notable for their relative moderation. There is little cross-national variation in attitudes towards extra-marital sex. However, Germany (both East and West) is significantly more liberal than other countries, although, even in Germany, over four out of five disapprove.

Column (4) of Table 3.3 shows the percentage who favour abortion if, for any reason, the woman chooses not to have the baby. In Ireland, there has been much recent public discussion of the abortion issue. The European Court ruled that Ireland's attempt to restrict information on abortion was an infringement of individual rights. However, abortion is still banned in Ireland, unless the mother's life is in danger, and those who wish to procure an abortion, and have the means to do so, must travel abroad.

TABLE 3.3. *Attitudes towards sexual morality, abortion, and gender roles by country, ISSP 1994*

		% disapproving			% agree	% disagree	
		pre-marital sex (1)	homosexual relations (2)	extra-marital sex (3)	allow abortion (4)	husband should earn, wife stay home (5)	child suffers if mother works (6)
Britain	Men	16	70	89	47	57	38
	Women	15^{ns}	57***	92^{ns}	54*	61^{ns}	48**
USA	Men	33	76	92	46	53	38
	Women	46***	72^{ns}	95*	45^{ns}	64***	51***
Ireland	Men	41	78	92	29	48	40
	Women	45^{ns}	76^{ns}	94^{ns}	27^{ns}	58**	45^{ns}
West Germany	Men	7	57	80	57	43	16
	Women	8^{ns}	47***	84*	62*	53***	20*
East Germany	Men	1	63	79	90	76	45
	Women	5**	57^{ns}	87**	88^{ns}	80^{ns}	56***
Sweden	Men	4	67	90	79	69	43
	Women	7*	56***	96***	77^{ns}	72^{ns}	54***
Poland	Men	22	83	85	49	16	24
	Women	30***	80^{ns}	90*	49^{ns}	25***	25^{ns}

^{ns} Not significant.
* $p < 0.05$.
** $p < 0.01$.
*** $p < 0.001$.

In Poland, abortion had been legalized since 1956 but in 1993, a bill was passed that effectively bans abortion except in the case of rape or on stringent medical conditions. So although Polish attitudes are very much in line with those of Britain and the United States, they remain out of step with the current national policy. Following the reunification of Germany, abortion was one of the most contentious policy issues that had to be resolved. Before reunification, East Germans, like the Swedes, had ready access to abortion on demand, whereas in West Germany abortion, although permitted, required a doctor's certificate of necessity, even in the early months of pregnancy. The new compromise law embodies an uneasy contradiction, with early abortion being an unlawful but unpunishable offence. There is a staggering range of opinion on the abortion issue, both across as well as within nations, and there is no indication that this is an issue that the policy process is likely to resolve, because it taps into such fundamental moral conflicts, with both sides viewing their cause as sacred, and perhaps both being right (Steiner 1981).

Columns (5) and (6) of Table 3.3 show the percentage who take a pro-feminist stance regarding traditional gender roles and whether pre-school children suffer if their mothers go out to work. As with abortion, it is difficult to make sense of the spread of public opinion without taking into consideration the different national policies that are adopted for reconciling the demands of family and the labour force participation of women. With the exception of Poland, there is substantial rejection of the traditional gender-role ideology which specifies that a husband's job is to earn the money and a wife's job is to look after the home. However, the public tends to be much less sanguine about changing gender roles when it comes to the well-being of young children. Such concerns are widespread even in nations like Sweden or the former East Germany, where state childcare provision was very high. Significant gender differences are more common on this issue than for any of the others, with women far more likely than men to reject the notion that children will suffer if their mother works. Perhaps women are more conscious of the complex economic and social realities of child-rearing in this modern era and recognize that children's well-being is not simply a matter of maternal attention. Yet, in the main, there is public scepticism of the idea that maternal employment is in the best interests of the child.

DISCUSSION AND SUMMARY

What has this survey of attitudes shown? There have been clear changes over time in British and American attitudes. There is far greater acceptance of pre-marital sex. Although attitudes and behaviour are not always in line, the rejection of the traditional stance—that sexual relations belong only in marriage—has its counterpart in dramatic demographic trends concerning cohabitation and extra-marital births, especially among the young. Yet it would be wrong to conclude that marriage itself is no longer seen as having any influence on sexual behaviour. Belief in fidelity within marriage is extraordinarily consistent, over time and across nations. Behaviour may not always live up to ideals with regards to extra-marital sex, as divorce statistics citing adultery indicate, but the traditional ideal of 'forsaking all others' is clearly endorsed. Attitudes towards sexual relations between same-sex adults have also been subject to change. Although attitudes were subject to a temporary setback because of the AIDS scare in the 1980s, tolerance of homosexual relations has increased. In Britain, the change has mainly been among women, but in the United States tolerance has increased among both sexes.

There has also been a marked increase in approval of abortion among British women. In contrast, British men's attitudes have remained relatively stable over the past decade. In the early 1980s, men were more likely than women to consistently approve of legal abortion in a variety of circumstances. By the mid-1990s, women had become more approving of abortion than men. Among women, attitudes to abortion have been shifting much faster in Britain than in the comparable period in the United States. One plausible interpretation is that approval of legal abortion might be linked to rising expectations about the control of reproduction, rising costs of unwanted pregnancies, and rising concerns about the economic and social plight of single mothers. Although the conditions which would increase support for abortion are common to both nations, there is an important difference. In the United States, the New Right ideology has been coupled to a fundamentalist religious fervour that has brought a strong anti-abortion backlash. Although the so-called Moral Majority only enjoys a small minority of support, it has been far more vocal and politically active in the United States than in Britain.

In marked contrast to abortion attitude trends, the change in gender-role attitudes has been quite slight in Britain and due mainly to the slow but steady process of cohort replacement, where the earlier, more traditional cohorts are replaced by recent cohorts who tend to adopt more egalitarian attitudes. Some strands of social theory have emphasized how, in this age of new individualism, ascribed gender roles are undermined. Many feminist activists and academics are more sceptical about the extent of change. Our data suggest that, as far as attitudes are concerned, there has been change, but that this change is far from revolutionary. Attitudes favouring the traditional gender division of labour have largely been overturned, probably, in part, because a dual income is widely perceived to be necessary in order to maintain a reasonable standard of living. At the same time, there is also a widespread belief, especially among men, that women should put the responsibilities of motherhood first.

Cross-national attitudes differ markedly on issues concerned with gender relations and family choices. Yet in the six nations examined here, there was remarkable agreement about the relative culpability of different sexual behaviours and there was also the same gender difference, with women tending to be less approving of extra-marital sex and pre-marital sex than men, but more tolerant of homosexuality. The pattern of national differences in attitudes was, on the whole, in line with differing national policies. On abortion, for example, there are marked national differences in attitudes, with Ireland by far the most traditional and East Germany and Sweden by far the most liberal. The pattern is similar with respect to pre-marital sex. Poland, despite the dominance of the Catholic Church, is fairly moderate on abortion and pre-marital sex, but highly traditional on gender-role ideology and intolerant of sexual relations between adults of the same sex. The United States is very much tilted towards a more traditional stance, both for sexual morality and abortion, whereas Britain conforms to the 'grey' stereotype of British moderation and national attitudes, on average, never veer to either extreme.

Even for the most liberal of nations, however, it would be wrong to assert that old proscriptions and prescriptions about sexual morality and gender roles have been abandoned. Extra-marital sex is almost universally condemned. Homosexual relations are regarded by the majority as wrong. In all six nations, most people view maternal employment as harmful to young children. Certainly, there has been change over time, as our examination of Anglo-American attitudes over the past decades has demonstrated. Only a small minority now condemn pre-marital sex; support for legal abortion has risen quite markedly; support for a rigid gender-role division is increasingly rejected.

Truths go in and out of favour. The tide now seems to be towards emphasizing change. Talk of revolutionary changes in the sexual and family domains has a momentum of its own and catapults us into believing that there is an almost limitless range of acceptable choice. It is easy to understand why such a representation appeals to intellectuals, academics, and social researchers who want to tell an exciting story. But is it really the case? Has there been a revolutionary change in familial and sexual values? It has become fashionable among family historians and demographers to do some debunking of the nostalgic myths about 'the way we never were' (Coontz 1992). I would argue that there is a new myth that needs debunking: that we live in an age where new individualism has overturned traditional family constraints. This cross-national analysis of attitudes suggests that the demise of traditional values has been exaggerated.

NOTES

1. The British Social Attitudes Survey (BSA) is a nationally representative sample of adults interviewed in person by Social and Community Planning Research (SCPR).
2. Statistical techniques to arrive at the resolution of this identification problem have been proposed and debated elsewhere (e.g. Mason and Fienberg 1985; Firebaugh 1989; Alwin and Scott 1996; Heath and Martin 1996).
3. Data from 1984 and 1985 are combined to increase sample size and make estimates more stable.
4. The mean change is not weighted to take account of the different numbers in each age group. Otherwise it would be the exact equivalent of the percentage shift across the relevant years shown in Figs. 3.1*a* and 3.1*b*.
5. Only respondents who answered at least 5 items are included in the analysis.
6. If the medical circumstances for abortion are placed first, then approval for abortion for elective reasons is depressed. The most plausible explanation is that this ordering establishes a contrast effect whereby some people feel more free to express their reservations about abortion for relatively 'trivial reasons', once they have indicated approval for the more serious circumstances.
7. For abortion, data from 1983 and 1985 are combined to increase sample size and make estimates more stable; 1984 data are not used because of the change in question order.
8. The relatively small amount of change among the immediate post-pill generation of women is puzzling, as it seems unlikely that they would be less liberal than the pre-war generations. This unexpected lack of support for abortion among these cohorts (those in their 30s and 40s in the early 1980s) is not replicated by the responses to the 1994 ISSP self-completion questionnaire, which was administered to the same sample. In the self-completion questionnaire, the post-pill generations, as expected, were considerably more liberal than the oldest generations.

APPENDIX: EXACT WORDING OF SURVEY QUESTIONS

British Social Attitudes Survey

Sexual Morality

- If a man or a women have sexual relations before marriage what would your general opinion be? Would it be always wrong, mostly wrong, sometimes wrong, rarely wrong or not wrong at all?
- What about a married man having sexual relations with a woman other than his wife? (1983 only)

- What about a married woman having sexual relations with a man other than her husband? (1983 only)
- What about a married person having sexual relations with someone other than his or her partner? (1984 onwards)
- What about sexual relations between two adults of the same sex?

Abortion

Here are a number of circumstances in which a woman might consider an abortion. Please say whether or not you think the law should allow an abortion in each case.

- The woman decides on her own she does not want to have the child
- The woman is not married and does not wish to marry the man
- The couple can not afford any more children
- There is a strong chance of defect in the baby
- The woman's health is seriously endangered by the pregnancy
- The woman became pregnant as a result of rape

Gender Roles

Do you agree or disagree:

- A husband's job is to earn the money, a wife's job is to look after the home and family
- A pre-school child is likely to suffer if his or her mother works
- All in all family life suffers when the woman has a full-time job
- Having a job is the best way for a woman to be an independent person

International Social Survey Programme 1994

Sexual Morality

- Do you think it is wrong or not wrong if a man and woman have sexual relations before marriage? (always wrong, almost always wrong, wrong only sometimes, or not wrong at all)
- What about a married person having sexual relations with someone other than his or her husband or wife?
- And what about sexual relations between two adults of the same sex?

Abortion·

Do you agree or disagree:

- A pregnant woman should be able to obtain a legal abortion for any reason whatsoever, if she chooses not to have the baby.

Gender Role

As in British Social Attitudes Survey above.

4

Forecasting British families into the twenty-first century

Mike Murphy and Duolao Wang

INTRODUCTION

This chapter forecasts the numbers of adults and children who would be living in single, married, cohabiting, divorced, or lone-parent families under alternative scenarios of the trends in family formation and dissolution. In order to derive these scenarios, it is necessary to set the scene, since future trends, especially in the short term, reflect an evolution of current trends. Over recent decades, a number of major changes in people's living arrangements have been experienced to some extent by all Western developed societies (van de Kaa 1987). Examples include fewer marriages and more living alone, cohabitation, marital breakdown, and childbearing outside marriage. Over the period from the early 1970s to the mid-1990s, the following changes occurred in Britain:

- the numbers of people marrying for the first time fell by 40 per cent, about 300,000 fewer annually, and the number of widowed people remarrying more than halved;
- the annual number of divorces in England and Wales doubled—over 40 per cent of marriages will end in divorce at current rates; however, the number remarrying has remained constant since 1981;

Thanks are due to the ESRC, who funded this work as part of a project, *Formal Modelling of Households, Families and Kinship*, Grant No. L315253017. Thanks are also due to the Office for National Statistics for permission to use the SARs and the LFS data. The data used from the SARs were provided through the Census Microdata Unit of the University of Lancaster with the support of ESRC, JISC, and DENI and used with the permission of the Controller of The Stationery Office. BHPS and LFS data were made available through the ESRC Data Archive; BHPS data were originally collected by the ESRC Centre on Micro-social Change at the University of Essex. Neither the original collectors of the data nor the Archive bear any responsibility for the analyses or interpretations presented here.

- the proportion of births outside marriage rose by a factor of more than four, from 8 per cent in 1971 to 36 per cent in 1996;
- cohabitation became much more common, rising from 11 per cent of non-married women aged 18–49 in 1979 to 26 per cent in 1996; and
- the proportion of families with dependent children which were lone-parent families almost trebled, from 8 per cent in 1971 to 21 per cent in 1996.

The trend in fertility is more ambiguous, with a general tendency for a long-term decline in fertility rates, but with some fluctuations (Council of Europe 1997; Coleman and Chandola, Chapter 2 of this volume).

Demographic events which occur (or fail to occur) at an earlier point in a person's life can have a lifelong effect. For example, the proportion of 75–79-year-old women who were never-married in 1981 was 14 per cent; in 1991, the corresponding figure for this age group was 9 per cent (OPCS 1993). The older group entered the main marrying ages during the 1920s when rates were low for a number of reasons, including the slaughter of men in World War I and higher rates of emigration by men than by women. In contrast, later birth cohorts entered the marriage market at a more favourable time and this is reflected in their higher levels of marriage as they now enter the elderly phase of the life course.

While we are now able to trace the behaviour of these older groups, we cannot yet predict the experiences in the twenty-first century of those who entered the marriage market in the 1980s, but it is likely that these younger cohorts will continue to have very different life experiences from those who entered this phase in the 1960s, an historically unprecedented period for the popularity of marriage.

Some aspects of the future are more predictable than others and may therefore be forecast with greater confidence. Cohabitation, for example, is usually a relatively short-term state (although the average length has been increasing, especially in the recent past). Thus, forecasts of the numbers who will be cohabiting in future years depend largely on the numbers who will enter cohabitation in years to come rather than on the numbers currently cohabiting. On the other hand, the average length of time that a divorced person spends in that state is much longer. Therefore, the divorced population in years to come will be determined at least in part by the number of people now divorced, and will not depend solely on what will happen in the future.

Changes in the numbers in a particular state are determined by the flows into and out of the group, which depend in turn on changes in the composition of other groups. If those in one state have a high propensity to move into a second state, then an increase in the former group will lead to an increase in the second group. It is difficult to predict what may happen. Indeed, some of the findings may be counter-intuitive at first sight; for example, increases in cohabitation would lead, ceteris paribus, to decreases in the number of single-parent families and increases in the numbers married (Murphy and Wang 1997*a*).

In this chapter, we set out the main demographic trends in family patterns, discuss the data on which these trends are estimated, and consider how these might evolve. First, we summarize the main trends in living arrangements over recent decades and consider the ways in which they may be described. This sets the context within which we will consider what sorts of patterns of living arrangements may develop in years to come. In the second section, we describe the multi-state household projection method that we use to undertake the formal modelling of family change, and discuss how appropriate data are constructed. The third section shows the results of this process, based on two scenarios which show what would happen under different assumptions in terms of the life experiences of cohorts as they pass into the first decades of the twenty-first century, and discusses the implications of these findings for the likely experiences of the British population in future years. We end with a brief methodological postscript.

MAIN CHANGES IN LIVING ARRANGEMENTS OVER THE PAST QUARTER-CENTURY

Marriage

Marriage has been in steady decline since the early 1970s; overall, marriage rates are falling by 3 to 4 per cent per annum (Figure 4.1*a*). Compared with 1971, 293,000 fewer people married for the first time in 1995 in England and Wales. First-marriage rates dropped by 90 per cent for teenage women and by 80 per cent for those aged 20–24 (Table 4.1). Over this period, the median age at first marriage increased substantially from 23.4 to 27.9 years for men and from 21.4 to 26.0 years for women; the proportion of first marriages to women under age 20 decreased from nearly one-third to just 5 per cent (ONS 1997*d*). While part of the fall in marriage is due to a move towards later age at marriage—a shift in behaviour which would not necessarily mean that fewer people would ultimately marry (Ryder 1964; Cooper 1991; Murphy 1993*a*)—it seems implausible that all of those who have not been marrying at young ages will do so at older ages and we expect that considerably higher proportions of people now in their twenties and thirties will never marry than was the case for their contemporaries two decades earlier. We do not foresee any changes in the next decade or so which would lead to a reversal of these marriage trends, and

TABLE 4.1. *Marriage rates, females, England and Wales (per 1,000)*

	Year	Age			
		15–19	20–24	25–29	30–34
Single	1971	93	246	167	76
	1984	30	115	118	67
	1995	9[a]	50	83	62
Divorced	1971	—	467	359	233
	1984	—	227	171	120
	1995		112[b]	98	86

[a] Age 16–19.
[b] Age 16–24.
Sources: OPCS (1984) and ONS (1997*d*).

given the lack of any tendency for the decline in marriage to be arrested, it is likely that marriage rates will continue to fall, at least in the short and medium term. We therefore consider what would happen if the current levels were to persist, and if the recently observed declines were to continue.

Remarriage

While first-marriage rates have fallen over recent decades, the decline in remarriage rates has been even more pronounced. The great majority of remarriages, nearly 90 per cent, now involve divorced people; for divorced men, the rate of remarriage has fallen by three-quarters since 1971. Recently, overall remarriage rates for divorced women have fallen for the first time to a similar level to those for single women, indicating that those who have experienced marriage are no keener to do so again than those who have never done so, whereas in the early 1970s, they were twice as likely as single people to marry (Figure 4.1*b*). Remarriage rates for widowed people have also fallen sharply, having more than halved since 1971 among a much older population than those who are single or divorced at marriage. Again, we see no factors which would tend to reverse these remarriage trends.

Cohabitation

A trend associated with the decline in marriage in recent decades has been an increase in extra-marital cohabitation. Although living together without formal marriage had not been uncommon in some working-class communities in the past, it attracted little attention and the overall proportions

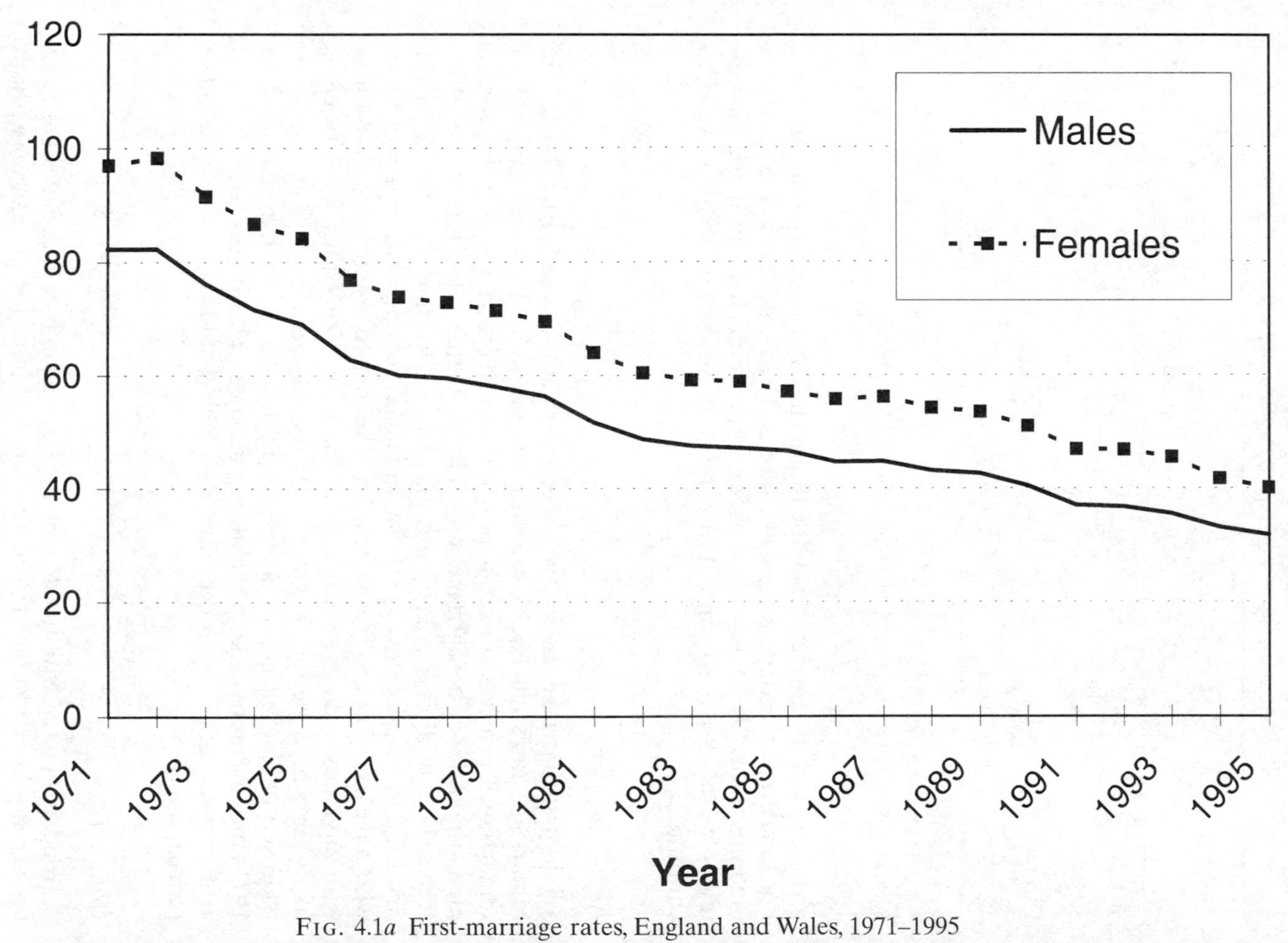

FIG. 4.1*a* First-marriage rates, England and Wales, 1971–1995

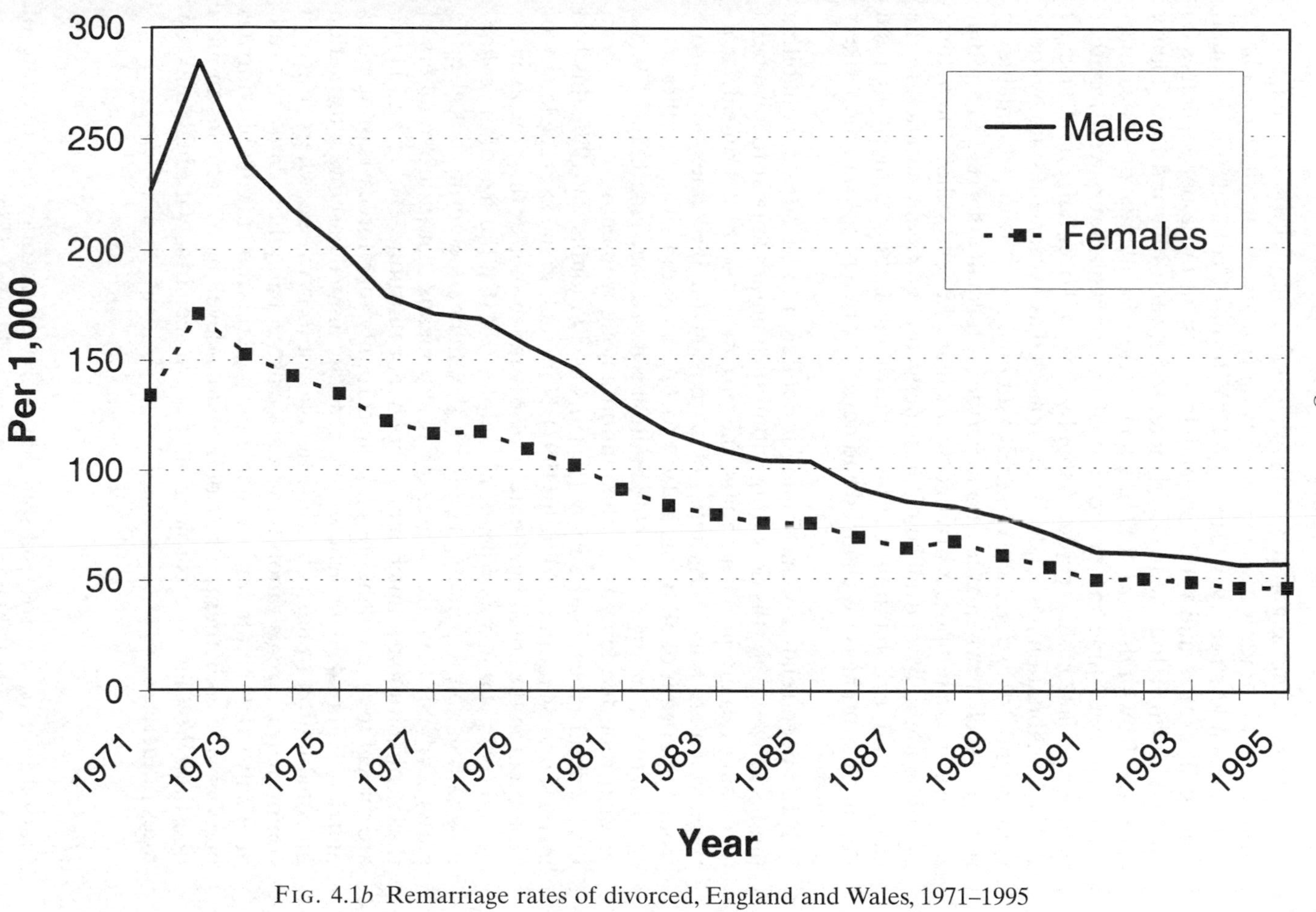

FIG. 4.1*b* Remarriage rates of divorced, England and Wales, 1971–1995

recorded as cohabiting were small in the 1960s (Dunnell 1979). Figure 4.2*a* shows annual trends for women not currently married for which data have been available since 1979. This 'modern' form of cohabitation is found among all groups, and with very similar trends; all those between ages 20 and 50 showing a four- to five-fold increase between 1979 and 1995 (Figure 4.2*b*; see Rowlands *et al.* 1997). Cohabitation frequently precedes marriage, and over time the proportion of people who have lived together before marriage has increased, so that by now well over half do so (Haskey 1997). Cohabitation has tended to be regarded as a transient state by those who intend to marry, and especially among those who are unable to remarry (such as when at least one partner is formally married to another person), or as a temporary arrangement. Figure 4.2*c* shows how the pattern of cohabitation by marital status has changed over recent decades. In the early period, cohabitation was more prevalent among formerly married people, but this has now changed and never-married people are more likely to cohabit.

It has been relatively uncommon for children to be born in cohabiting unions. However, births occurring within such unions appear to have been increasing rapidly in recent years; the proportion of births outside marriage which are jointly registered by parents giving the same address rose from 14 per cent of all births in 1989 to 20 per cent in 1996. Another indicator of the changing role of cohabitation is its average length. In 1979, the median reported length of cohabitation among women aged 18 to 49 in the General Household Survey (GHS) was 20 months: by 1995, this had increased to 34 months (Murphy 1997). Nonetheless, the average length of time spent in the cohabiting state is clearly much shorter than the average period spent within a marriage. This emphasizes that the size of the cohabiting population depends not only on the numbers entering but also the patterns of exit from that state, and it also means that future numbers of those cohabiting are much more dependent on future events, and hence are subject to much higher levels of uncertainty, than forecasts of numbers married. Figure 4.2*a* also shows that accurate annual baseline information on cohabitation trends is lacking. In contrast to marriage, where long-run comprehensive registration trend data exist, cohabitation data are available only from sample surveys. While the general trend in cohabitation has been upwards, whether this rate of increase is levelling off remains an open question. We therefore consider alternative scenarios with high and low rates of increase.

Divorce

Marital breakdown rose substantially in recent decades, but the rate of increase is now less than in the 1970s and early 1980s (Figure 4.3). In part,

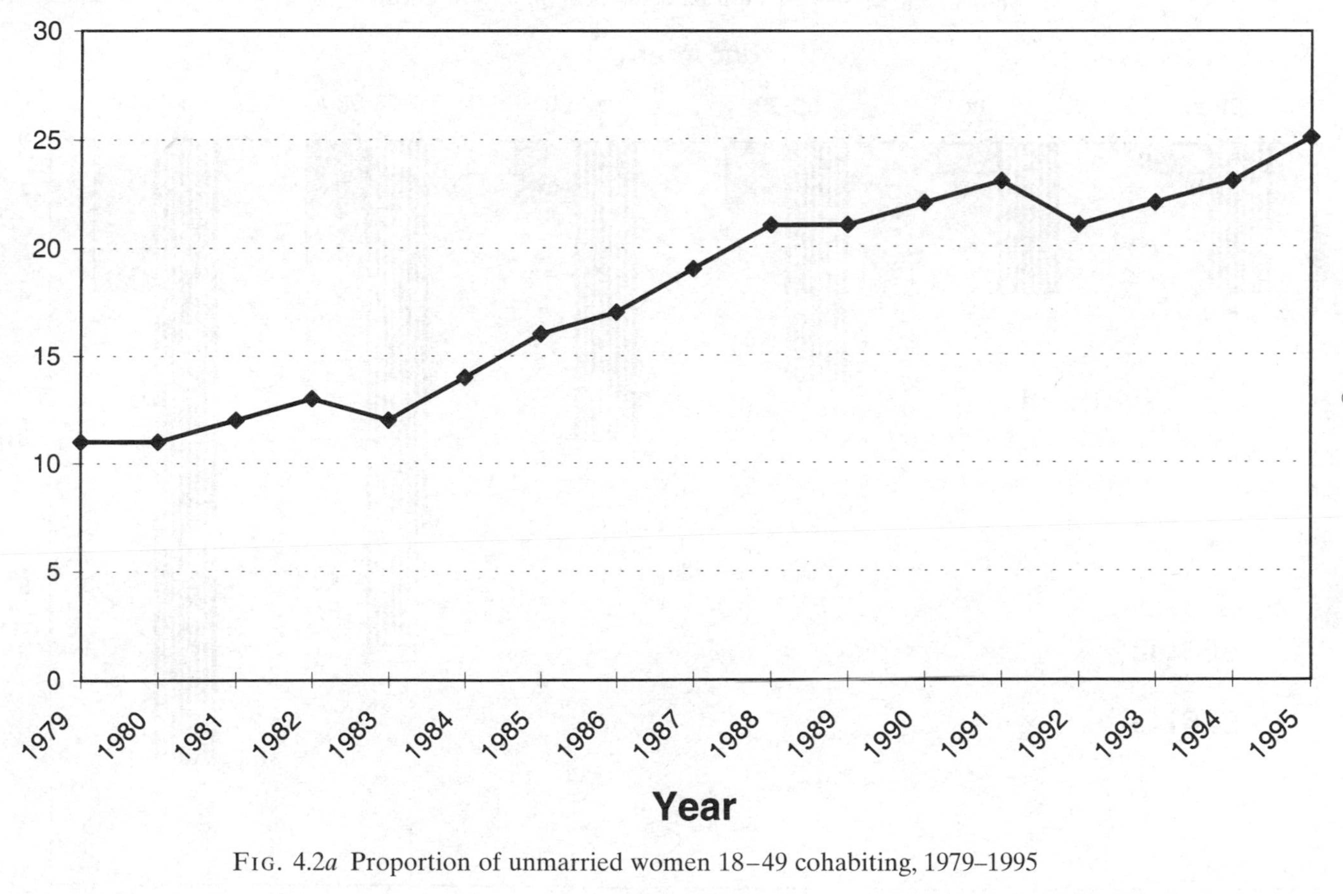

FIG. 4.2*a* Proportion of unmarried women 18–49 cohabiting, 1979–1995

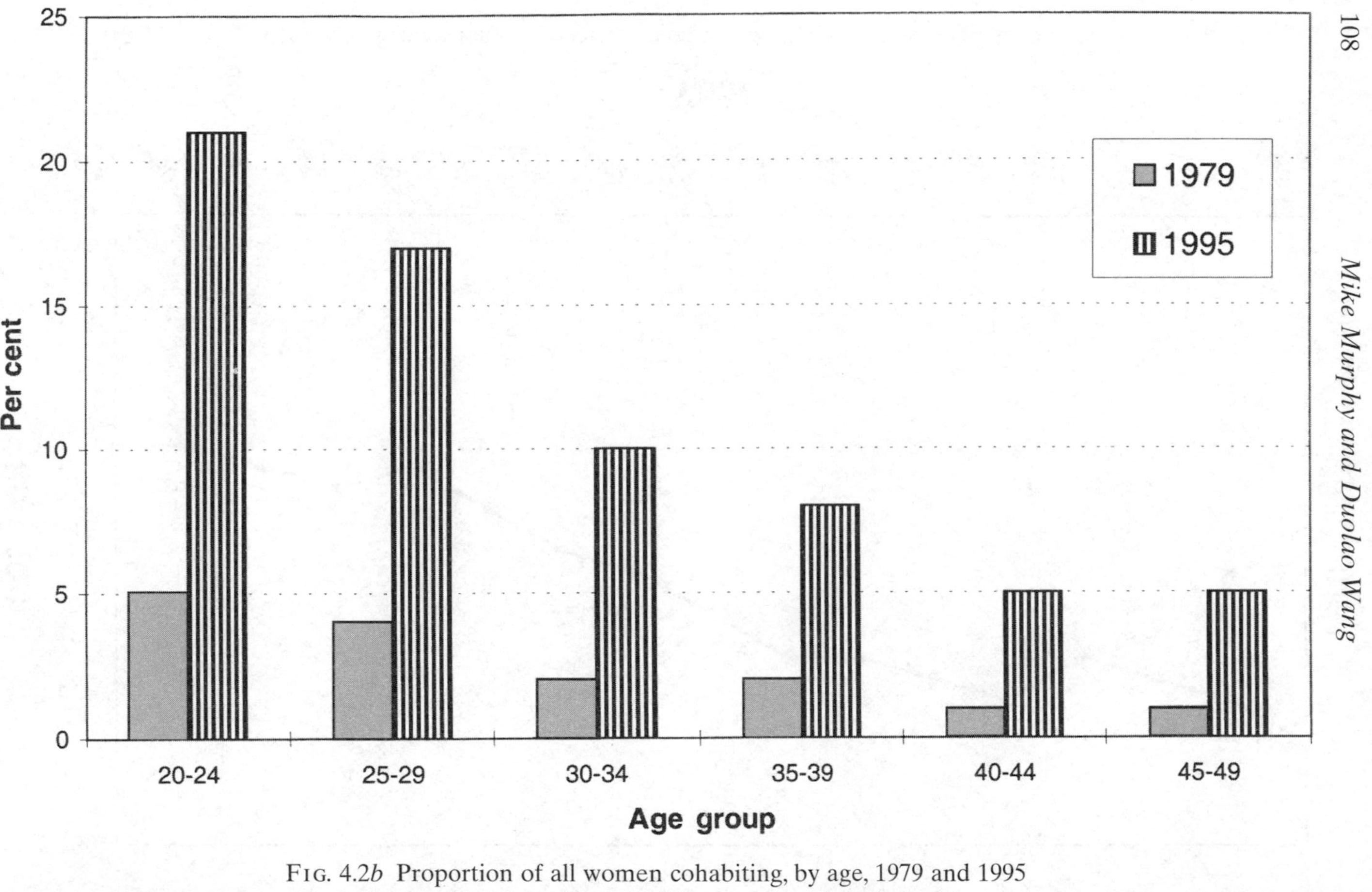

FIG. 4.2*b* Proportion of all women cohabiting, by age, 1979 and 1995

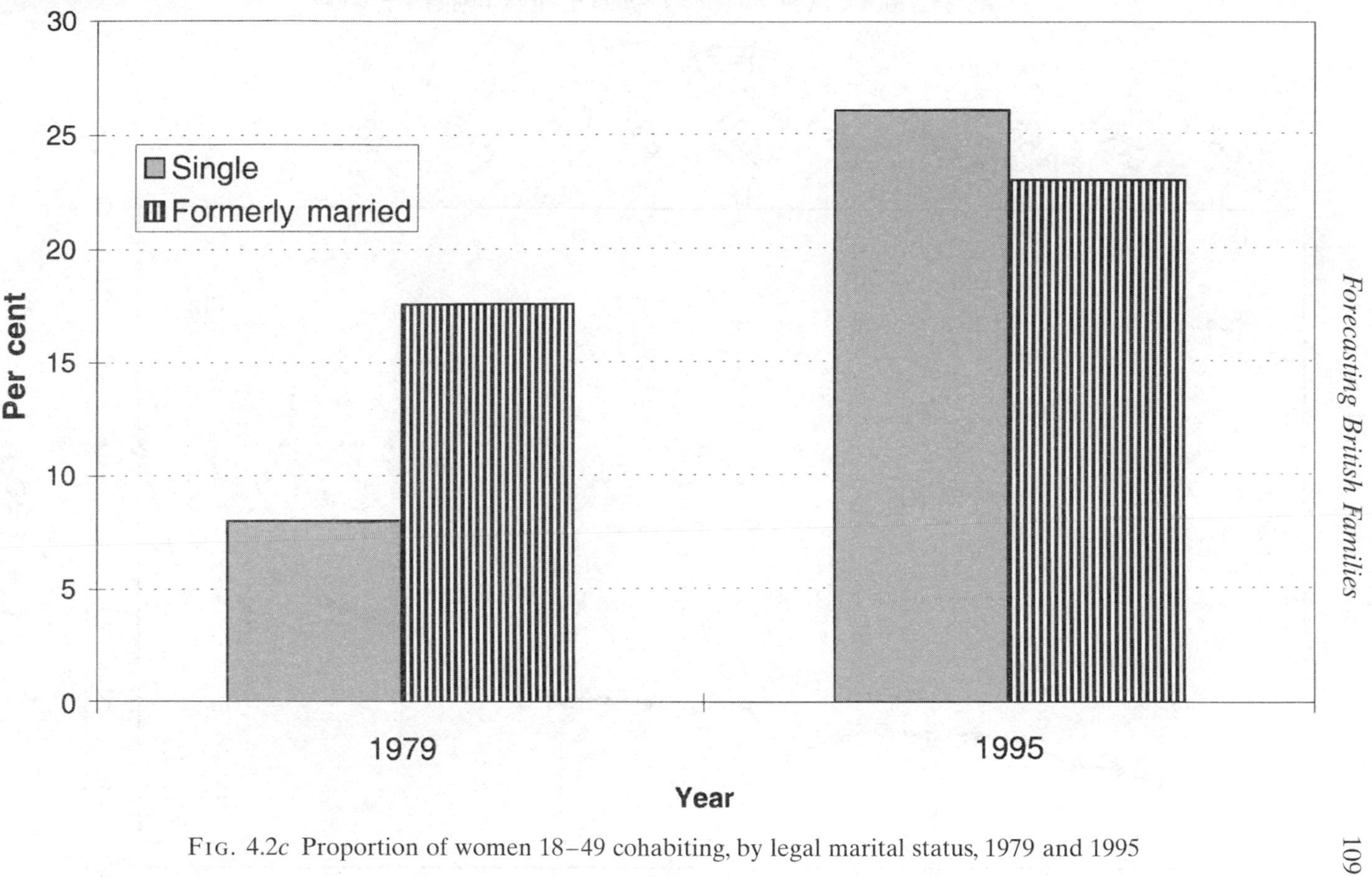

FIG. 4.2*c* Proportion of women 18–49 cohabiting, by legal marital status, 1979 and 1995

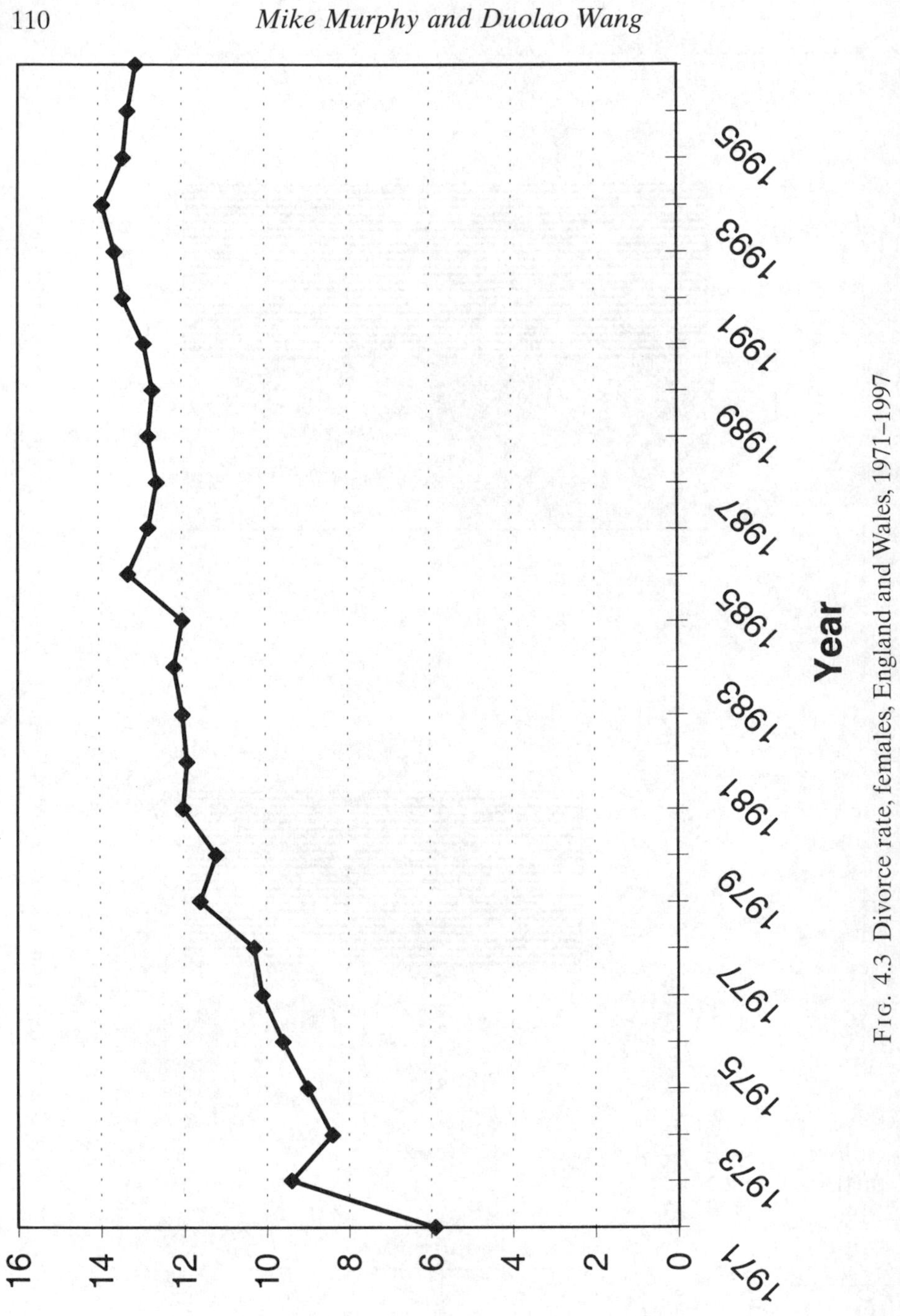

FIG. 4.3 Divorce rate, females, England and Wales, 1971–1997

this deceleration in divorce rates may be because the married population now contains fewer of those at high risk, such as teenagers (Table 4.1), who have very high divorce rates (Murphy 1985). While some increase in divorce may occur, this is likely to be modest: divorce rates are low in Britain compared with the USA but high in European terms, and at current rates over 40 per cent of marriages will end in divorce (Haskey 1996*a*). We therefore assume that divorce rates will remain at about their current levels. In practice, separation rather than divorce is the more relevant determinant of people's living arrangements and this can happen to cohabiting as well as married couples. However, as noted above, we have little reliable information about such informal events since information is available only from sample survey data.[1]

In the absence of clear indications about the trend in union dissolution, we have retained the current values. However, since the proportion of unions which are cohabiting as compared to married is increasing and dissolution rates are generally higher in the former, this compositional effect will lead to increasing overall levels of breakdown.

Lone-parent families

Changes in partnership arrangements have profound implications for children (Haskey 1996*b*). Over the past quarter-century, the proportion of families with dependent children which are lone-parent families has more than doubled, from 8 per cent to 21 per cent (Thomas *et al.* 1998). Initially, the rise was mainly among divorced lone parents as divorce rates rose and remarriage rates fell in the 1970s (Figure 4.4). Since the second half of the 1980s, the main growth in lone parents has come from never-married lone mothers, a consequence of factors including lowered marriage rates and a sharp increase in births outside marriage, from 13 per cent in 1981 to 36 per cent in 1996 in England and Wales. The proportion of widowed lone parents declined, as mortality rates improved over the period and age at last birth fell (Murphy and Grundy 1996). This shift is likely to have implications in a number of areas, and the pattern is likely to intensify if present trends continue. Data on the number of never-married lone parents, however, considerably overstate the extent to which young women bring children into the world without a partner present. In 1971, over half of births outside marriage were registered by the mother alone, whereas by 1996 this had fallen to 22 per cent (ONS 1997*d*). In cases of joint registration of births by both parents, information on whether they give the same address has been available from 1983. Over this period, the proportion of joint registrations for which the parents give the same address has been about 70 per cent (74 per cent in 1996) and this figure is often used as a proxy for births which occur to cohabiting couples. Indeed, the number

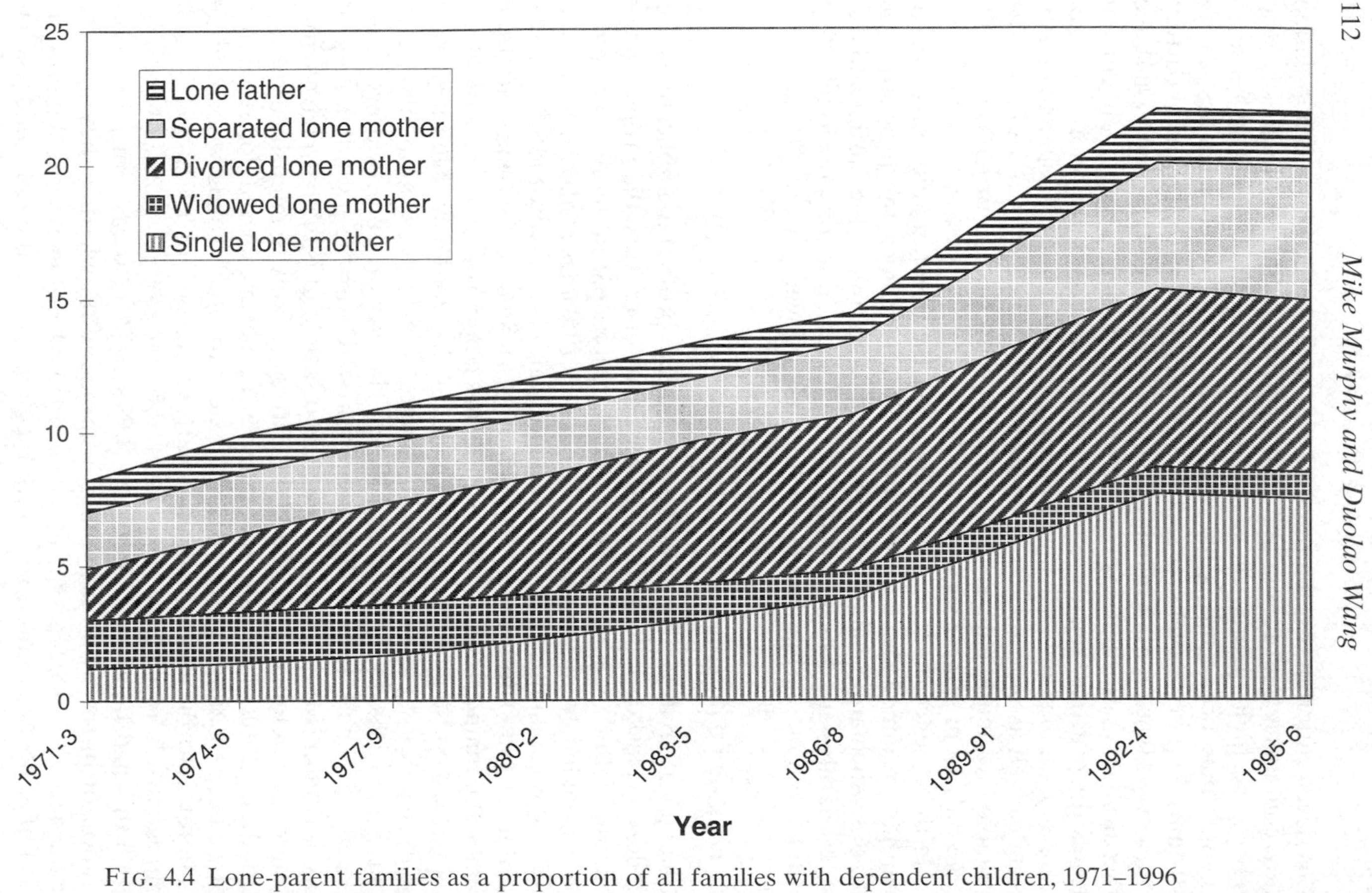

FIG. 4.4 Lone-parent families as a proportion of all families with dependent children, 1971–1996

of sole registered births only increased from 36,000 to 51,000 between 1971 and 1996 in England and Wales, an increase of one-third, whereas the proportion of families with dependent children which were single-mother families rose from 1 per cent in 1971 to 8 per cent in 1995 in Great Britain (Rowlands *et al.* 1997). Thus, the increase in lone parenthood is not only due to increases in women having children without a partner present, but also to other, possibly more important, factors such as breakdown of cohabiting unions and the reduced propensity of such mothers subsequently to marry or live with the child's father. These changes in lone parenthood mean that lone parents now tend to be younger and to have younger children and smaller family sizes than was the case in the past, when widowhood was the main reason for becoming a lone parent. As discussed later, we forecast the numbers of children living in lone-parent families from the forecast number of lone parents in order to ensure consistency between the numbers of parents and children in these different family situations.

Fertility

Trends in fertility have received less attention than those in family living arrangements, and the widespread decline in fertility in Western countries in the early 1990s has received surprisingly little comment. Britain has a relatively high level of fertility compared with most developed countries, including its EU partners (Coleman and Chandola, Chapter 2 of this volume). Fertility in England and Wales rose from the low point of a total fertility rate (TFR) of 1.66 in 1977, to remain in a fairly narrow band between about 1.80 and 1.84 until 1992. It fell in early 1996 to 1.69 (close to the lowest fertility ever recorded in England and Wales), but then increased sharply to 1.78 at the end of 1996 (ONS 1997*d*), emphasizing the difficulties inherent in forecasting fertility. We attribute this recent rise mainly if not wholly to the pill scare in November 1995, rather than to more distal socio-economic factors.[2] Whether the response will be relatively short-lived, as in 1971 and 1983, or longer-lasting, as in 1977, remains to be seen. While the possibility that fertility could be at a level equivalent to a TFR of 1.6 births per woman is one that deserves serious consideration, we have retained the assumptions made in the 1992-based official projections (Government Actuary 1995), which expects British fertility to be at a long-term TFR level of 1.8.

A major aspect of fertility change over recent decades has been the shift towards later ages at childbearing, with births at ages below 30 falling substantially but with rates above age 30 tending to remain relatively stable. Over the last quarter-century, there has been a steady rise in the average age at childbearing, from 26.2 in 1971 to 28.6 in 1996 in England and Wales.

A continuation of this rise in itself will tend to keep period fertility measures such as TFR low, a related aspect being that the proportion of women under age 30 who are not married has increased, and married women have higher fertility than unmarried ones. At present, well over half of births to women under age 25 are outside marriage, and nearly one-third of those to women aged 25–29. As the proportions married in their 20s and early 30s decline, this will have interactions with the level and age of childbearing which should not be ignored. The rest of this chapter is concerned with such interactions.[3]

FORECASTING METHODS FOR FAMILIES AND HOUSEHOLDS

Criteria for groups selected

Before forecasting family types, a decision is needed on the types of families to be analysed. More disaggregated models give greater detail but are more difficult to specify and fit, and possibly more unstable. There is, therefore, the empirical question of the appropriate level of disaggregation. For the trends set out above, there is a clear interest in the evolution of aspects such as lone parenthood and cohabitation which have become an increasing topic of public interest for a number of reasons: both have recently become more prominent; they are increasing rapidly; and both carry wider socio-economic implications. For example, expenditure on lone-parent Social Security Benefits in the UK in 1996–7 was £10.0 billion, compared with £0.7 billion in 1979–80 and £5.6 billion in 1991–2 (DSS 1994, 1997). The implications of these patterns for both the children involved and society in general have been extensively discussed and we therefore concentrate on estimating how children's living arrangements may evolve as a result of their parents' behaviour. For reasons discussed earlier, there are clearly different trends, characteristics, and underlying mechanisms at work determining the number of lone parents of differing marital statuses. We have therefore analysed single, separated or divorced, and widowed lone parents separately. We have considered married and cohabiting couples with and without children separately because they also have different characteristics (Haskey 1996*b*). These considerations yield fifteen family situations for those living in the private household sector (space precludes discussion of the non-private household sector; see Murphy and Wang 1997*b*). The set of family types comprises five de facto marital statuses, subdivided for adults by whether they have dependent children present or not, and for children by the type of family unit they live in. The criteria we used for selection may be summarized as follows: groups must be

- socially important;
- important for modelling population flows;
- easily 'forecastable', for example, age and sex groups;
- homogeneous;
- relatively large in number; and
- capable of providing robust estimates.

Table 4.2 provides a summary of the groups used in analysis and indicates baseline population numbers. This baseline population distribution was derived from the 1991 one per cent Sample of Anonymised Records (SARs), in order to provide a population of sufficient size, since typical sample survey sizes are inadequate for this purpose. These values have been grossed up to the 1991 private household population numbers.

TABLE 4.2. *Summary of groups used*

Type of unit	Number (000s)	%
One person (not in family or non-dependent child)		
One person, single (never-married) (Si0)	7,906	15
One person, divorced/separated (DS0)	2,064	4
One person, widowed (Wi0)	3,530	7
Families with and without children		
Couples:		
Married, no child (Ma0)	14,253	27
Married, with child(ren) (Co+)	9,895	19
Cohabiting, no child (Co0)	1,563	3
Cohabiting, with child(ren) (Co+)	741	1
Lone parents:		
Single female (Si+)	428	1
Divorced/separated female (DS+)	742	1
Widowed female (Wi+)	83	—
Dependent child living with parents(s):		
Married couple (CMa)	9,189	17
Cohabiting couple (CCo)	630	1
Single (never-married) parent (CSi)	619	1
Divorced/separated parent (CDS)	1,373	3
Widowed parent (CWi)	125	—
Total	53,140	100

— Less than 0.5%.

In this classification, we treat adult (that is, non-dependent[4]) never-married children living with their parents as separate units, rather than as members of the parental family as is normally done in the Census and major surveys such as the General Household Survey (GHS). This is because for many purposes, such as eligibility for social security benefits, they are treated separately. In fact, we are simply returning to the form of classification of families used in the 1951 Census of Britain, in a number of other countries at present, and in schemes which have been advocated for general purposes (van Imhoff and Keilman 1991).

The way in which cohabiting couples are identified is discussed elsewhere (Murphy 1996*b*). There are a number of problems in constructing consistent estimates. The proportion of children under age 1 reported as living with cohabiting couples in the 1991 Census is much smaller than the proportion of births registered in the previous twelve months by non-married parents at the same address. The treatment of those whose cohabiting unions have broken down is unclear: formally their marital status should be their legal marital status, but it could be argued that those with disrupted cohabiting unions should be classified as 'separated or divorced' rather than 'single' (if that is their formal status). Many of those whose cohabiting unions have broken down, especially those who retain any children of the union, describe themselves as separated or divorced, but some give their formal status as single. However, it seems unlikely that, for example, a man who lived in a short-term childless relationship some years earlier would describe himself as separated or divorced. This remains a grey area since there is a lack of consistency between data sources and in how people may record themselves at different time points in the same survey. We have therefore made a number of ad hoc adjustments to our data which space precludes from describing, but we note that there are no definitive estimates of the population broken down by de facto marital status, and indeed the official estimates of de jure marital status for 1991 were only published in late 1997.

Methods for forecasting populations and population subgroups may be broken down into two main groups, ratio (static) and transition-based (dynamic) models. Both methods are used in official projections and the reason why we use the second of these two approaches will therefore be discussed.[5]

Ratio methods

Ratio methods (Shryock *et al.* 1976) have been used as the basis for demographic projections, such as household, economic activity, urban–rural, and subnational ones (Bogue *et al.* 1993). They apply a projected estimated proportion, or 'splitting fraction', to the corresponding projected population aggregate, typically produced by a different method. For example, in household projections, the number of households headed by 30–34-year-old married men may be obtained by multiplying the projected headship rate for this group by the overall projected population in the group (the headship rate is the proportion of people designated as 'head of household' or 'reference person' in the relevant sex, age, and family category) (Kono 1987). The projected headship rate may be obtained by extrapolation from, for example, a series of values from recent censuses (Corner 1985, 1989; Capron and Corner 1990). The total number of projected households is obtained by summing the projected numbers over all types of heads of household, but this method also gives the distribution of households by the age, sex, marital status, and other characteristics of the household head (DoE 1995). The types of category used in the official household projections, such as lone-parent families and cohabiting couples, are broadly similar to those considered here, and therefore would a priori provide a suitable basis for forecasting. However, although ratio methods require only very limited data, there are a number of limitations to this approach:

- they are often based on mechanical extrapolation of time trends and therefore do not allow the role of the factors which determine change to be assessed;
- there is a problem of ensuring internal consistency: for example, projections of families with children may not be consistent with fertility forecasts;
- the approach fails to model the actual processes of change.

Dynamic models

A conventional and convenient way to make population projections is to apply fertility, mortality, and migration rates to a base population broken down by age and sex (Shryock *et al.* 1976). This approach is used for official national and subnational population projections in Britain because it provides an accurate and realistic mathematical model of the real world (that is, the population changes by births and deaths; different age groups have different probabilities of dying, moving, marrying, or divorcing; only women within certain age groups give birth). The model is based on rates that should move in a more predictable way than would happen, for example, by using raw numbers of births and deaths. Assumptions can be formulated more easily (for example, incorporating the effects of mortality improvement or reductions in nuptiality); and unlike mathematical extrapolation methods, details of the process, such as annual numbers of births, deaths, and marriages by age, are provided as an automatic by-product. Finally, there is considerable scope for using specialized knowledge in formulating assumptions (for example, cohabitation, old age, mortality, or fertility change).

Such a model applies transition rates (or 'jump intensities') to a base population in order to produce an updated population year by year on the transitions made by cohorts, such as those born in a particular year. The steps in making projections are as follows: estimate the baseline populations; estimate the transitions for each sex and age group between the initial and final stages; estimate the transition probabilities in the first interval of projection; specify a scenario for the rest of the projection period by making assumptions about the intensities for each interval. The model is sometimes referred to as a stock and transition flow, demographic component, or cohort component method, and it assumes that individuals in a particular category are subject to the same transition rate probabilities irrespective of how long they have been in that category or their previous state. This Markovian assumption is not wholly valid (Land and Rogers 1992) and it may be relaxed, for example, by making the transition rates dependent on time spent in the state (Wolf 1988); but this leads to massive increases in the number of parameters required and it is unfeasible in most cases. We have attempted to minimize this problem by having a large number of categories and by imposing a number of constraints on the system (see below).

When the population can move backwards and forwards between different states, the model is referred to as a *multi-state population projection model*. The benefits of such a model are:

- it is easily updatable and non-negative population values are guaranteed;
- it automatically generates a set of internally consistent projections without further ad hoc adjustment, such as to a control total (although as discussed later, when this approach is extended to family units, some additional constraints are required);
- it allows the construction of useful measures, such as the expected future number of years to be spent in each state of the system according to the state individuals are in at any particular age.

The multi-state family projection model and its data requirements

Thus, given an initial base population, a set of relevant intensities, and assumptions about the future trends in these rates, it is possible to project the population in the various family situations such as those of Table 4.2 using a multi-state household projection model. The benefits of a transition-based model would appear to be substantial, but in the particular context of forecasting families, there are some additional points that need to be considered: because of constraints within the system, such as that the number of men who marry must equal the number of women who do so, the specification and fitting of such models is much more complicated than the case of regional projections where individuals do not interact with each other. Data requirements are also substantial. A model which is used for annual forecasting needs single-year-of-age populations: for ages 0 to 100+, this requires 102 matrices of transition rates for each sex. With an average of about fifty possible transitions at each age between the various states in Table 4.2, about 10,000 separate transition rates are required for each year for which a projection is made. Further, it is difficult to model events which link the situations of individuals in different cells of the model (for example, parental marital breakdown should automatically alter their children's situation as well, but this is difficult to implement). The topic of data availability will now be considered in the light of these points.

We undertake the projections for five-year age bands to simplify the analysis (single-year data are covered in Murphy and Wang 1997*b*) and therefore results are available at five-year intervals ahead of the base year. The model has fifteen separate categories, leading to a maximum of 210 possible *internal* transitions between these states for each age group and sex (although this only holds for age groups 10–14 and 15–19 since for adults there are ten, and for children only five, possible states). The population analysed is the private household population, and entry is assumed to occur only at birth and exit only at death. Migration, therefore, is ignored (including to and from the institutional sector as well as abroad) because no suitable data exist. Since information on de facto statuses is required, survey data must be used in some cases. For the five marital status groups analysed, thirteen out of the twenty off-diagonal internal cells may be non-zero (Table 4.3).

Forecasting cohabitation rates is particularly problematic for several reasons: the numbers involved are large; there are more transitions into and out of cohabitation than other categories; there have been substantial changes in the pattern of cohabitation in recent decades; data are available only from sample surveys; and there are problems in establishing precise estimates with sample sizes such as those of the GHS or the British Household Panel Study (BHPS).

Construction of rates

For *internal transition rates*, we use the basic pattern of transitions given by the BHPS. To increase the effective sample size, the numbers of transition events were aggregated from Waves 1 to 5 of the BHPS conducted between 1991–2 and 1995–6. Average annual sample sizes of those present

TABLE 4.3. *Allowable and forbidden direct (instantaneous) transitions between marital status groups*

	To					
From	Single	Cohabiting	Married	Widowed	Separated/ divorced	Dead
Birth	✔					
Single	*	✔	✔			✔
Cohabiting	✔	*	✔	✔	✔	✔
Married		✔	*	✔	✔	✔
Widowed		✔	✔	*		✔
Separated/ divorced		✔	✔		*	✔

✔ possible event.
* the diagonal.

at the beginning of the interval who were also interviewed twelve months later, and aggregated average annual number of events, are shown in Table 4.4.

There are two major problems which mean these data cannot be used in a transition-based model without substantial processing. First, the number of sample events is very small when the number of events in Table 4.4 is distributed between five-year cohorts within each sex and the multiple outcomes possible. With forty age/sex groups, and an average of six outcomes for a transition from a particular state, about 2,000 separate transition rates need to be estimated from an annual average of 1,100 events. As indicated in note 1, even with much larger numbers of events, there is substantial imprecision in making such estimates. Secondly, the recorded events are subject to various biases. To illustrate this point, Figure 4.5 shows the annual estimated percentage change in the numbers of adults. The cross-sectional distributions have been aggregated over Waves 1 to 4 and 2 to 5 respectively, and the cross-sequential data are based on aggregating matrices for Waves 1 and 2, Waves 2 and 3, Waves 3 and 4, and Waves 4 and 5. Thus, the transition (cross-sequential) data are based on those individuals present at two successive waves, and the cross-sectional data on those present at any wave. These two data sets indicate very different trends, especially for cohabiting family types. The transition data show a *decline* over time at an annual rate of about 2 per cent per annum, and the cross-sectional data show an *increase* of about 10 per cent per annum. This may be because cohabiting unions are of shorter duration on average so that many of those cohabiting in the cross-sectional sample will not be present in the previous or subsequent year. Thus, to use such transition data would give the misleading impression that cohabitation is declining.

TABLE 4.4. *Numbers in sample and of transitions: average of BHPS Waves 1–5*

	Sample size[a]		Number of transitions in year	
	Frequency	%	into group	out of group
Dependent child living with:				
Single (never-married) parent (CSi)	94	1	15	13
Cohabiting couple (CCo)	180	2	48	40
Married couple (CMa)	2,163	18	207	52
Separated/divorced parent (CDS)	329	3	75	65
Widowed parent (CWi)	47	—	11	7
Adult:				
Single (never-married) person (Si0)	1,691	14	136	215
Single, with child(ren) (Si+)	84	1	12	18
Cohabiting, no child (Co0)	464	4	137	109
Cohabiting, with child(ren) (Co+)	205	2	48	57
Married, no child (Ma0)	3,062	26	149	228
Married, with child(ren) (Ma+)	2,310	19	166	136
Div/sep, no child (DS0)	405	3	51	78
Div/sep, with child(ren) (DS+)	183	2	37	39
Widowed, no child (Wi0)	694	6	16	52
Widowed, with child(ren) (Wi+)	23	—	4	4
Total	11,934	100	1,111	1,111

[a] For those present at start and end of 12-month period at any wave.
—Less than 0.5%.

On the other hand, the cross-sectional data are not nationally representative because the sample design means that it adds and removes people non-randomly (Murphy 1996*b*), and, of course, all sample surveys are subject to biases from non-response. Re-weighting the sample is not an answer because accurate weights can only be obtained if the true values are known, and if there were such a definitive source it would presumably have been used in the first place. GHS data suggest an annual increase of about 1 per cent per annum over this period.

Because of variability in the sample data, whenever possible we use data where coverage is complete for estimation of jump intensities, such as vital registration data for births and deaths. These have had to be allocated to the various dimensions of our state space (for example, deaths are not recorded by cohabiting status; further details are given in Murphy and Wang 1997*b*). These are also *externally constrained* to the values projected in the 1992 Official Population Projections (Government Actuary 1995); for example, fertility has a long-term TFR value of 1.8. For internal events, jump intensities are based on the pattern from the BHPS data. We have adjusted the transition-based data matrices to make them consistent with

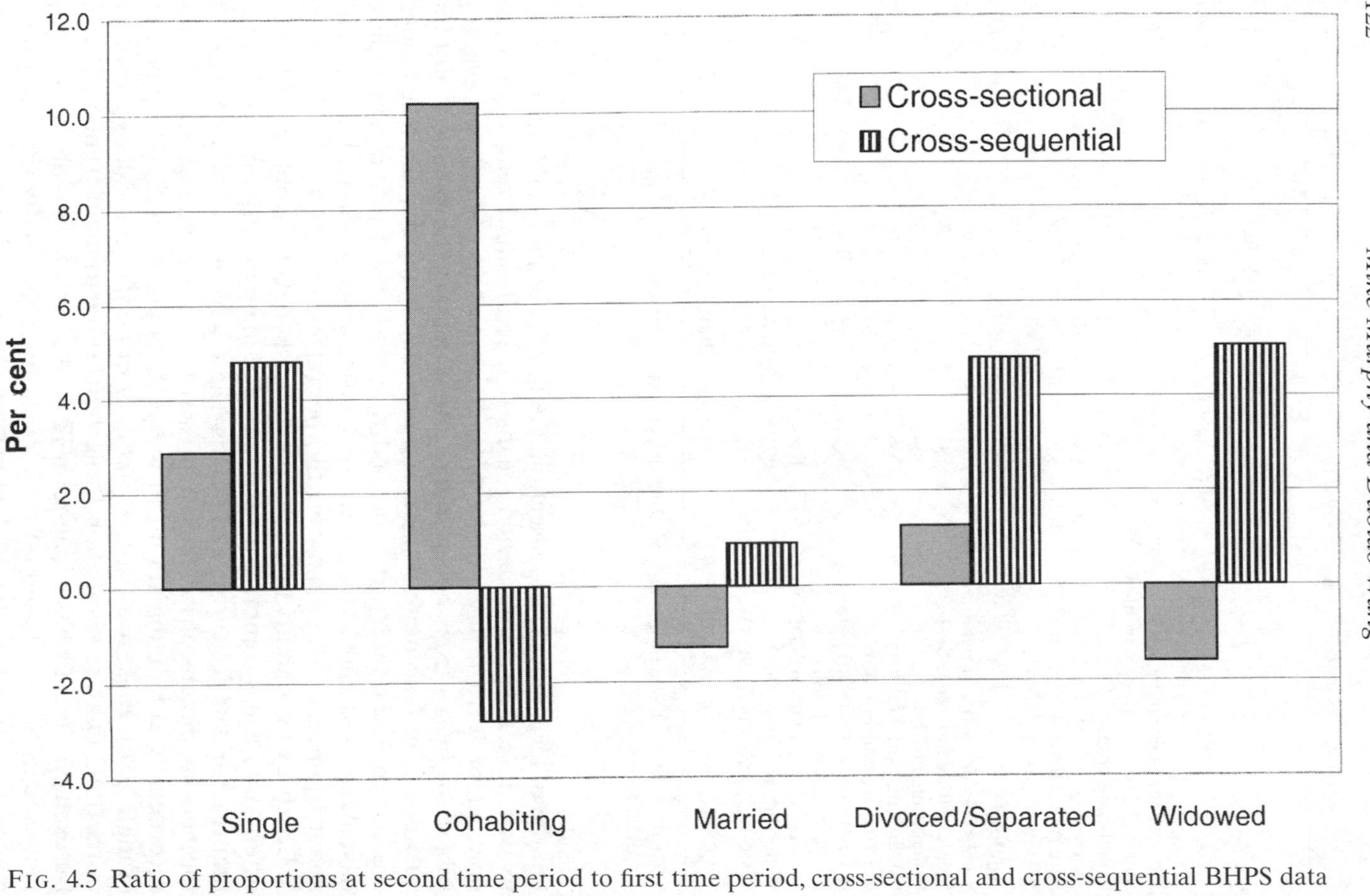

FIG. 4.5 Ratio of proportions at second time period to first time period, cross-sectional and cross-sequential BHPS data

the distribution of the base population (the method used is discussed in Appendix A). Thus, the result of this adjustment process is to produce a set of adjusted transition values which are used as the basis of our scenario assumptions.

Model-fitting considerations

Two-sex models

Rates cannot be applied independently to men and women since there are a large number of constraints that exist. The number of men who marry, for example, must equal the number of women who do so in any time period. In order to achieve this, we use age-specific rates for males and females applied independently, but subsequently made consistent with each other by mutual adjustment. We implicitly assume that marriage, cohabitation, and divorce are based on joint decisions and so are in the form of 'active' constraints where the mutual adjustment process is used. In contrast, events such as the change of status by the surviving spouse from married to widowed following the partner's death is a consequence of the death and is therefore a 'passive' constraint.

Treatment of children

Children's family status may be projected in two main ways. The first approach projects the child's status within each sex and age cell using transition rates for the child. This has the same problems as found with the separate projection of males and females in the standard population projection model, in that the values for males and females will in general diverge. Separate projection of children and parents may lead to unrealistic family sizes, and so we prefer to use an alternative method that treats the child's status as dependent upon their parents' transitions. This involves a passive constraint in that, for example, if a couple separate, the children of the family move in consequence from being in a couple to being in a lone-parent family. The children could move to some other form of living arrangement, such as living with a grandparent, but such events are rare in Britain and we assume that children remain with one or the other natural parent. It is necessary for such children to be distributed to both mothers and fathers, although the great majority remain with the mother. This reallocation of children is achieved by transferring the average number of children in a family that experiences the parental event.

There remain a large number of difficulties in modelling transition rates for dependent children. Examples include that of a male lone parent with one child who marries or lives with a woman in a similar situation, which means that both make the transition to being a couple with two children;

another is that of a child living with a separated mother who moves to live with his or her father on his remarriage. These issues are considered in more detail in Murphy and Wang (1997*b*).

A DYNAMIC MULTI-STATE PROJECTION OF FAMILY TYPES OVER THE NEXT FIVE DECADES

Forecasts are made using the LIPRO model devised by Evert van Imhoff and Nico Keilman at the Netherlands Interdisciplinary Demographic Institute (NIDI) (van Imhoff and Keilman 1991; van Imhoff 1994; Murphy and Wang 1996). A brief description of the model is given in Appendix B. Among the reasons for this choice are that the model permits the calculation of rates which are subject to the arbitrary control constraints, and allows consistency constraints for the two-sex model to be imposed in order to produce internally consistent results.

Specification of assumptions

As will have become apparent, we do not have defensible estimates of the level or trend of some of the main demographic variables in our model. Moreover, theoretical and/or empirical results, whether from detailed qualitative studies or quantitative econometric/statistical analyses, have proved to be of little or no benefit for forecasting purposes. This is not to imply that such work is without value; rather, whatever insights such work provides in improving our understanding of the past, as the chapters in this volume illustrate, they provide little useful information for assigning quantitative values to what may happen in the future. Therefore, we have set up what we regard as two plausible scenarios, which may be contrasted with a 'no change' scenario showing what would happen even if there were no behavioural changes in the future. These scenarios broadly continue the trends that have been observed in recent years into the next five decades or so. Extrapolation is neither objective nor unique. This is illustrated by Figure 4.6, which shows the results of extrapolating the proportion cohabiting by means of two widely used trend curves, exponential and Gompertz forms. The former extrapolates the observed constant rate of growth, and the latter fits a 'sigmoidal' or S-shaped curve which has the more realistic long-term behaviour of moving towards an asymptotic value and therefore need not go above 100 per cent as in the former case. On the basis of past performance, there is little to choose between them, but they lead to values differing by a factor of two by 2011. While we could use more sophisticated approaches such as Bayesian averaging (Wang and Murphy 1997) or ad hoc ones such as mixture models, these would not overcome the basic lack of data on de facto statuses.

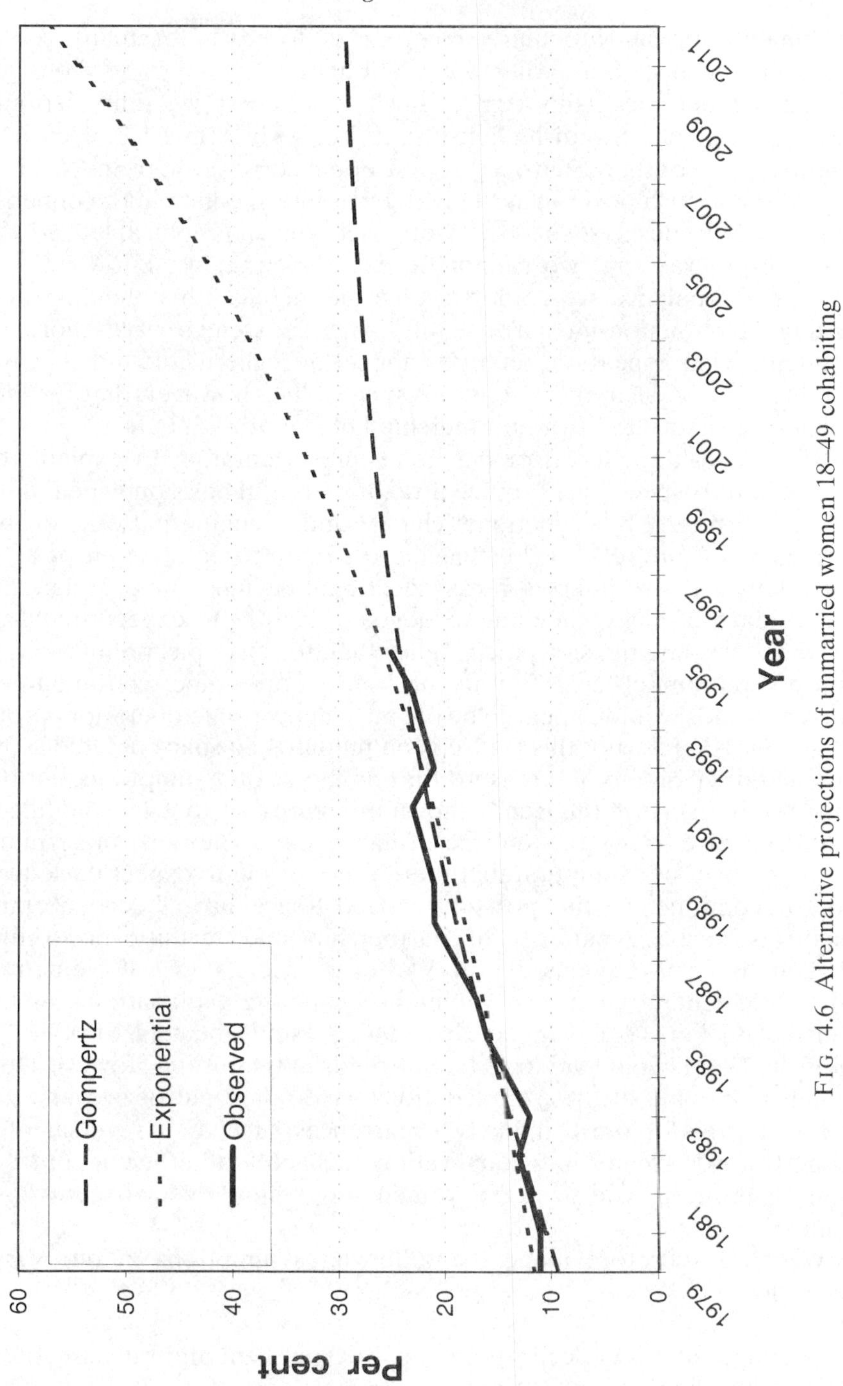

FIG. 4.6 Alternative projections of unmarried women 18–49 cohabiting

Cohabitation is particularly complex to forecast, for many reasons, including those set out earlier. We might hope to gain insights from international experience—this comes down to whether we think Britain is moving along the Swedish/Danish path but with a time lag. Clearly, the countries of Southern Europe are not doing so at present and we might regard the British position as likely to be as intermediate in the dimension of public attitudes to sexual behaviour as it is in geographical latitude. This is simply to say that we cannot be confident that we know what will happen. On balance, we do not foresee the increases in cohabitation offsetting the reductions in marriage rates, since the trend towards more independent living appears to retain its appeal over the whole life course (cf. Chapters 9 and 11 in this volume). We speculate, however, that fertility is becoming dissociated from partnership behaviour.

While considerable effort has gone into attempting to explain these trends in retrospect, they provide little or no useful basis on which to forecast the future. While ideational change and changing patterns of living arrangements are related (Lesthaeghe 1995), for forecasting purposes this is irrelevant if we cannot forecast ideational change. Thus, by default, in the absence of any compelling evidence to lead us to expect any change in trend, or some quasi-mystical belief that, for example, populations will enjoy replacement-level fertility at some future time, continuation of current trends would appear to be the most appropriate operational course of action. The focus of this article is on methods, so space precludes more detailed discussion of the reasons for our choice of assumptions, but these are based largely on the trends shown in Figures 4.1 to 4.4 as modified by our subjective views of how these may evolve. They are underpinned, however, by the assumption that there is no reason to expect these trends *not* to continue. In the post-war period, there have been substantial reversals in both patterns of partnership and fertility, not only in Britain, but more generally in Western societies (see Coleman and Chandola, Chapter 2 of this volume). Competing explanations for these trends (Becker 1981; van de Kaa 1987; Lesthaeghe and Surkyn 1988; Murphy 1993) could lead to different trends in the future. However, to the extent that some of these explanations have fallen out of favour or that reversal would require unlikely occurrences such as a reversal of the trend towards greater individualization, less access to efficient contraception, or reduced paid work by women, any major reversal seems highly implausible.[6]

We have therefore made the following assumptions in our varying scenarios:

- marriage rates will decline annually by 3 per cent and rates of entering cohabitation will increase annually by 0.5 per cent;

- marriage rates will decline annually by 2 per cent and rates of entering cohabitation will increase annually by 2 per cent.

The first scenario contains our estimates of current rates and of a continuation of these trends. The second is based on a rather lower rate of decline in marriage than the one of about 3.5 per cent per annum found recently, and on a continuation of high increases in cohabitation. It is assumed that rates of divorce and separation will remain constant. The effects of these assumptions are not straightforward (which is why we require a relatively complex forecasting model). For example, since most marriages are now entered from the cohabiting state, declining marriage rates will lead, ceteris paribus, to increases in the proportions cohabiting. This would occur because exits from the cohabiting state would decrease and so the average length of time spent cohabiting would increase. As a consequence, the proportion of people cohabiting at a given point in time would increase without any necessary increase in the numbers of people entering cohabitation each year (although we expect this to happen as well).[7] Thus, increases in cohabitation are due to 'deepening' as well as 'broadening'. These issues are considered in more detail in Murphy and Wang (1997*a*).

Results of the projection

The two scenarios described above, together with the stationary (no change) situation results, are shown here. These scenarios are based on a continuation of current trends into the future. Space precludes discussion of the important area of the assessment and presentation of errors in population forecasts, and there are a number of studies which have considered this aspect, although not in the context of the complex models used here (see, for example, Murphy and Wang 1997*a*). We do not present measures of error for our forecasts, but rather use the two scenarios to show the differences that would be obtained under alternative assumptions. One of the problems with attempting to illustrate the variability of these forecasts is that individuals in any group may have been through many earlier transitions, and even if one regarded, say, marriage rates as reasonable, the married population will depend on cohabitation rates as well.

What these scenarios do, however, is to show how sensitive each of these groups is to changes in rates in the future. Some groups may be shown to be relatively insensitive and therefore one would have greater confidence in the accuracy of such a forecast compared with groups whose future numbers are more dependent on what will happen in the uncertain future.

Turning now to the results, we find that if the trends and patterns observed in the first half of the 1990s with these illustrative rates were to apply to future decades, the population structure in the different family types in Great Britain would undergo a number of changes.

- an increase in the number of adults not living in a family from 7.9 million to 9.2 million;
- a decrease in married persons from 24.2 million to 22.3 million;
- a growth in the number of consensual unions without children from 1.6 million to 2.9 million, and for those with children, from 740,000 to 1.1 million;
- births within marriage would fall from 530,000 to 360,000;
- births outside marriage would increase from 240,000 to 360,000.

Figure 4.7 shows the projected number of adults in the three cases. With the stationary scenario, changes are due to the changing age structure, which would mean more widows and child-free married couples (as the population ages) and fewer married couples with children as the low-birth cohorts of the 1970s and 1980s reach their thirties and forties. If current trends in family formation and dissolution continue, the numbers single in the first scenario would increase by about 1.3 million, but with the second scenario, which has higher cohabitation rates, the numbers single would remain constant (one reason we prefer the first scenario). The effect of these scenarios would be to increase the numbers cohabiting without children by a factor of two, from 1.5 to 3 million, and an increase of about 400,000 in cohabiting couples with children. The fall in married couples with children would be substantial in the second scenario, about 2.4 million, or about twice the fall in the first scenario (although both of these include the age-compositional effects already mentioned in the context of the stationary scenario). Under these assumptions the number of single lone parents and divorced, separated, and widowed people would remain relatively stable.

While we do not discuss the results for 2041 in detail since such projections are highly speculative, Figure 4.8 shows projected population pyramids for that year. The decline in marriage would continue, especially under the first scenario. This also shows that there is substantial momentum in the system in that the relatively modest change in married couples without children is due to the large number of older married couples who have low rates of marital breakdown and lowering mortality rates over time, which tends to keep their numbers up. However, the pattern among younger adults is much more variable. At ages 20–49, when the bulk of cohabitation occurs, the numbers cohabiting are close to those at all ages. However, with these scenarios the number living as married couples without children would drop by about one-third between 1991 and 2016, and those with children by 2.3 million in the first case and 1.4 million in the second. The proportion of unmarried people aged 20–49 who are

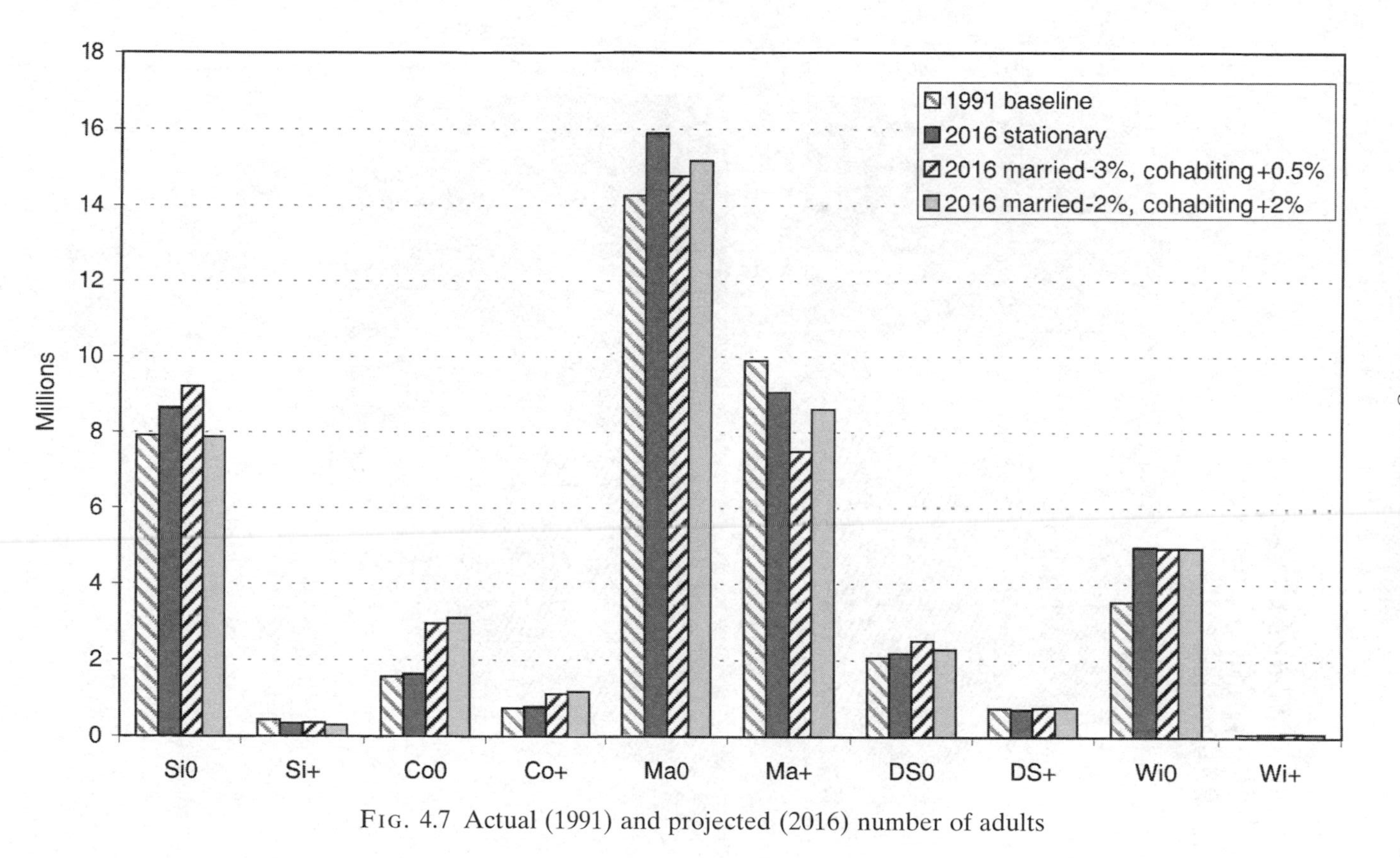

FIG. 4.7 Actual (1991) and projected (2016) number of adults

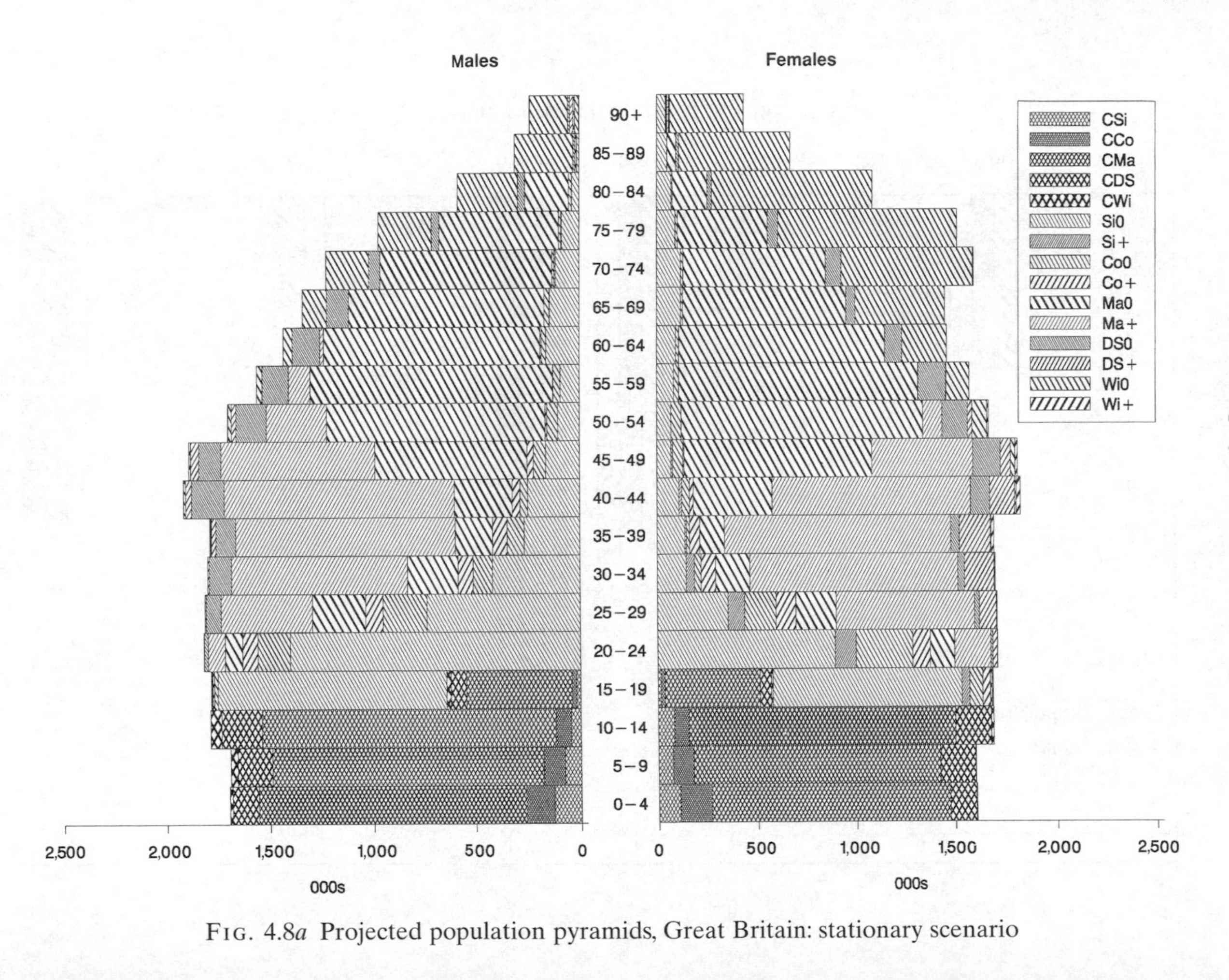

FIG. 4.8*a* Projected population pyramids, Great Britain: stationary scenario

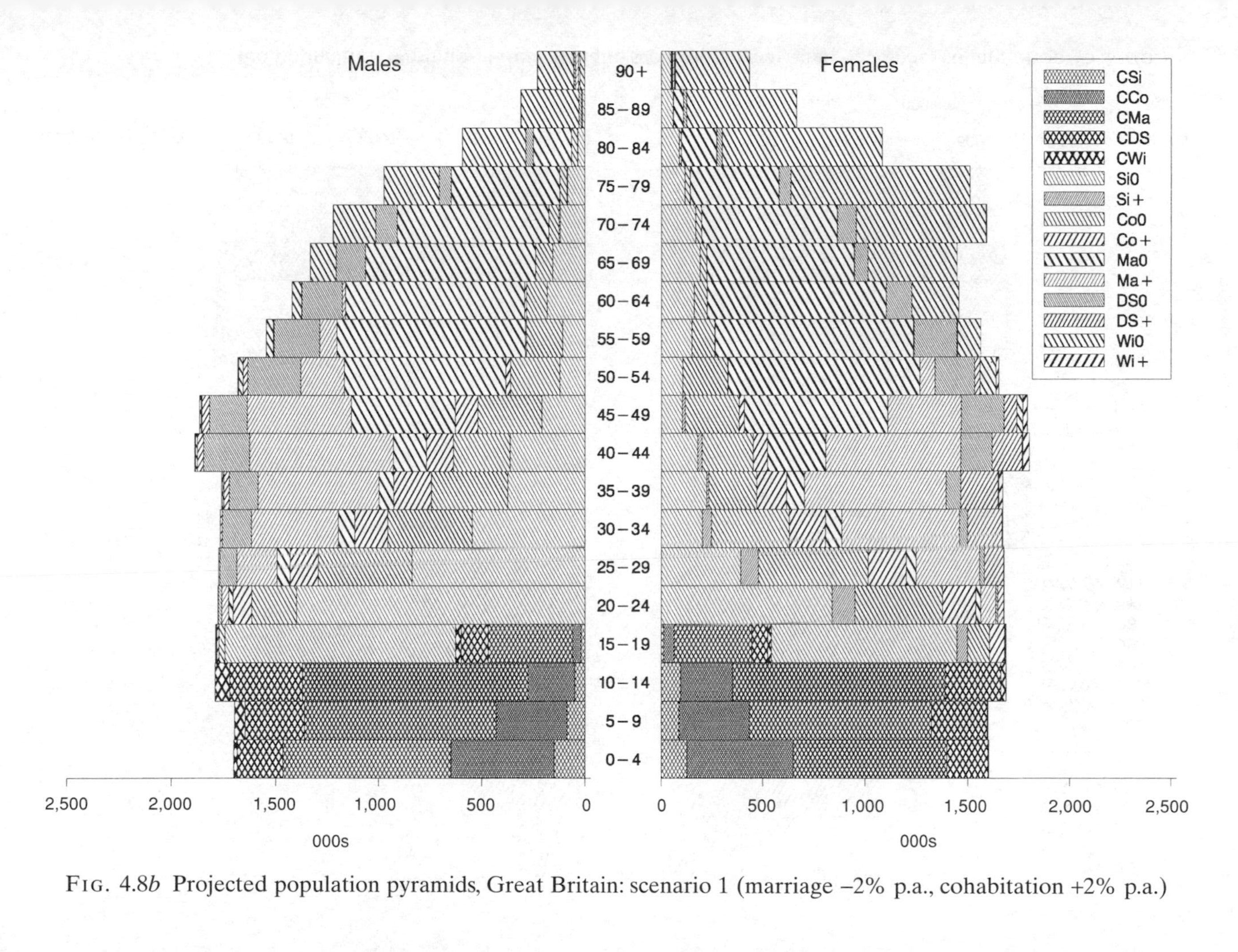

FIG. 4.8*b* Projected population pyramids, Great Britain: scenario 1 (marriage −2% p.a., cohabitation +2% p.a.)

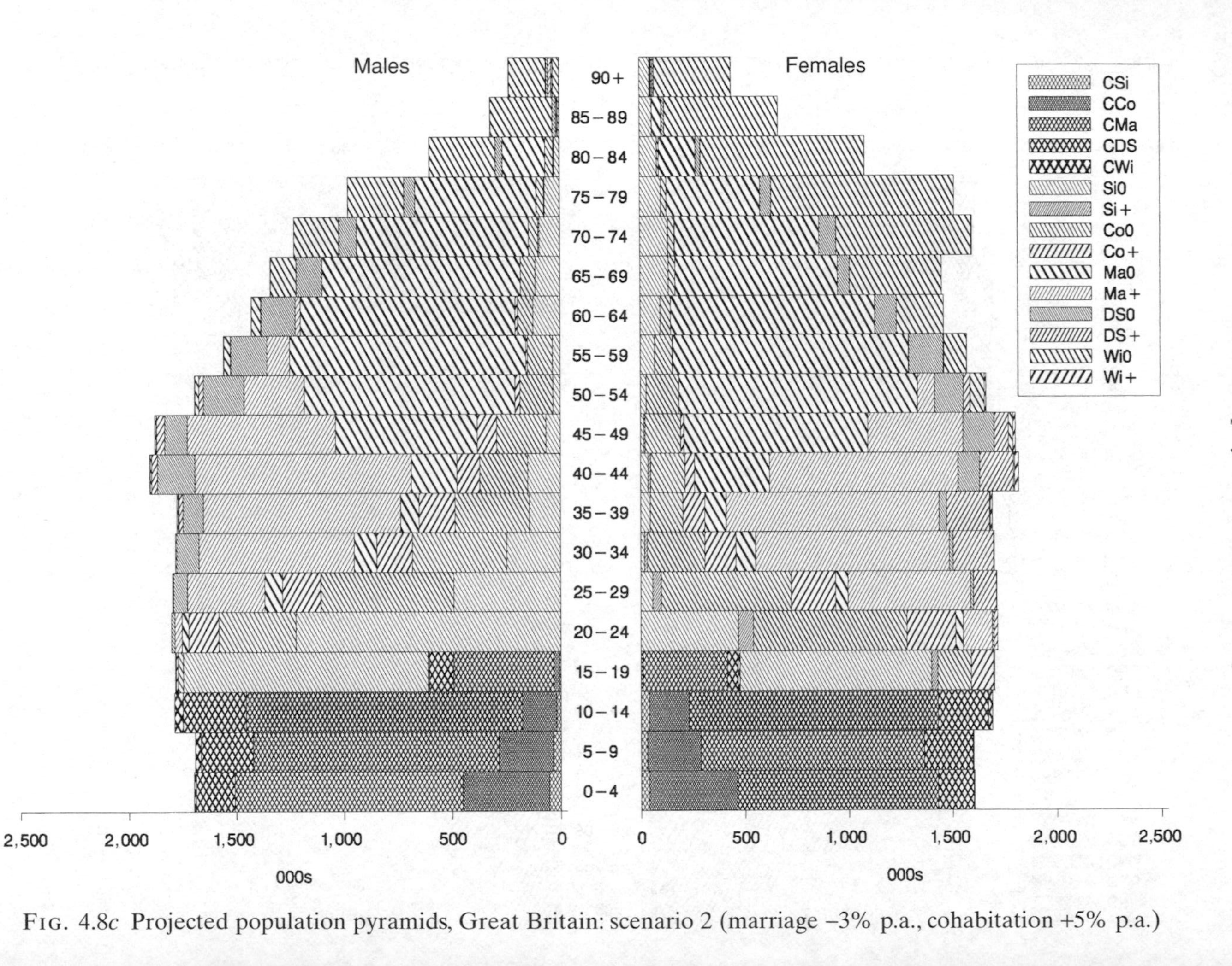

FIG. 4.8*c* Projected population pyramids, Great Britain: scenario 2 (marriage −3% p.a., cohabitation +5% p.a.)

cohabiting would rise from 22 per cent in 1991 to 31 per cent by 2016 in the first case, and to 53 per cent in the second scenario. However, even in the second case, there would still be nearly twice as many married in this age group as cohabiting, and 57.5 per cent of the overall group would be married.

We may also examine how the population evolves in terms of the number of events experienced each year. At present, we estimate that in the early 1990s, about 660,000 entered marriage each year (mostly from the cohabiting state) and about 420,000 entered cohabitation (although this latter estimate is subject to error). Under both of our scenarios, there would be more entries into cohabitation than marriage by 2016, and under the first scenario, fewer would then convert this into marriage. These data also indicate how patterns of childbearing may evolve. In the early 1990s, 31 per cent of births were outside marriage. Under our first scenario, this would rise to 50 per cent by 2016, and to 44 per cent under the second scenario. This change would be due almost entirely to increases in births within cohabiting unions.

While the main focus of this paper is on family living arrangements, this does interact with fertility trends. For example, the recent official projections foresee a fertility level of about 1.8 children per woman from the year 2000. Fertility rates are higher among married than unmarried women and if the latter group form a larger proportion of the fertile age groups, then this would mean that the separate fertility rates for married and unmarried women would have to increase at a higher rate to offset the changing composition of the fertile age groups. Thus, changes in fertility will depend to some extent on changes in partnership patterns. A second and related aspect of an increase in the proportion of unmarried women would be that even with no change in the fertility rates of married and unmarried women, the proportion of births which will occur outside marriage would also increase as a proportion of all births.

POSTSCRIPT

The life table has correctly been defined as the unifying concept in demography (Keyfitz 1985). It might, therefore, appear surprising that it is used so rarely in the analysis of contemporary family patterns. Quantitative approaches are overwhelmingly likely to use statistical techniques such as logistic regression to analyse differentials between sub-populations in a particular transition such as marriage or divorce.[8] The primary focus in such analyses is on the relative values for the groups studied, and often little attention is paid to the level of the transition. Such analyses do not give information about implications at the population level, nor do they show how the effects of a particular transition reverberate through the system.

The system discussed here is impossible to analyse without a life table framework, and the LIPRO model is the most satisfactory one for this purpose. Such modelling can show unexpected results. For example, an increase in cohabitation rates would, ceteris paribus, lead to an increase in marriage (since the pool of those who are most likely to marry would be increased) and a reduction in single lone parenthood (since cohabitation is a major route out of lone parenthood). Such models emphasize the importance of studying the cohort life course experiences, since the distribution of, say, 50-year-olds is determined by their experiences over earlier decades rather than their current socio-economic situation.

It will also have become clear that data are lacking on many of the key elements necessary for the proper evaluation of trends in living arrangements. Although there have been many developments in recent years, progress will require the better use of the range of current data sources, which are often incompatible, and ultimately the collection of relevant data from larger samples or in a more consistent way from existing sources. This remains an area for further development that would have considerable benefits in conjunction with recent advances in the methodologies for the analysis of living arrangements such as those described here.

NOTES

1. Apart from the fact that survey data are subject to non-sampling errors such as non-response, the number of events recorded is small. For example, the number of marriages reported in the General Household Survey in a 12-month period is under 150. If marriage rates were declining at, say, 7% per annum, this would mean that rates were halving every decade, and the following year about 140 marriages would be recorded. To obtain an estimate close to the true value, the *difference* should be measured to within 20%, or 2 events, of the true value, giving an estimate of between 8 and 12. In fact, with this sample size—which is twice that of the British Household Panel Study—the likely imprecision in this difference due to sampling variability is of the order of 35 events. Since information is required not only for overall numbers of events, but also for individual age and other groups, it is clear that such surveys, which are an indispensable source of information for many purposes, are not capable of providing usable up-to-date information on trends in experience of most types of life events.
2. One of us has argued in the past that such events provide a much better explanation of short-term fertility movements than, e.g., economic trends (Murphy

1992, 1993*a*). These recent happenings would appear to confirm this suggestion. While the alarm associated with low-dose pills may have been misplaced, the potency of the media in transmitting such messages may be illustrated by the fact that one of us (Murphy), who was in Cappadocia in Central Turkey when the story broke in Britain, noticed that a Turkish-language paper splashed it across almost a full page on the next day. See also Wood *et al.* (1997).

3. Official fertility projections do not consider trends in union formation. While there are good operational reasons for this and it possibly results in some improvements in forecasting accuracy, they cannot give any insight into the evolution of, say, extra-marital childbearing.
4. 'Dependent' is the usual definition of a child under age 16 or aged 16–18 and in full-time education.
5. A distinction is sometimes made between projections and forecasts: 'what if' and 'what's likely'. The methods used are the same in both cases, but the assumptions used will differ.
6. Such statements are not made without considerable risk and have provoked merriment: in the late 19th century, it was said that all that was left for successive generations of physicists was to measure physical constants to higher precision, a few years before relativity and quantum mechanics were discovered. If incorrect, at least statements such as these will provide some innocent amusement to those with the benefit of 20/20 hindsight.
7. This is simply the distinction between incidence (the number of events in a specified time period) and prevalence (the frequency of the state at a specified time). Unfortunately, these two distinct concepts are frequently confused.
8. This is not to say that such analyses are unimportant or intellectually unrewarding; rather, such studies have come to dominate discourse (Murphy 1996). There is far more work undertaken on the process of entry into lone parenthood compared with exit, and even less on the determinants of the numbers: the last topic is probably of the greatest public and policy interest.

APPENDIX A:

Method of constructing baseline stationary rates using the IPF method

Preliminary analysis showed that applying the observed transition rates, such as those shown in Table 4.4, leads to implausible results. Therefore, we constructed our basic set of transition rates for a given age group, for example those aged 20–24, by adjusting the observed empirical BHPS-based transition rates to generate rates which, when applied to the population distribution of the 20–24-year-old group in the 1991 baseline population, replicated the population distribution of the 25–29-year-olds in the 1991 baseline population. We do this by adjusting the matrix by using the iterative proportional fitting (IPF) method (Friedlander 1961; Murphy 1991), which controls the marginal values of the matrix to be consistent with the baseline while preserving its internal structure as far as possible (formally, it retains the cross-product values of the cells). For example, zero values are still zero, and large values tend to remain large. These 'stationary' rates have the property that when applied to the stationary (or life table) 1991 population distribution they produce the same values in subsequent years. Thus, they form a suitable basis for examining deviations from such behaviour, since the properties of these rates are known and they provide consistent results (further details and results are given in Murphy and Wang 1997*a*). It should be noted that these rates are not current rates, but rather contain an element of reversion in that, for example, the numbers divorced at age 55–59 in 1991 are determined by the rates of demographic processes, including marital breakdown, which they had experienced over the previous forty years.

APPENDIX B:

Brief summary of multi-state life table models.

$\mathbf{l}$(sex, age, time) is a row vector of dimension d which gives the number of people of a given sex and age at a particular time who are in each of the d internal states of the system, in this case $d = 15$ (the sum across all values of the state space gives the overall population in the sex and age category).

$\mathbf{M}_i$(sex, age, time) is a $d \times d$ dimension matrix that gives the intensities for internal events.

$\mathbf{M}_e$(sex, age, time) is a column vector of dimension d which gives the intensities for exits. (In this case there is only one mode of exit, namely death; if others, such as emigration, were possible the vector would be replaced by an intensity matrix of suitable dimension.)

$\mathbf{M}_b$(sex, age, time) is a $d \times d$ matrix of birth intensities, the (a, b) elements of which give the intensity that a woman in state a gives birth to a child of a given sex in state b. (In our case, children can be born to a mother in any of the ten possible adult states in Table 4.1, and the child will be in one of the five child categories.)

If a new matrix $\mathbf{M}$ (sex, age, time) is defined as follows:

$$\mathbf{M}(\text{sex, age, time}) = \mathbf{M}_i(\text{sex, age, time}) - \text{Diag}\ [\mathbf{M}_i(\text{sex, age, time}) \cdot \lambda^T + \mathbf{M}_e(\text{sex, age, time}) \cdot \lambda^T],$$

where λ is a row vector of dimension d consisting of 1s, the formula for updating the population becomes:

$$\mathbf{l}(\text{sex, age} + \tau, \text{time} + \tau) = \mathbf{l}(\text{sex, age, time})e^{\mathbf{M}(\text{sex,age,time})\tau}.$$

Generalizations of the usual life table functions may also be derived for this model; for example, the vector of person-years experienced by a cohort in a given state over the following h years is (assuming a linear change over the period):

$$\mathbf{L}(\text{sex, age, time}) = \tfrac{1}{2}\, h\{\mathbf{l}(\text{sex, age, time}) + \mathbf{l}(\text{sex, age} + h, \text{time} + h)\}.$$

Further details are given in van Imhoff and Keilman (1991).

PART II
Kinship in the 1990s

5

Kinship and friendship: attitudes and behaviour in Britain, 1986–1995

Francis McGlone, Alison Park, and Ceridwen Roberts

INTRODUCTION

The family is seldom out of the news. Politicians, journalists, and interest groups all discuss, in various ways, the structural changes that families are experiencing and their likely social consequences. Yet, what is often missing from this debate is attention to wider kin. The 'family' most commonly under the microscope is the nuclear family, with its two parents (or, increasingly, one parent) and dependent children, and not the extended family. Grandparents, siblings, uncles, aunts, and cousins are hardly ever mentioned.

This is rather surprising, given the large, if scattered, body of evidence about wider family contact and support. The 1994 General Household Survey (OPCS 1996*a*), for example, found that over three-quarters of elderly people aged 65 and over saw relatives or friends at least once a week. Only 3 per cent said that they did not see relatives or friends at all. Moreover, research shows that relatives (in particular, grandmothers) are an important source of child care for working mothers (Martin and Roberts 1984; Meltzer 1994). But the most important evidence of extended family contact and support comes from actual studies of kinship.

One of the earliest attempts in this country to investigate the importance of kin outside the nuclear family was by the anthropologist Sir Raymond Firth (1956). In a study of a working-class district in South London, Firth found that people could count anywhere between 37 and 246 people in their 'kin universe' (with an average of 146). Of the households studied, knowledge of kin was usually greater among women than men. Women were pivotal to the kinship system. Unlike the kinship systems of 'primitive' societies, Firth's sample demonstrated a high degree of personal selectivity in the choice of kin with whom people had close personal relationships. The basis of this personal selectivity was emotional attachment rather than formalized ties. The exchange of personal services outside the household followed this pattern of personal selectivity, and in turn, influenced relationships between kin. The services a person could offer, or needed from, kin reinforced kinship ties.

Young's and Willmott's (1957) often-quoted study of family and community life in Bethnal Green, East London found a particularly close relationship between mothers and daughters, who in many cases lived nearby. The relationship was based on mutual aid and support, with the daughter receiving help with the care of her children and reciprocating when the mother was old and in need of care. Young and Willmott followed their Bethnal Green study with an investigation of kinship in the middle-class London suburb of Woodford (Willmott and Young 1960). Here kinship ties were much looser and the mother–daughter tie not so tight, although women were still often seen as the centre of the extended family. The three-generation family in Woodford lived further apart than in Bethnal Green but access to telephones and cars helped family members to keep in touch.

Later research painted a similar picture of family life. Rosser and Harris (1965, 1983) in their study of family and social change in Swansea, found only rare cases where people were entirely isolated from kin, although there was great variation in kinship behaviour. The extended family was more widely spread than in Bethnal Green but this was balanced by improvements in communication, especially the growth in car ownership. The 'core family', according to Rosser and Harris, was not simply the nuclear family but also the two sets of grandparents. The kin relationship in the extended family therefore consisted of wife's mother/wife to husband/husband's mother. The family structure in practice was 'built around this central balance between the two sides of the family, linked through the marriage to a common set of grandchildren' (Rosser and Harris 1983: 226). The wife's side of the family was dominant, reflecting the stress on women's role in the family and relationships.

Bell's (1968) research into mainly middle-class families showed that although they lived some distance from relatives, and had little day-to-day contact, kinship still played an important role in their lives. Most of his sample was in the 'house-making' and 'child-rearing' stages of family life (the two stages in the family life-cycle of greatest expenditure and lowest income) and received considerable aid from relatives. Often this help was financial and there was therefore no need for geographical proximity. Qualifying the work of Willmott and Young (1960) and Rosser and Harris (1965), Bell argued that among the geographically mobile middle class, where frequent contact between mother and daughter was not possible, greater stress should be laid on the relationship between father-in-law/father to son/son-in-law because through this flowed financial aid.

Since Bell's work, little detailed research has been carried out into the role of the extended family within modern society. In 1986, however, as part of the International Social Survey Programme (ISSP), SCPR's British Social Attitudes Survey carried out the first national survey of kinship and friendship in Britain. That survey examined people's contact with their relatives and friends, and the extent to which they feel able to call upon family, friends, and others for help in a variety of different situations. The main emphasis of the published results was a comparison of Britain and the six other ISSP nations (Finch 1989*b*). Consequently, little in-depth analysis of the British data was undertaken and the 1986 survey remained a relatively under-utilized resource. Nonetheless, the results showed that most people in Britain do keep in regular contact with relatives (other than those with whom they live) and that, when it comes to asking for help, parents or adult children are the most popular sources of help after spouses or partners.

Over the nine-year period since the British Social Attitudes Survey first investigated social networks in Britain, there have been a number of important demographic, economic, and social changes which are likely to have affected attitudes and behaviour regarding the family. Overall, the population of Britain has aged. Increasing proportions of women are entering the labour market. Government policies have shifted in focus, with many policies attempting to make families more responsible for the care of their elderly and disabled members (as illustrated, for instance, by 'care in the community'). Family structures have continued to change, with a growth in cohabitation and comparatively high levels of divorce being accompanied by increasing numbers of children born outside marriage and an increasing proportion of lone parents.

These changes raise many questions which much British research has so far been unable to answer. Does the extended family matter in the 1990s? Have divorce and cohabitation increasingly weakened kinship ties? What impact has the growing proportion of women in the paid workforce had on the extended family? What makes the answers to these questions particularly pressing is the central importance that social networks have in every society, particularly when it comes to the provision of support and practical help. With increasing pressure on state welfare budgets, public policy interest has turned to this informal sector and to how it can be encouraged and strengthened. Most recent British research in this area has been indirect, focusing on the informal care of specific groups. Consequently, we know a lot about the family care of, say, disabled or older people, but very little about the support provided by (or to) relatives in general. Nor do we know much about the day-to-day contact that people have with their relatives or their attitudes towards their wider kin.

To begin to address these issues, the 1986 questions were repeated and extended in the 1995 round of the British Social Attitudes Survey. As in 1986, the aim was to establish how closely people live to their relatives, how much contact they have with them, the importance they attach to these networks, and whether or not they feel that they can be called upon as sources of help and advice.

THE BRITISH SOCIAL ATTITUDES (BSA) SURVEY

The BSA Survey is designed to yield a representative sample of British adults aged 18 or over. Each year around 3,600 adults are interviewed in England, Scotland, and Wales. The sampling frame for the survey is the Postcode Address File, a list of addresses (or postal delivery points) compiled by the Post Office. One adult is randomly selected at each address for interview. For practical reasons, the sample is confined to those living in private households.

The 'kinship and friendship' module was administered to a random two-thirds (around 2,100) of the 1995 BSA Survey sample. The questions were contained in a self-completion questionnaire given to respondents after the main face-to-face interview. In addition to the questions asked as part of the 1986 module, a number of new questions were added, covering any related day-to-day assistance that people might give or receive, attitudes towards keeping in touch with family members, the relative importance of family and friends, and family obligations.

THE EXTENT OF FAMILY NETWORKS

Contact with relatives

In 1995, as in 1986, substantial proportions of adults shared their home with one or more adult relative. One-third, for instance, lived with an adult child. However, the proportions living with relatives have fallen since 1986, with a 6 percentage point drop in the proportion living with an adult child, and a similar drop in the proportion living with a mother or father. The key factor behind this decline is that the group who have always been the most likely to live with a parent (18–24-year-olds) seem to have changed their behaviour in the intervening period. For instance, while around two in three 18- to 24-year-olds lived with a parent in 1986, less than half did so in 1995. This appears largely to reflect the rapid increase during this period in the numbers of young people leaving the parental home to go to university. Certainly, among older age groups there has been no change in the proportion living with a parent.

Despite these changes, most people (around 60 per cent) still live within one hour's journey from at least one close relative—and between a quarter and a third live less than fifteen minutes away. Most commonly, the family member in closest proximity is an adult child. In fact, two-thirds of parents with grown-up children live less than an hour's journey away from at least one of their sons or daughters, and around half of these live less than fifteen minutes away. Here too, however, there has been a small decline over the last decade. While in 1986, 70 per cent of people lived within an hour's journey from their mother, this figure had dropped 5 percentage points by 1995.

Physical proximity, of course, is not the whole story. More important, perhaps, is the extent to which people stay in touch with family members, either by visiting them or by telephone. Here the data show that most people do maintain regular contact with close relatives, with, for instance, nearly half of those with a non-resident mother seeing her at least once a week. However, contact with fathers is slightly less frequent. Of those who do not live with their father, around 40 per cent see him every week. What is most striking about contact with fathers, however, is the proportion of respondents—1 in 10—who never see their father. The comparable figure for mothers is 1 in 33 (Table 5.1).[1]

The parent–child relationship is by far the most dominant as far as contact with relatives is concerned. Around 6 in 10 parents with a non-resident adult child see him or her at least once a week (including 1 in 10 who see this son or daughter every day). Only 1 per cent report never seeing their adult child. Far less likely to see each other regularly are adult siblings, with around 3 in 10 people with non-resident siblings seeing them at least once a week, and 45 per cent seeing them less than once a month. In fact, adult siblings are less commonly visited than relatives by marriage (such as mothers-in-law). Not surprisingly, close friends are seen more often than most relatives. Nearly 6 in 10 of those with close friends see their 'best friend' on a weekly basis.

TABLE 5.1. *Frequency of seeing non-resident relatives/friends (% of respondents)*

	Daily	At least once a week	At least once a month	Less often	Never	N[a]
Mother	8	40	21	27	3	1,026
Father	6	33	20	29	9	822
Adult sibling	4	25	21	45	4	1,702
Adult child	10	48	16	18	1	812
Other relative	3	31	26	37	1	1,796
'Best friend'	10	48	22	17	—	1,768

[a] Bases exclude those without the relative/friend in question, as well as those living with this relative/friend.
—Less than 0.5%.

People also maintain a high level of contact with relatives by telephone. For instance, nearly 3 in 4 parents speak to an adult child by telephone at least once a week.

Families with dependent children

People living with dependent children (that is, children aged under 16) are more likely to see relatives than those with no dependent children. The notable exception to this is seeing mothers, with roughly similar proportions of both groups (around a half) seeing their mother every week. However, having a dependent child is linked to increased contact with fathers, siblings, and other relatives. More than a third of people with a dependent child see a sibling at least once a week, compared with a quarter of those without dependent children, while the proportion of those with dependent children who see their father each week is 10 percentage points higher than the equivalent proportion among those without children. The age of the dependent child also makes a difference, with weekly contact being slightly more common among those with children aged under 5 than those with children aged between 5 and 15.

Only a tiny proportion of parents of dependent children (around 3 per cent) report that they never see their relatives, although 8 per cent never see their father. The comparable figures for those without a dependent child in the household are 4 and 11 per cent, respectively.

People with a dependent child do tend to live closer to their relatives and this may, in part, explain the differences in family contact, but even taking distance into account, those with a dependent child in the household are still more likely to see most relatives regularly than those with no dependent child in the household.

Declining contact: 1986–1995 compared

Is contact with the family more limited today than it was in the past? Some research certainly suggests that it is. For instance, by comparing the data from various local studies on married women's contact with their mothers, Willmott (1986) found that the proportion of women seeing their mothers once a week had clearly fallen since the 1950s. And when we compare our own findings with those of 1986 (Table 5.2), we find that contact with all types of relatives appears to have fallen even in the last decade, and this is particularly true of contact with parents and children. For instance, in 1986, 60 per cent of people with a non-resident mother saw her at least once a week; by 1995, only around half did so (49 per cent). The fall in contact with fathers and children is of a similar magnitude. This is not because relatives are being supplanted by friends, as the proportion of people who see their 'best friend' on a weekly basis also fell over the same

TABLE 5.2. *Frequency seeing relative/friend at least once a week*

	1986 (%)	N[a]	1995 (%)	N[a]
Mother	59	643	49	1,026
Father	51	477	40	822
Sibling	33	1,092	29	1,702
Adult child	66	420	58	812
Other relative	42	1,218	35	1,796
'Best friend'	65	1,224	59	1,768

[a] Bases exclude those without the relative in question, as well as those living with this relative.

period. So it appears that people have generally become less likely to visit, or be visited by, anyone at all. Contact with relatives has also fallen among those with a dependent child in the family. Weekly contact with all types of relatives has declined by between 5 and 9 per cent, and this is most marked among those with a child under 5, where weekly contact with the respondent's mother (the child's grandmother) has fallen by 11 per cent.

Contact with relatives is clearly related to geography. If people are tending to live further a way from their kin than they did in the past, we might expect to find a fall in how often they visit each other. Certainly, the data show that those who live closer to relatives tend to see them more often than those who live further away. However, since average journey times between relatives have increased only very slightly since 1986, this is unlikely to be the only reason for the scale of the decline in family contact that we have noted. In fact, contact has declined even if we take into account geographical proximity. An alternative explanation is that contact with relatives has fallen because friends have replaced kin as 'families of choice' (see, for instance, Weeks *et al.* 1996, Chapter 12 of this volume). This is just as unlikely, for—as already noted—contact with friends has dropped alongside contact with family members.

A more plausible explanation for the change is the continuing transformation of the role of women in society and, in particular, the increasing proportion of women who now work outside the home. Although women remain considerably more likely than men to keep in contact with relatives, their contact has fallen since 1986. Furthermore, this fall has been most marked among women in full-time work. In 1986, around two-thirds of women in full-time work (and one-half of men in full-time work) saw their mother on a weekly basis (Table 5.3). Now, men and women working full-time are almost indistinguishable in this respect, with 46 and 45 per cent respectively seeing their mother each week. So, whereas among full-time working men there has been virtually no change over the nine-year

TABLE 5.3. *Frequency seeing non-resident mother at least once a week*

	1986 (%)	N	1995 (%)	N
Men				
All	50	308	42	450
In full-time work	49	266	46	314
Women				
All	65	355	53	576
In full-time work	64	97	45	177

period, among full-time working women there has been a drop of 20 percentage points.

Since we are comparing here only those men and women who are in full-time work, we cannot argue that a decline in family contact is due to more women working full-time. Rather, it is plausible that over the last decade the nature of women's full-time work has changed more than men's, and that the sorts of women entering the full-time workforce in the 1990s differ from those in the 1980s. In any event, male and female full-time workers are becoming more like one another in their kinship roles than they used to be, and this is not because the roles of men have changed.

TO WHOM WOULD YOU TURN FOR HELP?

We asked respondents to whom they would turn with the sorts of 'problems that can happen to anyone'. The situations covered were: help with household and gardening jobs; help while ill in bed over several weeks; needing to borrow a large sum of money; being upset about a problem with a husband, wife, or partner; and feeling depressed (Table 5.4). Most people would naturally rely on the help of a spouse or partner for the more routine tasks specified. Other relatives, particularly parents, come into their own for help with less routine problems for which a spouse or partner may well be inappropriate—such as borrowing money or talking through marital problems—although in the latter case, friends are more important than other relatives.

With one exception, few respondents mentioned professionals such as social workers or GPs as a first source of help. For instance, only 2 per cent mentioned marital counselling as a source of help with marital problems, and a similarly small proportion mentioned the Church. On the other hand, when the hypothetical problem was a financial one, the most common response was a bank or a building society.

TABLE 5.4. *People turned to for various problems (% of respondents)*

	Household job	Help while ill	Borrowing money	Marital problems	Depression
No one	1	1	7	8	3
Spouse/partner	58	61	21	9	47
Parent	8	13	20	15	8
Child	13	11	6	17	7
Sibling	4	3	4	12	6
Friend	7	5	2	27	21
Bank/building society	n.a.	n.a.	32	n.a.	n.a.

n.a. = not applicable.

Notes: N = 2,077.

Who people would turn to for help varies, of course, with age and circumstance. Not surprisingly, the most popular initial port of call for those who are married or living as married is their spouse or partner—around two-thirds said they would do this if they were depressed, with 13 per cent saying they would talk first to a friend. The most popular source of help for those who were separated or divorced was a friend (with 44 per cent giving this answer). Similar proportions of those who were single said they would turn first to a friend, whereas for the widowed the most popular initial source of help was a child, with 42 per cent saying they would do this. Notably, siblings do not feature very strongly as sources of emotional support for any of these groups.

The importance of the spouse or partner is even more notable when there is a dependent child in the household. For instance, 4 out of 5 people with a dependent child would turn first to their spouse or partner if they were ill or needed help around the house. The comparable figure for those with no dependent child is around a half. As those with children are more likely to have regular partners than those without, this is not an altogether surprising finding.

The sources of help people cited also varied according to sex in a way that suggests that notions of traditional male and female roles remain widespread and far-reaching. Thus, men were more likely than women to rely on their spouse or partner to nurse them through a sickness, while women were more likely than men to rely on friends or children in such circumstances. By the same token, women were more likely than men to turn first to their spouse or partner for help with a household job or for borrowing money.

With one exception, responses to these questions have not changed markedly since they were first asked in 1986. The exception concerns the role of friends, who are now more likely than they were to be cited as a first source of help in marital problems or depression. This appears to be at the expense of turning, as a first choice, to spouses or partners and not at the expense of other relatives. On the other hand, the unmarried are also more likely now to turn to friends than family members for emotional support.

EXPERIENCES OF HELP AND HELPING

Of course, people's answers to these sorts of hypothetical questions may merely reflect their notions of appropriateness rather than portraying what would actually happen if an actual situation arose. In order to assess this, we asked respondents whether they had either provided or received regular help from specific sorts of people over the last five years 'because of pregnancy, an illness, disability or other problem'. Everyone who said that they had provided help was asked for details of the recipient, while those who had received help were asked to identify the provider. As this was the first time these questions were asked by the BSA Survey, we will have to wait for future rounds to look for evidence of change.

Around 2 in 5 people said they had provided regular care for an adult at some point during the past five years, and around 1 in 5 had received such care at some point. Not unexpectedly, women were much more likely than men to have provided care (48 per cent; 34 per cent), but they were also more likely to have received care (26 per cent; 17 per cent). This difference stems largely from the above-average tendency of women between 25 and 34 to have received care, presumably during pregnancy or following childbirth.

The most common person to whom care was provided was a parent, around one-third of all cases. Around 1 in 5 had provided care for a partner or spouse and a similar proportion had provided care for another family member. The most common recipients of care provided by men were spouses or parents (29 per cent and 31 per cent respectively), whereas the most common recipients of care provided by women were parents and other family members (36 per cent and 25 per cent respectively). When we looked at those receiving care, we found that men were more likely than women to have received care from their spouse or partner, with women being more likely than men to have received it from a parent or another family member. Only around 1 in 10 respondents (mainly men) had received care from a friend or neighbour, and other sources of care hardly featured at all. The most likely source of care for those with a dependent child was also a spouse or partner, but parents and parents-in-law figured more commonly as sources of care for those with dependent children than for those without dependent children.

We also asked respondents whether they had provided or received help with money over the last five years. Around a third (31 per cent) had lent or given a sum of £100 or more during this time and around the same proportion had received such help. Men were slightly more likely than women to have helped out in this way (34 per cent and 29 per cent respectively), with the beneficiary most likely to be another family member (usually a son or daughter). Sixteen per cent of people had lent or given a sum of £100 or more to a friend. Similarly, of those who had received a gift or loan of £100 or more, the source for the majority was a parent or parent-in-law (these two sources accounted for 59 per cent of the cases). Parents and parents-in-law appear to be particularly important sources of help with money for young families. Of those respondents with a dependent child who had received help with money in the last five years, 7 in 10 received it from a parent or parent-in-law. This corroborates earlier research showing that wealth tends to travel down the generations (Bell 1968).

The data suggest that there are no significant class differences in the provision and receipt of care. However, the middle classes (or non-manual workers) are more likely than manual workers to have provided help with money, with 35 per cent having done so (as opposed to 27 per cent of manual workers). This may, of course, reflect nothing more than the greater access to financial resources among the middle classes in general.

ATTITUDES TOWARDS RELATIVES AND FRIENDS

We turn now to people's attitudes towards the family, and the extent to which these substantiate our findings so far. How much do people believe that the family should have a role as a source of care and support? Are friends seen as being more, or less, important than relatives? To assess this, we asked respondents how much they agreed or disagreed with a number of positive or negative statements about the family. The answers show that most people are indeed 'family-centred', believing it important to keep in touch both with close relatives and the extended family—including members with whom they have little in common (Table 5.5). So, 7 in 10 people support the view that 'people should keep in touch with close family members, even if they don't have much in common', falling to 55 per cent when the relatives are 'aunts, uncles and cousins'. In both cases, only around 1 in 10 people actually disagreed with these views.

The family is also seen as overwhelmingly more important than friends—by a margin of around 11 to 1. Seven per cent of people agree that 'on the whole, my friends are more important to me than members of my family', with three-quarters (76 per cent) disagreeing. Similarly, when asked to respond to the statement 'I'd rather spend time with my friends than with my family', 13 per cent agreed and 59 per cent disagreed.

The most dominant family tie is that between parents and children, even after children have left home. Nearly three-quarters (72 per cent) of people disagree with the view that 'once children have left home, they should no

TABLE 5.5. *Attitudes towards the family (% of respondents)*

	Agree	Neither agree nor disagree	Disagree
People should keep in touch with close family members even if they don't have much in common	70	18	10
People should keep in touch with relatives like aunts, uncles, and cousins even if they don't have much in common	55	31	12
People should always turn to their family before asking the state for help	48	19	29
I try to stay in touch with my relatives, not just my close family	46	22	27
I'd rather spend time with my friends than my family	13	23	59
Once children have left home, they should no longer expect help from their parents	12	13	72
On the whole, my friends are more important to me than members of my family	7	12	76

Note: N = 2,077.

longer expect help from their parents'. In contrast, a much smaller proportion (48 per cent) supported the view that 'people should always turn to their family before asking the state for help'. The implicit reference to financial help in this statement may well have had some effect on the response. Nonetheless, while many people believe that staying in touch with their family is important, they do not necessarily see the family as the most appropriate first port of call in times of need.

To find out what sorts of people are most and least likely to be family-centred, we placed people on a continuum, based on the answers to the key questions on this subject. In essence, we calculated a single score for each respondent from 1 to 5 on an index, where high scores indicate a more, and low scores a less, family-centred outlook (see Appendix).

The extent to which one has a family-orientated (or family-centred) outlook turns out to depend primarily on one's age, with those aged 45 or older being substantially more family-centred than their younger counterparts. The strength of the relationship is illustrated by responses to the statement about the importance of the extended family. While 41 per cent of 18–34-year-olds agree that 'people should keep in touch with relatives like aunts, uncles, and cousins, even if they don't have much in common', some 54 per cent of those aged 35–44, and 68 per cent of those aged 55 or over, agree with the statement. At first sight, women seem more family-centred than men, but this difference varies with age. Women and men who are under 45 barely differ in their degree of family orientation.

It is women over 45 who are substantially more family-centred than their male counterparts.

People with a dependent child, however, are slightly *less* family-orientated than those with no dependent child. This again is largely a function of age: those with a dependent child are more likely than those without to be under 45. For instance, respondents with a dependent child are less likely to agree that people should keep in touch with close relatives than respondents with no dependent child (68 per cent as opposed to 74 per cent), and this gap increases for more distant relatives like aunts, uncles, and cousins (49 per cent as opposed to 59 per cent). Similarly, fewer of those with a dependent child admit to making the effort to keep in touch with more distant relatives (43 per cent as opposed to 50 per cent), though there is very little difference when it comes to ranking the importance of family over friends.

There are two ways of interpreting the relationship between age and attitudes towards the family. The first is that we are seeing a general shift in attitudes, with younger generations becoming less family-centred than previous generations. If so, as these generations replace older cohorts, society is likely to become less family-centred. Alternatively, if one's sense of family responds more to the stage in the life-cycle that one happens to have reached, then we can expect no major overall change over time, merely a continuing generation gap as now. Thus, people would simply become more family-conscious as they acquire families of their own and, as a consequence, begin to value the help and support that an extended family network tends to provide.

In the absence of trend data on these particular questions, it is not possible to assess these competing theories rigorously. However, when we examined the relationships between certain life stages and family-centredness to see, for instance, whether being married or having children does make a difference to people's sense of family orientation (something we would expect), it was found that once age is taken into account any differences vanish. Thus, it seems that age, rather than stage in the life-cycle, has the strongest influence on one's degree of family orientation and, as a consequence, attitudes to the family are likely, we believe, to change over time.

Family orientation also varies according to more general values. Those who are religious (and particularly those who attend church, or its equivalent, regularly) are more family-centred than those who are not religious or who only attend church occasionally. Notably, these associations hold true even after age has been taken into account.

Finally, drawing on a 'libertarian–authoritarian' scale included regularly in the BSA Survey, we found a strong positive relationship between an 'authoritarian' outlook and being family-centred. This holds true even when age and religion are taken into account. A likely explanation for this correlation is the fact that many debates about the family link its supposed decline and fall to a number of popular authoritarian concerns such as law and order and 'traditional values'. Consequently, we might expect those who share such concerns to score higher than average on a measure endorsing notions of family duty and durability.

DISCUSSION AND CONCLUSION

What do our findings show? They show that in spite of its many detractors, family life in Britain continues to thrive. Most people are in regular contact with their immediate family, and it seems that these family members remain of primary importance in people's lives. The data also show that the mother–daughter tie, identified in earlier research (Young and Willmott 1957), still appears to be very much alive. Yet if measured in terms of contact, the importance of the family does appear to have declined slightly over the last decade. However, the idea that this represents some sort of crisis for the family seems to be a gross exaggeration. After all, as many as around one-half of adults whose mother is alive see her at least weekly.

Moreover, since contact with friends is also lower than it was a decade ago, our data indicate that it is social contact rather than family contact alone that is suffering from competition from other commitments, such as work. Certainly, as far as women in full-time work are concerned, their reduced role in sustaining family contacts might well be related to the changing nature of, and pressure from, their jobs and to a rise in their commitment to work. It is not surprising, therefore, to find that full-time working women are nowadays little different from their full-time male counterparts in the amount of family networking in which they engage. Nevertheless, this should not distract us from the fact that women are still considerably more likely than men to keep in frequent contact with relatives.

Our data on informal support and care suggest that the family remains an important source of help, especially for young families. But friends also matter when it comes to care, in particular for the single and divorced. As earlier research has found, friends are indeed an important source of practical, often long-term, help in times of crisis, typically to people they have known for a long time (O'Connor 1992). Friends in this respect become 'fictive kin'—'She's like a sister to me. I can always turn to her' (Allan 1989). Since these questions about actual examples of help given and received were asked for the first time in the 1995 British Social Attitudes Survey, we will have to wait for future rounds to look for evidence of change.

People's attitudes towards family life correspond largely to their behaviour. Most people believe—in principle and in practice—that one should keep in touch with both immediate and extended family members. There is, however, a close association between strong family-centred attitudes and age, and to a lesser extent, gender. The older one is the more one adheres to the desirability of contact with the wider family, suggesting that for the young, the family is increasingly in competition with other aspects of both social life and work and that its dominance as a social force will diminish over time.

It is, of course, important to keep these secular trends in perspective. For the bulk of people, their family continues to be a central and enduring part of their lives—as secure as can be expected against the supposed threats from social, cultural, and even occupational pressures.

APPENDIX:

BSA Attitude scales

The BSA survey includes a number of attitude scales that aim to measure underlying value dimensions. A useful way of summarising the information from the questions that make up these scales is to construct an additive index (DeVellis 1991; Spector 1992). This approach rests on the assumption that there is an underlying or 'latent' attitudinal dimension that characterises the answers to all the questions within each scale. If so, scores on the index are likely to be a more reliable indication of the underlying attitude that the answers to any one question. Each of the scales consists of a number of statements to which the respondent is invited to indicate agreement of disagreement.

The 'libertarian-authoritarian' scale referred to in this chapter is one of the most commonly used scales. For analysis purposes, the sample was divided into roughly equal quintiles from the most authoritarian to the most libertarian. The 1995 survey also included a series of questions that aimed to tap 'family-centredness', three of which were used to form the family-centredness index used in this chapter. These are:

- People should keep in touch with close family members even if they don't have much in common.
- People should keep in touch with relatives like aunts, uncles and cousins even if they don't have much in common.
- I try to stay in touch with all my relatives, not just my close family.

NOTE

1. All differences between groups cited in the chapter are significant at a 95% confidence level.

6

Living away from relatives: kinship and geographical reasoning

Jennifer Mason

'THINKING ALOUD' ABOUT KINSHIP AND GEOGRAPHY

Living near relatives can be a mixed blessing. The warmth and security which can come from feeling that you are a member of a local kin network can also make you feel too close for comfort. Living near enough to provide or receive help can mean being expected always to be the first to help, or can feel like a compromise of your own or someone else's independence. Local and everyday familiarity with each others' lives can feel intrusive as well as friendly and supportive. Yet living far away is problematic too. Independence may feel easier to establish and maintain, but it is easy also to feel too far away, especially in times of crisis or need. Distance can provide a space in which you can conduct your daily life and relationships away from the gaze of relatives, yet the same distance makes it much harder to achieve the kind of comfortable familiarity which comes from regular acquaintance with the detail of each other's everyday lives. Family visits or 'get-togethers' for those living at a distance from each other can feel too formal, too short, too infrequent, too long, or just too morally and emotionally loaded. The twice-yearly weekend visit where so much seems to hinge on how everyone gets on can seem inferior to the supposed (correctly or otherwise) casual and relaxed relations between neighbouring or even co-resident relatives.

These are examples of a familiar geographical discourse about the morality of kinship. It is *geographical*, and about *kinship*, because it

I am grateful to my colleagues on the ESRC-funded project on 'Migration, Kinship and Household Change' (Grant No. L315253007): Lynn Hayes, Robin Flowerdew, Richard Davies, Alaa Al-Hamad, and Janet Finch. I am especially grateful to Lynn Hayes for her very significant role in the collection and analysis of the data on which this chapter is based.

invokes ideas about what distance does to the operation of kin relationships. It also suggests that kinship can modify people's sense of distance, making a few miles or a few hundred miles seem too far or not far enough, and of course that distance can modify kinship. It is about the *morality* of kinship in so far as it is a vocabulary of how kin relationships should work, or about what is good or bad in them. It suggests both that geography and kinship are inextricably linked, yet also negotiable in their relationship and subject to change and to multiple interpretations.

The connections between kinship and geographical distance or proximity have been studied by family sociologists—gerontologists in particular—for some time and in various ways, from, for example, Rosenmayr's and Kockeis's (1963) articulation of the phrase 'intimacy at a distance' to Wenger's studies (1989, 1992) of the local support networks of elderly people. Yet, arguably, a geographical discourse of kinship is becoming a more central feature of everyday life in the late 20th century and into the new millennium, as family, kin, and personal relationships on the one hand, and patterns of migration, residence, and co-residence on the other, are said to be becoming more complex, more variable, and less predictable (Beck 1992; Giddens 1992; Finch and Mason 1993; Buck *et al*. 1994; Beck and Beck-Gernsheim 1995). Family and kin relationships, and what they mean among other things, are being negotiated and renegotiated in the light of important social changes (Finch 1989; Finch and Mason 1993; Smart and Neale, 1999), and we are living in an era when people are likely to be 'thinking aloud' about the ways in which geography and kinship connect up in their lives.

It is this process of 'thinking aloud' which I explore in this chapter. I examine the operation of this kind of discourse in the lives of people interviewed as part of a project on migration, kinship, and household change.[1] Specifically, I explore how people make sense of living a long distance away from kin, how people who have lived away reason about distance, proximity, and kinship, and what being at a distance does to the significance of kin relationships. I draw in particular on data from three contrasting case studies involving people who have moved a long way away from relatives, especially parents, under rather different circumstances. The distance between these people and their relatives was a consequence of their own mobility rather than that of their kin which, as Warnes (1986) notes, is the common pattern between parents and their adult children nationally.

Although I focus on people who have lived away, each of these three people also had experience of living near or with relatives, and the ways in which they reasoned about distance and kinship were grounded within those experiences. All of the fifty-seven interviewees in our study had experienced living at a distance from at least some relatives, as well as living nearby, although not all had themselves moved away. Their experiences varied from living in a different region or country from most of their kin for a significant part of their adult lives, to living away for a temporary period, to having one or more kin living in a different region of Britain or overseas. Similarly, living near relatives could mean living in the same neighbourhood as a sister or having most of one's kin 'just around the corner' in the same street. Perhaps surprisingly, since we were not targeting it as a *majority* experience in our sampling strategy, forty-eight of our interviewees also had experience of living with one or more relatives (other than a spouse or cohabitee and not including dependent children living with one or more parents in intact or 'reconstituted' families). Again though, their experiences varied from lodging temporarily with parents following separation or divorce, or with a sister and her family in between the sale and purchase of a house, to couples buying houses with one or other elderly parent or grandparent as a more or less permanent arrangement.

It is not so much the distribution of these experiences that is important for the current discussion as the ways in which they come together in individual biographies over time, and what we can say about their influence on people's reasoning about kinship, distance, and proximity. This is what I explore in the following case studies, focusing on how different people reason about putting a long distance between themselves and their kin.

CASE STUDY 1: MOIRA HENDRY AND HER KIN[2]

None of our interviewees had always lived a long distance from their kin. For a small minority, however, living far from most of their kin was a significant feature of their adult lives. Moira Hendry, a single professional woman in her thirties of working-class origins, was one of these. When we interviewed her, she was living more than 150 miles away from her widowed elderly mother and her sister Amy Gorman, whom we also interviewed and who lived about forty miles from their mother. Their only brother had died in his thirties. Moira's first move away from her parental home in Scotland was to go to university about forty miles away. She returned home on a short-term basis after that and later between jobs, but had spent most of her adult life living and working first in the South of England, then in the North-west. Moira's working-class parents had always lived in the same town. They had been very supportive of her living and working at a distance from them and 'making her own way in the world'. Although there was a long distance between them, Moira and her parents stayed in close contact through regular visits to each other and telephone calls. Her parents made light of the distance: 'they loved the fact that I was in London because they loved London, you know, so they used to come and visit and stay. Or go to Paris and pop in on the way, yes.'[3]

Although she had mostly lived alone or in flats shared with friends, including a boyfriend, since leaving her parents' home, she had spent a few months when she first went to university living with her sister and her husband and first child, and later had moved in with her sister-in-law and her children for nine months following the death of her brother. This latter arrangement prompted Moira's move from the south of England to the North-west. She had been unsettled and in temporary employment, and the move (which was intended to be short-term and temporary) felt mutually beneficial at that time.

From there, Moira found a permanent job in the North-west and another flat share with friends. She then moved to a different job, and a couple more shared houses, before finally buying her own house, with a little financial help and a lot of encouragement from her father (who had always lived in local authority housing). At the time of our interview, Moira was planning shortly to embark upon another long distance move which would take her back to Scotland and closer to her mother and sister (although still sixty or so miles away, but a straightforward car or rail journey). The move was to be partly because of a job opportunity, but mostly because of a desire to move to a particular city to which she felt socially and culturally attracted. Although this city was some distance from where she had been born and brought up, Moira articulated this in part as a *return* and in part as a new start. In a sense, she was self-consciously moving to find a different way of life. Moira considered that being closer to her mother and sister would have advantages, especially as her mother was ill with dementia. The move would enable her to visit her mother more frequently but for shorter and less intensive periods than the weekend stopovers she was currently doing. She also felt some pressure from others to move nearer. But she was clear that her mother's need for care did not form the only or the main impetus to go:

> Then there's secondary things. My mother, giving my sister more support with my mother, and I want to spend more time with her while she still recognizes me . . . There's a lot of pressure on me to come back. The home help said something about there being a job locally and 'Oh you can live at home' says the home help.

Moira's sister Amy's history was rather different. In her early twenties she married and moved away from her parents' house to a rented house in the same town. Both she and her husband were in middle-class occupations when a job opportunity for her husband and a job transfer for her took them to a large city about forty miles away. At the time of the interview, they still lived in that city but now in a larger house. She had subsequently gained a higher education qualification as a mature student. Some years ago, her husband had turned down a job in a town about 130 miles away (but not an easy car or rail journey) because the move would have taken them too far away from Amy's parents. When we interviewed her, Amy had two children aged 16 and 13.

Although neither sister now lived in the same locality as her mother, Moira was the one who had moved a very long way away in her lifetime, whereas Amy, the older sister, had stayed closer. It is interesting, therefore, to compare Moira's reasoning about distance and kinship with that of Amy. At the time of our interviews, their mother still lived in the town where they were brought up, adding to both sisters' sense of stability in their origins or 'roots'. Their mother had dementia and their father, who had been caring for her for some time, had died suddenly three years ago. Since that time, their mother's health had deteriorated but also her need for care and support had become more visible to the daughters because their father was no longer around to 'hold things together'. Their mother had several brothers and sisters living nearby, but none who provided the kind of daily support and care which Moira and Amy were beginning to realize was needed. One or other of them visited their mother most weekends, although Amy tended to go more often and had taken the major responsibility so far for organizing what was quite a complex package of domiciliary and day care for her, 'because I was the closest, you know, even though I'm quite far away, I was much closer'. Their mother's neighbours provided limited support and had telephoned Amy in the past in times of crisis or greater need.

When we interviewed them, Amy and Moira had just taken the decision to find a place in a nursing home for their mother and were trying to work out the best thing to do. Their mother was not particularly happy about this prospect, and it was clearly a difficult time for all of them. The sisters had virtually decided that they themselves would have to choose the nursing home because of their mother's reluctance to participate in the discussions and what they felt was her unrealistic desire to stay at home. Given that their mother, Amy, and Moira all lived some distance apart, this was raising difficult questions for them about geography; among other issues, where should the nursing home be? Amy put it like this:

> We're [herself and her sister] having a bit of a discussion about that because I think there is a nice one just over the bridge from me, and I've been to see it and it's quite, it's not brilliant, but it's quite nice. And I thought it would be ideal if my mum was there because then I could pop in even for just five minutes every day and see her. And so I said that to Moira but Moira doesn't think she should be taken away from her roots. And I can see that too—if she was going to be able to go about on her own on an independent basis. But I don't think she's going to be able to be left to go about on her own in an independent way.

Amy was rather more dismissive than was Moira of the significance or practical value of her mother's roots in her home town and explained that although her mother had brothers and sisters living nearby, 'they don't visit her in her house, so I don't know if they'll visit her' in a nursing home. Because they were pulling in different directions about the issue of location when we spoke to them, Moira and Amy had reached the rather uneasy conclusion that they should look at nursing homes in both of the towns where Amy and her mother lived, and make their choice on the basis of which establishment seemed to be the best. The possibility of a nursing home in the town where Moira was to live had not entered the discussions at that stage.

Overall then, Moira's story was one of geographical mobility coupled with highly significant kin relationships. Despite the geographical distance, she had maintained a close relationship with her mother, sister and family, and sister-in-law and family, just as she had with her father and brother before their deaths. She had moved to live with kin at various points in her life and had been involved over the years in negotiations about family relationships and responsibilities. The current preoccupation that she and her sister shared with the question of how to look after and support their mother demonstrated that she felt a strong sense of commitment, although she had different views from her sister about how that commitment should be fulfilled. By her own account, her sister had taken the greater responsibility for their mother.

In Moira's reasoning about all of this, distance assumed a *malleable* quality in at least two senses. First, Moira gave a sense of making kin relationships work over long distances and of seeing that as an entirely normal activity. It was a 'can-do' attitude to distance and kinship, which not all of the interviewees in our study shared. It was possible for her to live at a distance not because kin relationships did not matter, but because distance did not prevent their relationships from functioning. For Moira, it was possible to conduct good kin relationships over long distances. Indeed, she maintained a close relationship with her parents not least because of their support and encouragement for her independent lifestyle and her career. In other words, the fact that they had encouraged and supported her geographical mobility, and were prepared to visit her as well as to encourage her to visit them, in some ways added significance to their relationship rather than subtracting from it. Moira's professional employment and consequent income undoubtedly helped to provide the resources necessary to finance and maintain the telephone calls and visits associated with long-distance relationships.

Now that her mother needed practical care of the kind which was difficult to provide or arrange over the telephone, there was some evidence that Moira's views of distance were being scaled down a little, but she nevertheless still viewed living, say, sixty miles apart (as she would soon be from her mother) as living fairly close. If her mother were to move into a nursing home in her home town, Moira felt that she and her sister would be close enough to visit frequently and provide support when they were living sixty and forty miles away, respectively. For many of the interviewees in our study, these would have been viewed as prohibitive distances.

The second way in which Moira constructed distance as malleable was in her readiness to move for a range of reasons. For Moira, moving was always a possibility which she would be ready to consider in response to different sets of circumstances, and so far no move had been seen as being permanent. However, she was clear that it was wrong to move for only one reason such as a job or a family need, because of her view that anyone's life, including her own, should be multi-faceted and that one's own interests and the interests of those needing support should be balanced in some way:

> I've done enough moving for the wrong reasons, moving for, er, just going for a job and finding how hard it is to have a life living on your own somewhere where you don't know anybody and all you've got is your job. It's just a disaster because you end up wanting much more from the job than the job can possibly give you because you basically haven't got anything else in your life. So I've learned those lessons. And I moved for family reasons when I moved to [town in North-west] and then I realized that my sister-in-law couldn't give me everything, [town in North-west] couldn't give me everything. But you can't, there's a sort of false altruism you know, you might think 'Oh this is the right thing to do', you know, 'people will approve of this.' But that's not enough. You've got to maybe be selfish and look after yourself. No, *it'd just be a disaster if I moved simply to be near my mother* [emphasis added]. And I know that I might end up when she dies living with the guilt of it. But it's better than being driven to murdering her [laughs]. Oh I'd just go insane if I was living with her.

For Moira, the elements relevant to a decision to move involved not just jobs or family needs, but also her own needs—her needs for support, for friends and social networks, and for a culturally conducive environment. Her ideas about location were currently being expressed as a feeling that it would be nice, although not essential, to get back to her roots. But because moving was always a possibility, distance was not prohibitive in relation to kin or indeed other social relationships, since it could always be reduced.

In these ways, Moira came across as what I would call a *distance thinker* in her kin relationships, and she was more of a distance thinker than was her sister. Amy had moved less frequently, had avoided moving 'too far' away from her parents over her lifetime and, in relation to their current dilemma, felt that her mother would be best located in a nursing home local to herself rather than in the town where her mother, and some of her mother's siblings, currently lived. In part, these differences were a consequence of the different migratory and kin biographies of the two sisters, and in part they contributed to those different biographies. Where Moira had an image of herself as a mover and a relatively autonomous actor, Amy's sense of self was more about stability and local connection to others, including her husband and children, but also in more recent years her mother and father. It was likely that they had each received a different form of parental encouragement too, as Moira hinted: 'my dad was a bit peculiar because he always saw marriage as being Amy's vocation, marriage and kids, and he always saw me as being independent'.

Amy's views about distance and kinship were grounded in her experience of exchanging more face-to-face practical support with kin than Moira, and in a close-up knowledge about how her mother's local support network did or did not function. In Amy's experience, her mother's siblings did not visit her very much in her own home, so she was a little sceptical about how much they would visit if she were in a nursing home nearby. Furthermore, although her mother's neighbours were helpful and supportive, they would telephone Amy when there was a crisis or the need for support was great. So, to a great extent, Amy *was* the local support network.

CASE STUDY 2: LINDA SHARPE AND HER KIN

Moira Hendry had lived a long distance from kin for most of her adult life, but it was more common among our interviewees who had lived away from kin to have done this for shorter periods or only temporarily. Linda Sharpe, a married, middle-class woman in her late thirties, was one of these, and had spent most of her life living in the north-west of England, where her middle-class parents, married brother, parents-in-law, and brother-in-law also lived. However, Linda and her husband Brian (whom we also interviewed) and more recently their three children (aged 13, 11, and 9 at the time of our interviews) had moved around the region, mostly following job opportunities for Brian in his middle-class occupational career, with Linda picking up part-time office work locally. Linda's parents, too, had moved within the region and although they currently lived in the same neighbourhood as Linda and her family, there had been quite lengthy periods during which she lived at least sixty miles from them albeit within the region. Indeed, her parents were shortly planning to move, again within the region, but this move would take them forty or so miles away. Linda's in-laws had stayed in the same town in the North-west, which was around thirty-five miles from Linda's and Brian's current household. Most of these distances were relatively easy car journeys, as the region is served by a fairly good motorway network, but the journeys were significantly more complicated on public transport.

Along with their three children, Linda and Brian lived with his elderly grandmother, who had previously lived adjacent to Brian's parents. Anticipating her need for care, and in view of their own need for a larger house than they could afford at the time, Linda and Brian had bought their current house three years ago with a financial contribution from his grandmother, and also with 'bridging' money from Linda's parents pending the sale of their previous house (still unsold at the time of our interview). Linda and Brian both said that they had a very close relationship with her parents, but a difficult one with his. They had a strong relationship with his grandmother, but this had become a little strained during their period of co-residence. Linda had an unequivocal sense of responsibility to support her kin, in particular her parents but also Brian's grandmother, and this extended to her feeling that Brian's mother (and father) should have done more to support his grandmother when her need for care became most acute and they were living nearby:

> She's disabled, she can't walk, and she got to the stage where she couldn't look after herself and, um, her daughter, my mother-in-law, wasn't interested in looking after her so it was either go in a home or come and live with us . . . They actually lived back door to back door and she wasn't very interested in making her a cup of tea or anything but you know, it was difficult as well, but without being unpleasant to my mother-in-law about it, she just didn't want to have the responsibility.

The difficulties Linda referred to included not only the fact that the care situation and the relationships involved were demanding and difficult, but also that her parents-in-law lived in a small house and had their other, unemployed son living there too. The consequence, however, had been that the grandmother-in-law had moved some thirty-five miles away from her home town and her daughter to reside with Linda and Brian, who had become her only local source of support.

Linda's regional migratory biography was interrupted by a period of around eighteen months when she and Brian and their first two children lived in the south-west of England. Until then, they had lived in their first marital home in a town chosen because it was 'close enough' both to their parents' homes (around twelve miles from her parents and six miles from his, both easy car journeys) and to the town where Linda worked and Brian was training (around twenty miles, although a less easy car journey), and because it had houses in their price range. The move to the South-west was prompted by the offer of a post-qualifying job for Brian and a lack of similar opportunities more locally. Linda was doing a few hours a week bookkeeping in between looking after the children and was prepared to give that up.

However, what was significant about the way Linda, and to a lesser extent Brian, talked about that move was the role of her parents in making it happen. Neither Linda nor Brian were keen to move south and may not have done so had it not been for Linda's parents' encouragement and support, and the fact that Linda's father travelled south regularly with his work, which meant that this could be combined with family visits. Importantly, her parents were not fazed by the idea of Linda and Brian putting a distance of over 200 miles between them:

At the time my father had to attend lots of conferences in London, once a month at least, and he used to come and stay with us. So we saw my parents nearly as much as we'd seen them before . . . We talked to them a lot about it [the potential move] and they were very pleased that my husband had actually got a job. His parents weren't happy because they didn't want to not have their grandchildren around . . . They don't go out very much and to them it would be the other end of the world, whereas for my parents it's just a train or a motorway journey.

The experience of this particular long-distance move helped to cement an image of Linda's parents as people who were prepared to make kin relationships continue to work over long distances—a can-do attitude to distance and kinship—in contrast to Brian's parents, who were seen as being inflexible and overly constrained in their views of how distance impinges upon kinship. What is particularly interesting about this contrast is that although Brian's parents wanted them to continue living nearby, they were seen as taking kin relationships less seriously and according them less significance than they might because they were not prepared to work at them over a long distance. Also implicit in Linda's remarks was the view that they had not worked hard enough at maintaining even local kin relationships, most notably with Brian's grandmother.

After the 'interlude' in the South-west, Linda and Brian readily returned to the North-west as soon as they were able, that is, as soon as a job opportunity arose for Brian. From that point began their history of living and moving within the North-west. It is clear in both of their accounts that kinship, and especially the relationship with Linda's parents, was a strong pull, as was a sense for both of them, but particularly for Brian, of being *rooted* in a particular region of the North-west. Brian began looking for a job which would facilitate a move *home*, while tolerating short-term (although for the most part career-friendly) moves elsewhere in the country or, indeed, in the North-west because of the practical need for employment and an income:

It was a long way from home, that was the thing. A long way from parents, not just my parents but Linda's parents as well and you know, we'd one young baby and another one on the way sort of thing, so we were going to be a long way away. And I suppose I saw it as a temporary thing. I wasn't going to stay down there. We were going to move back north again at the first opportunity . . . It's not because I've any great sort of longing to get back to my parents or anything like that. Or even that I have a fantastic close relationship with my parents. I don't. But it's just I like sort of to be in that area, you know, it's where I grew up and I know people and that and so I always, and of course Linda's parents were in the same area, so I always thought, you know, this was where I wanted to get back to.

Now that they all lived broadly within the same region, Linda saw her own parents, and especially her mother, several times a week and was involved in frequent exchanges of support with her, although the everyday nature of this was likely to change soon when her parents would move forty miles or so away. Linda was not worried about their ability to maintain a close relationship across the region, undoubtedly because of their successful experience of doing this over many years. Linda and Brian saw his parents every two or three months and exchanged little or no support with them, nor did they feel that his parents made a contribution to the care of Brian grandmother. She, however, had contributed financially and in practical terms to Brian and Linda's household. It was a bone of contention that Linda's parents-in-law were 'not prepared to travel' the thirty-five miles or so to visit her or them, and this continued to be a major issue in their difficult relationship.

Linda's story, then, was one in which kin, and especially her parents, were highly significant. Brian's relatives were significant to Linda too: his grandmother in a very direct sense and his parents less directly, not least because Linda and Brian felt continuing disappointment in them and with what they saw as their lack of commitment to kin relationships—their failure to take long-distance relationships in their stride provided a strong example of this. Although on the face of it, it might appear that Linda and Brian's residential history was dictated by his employment, in fact kin relationships and the sense of having roots or a 'home' in a particular region was highly influential in decisions about whether and when to move, as well as where to live.

Linda, just like Moira Hendry, was someone for whom kin relationships were important and were *made to work* whatever the geographical distance between herself and those involved. She also had a view of distance as malleable, although this was not unconditional. So, for example, although Linda was prepared to live a long distance from her parents, she would have preferred to have been closer, especially when her children were very young and she felt in need of their support. Having lived such a long distance away, Linda had now come to see regional distances of the order of thirty, forty, or fifty miles as quite short and easily workable for kin relationships. However, we always got the sense that she would have preferred really local relationships, if that were possible. Her migratory biography had developed through her co-ordination and balancing of the different agendas of kinship (her need and desire for close contact with her parents in particular), jobs and career (her husband's jobs in particular, since Linda had subordinated her career to his and had been more easily able to find work locally), children's educational and social needs, and their desire to return to local/regional roots, for her husband in particular. Unlike Moira, Linda was trying to balance her husband's and children's needs too, and it is interesting that friends do not figure at all in Linda's account, whereas for Moira friends were rather significant players.

Linda emerged from all of this as what I would call a *reluctant* distance thinker, who was willing to think regionally in relation to her kin and over longer distances on a temporary basis, if that was what was required in order to achieve the best balance between these different agendas. It is easy to see in Linda's case how the largely positive, and temporary, experience of having moved away had helped to develop her distance reasoning. Various factors came together to do this, including: the admired and positive response of her parents to the move and their easy acceptance of the 'need' to move from one region to another for employment (and, indeed, to think about work as operating within a national rather than strictly local context); the willingness of her parents (although not her in-laws) to make the relationships work despite the distance, including being prepared to visit frequently; and the fact that Linda and her relatives for the most part had access to the resources necessary to maintain supportive distance relationships.

CASE STUDY 3: MARK MARPLE AND HIS KIN

Not everyone who has had the experience of living away from kin goes on to become a distance thinker. My final case study is such an example. Mark Marple, a divorced 40-year-old working-class man, had spent most of his adult life living very close to relatives, including his parents, two married sisters, grandparents, aunts, uncles, and cousins. He had spent some lengthy periods of co-residence with his parents (or his mother, as he put it, since it was she who orchestrated these periods of co-residence, and with whom he had a particularly close relationship). At the age of 17, however, following arguments with his father, he had packed a bag and left the home in North-west England where he lived with his parents and two sisters, hitching a ride to the South of England, where he found a job, rented a flat, and stayed for more than a year. Although this turned out to be a relatively short stay in the South, Mark had not seen it as temporary when he embarked upon it. In fact, it really was not planned at all:

Mark: I went living down [town in the south of England]. I thought 'There must be more to life than this'. Off I went, see, to London, but I actually thumbed a lift and the bloke was going to [town in the south of England] so I went there. And I liked it so I got a flat and I got a job at 17 and—
Interviewer: So you didn't have any friends down there, you just literally—
Mark: No, just me. Up and off.
Interviewer: And what made you do that?
Mark: Arguments. Family arguments with me dad.

Mark's experience of moving far from kin, therefore, differed quite significantly from that of Linda Sharpe, for whom the move to the South was a planned, albeit relatively short, interlude, and of Moira Hendry, for whom living away had been a more or less permanent feature of adult life. Whereas both Moira and Linda had received parental support and encouragement in their moves, Mark moved as a response to a difficult relationship with his father. Similarly, the level of contact differed, with Mark barely keeping in touch and his parents never visiting him, whereas Linda and Moira both had frequent contact by telephone and face to face. The circumstances surrounding Mark's return to his parents' home a little over a year later were a bit ambiguous. He suggested that they had some (unspecified) need of him and that he returned in a casual, almost accidental, way:

Mark: I sent cards for me mother's birthday and at Christmas. But I never come, I didn't come home at all. And then I just, well, they were going through a bad time, so I came home, and met the girl who I later married.
Interviewer: So when you say you came home, did you come back to live here?
Mark: I came back up to visit. Came back to visit and I just, er, stopped. I went out for a drink and met all the old gang, you know.
Interviewer: Where did you live, back with your mum and dad?
Mark: Well, at first, the first week I stopped at a friend's house round the corner because his mum and dad was away, and then when his mum and dad were coming home, and me mum said 'Your room's upstairs, you know, move back in.' So I went down to [town in the South], got me stuff and came home on the same, you know, overnight coach.

Mark had again moved out, but was living locally, when about a year later his girlfriend became pregnant and they put their names down for a council house. In the meantime, they moved back in with his mother:

My mother said, 'Well, while you find something, come here'. You know, and I can't fault her that way, you know, she were right sound, and she's still sound to this day. She's brill you know, she really is brilliant, but the other one you've got to take with a pinch of salt, you know, the old fella [his father].

Mark and his wife lived in his room in his 'mother's' house, but moved about a year later to his wife's parents' (again, he says 'wife's mother's') house because it was within walking distance of his workplace and he was tired of the four- or five-mile motorbike journey (in the rain) from his mother's. They stayed there only a few months, and then moved into one of the newly built council houses on a nearby estate. After a few years, and the birth of their second child, they bought a house nearby, again within walking distance of their jobs and the children's school, and lived there together for ten years until their traumatic separation and divorce. His wife had started a new relationship, and Mark gave up his job and left his wife and children in the marital home, to live in a succession of rented rooms in the same locality. He describes this period as 'being on the skids', and as a very low point in his life. Eventually, he moved in with a friend and began to put some order back into his life, but the living arrangement was only temporary. He wanted to stay local, particularly to be near his children, but also it was clear that moving out of the region simply was not an option which occurred to him at that time:

> So I came up here [his mother's house] one night and watched the TV and I fell asleep on the settee, so me mum left me there and the night after she said 'Come on, come and get yourself back here.' Went full circle really . . . I thought I can't be doing with this again, you know, sort of four moves in twelve months, I couldn't be doing with it so you know I came here and I've been here since and me and my mum get on great. Mum, she's a star.

Over his lifetime, then, Mark had left his parental home ('my mum's house') and returned three times. Although Mark viewed his first return as being partly about reciprocal need and support, he was clear, not least in his praise of his mother ('she's a star', 'she's brill', 'I can't fault her'), that these arrangements had been mostly about his mother providing support for him. He saw her as having literally rescued him on several occasions and as always being there to do so. In her interview Doreen, his mother, characterized his three returns home as being based on *his* need for a home and practical and emotional support. In her account, he had actively 'hinted' that this was what he wanted and she had agreed. She has also helped find him work by persuading her two brothers to employ him as a labourer, and helped him keep in touch with his children following his divorce by providing practical support.

Mark was unemployed and still living with his mother when we interviewed them, although he had previously done various labouring and driving jobs. His two children and former wife still lived locally. One daughter, now aged 14, lived with his ex-wife. The other, aged 21, lived with her boyfriend and their baby, making Mark a grandfather. He spoke about his daily life and relationships in very local ways, using the language of street names and neighbourhoods and referring to different districts a few miles apart in the same town as being 'a long way'.

In all these ways, Mark came across as a *local thinker* in relation to kinship. For him, kin relationships were highly significant, especially the relationship with his mother, on whom he depended, but they simply did not work over long distances. Local relationships with friends were important too. During his time in the south of England, he was effectively cut off from kin contact and support and, indeed, for most of his life he has not had easy access to the resources necessary to maintain distance relationships. His frame of reference in relation to kinship was now very local, and co-residence with his mother had become a normal and more or less permanent feature of his life. Although he had provided help and support to his parents in the past, he had needed quite intensive support himself over much longer periods and this had been provided mostly by his mother. By contrast with Linda Sharpe's parents, Mark's appeared to be local, not distance, thinkers. His mother, in particular, was tied closely into a local kin network which included most of her kin and over the years had had many relatives live in her household for temporary periods. She talked of geographically more distant kin, whether they were in Australia as was her sister or only thirty miles away, as all being 'not here' and 'a long way away'. For her, it was being 'not here' which was significant and frowned upon. She and Mark shared a view that proper or effective kin support was only possible locally and, sometimes, only within the same household. This differentiated Mark's parents from Moira Hendry's, for example, because although both had similar experiences of always living within a tight geographical region, Moira's parents saw moving and the maintenance of long-distance kin relationships as entirely appropriate for their daughter if that was what she wanted to do; whereas for Mark's mother, local kin relationships were always the most appropriate.

REASONING ABOUT PROXIMITY, DISTANCE, AND KINSHIP

I have argued that the three people whose stories I have examined in depth in this chapter each developed distinctive styles of reasoning about proximity, distance, and kinship. Moira Hendry was a distance thinker; Linda Sharpe was as well, but a more reluctant one than Moira; while Mark Marple was a local thinker. A distance thinker, I want to suggest, is someone who reasons that it is possible to conduct kin relationships over long distances. This might be either because they do not see geographical distance as necessarily incompatible with the development of meaningful and supportive kin relationships, as in the cases of Moira and Linda, or because they do not see kin relationships as particularly significant to their own lives, and we did have a minority of interviewees to whom this description applied. A distance thinker may well see living in the same neighbourhood as relatives as 'too close for comfort'. A local thinker is someone for whom kin relationships simply do not work in any meaningful sense over long distances. I should say that thinking or reasoning about distance in these ways should be distinguished from action: it is possible to be a distance thinker yet to live near to kin, or to be a local thinker and live away.

Intuitively, however, one might suppose that living at a distance from kin will produce distance thinking, but a comparison of the cases of Moira, Linda, and Mark shows that this is not necessarily the case. Linda's distance thinking was reluctant and Mark was very much a local thinker, despite their periods of living away from kin. Living away from kin had been influential, but not straightforwardly so, and for Mark at least it was partly because his experience of living away was negative that he became a local thinker. Similarly, in the rest of our data set, although there is a tendency for those who have lived away from kin because of their own mobility (twenty-five cases) to be more likely to become distance thinkers, almost half did not. There are other elements in the experience of living away from kin which can be teased out of the three detailed cases, and which suggest a more complex picture of the ways in which experiences of living away from kin get channelled into reasoning about kinship, proximity, and distance.

First, *legitimacy of purpose* in moving away or living at a distance was clearly relevant, and for our interviewees this meant legitimacy not only in their own eyes, but in the eyes of significant others. Moira and Linda were both confident that they were moving away for legitimate reasons and, crucially, their parents and Moira's sister were convinced of this as well, although there were suggestions that should Amy have wished to make a similar move, it might not have been accorded the same legitimacy. That Linda's in-laws did not approve was seen as yet another example of their own shortcomings in relation to kinship rather than a serious questioning of the legitimacy of the move. On the face of it, Moira's and Linda's reasons for moving might seem inherently more legitimate than Mark's: Moira was moving to make her own way in the world; Linda to pursue her husband's career and income potential at a time when they had a growing family; Mark was 'drifting', by his own account. However, I think it is much more likely that whether or not a person persuades others that their reason for living away is legitimate depends more upon their negotiating position within their family and their own sense of how family responsibilities should be fulfilled, and less upon any objective definition of what is and what is not a legitimate reason.[4] So, for example, if Mark had held a stronger negotiating position within his family, and he had been more convinced of the legitimacy of his own move, he might also have been able to get his actions interpreted as 'making his own way in the world'.

Gender is clearly important in this process, although again not straightforwardly. Certainly, if Linda's husband had moved to support her career rather than the other way round, her parents might have seen this as less legitimate than they did, and his parents most certainly would have. Linda had an identity as a carer and almost-full-time mother in the eyes of her family, whereas Brian's identity was tied up with his employment and he had the greater earning potential. But people's notions of gender are not necessarily so clear-cut and stereotypical as this. Moira's professional career progression seemed to be seen as entirely legitimate by her parents and, indeed, by her sister, even though she was a woman—although it is not insignificant that Moira was single and childless, nor that her sister Amy, married with children, was seen by her father in a more stereotypical light. Furthermore, Moira's and Amy's only brother had tragically died, so there was no longer a son to be the repository of any parental career aspirations.

Moving a long distance to follow a husband's (or male partner's) job, as Linda did, was a much more common experience in our data set than moving to follow a wife's. There were nine people in our data set who had done the former, and one Asian woman who moved on marriage to live in her unemployed husband's parents' home. There were no examples which can clearly be interpreted as the latter, however, although we do have examples where moves were related to the jobs of both partners. Moves to follow a husband's job were not always seen as legitimate by the movers or their relatives, and we had three cases, for example, where divorced women reflected back on moves made for former husbands' jobs with strong disapproval. One woman said, disparagingly, that the many long-distance (and some international) moves that she and her former husband had made to follow his career had 'all been part of his grand plan', and that he had paid little heed to their kin relationships or children's needs. Since their separation and divorce, she had remained living at a distance from her widowed mother, who was now terminally ill and living in a nursing home. She had become a local thinker: her relationship with her mother now involved little contact and no support other than occasional liaison with Social Services. This was clearly something she regretted but, significantly, she felt it was simply impossible to do any more over several hundred miles and she was not prepared to move—not least because of her own and her children's local social and personal networks. Moira Hendry's thinking that one reason is never enough to make a long-distance move was strongly echoed in this case and in the rest of the data set, so that moves which were interpreted as having been solely for career advancement, or indeed for any other single reason, did not gain widespread approval.

The *encouragement of relatives*, and particularly parents where they exist, for living away was very important in the development of distance thinking, as I have suggested throughout this chapter. This was tied up with, although not the same as, legitimacy of purpose, but certainly in the three cases discussed in this chapter, legitimacy in the eyes of parents and their willingness to make relationships work over long distances seemed fairly crucial to the development of distance reasoning. This was reflected in the rest of the data set, especially in the accounts of people in their 'middle years' (thirties, forties, and fifties). This may be affected, of course, by the parents' own geographical mobility or stability (although remember that Moira's supportive parents had themselves been residentially stable). Certainly, in some families there was a sense of a culture of moving, and in others a culture of stability, which, although not directly transmitted down the generations, formed a backdrop of 'normal' behaviour. This was likely to be related to, although again not the same as, the geographical dispersal or concentration of one's kin and, indeed, the shape and composition of the group one regards as kin.

The *'need' for practical support* for oneself and other kin which arises while one is living at a distance was also crucial in how people reasoned about living away. Linda was a reluctant distance thinker, partly because although she and her kin had successfully made relationships work over long distances, she missed the everyday practical support that her mother might have provided when she had young children. She and Brian both defined this as a particular period of need, and some such periods are related to more or less predictable life-course stages, such as when children are young or when parents are elderly and may be in greater need of everyday practical support. Mark experienced fairly acute needs for practical support which prompted his move back to his mother's house. It is, undoubtedly, easier to become a distance thinker if one's time living away from kin does not overlap with any period of intensive need of one's own or of kin for whom one feels a responsibility. It is also likely to be easier if, like Moira with her sister Amy, there are others who do live relatively near the person needing the practical support who are prepared to provide it.

Finally, *access to resources* and *social class* were both related, relevant issues. Maintaining supportive kin relationships over long distances can cost money and require access to resources, such as a car. This clearly differentiated Moira and Linda from Mark, who for much of the time simply did not have sufficient resources to make frequent visits and telephone calls 'home', for example. Therefore, it is easier to develop distance thinking if you have plenty of money, although I should point out that not all of our apparently well-resourced interviewees did develop distance thinking. The connections with social class are more tenuous, and although it is tempting to suggest that 'long-distance kinship' is a middle-class phenomenon, in fact it is not, since many of our local thinkers were middle class and some—although fewer—of our distance thinkers were working class (loosely defined). The experience of, say, a young adult leaving home to go into higher education, as Moira did, was certainly formative in that it made kinship at a distance seem possible and tended to be seen as a 'legitimate purpose' for a young unattached person. We already know that this experience makes a significant impact on the process through which young adults gain independence from their parents, and on what that independence looks like (Jones 1987). But of course, this is not solely a middle-class experience.

To conclude, living away from kin does not mean that kin relationships are insignificant, and there is a very real sense in which many people are prepared to contemplate, and to put into practice, 'long-distance kinship'. The ways in which people reason about distance and kinship are quite complex and, as I have said, are not necessarily the same as the actions people take or a direct reflection of whether or not they have lived away from kin. It would also be wrong to suggest that different styles of reasoning govern what people do in any strategic sense. They are significant, however, because they express something of the ways in which people are 'thinking aloud' about changing kinship in a changing Britain, and because they provide analytical handles on the multi-layered significance of people's past and present experiences for the current ordering of their lives, aspirations, and responsibilities.

NOTES

1. As well as secondary analysis of large data sets, reported in part by Flowerdew *et al.* in Chap. 18 of this volume, the project involved detailed interviews with 57 people, sampled theoretically, about their residential histories and kin relationships. Twenty-six of these people had relatives in the study and thus we have been able to construct kin case studies with data from the perspectives of different relatives. This chapter draws on 3 such cases, and on material from the rest of the qualitative data set.
2. All names of interviewees in this chapter are pseudonyms and some personal details have been changed.
3. In all excerpts from transcripts, '. . .' indicates that some text has been edited out; a dash indicates interruption; words and phrases in square brackets are editorial insertions.

4. A similar point is made in Finch and Mason 1993, where it is argued that the legitimacy of a person's 'excuse' for not providing help or support for a relative (including being geographically 'too far away') has more to do with their negotiating position within their family, and their own sense of commitment to specific individuals within their family which has developed in relationships with those individuals over time, than with the legitimacy of the excuse itself in any objective or measurable sense.

7

The transnational character of Caribbean kinship in Britain

Harry Goulbourne

INTRODUCTION

This chapter is concerned with aspects of transnational kinship characteristics among British families of Caribbean backgrounds. While some other features are mentioned, the discussion principally focuses upon two key aspects of Caribbean transnationality: first, the provision of care and support across national boundaries and, second, the sense of self and national identity that is expressed through kin membership and participation. The purpose of the chapter is to increase academic and public understanding of forms of Caribbean living arrangements through an empirically informed discussion of issues which have significant theoretical and policy implications. The policy implications are beyond the scope of this discussion and not entered into here. Rather, the chapter advances the argument that Caribbean family and communal life in Britain cannot be fully understood without an appreciation of the continuing kinship links across national boundaries which both provide support for members and impose duties and responsibilities on them. A necessary starting point of such a discussion, however, is the theoretical and methodological context of the research from which data are drawn for the interpretation advanced here of the meaning and function of Caribbean transnational kinship.

The full title of the project was 'Living Arrangements, Family Structure and Social Change of Caribbeans in Britain'; ESRC grant no. L31523009, held by Harry Goulbourne and Mary Chamberlain. The research team also included Dr Dwaine Plaza (for 15 months) and Dr David Owen (for 6 months). In preparing this chapter, I have benefited greatly from discussions with colleagues on the research team, particularly Mary Chamberlain; my thanks are due to them and also to Susan McRae.

THEORETICAL AND METHODOLOGICAL CONSIDERATIONS

In general, kinship systems combine descent by blood or genealogy—comprising the primary or core nuclear unit of the family—with wider networks of social relations based on affinity through marriage, cohabitation, co-residence, and/or fictive relations. Kinship involves the ascription of individual and collective rights alongside reciprocal obligations and responsibilities. It is partly through the kinship system that a society sanctions acceptable forms of social behaviour and prohibits others (for example, incest). Kinship also provides the social context for procreation both within and outside the framework sanctioned by law, and it is partly through the kinship system that the transmission of values, customs, and culture occurs. Within this network, individuals receive primary care and are socialized—the necessities for life in the wider social order—and develop a sense of belonging to discrete bio-social, or consanguineal and affinal, units. It is not surprising, therefore, that in sociological and anthropological discussions kinship networks are generally referred to as *systems* because they are identifiable institutions with a number of functions that are considered (for example, by M. G. Smith 1962; Malinowski 1963) to be primary to the larger society.

While all human societies have established family and kinship systems, these differ and each has to be understood in its own terms rather than through any extraneous overarching structure, functional schema, or value system. Awareness of such specificities need not be as relativistic as this statement may sound, because in practice societies are more similar in their broad structures, functions, and values than they are distinct. It is, however, more usual to stress the differences than the similarities between kinship systems.

These general remarks are as apposite for the indigenous as they are for the new minority communities in contemporary Britain. In several respects, however, Caribbean families differ from the majority as well as other minority ethnic communities. For example, work on the 1991 Census supports the observation that there is a greater tendency in British Caribbean communities for marriage or cohabitation to be exogenous than is the case with other communities (Berrington 1996; Owen 1996; Modood *et al.* 1997). Berrington sought to explain this in terms of the relative sizes of minority ethnic communities, their density, and the preponderance of the white population (Berrington 1996: 198–9), but there are other, more relevant correlative factors such as the already mixed lineages and linkages of Caribbean families and kinship. There is a tendency, moreover, for Caribbean culture to be outward-looking. The important point here, however, is that the general willingness to form unions with individuals outside the ethnic or national community gave, and continues to give, rise to kinship patterns that transcend the boundaries of the nation-state. Expressed another way, it may be said that Caribbean families in Britain more than others exhibit, and live within, multi-ethnic and multi-cultural contexts.[1] Migration and family reproduction in Britain have given a new dynamism to this process, but it was one which began within the Creole societies which developed out of the slave and plantation systems in the region (Patterson 1967; Brathwaite 1978, 1997).

A more significant difference between families of Caribbean backgrounds and the indigenous and other minority communities is the fact that over 50 per cent of mothers of Caribbean backgrounds are lone parents (cf. Owen 1993) and that fewer than half of all Caribbean families are thus nuclear families,[2] contrary to the observation of high rates of marriage during earlier decades (cf. Rex and Tomlinson 1979: chap. 3; also Barrow 1982). The prevalence of lone-mother households and the resurgence of a Caribbean kinship system that places greater importance on consanguineal than on conjugal ties can be easily misunderstood to suggest that the Caribbean family is dysfunctional or weak. This line of argument soon leads to the conclusion that Caribbean families are unable to provide the necessary support required by members and therefore encourage such social 'pathologies' as welfare dependency and male marginality (see, for example, Dench 1992, 1996*a*). But the tendency to reach such hasty conclusions is not new in Britain (see, for example, Pryce 1979: 15 ff.; Rampton 1981: 15; also cf. Barrow 1982). As Raymond Smith (1996: chap. 6) has argued, this mistaken conclusion has been a common view in the Caribbean itself, at least since the influential work of Simey (1946) on welfare and planning in the West Indies in the 1940s.

Our research into the living arrangements and family structures of Caribbeans in Britain, therefore, sought to test the hypothesis that contrary to the view of dysfunctionality and dependence, it has been the strength and resilience of Caribbean family and kinship groups in unfavourable conditions which has provided them with the wherewithal to establish communities and to sustain and reproduce themselves. With regard to the articulation of public issues and participation in political action, these groups' strength and resilience has been variously described (see, for example, Fitzgerald 1988, 1990; Sewell 1993; Goulbourne 1998*a*). In the private world of the family, the accounts of mutual support across distance, the closeness between members, and the ways in which knowledge and values are transmitted all suggest that the kinship system provides the emotional and material factors necessary for meaningful individual and family life. Our research suggests that families tend to utilize their kinship networks as primary institutions for equipping individual members for fulfilled lives in a competitive and generally hostile world. Where what M. G. Smith (1974, 1988*a*) called *differential incorpo-*

ration into the social fabric is involved, as with Caribbeans in Britain, family and kinship links and obligations may be of particular importance. Education, the building of confidence, the acquisition of collective self- and community awareness (which do not necessarily find support in the public domain), a sense of individual well-being and happiness, and the devising of survival strategies are all vitally important functions of kinship networks. Our data suggest that maintenance of transnational kinship in the Atlantic world is central to these functions in Caribbean communities in Britain in the 1990s. In other words, what Sheila Patterson recognized among Caribbean settlers in Brixton in the early 1960s as 'the close trans-Atlantic consanguineous links between migrants and their kin at home' (Patterson 1965: 261) have remained constant, as the discussion in the second half of this chapter illustrates.

However, Caribbean families do not, nor have they sought to, live in isolation from the wider British social system and survive exclusively through their kinship groups. Caribbean kinship networks do not account for the total social incorporation of individual members, because kinship groups operate within the wider social systems of the national labour market, educational institutions, and judicio-political units of the British state. Thus, for example, we found relatively little in the histories of the families studied to suggest that their kinship networks could provide employment for members, or that kinship was used with respect to the political system. While there was evidence of individuals taking limited advantage of the economic opportunities provided by the international kinship system, in general these opportunities had not been fully exploited by members of these networks.[3]

The second hypothesis which guided our research asserted that Caribbean families and kinship networks exhibit modernist features to an unusually high degree. This is most clearly seen in the tension in each family between collective control and the freedom of individual members. The overall value system which informs Caribbean societies is not discordant with the dictates of the impersonal, contractual rules which characterize and mark off modern societies from earlier social formations and which the founding figures of sociology such as Marx (1974), Durkheim (1933), and Weber (1995) stressed. At another level within these social orders, a variety of modifications have occurred, combining patterns of resistance and innovations which draw on pre-Colombian and African roots, but in ways not clearly recognizable as African or otherwise. In short, the tension between the desire to control or restrain individual behaviour through kinship ties and obligations and at the same time strongly assert individual freedom reflects an absence of traditionalism (Mintz and Price 1992; Mintz 1993; Goulbourne 1998*b*).

Although not explored in depth here, our data provide ample evidence of this tension between individual autonomy and the burden of collective obligation which Durkheim (1933) saw as a fundamental problem at the root of modern societies and which continues to be problematic (cf. Finch 1989*a*). For example, nearly all our respondents who were brought up in the Caribbean spoke about the severity of the physical punishments they received, usually from their fathers; respondents tended to speak about their fathers' strictness and their mothers' sternness, reflecting moral codes to which they came to adhere. While parental authority was exercised through the threat or use of physical force, respondents felt that such punishments were administered not out of hate, malice, or cruelty but from a deep concern for the long-term well-being of children in the hostile world of a wider society marked by social inequalities based on dominant perceptions of racial differentiation. Sometimes punishment was justified by reference to more moderate rules such as learning 'good manners' and the need to be 'presentable' (that is, to behave and to dress in acceptable ways) in the perception of the wider world. There was always a concern over whether the behaviour of the individual would bring shame on the family or the larger network of kin, or make them collectively feel proud.

At the same time, there has been, and continues to be, a profound respect for the individual's freedom to act, even where the rules and boundaries of good behaviour are breached. This is perhaps most clearly expressed over the deep fear about girls becoming pregnant prior to marriage, cohabitation, or a clear signal of commitment by a male partner. Consequently, girls are kept on a short leash, particularly by mothers who are generally responsible for the upbringing of children. Once children arrive, however, they are warmly welcomed as members of the family and kinship group, with the girl's mother exuding pride at becoming a grandmother, the grandfather radiating confidence and warmth even when a sense of failure lingers in the memories and narratives of family members. This is consistent with several points made in classic studies of family and kinship among African and mixed populations in the Caribbean (Henriques 1953; Clarke 1957; Blake 1961; M. G. Smith 1962; R. T. Smith 1988*b*; see also Mohammed 1988 and Barrow 1996). Even where the nuclear family continues to exhibit hostility or reserve toward the mother and child, often members of the wider kinship network will assume responsibility, and with time the child is likely to be endowed with the same rights as children born within wedlock.

The research on which this chapter is based includes 180 transgenerational interviews with 60 families with backgrounds in Barbados, Jamaica, and Trinidad and Tobago, although only a limited number of these interviews are drawn upon here. Our starting point for research was the UK, where respondents presented us with material covering the memories, perceptions, and experiences of four, and sometimes five, generations of their families. While we collected statistical data in both Britain and the Caribbean, our main methodological tool was the life-story approach (Vansina 1965; Thompson 1978), which, unlike more conventional in-depth interviews, seeks to capture the longer perspective of a person's life, including its rhythm, cycles, and changes. While the conventional in-depth interview technique generally focuses upon specific instances and events, and is particularly useful for conducting research among organizational, corporate, or political leaders, the life-story approach seeks to capture the lived experiences of ordinary individuals and communities, whose lives are part of the day-to-day fabric of social structure and action. The life-story approach, therefore, is particularly suited to the study of family and kinship systems because the social investigator places the emphasis on the micro- and subjective dimensions of social and political life as distinct from the macro- and aggregate aspects. This approach helped us to avoid what Gundar Myrdal (1944, 1969) and Frantz Fanon (1968) saw in their different ways as the error of using objectivity against the interests of the excluded and the colonized. The extensive questionnaire guideline we constructed covered matters such as childhood, education, work, aspiration, ageing, and the home from the subjective perspectives of actors. While this may be seen as a limitation because the merits of sociological observation and the partial participation in community life by the social anthropologist are missing, it should be borne in mind that our questionnaire guideline also enabled us to come closer to the individual's understanding of the relationships between parents, grandparents, siblings, lineal and affinal aunts and uncles, cousins, and other members of the kinship network across generations and distance.

The theme of transnationality that is explored in the remainder of this chapter is not new but has not hitherto been properly focused upon. Since the 1980s, but particularly in the 1990s, the work of Goulbourne (1980), Thomas-Hope (1980, 1992), Western (1992), Olwig (1996), and Chamberlain (1997) has added to earlier migration studies, such as those by Roberts and Mills (1958) and Peach (1968), by explaining the meaning of the trans-Atlantic experience for those who migrated from the Caribbean. There is also a relatively small body of literature which describes particular aspects of Caribbean settlement in Britain and other European countries (for example, Foner 1979; Brock 1986; Cross and Entzinger 1988; also Carter 1986). In Britain, however, there is less scholarly attention to the consanguineous links across the Atlantic that Patterson observed in the 1960s than appears to be the case in the USA (cf Foner 1987; Sutton and Chaney 1987).

But there are several other practical links across the Atlantic which provide a general context for the consanguineous ones which are maintained over distance and time. For example, since both Commonwealth

Caribbean states and Britain respect dual nationality, becoming British or residing in Britain does not mean that family members have also to cut formal links with their country of birth or their parents. Voting and property rights can therefore be enjoyed within the normal framework of the law in these societies, and the high levels of citizens and their families returning to the region, particularly to Jamaica, Barbados, and St Lucia, suggest long-standing and regular contact often involving investments in future homes. The popularity of Caribbean music (such as reggae or soca), as well as food and beverages, complement the work of island and Caribbean-wide organizations to maintain close and continuing links between the region and Britain (see, for example, Goulbourne 1991*a*; also Foner 1979, 1987).

Two features of transnationality across the Atlantic are described in the remainder of this chapter. These are, first, the care and affection which members provide for each other and, second, the sense of self and of national identities which are expressed through their kinship network across the Atlantic. The discussion focuses upon the experiences of three families: the Forbishers, who are in the main Barbadians; the Whaiteses, with backgrounds in Jamaica; and the Smiths, who are predominantly Trinidadian. Each family exhibits several of the features discussed here but in unique ways which cannot be compressed into a general story without losing the nuances which make their narratives distinctive and meaningful. Figures 7.1, 7.2, and 7.3 illustrate the formal structural relationships between parents, between parents and children, and between siblings themselves; these figures also indicate family size and gender distribution, but cannot portray the importance of residence, occupation and class, gender, and generational relationships. It is hoped that the following discussions of the experiences of selected members of each family will convey the powerful meanings that they give to the transnational dimension of their individual lives as well as to their respective kinship groups.

CARE AND AFFECTION ACROSS NATIONAL BOUNDARIES

Family and kinship networks are maintained through the regularity and frequency of visits, or what the Forbishers variously describe as the 'back and forth' movement of kin members. Thus, Annie Forbisher's seafaring maternal uncle, James, who had traversed the seas before settling in Nigeria in the 1960s as a businessman in the construction industry, decided to resettle in London with his wife, a widow whose first husband was an Indian who died young after they had had a daughter. A number of Annie's siblings received their occupational training in England[4] and her family of creation has had frequent visits from members in Barbados and North

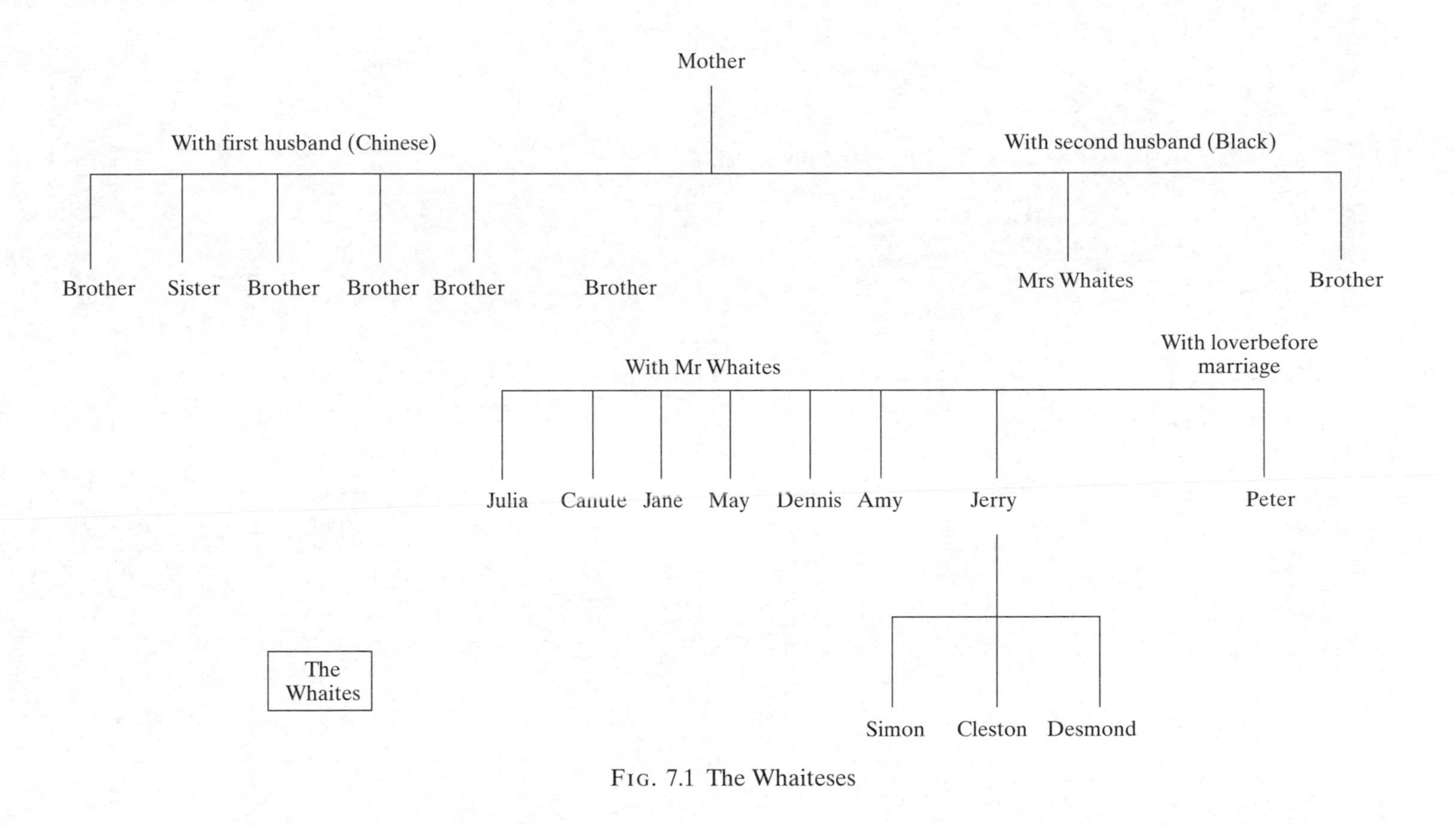

FIG. 7.1 The Whaiteses

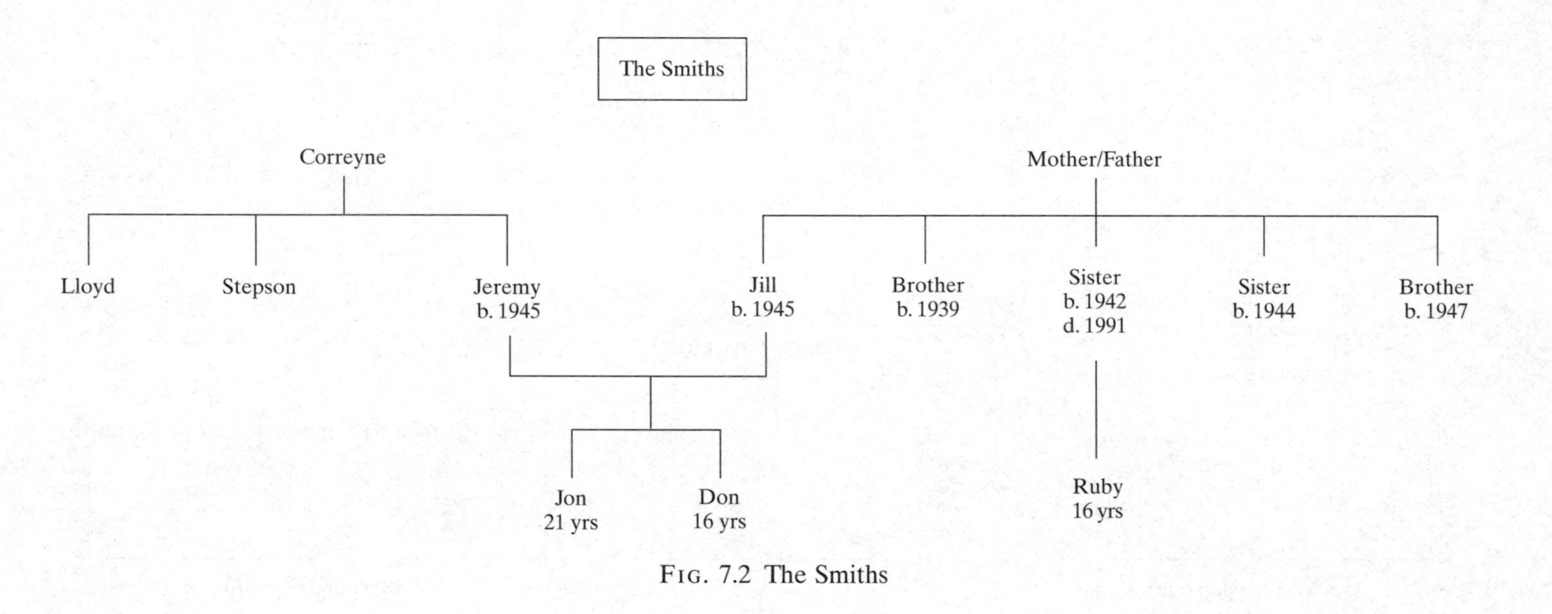

FIG. 7.2 The Smiths

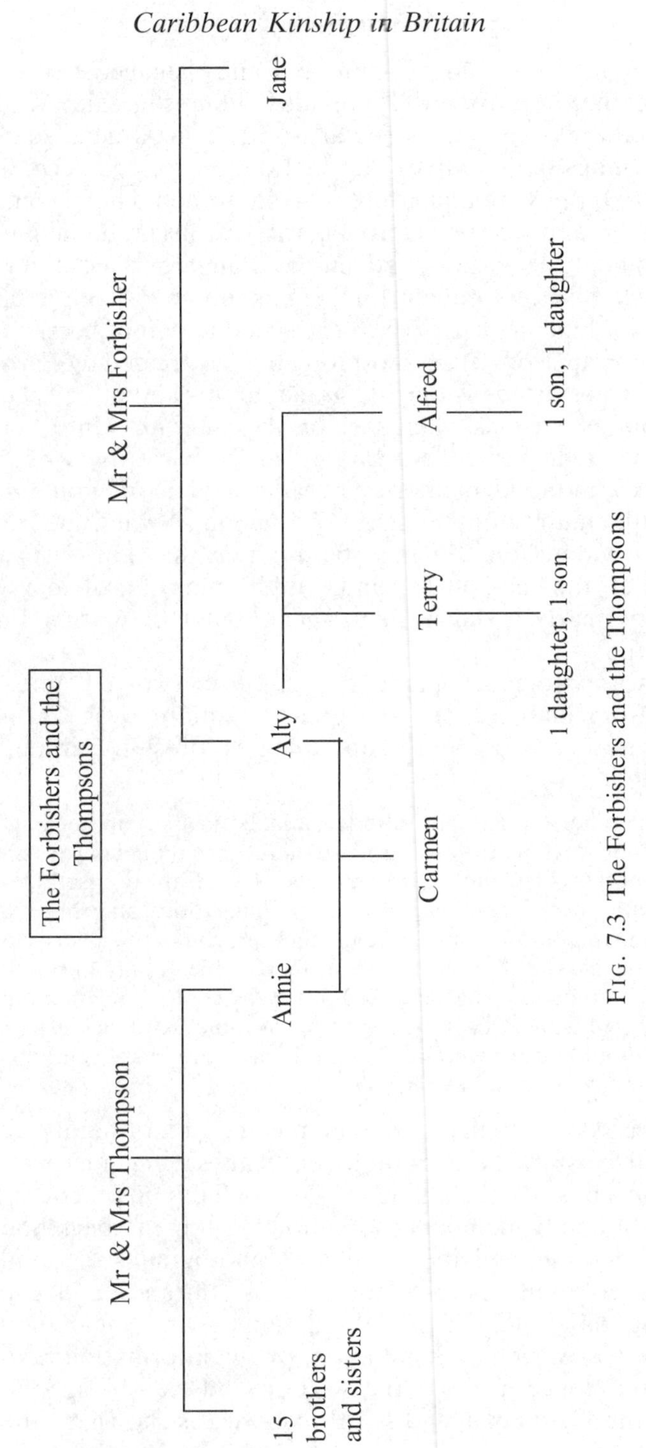

FIG. 7.3 The Forbishers and the Thompsons

America. When, in London, Annie fell and damaged her ankle, her lay preacher father in Barbados, Theophilus Thompson, said, 'Well, Carmen is in school, the husband has to be at work, so she'll need somebody. So, I pack my things and went to her, in London for the second time' (BG 120/1/2/A/p9).[5] His great pleasure was that he could be of some help to his eldest child's family by being around, carrying his granddaughter, Carmen, on his shoulders. He also visited another daughter, Jane, and her family in Ottawa, where after praying for her neighbour's diabetic child, experienced how a kind act can help to transcend apparent barriers of race.

The importance of visits is most forcefully expressed by Carmen, Annie's daughter, who started visiting her grandparents and other relatives in Barbados from as early as when she was 4 years old.[6] Until her fourteenth birthday, Carmen visited her kinfolk in Barbados every summer. As a result, her childhood memories became as full of moments when she played with children on her street in London as when she romped in the sand in Barbados. Consequently, she could say that 'I mean, by now, I know Barbados off the back of my hand. And it's almost as if, in a way, I feel as if I'm very nearly a Bajan, so to speak, but I know that I'm not' (BG 091/3/1/A/p8).

There was also much practical assistance involved here. The family suffered from diabetes, and the greatest sufferer was Carmen's grandmother, who lost two children and a leg as a result. Carmen says of her grandmother:

> I used to help her on with her false leg, and, basically, help her out, get a magnifying glass, and all those little things. And there's one thing I always used to remember about her, was her mole, on her, on her face. I always used to sit on her lap and play with her mole, and she used to tell me stories, and things like that. And she was, I mean, she was almost like my mother, you know, a very close bond with her. So when she did die, and I was not there, which really hurt . . . it was . . . oh, it was a very strange feeling, because I felt, 'Why couldn't my mum have taken me with her, so that I could see my gran for the last time?' But luckily in a way, because unlike my other cousins who live here, I, I was there every year, up to her death, in the summer, whereas they only saw her about four times. (BG 091/3/1/A/p7)

These visits also helped to maintain continuity of family traditions and customs such as the laying of table for meals, saying grace, eating together at points in a busy day, retaining religious beliefs and practices, and seeking the views of family members and kinfolk. 'Talking to back home' over the telephone, writing, and the sending of photographs of family members reinforced continuity and bonding across distance and came close to influencing day-to-day activities, thereby giving meaning to Castells' (1996) *network society* brought about by the information revolution.

The same concern about the welfare and well-being of their kin in England, the Caribbean, and North America is shown by the Whaiteses.

But their kinship network went beyond the Atlantic world. For example, Jerry, the family historian, found that some cousins from Jamaica were living in Japan. He explained that a cousin worked in the tourist industry in Jamaica and that on one occasion she was involved in ushering a group of Japanese tourists:

> and one of the guys took a liking to her, and it developed from there. Took her back to Japan, married her. And one of her brothers followed her up, well, two of her brothers followed her up, to visit, as members of the family. One of them stayed and married a Japanese girl, and he is still living there. (JF 022/2/1/A/p9)

This young man, Kris, appears to have started a business in Osaka marketing Jamaican health foods.

Jerry also had a keen interest in travelling and was planning to visit his cousins and their families in Kyoto and Osaka. The family depended on Jerry to keep members of the network in touch with each other, and he actively encouraged them to visit each other in different countries. He personally had a strong urge to visit Jamaica, which he had left reluctantly in 1966 to join his parents in London. Although Jerry went on to become the first black head boy of his school and had the opportunity of having a career as a sprinter, coming to England had been traumatic for the 12-year-old boy and he longed for home. He expressed the point thoughtfully when he said:

> I decided . . . if ever I'm going to go home, I'll have to do it myself, because initially, I was sent for, and it's as if, subconsciously, I was waiting to be sent back, you know. And I thought, no, well, obviously my parents are not going to send me back, so if I want to go, I'm going to have to do it. (JF 022/2/1/A/p3)

Jerry first visited Jamaica in 1979 when he was 25 years old, paying for his ticket in instalments to a local travel agency. Although we do not know what impressions this first visit had on Jerry, we may surmise that it was important, particularly because, when confused and bewildered by life in England, it is to Jamaica that he turned as a way out of his problems. At the age of 19 he had made 15-year-old Yvette pregnant. A white, ex-colonial family was to take care of the baby, Simon, because Jerry and Yvette and their respective families could not cope with the situation. After a year, baby Simon joined his parents and paternal grandparents in the family home. Some years later, however, Jerry set up house with a second woman, Thelma. But his conscience got the better of him, and he returned to live with Yvette and Simon at his parents' home. Six months later, he learnt through a friend that Thelma was in hospital, and rushed there to discover that he had fathered another son, Desmond. Thelma had learnt from friends that Jerry had had a son with Yvette, and Jerry now wished to avoid this embarrassment being repeated and therefore informed Yvette about his son with Thelma before Yvette could hear of him from others. Both Jerry and Simon told us that Yvette was deeply upset by this news. Simon did not know it, but so too was his father, Jerry, who was caught between the mothers of his two sons, and could see no clear way forward. In 1983–4 Jerry decided that he

> had to go and chill out and sort out what I was going to do, you know . . . that's one of the reasons why I went to Jamaica for the year, because I was being pulled like here, and pulled out there, and everybody's hurt, apart from me. And I'm thinking, 'No, this can't work. I've got to go away and clear my head and sort myself out.' (JF 022/2/2/B/p5)

Jamaica is not only the home longed for; the island becomes a refuge, a resource to be depended upon in time of deep psychological or spiritual need. Jerry spent a year there, working for a maternal uncle who had a number of small businesses. Failing to secure long-term work in Jamaica, Jerry returned to England, after deciding to settle down with Yvette and his first son, Simon. Jerry and Yvette cohabited for some years before their spontaneous marriage during Yvette's first visit to Jamaica for the wedding of one of Jerry's cousins.

Apart from visiting his maternal grandfather and meeting a number of cousins in Canada, Simon was keenly aware of his father's feelings about the need to maintain family contact across generations and across countries. He was 'very proud of his Jamaican heritage, and that' (JF 021/3/1/A/p2). In 1979, Jerry had planned to take Simon to Jamaica, but this did not happen, so that 'when he [Jerry] actually left, I remember crying at the airport, because I wasn't going with him' (JF 021/3/1/B/p1). But separations were part of the family's recent history. Jerry said that when 'my father left, it is sad, everybody was sad, you know' (JF 022/2/1/B/p1). This unhappiness was repeated later when their mother left to join their father in London, particularly for their mother, who was leaving her young children behind and entering an uncertain future. The theme of sadness was accepted as part of the experience of migration, but for Jerry and other members of his family and kinship group, the opportunities offered by migration appeared to balance their feelings of dejection as a result of temporary separations. Jerry told us:

> I remember once, one of my uncles went to the States for a while, and he came back. And the thing that struck me was the type of clothes he wore, the belts he wore, the watch he wore, the shoes he had, you know, the trousers he had. I mean, it's a visual thing, because, I don't know, maybe because the Caribbean is lots of bright colours and stuff, you pick up on these things that are different, you know. And some of the stuff was new and smelt good, and, you know . . . those are the things that, you know, stuck in your mind, or stuck in my mind, anyway, you know. So I wanted to experience some of these things,' cos, although they were telling

you stories about it, you wanted your own experience. I mean, as young as that, I was thinking those sort of things. (JF 022/2/1/B/p1)

This was the magic of travelling—the allure of experiencing difference and new opportunities which has never left Jerry. Indeed, his love of travel has become intertwined with family responsibilities and the need to keep members of his transnational kinship network in touch with each other.

But in addition to the sadness of family separation, the demands of family and kin when spread over vast distances can take their toll on the nuclear family unit. When Jerry and his siblings arrived in London to be reunited with their parents, the newcomers were faced not only with a new youngest brother, Denis, who was demanding the attention of their mother, but also with his hostility. Jerry expressed the experience as follows: '[so when] evening comes, he [Denis] said, Mummy, you're not going to let these, these children stay here. They're not . . . you have to send them back to their mummy. They can't sleep here!' (JF 022/2/1/A/p12). But mutual readjustments came with the family being together again. Unfortunately, this was to be fractured through the dual pull of kinship responsibility and potential new opportunities. After having secured a job as an assistant at a medical research laboratory, Mrs Whaites had to rush to New York to help her sister-in-law take care of her mother, who was suffering from diabetes and high blood pressure. On arrival Mrs Whaites discovered that her sister-in-law was also ill and in serious need of help; additionally, she was keeping the three children of her sister who was ill in Jamaica and who in desperation had sent her children to New York. Mrs Whaites postponed her return to London and turned to cooking, washing, and taking care of her in-laws and their children. Not surprisingly, Mrs Whaites lost her job in London, although she secured illegal employment in New York as a home nurse with an elderly Jewish family. The stay in New York lasted three years, by which time (we learn not from her but from her son Jerry) she was hoping to get her green card, stay in the US, and later send for her family. During her absence, her husband had to manage as best he could with the family, and felt that it was his failure that one of his daughters became pregnant in her early teens and that his son, Jerry, had had a baby with Yvette when she was an under-age schoolgirl. From all accounts, the family suffered as a result of Mrs Whaites's long absence and her return provided the family with a vital missing element.

Unlike the Forbishers and the Whaiteses, the Smiths wished to avoid their kin but nonetheless were pulled into the sharing of responsibilities and the use of the network as a resource from time to time. Thus, although his mother does not tell us, Jon recalled and his grandmother confirmed that there was a time when Jill and Jeremy were in such need of help that they sent Jon to Trinidad to stay with relatives for the better part of a year.

Jon's memory of that period was understandably vague, but it was a time with the wider family network that he looks back on with some nostalgia. Moreover, when Jill's eldest sister died in 1991, Jill and Jeremy decided to take care of Ruby, the sister's 10-year-old daughter. Ruby was taken to London and brought up as a member of the family alongside Jon and Don and in 1996 was preparing for her GCSE examinations at a reputable school in North London. In addition, the Smiths, like the other families, made frequent visits 'back home', so that the children could meet their kin and feel that they were part of the kinship network. Again, like the other families, some members of this network lived in North America, particularly the USA.

The Smiths were a multi-ethnic and pan-Caribbean family, with a long history of migration between islands in the Eastern Caribbean. Jon's grandfather and grandmother met in Trinidad, but they were both Grenadians whose parents had migrated with them to that island. When Jeremy's mother was pregnant with him, and her lover left Trinidad to train as a dentist, family circumstances obliged her to return to Grenada so that the boy was born there. His father returned to Grenada, where, according to Jon, who visited and established his own independent link with his grandfather, he rose to public prominence and wealth with his wife, who was described as being from a half-white, Creole family. Jill said of her mother, 'She's mixed with Portuguese and African Negro, that's not really politically correct! I don't know what to say. Negroid. And then my father, he was mixed with Chinese and Negroid, so there's three different mixtures. Three different races, rather' (TA 001/2/1/A/p1).

TRANSNATIONALITY OF SELF AND NATIONAL IDENTITIES

The second example of kinship maintenance across national boundaries is expressed through a strong sense of self- and national identity which persists through time and across distance. Overt, expressive nationalism is relatively muted in the Commonwealth Caribbean, and this is perhaps more evident in Barbados than in some of the other islands. There is, however, a strong and confident and therefore relatively calm feeling of national identity and commitment to the country. Our Barbadian respondents, representing different generations, expressed this deep sense of national identity which posits that it does not matter where a person is born nor where they live: if there is a Barbadian connection, then this is what matters. National identity is least strong in Annie Forbisher, but she too expressed a view about such matters. After having enjoyed a relationship with a Kenyan Asian for seven years, his family arranged, unbeknown to Annie, his marriage in Nairobi, bringing the relationship to an abrupt and 'very heart-breaking' end. It is not mere rationalization that led her to say, 'Well, I don't regret it, looking back now, because I'm glad I stuck more to my culture, you know' (BG 070/2/3/A/p4); a point expressed by her father (Mr Thompson) in Barbados, who was aware of the pain the break-up had caused his eldest daughter. In his view, it was not so much a matter of where a person lived or was born; of greater significance was the person's culture. Love for one's own, or one's parents', place of birth came first in the individual's sense of identity; to disregard this was to jeopardize the well-being and happiness of the individual and the children who would result from the union. The objection was to do with culture and religion, not race. The arranged marriage was something they could no doubt understand, because the Thompsons, although predominantly black, had both European and South Asian predecessors, and indeed, Mr Thompson's marriage had been an arranged one in the Hindu tradition. Mr Thompson was also of the view that a wife should follow her husband's lead, and, he believed, this would have resulted in a great deal of pain for his daughter had she married into an Indian family. Indeed, Mr Thompson expressed most clearly the sense of being Barbadian, in terms that would be understood readily by nineteenth-century European Romantics who reacted against the cosmopolitanism of the Enlightenment. He opined, in terms that the German Romantic and humanist poet Herder (see Berlin 1976: 160 ff.; Kedourie 1985: chap. 5; also Goulbourne 1991*a*: chap. 4) would approve, that:

> Now, see the point now. If you went now, and went to the utmost, let me say you go to Germany, you might see a girl, and everything as of her appeals to you, everything. But for me, now, I'm saying it's not wisdom to make her a wife. And this is the thing now, that I showed her [Annie]. Every person that comes up at a certain level, he thinks his land to be the land. And he so yearns for it, the more he goes into old age. I can't speak with authority, but this is feeling, that the majority of people always wish they could return home, see. Now, if you marry a German woman, she has that same thing for Germany. And then you make children, see? You raise them in Germany or you raise them in Trinidad. If you raised them in Trinidad, the tendency will be Trinidad. But the mother's journey is Germany, and then you're tearing her apart when she would love to go to Germany. But then you love Trinidad. And the children now, is torn. They love you, they love her. Who must we cater to? So those are things that I show her. I said, 'The Indian, whenever he's coming up to old age, he is going to desire India'. I says. 'And not only that, as the man, you've got to give reverence to him. And he, not knowing the true God, but has a love for what is not God, but is God for him,' I says, 'he's going to want his children to be trained that way. And if you are not going to have quarrels and fight and things, you gonna have to give way to him, sending your children to what is no God, and selling him. Because if you resist him . . . without his permission, then you're breeding thing.' And she saw it. (BG 120/1/2/A/pp8–9)

Several emotions or feelings about identity, conservation and perpetuation of self, a sense of care for the future and the well-being of family and kin are involved in this expressive statement, which dismisses the challenges and opportunities of social participation that transcend mono-culturalism or the assumed cultural singularity perceived to be the basis for the nation-state. But the location of the statement within the contention between Enlightenment and Romanticism is not the point here. It is sufficient to note the passion expressed about belonging to a community through family and kin that even unassuming nationalists within an outwardly oriented culture can articulate in order to preserve their kin.

For Carmen, Annie's daughter and Mr Thompson's granddaughter, the tension involved in maintaining an identity across national boundaries is obvious. Brought up in an ostensibly multi-cultural Britain, she is far better equipped than either her grandfather or her mother to understand the world of ethnic and racial pluralism, and is at relative ease within it. Complex questions about mixed unions can be answered by reference to her kinship network across the Atlantic. As she stressed,

> Well, I mean, okay, you can't choose who you fall in love with, put it that way. I mean, if it happens, it happens, whoever it's with, whether it's with a white guy, or an Indian guy, or a Chinese guy or an actual black guy. But there is, you've got to, people who are in mixed relationships, you've got to have a very strong personality to put up with what people say, because one of my friends, she had a white boyfriend, and she said that people used to ring her house and just abuse her, saying, 'What are you deserting your race for?' And all this . . . [and] she really liked him, and he liked her too, but . . . she couldn't take the pressure no more, so she just ended it. So, I don't know, you've got to be able to, you've got to know that you're going to get that sort of thing, just on the street when you're walking, I mean. (BG 091/3/2/A/pp4–5)

When asked if it would bother her if one of her family were involved with someone from another race, Carmen responded:

> I don't think it does, because my Auntie Jane, she, she was married and she divorced, and she was bringing up her four kids by herself, and she was, she married, I think it was two years ago, to a white guy, a white Canadian, and, I mean, I don't . . . well, he's Uncle Tim, and I don't see him any different. I mean, he fits in so well, because he has such a strong personality, and everyone warms to him. And she is happy, which is the main thing. And the bonus is that we all get along with him. So it doesn't really bother me. I mean, it would only bother me with it, any of my cousins, if it wasn't a person who could, you know, fit in with us. I mean, the point is, our family in Barbados, we're very strong, very close-knit, and if someone . . . you've got to be able to get on with everyone, you've got to have . . . not a musical interest, but you've got to be able to adapt to surroundings. I mean, we're a very close lot. So you've got to be someone who will fit in, otherwise you'll be left on the side. (BG 091/3/2/A/p5)

Carmen, not unlike other young persons of Caribbean background in Britain, felt that she was 'black Caribbean', because of her parents. Not being white, Carmen did not feel that she was English or British, even though she was born and brought up in London and is a British citizen. Parentage and colour marked her off from her white mates; she was also conscious that she was somewhat different from other young people of Caribbean background whose parents came from the same island, and suggested that the integration of families from different islands was 'going to be pretty hard. People are going to have an identity crisis.' If it had not been for her kinfolk in Barbados, she said, 'I wouldn't have much of a family really, if I think about it' (BG 091/3/2/A/p5). Although, as noted earlier, she knew she was not Barbadian, she nonetheless looked forward to migrating to the island that her mother had left for England—the country that her grandfather saw as a great opportunity for his eldest child in the struggle for self- and social improvement.

Jerry Whaites, the family historian, is also a Jamaican patriot, but his patriotism is not an exclusive kind. It led him to insist that Yvette visit St Vincent, where she was born, before she visited Jamaica, and with Yvette's mother they went on a two-month tour to meet her kin and acquaint themselves with St Vincent. Indeed, Jerry had set it out as a condition of their being together that Yvette would visit St Vincent to renew links with her roots. He insisted that

> if she was going to be my partner, she would have to travel also. And one of the things that I insisted upon was that she went home, wherever it was she came from, she had to go back there to be at peace with herself, settle some of the memories she had from home, instead of just thinking about it, the way I found whatever it was I was looking for at home. So I didn't want her to come to Jamaica, initially, until she'd actually gone home first. (JF 022/2/2/B/p7)

These are sentiments with which the Barbadian Mr Thompson would agree; the migration process appears to require a return, a journey back to the point of departure. Travelling and meeting relatives in the islands clarified and gave coherence to the relationship between Jerry and Yvette. The journey back to their roots seemed to have consolidated their relationship and allowed them to move from an informal living arrangement to a formal marriage. It was as if there was a deep, unspoken matter regarding kinship affinity, self-identity, and wider national or communal solidarity to be settled. A Durkheimian solidarity is achieved not through a guild or occupational group, but through the repeatability of return and the renewal of affinity. Like Carmen and her parents, Jerry felt that

> It's all well and good asking me how I see myself; especially in this society, it's how people see you. They see me as a black person, you can't hide, right? I see myself as a human being first, and as a black person of Afro-Caribbean descent. I've

become a British person through rules and regulations, but I can never ever be English. Not even my sons who were born here, they might be English on paper, but they will not, they will not be regarded as such. They will always be Afro-Caribbean, or West Indian . . . or black, yes. And this is why I'm, I'm insistent about them learning about where their parents are from, right? Taking Cleston and Simon, and even Desmond's been back to the Caribbean, so at least they've got an idea of where their parents are from, which I think is very important, you know. I mean, I always thought that we've got this escape hatch in the back of our minds, those of us who are not born here, where we can always go back to. But those who are born here haven't got that, it's just stories to them, you know. (JF 022/2/2/B/p7)

For Jerry, the Caribbean background, like the more distant African past, is a resource for Caribbean families in Britain, but there is a responsibility on the part of parents to ensure that their children experience this heritage through deliberate and direct exposure, and not be left with 'just stories'.

The crucial question that released Jon Smith from an English reserve to express his frustrations with being British of Trinidadian background was this: 'What about other young black people in England—do you think that it's difficult for them to get on in Britain?' To which he responded:

Yeh. It is difficult to get on in England. It kind of creates a . . . well, my theory is that the reason there are a lot of black people in mental institutions, a higher proportion than in the normal population, 'normal', well, indigenous population, is that you have to, you don't have to, but you find yourself having to divide your mind. And you're working in a white environment, living in a white environment, and then you find yourself in a black environment with your family and your friends, so that creates, that creates a lot of pressure for people, and they find, like, they're not accepted in the white community fully. I mean, they're accepted. But there's always the odd slight, or the odd patronizing remark, or outright discrimination. And in the black community, there's people who still, who, like, retreat into the bunker to cope with the problems in Britain, and they see a white person and they just cut them dead. So a person who has been in a white environment with white people, if they see you're like that, then they'll cut you dead, and that creates a stress in people's minds, so that sends them over the edge. So, I think that's why it's difficult for black people, because they have to try and assimilate, not assimilate, kind of get on in the white environment, because those are the people who control everything in Britain. But at the same time they want to stay, you know, you have to stay true to your roots, so that creates a big pressure. (TA 015/3/1/A/p14)

It was never explicit but nearly always implicit in the discussion with the Smiths that in order to succeed it was necessary to maintain some distance between the nuclear and extended families. Consequently, their transnational kinship network was not seen as a resource, but more as a drain on the nuclear family or as a constraint on the accumulation possible within the smaller unit. For example, in multi-cultural Britain Jon interpreted his inherited pluralism as a drawback: 'when I go home it's always reinforced that you're black and Trinidadian, West Indian, and you know, it's just, it's embedded into your head that, you know, you're different. I can't really explain it' (TA 015/3/1/B/p8). Like his parents, Jon felt that he had always been committed to the ideal of the nuclear family. He could not, therefore, understand his paternal grandfather, who did not see his son, Jeremy, until the latter had become an adult and sought out his father. But, then, Jon admitted that he had 'always been fed . . . my grandmother's line, you know, that he [his paternal grandfather] ran off or whatever, he treated her badly' (TA 015/3/1/B/p4). Jon was always concerned about meeting this prominent Grenadian figure who had made his name as a professional man, with whom he managed to get on well even though he found him to be 'quite fierce, he's quite an intimidating person' (TA 015/3/1/B/p5). Would-be monogamous Jon had learned that his grandfather had 'other children sort of dotted around, you know . . . and plus he married somebody else, and had children. He's got grandchildren from that wife, yes' (TA 015/3/1/B/p6).

Additionally, and more confusingly, Jon had a steady white girlfriend, but he felt that her family was less than comfortable with him. Jon described them in the following terms:

> Her parents, I think, although they're polite, I still think they're a bit, I don't know whether they're used to it now, but at first they were a bit uncomfortable with it. Not disapproving, just worried about what I'd be like, you know, they're very . . . I still find them quite formal when they're with me, sort of desperate not to put their foot in the wrong place, offend. (TA 015/3/1/B/p6)

Jon had a close understanding of the British youth scene, but was keenly aware that he was not English 'because England isn't home'. He always thought of himself as being Trinidadian, although he was born and brought up in London. His parents were of the view that Jon saw himself as English, and his mother wanted her children to adapt to British society. However, Jon himself said that he

> always felt blood is, blood is what you are, not really the type of . . . not really the place where you are born, it's more blood, blood-related, I think is what you are. And I've always been Trinidadian, Trinidadian especially, as opposed to West Indian, because in Britain, everyone's a Jamaican it seems! [laughs] So I've always been quite strong on this, like, people say, 'Are you Jamaican?' I say, 'No, no, I'm not. I'm Trinidadian'. I've always been quite proud of that, yeh. So I'd say half, half British, half Trinidadian, yes. Yes. (TA 015/3/1/B/p8)

Many of the sentiments expressed here reveal tensions caused by the wider social order for families and kinship groups, and these straddle the public and private spheres of life in ways that cannot be explored here. What is clear, however, is that these tensions generate new questions about what is seen, not uncontentiously,[7] as a multi-cultural, post-imperial Britain (cf. Favell 1988; Goulbourne 1988*b*).

CONCLUSION

It is within this general context of a changing multi-cultural society that the discussion here has emphasized one dominant theme in the living arrangements of Caribbean communities in Britain, namely, the transnational dimension of kinship and the care provided to members as well as the maintenance of self- and communal identities. Although these features are not unique to the Caribbean segments of British society, the characteristics described may be more pronounced where Caribbeans are concerned. It is therefore necessary to take this powerful feature into account when assessing development and continuity in communities in Britain which have backgrounds in, and continuing dynamic links with, the Caribbean. The variety and complexity of kinship networks suggested in this discussion should serve as a caution against hasty conclusions about the capacity of these communities to provide the wherewithal for their survival and well-being. No doubt, as with other segments of society, there will always be families in Caribbean communities who require public assistance, but this need not always be explained by reference to some supposed deficit in the structure and function of family and kinship. The trans-Atlantic character of family and kinship in Caribbean communities appears as a significant aspect of a strategy for survival within the wider British social system in which Caribbeans are differentially—and this means inequitably—incorporated.

NOTES

1. For a definition and discussion of the ideals of multi-culturalism in Britain, see Swann (1985: 5 ff.) and Goulbourne (1988*a*: chap. 1).
2. The much-commented-upon national trends toward divorce and delayed first marriage (Newman and Smith 1997: 16–17) would appear both to reflect and reinforce practice in the Caribbean and British-born offspring of Caribbean migrants.
3. Caribbean firms and governments have, however, been showing renewed determination in the 1990s to exploit the export and investment opportunities made available by the vitality of the Caribbean trans-Atlantic community (see McLeod 1991).
4. Subsequently, a family myth developed (or was reinforced) that English training is superior to Canadian training, at least in the nursing occupation.

5. In references to interviews of individual family members, (1) the first letter refers to the country under which the interviewee is classified due to birth or descent (thus B = Barbados, J = Jamaica, T = Trinidad); (2) the second letter refers to the family interviewed; (3) the first number indicates the chronological position of the interview in the total series of interviews conducted during the project (thus 120 = the 120th interview); (4) the second number refers to the generation (chronologically ordered) of the person interviewed; (5) the third number refers to the tape of the interview; (6) the final letter refers to the side of the tape from which the quotation comes; and (7) the page number refers to the page of the transcription. The data will be lodged with the ESRC Qualidata at the University of Essex and in due course will become available to the academic research community.
6. Of course, this kind of arrangement between kin members is not unusual in the Caribbean (see, e.g., Gordon 1996).
7. What may come readily to mind is Lord Tebbit's attack on the multi-cultural society at the Conservative Party's 1997 annual conference. But his antipathy has been frequently expressed since at least the late 1980s (see, e.g., Tebbit 1990; also Mishan 1988; cf. Goulbourne 1991*b*).

PART III
Older People's Lives

8

Intergenerational perspectives on family and household change in mid- and later life in England and Wales

Emily Grundy

INTRODUCTION

In many developed countries, people aged 50 or more now account for a large and growing proportion of the total population. In England and Wales in 1994, for example, 31 per cent of the population were aged 50 or over, and by 2021 this proportion is projected to reach 41 per cent (OPCS 1996*b*). As the household is an important consumption unit, the household arrangements of such a demographically substantial group have major social and economic implications. The household also remains an important unit for the production and exchange of essentials, including meals, personal care, emotional support, and companionship, and is to an increasing extent the locus of leisure activities. This is particularly true for older people, who spend a large proportion of their time in home-based

The work reported here was supported by ESRC Grant No. L315253010. Data from the ONS Longitudinal Study (LS) were made available by ONS; data from the National Survey of Health and Development were supplied by Michael Wadsworth, University College London; from the British Retirement and Retirement Plans Survey and the British Household Panel Survey by the Data Archive (United Kingdom); and from the US Health and Retirement Survey by John Henretta, University of Florida at Gainesville. Karen Glaser, King's College London, and Kevin Lynch of the Centre for Longitudinal Studies, Institute of Education, London, provided considerable help with abstracting relevant tabulations. The LS support team at the City University is supported by ESRC Grant No. H/507/26/5001. This chapter is based on a paper given at the 1997 Annual Conference of the British Society of Population Studies, Exeter. The plenary papers at this conference were presented by former students of Professor (William) Brass in honour of his contribution to demography. The inspirational training in demography provided by Professor Brass is gratefully acknowledged. Finally, thanks are due to Basia Zaba for helpful comments on a draft version of this chapter.

activities (Altergott 1988). The supply of intra-household resources has a potentially large effect on the extent to which such resources may be sought elsewhere, either through the provision of extra-household support or through forming or joining another household. Gierveld *et al.* (1991), for example, showed that differentials in the availability of transferrable (money) and non-transferrable (domestic services and care) resources in the households of mid-life parents were associated with differences in the home-leaving behaviour of their children. For those in older elderly groups in need of support as a result of disability, the availability of intra-household help influences demand for help from outside, including formally provided services (Cafferata 1987; Arber, Gilbert, and Evandrou 1988), and, for the more seriously disabled, the viability of remaining in the household. Elderly people who live alone, for example, are much more likely than those who live with a spouse to enter institutional care (Dolinsky and Rosenwaike 1988; Grundy 1992*b*).

A further reason for interest in changes in the household arrangements of older people is that they may be indicative of broader changes in intergenerational relationships and exchanges. In this context, it is important to remember that household, family, and kin groups constitute separate, if overlapping, entities and that, as Anderson (1971) noted, 'kinship does not stop at the front door'. Numerous studies have shown that older adults maintain close links with non-co-resident adult children and other relatives, and that, for parents, geographical proximity to at least one child is common (Warnes 1986; Clark and Wolf 1992; Lin and Rogerson 1995). However, living *close* to a child implies a different type of relationship to living *with* a child. Moreover, co-residence generally involves a greater exchange of resources; thus adult children living with a parent provide more help, both financial and care-related, than children living elsewhere (Hoyert 1991).

Changes in the household arrangements of those in older age groups therefore have a number of important implications, and in recent decades the extent of such change has been substantial—this is the broad topic considered in this chapter. I focus particularly on changes in the extent of residence in multi-generational households or households including members other than the nuclear family (complex households) and thereby on the age groups in which intergenerational residence is most common—later mid-life (50–59) and later old age (75+).

CHANGES IN LIVING ARRANGEMENTS

The post-war period in many developed countries has seen dramatic increases in the proportions living alone and decreases in the extent of co-residence in complex or multi-generational households (Kobrin 1976*b*; Pampel 1983; Keilman 1987; Sundström 1994). Although in Britain, other North-west European countries, and North America, co-residence between married couples of different generations seems always to have been unusual (Laslett 1972; Smith 1981; Wall 1990; Hareven 1992) except as a temporary response to housing or other constraints (Holmans 1981), co-residence between unmarried parents and married children, or married parents and never-married children, was much more common in the past than it is today. In the USA in 1910, for example, only 10 per cent of widows aged 65 and over lived alone compared with nearly 70 per cent in 1990; most of this change occurred in the post-World War II period (Kramarow 1995). Changes in the household arrangements of widows in Britain have been similarly marked—and remarkable—in that the extent of recent change stands in counterpoint to a previous long period of relative stability (Wall 1984, 1995). The proportion of elderly people with a never-married child at home was also much higher in the past (Wall 1995). This particular change reflects shifts in the relevant demographic parameters—in this case age at completion of childbearing, life expectancy after the age of 65, and the age composition of the elderly population—and demographic change is one of the three main explanations advanced for period changes in household patterns, including those of the elderly population.

EXPLANATIONS FOR PERIOD CHANGES IN LIVING ARRANGEMENTS

Availability of kin

Most of the research on demographic influences on household arrangements of the elderly population has focused on the availability of kin, particularly spouses and children, with whom to co-reside. Numerous studies have demonstrated strong associations between marital status and living arrangements in later life, and changes in the timing and duration of widowhood are an important potential influence on household type in older age groups. In Britain during the 1980s, for example, the proportion of women in their sixties living in married-couple households rose, largely reflecting a narrowing of sex differentials in mortality and cohort differences in nuptiality (Murphy and Grundy 1993). Early work on the availability of children based on aggregate analysis (Kobrin 1976*b*) has been substantially extended by more recent research based on micro-data (see Wolf 1994 for a review). Many, but not all, of these studies show relationships between variables such as number of children and the demographic characteristics of children (gender and marital status) and both the living arrangements of elderly people at one point in time and their transitions between types of household (Wolf 1984; Wolf, and Soldo 1988; Soldo, Wolf, and Agree 1990; Wolf 1990). Apart from these largely empirical studies, analytic and simulation models have been used in estimation of kin and the effects on households. The former approach is exemplified in Brass's (1983) seminal paper, which demonstrated the predominant role played by fertility in determining household size and formally identified the other relevant analytic parameters.

Economic and attitudinal change

The other two main explanations for period changes in household patterns, including the living arrangements of elderly people, are economic changes allowing higher proportions to purchase privacy (Michael, Fuchs, and Scott 1980; Ermisch 1985); and cultural or attitudinal changes, including those associated with a convergence of age and gender roles, a growing emphasis on individual autonomy, and the rise of 'post-materialist' values (Burch and Matthews 1987; van da Kaa 1987; Inglehart 1990; Pampel 1992). Studies of differentials in the living arrangements of particular populations lend support to both hypotheses. A wide range of research, predominantly although not exclusively from the USA, has shown relationships between income and living arrangements, with higher income being associated with a greater probability of living alone and reduced chance of co-residence with relatives (Crimmins and Ingegneri 1990; Soldo, Wolf, and Agree 1990; Hoyert 1991; Mutchler and Burr 1991; Spitze and Logan 1992; van Solinge 1994). Some studies from Canada and England and Wales have reported a contrary trend, with co-residence being higher in the more socio-economically advantaged groups (Béland *et al.* 1987; Grundy and Harrop 1992; Grundy 1993), but these were based on work in which differentials in kin availability could not be allowed for. Macro-economic changes, allowing increases in the availability of housing (Ermisch 1985) or in the provision of health and support services, may also be important.

The evidence for cultural and attitudinal differences in living arrangements, including the extent of co-residence, comes largely from cross-national comparative work and studies of within-country differences between ethnic or social groups and regions. The living arrangements of elderly people both between and within European countries, for example, show considerable diversity (Grundy 1987; Wall 1989; Bartiaux 1991; Pampel 1992; van Solinge 1994). There are also large variations within Europe in the marital status of elderly populations and the extent of childlessness (Grundy 1996*a*), but national differences cannot be wholly explained by variations in kin availability. Ireland, for example, has an extremely high rate of childlessness in the elderly population, but in comparison with other Western European populations also has a very high proportion of elderly people who live with a child. Many studies have shown marked differences in the living arrangements of elderly people by ethnicity (Burr 1990; Angel, Angel, and Himes 1992; Kamo and Zhou 1994). In the US, for example, a significantly higher proportion of elderly people aged 65 or over of Southern, Central, or Eastern European origin live with close relatives, even when socio-economic factors are controlled for, when compared with those of North-western European origin (Clark and Neidert 1992). Similar differences by ancestry have been found in Canada (Thomas and Wister 1984).

Although these three explanations for change in household patterns are sometimes treated as alternatives, in reality all three, and interactions between them, are likely to be important. Thus, cultural and economic factors may influence the degree of consanguinity and propinquity considered to confer kinship obligations of a particular kind. In this sense, the availability of kin may contract even in the absence of demographic change, if, for example, the expectations of aunt–niece or mother–daughter relationships change.

LIFE-CYCLE, AGE, AND COHORT INFLUENCES ON HOUSEHOLD ARRANGEMENTS

Period changes in household patterns, of course, imply differences between cohorts in living arrangements at particular ages. Surveys and censuses from a range of European countries with predominantly nuclear family household structures show strong relationships between increasing age (in elderly age groups) and likelihood of co-residence with kin outside the nuclear family (Grundy 1987; Wall 1989; Bartiaux 1991; van Solinge 1994). Decrements in health status are an important reason underlying this association, and numerous studies have found relationships between health and household type, and health and transitions between different types of household (Magaziner *et al.* 1988; Borsch-Supan 1990; Crimmins and Ingegneri 1990; Stinner *et al.* 1990; Speare *et al.* 1991; Prohaska *et al.* 1993; Glaser *et al.* 1997). Although long-term trends in the health status of elderly people are hard to determine, recent trends in Britain, some other European countries, and the United States suggest some decline in the extent of the most serious types of disability (Boshuizen and van de Water 1994; Manton and Stallard 1994; Grundy 1996*b*) and it is possible that improvements in the health status of successive cohorts at given ages may partly account for period changes in living arrangements. Cohort differences in nuptiality and fertility, including timing of births, have also been associated with period changes in some aspects of intergenerational co-residence. Partly for these reasons, Wall (1995) has suggested that cohort, rather than period, analysis may be the most appropriate way to study change over time in the living arrangements of elderly people. This approach has been adopted in some research (Bracher and Santow 1990). Weinick (1995), for example, used retrospective data from the US National Survey of Families and Households to examine cohort differences in the probability of co-residence of adult daughters and parents. His results showed surprisingly little change between birth cohorts (1900–14 to 1960–9) in the probability that an adult daughter of any age experienced a parent living with her although, of course, this is compatible with substantial changes viewed from the parents' perspective.

GENERATIONAL PERSPECTIVES

The foregoing illustrates one of the difficulties of studying household-level change: the need to consider changes in the behaviour or characteristics of more than one individual, and often more than one generation, concurrently. Differences in the size of *parent* and *child* generational groups mean that the proportion of elderly people living with an adult child is much higher than the proportion of adult children living with a parent; US cross-sectional data indicate that the former was 15 per cent in the late 1980s while the latter was only 2 per cent (Weinick 1995); British data show a similarly large difference depending on the generational viewpoint (Grundy and Harrop 1992; Grundy 1993). Reductions in average family size may be associated with a fall in the proportion of elderly people living with a child (as opportunities for this kind of co-residence will be reduced) while from the child's perspective, they will tend to increase the probability of co-residence with a parent. Similarly, while a later age at childbearing implies that parents will be older when their children leave home, it is also associated with an earlier age at orphanhood for children. This is illustrated for near-contemporary Britain (1982) by data drawn from the British National Survey of Health and Development (a cohort study of a sample born in 1946) which shows that at the age of 36, 83 per cent of sample members had a surviving mother and 64 per cent a surviving father. These proportions varied substantially, as expected, according to parental age; a third of those fathered by 30–34-year-olds, and over half with fathers aged 35 or over at the time of their birth, had lost their father compared with only a fifth of those fathered by men aged 20–24. This implies that, while later childbearing may increase the chance of parental co-residence with a child in later mid-life and early old age, from the child's perspective it will reduce the probability of co-residence with a parent.

If a three-generational perspective is adopted, unravelling the relationship between demographic change and the household arrangements of older people becomes even more complex, as for middle-generation adults the needs of children and parents may compete. Grundy and Harrop (1992) reported that in England and Wales, rates of co-residence with an elderly parent among 35–54-year-olds were lower for those who had dependent children, presumably because of pressures on both space and time. Wolf (1995), in an analysis of macro-data from twenty-one European and North American countries, found that the proportion of elderly women living alone was positively associated with the ratio of elderly mothers to daughters (inferred from age structure) but negatively associated with the grandmother-to-granddaughter ratio. Wolf speculated that this might reflect the negative effect of potential household crowding on co-residence and that recent falls in fertility (lowering the grandmother-to-granddaughter ratio) might have the effect of slowing down the increase in solitary living among elderly women.

In the following sections of this chapter, I consider recent changes (since 1971) in the household patterns of older adults, with a particular focus on changes in households including members of different generations or members who do not constitute a nuclear family group.

DATA SOURCES

The major data source used here is the ONS Longitudinal Study (LS). This is a record-linkage study based on 1 per cent of those enumerated in the 1971 Census of England and Wales. Sample members were traced in the National Health Services Central Register and record linkage used to add information from the registration of vital events such as death, and data from the 1981 and 1991 Census records of surviving sample members. The 1971 Census included a section on marital, and marital fertility, history completed by ever-married women aged 16–59. As information on subsequent births (both marital and non-marital) has been added to the data set, this means that fertility history data are available for women aged up to 79 in 1991, provided they were present in the 1971 Census. The LS sample has been maintained through the addition of 1 per cent of births and of immigrants; further details, including linkage rates, are given in Hattersley and Creeser (1995). Some use has also been made of data from the British Household Panel Study, which since 1991 has followed at yearly intervals members of some 5,000 households (Buck *et al.* 1994).

Definitions

The definitions of household and family used here are, for the most part, the standard ones employed by the Office for National Statistics (ONS) and other statistical offices. Households are defined as co-resident groups with some common housekeeping; families are categorized as couples (married or cohabiting), couples or lone parents with never-married children (of any age), or grandparents with never-married grandchildren where the intermediate generation is absent. In some parts of the analysis, I distinguish between those living just with a spouse and those in families including a never-married child. The classification of elderly people's living arrangements used here is based on consideration of the family *and* household circumstances of sample members. Particular attention is paid to the proportions of old people in complex family/households, defined here as households including only individuals who are not in a nuclear family (although in most cases they are related to each other) or households including two families. Reference individuals (LS members) living with others, none of whom are members of their nuclear family, have also been assigned to this category, even if some or all of these co-residents constitute a nuclear family themselves. Thus, a widow living with her married daughter and son-in-law has been categorized as living in a complex family/household, whereas the daughter and son-in-law would be classified as a 'married couple and others'. A further distinction is between 'non-private' and 'private' households; the former largely comprise communal establishments such as hospitals, nursing homes, and residential homes.

CHANGES IN INTERGENERATIONAL CO-RESIDENCE, 1971 AND 1991

Intergenerational co-residence between mid-life or elderly parents and their children may arise because of the needs of either the child or the parent, or in some cases both, as illustrated schematically in Table 8.1. Among those in their fifties and early sixties, two-generational households

TABLE 8.1. *Pathways to parent–adult child co-residence*

Child not yet reached home-leaving stage	↘	
Child disabled, remaining for care	→	Child has never left parental home
Parent disabled, child remains to care	↗	
Child needs support (e.g. after divorce)	↘	Child returns to parental home
Parent needs support (e.g. disability)	↗	
Parent needs support (e.g. disability)	↘	Parent moves to child's home
Child needs support (e.g. lone parenthood)	↗	

are most commonly the result of the presence of never-married children who have not yet left home, whereas among those in the oldest groups intergenerational co-residence will more usually be the result of living with a married child.

Figures 8.1 and 8.2 show the distribution of the private household population of England and Wales in 1971 and 1991 by age group and the number of generations in the households of LS sample members. In both years, intergenerational co-residence among those aged 50 or more was highest at the bottom and top of the age ranges shown, reflecting different pathways to this type of household. Marked differences are shown between 1971 and 1991 in the extent of intergenerational co-residence among those aged 70 and over, particularly in the oldest age group shown, those aged 85 or more. In 1971, 29 per cent of men and 34 per cent of women in this age group lived in two-generational households (and 9 per cent and 8 per cent in three-generational households) compared with 12 per cent and 17 per cent in two-generational households (and 3 per cent and 4 per cent in three-generational households) in 1991. Changes between 1971 and 1991 among those in their fifties, in contrast, appear relatively slight. However, as the demographic histories of the cohorts who comprise these age groups in 1971 and 1991 vary so markedly, this apparent stability may mask important changes in the age- or parity-specific probabilities of intergenerational co-residence.

Women in later mid-life: demographic influences on intergenerational co-residence

Figures 8.3*a* and 8.3*b* show the proportion of parous women aged 50–54 and 55–59 living with a never-married child by parity in 1971, 1981, and 1991. In 1991, the proportions co-resident with a child among those with more than one child were substantially lower than for women of the same parity in either 1971 or 1981. However, these differences are not reflected in an equivalent reduction in the overall proportion of 50–59-year-old women living with a never-married child, because as shown in Table 8.2, the composition of the cohorts who were in their fifties in 1971, 1981, and 1991 varies so markedly. The achieved fertility of the later cohorts, who were in their fifties in 1991, was much higher than that of the earlier ones. Twenty-three per cent of women born in 1912–16 were childless, according to the fertility history data collected in the 1971 Census;[1] the estimate of childlessness for the latest cohort shown—those born in 1937–41—was nearly 50 per cent lower.[2] The proportion of multiparous women, by contrast, was much higher in the later cohorts: 73 per cent of those born in 1932–41 had at least two children compared with only 53 per cent of the 1912–21 cohorts. As well as higher fertility overall, the later cohorts started

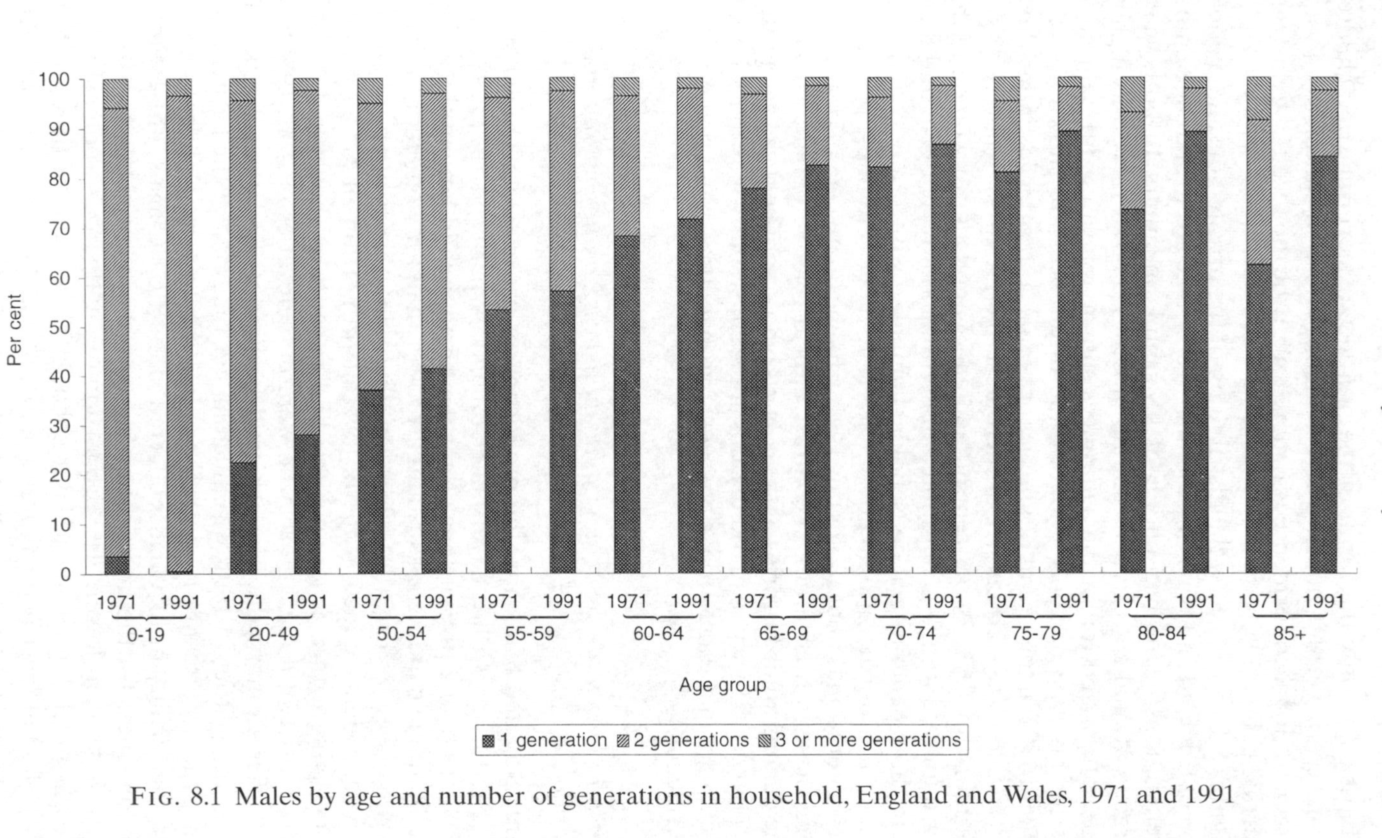

FIG. 8.1 Males by age and number of generations in household, England and Wales, 1971 and 1991

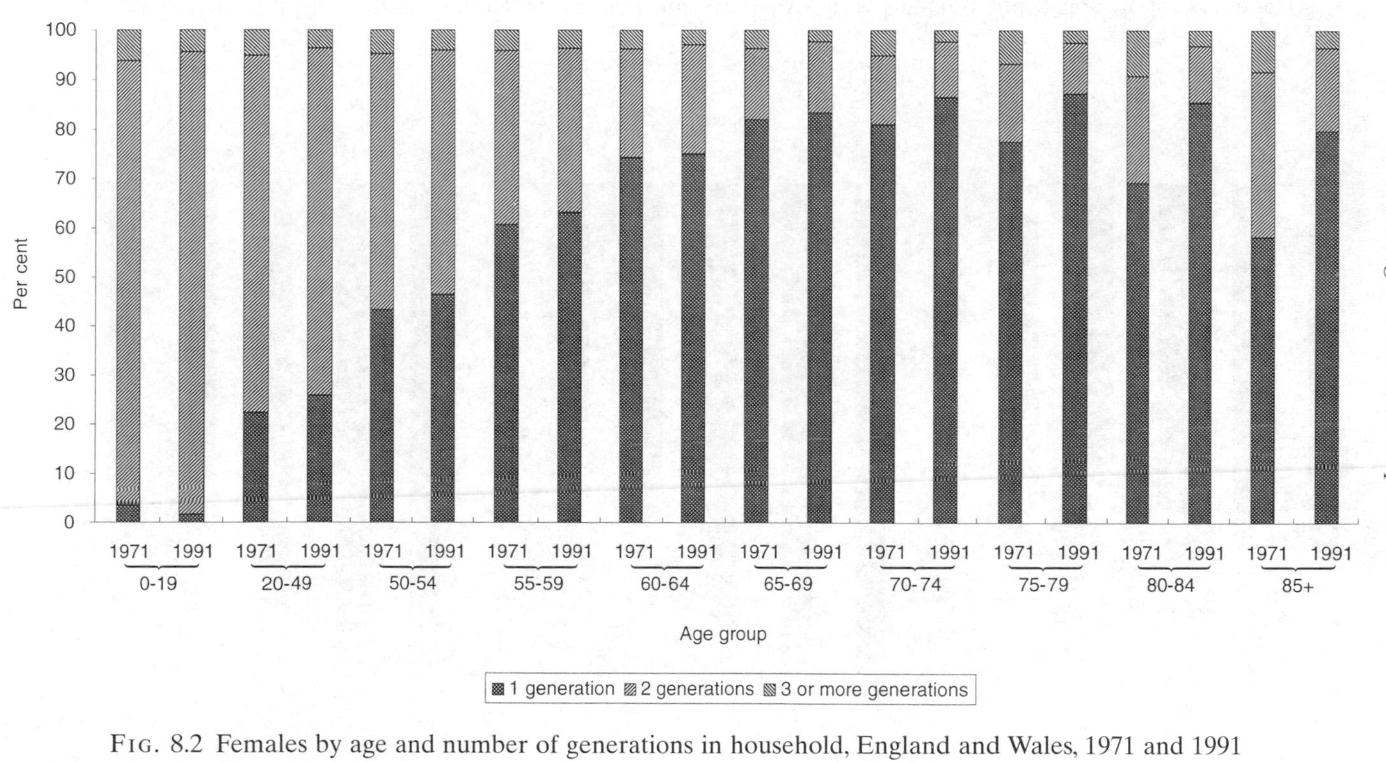

FIG. 8.2 Females by age and number of generations in household, England and Wales, 1971 and 1991

FIG. 8.3*a* Women aged 50–54 living with never-married child(ren), by parity, England and Wales, 1971, 1981, and 1991

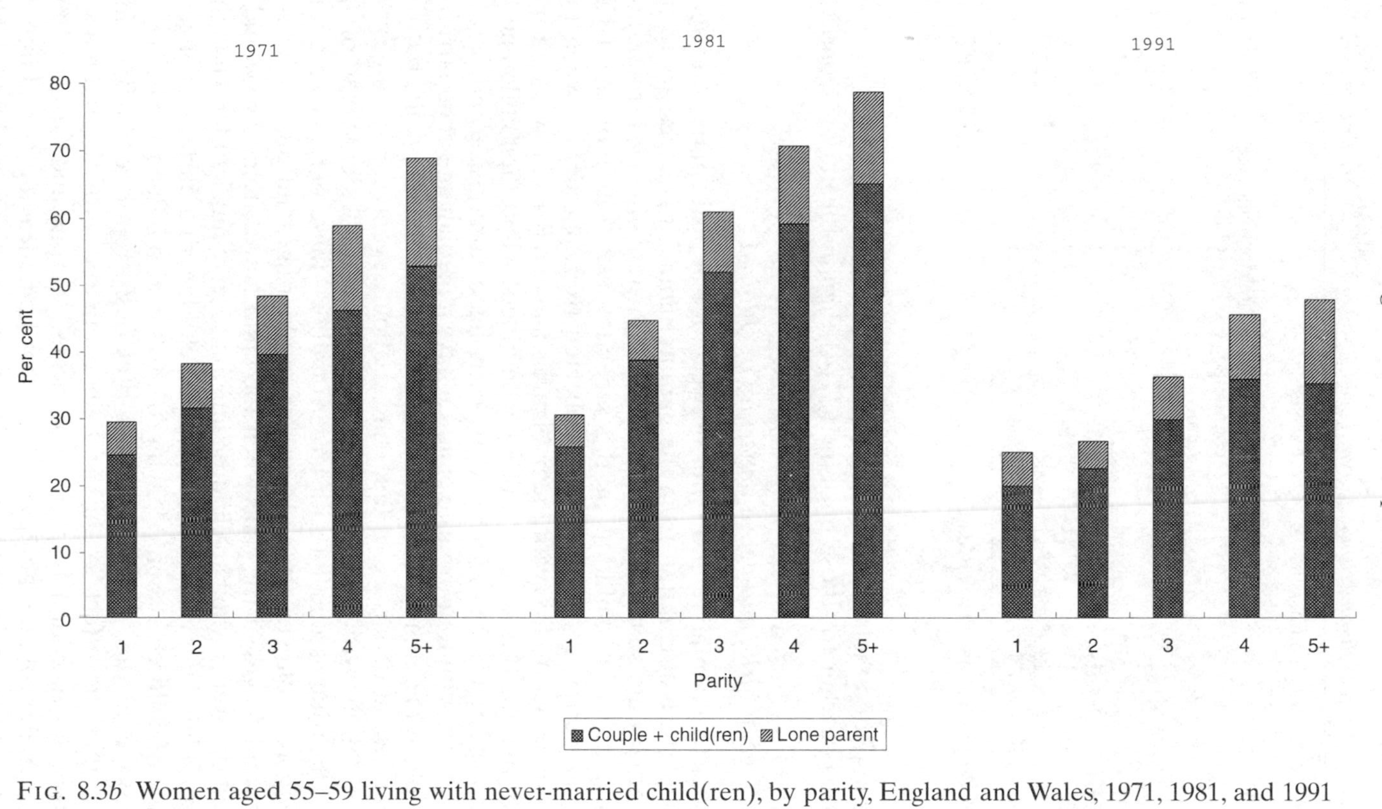

FIG. 8.3*b* Women aged 55–59 living with never-married child(ren), by parity, England and Wales, 1971, 1981, and 1991

TABLE 8.2. *Fertility characteristics of women aged 50–59 by birth cohort, England and Wales*

Birth cohort	Nulliparous %	Parous		
		Mean completed family size	Mean age at first birth	Mean age at last birth
1912–16	23.2	1.8	26.7	32.1
1917–21	20.3	1.9	25.9	31.1
1922–26	19.1	2.0	25.4	30.9
1927–31	17.2	2.1	24.9	30.5
1932–36	13.9	2.3	24.4	29.1
1937–41	11.8	2.3	23.5	27.0

Source: ONS Longitudinal Study data.

and completed their childbearing much earlier. Mean age at last birth was five years earlier for those born in 1937–41 than in the earliest cohort.

Parity, age at birth, and age at departure of children

In order to examine relationships between age at birth, parity, and age at the departure of children from the parental home, it is necessary to turn to another data source, as the LS does not include direct information on the departure of children. In the second wave (1992) of the BHPS, however, retrospective data were collected from parents on when their children ceased to live with them. Figures 8.4*a* and 8.4*b* show the proportion of parents (fathers and mothers combined) whose first child and last child respectively had left home, by completed family size and parental age. Parents with four or more children have a median age at departure of last child some eight years older than parents of only one child, but their median age at departure of first child is about seven years younger than that of parents with only one child. This reflects the wider spread of ages at childbearing associated with larger families—these parents start childbearing at a younger age and finish at an older age, and this is echoed in the parental ages at the time when the child leaves home. As would be expected, parents who had children late in life were much older when their last child left than those who completed childbearing earlier. Changes in the age of children at home-leaving, of course, also influence parental age at passage to the 'empty nest', but previously reported analyses have shown that the effect of this is slight compared with the influence of parental age at completion of childbearing (Murphy and Grundy 1996). However, the countervailing trends of later home-leaving by children and earlier completion of childbearing among parental cohorts have resulted

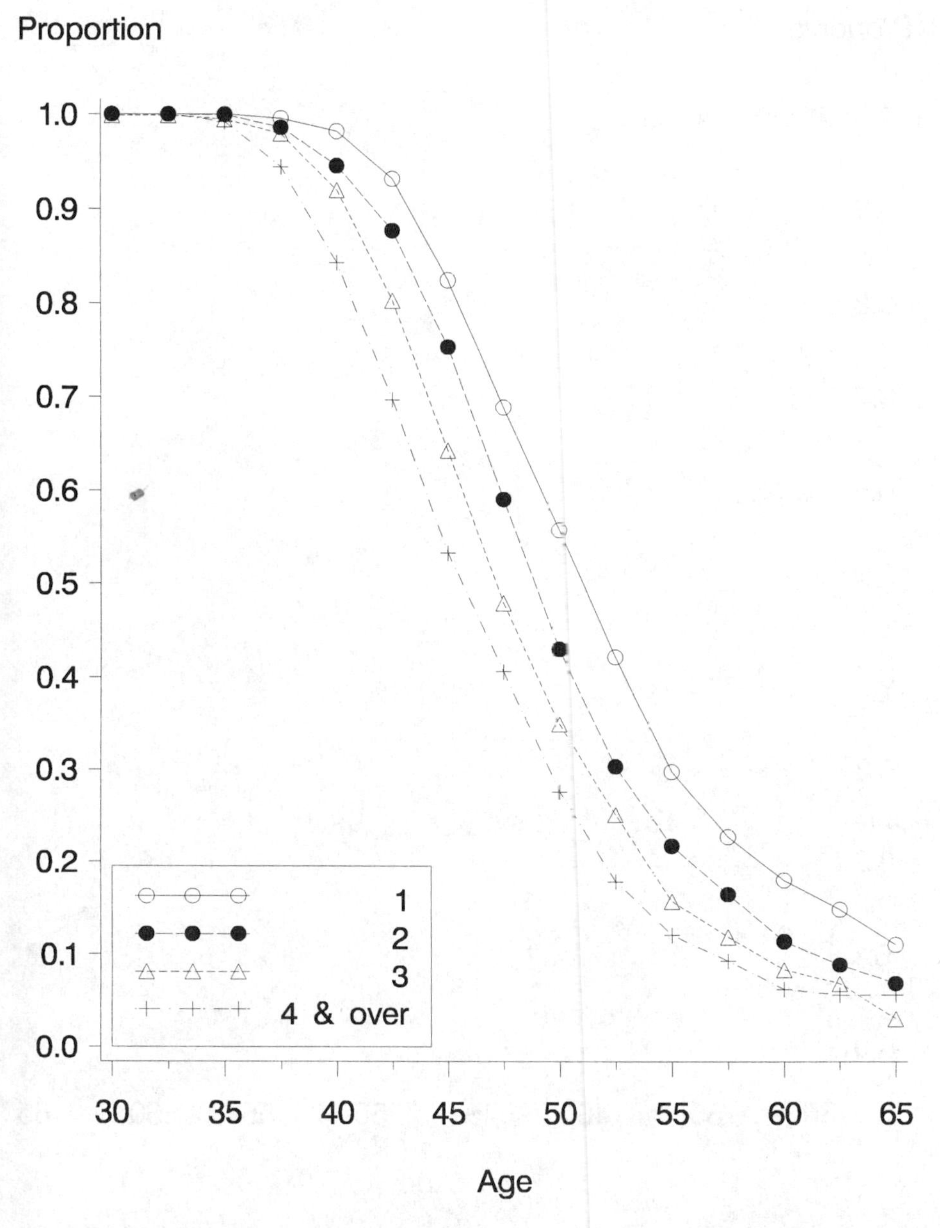

FIG. 8.4*a* Proportion of parents with first child having left home, by parent's current age and family size, Britain, 1992

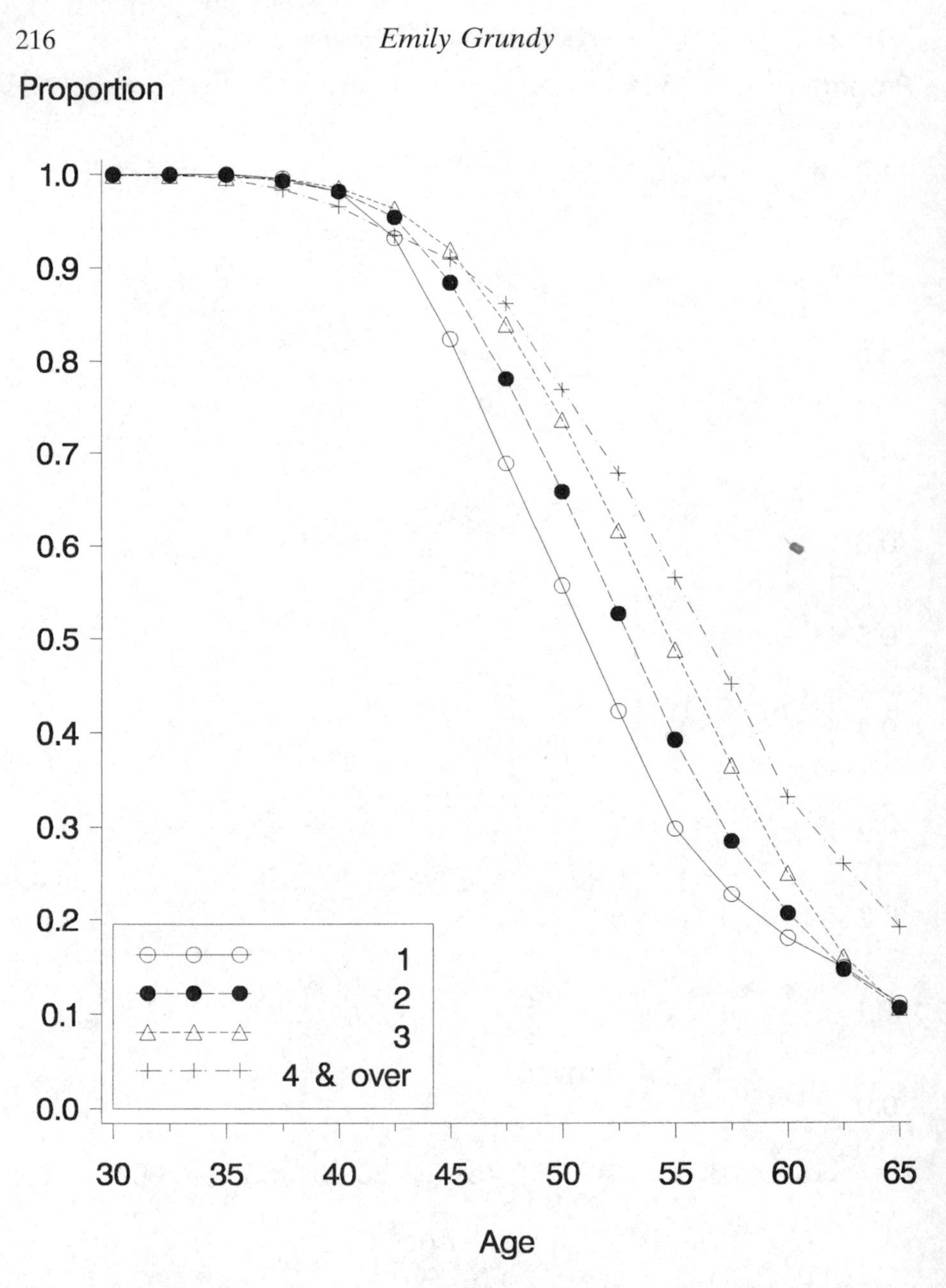

FIG. 8.4*b* Proportion of parents with last child having left home, by parent's current age and family size, Britain, 1992

in some changes in the age distribution of children still in the parental home (Grundy 1992*a*; Murphy and Grundy 1996).

Parents and children of women in later mid-life

The LS and BHPS results presented above show the important influence of parental age at childbearing on co-residence with children in late mid-life. Intergenerational co-residence for women in later mid-life may also arise as a result of living with parents. Obviously, this is only a possibility if at least one parent is still alive; similarly, the availability of either both parent and child, or both child and grandchild, is a necessary prerequisite of residence in a three-generational household. Cohorts now reaching mid-life in Britain include higher proportions with children and have higher overall fertility than their predecessors. Lower rates of mortality in older age groups also imply an increased probability of mid-life adults still having a surviving parent. The effect of differences in demographic parameters on the proportion of women in later mid-life who have both surviving parents and children can be illustrated by comparing the USA and Britain. The levels of fertility reached during the baby boom in the USA were much higher than in Britain; thus in the USA, the total fertility rate (TFR) reached 3.7 in 1965 compared with 2.7 in Britain.[3] Currently the USA also has a lower level of late-life mortality than Britain (Manton and Vaupel 1995). Table 8.3, based on data from two very similar surveys conducted in Britain in 1988 and the US in 1994, shows that these variations are reflected in dramatic differences between the two countries in the distribution of women aged 55–63 by numbers of surviving parents and surviving children. Twelve per cent of British women had no children and no surviving parent, compared with 6 per cent of US women. At the other end of the distribution, 35 per cent of the US women had at least one living child *and* a surviving parent compared with only 19 per cent of the British women. It is worth noting that despite these differences in the survival of parents, more of those women who *had* a parent lived with them in Britain

TABLE 8.3. *Distribution of women aged 55–63 by whether or not they had surviving parents(s)/child(ren): Britain, 1988, and USA, 1994 (%)*

Women with:	Britain	USA
At least one child and at least one surviving parent	19	35
At least one child, no surviving parent	65	57
No children, at least one surviving parent	4	3
No children, no surviving parent	12	6

Sources: Retirement and Retirement Plans Survey (GB); Health and Retirement Survey (USA).

than in the US, so the overall proportion of women living with a parent was very similar in the two populations (4 per cent in Britain and 3 per cent in the US). Differences in the extent of co-residence with at least one child were also relatively slight (30 per cent in the US, 26 per cent in Britain).

HOUSEHOLD ARRANGEMENTS AMONG THOSE AGED 75 AND OVER

Intergenerational co-residence among those in their fifties is most likely to reflect the presence of never-married children who have not yet left home. In elderly age groups, however, and more particularly among the very old, pathways to co-residence are more likely to be of the second or third type shown in Table 8.1 and involve one party moving to join the other (cf. Flowerdew *et al.*, Chapter 18 of this volume). The majority of adult children in these types of household are, or have been, married: 61 per cent of adults aged 35 or more who lived with an elderly parent in 1981 were married, divorced, or widowed (Grundy and Harrop 1992). In the following sections, I examine changes in the household arrangements of those aged 75 and over, with a focus on residence in complex households.

Cross-sectional trends

Table 8.4 shows the living arrangements of men and women aged 75 and over in 1971, 1981, and 1991. Over these two decades, the proportions living alone or just with a spouse increased. Co-residence with a spouse is, of course, only possible for the currently married and the increase in the proportions in this type of household partly reflects cohort differences in nuptiality and a recent narrowing of sex differentials in mortality in older age groups resulting in a later age at widowhood (Grundy 1996*b*). Obviously, as the proportions in simple, one-generation households (solitary or married couple only) have increased, so the proportion in other household types has fallen. The decrease in the proportion living in complex households, particularly among the very old, is striking. In 1971, 27 per cent of men and 31 per cent of women aged 85 or more lived in this type of household, compared with only 9 per cent of men and 13 per cent of women twenty years later. Overall declines in the proportions living with spouses and children (including ever-married children) or in lone-parent families with a never-married child (but no spouse) similarly point to a continuing trend towards smaller and simpler households. The proportions in non-private (institutional) households decreased between 1971 and 1981, but

TABLE 8.4. *Men and women aged 75 and over by family/household type, 1971, 1981, and 1991 (%)*

Age	Year	Family/household type[a]						Total[b] (N)
		Solitary	MC only	MC + ch/others	LP	Complex	NP	
Men								
75–79	1971	17	51	10	3	14	5	4,289
	1981	19	58	7	2	10	3	5,631
	1991	22	61	7	2	6	3	6,794
80–84	1971	19	39	10	6	18	9	2,275
	1981	27	46	6	4	13	6	2,589
	1991	29	52	5	2	7	6	3,817
85+	1971	20	24	6	8	27	15	1,102
	1981	29	31	5	5	20	11	1,213
	1991	32	36	3	3	10	16	1,843
Women								
75–79	1971	41	20	3	8	23	6	7,838
	1981	50	24	2	6	14	4	9,704
	1991	52	28	3	5	9	4	10,817
80–84	1971	39	11	2	9	28	11	4,932
	1981	51	13	2	7	19	9	5,906
	1991	55	17	1	5	10	11	7,408
85+	1971	30	5	1	12	31	22	3,125
	1981	42	5	1	8	25	19	3,913
	1991	49	6	1	5	13	27	5,823

[a] MC = married couple; MC + ch/others = married couple and child(ren), with or without others, or married couple with others; LP = lone parent (includes LP + others); NP = non-private household; for definitions see text.
[b] Total number includes, living with a parent never-married child.
Source: ONS Longitudinal Study data reported in Grundy (1996*b*).

among those over age 85 this proportion then increased between 1981 and 1991. In 1971, the size of the population resident in complex households was substantially larger than the number resident in institutions in all the age groups considered here. By 1991, however, this situation had reversed in the oldest group. Thus among the oldest women, the ratio of those in non-private to those in complex households rose from 0.71 in 1971 to 0.75 in 1981 and 2.0 in 1991. These cross-sectional data suggest some substitution of institutional care for intergenerational co-residence, an issue which can be better examined using longitudinal data to look at transitions between different types of household in 1971 to 1981 and 1981 to 1991.

Cross-sequential changes, 1971–1981 and 1981–1991

In Table 8.5, the household type of sample members in 1981 is shown by household type ten years earlier; Table 8.6 presents equivalent data for the 1981 to 1991 decade. These tables allow transitions between different types of household to be examined—although the ten-year gap between obser-

TABLE 8.5. *Family/household type in 1971 by family/household type in 1981, men and women 65+ in 1971 (%)*

Age in 1971	Family/household type, 1971	Family/household type in 1981[a]						Total (N)
		Solitary	MC only	MC + ch/others	LP	Complex	NP	
Men								
65–74	Solitary	**76**	8	—	—	9	7	705
	MC only	18	**74**	1	—	5	2	4,617
	MC + ch/others	8	44	**32**	9	5	1	1,325
	LP	23	7	2	**50**	17	3	120
	Complex	17	14	3	1	**59**	6	690
	NP	10	31	2	2	5	**50**	125
	All	22	55	7	3	10	3	**7,598**
75+	Solitary	**69**	5	0	1	13	13	191
	MC only	27	**54**	1	0	10	8	588
	MC + ch/others	7	16	**40**	24	10	4	110
	LP	4	2	2	**62**	13	16	45
	Complex	11	2	0	0	**70**	17	145
	NP	5	10	5	0	15	**65**	20
	All	29	32	5	5	19	11	**1,099**
Women								
65–74	Solitary	**85**	1	0	1	7	7	4,469
	MC only	43	**46**	1	1	7	3	5,457
	MC + ch/others	17	22	**23**	26	11	1	1,117
	LP	21	—	—	**67**	8	3	784
	Complex	29	2	1	1	**61**	6	2,158
	NP	25	8	0	3	10	**55**	228
	All	50	20	2	6	15	6	**14,247**
75+	Solitary	**69**	—	0	—	11	20	1,465
	MC only	42	**26**	1	—	14	17	655
	MC + ch/others	19	6	**19**	33	12	9	114
	LP	7	0	0	**76**	11	7	306
	Complex	20	—	1	1	**65**	14	831
	NP	13	0	0	1	9	**76**	106
	All	43	5	1	8	25	18	**3,478**

[a] MC = married couple; MC + ch/others = married couple and children, with or without others, or married couple with others; LP = lone parent (includes LP + others); NP = non-private household; for definitions see text.

— Less than 0.5%.

Source: ONS Longitudinal Study data.

TABLE 8.6. *Family/household type in 1981 by family/household type in 1991, men and women 65+ in 1981 (%)*

Age in 1981	Family/household type, 1981	Family/household type in 1991[a]						Total (N)
		Solitary	MC only	MC + ch/others	LP	Complex	NP	
Men								
65–74	Solitary	**80**	7	—	1	6	6	1,097
	MC only	19	**75**	2	0	2	3	6,191
	MC + ch/others	7	47	**32**	8	4	2	1,376
	LP	29	6	4	**48**	10	3	144
	Complex	22	18	4	1	**45**	9	584
	NP	3	10	0	0	7	**80**	59
	All	24	58	6	2	6	4	**9,473**
75+	Solitary	**67**	1	1	0	6	24	311
	MC only	29	**55**	1	0	5	11	1,027
	MC + ch/others	8	20	**39**	18	7	8	119
	LP	13	0	0	**58**	13	16	38
	Complex	18	7	4	1	**48**	21	165
	NP	6	11	0	6	6	**72**	18
	All	33	36	4	3	10	15	**1,680**
Women								
65–74	Solitary	**85**	1	0	1	5	9	5,508
	MC only	43	**48**	1	—	4	5	7,087
	MC + ch/others	17	26	**25**	22	7	3	1,133
	LP	23	0	0	**64**	9	3	786
	Complex	34	5	1	1	**50**	7	1,572
	NP	8	1	0	0	6	**85**	112
	All	53	24	2	5	9	7	**16,228**
75+	Solitary	**65**	—	0	1	6	28	2,690
	MC only	49	**23**	—	1	6	21	1,139
	MC + ch/others	18	17	**11**	32	14	9	132
	LP	10	0	—	**68**	5	17	312
	Complex	24	1	—	1	**51**	23	754
	NP	2	0	0	0	0	**98**	94
	All	50	6	—	5	13	26	**5,123**

[a] MC = married couple; MC + ch/others = married couple and children, with or without others, or married couple with others; LP = lone parent (includes LP + others); NP = non-private household; for definitions see text.
— Less than 0.5%.
Source: ONS Longitudinal Study data.

vation points means that many transitions made within the decade cannot be captured, especially as attrition through mortality is high in the age groups considered here. Cohorts are identified by their age at the start of the interval. The proportions in the same type of household in both Censuses (the diagonals) have been highlighted. As might be expected, in the group aged 65–74 at the start of each decade, stability—being in the same type of household at the beginning and end of the decade considered—was highest for those initially living alone. Thus, 85 per cent of women who lived alone in 1971 and were then aged 65–74 were still living alone ten years later; the equivalent proportion for the later decade was also 85 per cent. A small proportion of those initially living alone were living in a married couple at the next Census, reflecting (re)marriage. The higher remarriage rates of elderly men, compared with those of women, are reflected in higher proportions of men than women experiencing this type of transition. In the older age group, those living alone—and in 1971–81 but not 1981–91, those in complex households—were the most stable groups. The highest rates of transition from particular household types were from living with a spouse and others or just with a spouse. This pattern reflects the continued departure of children (including ever-married children) from the parental home and the impact of widowhood.

Transitions *from* complex households were higher in the second decade than in the first, and transitions *to* this type of household were markedly lower from solitary, married-couple, and, in the younger age group, lone-parent households. This partly reflects an increase in transitions to institutions (non-private households). I have shown elsewhere that the risk of transition to an institution was 43 per cent higher for men and 52 per cent higher for women in 1981–91 compared with 1971–81 after controlling for age, marital status, and housing tenure (Grundy and Glaser 1997), an increase undoubtedly influenced by policy changes which had the effect of increasing the availability of institutional care paid for by the state during the 1980s.

Clearly, the probability of transition from one type of household in these age groups is likely to be associated with variables such as age, marital status (and change in marital status), and health. The literature also suggests that differences by availability of children and socio-economic characteristics might be expected.

The 1991 Census (but not preceding ones) included a question on limiting long-term illness and, as shown in Figure 8.5, women living alone in 1981 were less likely to be still living alone in 1991 if by then they had a limiting long-term illness. A much higher proportion of the 'ill' group were resident in a non-private household (institution) by 1991; among those then aged 85 or more (but not in the younger group) the proportion in complex households was also slightly higher among those with a limiting long-term illness than among those without one.

For women aged 65–69 in 1981, it is possible to examine differentials in transitions to complex households by parity, as well as by health status and other variables. Table 8.7 shows the proportions of women who in 1981

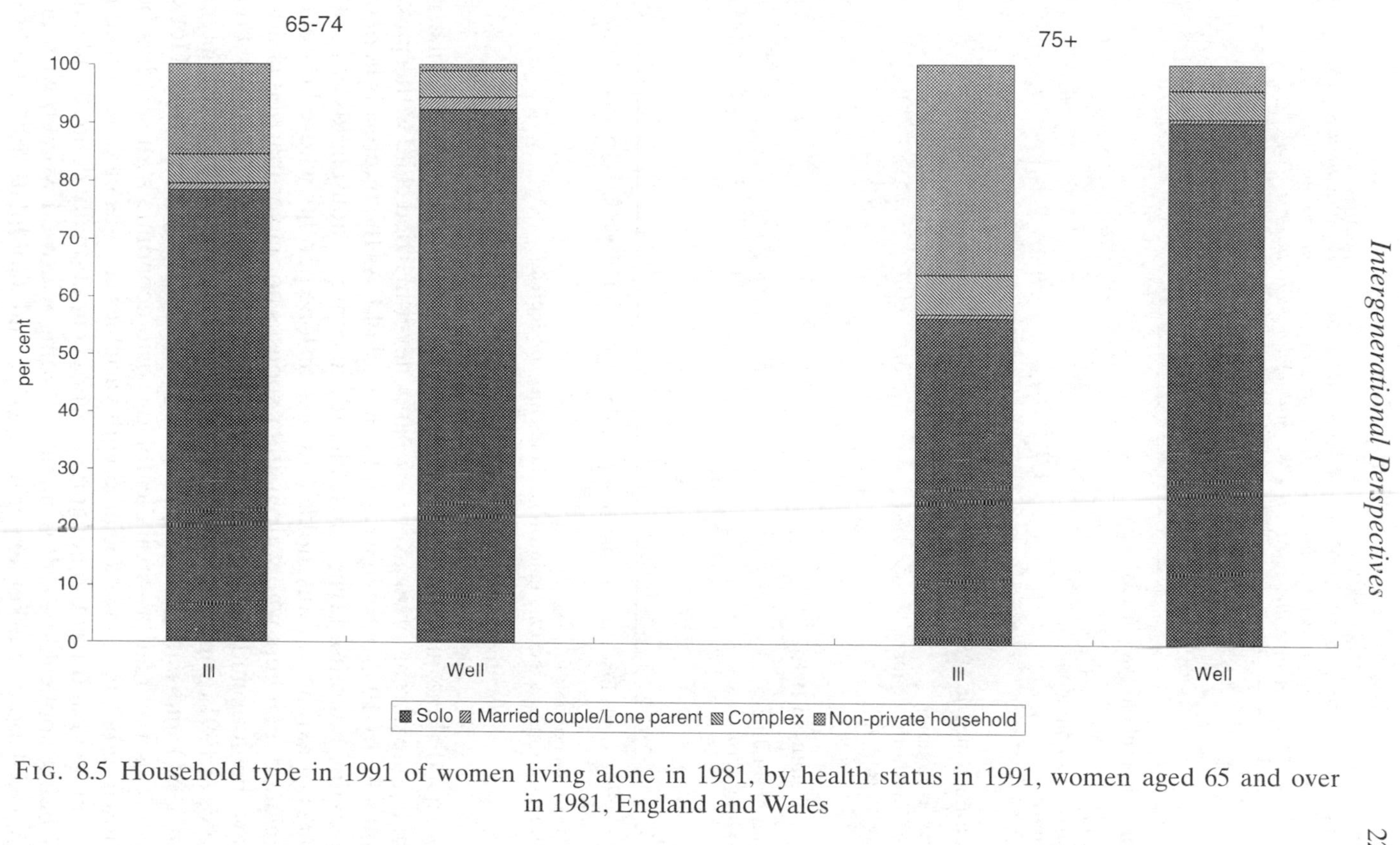

FIG. 8.5 Household type in 1991 of women living alone in 1981, by health status in 1991, women aged 65 and over in 1981, England and Wales

TABLE 8.7. *Women aged 65–69 in 1981 who were living alone, with a spouse, or in a family in 1981 but in a complex household in 1991, by family/household type, housing tenure, and parity in 1981, and health status in 1991 (%)*

	Number of children					
	0	1	2	3	4+	All
Family/household type in 1981						
Solitary	4	5	5	4	4	5
Married couple alone	2	4	3	5	4	3
Family[a]	17[b]	3	6	6	9	6
Housing tenure in 1981						
Owner occupier	4	4	4	4	5	4
Local authority tenant	3	3	4	5	6	4
Private renter	5	2	3	4	5	3
Health status in 1991						
Long-term illness	4	5	4	5	6	5
No long-term illness	4	3	4	4	5	4
All[c]	4	4	4	5	5	4

[a] Married couple/lone parent with never-married child(ren); never-married child living with parent(s).
[b] Denominator < 50.
[c] Total for those in the 1981 family/household types considered.

had lived alone, just with a spouse, or in a family (couple and never-married child, lone parent, or, in a very few cases, never-married child with a parent) and who by 1991 were in a complex household. As the interest is in people changing household type, those already in complex households or in other types of extended households (couples or lone parents whose households included members who were neither spouses nor never-married children) have been excluded. The table shows the proportions in complex households in 1991 by initial family/household type and parity; by housing tenure (in 1981) and parity; and by health status (in 1991) and parity. Housing tenure is included as an indicator of socio-economic status; it has been shown to be strongly associated with variables such as income and educational level and has the advantage over occupationally defined indicators of being applicable to all women, including widowed women with no or limited labour market experience (Fox and Goldblatt 1982; Goldblatt 1990; OPCS 1994). The table shows that those initially living with a spouse had the lowest, and those living in a family the highest, rate of transition to a complex household in all parity groups. Tenants of privately rented accommodation and those with no long-term illness appear to have slightly lower, and women with parities of three or more slightly higher, transition rates than other groups.

Family/household type, parity, health status, and housing tenure are all associated, so multifactorial analysis is needed to disentangle the relative contributions of each, and of any interactions. A series of models was therefore fitted to the data using a logit transformation of the proportion in complex households by 1991; the package GLIM was used for this analysis. The top panel of Table 8.8 shows the scaled deviance and associated degrees of freedom for models fitted, together with changes consequent on adding specified terms. It can be seen that the only variable associated with any significant change in the deviance was initial family/household type. The other variables had little effect, and adding them, or various interaction effects, to a model simply including the family/household term did nothing to improve the fit of the model. The parameter estimates and associated odds ratios for the model including only this term are shown in the second panel of the table; this demonstrates the higher 'risk' of transition for those living in a family and the lower 'risk' for those initially living with a spouse. However, it should be noted that the overall fit of this model is not very good and clearly there are other important factors which I have not been able to specify.

TABLE 8.8. *Results of regression models of the proportion of women aged 65–69 in 1981 who were in solitary, married-couple-only, and family households in 1981 but in complex households in 1991*

A Model

	Scaled deviance	df	Change (from null)	
			D	df
Null	129.6	89	—	—
Family/household type	108.3	87	−21.3	−2
Parity	126.6	85	−4.0	−4
Health status	126.5	88	−3.1	−1
Tenure	128.2	87	−1.4	−2

B Model including family/household type

	Parameter	S.E.	Odds ratios	95% confidence interval
Married couple alone	−0.3427	0.1301	0.71	0.55–0.92
Family	0.3799	0.1591	1.46	1.1–2.00

The failure to find any association between transitions to complex households and either parity, health status, or housing tenure is surprising given the large literature on the influence of these factors on household transitions. There are, of course, some problems with the covariates used; in particular, the measure of health is a very general one. The parity variable, too, is not a precise measure of children currently available, as it includes children who may have died and excludes non-marital births prior to 1971. However, given the low levels of child and young adult mortality in the relevant cohorts and the low levels of extra-marital childbearing prior to 1971 (and high rates of adoption), the effect of these errors would be slight. A further important limitation is that, as parity data are only available for those aged up to 79 in 1991, I have been unable to consider the oldest age groups, among whom residence rates in complex and multigenerational households are the highest; it may well be that relationships in the expected direction do exist in these elderly age groups but are not discernible among those still in their seventies.

DISCUSSION

Those in mid-and later life form a large and increasing proportion of the total population in Britain and other developed countries, and the household patterns of these groups have a number of important implications, as well as perhaps providing clues about broader issues of great importance, such as intergenerational relationships and exchanges. A number of issues complicate the study of such patterns, including the need to consider trends from the viewpoint of more than one generation. In comparison with earlier cohorts, those in their fifties and early sixties include far lower proportions of nulliparous (childless), and far higher proportions of multiparous, women—this has not, however, resulted in increased parent–child co-residence in these age groups because of the far earlier completion of childbearing in the relevant cohorts. These cohorts have also had higher levels of nuptiality than their predecessors, experienced or will experience widowhood later, and as yet include only small proportions of divorced people (Grundy 1996*b*). However, it is unclear whether the higher levels of kin resources among these cohorts will affect their living arrangements later in life, particularly in later old age, when requirements for support may be greatest, or whether the potential effect of having more children will be offset by changes in the extent of intergenerational support and contact.

As is clear from this chapter, the extent of intergenerational co-residence has declined markedly among those who are currently in later old age. For the 1980s, this seems partly to reflect a growing use of institutional care; by 1991, there were more very old people in institutions than in complex households, in marked contrast to the situation prevailing twenty years earlier. The aim of the 1990 Community Care Act, which came into force in 1993, was to reverse this trend by removing perverse incentives to enter nursing homes and other institutions which existed in the 1980s (Laing 1993). However, if the views of both older and younger people about the kind of care best provided by family and that best provided by formal services, including institutions, have changed, then a complete reversal may prove difficult. Analyses of differentials in transitions to complex households failed to find a relationship with parity, the health status indicator available (long-term illness), or the socio-economic indicator used (housing tenure). However, initial family/household type was associated with transitions to complex households. These rather surprising results may indicate that relationships between family size and living arrangements either do not exist at all in contemporary Britain or exist only in very old age groups.

Cohorts born since the mid-1950s have not replicated the high-nuptiality and high-fertility patterns of those born in the inter-war decades and will include higher proportions of never-married, divorced or remarried, and childless people (although levels of childlessness projected for cohorts born in the 1960s and 1970s are still lower than those for cohorts born at the start of the twentieth century and in some earlier periods). However, as mortality rates in later old age are declining, more of those in these age groups will have surviving parents. Already in the US, 37 per cent of 55–63-year-old women have a surviving parent, compared with only 23 per cent of women of the same age in Britain; further falls in mortality will tend to increase this proportion, although changes in the age distribution of parents at the birth of their children also need to be taken into account.

There are several implications of this. More children will have surviving grandparents potentially available to provide support. More women (and men) in late middle age and early old age will have both upward and downward generational ties and families of four and even five generations will become more usual. What is far less clear is how this vertical extension of the family will affect patterns of intergenerational exchange and, critically, how such patterns of exchange may alter for other reasons. Some have hypothesized that recent changes in demographic behaviour are the results of changing aspirations and orientations, including a shift towards more individualistic, and less family-oriented, values (van da Kaa 1987). The declines in intergenerational co-residence shown here are consistent with such an interpretation, which, if it is correct, implies a major increase in the demand for formal, rather than kin, provision of services for frail elderly people. However, changes in co-residence patterns represent only one part of the continuum of intergenerational exchange. It is possible that co-residence has declined because 'intimacy at a distance' has become more available due to higher incomes and better communication systems. However, it is also possible that decreased co-residence is an indicator of a more general decline in intergenerational support and exchange. If so, this would have far-reaching implications for the providers of formal services. What we now urgently need is more information on support exchanges between non-co-resident kin, in order to see which of these processes is the predominant one.

NOTES

1. As these data excluded births before marriage this estimate is slightly too high, but the extent of non-marital childbearing in the pre-World War II period was low (less than 5% of all births). Moreover, adoption was then a common response to non-marital childbearing.
2. This estimate may also be slightly too high because of the exclusion of women who immigrated to England and Wales after 1971.
3. TFR is a measure of how many children, on average, a woman would bear if she experienced current age-specific fertility rates throughout her reproductive life.

9

Older people in three urban areas: household composition, kinship, and social networks

Chris Phillipson, Miriam Bernard, Judith Phillips, and Jim Ogg

INTRODUCTION

The research reported here examines changes to the social and family networks of elderly people in three urban areas of England: Bethnal Green, Wolverhampton, and Woodford. The areas were the locations for major research studies in the 1940s and 1950s which provided rich material about the lives of elderly people (Sheldon 1948; Townsend 1957; Young and Willmott 1957; Willmott and Young 1960). These studies were carried out during a period when major concerns were being raised about the growing numbers of elderly people in the population. A variety of reports focused on the problems associated with population ageing, specifically its impact on economic growth, and expenditure in areas such as pensions and health (Royal Commission on Population 1949). Closely related to this was an increasing anxiety that the successful development of a welfare state might undermine the willingness of the community (and members of the family, in particular) to provide care and support to older people. Such views set a clear agenda for a number of research projects in the period after the Second World War.

The original studies examined the thesis that, in the context of a developing welfare state, families were increasingly leaving the old to fend for themselves. Their findings, however, suggested a different picture. Most of the studies demonstrated the continuing importance of kinship and family life in post-war Britain. Sheldon (1948), for example, describes Wolverhampton society as one in which the old are an essential part of family life. He questioned whether the phrase 'living alone' was in fact of any value in Wolverhampton, given the high degree of residential proximity of kin to elderly people. Townsend (1957) reports as well on a community that, despite the devastation suffered during the war, appeared to be remarkably successful in its provision of support to older people.

Alongside this, however, the studies also stressed the desire of older people to sustain an independent life: a desire which earlier generations of elders would have recognized (Laslett 1984), and which future generations have maintained. Similarly, it was the concern of Willmott's and Young's (1960) study of Woodford to explore the extent to which geographical and social mobility may have loosened ties between generations. In fact, what they referred to as the 'surprise' of their study was the degree of similarity in many important respects between middle-class Woodford and working-class Bethnal Green. In terms of regular contact and geographical proximity, they were led to the conclusion that 'The old people of the suburb are plainly as much as in touch with children, measured in this way, as those in the East End' (Willmott and Young 1960: 38). There were, though, some important differences between life in a working-class inner city community and that in a more affluent suburb. One was that, in the former, the generations lived side by side throughout life; in the latter, this tended to follow on from a bereavement. Increasing mobility, while not preventing links between the generations, did tend to loosen traditional obligations. Forty to fifty years on from these original investigations, the current study ('the Keele study') set out to explore how the lives of older people had changed in the intervening years.

Between them, the baseline studies represent three different types of urban setting: inner city (Bethnal Green), Metropolitan Borough (Wolverhampton), and suburban (Woodford). These locations also illustrate different pathways regarding urban development. In the case of Bethnal Green, redevelopment in the 1950s and 1960s amounted to a rebuilding of the community, with a scattering of at least some of the population to outlying suburbs and beyond (Porter 1991). In Wolverhampton, there was also substantial redevelopment and slum clearance, but with the population affected moving relatively small distances (at least in geographical terms) to newly built estates. For the suburbanites of Woodford, the process was one of consolidation rather than change, with a slowing down in the rate of development from the inter-war years.

These pathways offer different contexts within which to build relationships in old age, and suggested at least two questions worthy of further exploration. First, what is the experience of ageing in the context of urban change? Secondly, given these urban experiences as a backdrop, what is their impact on the social and family networks of older people? In relation to the first question, we are arguing that age is an important element in the social divisions running through city life (Pacione 1997). Beyond this, the study is contributing to the development of what may be termed an urban sociology and social geography of ageing. With respect to the second question, our study is concerned with examining how these differing urban environments influence the kind of networks which people construct and maintain during old age, and whether these structures vary in response to the social and economic relations within which they are located. In order to explore these issues, the study adopted a specific type of network methodology and a typology of kinship systems. The background to this will now be reviewed.

METHODOLOGICAL ISSUES

Trying to measure change over a forty- or fifty-year period clearly raises significant issues and problems. In our case, the studies concerned had used different approaches and questions, and had been shaped by different agendas as to the reasons why they had been carried out. Simply replicating the previous research was not, therefore, a viable option. Nor was it desirable, for at least two main reasons: first, social science methods have moved on and different approaches are now available for exploring the main research questions; secondly, repeating particular questions itself raises issues of comparability of response between different time periods.

The approach decided upon was to draw out some key findings from the baseline studies, and explore the extent to which these still seemed characteristic of the family and community lives of older people in the 1990s. In the 1940s and 1950s, research focused on people living within what Frankenburg (1966) was to term an 'environment of kin'. In the studies of the late 1950s and 1960s, however, there was a shift in the sociological debate regarding the networks surrounding older people. Rosser and Harris (1965), for example, in their study of Swansea, suggest a fragmentation in the bonds connecting older people to family members: a move from generations 'living together throughout life' to (sometimes) 'joining when parents grow old' (Willmott and Young 1960: 38).

This change has been interpreted in different ways in the research literature. On the one hand, despite recognition of changes to family relations, sociological and policy perspectives still view support for older people within the context of kinship; this is seen as reflecting the preferences of older people as well as more traditional solidarities. On the other hand, a more recent view suggests a move towards a more individualized family, with relationships 'based on individual "commitments" rather than "fixed obligations"' (Finch 1989, 1995: 61).

Our research provides one way of examining these two approaches. The assumption we make is that the original studies made an important statement about a particular form of solidarity or mutual aid: in particular, that which was built around kinship and locality. The question we want to pose is what kinds of solidarities have been maintained in the same communities fifty years on. To explore this question, we have utilized the concept of the social network in attempting to understand social relationships in the three localities.

The idea of the social network has had an extensive pedigree within the social sciences, with its development in social anthropology from the early 1950s (Barnes 1954; Frankenburg 1966; Mitchell 1969). Subsequently, Bott's (1957) research on the impact of network structure on marital relations was important in spreading the influence of this approach (Bulmer 1987; Crow and Allen 1994). The application of the network idea has been extensive, varying from locality-based studies (Fischer 1982; Wellman 1990) to research on the personal networks of parents and their children (Cochran *et al.* 1990) and studies of older adults (Wenger 1984, 1992, 1995; Antonucci and Akiyama 1987; Bowling *et al.* 1991; Lang and Carstensen 1994; Knipscheer *et al.* 1995).

The network approach provided a number of advantages for our research. First, network perspectives (in theory at least) make no assumption about the nature of the network in which people are involved. The extent to which this is dominated by kin, or by a variety of relationships, itself becomes the focus of investigation. Secondly, social network perspectives offer a practical and flexible method for exploring community life, and enable researchers to work with dynamic notions of what 'community' means to people (Crow and Allen 1994). Thirdly, the network approach can be used to examine issues related to personal change over time (Antonucci 1985; Kahn and Antonucci 1980), and within different settings. Finally, networks can be viewed as providing resources which may serve different functions at different points of the life course and, in terms of our concerns, may have an important part to play in supporting people in old age.

Measures of social networks have typically been focused around three types of research questions: first, the *exchange question*, exploring people who might have performed a service of some kind for the older person (McCallister and Fischer 1978; Wenger 1984); secondly, the *role relation question*, focusing on people who are related to the individual in some formalized or prescribed way (Cochran *et al.* 1990); and thirdly, the *subjective question*, about those who are nominated as 'close to' or on 'intimate terms' with the person concerned (Kahn and Antonucci 1980).

In terms of our interests, all of the above suggest significant issues for exploring family ties in old age. However, bearing in mind the thrust of the original studies which were the basis for our research, we took the *subjective* dimension as the key measure for investigating the characteristics of networks in each of the areas. Rather than consider a variety of supportive relationships, our study examines those whom the older person defines as having a central place in their life (what may be termed their 'affective' network). The approach taken was to ask older people to make their own assessment about, first, who was most important in their lives and, secondly, the role such people play in the provision of support. The method adopted makes no a priori assumptions about the nature of the network in which people are involved. Traditional bonds may be important; equally, other relationships may be significant—these serving different purposes for the individual. The technique used in the study, originally devised by Kahn and Antonucci (1980; see also Antonucci 1995), collects information about people who stand in different degrees of closeness to the individual. Data are collected by presenting the respondent with a diagram of three concentric circles, with the word 'you' written in the innermost circle. Respondents are asked to place in the innermost circle those persons who are 'so close and important' to them that they 'cannot imagine life without them'. Those considered less close but still important are listed in the middle and outer circles. Respondents are subsequently asked about a variety of support functions that network members provide or receive.

Evaluations of the technique suggest that it is especially useful for measuring long-term as opposed to short-term relationships (Sonderen 1990); that it maximizes the opportunity for people to participate in the network assessment (Antonucci 1995); and that it can generate rich network data (House and Kahn 1985: 100). Van Groenou and van Tilburg (1996) also note that it has proved to be a useful method of yielding similar types of networks in different samples. Typically, measures of affective networks suggest that they are relatively small in size (usually comprising between five and nine members), with a large proportion of these (up to 80 per cent) being (close) kin. In their US national sample of men and women over 50 years of age, Antonucci and Akiyama (1987) report an average of 8.9 network members. Size of network did not differ across age groups.

Sampling

The research reported here was carried out in two main phases. The first phase of the project consisted of a questionnaire survey of 627 older people in the three urban locations. This was based on the selection of a random sample of people of pensionable age, drawn from the age–sex registers of General Practitioners in the three areas following approval of the project by the respective District Research Ethics Committees. The size of the achieved samples in the original studies was 203 individuals in Bethnal Green, 210 in Woodford and Wanstead (older people only), and 477 in Wolverhampton. Thus, the Keele survey aimed for around 200 interviews in each area, achieving 195 in Bethnal Green, 227 in Wolverhampton, and 204 in Woodford. The questionnaire survey itself was designed to explore general issues of social and family change since the original studies, and the fieldwork was undertaken by Social and Community Planning Research (SCPR) in July and August 1995.

The second phase, conducted approximately one year later, comprised a series of semi-structured tape-recorded interviews with 62 people over the age of 75 who had indicated at the survey phase that they would be willing to participate further. The purpose of these interviews was to examine the issue of change from the standpoint of a possibly more vulnerable group of older people. The interviews were carried out by the Keele team during the second half of 1996; this chapter focuses on results from both these quantitative and qualitative phases.

In addition, we also conducted interviews with members of the 'younger' generation whom the older people nominated as being important in their networks. A total of 19 such interviews were achieved, together with a further 35 interviews with Punjabi and Bangladeshi elders in Wolverhampton and Bethnal Green, and two group interviews: one with a Bangladeshi carers' group in Bethnal Green and one with the Asian interpreters and social workers with whom we had worked in Wolverhampton.

CHANGING AREAS, CHANGING HOUSEHOLDS

In terms of setting the context for the findings reported here, it is important to note that each of our areas experienced population decline in the period between 1951 and 1981: in Wolverhampton and Woodford these were relatively small percentage decreases, compared with a decline of almost half in Bethnal Green. Damage to housing in inner city London before 1950, and subsequent demolition and clearance over the succeeding decades, obviously accounts for part of the differences between the study areas. However, Wolverhampton's population decline has been recent, compared with the other two areas. Indeed, Bethnal Green and Woodford have shown an upward trend from the 1980s onwards.

With regard to the older age groups, we can observe that, in 1951, Woodford was the 'oldest' of our three areas: 15 per cent of its population were of pensionable age, compared with 14 per cent in Bethnal Green and 12 per cent in Wolverhampton. In the intervening forty years, all three study areas experienced a marked ageing, so that they now (1991 Census) have figures of 20 per cent, 18 per cent, and 19 per cent respectively. This compares with a national figure for the UK of 18 per cent of the population over pensionable age, and shows that while Woodford is still our 'oldest' study area, Wolverhampton has in fact experienced the greatest percentage increase. Bethnal Green on the other hand, while ageing, has also experienced both increasing ethnic diversity and rising proportions of children in its population, in common with a number of other East London boroughs (Rix 1996).

These figures mask some specific changes. First, the pensionable population in each of these areas is itself ageing, with substantial increases in the population aged 85 and over. Secondly, there has been a growth of minority ethnic groups, notably Bangladeshis in Bethnal Green and Indians in Wolverhampton. In the case of Bethnal Green, 8 per cent of the pensionable population is now over the age of 85 (compared with only 3 per cent in 1951), while 38 per cent of the population is drawn from minority ethnic groups (Bangladeshis represent 54 per cent of the ethnic minority). In Wolverhampton, those over age 85 account for 8 per cent of pensioners (compared with 3 per cent in 1951), and 24 per cent of the population are from minority ethnic groups (of which 59 per cent are Indians). Woodford has 9 per cent of its pensionable population over age 85 and a much smaller minority ethnic population, at just 12 per cent of the total (with Indians being the majority group).

Some of these population changes are further reflected in alterations to people's living arrangements. Nationally, there has been a marked growth in the proportions of older people living alone or with a spouse/partner, together with a decline in 'complex' households, that is, those consisting of more than one generation (Glaser 1997). Table 9.1 illustrates these trends for our three areas and makes comparisons with the baseline studies in the case of Bethnal Green and Wolverhampton.

These figures confirm that the present-day households of older people are substantially different from the early post-war period. The contrast is between an old age spent with others and one where it is experienced alone or with one other person (usually a spouse). Middle-class Woodford, in fact, represents what may become the norm, with not far short of 50 per cent of pensioner households comprising spouse and partner only. Bethnal Green, with the influence of minority ethnic groups, still shows the importance of multi-generational households in inner city areas in particular: over a quarter of households (26 per cent) being of two generations or more (these drawn predominantly from the Bangladeshi families in our sample). The comparable figure in Townsend's study was 41 per cent, so the change here is considerable but not as great as might be imagined. In suburban Woodford, on the other hand, just 13 per cent of pensioner households are of two or more generations.

The existence of multi-generational households is best illustrated by the two main minority ethnic groups in our samples—Bangladeshis and Indians. The Bethnal Green sample included 23 respondents originating from Bangladesh, 21 of whom had a child or children living at home. Fifteen Bangladeshi households (65 per cent) contained five or more

TABLE 9.1. *Household type in three urban areas: women 60+, men 65+ (%)*

Number of generations	Relatives present	Bethnal Green		Wolverhampton		Woodford
		1954–5[a]	1995[b]	1945[c]	1995[b]	1995[b]
One	Lives alone	25	34	10	37	35
	Spouse/partner only	29	38	16	41	48
	Other relatives	4	2	8	1	2
	Other non-relatives	0	1	15	1	1
Two	Single/widowed/divorced/separated/child(ren)	24	14	29	12	10
	Married child(ren)	4	2	9	2	1
	Other relative(s)	3	2	0	0	0
Three	Single/widowed/divorced/separated/child(ren) + grandchild(ren)	2	1	0	1	0
	Married child + grandchild(ren)/grandchild(ren) only	8	5	13	5	1
	Other relatives	0	1	0	1	1
Four	Single/widowed/divorced/separated/child(ren) + grandchild(ren) + great-grandchild(ren)	0	1	0	0	0
N		203	195	477	228	204

[a] From Townsend (1957: 36).
[b] From Keele survey (1995).
[c] Derived from Sheldon (1948: table XXXVI).

people (a similar figure to that reported for all Bangladeshi households in the 1991 Census). Only 2 out of the 23 households were solo or spouse only, the rest including married as well as single children (9 of our respondents were living with married children and grandchildren or some combination of a three-generation household). The following are illustrative:

Mr Hussein is aged 70 and lives in a four-bedroom flat on the third floor of a council block in Bethnal Green. Mr Hussein came to Britain from Bangladesh in the late 1950s, living first in Birmingham and moving to London in the mid-1980s. There are ten people in the flat: Mr Hussein (who rents the flat), his wife, his mother-in-law, four sons, two daughters, and a grandchild. Mr Hussein also has a nephew living in the same block. He has three sisters and one brother also living in East London. The grandchild living with him was married in Bangladesh twelve months prior to the interview and she is waiting for her husband to join her from Bangladesh.

Mr Ali is aged 69 and lives with his wife and seven of his eight children (all of these still at school). He arrived in London from Bangladesh in 1957 and has been living in various parts of the East End of London since that time. The family lives in a ground floor flat with five bedrooms. Their other child (a daughter) lives in a flat above them with her family. Mr Ali's flat is a converted laundry which was once attached to the housing estate for the use of its residents. He has three brothers living in Leeds, Bradford, and Birmingham.

The combination of generations was also important amongst some of the Indian households:

Mrs Kaur is aged 60 and lives in a three-bedroom house in Wolverhampton with her husband, two of her sons, her daughter and son-in-law, and their four children. Her husband is diabetic and has a heart condition. During the day, Mrs Kaur looks after her grandchildren.

Mrs Koshla is aged 77 and lives in a very large house in Wolverhampton. She lives with her husband, a handicapped daughter aged 40, a son and daughter-in-law, and their two children. She also has other daughters living close by in Wolverhampton.

Some of the characteristics of the Bangladeshis reflect findings from the 1991 Census which showed this group to be in very poor living conditions, with a high degree of overcrowding. Eade *et al.* (1996) reported that nearly a fifth (19 per cent) of Bangladeshi households lived at the highest density given by the Census of over 1.5 persons per room, compared with less than half of one per cent of the total resident population and 8 per cent of Pakistani households. The situation of the Bangladeshis is reminiscent of the family groups described by Sheldon and by Willmott and Young in the 1940s and 1950s.

In addition, it is important to note that the general trend towards solo living or living in married pairs, as illustrated in Table 9.1, conceals some interesting variations. First, although only 27 of our households include a married child, 79 (13 per cent) contain a never-married child. Of these, 31 (16 per cent) are in Bethnal Green, 27 (12 per cent) in Wolverhampton, and 21 (10 per cent) in Woodford. Secondly, the households in the survey also reflect the needs of individuals for different kinds of economic and social resources. In this context, there were important differences between the areas. Overall, 47 households (7 per cent) contained at least one person in full-time education (mainly children under 16), with 28 of these in Bethnal Green (mainly but not exclusively in Bengali households). There were also 21 households with at least one person unemployed (excluding spouses or partners), 17 of these in Bethnal Green. Furthermore, Bethnal Green households were much less likely than those in other areas to contain someone in full- or part-time employment: of the 63 households (10 per cent) overall with an employed person, 30 were in Wolverhampton, and 20 in Woodford. Although the numbers here are relatively small, the circumstances of the households reflect some of the social changes over the period since the original studies.

Another important issue concerns the impact of widowhood on living arrangements. Here, there was a marked change from the baseline studies. With the exception of Asian households, fewer widowed respondents were living with adult children. Most were living alone (an average of 78 per cent across the three areas). In Bethnal Green and Wolverhampton, however, the proportions of households where widows and widowers live with others was greater than the national average (20 per cent in the 1991 British Household Panel Survey), again reflecting the higher proportion of Asian households in the two localities. In almost all cases where older widows and widowers were living with married children, the householder was the adult child and not the older parent (a development foreshadowed in the original Woodford study), reflecting the fact that it was the widowed parent who had joined the married child's household.

CHANGING NETWORKS, CHANGING RELATIONSHIPS?

While our overall findings confirm that children (as well as other relatives) tend now to maintain separate households, the issue next considered here concerns the interrelationship between these households and the social networks of our respondents. Working from what we took to be a central finding from all three of the baseline studies, namely, that the older people in these communities were surrounded by people with whom they had close and supportive relationships, we were interested in the extent to which this had changed in the intervening period of forty or more years.

As noted above, respondents were asked to make their own assessment about who was important in their lives; in the network measure adopted, they could name up to 20 people. The 627 people we surveyed generated a total of 5,737 network members. This yielded a mean network size of 9.3 (SD 5.4) per person, with Bethnal Green showing a slightly lower figure (8.3, $p < 0.001$) than Wolverhampton and Woodford. Although there was a slight decrease in network size with age, this was not found to be statistically significant and there were no statistically significant differences between the areas. Women reported larger networks than men (10.02 compared with 8.18, $p < 0.001$) despite the fact that very elderly women in particular are less likely to have a spouse to nominate in their networks. Again, this pattern held across all three areas.

Overall, the majority of the elderly respondents could identify a number of people whom they viewed as close and important in their lives: just 7 out of the 627 people interviewed could think of nobody they could describe in this way. Few older people, therefore, would appear to be isolated, in the sense of lacking close relationships—a finding which held for all three areas and which may be taken as representing at least some degree of continuity with the previous studies. On the other hand, a minority could be said to have small personal networks. Defined as five people or fewer, small personal networks were characteristic of 30 per cent of those interviewed, fluctuating between Woodford, with 24 per cent having small personal networks, and Bethnal Green and Wolverhampton (39 per cent and 38 per cent respectively). Among respondents with very small networks, men appear more frequently than women: for example, 5 per cent of men have networks of just one person or less, compared with 2 per cent of women, and these men are to be found in all three localities.

To illustrate some general features of our respondents' networks, Table 9.2 divides the relationships identified according to four categories: immediate family; other relatives; non-kin; and care-related. Leaving aside partners or spouses, it is clear that friends and children are the dominant groups. Other relatives and neighbours appear as much less important on the type of measure we have used. Overall, the personal networks of older people are dominated by kin, who form nearly three-quarters (73 per cent) of the total. Twenty per cent of network members are children, but with relatively small numbers in each network: the average number of children per network was 1.9 overall, with 2.1 in the case of Wolverhampton, and 1.8 in Bethnal Green and Woodford.

The numerical importance of kin—and children especially—is matched by the way in which they also provide the emotional core within the network (comprising the bulk of those listed in the inner circle). Qualitative interviews with the age 75-plus group may be used to illustrate the point. Mr Green is aged 75 and lives with his wife in Bethnal Green. They have one son, who now lives in an adjoining borough. Mr Green expresses as follows the way in which he feels secure in the support provided by his immediate family:

> Oh, I think that family life is 100 per cent important. In every way because I mean for myself now this, I have only got one son right, there is peace of mind, I am under the weather, the wife had a very bad spell and so family life then was, it showed family life, you know what I mean, it showed family life, everybody was prepared to, I mean at the drop of a hat they would be there, anything on the phone, I mean my son has got a car . . . and we have got their home phone

TABLE 9.2. *Networks of older people: social and family characteristics*

Domain and type	N	Domain and type	N
Immediate family		Non-kin	
Partner or spouse	316	Friends	1,323
Ex-wife/husband/partner	3	Neighbours	119
Father/mother	18	Work-related	6
Son/daughter	1,134	Leisure-related	2
Brother/sister	576		
Grandson/granddaughter	787		
Son/daughter-in-law	349		
Son's/daughter's partner	5		
Stepson/step daughter-in-law	28		
Foster daughter	1		
Other relatives		Care-related	
Niece/nephew	315	Home help	5
Brother/sister-in-law	310	Carer	10
Cousin	110	GP	17
Uncle/aunt	32	Dentist	1
Great-grandson/daughter	39	Priest/vicar	23
Great-niece/great-nephew	35	Wife of priest/vicar	3
Niece's husband/wife	25	Warden	3
Father/mother-in-laws	12	Church visitor	2
(Including Stepfather/mother-in-laws)		Hairdresser	2
Cousin's husband/wife	13	Nuns/sisters from hospice	6
Other	56		

Notes: N = 5,735; number of networks = 627.

numbers, posted up down there and that to us is . . . it doesn't matter what time of the day or night, if there is a problem, pick the phone up. I mean they have got, my son has got us the pre-programmed phone, they programmed them in so that the wife doesn't even have to dial, you know we have got the individual buttons so that all you do is press the button. To that extent they have even put an extension in here for us . . . so you know family life is very, very important.

Mr Barker is 76 and also lives with his wife in Bethnal Green. They had five children and two of their daughters still live in the area. Mr Barker suffers from chronic depression and gets support for this mostly from within his family. They live in the large flat (bought for them by one of their sons) where they brought up their family. The lounge is filled with photographs of children and grandchildren as well as various weddings. Although they still have children close by (with whom they are in close contact) both Mr Barker and his wife expressed a sense of 'grief' at the physical separation from their children:

Mr Barker: This place was alive [when the children were here] . . . I mean you go into the bedrooms and they are so empty.

Mrs Barker: Oh they are so empty when they go, it is dreadful. After having rooms full of children and their friends, suddenly it all goes and you think what was it all for, the worrying and the fussing and the cooking and the washing and the cleaning, what was it all for because now they have all gone.

Mr Barker: You don't realize it when you do it. When you leave your parents it doesn't even enter your head, it is only when your children leave you that we think of these things, how your mum and dad might have felt when you left, you know . . . And yet they only moved, Anne only moved just down the road and yet the house is empty.

As a contrast to this, the importance of maintaining a sense of independence was also expressed by many of our respondents, but was often given particular emphasis amongst some of the middle-class elderly people in Woodford. Mrs Lennon is 81 and has lived alone since being widowed in 1983. She has two children, who live some distance from her but who are in regular contact on the telephone. Her son recently moved further away and visits infrequently but she sees her daughter on a regular basis:

I see my daughter once a fortnight, because as she comes home from Stratford where her firm is, she calls and has dinner with me once a fortnight. Or she takes me to a garden centre if I want plants for the front. I don't expect to see them too often, they have got their own lives to lead, haven't they? But I do see her once a fortnight.

Mrs Chater is 78 and lives with her husband. They have two daughters, neither of whom are living in the area. The youngest daughter usually comes to visit every Saturday and Mrs Chater describes her relationships with her children as 'very close'. She is clear, however, on the boundaries which surround these relationships:

we don't live in each other's pockets but we are always available if there's something needed, that sort of . . . we're very independent people really . . . I help my younger daughter out with cooking sometimes . . . obviously she's working full-time and she spares time to come here; she's very limited really with her time. My other daughter is also Captain of the Girl's Brigade Company as well, and very interested in the Baptist Church now and so her time is taken up very much.

The overall significance of kin varies, however, according to whether children are cited in the network. For those respondents who did not place any children in their networks (N = 137), the largest substitution was from the category of friends: friends represented 39 per cent of the networks of respondents with no children compared with 20 per cent of the networks of those with children. These differences were consistent across the areas, although the importance of friends for childless respondents was most notable in Woodford, where almost half (49 per cent) of the personal networks of such respondents consisted of friends. Indeed, our findings suggest that this cohort has maintained active links, often with friends in the immediate area. These ties are important in sustaining leisure and social activities in retirement, although in many cases (again as the Willmott and Young 1960 study suggests), this represents a continuation of a pattern established much earlier in life. Excerpts from our qualitative interviews may again be used as illustration.

Mrs Hope has lived in Woodford for over forty years and was widowed twelve months prior to the interview. She and her husband had no children but she maintains close links with her sister and with a friend in Woodford:

> Well, emotional support, I suppose mainly from my sister. People will say 'How are you?', and I will say, 'Oh, I am all right', which of course you have got to say, haven't you. I have got a very good friend who lives in Woodford, she lost, as I say she is one of those that lost her husband last May and although she has got three daughters who live locally, well at least one does, she is one of these people who will do anything for you if you wanted it, if you were to ring up and say, 'Oh I am in a terrible state', then she would come. She is reliable. I see her every Tuesday because we all go to the WI handicraft class and we ring one another up. I went one morning last week to have coffee together. It is not a long walk but it's just over the railway bridge not far, so I know a lot of people in that respect, but apart from herself she is the only person who I can think of who lives near here. So many of them . . . don't live anywhere near, they live the other side of the [railway] line or somewhere like that. Well one lives, well there is another one who lives near but we mainly communicate by telephone.

Mrs Craig is 80 and lives with her husband. She has two children. Friends also feature prominently in her network. She has been a member of the Red Cross for over thirty years, with a lot of her friends coming from this organization. She describes how she met one of her closest friends as follows:

> Well, years ago I knew her daughters, her daughters were my cadets when I was in the Red Cross, that's how I got to know her really and then when her children grew up I met her up at a Flower Display at Korkey Hall and she told me about the flower club and she said, 'Well come along next month, you know, and you might like it.' We didn't know each other at all then, and then I used to go to the flower club and then it got to the stage when I used to give her a lift home. She lives in Wanstead, and eventually we got quite close. I mean we very often, I go there every Tuesday. I very often get shopping for her on a Tuesday morning, take it in because she's a widow and she doesn't drive or anything so she's glad to have the bulkiest ones taken in sort of thing but, er—I mean knowing her has changed my life. Something, we go to the flower club, and through the flower club I made quite a lot of friends, you know, sort of casual friends more . . . not close.

CLOSE, BUT NOT NECESSARILY CLOSE BY?

Our findings also suggest that people defined as close or important may not necessarily be living in the immediate community. The baseline studies had demonstrated that children and other relations were both supportive and living either in the same locality or close by (part of what Frankenburg 1966 termed an 'environment of kin'). To what extent, we wondered, was this still the case today? Our information comes from data collected about the first five people whom respondents listed in their network. The majority of these are recorded in the inner circle, which means that, in terms of our model, they are the most important providers and recipients of support: those people to whom the focal person feels very close (Antonucci and Akiyama 1987). Table 9.3 illustrates the proximity of the nearest person in this group (excluding those living in the household). The majority of respondents have their nearest network member living within four miles. This is particularly the case in Wolverhampton, where 80 per cent of network members live within four miles. In contrast, one-fifth of Woodford respondents and nearly one-quarter (24 per cent) of Bethnal Green respondents have their nearest network member living at a distance of ten or more miles.

Table 9.4 looks at proximity in a different way by taking the nearest child in the first five listed people (including children living within the household). This table also provides findings from studies from the early 1950s onwards where the data are similar, if not strictly comparable, to our own. The Bethnal Green and Swansea studies in the 1950s reported high numbers of older people with their nearest child either in the same household or in the same district (85 per cent for Bethnal Green and 68 per cent for Swansea). Abrams' (1978) Four Towns study in the mid-1970s confirmed the extent to which children had moved out of the household, but showed a substantial number still having close access to their children. The Keele survey figures confirm that, for older people who cite a child in their network, the majority of these live either within the household or within four miles (the consolidated figure for the three areas is 65 per cent).

TABLE 9.3. *Proximity of nearest network member (%)*

Distance	Wolverhampton	Bethnal Green	Woodford
4 miles or less	80	67	67
5–9 miles	10	10	13
10 miles or above	10	24	20

TABLE 9.4. *Proximity to elderly parent(s) of nearest child, England, 1954–1995 (%)*

Location	Date	Same household	Same parish	Elsewhere	N
Bethnal Green	1954–5	52	33[a]	15	167
Swansea	1960	50	18[a]	32	327
Britain	1962	42	24	34	1,911
Four Towns	1977	14	35[b]	51	1,646
Bethnal Green[c]	1995	31	33[a]	36	144
Wolverhampton[c]	1995	21	50[a]	29	191
Woodford[c]	1995	16	44[a]	40	156

[a] Under 4 miles.
[b] Under 5 miles.
[c] Children placed in the network.
Sources: Wall (1992); Keele survey (1995).

Despite the existence of children in the immediate locality, they were certainly more generally dispersed than in the 1950s, as Table 9.4 suggests. Our three areas varied both in the extent to which networks were geographically stretched and the impact of this on the lives of older people. In Wolverhampton, the chance of having at least one child remaining in the locality was relatively high and was confirmed in the qualitative phase of the research: of the 17 people aged 75 and over who had married and had children, the majority (13) still had at least one child living within the town. For those in Bethnal Green, however, the dispersal of children was more noticeable. Of the 18 people aged 75 and over who had married and had children, only five had at least one child still living in Bethnal Green itself, with many in the group speaking of the difficulties of managing and contacting a more scattered family group. In Woodford, too, children had often tended to move away although our older respondents were themselves more mobile (65 per cent owned or had use of a car) and therefore were generally better placed to cope with changes to their personal networks.

This illustrates some of the ways in which social networks vary in their capacity to handle what Fischer (1982) refers to as the freight of distance. For some groups, notably our predominantly working-class older people in Bethnal Green, managing the distance between close kin can pose great problems especially when one is reliant on public transport (fewer than one in five respondents in Bethnal Green owned or had use of a car). However, while illustrating changes from the baseline studies in respect of proximity and geographical mobility, our findings also confirm the extensive levels of contact with key network members. Excluding those living within or sharing the household with the older person, 70 per cent of respondents had been in touch within the previous 24 hours (by telephone or face to face) with somebody who was close to or intimate with them (72 per cent in the case of Wolverhampton, 71 per cent in Woodford, and 65 per cent in Bethnal Green).

DISCUSSION AND CONCLUSION

What does this review of our findings tell us about the family and social networks of older people in the three areas in the 1990s, in contrast with the 1940s and 1950s? Broadly speaking there are, first of all, important continuities. Kinship remains, not surprisingly, central in terms of the social ties of our respondents. When asked to name who is important to them, most older people identify kin as being the main group with whom reciprocal relations are maintained, and the bonds of kinship therefore remain of major consequence in urban areas.

On the other hand, there are notable differences between the earlier period and the Keele study. One way of illustrating this point is by examining the three areas using Willmott's (1986) classification of kinship systems into four types: the local extended family; the dispersed extended family; the dispersed kinship network; and the residual kinship network. Of the three areas today, it is Wolverhampton which perhaps best approximates to the local extended family. Here, older people are likely to have access to relatives living close by, though rarely in the same street or immediate district as in Sheldon's time. Strong local networks seem to characterize predominantly working-class towns such as Wolverhampton, which have experienced rather less external migration in the post-war period than is the case with inner city areas.

In Bethnal Green, it is difficult to identify a particular family type which could be said to be dominant. Dense, locally based networks are still flourishing—at least among the Bangladeshi families we interviewed. In many cases they live in considerable deprivation and in housing conditions which would have been recognizable to Ruth Glass in the late 1940s (Glass and Frenkel 1948) and to the researchers from the Institute of Community Studies in the 1950s. Dispersed extended families were a feature of the lives of our white elderly respondents, with a typical situation perhaps that of having at least one child close by (perhaps in an adjoining borough), but with others scattered around Essex and beyond. On the other hand, there were also examples of the dispersed kinship network, with visits from kin who often came from considerable distances. Finally, there were certainly one or two examples of people with a residual or non-existent family network: individuals living in circumstances of immense social isolation.

Woodford, meanwhile, represents examples of the dispersed extended family, where regular contact (weekly or more often) is maintained, crucially through the motor car and the telephone. The latter in fact was one of the biggest changes which we might suggest from our study: telephone ownership is now virtually universal (although it should be noted that 13 per cent of respondents in Bethnal Green did not have access to a telephone compared with 9 per cent in Wolverhampton and 3 per cent in Woodford). The telephone was a symbol of the contact which could be maintained with children and siblings often dispersed at considerable distances (overall one in three of our respondents had last been in touch with someone in their network via the telephone).

In terms of personal networks, our findings also suggest that those who are significant to older people are either their own age (partners, friends, and siblings especially) or the next generation down (mainly children). Fewer than one in five of those we interviewed placed themselves within a network which stretched beyond two generations. In this context, we would suggest that relationships in old age are perhaps more focused than in the past, with children and friends the centre of attention. Today, the extended family group appears to be rather less significant in terms of its impact on daily life. Of course, relationships extend beyond those with children (many of whom may be elderly themselves): siblings, grandchildren, and great-grandchildren are also present within the family system. But our research brings out the point that in terms of close and supportive relations, most people draw upon a small and rather selective group.

Finally, the findings reported here raise a number of issues about the nature of older people's social networks. First, our results are consistent with those of Kahn and Antonucci (1987) in showing that in terms of significant relationships, network size does not appear to decrease with age. This suggests that in old age and late old age, emotional ties are maintained and may indeed become increasingly central as other relationships fall away (cf. Lang and Carstensen 1994). Secondly, as the work of Pearlin (1985) and others suggests, networks may vary in terms of the resources which they provide for their members. An important finding from our work suggests that inequalities within localities may interact with differences between personal networks and produce new forms of social stratification in old age. While our results confirm that older people are surrounded by a 'convoy' of intimate relationships, these may vary not just in terms of their number and proximity, but also as regards ease of access for the exchange of support and assistance. Thirdly, our work confirms the important role of friends in the social networks of older people. They appear especially important for older people without children, but they may also play a more general role in substituting for family in situations where other relatives are unavailable. Neighbours, on the other hand, appear much less prominently in the personal networks of older people, although this may be a by-product of the kind of instrument used in this research.

In conclusion, this chapter has reported on selected findings from the Keele study and has focused on describing the characteristics, first, of the pensioner households in three localities studied in depth in the 1940s and 1950s, and, secondly, the family-based networks within which these households are located. Our research complements other network studies which have focused mainly on national or regional samples, and highlights changes as well as continuities in the experiences of older people. Overall, our findings confirm the continued importance of the family (and particularly the immediate family) in the lives of older people. It is, however, a different type of family than that which was characteristic of the 1950s. Indeed, an important observation from our research is that it is much less easy now to talk about *the* family life of older people. There are many more types of elderly people than was the case in the 1950s, and more types of family (not least because we are living in a multi-cultural society). But the family in some form is central as regards the social relationships of older people, even if it is focused around a relatively small number of network members. In general, the diversity and variety in the family and community lives of older people is an important theme of our study.

10

The impact of family change on older people: the case of stepfamilies

Joanna Bornat, Brian Dimmock, David Jones, and Sheila Peace

And it was just that I wanted to drop me stepmum a line to say, you know, if she's ever down, or she wants to come back for a visit or—I believe in keeping the door open . . . my stepmother would be about 61, 62—mind you, she dresses very young—and the gentleman friend she's gone off with is only 35. And good luck to her. If it makes her happy . . . But, I'd like to leave it that, if things don't work out . . . that she could come back to Luton, and she'd be welcome. My little girl thinks of her as a Nan. And she's never done her any harm . . . My husband's quite agreeable. I can write to her, and if she comes to visit me, that's all right. Doesn't get on so well with my Mum.[1]

You can replace a husband but you can't replace a child.[2]

INTRODUCTION

Centre stage in debates about family and society in Britain today is taken by two concerns: the ageing of the population and the rate of family change through divorce and separation. By the mid-1990s, the proportion of the population over the age of 65 had reached 15 per cent, while four in every ten marriages in England and Wales were expected to end in divorce (Haskey 1996*b*; OPCS 1996*a*; ONS 1996). The quotations above come from a study carried out in Luton during 1995–6 which investigated the impact of family change on older people. They represent some of the hopes and fears which surface in debates about the future of family life at the end of the twentieth century.

An ageing population, together with evidence of high rates of divorce, separation, and cohabitation, suggests that the nature of intergenerational relationships within families might be changing. There are two alternative views implicit in the quotations with which we began: first, the scenario of post-modern optimism, with a shift away from the restrictive confines of normative roles and a move towards more equitable family relationships; and secondly, the nightmare scenario which foretells moral decline and social fragmentation, where the most vulnerable in society, older people especially, come off worst in an individualistic struggle for survival (Giddens 1991: 176–7). To assess these alternatives, we identified three key issues: the nature of intergenerational ties, the care of frail older people, and inheritance. This agenda was largely set by concern that the nightmare scenario could leave large numbers of older people without contact with grandchildren or family carers, and that transfers of resources between family members may change or reflect new loyalties following family reconstitution. In carrying out the research, we chose a method, the in-depth life history interview, which allowed people to use their own language in describing changes which they had experienced. This meant not only identifying meanings attributed to family over people's lifetimes, but also that we were not bound at the outset by any one definition of 'stepfamily'.

In this chapter, we consider these issues in the context of a range of relevant literatures, outline the research methods adopted, and go on to describe the data which ensued, ending with a discussion of the findings.

BACKGROUND LITERATURES

The literatures which concerned us tend to be problem-focused: for example, who will care for older people, the changing quality of intergenerational relationships, and definitions of 'stepfamily' in ongoing research. Despite the fact that over 40 per cent of carers of older people are themselves over age 65 (Allen and Perkins 1995: 24) debates about 'who will care' tend to be focused on the changing roles and expectations of younger family members (Finch and Groves 1983; Ungerson 1987; Qureshi and Walker 1989; Dalley 1996). This is now a substantial literature but with a tendency to reflect less on gendered aspects of the care 'burden' and more on the reciprocities of care relationships within family networks (Finch and Mason 1993; Cotterill 1994; McGlone and Cronin 1994; Allen and Perkins 1995; Jerrome 1996*b*; Twigg 1998). As Jerrome (1996*a*) has pointed out, such studies take a narrow view of older people's family roles, emphasizing the care relationship at the expense of other relationships which may be just as significant, for example, continuing parental roles in old age.

Studies of the reciprocal roles of older people within family and intergenerational relationships have been far less frequent in Britain than in North America (see, for example, Hagestad 1991; Bengtson and

Achenbaum 1993; Bengston *et al.* 1995; Soldo 1996). In North America, interest in grandparenting has been sustained through a developing interest in changing roles and responsibilities for grandparents during phases of family change (Brubaker 1985; Cherlin and Furstenberg 1986; Johnson 1988; Connidis 1989). At the time we embarked on our research, a similar literature was not evident in the UK, where studies of grandparenting tend to focus more on emotional, affective, and legal ties with youngest family members (see, for example, Douglas and Lowe 1990; Thompson *et al.* 1990; Bamford 1994). The result is that the grandparental role at times of family break-up and reconstitution is seen largely in terms of servicing other family members during periods of high dependency for young and teenage children. Beyond caring reciprocities, there are also the roles which grandparents are seen to play in providing material support, even surrogate parenting, at times of crisis (Finch 1989*a*; Finch and Mason 1993; Finch and Wallis 1994; Dench 1996*a*; Gorrell Barnes *et al.* 1998). Our interest lay in discovering continuing roles for older people beyond caring and grandparenting, in particular their position as parents with a longer time perspective from which to view intergenerational relations. This does not appear to have been included in existing investigations into the lives of older family members.

British literature on stepfamilies also demonstrates a bias in its focus away from the perspectives of older family members. This literature has expanded considerably in the last twenty years (Burgoyne and Clark 1984; Ferri 1984; Gorrell Barnes 1992; Robinson and Smith 1993; Batchelor *et al.* 1994) and has been far more influenced by American research (Pasley and Ihinger-Tallmann 1987; Papernow 1993; Visher and Visher 1996) than by European (Meulders-Klein and Thery 1993; Dumon 1992). Although some British research has a broad sociological focus (Burgoyne and Clark 1984) the research agenda has focused on three main areas: (1) the 'problems' of stepfamilies (McGoldrick and Carter 1989; Kiernan 1992; Batchelor *et al.* 1994) and the 'spoiled identities' arising from step-relationships, particularly the myth of the 'wicked stepmother' (Burchardt 1990; D. Smith 1990; Gorrell Barnes *et al.* 1998), with a dominant concern arising from clinical studies, particularly with respect to children (Ferri 1984; Furstenberg 1987; Amato 1994; Collins 1995); (2) attempts to understand stepfamilies by exploring how they differ from the 'normal' family, using terms such as 'reconstituted', 'reformed', and 'blended' (Robinson 1980); and (3) the counting of stepfamilies (Haskey 1994*b*).

A fourth literature, significant for our study, is that which relates to family resources. We were interested to see to what extent family change might affect attitudes towards the disposal of family assets. Given changes in relation to the funding of care late in life, questions of family money are now increasingly significant within families. Rising levels of owner-occupation, particularly among those over 65 years of age, in conjunction with rapid house price inflation during the 1970s and 1980s, has led to a huge interest in housing wealth and housing inheritance (Hamnett 1995). Controversy has surrounded the debate about the effect that home ownership—and its potential for wealth accumulation and transfer through gifting and bequeathing—has upon patterns of social inequality and the ability of families to reproduce themselves and to maintain or enhance their social position (Saunders 1990; Hamnett *et al.* 1991). While it is true that 'probably for the first time "modest income earners" have had an asset to hand on the next generation on death' (Thorns 1994: 473), it is also likely that housing wealth transfers will result in 'deeper wealth divisions in the longer term between those who own houses and those who do not' (Munro 1987: 435).

The impact of family change on such transfers and on the dynamics of will-making practices is not yet well understood. Finch and Wallis (1994) suggest that bequests follow a pattern of transfer from parents to children rather than to grandchildren, and that 'care bargains' tend not to influence preferences for 'fairness', and 'equity' among children. More recent research suggests that blood-ties remain the strongest determinant of who will inherit and that step-relatives receive a tiny proportion of bequests (Finch *et al.* 1996; Burgoyne and Morrison 1997). We were interested in probing further through interviews to see what meanings and practices are attached to inheritance in families where there has been divorce and other kinds of change.

A continuing problem for anyone interested in researching the area of family change is definition of terms. Research has been shaped by different definitions of 'stepfamily', which makes comparisons of outcomes extremely hazardous (Batchelor *et al.* 1994). For example, the Office for National Statistics defines a stepfamily as a married or cohabiting couple with dependent children living in their family, one or more of whom are not the biological children of both the man and the woman (Haskey 1994*b*). This definition fails, however, to encompass the household of the absent biological parent, who may also be cohabiting or married, creating another stepfamily household. It would also include those families where children are the result of fertility treatment which involves the use of donated sperm or eggs, while excluding families with same-sex couples.

A broader definition of a stepfamily is that it is created when a parent takes a new partner, whether through cohabitation or divorce. Some work has been done which supports the need for such a wider definition, as many people define themselves as living in a stepfamily even if their dependent children are not resident (Batchelor *et al.* 1994). The term can encompass families where a non-biological parent (usually the man) has been a parent figure for the child since it was a baby, right through to the large number of brief cohabitations which last less than a year (Ermisch and Francesconi 1996). There is, however, little evidence that the term is widely used in society, and plenty of evidence that considerable stigma remains attached to the 'step-' prefix with respect to any relationship (Ribbens *et al.* 1996). The term disguises enormous diversity (Furstenberg 1987; Batchelor *et al.* 1994) and little is known about the extent to which it has a common meaning across cultures and ethnic groups (Crosbie-Burnett and Lewis 1993; Hylton 1995). Indeed, in summing up their recent research, Gorrell Barnes *et al.* (1998: 271) argue that they 'would see any attempt to describe stepfamilies as if they were one single discrete and definable family form as highly misleading and limiting'. Our study, which overlapped in time with that of Gorrell Barnes *et al.*, took this conclusion as a starting point. For all the reasons just cited, we sought to explore the meanings which people give to 'family change' rather than to begin with the term 'stepfamily'.

RESEARCH METHODS

Although we were keen to interview people who had experienced some form of family change, we tried not to attract people who might have strongly formed points of view or organizational involvement in family 'politics' (Batchelor *et al.* 1994: 10). This was partly because we were aware that the language of family change is as yet unfixed; it also seemed appropriate given that throughout the period of our research 'family breakdown' was constantly in the news as a chosen focus for media attention, judgement, and concern. We decided, therefore, against advertising for volunteers. Instead, we constructed a sample for interviews from a screening questionnaire delivered on an area basis. The sample was to be purposeful (non-probabilistic) while at the same time without systematic bias on the one hand or eclecticism on the other (see Bornat *et al.* 1996 for a more detailed description of the research methodology adopted).

Our aim was to obtain data which enabled us to hear how people talk and make sense of family change. The use of a life history perspective enabled the people interviewed to reflect on their own lives over time and it became clear, as the interviews accumulated, that for many this was a first opportunity to make sense of past experience (Portelli 1981; Denzin 1986; Rosenthal 1993). People were searching for the right words and language to explain family change and decisions related to partnering. The results are narratives which include moral, as much as social and political, explanations for behaviour and which enable us to see how action recorded in larger data sets is explained and justified at an interpersonal level. Qualitative data of this type may also, as Dench (1996: 2, n. 6) suggests, challenge researcher bias by revealing unexpected, even unappealing, beliefs and preferences.

The town chosen for our study, Luton—an average-sized town in the south-east of England with a population of 171,671 at the 1991 Census—has witnessed economic change within both long- and newly established industries (motor, millinery, light engineering, chemicals). It is also a town which has experienced population growth through migration, both from within the British Isles and from the Indian subcontinent and the Caribbean.

The sample was obtained through a three-stage process. Screening questionnaires inviting people to identify themselves as having experienced some form of family change—defined in terms of divorce, separation, or widowhood—were distributed in three socially contrasting electoral wards in Luton. Responses were followed up and, together with contacts resulting from a parallel activity involving talking and listening to community groups of older people, a total of 60 interviews were arranged. A number of these included couples, yielding a final total of 72 people, 28 men and 44 women.

Because we were interested in gaining the views of people from different generations, our interviewees include people ranging in age from their early twenties to their late eighties: 8 *younger* respondents, that is people under 30 years of age with and without dependent children or living parents and grandparents; 33 *middle-aged* people between 30 and 59 years of age with and without dependent children and dependent parents; and 31 *older* people over 60 years of age with children and grandchildren but no living parents. In terms of experience of family change these 72 people fall into four groups:

- Twenty-four who had lived in a step-household (9 as a child, 7 as the partner of a step-parent, 8 as a step-parent).
- Twenty-one who had experienced the formation of a step-household within their kin group.
- Eighteen who had experienced the formation of step-relationships (but not step-households) within their kin group.
- Nine who had experience of separation but not repartnering within their kin group.

The life history interviews were relatively unstructured, although the interviewers probed areas concerning the project topics: intergenerational relationships, caring arrangements, and transfers of family resources. All the interviews were transcribed and analysed using a grounded theory approach (Glaser and Strauss 1967; Gilgun 1992) which identified underlying themes within the data as well as a focus which emphasized consideration of the language used in relation to family change.[3]

FINDINGS

In presenting our results, we focus first on the ways in which our respondents use the term 'step-' in their discussions of family life.

The language of step-relationships

The many different definitions of the term 'stepfamily' currently in use (Batchelor *et al.* 1994; Haskey 1994*b*; Dimmock 1997/8), including those provided by dictionaries, are significant in two ways: first, because, as we have seen, they vary; second, because the effort which has gone into these definitions seems, so far, to have had little impact on Luton residents. Only one respondent used the word 'stepfamily'. Even the use of the 'step-' prefix is infrequent and then only reluctant. Gerald Marsh,[4] now in his late seventies, married a war widow with a daughter; later they had a son together. He explains: 'I'm a great-grandfather step! But I don't—the word "step" doesn't come into my vocabulary now, so that's how far removed I am from it. I take it as a natural course, they're my children, and grandchildren, and great-grandchildren. I take it as a natural course of events.'

Many of our respondents talked about step-relationships without reference to the term 'step-' at all, although from the quote above it seems that some people may need a term without liking it, even with respect to grandparenting. The incidence of such spoken dilemmas illustrates the great difficulties facing many of the people we interviewed. The lack of a well-understood and stigma-free language to describe post-divorce or separated, or simply successive, family lives creates many difficulties when giving an account of events. What is clear is that neither the word 'stepfamily', nor the use of the 'step-' prefix, is being embraced by our respondents. Moreover, no clear difference emerged between generations in our sample, and little evidence that younger respondents find it any easier than older ones to use these words. Sian Rakulla has had two arranged marriages, the first ending in divorce. She and her second husband each brought children to the new marriage:

> But we do not like to use the word 'step-parent' in our culture. We want to see the family together bonding. Although this 'step-' was being used in the beginning, but I'm afraid that was terribly upsetting for myself, and for my son, who hadn't been brought up to use the 'step-' word at all. He was just put into this family, saying: 'This is your new father.' Because he was old enough to understand it . . . And 'He is the man you've got to respect. Any problems, you come back to us.' That's the same from my parents. So he never used the 'step-', and he knew that if he did he would get told off very badly. Whereas I'm afraid I was getting that from the girls. It was always 'the step-mother', or 'step-brother', or no brother at all. And

'step-grandparents'. But we did have to put a stop to that. That was jolly difficult, I must say.

Our respondents were not just describing their experiences, they were exploring and reflecting as they spoke. In general, they did not seem to want to have their experiences labelled nor made subject to generalizations. It may be helpful to have a name or label to attach to relationships, but many people are very cautious about the term 'step-'. It seemed as if each was describing what felt to them like an individual and unique experience. Indeed, the relationships and families were highly diverse and this may account, to some extent, for their lack of use of the word 'stepfamily'.

Intergenerational relationships

The general pattern which emerged from our interviews was that members of families where there had been some process of change expressed intentions and described patterns of relationships between the older generations which demonstrated a range of different types of contact. Older people and younger members of such families talked about family ties in ways which were suggestive of emotional involvement and mutual interest and support, but which were lived out in the expectation that households would be separate and that non-interference was a measure of successful family relationships. This was true even when families lived close by each other. In this, they seemed not to differ from a traditional Northern European cultural pattern of 'intimacy at a distance' (Rosenmayr and Kockeis 1963), a preferred independence already identified in other studies (Laslett 1983; Thompson *et al.* 1990; Arber and Ginn 1991; Allen *et al.* 1992; Allen and Perkins 1995; Phillipson *et al.*, Chapter 9 of this volume).

The intergenerational tie is maintained by older parents throughout times of family change by providing financial and personal support, sometimes by withholding judgement, always by expressing independence yet gratefulness for contact:

We've been lucky. We've been down there a couple of times. She [a daughter who had divorced and remarried] was up this last weekend, because of something they wanted to do . . . business she'd got. (Man aged 74, married with two daughters and a son)

I like it, just to know they're there. As I say we only see them once a week, don't we? (Couple in their seventies, she married twice, to two brothers, two children by first husband, daughter divorced)

I mean I know that they're all right and that if there's anything to tell me they'll get in touch. And there's no point in being jealous. (Woman in her late seventies, divorced, whose daughter-in-law had remarried and was then murdered by her second husband)

These oldest parents are describing a continued link built around compromises as they adjust to new relationships with, and within, their children's generation.

We began the chapter with a quote from one of our *middle-aged* respondents. The qualified inclusiveness of her language is typical of the children's generation. She'll be 'keeping the door open' so long as her husband approves. Another of our respondents, a divorced man, in his late forties and married to a widow, childless by choice, describes maintaining relationships at a distance with three sets of parents: his own, his new wife's former mother-in-law, and his new parents-in-law. These new *divorce-extended families* set challenges for couples. Nevertheless, however new relationships are managed, when family help and support are mentioned it is always in the context of the parents' independence and the children's commitment to the succeeding generation of grandchildren.

In analysing our data we found useful the theory of 'intergenerational stake' or 'developmental stake' as first developed by Bengtson and Kuypers (1971; quoted in Giarusso, Stallings, and Bengtson 1995: 228). Their suggestion that parents' descriptions of their relationships with their children are more positive than those children's accounts of their relationships with their parents seems to fit with our data. Finch and Mason (1993: 168) found a similar imbalance, with parents' responsibility to help children 'stronger than the reverse'. However, both these approaches locate explanation in what seems to us as calculative, exchange-based behaviour rather than in terms of emotional attachment. Indeed, we have argued elsewhere (Bornat *et al.* 1997) that adult attachment has been underused in explaining parent–child relationships in later life.

In so far as grandparental relations are concerned, we found no examples of grandparents left 'mourning' after having lost touch with grandchildren following divorce, although we did encounter older parents who expressed bereavement following a child's emigration. From their own accounts, our respondents were not the victims of divorce (Johnson 1988). In taking a sometimes quite moral attitude to their own children's actions, some grandmothers were able to maintain close contact with their sons' ex-partners. Jane Minder is 33 and has three children, She is separated from her husband, who was judged to be at fault by his mother: 'My mother-in-law. Yes, she's brilliant . . . she's been more of a mum to me than my mum has. She treats me like one of hers. She always has done. And even my ex-husband . . . he feels he can't talk to her, you know. He can't confide in her.'

In such situations, those likely to be most at risk are the fathers and we found that grandfathers least in contact with their families were those who had not maintained a relationship with their children at the time of divorce or separation. From our research, it seems that the persistence of good-quality relationships was a product of gender; that is, ties remained strongest where a grandmother or grandparents as a couple were involved.

Caring relationships

Although independence and mutual respect of each other's lifestyles may be expressed, this preference may be subject to other pressures once circumstances change. When asked what would happen if a parent became ill or needed help, the *middle-aged* group tended to emphasize the importance of family ties and the need to be available to help when necessary, even when their parents had been distant or absent following divorce or separation. However, with few exceptions they also operated a system which allowed them to put their own or their children's needs first, sometimes redefining 'family' in the process. Jack Albright is a 45-year-old man living with a divorced woman; they are both parents but have no children co-resident:

> You have to live your own life. It becomes your responsibility. My mum and dad's not my responsibility. But if I can help them and love them and care for them—but I've got a family to look after as well . . . I'd make the choices which seem appropriate when the time came . . . I would make the decision. I wouldn't say they can come and stay with me, and then cause the breakdown of our family. Or, if it had to be a hard decision to make, to put them in a home. I could do that. Because I believe sometimes we've got to make hard decisions in life.

Thelma Gordon is in her late twenties. She has cohabited with two successive partners, with a child from each relationship, and was brought up largely by her grandfather. She outlines her dilemma. She says she would have him to live with her, but 'obviously I've got to put my family first, which is an awful thing to happen [though] I would have him here if I could.'

Dennis and Zena Cosh are in their thirties, his parents divorced. This is his second partnership and, by deliberate choice, they have no children of their own. She says:

> I owe it to my parents to look after them because they would look after me . . . If the worst came to the worst I think we would have to up sticks and go, wouldn't we? . . . I would never be able to employ somebody to look after my parents. No way. I couldn't live with that, no . . . We'd have to reconsider. I mean we can't just give up our life.

Emotional commitment seems to be strong, but emotions may conflict, as may choices about lifestyle and identities. And, of course, these middle-aged and younger generations are developing the ground for their own intergenerational stake. Robert Kent is aged 48, divorced from his first wife and married to a second partner, who was a widow. Neither has any children from this or any previous relationship. He described how at a low point he had considered taking demotion to move in with his parents, but now he has a new partner who visits them regularly and 'I would be abandoning the whole of my career for perhaps two extra years for her [his mother], and who knows whether she is anyway more comfortable, because she's fairly remote from the world now anyway. So I guess, yes it's going to have to be residential care for her.'

Johnson (1993: 36–7), in her analysis of intergenerational relations in American divorced and reconstituted families, argues that there are three types of 'solidarities' following divorce and reorganization: 'increased emphasis on the solidarity of the generational bond'; the development of a separate 'private, bounded, but abbreviated nuclear family'; and 'loose-knit social networks of permissive and flexible individuals'. Her typology is appropriate for describing situations in which grandparents are relatively active and able to maintain independence if that is their preference. Extending her typologies into later life, it appears that relationships renegotiated at the time of divorce may well determine the nature and quality of family care. Dick Lathwaite is one of our older interviewees who seems to typify Johnson's third type of solidarity. He has been married twice, but both wives have died. His second wife was divorced with children. He has one child from his first marriage and three stepchildren, nine step-grandchildren, and two grandchildren:

> my step-daughter. I see her more than all the others put together. And then my stepson, the eldest one. I see him—at least once a month he comes up. But I don't see as much of my daughter as I would like. But, as I say, they're always so busy. Because she's got a full-time job and often works on Saturday as well. So on Sunday she's got all the things to do in the house. So I can't really expect her to come ambling in here just to see me. And she gets on extremely well with my step-daughter as well. And she knows she keeps an eye on me, so. She says, I know [stepdaughter] will let me know if you're in any trouble.

The integrity of such typologies can, of course, be affected by sudden crisis, and at any rate may not extend generationally upwards as effectively as downwards. Josie Rycroft explained how she heard about her elderly father's accident from her stepsister, to whom she had not spoken since their parents' wedding twenty years earlier. Her stepmother had first phoned her own daughter rather than her husband's daughter. While her parents had been maintaining an 'abbreviated nuclear family' in good times, at a point of crisis generational bonds were revived but sustained separately. What this seems to suggest to us is that however loose-knit the network of the new extended family, the availability of care and support will depend on generational blood ties.

To what extent do such blood ties then become fixed through monetary links? In our next section we go on to look at the way the distribution of family money is affected by family change.

Money transfers and family change

We earlier highlighted work by Finch and Wallis (1994) which suggests that in most 'ordinary families' the urge to be seen as a 'good parent' tends to outweigh any likelihood that inheritance will be used strategically to maximize its material value. Even when one child has provided more care than another, this does not increase their chance of inheriting. In fact parents try to be 'fair' and deal with children equally. In this sense, people do not 'think any less' of different children, at least when it comes to inheritance.

These points are important for our study of family change. How might the impact of divorce, separation, and remarriage affect the process of inheritance? Can the older generation continue to be 'good parents'? Might some children become more favoured than others due to family reconstitution? Might it be more likely that 'skipping a generation' may be more common where the middle generation has experienced change? Are reconstituted families more likely to make wills? Evidence from the Luton interviews suggests that this remains a fraught area.

Our interviews suggest that despite experiences of family change, when it comes to issues of inheritance, people overwhelmingly resorted to the principle that blood is thicker than water. This occurred where there was housing wealth to pass on and where possessions were less financially valuable, and was also the case in relationships where bonds between older people and their stepchildren were strong. Doreen Cooper spelled out particularly bluntly the difference she feels towards her two 'blood' children compared to her husband's child (by a former marriage) when it comes to issues of inheritance: 'I think it's so delicate a subject we hardly mention it. We did think about it at first. But I think you all stick up for your own . . . I don't care what anybody says, your own always seem to come first.' Even though the oldest child in question was only 11, she was concerned about establishing fairness through wills. For her, it was fair that they should divide their estate equally between their two shared children since his son would 'Get everything from his mum'. In the end, they had been unable to discuss the issue further; fairness was too difficult to operate when blood lines crossed. When one party has access to greater wealth as a consequence of being a member of an extended family, then fairness conferred through parent status is corrupted in the eyes of other family members. Inequities introduced through repartnering were also noted by Julie and Alan Biggin, who are each divorced with their own grown-up children. They married each other when they were both 55 and have tried hard to maintain an equal balance of resources so that all their children inherit on an equal basis. But, as she explains: 'when older people remarry . . . it seems to me that if you get one family that is more—that is, more powerful than the other family or larger—then that family very often overrides the other side . . . either more members . . . or in money terms.

Ties of affection and a caring debt make no inroads into inheritance practices. Dick Lathwaite is clear that even though it is his stepdaughter whom he sees most:

> I've left everything to my daughter. And then I've left her a letter saying I'd like everything to do with the Air Force to go to my grandson—that's her son—because he's always been mad on it. I've got an old flying jacket upstairs. He can't wait for me to die so he can have that flying jacket.

Here we see that a blood daughter would be the 'natural' choice. He doesn't hesitate; it is not a question of one or the other. Rather, he demonstrates that sense of control over his own effects, passing responsibility down to his daughter in the form of a letter to carry out his wishes concerning his grandson. He is not going to relinquish this control while he is alive.

Not surprisingly, a will might feature as a weapon in families where there is conflict. Lorna Semper described how she had got on better with her father and stepmother than with her mother, and that her mother had threatened to cut her out of her will if she . . . 'had anything to do with your dad'. Although she defiantly expressed her contempt for this, she was concerned that there might be 'a lot of squabbling if anything happens to my mum because you've got two lots, stepbrothers and that . . . it all depends. If she's wrote a will and she's mother to all of them anyway.' She is anticipating that she can rely on her mother to adopt common practice so that parental fairness will finally prevail.

Our data suggest that families experiencing reconstitution follow rules similar to those of intact families. However, separations and repartnering may serve to make parents emphasize blood lines more prominently when considering their wills; otherwise, if the rule of fairness persists indiscriminately, then their blood children may find their inheritance shared among a greater number. Certainly, for our interviewees, repartnering meant that issues of fairness were clearly expressed and indeed 'fairness', 'shared', and 'equally' are words which accompany any discussion of wills and family wealth. David and Vi Crisp are cousins in their late seventies, both widowed with two children each. After they die, their house is to be sold and then it will be 'shared fours' for the children. Horace and Bertha Masters are in their sixties. Bertha had the experience of being left out of her mother's will and both are adamant that when it comes to their children, even though they have little contact with their 'born again' Christian daughter, 'It's down the middle' to be shared with their son. Only one of our older interviewees was making plans to favour a particular child. Mr Boot's son, who has a learning disability, is to have the proceeds of the house that he and his parents live in together. This was partly because his redundancy payment had gone into the house, but also because his father recognized that his son was likely to need extra support and that neither of his two daughters was prepared to look after their brother.

CONCLUSION

Our two epigraphs present something of a contrasting view of the family. We chose them because they represent the two most dominant themes which our study reveals. These are a continuing commitment to the notion of family alongside, and indeed intertwined with, a commitment to blood ties. Ideas of family and family relationships were clearly adjustable in terms of shifting commitments, endings, and beginnings. Families might grow to be more inclusive of step-grandchildren, added in-laws, and new step-parents at almost all life stages. At the same time, given certain specific demands, family might be defined in terms of more restrictive blood lines. At times of high dependency or in expectation of need, the parent–child relationship, most usually mother–child rather than couple–child, was identified as the default, the failsafe. Exercised on a gendered basis, such a line might therefore exclude or discourage paternal involvement.

For several of our older interviewees, these two familial strategies represented continuity with their own lives. Parents had separated, died, left home, or become incapacitated. They were experiencing a second or even third generation of family change. Nevertheless, there are changes which families in the late twentieth century are managing for the first time. More older people are surviving. Some of our middle-aged respondents mentioned more than two sets of parents or in-law relationships as a result of repartnering. Children seem to be more ready to replace partners as relationships break down, with the result that family structure and meaning might be redefined by younger generations. Opportunities for independent living appear to be greater as older members fund their own support through earlier house purchases, occupational pensions, and, sometimes, new partnerships.

Commitment to the idea of family as a set of flexible, interconnecting, and supportive relationships provides one way to ensure that these more recent changes are coped with, and indeed identified as beneficial by older family members. Maintaining the blood line works in tandem with such principles. At a broad, existential level, this may be a matter of colonizing the future (Giddens 1991)—a guarantee of immortality or continued identity after death. At a more prosaic level, it means maintaining into late life the parent–child relationship by invoking the emotions, attachments, and rewards with which it began at birth. This non-negotiable tie carries with it expectations which cannot easily be shed. At times of crisis and need, it may be summoned up as the key resource, for as one older woman explained: 'We've got nothing else other than our children and they're our jewels. Some are chipped, some are flawed. But they're still our jewels.'

The expectations which underlie such a statement may yet be fully tested as relations with the oldest generation come to compete with the growing complexity of life in families which have undergone change.

NOTES

1. Woman b. 1951, parents separated when she was a year old and both remarried. Both father and stepfather have subsequently died. She has 2 brothers and 8 step-siblings. Married with 4 surviving children.
2. Woman b. 1926, mother married twice, divorced her own husband and cohabited for 2 years with partner, now deceased; daughter's marriage unhappy.
3. A contribution to debates about the feminization of the family by Bornat, Dimmock, Jones, and Peace which draws on these data is published in Silva and Smart (1999).
4. All interviewees' names are pseudonyms.

PART IV
New Ways of Living

11

Living alone: evidence from England and Wales and France for the last two decades

Ray Hall, Philip E. Ogden, and Catherine Hill

INTRODUCTION

During the 1990s, living alone moved from being perceived as a somewhat marginal household type concentrated among older people to a more widespread phenomenon with wide-ranging policy implications. In 1991, 27 per cent of all households in Britain,[1] and a similar proportion of households in France, were made up of people living alone, compared to 18 and 20 per cent respectively around 1970. The continuing rapid increase of one-person households has been described as one of the most significant changes that will take place between now and 2020 in England and Wales: of the projected growth of new households in England, 80 per cent will be one-person. By 2020, more than one in three households will be made up of people living alone. Such changes have far-reaching consequences, in terms of both the physical provision for such households and the social implications of increasing numbers of people living alone (DoE 1995, 1996; Hall, Ogden, and Hill 1997).

Households are the basic units of society, the primary consumption units, and the units through which most people organize their lives. They are the juncture where a whole range of social and economic processes intersect. The increasing importance of one-person households reflects wider change in society; their growth is both a reflection of demographic changes and

We should like to thank ONS for allowing us to use the ONS Longitudinal Study (LS) and members of the LS Support Programme at the Social Statistics Research Unit (SSRU), City University, for assistance with accessing data. The views expressed in this publication are not necessarily those of the ONS or SSRU. We should like also to thank Dominique Rouault of INSEE in Paris for his invaluable assistance in producing tables from the EDP and Patricia Bardoux, also of INSEE, for help in preparing special tabulations from the French census.

closely interrelated with other geographical issues, particularly changing urban economies and societies. Processes such as professionalization of the labour force (Hamnett 1994*a*, *b*) and changes in the housing market, particularly gentrification, are associated with new types of households, including one-person households. At the same time, the household itself can stimulate other changes: 'the household exerts a major independent influence on both the demand for employment and housing as a result of changes in the rate and form of household fissions and formation' (Randolph 1989: 41). Processes leading to the emergence of one-person households are widespread geographically but are particularly evident in 'world cities' such as London, Paris, or New York which are undergoing rapid evolution both of physical infrastructure and socio-demographic structures (Sassen 1991; Feinstein 1994; Hamnett 1994*a*; Knox and Taylor 1995).

The planning and wider policy implications of the trend towards smaller households and one-person living especially are profound. The planning implications of these changes have been to the forefront recently, with discussions about where and how the extra households projected for England over the next few decades will be accommodated—on 'brownfield' or 'greenfield' sites? In particular, where will people living alone want to live (DoE 1996)? What are the wider social and economic implications of more people living alone? Do people living on their own have distinctive consumption patterns—not just of goods but also of services? And what are the implications for social relationships? Is one-person living a manifestation of lifestyle changes? Is it, indeed, a new way of living?

Although older age groups still dominate those living alone, the largest increase has been among those under retirement age. This chapter discusses the changing characteristics of such younger one-person households over the last two decades in England and Wales and France, with some suggested explanations for the changes. Understanding their characteristics helps to answer questions about future trends in one-person living, trends which are not necessarily amenable to straightforward projection since they are a function of a whole range of intangibles requiring qualitative as much as quantitative judgement. A two-country comparison may shed more light on such processes and enable us to set the British picture in a wider context. One of our specific concerns has been with the role of migration in the changing patterns of one-person households, which in turn raises other questions. Is there, for example, an increasingly mobile group emerging in society who are willing to migrate as new opportunities emerge? Are there gender differences in how these opportunities are perceived and hence gender differences in migration?

PROBLEMS OF DEFINITION AND DATA

A one-person household is defined by the United Nations as 'a person who lives alone in a separate housing unit or who occupies, as a lodger, a separate room (or rooms) of a housing unit and does not join with any of the other occupants of the housing unit to form part of a multiperson household' (Council of Europe 1990). However, census definitions may not always be entirely clear, as they vary among countries and sometimes between censuses within one country. There are several problems of meaning and definition associated with the one-person household. The person enumerated as living alone in a census may do so for only part of the time, perhaps living alone during the week and with someone else or their family at weekends. The term 'living apart together' (LAT) has been used to describe such a situation (Kaufmann 1993, 1994). Another problem is how far individuals living with other unrelated individuals regard themselves as living alone. There is, too, an inherent ambiguity about living alone—it has a connotation of isolation and solitariness; indeed, one-person households are sometimes referred to as 'solitaries'. However, rather than living alone being associated with isolation, quite the reverse may be the case, especially for younger adults, with those living in cities, for example, perhaps having extensive social networks (Bien *et al.* 1992; Kaufmann 1993).

The census and associated data sets for England and Wales and France have provided most of the data used in this research. The census for England and Wales has been used to look at changes in the characteristics of the population and households between 1981 and 1991.[2] However, tabulations from the British census using both the Small Area Statistics and Local Base Statistics provide only a limited range of information about people living alone. The Samples of Anonymised Records (SARs), made up of a 1 per cent household sample and a 2 per cent individual sample drawn from the 1991 Census, offer much wider opportunities for analysis (Marsh 1993). Here, we use the 2 per cent sample of individuals for a detailed investigation of the characteristics of people living alone in 1991.

The ONS Longitudinal Study (LS), a 1 per cent sample of the population of England and Wales, has provided us with a further valuable data source. We have used it both for cross-sectional comparisons of people living alone and for longitudinal analyses, particularly between 1981 and 1991, of household transitions and migration. The British Household Panel Survey (BHPS), an annual sample survey of some 9,000 people, offers possibilities for tracking people into and out of one-person households over the four waves so far available, and this source was also used.

Data sources for France are broadly similar and although there are some differences in the definitions of family and household, these did not greatly affect our analyses. The French censuses of 1968, 1975, and especially 1982 and 1990 provide rich data in published form and, while there is no French equivalent of the SARs, specific tables were requested from the 1990 Census. There is a French equivalent to the Longitudinal Study—the *Échantillon Démographique Permanent* (EDP) (Rouault 1994; INSEE 1995*a*)—which, although less well developed than its counterpart in England and Wales, has been able to be used in this study.

Censuses and their associated sources, of course, cannot show the full diversity of the ways in which groups of individuals organize their lives nor how people interpret their living arrangements, and for this we rely on twenty in-depth interviews with people living alone in London's Docklands which give some insight into attitudes towards living alone.

THE EMERGENCE OF LIVING ALONE

Around 1950, generally fewer than 3 per cent of the population lived alone in Europe and North America. The proportion has since increased three- or four-fold. From about 1970, the trend towards independent living has spread from the elderly widowed to younger adults (Kobrin 1976*a*; Michael *et al.* 1980; Pampel 1983; Roussel 1983; Santi 1988; Wall 1991). Santi (1988), examining American data for the period from 1970 to 1985, observed that more unmarried adults were choosing either to live alone or with non-relatives instead of living with relatives; for the period 1970–80 at least, he concluded that these trends were the result of real behavioural change and not just of changing age structures. Goldscheider and Waite (1991: 199) saw this 'rise of non-family living' as a clear indication of fundamental change in modern societies, particularly the declining importance of the family; 'a consequence of changes leading modern societies not to "new families" but to "non-families"'.

Household change is the outcome of both the demographic processes involved in family formation and dissolution—marriage, divorce, death—and of wider socio-economic processes (Ermisch and Overton 1985). Certain family or marital statuses are usually associated with particular household arrangements; being married or a single parent are both normally associated with living in an independent household. An unmarried adult, on the other hand, has a choice of household arrangements: either to remain in the family home, to cohabit or live with friends, or to live alone (Santi 1988). Similarly, a divorced or widowed individual without resident children has a choice of household arrangements. The extent of choice depends, of course, upon various other factors, including the availability of both other people to live with and suitable housing within the financial means of the individual.

One-person households may be a result of the deliberate choice of a permanent way of life or a response to a particular set of circumstances which the individual concerned views as essentially a temporary arrangement. Others, though, may have little or no choice. The increasing numbers of one-person households may therefore reflect the increasing numbers of transitory periods in an individual's life associated with, for example, changes in marital status or in employment opportunities. While younger one-person households are likely to be more transitory than older ones, overall it is likely that increasing numbers of people will live alone for some period of their lives, although the length of time spent living alone will vary by age and sex. A recent study of women in France (INSEE 1995*b*) demonstrates the transformation that has taken place during the life course in the periods which an individual spends in certain living arrangements, with a particularly marked increase in the time spent alone. In 1968, the average woman spent 0.6 years living alone when under 40 and 6.5 years after age 40; by 1990 this had increased to 1.8 and 9.8 years respectively. For men, the comparable figures were 0.9 and 2.1 years in 1968, and 2.3 and 3.8 years in 1990. We should note that while the proportion of the population living alone at any one moment may seem low (for example, around 10 per cent in both countries in 1990–1), three caveats are appropriate: first, the rate of increase has been substantial; secondly, seen from the perspective of the life course, many individuals are, as noted above, spending time living alone; and thirdly, in terms of households (and therefore dwellings) both the present level and the projected rate of increase is substantial.

Increases in numbers living alone result from three groups of factors. First, there are *compositional* factors, including more childless people, regardless of marital status, and changing age structures (which may reflect, for example, previous birth rates or greater longevity). Secondly, the changing *propensity* to live alone, which, as a chosen lifestyle, is likely to diminish with age (Van Hoorn 1994). The young may choose to live alone while older people may have no alternative. Thirdly, the economic *ability* to live alone; one-person households which are the result of personal choice may well be more affluent than those which are involuntary.

Figure 11.1 develops these ideas in more detail and shows the variety of immediate *demographic* processes that influence household change, together with changing patterns of *behaviour* and the interaction of the *job* and *housing* markets. In this way, the study of households is linked into the wider patterns of socio-economic change. A final element in Figure 11.1 is the mediating role played by *migration* both in producing and reflecting household changes and as a major contributor to their geography.

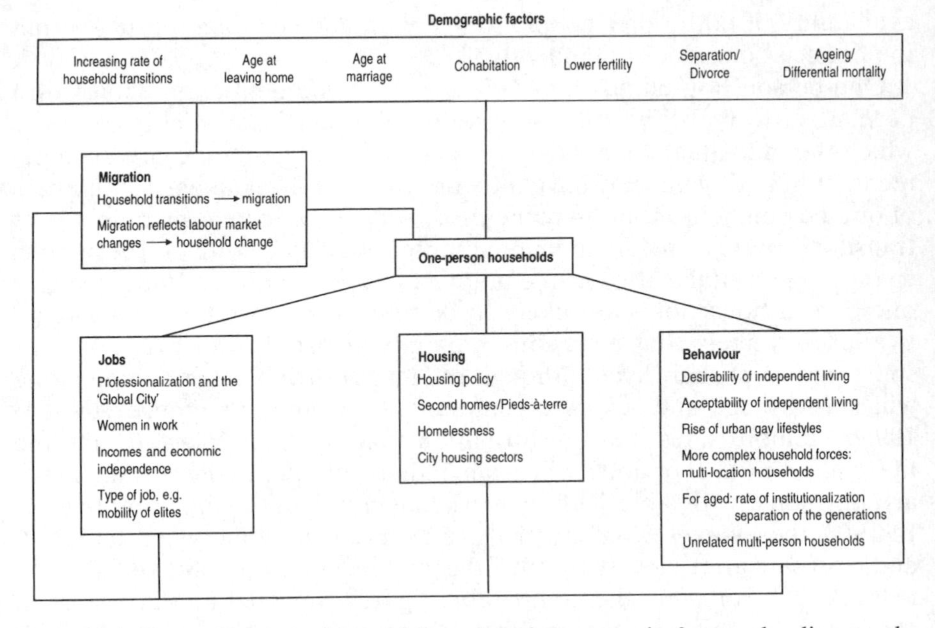

FIG. 11.1 Some demographic and broad socio-economic factors leading to the creation of one-person households

We measured the effect of *compositional* change versus increasing *propensity* by comparing 1981 and 1991 figures of those living alone in different marital status groups in England and Wales. This shows that both compositional factors and increasing propensity are important in explaining the increasing numbers of younger adults living alone. Table 11.1 shows that increases in the number of those single and divorced among both males and females has contributed to the growth in the numbers living alone and, at the same time, that there has been an increasing *propensity* of single men especially, together with divorced women, to live alone.

THE GEOGRAPHY OF LIVING ALONE

Living alone among younger age groups has a distinctive geography compared with the distribution of the elderly living alone. Younger one-person households are much more an urban phenomenon, particularly associated with large urban areas such as the capital cities as well as, for example, Manchester or Newcastle-upon-Tyne in England and Lyon or Bordeaux in France. It is, however, becoming a more diffuse geographical phenomenon than has hitherto been the case. Nonetheless, in both countries, the largest

TABLE 11.1. *Role of changing propensity and compositional changes in explaining increasing numbers living alone from 1981 to 1991, males and females aged 20–59 living alone (% share of increase)*

	PROPENSITY Components of growth 1981–91, keeping 1981 population number constant			COMPOSITION Components of growth 1981–91, keeping 1981 propensity in each marital status group constant		
Marital Status	Males	Females	Total	Males	Females	Total
Single	61	7	44	57	75	66
Married/separated	25	45	32	−3	−2	−2
Widowed	2	11	4	−2	−14	−8
Divorced	13	37	20	46	40	43

Source: ONS Longitudinal Study.

concentration of one-person households, and particularly of younger one-person households, is found in the capital city: 38 per cent of all households in London and 50 per cent in Paris are one-person.

If we examine the proportion of 20–49-year-olds living alone by district in England and Wales, the London boroughs emerge at the top of the list. The top ten local authority areas for younger females living alone in 1991 were London boroughs and ten out of the top eleven for men were London boroughs, with Brighton on the South Coast sixth in the list. Apart from London, other large urban areas were near the top of the list, including Manchester, Newcastle, Nottingham, Liverpool, and Sheffield. Gender contrasts in living alone at younger ages are also apparent from such an analysis. In every case, a higher proportion of males than females live alone. Only 30 districts have 7 per cent or more of the female population aged 20–49 living alone, compared with 30 districts with over 11 per cent of the male population living alone. Numbers of women living alone lag behind those of men for a number of reasons: they are more likely to have children living with them, for example, and less likely to have the financial ability to live alone.

The 1991 Census provides a detailed picture of the geographical distribution of persons living alone at that date and allows analysis of changes since 1981. Metropolitan districts and non-metropolitan districts in parts of Wales and both southern and other coastal areas have between 28 and 39 per cent of all households consisting of one person. The highest proportions of one-person households are, however, in London boroughs, rising to 48 per cent in Kensington and Chelsea. The largest percentage point change between 1981 and 1991 in proportions of one-person households was concentrated in and around large urban areas such as

Newcastle, Liverpool, Manchester, and Birmingham as well as in and around London. This contrast is reflected in Figure 11.2, which shows that younger and older one-person households each have a distinct geography. Figure 11.2*a* shows the concentration of pensioner one-person households both in often remote rural areas and in retirement areas such as those along the South and East Coasts. By contrast, Figure 11.2*b* shows that non-pensioner one-person households are a more urban phenomenon and are concentrated in London and other regional urban centres. Indeed, 85 per cent of the variation in the distribution of non-pensioner one-person households can be explained by density of population.

At the regional level in France, there is not a great deal of variation in the proportions of one-person households, from 22 per cent in Picardy to 32 per cent in the Île-de-France, not surprising given the wide diversity of places included within each region. The distribution by *département* shows the importance, first, of rural areas with aged populations and little tradition of extended households and, secondly, of urban areas with high numbers of younger people and of divorcees living alone. The greatest increases in one-person households between 1982 and 1990 were in the South-west, Corsica, Brittany, and the Loire although proportions are still relatively low. The urban population as a whole had both smaller mean household sizes and a larger proportion of people living alone than non-urban areas: at the two ends of the settlement spectrum, rural communes had 21 per cent one-person households while urban areas of over one million had 30 per cent.

As in England and Wales, the geography of one-person households in France varies considerably by age: while nationally, some 14 per cent of all households contained one person aged over 60, this figure falls sharply for the Île de France and other urban areas (Figure 11.2*c*). In the most rural areas, up to 65 per cent of those living alone were aged over 60. Younger one-person households were strongly associated with *départements* containing large cities, such as Gironde (Bordeaux), Rhône (Lyon), and Haute-Garonne (Toulouse) (Figure 11.2*d*).

The Paris region (Île-de-France) and Paris itself (the Ville de Paris) stand out as exceptional in many respects compared to the national pattern. The numbers of people living alone rose from 1 million in 1975 to 1,342,000 in 1990, accounting for 32 per cent of all households in the region by 1990. There is considerable variation within the region. Paris itself, defined as the 20 *arrondissements* of the Ville de Paris, has long stood out nationally and has been consistently ahead of London in proportions of one-person households: as early as 1901, a quarter of Parisian households were one-person (Coppée 1990). By 1990, this figure had risen more or less continuously to about 50 per cent, a considerably higher proportion than

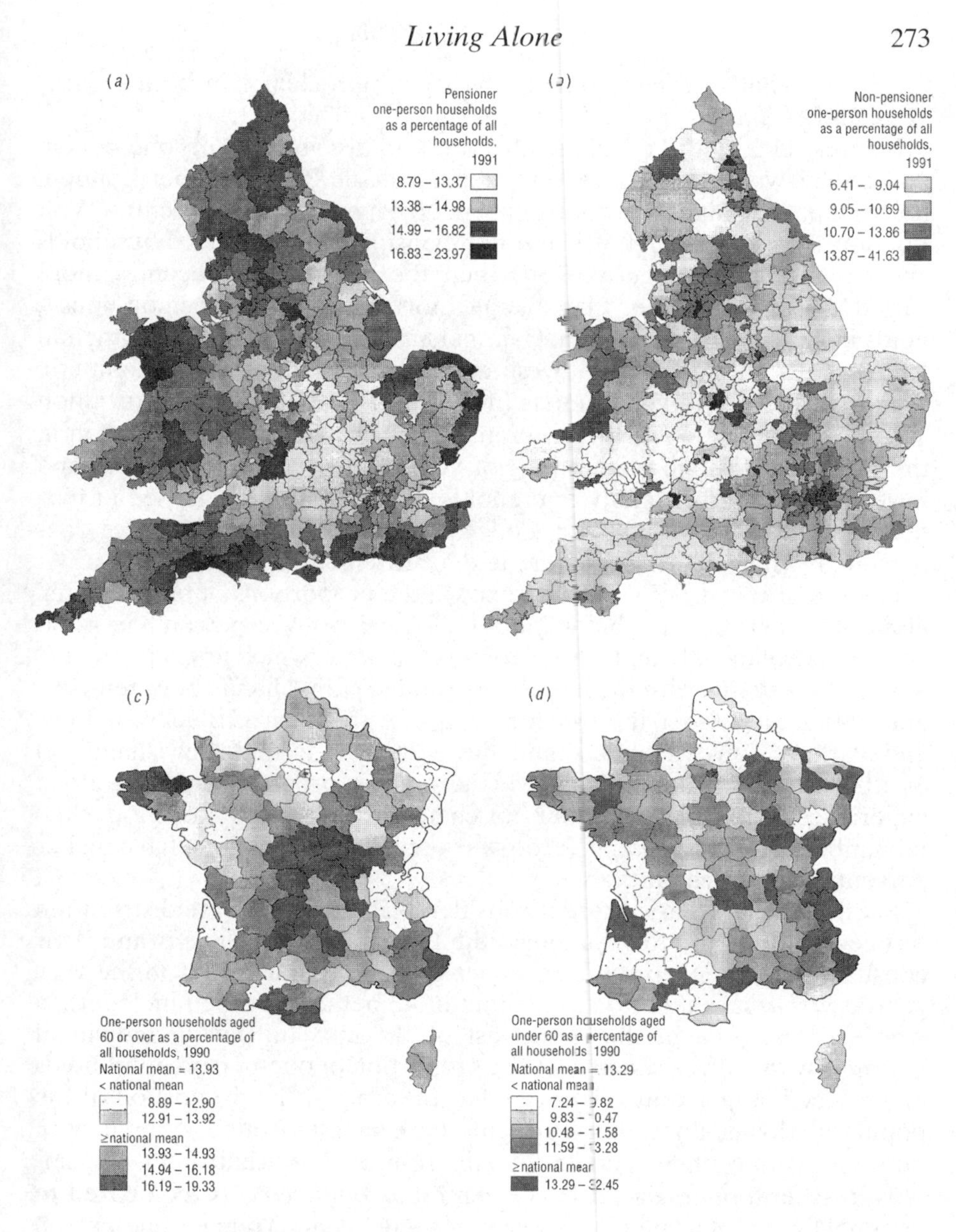

FIG. 11.2 Proportions of households in England and Wales, 1991, that were (*a*) pensioner one-person and (*b*) non-pensioner one-person; and in France, 1990, which were one-person aged (*c*) over 60 and (*d*) under 60

the 38 per cent in Inner London. Paris emerges clearly in both Figures 11.2*c* and 11.2*d*.

Figures 11.3 and 11.4 show the uneven distribution of one-person households within Inner London and the Ville de Paris. In Inner London, for example, the highest proportion of people living alone is in central West London (Figure 11.3*a*), but if the non-pensioner one-person households are separated out (Figure 11.3*b*) then the distribution becomes more varied. Areas with higher than average non-pensioner one-person households include parts of Camden, Hammersmith and Fulham, Haringey, and Islington to the north and west and wards in Lewisham, Lambeth, Wandsworth, and Tower Hamlets in the south and east. This distribution gives some indication of the different stages of parts of Inner London in the transition to high proportions of young one-person households and lower proportions of family households. Kensington and Chelsea in particular stands out, with 48 per cent of all households in 1991 being one-person, of which 70 per cent were under retirement age.

Geographical variations clearly exist in the proportions of people living alone in Inner London but Figure 11.3*c*, which gives percentage point change between 1981 and 1991, shows those areas which are catching up. Many of the wards with the largest percentage point change between 1981 and 1991 are located in the east, for example wards such as Blackwall, Bow, and Park in Tower Hamlets, and the easterly wards of Lewisham and Southwark. The areas which have the highest proportions living alone experienced the smallest amount of change, and in some cases a decline in numbers. Areas with relatively low proportions living alone have higher percentage point changes.

Similarly within Paris, there is considerable variation in the distribution of one-person households amongst the twenty *arrondissements* and their constituent *quartiers*: from over 56 per cent of all households in the very central *arrondissements* to a minimum of 42 per cent in the nineteenth, a working-class area in the north-east of the city. Indeed, in individual *quartiers* within *arrondissements*, the proportion of one-person households may exceed 60 per cent (Figure 11.4*a*). In terms of the proportion of the population living alone, this represents, for example, around 45 per cent of both men and women aged 25–29 and around 30 per cent of 30–49-year-olds in several *quartiers* of the six central *arrondissements* (compared to national figures of around 13 per cent and 8 per cent). Younger one-person households are particularly concentrated in the central *arrondissements* but there is also a northern and eastern concentration (Figure 11.4*b*) and the most rapid increase in one-person households has been in the outer *arrondissements*, both in the north and south (Figure 11.4*c*).

One-person households in both Inner London and Paris have distinctive geographies, showing marked central concentrations and a diffusion

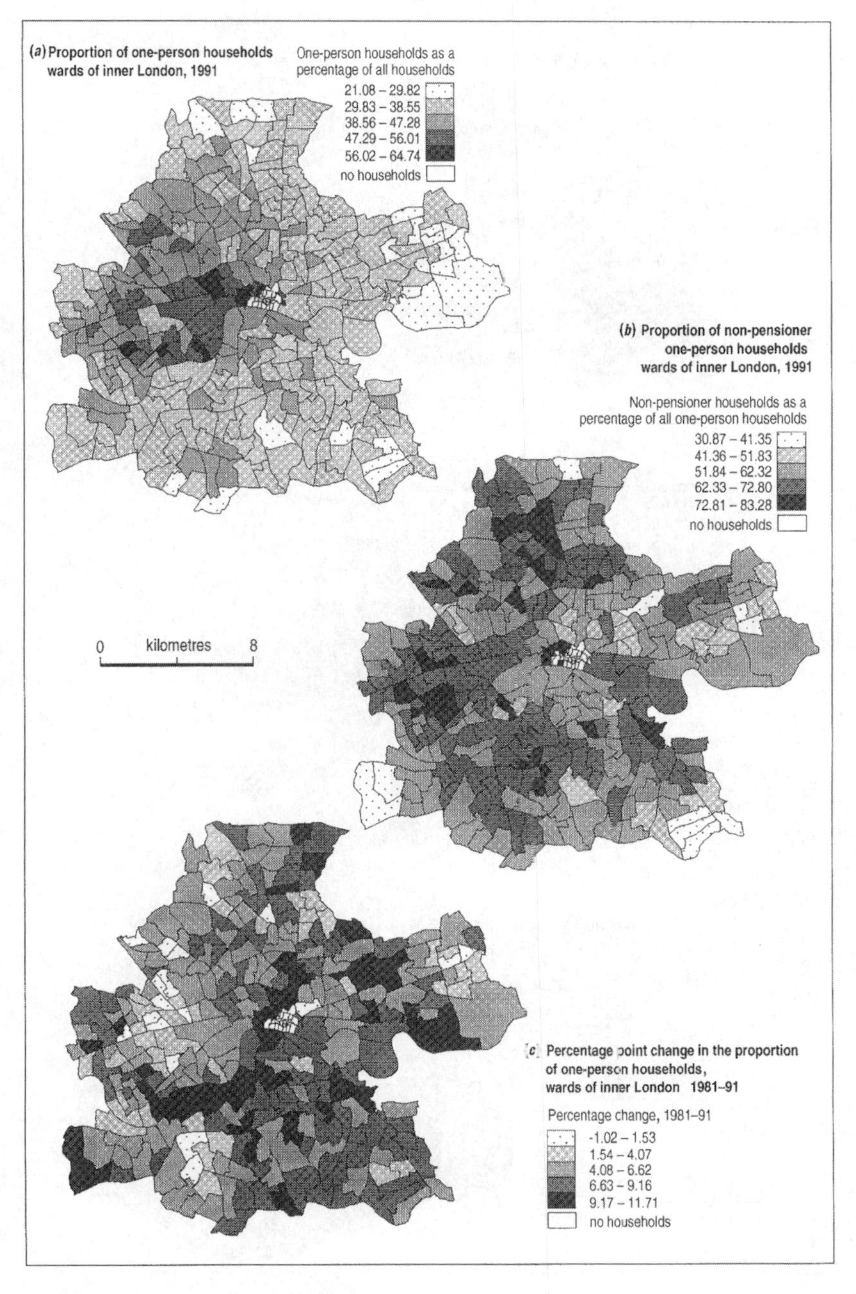

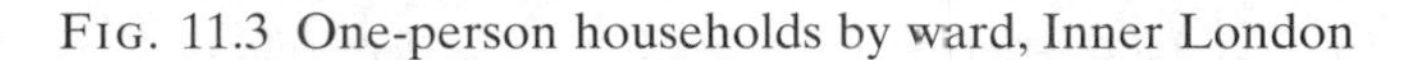
Source: 1981 and 1991 Census of Population: Small-Area Statistics.

FIG. 11.3 One-person households by ward, Inner London

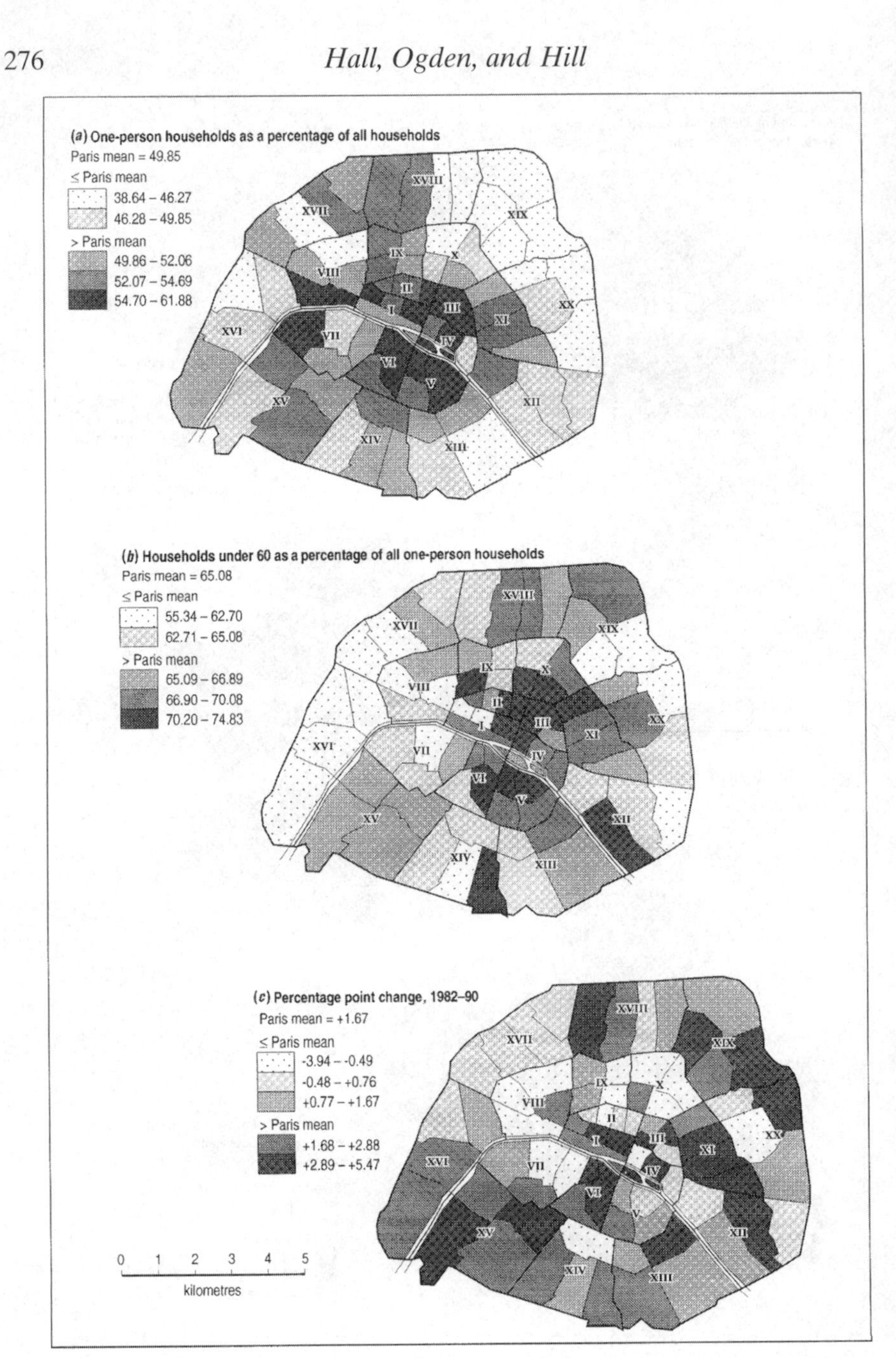

Source: Unpublished tables from *Recensement Général de la Population* 1982, 1990.

FIG. 11.4 One-person households by *quartier*, Ville de Paris

outwards during the 1980s. Areas associated with specific redevelopment or urban renewal in particular have seen a growth in numbers, such as north-eastern Paris or London Docklands. Not surprisingly, one-person households will be found where there is suitable accommodation. At the same time, the housing market is likely to respond to the demand created by more people wanting to live on their own. Large cities seem to be particularly able to respond to this demand.

WHO LIVES ALONE?

Age

The initial increase among people living alone after 1945 was among older people, especially women, but over the past two decades much of the increase has been among younger people (Figure 11.5). In England and Wales in 1971, 32 per cent of people living alone were aged under 60; by 1991, this proportion had risen to 40 per cent. In particular, there has been an increase in people under 40 living alone. In 1971, 10 per cent of all one-person households were aged between 20 and 40 years, a proportion which doubled by 1991. The increasing propensity for all age groups to live alone is particularly evident for younger males. Thus, while only 3 per cent of the 25–29 age group lived alone in 1971, by 1991 11 per cent were doing so. For females in this age group, the increasing propensity to live alone is less dramatic, with proportions of 25–29-year-olds increasing from 2 per cent to 6.5 per cent between 1971 and 1991 (Figure 11.6).

There are higher proportions of one-person households in the adult working-age groups in Inner London than nationally (Figure 11.7), particularly among younger women. In Inner London, the mean age of one-person households is 52 years compared with 57.2 years in Outer London and 59.3 years in England and Wales. Seventy-eight per cent of men and nearly half of all women living alone in Inner London are under age 60, compared with national figures of 69 per cent and 29 per cent respectively.

In France, too, there was a strong increase in proportions living alone at all pre-retirement ages between 1982 and 1990, although in 1990–1 the French figures are consistently above those for England and Wales for all ages under 60 (Figure 11.5). While in the most urban areas, particularly Paris, the majority living alone are under age 60, in the most rural areas up to 65 per cent of those living alone are aged over 60. While there is a considerable bias towards women living alone at older ages because of higher male mortality, there has been a much larger proportional increase in living alone among men, both generally and within the economically active population.

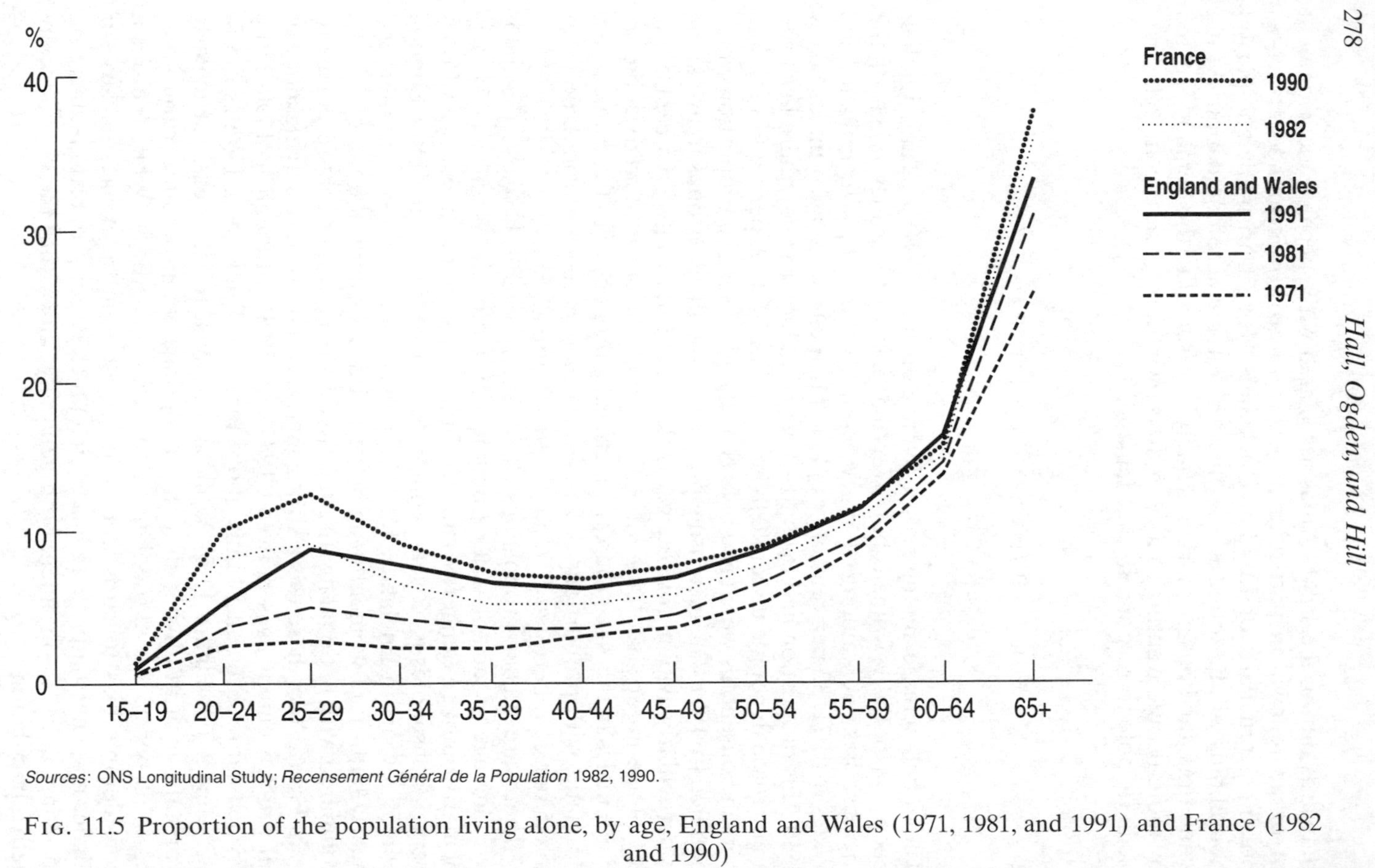

Sources: ONS Longitudinal Study; *Recensement Général de la Population* 1982, 1990.

FIG. 11.5 Proportion of the population living alone, by age, England and Wales (1971, 1981, and 1991) and France (1982 and 1990)

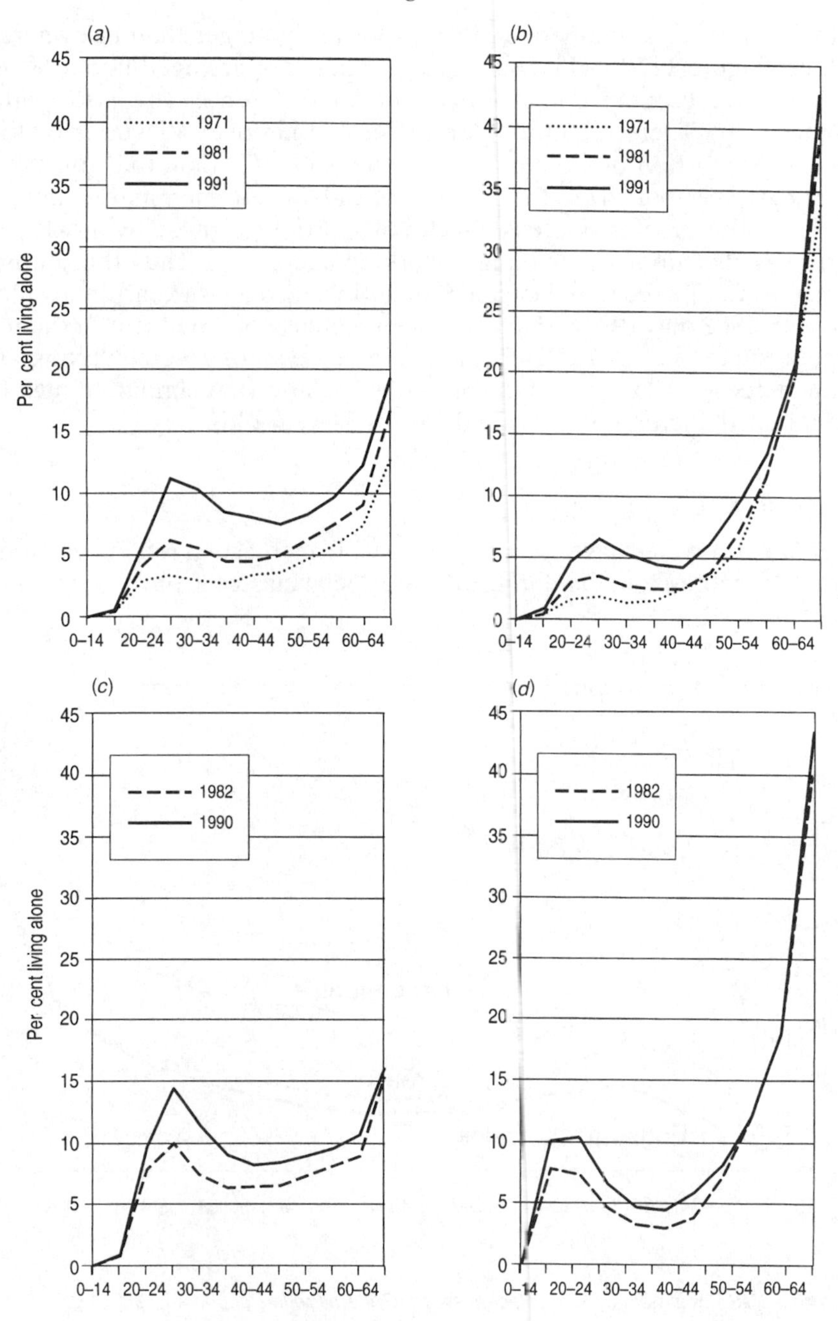

Sources: ONS Longitudinal Study; *Recensement Général de la Population* 1982, 1990.

FIG. 11.6 Proportion of the population living alone, by age, England and Wales (1971, 1981, and 1991) for (*a*) men and (*b*) women; and France (1982 and 1990) for (*c*) men and (*d*) women

In Paris as well, one-person households are younger than elsewhere in France (Figure 11.7). While nationally, 49 per cent are aged under 60, this rises to over 65 per cent in Paris. Gender differences are also evident (Figure 11.6). There are more men under 40 than over 40 who live alone, but the proportion of women living alone is greater than that for men in all age groups apart from the 25–39-year-olds, where men marginally take the lead. The greatest increase in the proportion of those living alone in Paris was also among the younger working-age groups. Thus, there was an increase of 21 per cent in the male population aged 35–44 years living alone between 1982 and 1990 (compared to an increase of 9 per cent in the total population at that age) and 43 per cent increase among women (compared to an increase of 23 per cent in the total population). A similar, though less pronounced, increase was evident for 25–34-year-olds.

Social class

England and Wales have seen a considerable increase in the proportion of people in professional and intermediate social classes: from 15 per cent of

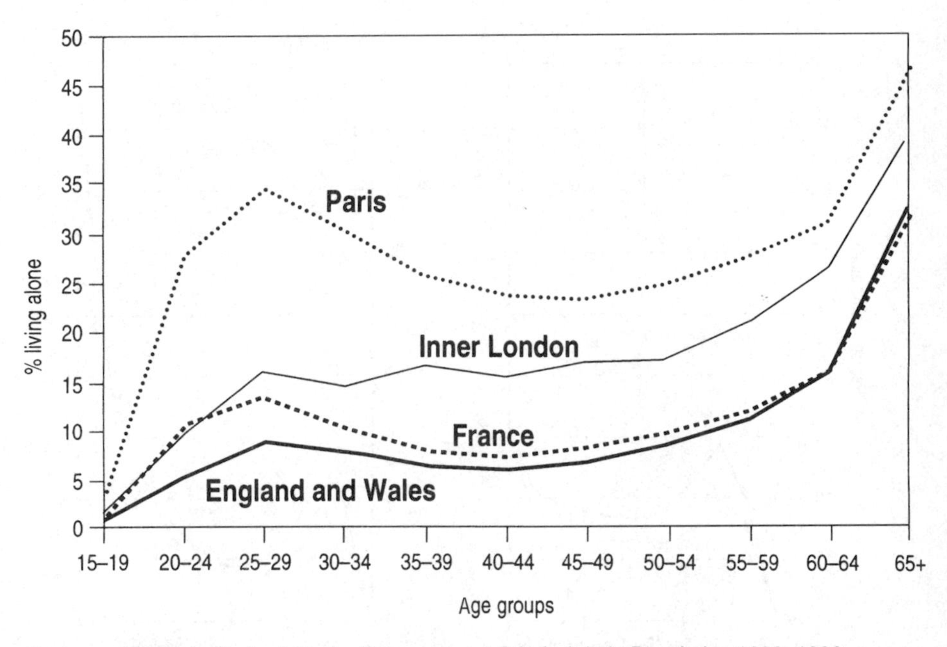

Sources: ONS Longitudinal Study; *Recensement Général de la Population* 1982, 1990.

FIG. 11.7 Proportion of the population living alone, by age, England and Wales and Inner London, 1991; and France and the Ville de Paris, 1990

the population aged under 60 in 1971 to 26 per cent in 1991, according to analyses based on the Longitudinal Study. Among those living alone, 24 per cent were in professional and intermediate social classes in 1971, a proportion which had risen to over 35 per cent by 1991. The increase in those living alone in the higher social classes was particularly rapid between 1981 and 1991: over that decade, there was a 70 per cent increase in the number of men aged between 20 and 59 living alone and a 94 per cent increase among men living alone in professional and intermediate social classes. For women, the figures were 53 per cent and 104 per cent respectively. Forty-two per cent of the extra men living alone in 1991 (compared with 1981) were in the professional and intermediate social classes and 53 per cent of the women. The increase in younger people living alone has been particularly concentrated among professional and intermediate classes. In 1971 in England and Wales, 6 per cent of those people aged 25–29 in social class I lived alone. By 1981, this figure had increased to almost 13 per cent, and by 1991 just under one-fifth were living alone.

While the difference in class structure for males living alone compared with the total male population is small, the class structure of females living alone is much more skewed to the upper end. The proportion of females in professional, managerial, and technical social classes who were living alone in 1991 was almost the same as for males living alone, even though women tend to be under-represented in these occupations. However, many more women than men living alone are in skilled non-manual occupations while many more men are in skilled manual occupations, reflecting more accurately male occupational distribution as a whole.

In France, census data reveal a similar pattern. The greatest increases in the number of one-person households were in the *cadres* and *professions intermédiaires* categories. Between 1982 and 1990, there was an increase of 34 per cent in the number of households whose reference person was in the *cadres* category and an increase of 74 per cent in the number of one-person households in that category. Comparable figures for the *professions intermédiaires* were increases of 13.5 and 40 per cent. If we look at the population living alone in each socio-professional category, we see that a great proportion of those in professional or intermediate professional jobs were living alone and this is especially so among women. Some 20 per cent of women in professional jobs were living alone in 1990.

Changing the scale to examine the class structure of one-person households in Inner London and Paris reveals some of the possible links between living alone and wider socio-economic and household changes. In both London and Paris, the 1980s was a period of significant socio-economic change. In Inner London, for example, the proportion of the total economically active population employed in professional and intermediate occupations increased from 25 to 40 per cent between 1981 and

1991. In contrast, all other occupational groups experienced a decline both proportionately and absolutely. Manual and partly skilled jobs declined most rapidly, by 31 per cent and 36 per cent respectively. These figures reflect the general pattern of occupational changes in England and Wales as a whole, although the increases at the top and decreases at the bottom of the scale were more pronounced in London. Similarly, in the Ville de Paris, there was a large increase in managers/professional occupational categories between 1982 and 1990, a smaller increase in intermediate professionals, and a decline in all other occupational groups. The increase in managers/professionals was particularly large among women (73 per cent), and the increase among intermediate professionals was concentrated almost entirely among women. It is within this context of occupational change that the increase in the numbers of one-person households took place: for Greater London from 26 to 32 per cent and for Inner London from 32 to 38 per cent of all households between 1981 and 1991. The comparable French figures are an increase from 30 to 32 per cent for the Paris region (Île-de-France) and from 48 to 50 per cent for the Ville de Paris between 1982 and 1990.

Thus, one-person households in the capital cities are of higher social status than one-person households in the rest of their respective countries, a characteristic which is particularly pronounced for females. Nearly 40 per cent of men and over 42 per cent of women under 60 and living alone in Inner London are in social classes I and II, compared with national figures for England and Wales of 34 per cent and 24 per cent respectively. In Paris there are clear links between the dramatic increase in younger women living alone and the changing social class composition of the city (Carpenter, Chauviré, and White 1994; Carpenter and Lees 1995). Among women, it is especially the high socio-occupational groups who live alone. In 1990, 36 per cent of women in professional jobs in Paris were living alone compared to 20 per cent of professional women nationally.

Marital status

In 1991 in England and Wales, at ages under 30, the large majority of people living alone were never-married (90 per cent); between the ages of 30 and 39 years, never-marrieds were still the largest group among those living alone, with divorced people making up 23 per cent. Between the ages of 40 and 59, the number of never-marrieds declines and that of divorcees increases, with never-marrieds making up 30 per cent, and divorcees 36 per cent, of the population living alone by ages 50–59. Inevitably, the proportion living alone made up of widowed people increases at older ages: by ages 50–59 to 23 per cent, while at ages 60 and over the majority of those living alone are widowed (73 per cent). The marital status of those living alone in Inner London is again rather different from the national picture, with fewer divorced and more single people.

In France, too, the majority of under 40-year-olds living alone in 1990 were never-married, with just over 7 per cent divorced. Among the over-forties, 23 per cent were never-married and 14 per cent divorced, with the widowed being the largest category at 57 per cent. The proportion of divorcees among one-person households is rather less in France than in England and Wales. The rise of divorce has certainly had an impact on the rise of living alone in both countries and, although remarriage frequently occurs, divorce increases the number of household transitions and, therefore, the frequency of living alone at least for short periods. Thus, for the age group 35–49 in France, a quarter of those living alone are divorced (Durr 1992).

Tenure

Living alone, especially among younger people, has traditionally been associated with living in rented accommodation. In 1971, just under half of people aged 20–59 living alone in England and Wales were renting compared with less than 20 per cent of the total population aged 20–59. By 1991, however, the proportion of those living alone in privately rented accommodation had declined to less than one-quarter, while owner-occupation had increased from around a third to just under 60 per cent. Inner London stands out from the rest of the country as having a much higher proportion of privately rented accommodation and a lower proportion of owner-occupied accommodation. In the past especially, one-person households in London have been associated with the privately rented sector, where maximum flexibility is possible. In 1971, only 10 per cent of those living alone in Inner London aged 20–59 were in owner-occupation compared with 24 per cent of the total population. Nonetheless, Inner London is following the national trend over the twenty-year period of declining proportions of privately rented accommodation and increasing proportions of owner-occupation. By 1991, 39 per cent of those living alone in Inner London were in owner-occupation, compared with 45 per cent for the total population, a much smaller gap between the two groups than for the country as a whole. Despite this, many more people living alone in Inner London live in privately rented accommodation and fewer are owner-occupiers compared with the national figures for those living alone. It can be argued that the type of housing available in Inner London plays a part in making living alone an easier option compared to other areas in England and Wales.

In the Ville de Paris, there has also been a general increase in owner-occupation (from 18 per cent in 1962 to 28 per cent in 1990) and a general decline in the rented sector. The Parisian housing market has undergone profound changes in its geography, with increased *embourgeoisement* in the last three decades (Carpenter, Chauviré, and White 1994) comparable with London and New York in some respects (Carpenter and Lees 1995). The average number of rooms per dwelling increased from 2.24 in 1962 to 2.49 in 1990; the average number of persons per room declined from 1.02 to 0.77. There was also a rise in *pieds-à-terre* in Paris: by 1990 this newly established census category of *logements occasionnels* recorded almost 10 per cent of dwellings in the central *arrondissements*, indicating an increasing number of households split between central Paris and the provinces. These overall trends are fully reflected among one-person households: by 1990, 27 per cent were owner-occupiers, and, like Inner London, this is a level only slightly behind all households taken together.

Inner London and Paris stand out from the national picture, with one-person households in both cities having distinctive characteristics: they are younger and more likely to be in higher social classes, while the contrasts with the national picture are particularly marked for women.

MIGRATION

If one-person households have distinctive patterns by age, sex, and geography, do they also have distinctive migration trends? Can we demonstrate that the new, young, urban population living alone is, as we might expect, also highly mobile both geographically and socially? In order to try to answer this question, we have analysed data from the Longitudinal Study (LS) for England and Wales and the *Échantillon Démographique Permanent* (EDP) for France which allow us to compare household status at the two censuses (1981–91 and 1982–90 respectively) and to see which individuals migrated between the two dates. The methodology we adopted in both countries was to select those aged under 60 at the time of the latest census for longitudinal analysis, with a particular emphasis on London and Paris (discussed more fully in Ogden and Hall 1998).

England and Wales

The majority (88 per cent) of people living alone in England and Wales in 1991 were not living alone in 1981 and so had experienced a household transition (or change in household status) between the two dates. We can hypothesize that there is likely to be a relationship between mobility and the growth of one-person households. In a more general sense, the greater mobility of society—social and geographical—is responsible for the growth of non-family living. The creation of a new household in many cases is accompanied by geographical mobility, as when a child leaves the parental home to form a new household, or when a couple parts and at least one partner leaves to establish a separate household.

Geographical mobility and household transitions are closely linked but difficult to investigate and many studies of household transitions have largely ignored their spatial dimension and geographical impact (Grundy 1992*b*). One-person households may be the result of labour market demands: particular jobs may have high mobility requirements at the early stage of career development. The housing market may also encourage mobility: particular housing types and lifestyle possibilities may be found in particular areas of the city, attracting younger single people to them who choose to live alone.

If we examine household transitions and geographical mobility for LS members aged under 60 in 1991 and also present in 1981, we see that different transitions have different levels of mobility. Household transitions are clearly associated with increased rates of geographical mobility, and people who moved to live alone have the highest rates of geographical mobility, slightly more so for men than for women (Table 11.2).

Inner London has the highest proportion of in-migrants living alone of any region, with slightly more male than female in-migrants living alone. During this period, Inner London was also attracting the highest proportion of long-distance migrants to live alone of any region in England and Wales. Nationally, the age structure of male migrants living alone is

TABLE 11.2. *Proportion of movers by household transition category, men and women aged under 50 in 1981, England and Wales, 1981–1991*

	% who moved	% who moved more than 50 miles
MEN		
All transitions	63	14
To living alone in 1991	77	16
No change in household status[a]	51	13
Stayed living alone	53	16
WOMEN		
All transitions	55	14
To living alone in 1991	71	15
No change in household status[a]	52	13
Stayed living alone	49	14

[a b] Excluding those who remained living alone.

Source: ONS Longitudinal Study.

similar to that of all migrants, while female migrants living alone are older. By contrast, in-migrants living alone in Inner London are much younger than nationally and there is no gender difference in age structure: women living alone are as young as men. Long-distance migrants are even younger.

Large proportions of male and female migrants living alone are in the highest social class, with no major differences between men and women, although there is a clear gender difference in the social class structure of all migrants. Migrants to Inner London are more concentrated in the highest social class, with even higher proportions of migrants living alone in the highest social class (62 per cent of men and 53 per cent of women). Improvements in social class were particularly associated with those migrants living alone in 1991. This was the case for Inner London, where all migrants as well as those living alone improved their social class rather more than was the case in the country as a whole; female migrants living alone in 1991 showed the greatest increase in social class (Table 11.3*b*). These results add a further dimension to the work reported by Fielding and Halford (1993).

France

In France, people living alone in 1990 had been markedly more mobile than other household types at certain ages and in certain occupational

TABLE 11.3. *Change in social class, men and women aged under 50 in 1981, all migrants and migrants living alone in 1991, England and Wales and Inner London, 1981–1991*

(*a*) ENGLAND AND WALES

	All migrants		Migrants living alone in 1991	
	Males	Females	Males	Females
Stayed in same social class	80	80	73	71
Moved upward	15	13	19	21
Moved downward	6	7	8	8

(*b*) INNER LONDON

	All migrants		Migrants living alone in 1991	
	Males	Females	Males	Females
Stayed in same social class	72	73	70	67
Moved upward	22	21	20	28
Moved downward	6	6	9	5

Sources: ONS Longitudinal Study.

groups. Migration was greater for younger than older adults and greater for those under age 60. Mobility was higher for the higher socio-economic groups (see also Bonvalet and Lelièvre 1989) and in each case, higher for those living alone. Men living alone had generally migrated more than women, although for young adults under 40 the rates were very similar.

In Paris, some 50 per cent of the population had been living in a different dwelling in 1982. This rises to 84 per cent among 25–29-year-olds and to 91 per cent of that age group who were living alone in 1990. The most mobile occupational group was those who were by 1990 in managerial and professional jobs: 63 per cent had changed dwelling between 1982 and 1990 and 68 per cent of those living alone in 1990 had done so.

The *Échantillon Démographique Permanent* (EDP) allows us to look a little more closely at those who had migrated between 1982 and 1990. In France as a whole, migrants living alone were much more strongly represented in the professional and intermediate professional categories and this was marked for women—particularly in Paris, where female migrants living alone in 1990 were more likely than all migrants to be in professional or intermediate professional jobs. Higher proportions of migrants living alone were in the professional categories in 1990 compared with all migrants, with the contrast between all female migrants and female migrants living alone being particularly pronounced. At the same time, those living alone in 1990 were especially associated with upward social mobility. The professionalization of women was particularly pronounced among women who had migrated to Paris and were living alone in 1990. Again, the social process seems similar in both France and England and Wales, with the capital cities demonstrating their distinctive role.

Migrants living alone do, then, emerge as a distinctive subgroup although the differences are most apparent among those migrants living alone in Inner London and Paris. In both cities, women emerge as a particularly distinctive group, both compared with all migrants and with female migrants living alone in other regions of the country. We can see how young, professional adults are able, and more likely, to migrate to Inner London or Paris to obtain better jobs offered by the city, and this is especially true for women. Migration emerges as a key link between professionalization and one-person households, with the large amounts of rented property in Inner London and Paris providing the flexibility of the housing market necessary for high levels of in-migration. Thus, large cities in particular may function as 'escalator regions' attracting 'many upwardly mobile young adults living in single-person households' and then encourage 'their out-migration in nuclear family or empty-nest households to other regions in later middle age or at, or close to, retirement' (Fielding 1993: 158). This is similar to the idea of Paris as a filter developed in the work of Bonvalet and Lelièvre (1991). Our results indicate, however, that the growing tendency to live alone in all adult age groups may upset at least some of the assumptions of this model, in that an increasing number may stay put in the city.

EVIDENCE FROM QUALITATIVE SOURCES

The more detailed motivations and attitudes towards living alone can only be surmised from data such as the Longitudinal Study. Other sources allow us to explore in more depth possible motives for, and attitudes towards, living alone. First, we look briefly at British Household Panel Survey (BHPS) data which give some indication of the reasons for migration before using material from in-depth interviews in London to illustrate the variety both of reasons for migration and of living arrangements which lie behind census figures.

Reasons for migration

The British Household Panel Survey asks panel members whether a move between waves of the survey was primarily for employment-related reasons, and to give the first non-employment reason for migration. A much higher proportion of migrants living alone under pensionable age gave employment as the primary reason for their move—24 per cent of both males and females—compared with all migrants. The sample size for Inner London is too small to draw any real inferences from the data; nonetheless, it is interesting that 37 per cent of men compared with only 15 per cent of women living alone gave employment as the reason for their move.

Although employment emerges as an important reason for migrating, especially for those living alone, it is not as important as is often assumed. An analysis of the first non-employment reasons given for migrating by all BHPS members and those living alone reveal a number of interesting points. Housing reasons, which include eviction, moving to a larger or smaller property, or buying their own property, are the most important reasons given by everyone, but particularly by women living alone. It is predominantly the purchase of, or the move to, their own accommodation which sets apart women living alone from both men living alone and all migrants: 22 per cent of women give this as a reason for their move—double the figure for men and more than three times that of all migrants. Comparing all men and women and those living alone who give housing as the first non-employment reason for their move shows highly significant differences among them in the type of housing reason given. More men than expected cite eviction, rather fewer men and women than expected give moving to their own accommodation or buying accommodation as a reason, whereas many more women living alone than expected give this as a reason. Over 19 per cent of all migrants give partnership change as the first non-employment reason for moving, while for those living alone around a quarter give a move to or from college as the first non-employment reason. Over 12 per cent of women living alone give environment and change of area as the first non-employment reason, compared with only 7 per cent of men living alone and around 9 per cent of the total population.

These data suggest that for males and females living alone, although job reasons are important for migration, housing and personal reasons are also important. Relationship breakdown is more important for males living alone, while moving to their own accommodation, buying accommodation, and moving to a specific place are more important reasons for migration for women living alone. This can be summarized by saying that for women, the move to live alone is associated to a greater extent with personal choice, whereas for men it is the result of a change in job or changing personal circumstances.

Reasons for migration: in-depth interviews

The broad-brush reasons suggested by the BHPS are confirmed and amplified by twenty in-depth interviews carried out in the London Docklands, in Wapping and the Isle of Dogs, with people under retirement age living alone now or, in the case of two respondents, until very recently. Respondents ranged in age from 24 to 60 years and two-thirds were women. Earlier results from a postal questionnaire had revealed the importance of these groups in this very distinctive example of gentrification (Hall and Ogden 1992). The people interviewed are by no means representative of all people living alone in Inner London but simply serve to illustrate the complex interaction between housing, employment, and migration for a specific group identified as significant in Inner London: younger, professional in-migrants. The interviews were used to investigate changes in their living circumstances, reasons behind moves (particularly the extent to which their changing household arrangements were a result of deliberate choice), and degrees of satisfaction with their present living arrangements.

The majority of those interviewed could be described as very migratory, having moved to London often over long distances, and sometimes away from London before returning again, and then moving frequently within London. Only one was born in Inner London, two in Outer London, and a further two in the south-east of England. Several had moved from Scotland. The two main reasons given for moving to London were to take up a job and to enter higher education; a few women moved either with a man or to join a man in London and then looked for a job after they arrived. Several had moved abroad for some time: five had worked in the United States for between one and two years, three of them in New York.

Within London, moves were often frequent, demonstrating the importance of the flexibility of the housing market. Some had moved five or six times within London before their move to Docklands, and some had moved within Docklands, responding to their jobs, changing needs, or changing relationships. As one woman said, 'I have always been quite . . . it's never been long-term, two years is probably the longest I have lived anywhere. There have always been reasons for leaving, whether it's travelling, or in the Earl's Court case, it was the rent, too much' (13F40)[3], or another, 'I moved with jobs' (18F38).

Most had shared accommodation before living alone, and indeed sharing was often a decisive factor in deciding to live alone—'to be in a flat with four others was a real nightmare' (20F20)—although they needed to be able to afford either to rent or buy on their own. For most, the move to living alone was deliberate: only one said 'I didn't consciously decide I wanted to live on my own; various things were happening in his life [the life of the man she was sharing with] and he wanted to move on' (10F43). For some, the precipitating factor leading to living alone was divorce or separation, although women, especially after a divorce, often shared before they could afford the move to live alone. Some women were able to move into housing association shared-ownership flats. For example, one who had first moved to Docklands with her long-term partner was able to obtain a housing association flat by the river after her separation: 'I didn't look at anywhere else, I didn't have any money. It was all I could afford and it's a shoe box' (12F41). Another woman in her early thirties, the only interviewee born in East London, left home when she gained a housing association flat. Since she wanted to remain in the area but was not eligible for a council flat and could not afford to buy on her own, she jumped at the opportunity of shared ownership. Only a few, all men, discussed the desire to ascend the property ladder as a motive for moving. For example, a single man aged 31 said: 'what I would really like to do is invest in something bigger and better. This is my first purchase and as far as I know you just have to keep the pace up when you are moving if you want to own a nice property in 20 years' time' (5M31).

The decision to move to Docklands was made for a number of reasons. Most of those choosing to live in Docklands worked near the area, and indeed proximity to work was an important reason in the choice of location for many: 'it's on the riverside and walking distance to work, a short walk to Tower Bridge and £7 by cab to Covent Garden' (16M40). By contrast, another man acknowledged that he was unusual: 'because I work completely the other side of London, but clearly it [Docklands] caters for a lot of people who are in financial industries working in the City' (1M51).

For the majority, environmental factors were important in choosing where to live, in particular, proximity to the Thames, which was mentioned by almost all respondents as a reason for selecting Docklands. A woman solicitor employed in the City moved to a flat in Docklands following her divorce (and after a short period sharing a house). She selected her flat for its location: 'it's right on the river . . . I can actually sit and look at the river . . . it was the quality of light . . . it just gives you a feeling of space' (14F35). A woman investment banker made the decision to stop commuting and move to London after previously moving from Scotland to Guildford after her divorce: 'I just came up here for a drive one day and I liked the atmosphere and it was just handy for the office really, but I liked the idea of the river and water' (19F47). One who described her flat as 'my shoe box' added 'I couldn't live here if there were no views of the river' (12F41). Others mentioned the value for money: 'value for money in terms of accommodation . . . I found that the environment that I could find . . . was unbeatable compared with what else you could find in London' (1M51); 'the thing that attracted me was the quality of accommodation that you could purchase' (11F32).

Although there were many contrasts among them, the women living alone emerged as a distinctive group in terms of their employment: many were in well-paid City jobs, others in professional administrative jobs, and two had been in highly paid jobs before deciding to change direction and take degrees. One, now in her forties, had paid off her mortgage before she did so. The majority of women saw themselves as independent and mobile: 'I don't think I would ever live with someone else again without having somewhere to escape or some way of escaping' (14F35), and one of the women who had recently begun to cohabit still owned her flat in Paris and said, 'I can imagine living alone again . . . there are lots of good points to living alone, you can do what you want when you want' (17F30). She had moved around France before coming to London and certainly envisaged further moves, with the next probably to Tokyo. Certainly, the interviews add weight to the themes that emerged from analysis of the LS data—people living alone seem to epitomize a professional, independent, mobile lifestyle, facilitated by the nature of the housing and labour markets in cities such as London.

Attitudes towards living alone

The in-depth interviews also allow some insight into attitudes towards living alone, which are revealed partly by some of the reasons people gave for living alone. These emphasize the importance given to independence and freedom by those living alone, whether divorced or single. A divorced woman in her thirties said, 'I wanted my own thing and freedom to do exactly what I wanted; just not having anyone to report to is quite nice' (14F35), and a single woman of similar age said almost the same: 'It was just like the freedom of it really, come and go as I like' (15F37). A woman in her early twenties who did not envisage herself living alone for ever still said: 'I just wanted to come and go as I pleased and do my own thing for a bit' (20F24). One woman aged 35, whose partner usually stayed with her at weekends but who saw herself very much as living alone, albeit with frequent visitors, said: 'as you get older you just need your own space' (14F35). Another described her flat as 'my bolt-hole' (12F41). A divorced woman in her late forties thought personality was important: 'I think it's an interaction, a personality variable, having the money to do it I think . . . I have always been a very independent person from a very early age (19F47). A single man in his forties said: 'nobody would live with me . . . probably too selfish to live with anyone, but there isn't anyone I want to live with anyway for that long a period' (7M44).

The positive aspects of living alone were emphasized by almost all interviewees, particularly the need for space and time alone. For example: 'I find I do need the time and space on my own, I thoroughly enjoy it . . . I feel frustrated and inhibited if people impose on my space and assume that because I am on my own that I must want company, and I don't' (1M51); or 'I have no desire to move in with anyone' (3F46); 'you can deal with the loneliness by doing things like that, whereas you can't get rid of the [pause] it's much more difficult to deal with people who irritate you by not being tidy and things like that' (11F32). The pleasure of living alone was summed up by one man: 'I love it . . . it's rather like going on holiday' (7M44).

Negative aspects of living alone were mentioned by very few respondents: 'the downside of living on your own, I think, is that you have to make efforts to socialize' (16M40). One divorced woman spoke of her fears of living alone: 'when I did move in though, and the first time I had to live in the place on my own, I was petrified. It took months for me to settle in . . . it was just a bare shell. I didn't have any money . . . it was just like a white shell . . . a year ago, I just stopped worrying and relaxed and got used to it, now I'm delighted' (8F34). The anticipated fears of others were not realized: 'I thought I would be much more frightened at night, but I'm not' (3F46). The extra costs of living alone were only rarely discussed and then only by women: 'living alone is expensive because there is no one else to share all the bills' (20F24). Another woman who enjoyed being alone still said, 'it's absolutely stupid at the end of the day because it costs you more and it has its difficulties because you have to do everything, you have to do absolutely everything' (18F38).

No one we interviewed found it lonely to live alone, and indeed many had important relationships and spent part of their time with a partner, although they still considered themselves to be living alone. One man regularly visited his partner in Paris and she would also come and stay with him. A woman had a partner in West London but had no plans to move closer to him. One married man lived in Docklands during the week and went home at weekends, and only envisioned this changing when he retired. Others talked of frequent visitors: 'people drift in and out all the time' (18F38). This same interviewee spoke about when she first started to live alone: 'it did not feel like living on my own even though I was on my own' (18F38). Even so, the development of a particular lifestyle was also evident from some interviews. One woman spoke of the change in her attitudes around the age of 30: 'until the age of 30 there was always a man in my life . . . but around the age of 30 it all started to change and work took over in a way . . . and by the age of 35 I had come to the conclusion that I should knock it on the head and concentrate on work' (19F47). Another, who had not deliberately chosen to live alone, said, 'I really enjoy what I've got, my lifestyle, my home, and my garden' (10F43).

One of the more ambivalent respondents spoke of what she considered to be the selfish aspects of living alone, seeing it as part of a trend 'amongst certain groups of people, like any form of, for want of a better word, commitment, or staying with somebody is just a no-no'; she added, 'I don't think most people would do it out of choice for a long period of time because I think it's a very selfish way of living. It means you . . . don't have to think about other people. You can come and go as you please', but also said, 'I think it's important to kind of be individual, I think there are too many people who are dependent upon other people' (18F47).

POLICY IMPLICATIONS

Living alone is a desired option for many people and the trend to more individual living is likely to continue. The projected increase in numbers living alone under pensionable age seems unlikely to diminish markedly. In England, such households are projected to increase from 2.2 to 4.4 million between 1991 and 2011 (from 16 to 27 per cent of households under pensionable age); while in France, the projected increase in one-person households under 65 is from 3.4 to 4.2 million between 1990 and 2010 (from 20 to 22 per cent of households under age 65) (DoE 1995; Louvot 1994). Such increases in numbers living alone at younger ages have wide-ranging policy implications for both countries, although the pressures on land for new housing might be seen as greater in more densely populated England and Wales than in France. Nonetheless, the choices made by people living alone of geographical location and type of housing will have profound implications for land-use planning in both countries. Younger people are likely to continue to repopulate decaying inner urban areas but may also continue to move to more peripheral urban locations if transport links are good. There may be considerable differences in housing preference by age and social status within the working population living alone and we should not assume a false degree of homogeneity based simply on 'living alone'.

One of the questions asked in the report *Housing Growth: Where Shall We Live?* (DoE 1996) was 'Will one- and two-person households be more willing to live in smaller homes, especially flats in or near town centres?' Further questions included 'To what extent should a greater diversity of housing be provided to meet the needs of young and elderly people and, in particular, one- and two-person households?' and 'Do we need to encourage a more flexible and varied supply of homes to suit people's increasingly varied patterns of living?' Large-scale surveys are needed to answer such questions fully but our in-depth interviews in Docklands highlight some aspects of housing seen as important by younger people living alone.

Security was mentioned as vitally important by all of the women interviewed: 'the first thing for me is security . . . it has video entry, security guard and there is 24-hour security, underground car parking' (8F34); 'my flat is very secure as it is a converted block of flats and there is only one entry . . . I think it is very safe . . . I think it is quite a secure area' (11F32); 'when I come home at one in the morning it feels very secure' (14F35); 'I feel safe compared with Tottenham' (where she had lived previously) (4F35). One interviewee said that she looked only at flats above ground floor because she did not want to live at ground-floor level or in a house due to security problems.

Ease of maintenance and care was also very important: 'my flat is very easy because it's brand new and easy to keep clean' (15F37); 'you just come home and it's like a nice little friend, it makes no demands' (19F47). Although a number of interviewees were living in one-bedroom flats, the majority had at least two bedrooms and indeed specified that they needed a spare room in order to accommodate frequent visitors. Our research, then, provides an answer to at least one of the questions posed in *Housing growth: Where Shall We Live?*: an increase in one-person households will not necessarily mean a decrease in the desired size of accommodation. Even those living in one-bedroom flats because they could afford nothing bigger expressed a desire for more space. The demands of one-person households will almost certainly require more diversity in housing type, with particular emphasis on security.

Other important issues included accessibility to work, especially for people working long hours. In general, they were willing to forgive Docklands' lack of amenities, although they acknowledged that there had been an increase in supermarkets, which made daily living easier. Our interviewees were people who had busy social lives and who ate out regularly, but at least some felt that the new housing developments had had little impact on the wider area: 'I couldn't live here if I wasn't always out. There is no infrastructure' (12F41).

The particular consumption patterns of one-person households, of retail, leisure, and other service sectors, are likely to contribute to changing local economies, albeit slowly, as shown in Docklands. The continued atomization of society into smaller households has wider societal implications. The interviews suggest different patterns of social interaction from those of family households. There was almost no social interaction within the local area: hardly any had friends living locally and only one had family nearby. Nevertheless, the majority had active social lives. The need to be on one's own was balanced by a need to go out: 'I can go out to other parts of London and have a lot of fun and then come back and be on my own and be peaceful and do my own thing—a bit of a retreat' (11F32).

CONCLUSION

In this chapter, we have shown the growing significance of one-person households among younger people in both England and Wales and France. These younger one-person households are particularly concentrated among the professional and managerial classes and more of them now own their own property rather than follow the traditional pattern of renting. We have also shown the particular geographies of these younger one-person households, with Inner London and Paris having the greatest concentration of such households, particularly among those under age 40 and in the highest social classes. There are gender differences in one-person living, with the trends being most pronounced among men. However, numbers of women living alone are also increasing, and such women are even more likely than men to be in higher social classes. One-person households have distinctive mobility patterns and they are particularly attracted to the capitals in both England and Wales and France. The in-depth interviews help to illuminate both reasons for migrating and for choosing to live alone.

Some sense of people's attitudes towards living alone can also be gleaned from this research. There was little sense of discontent with what for most was a chosen and, indeed, enjoyable lifestyle. A theme of many interviews was the flexibility and fluidity of household arrangements, where lifestyle rather than household structure dominated living arrangements. Choice, freedom, and independence were often mentioned by the women particularly; as one said, 'this is my choice of how I want to live' (3F46); or another, 'I don't think I would ever, ever live with someone else again without having somewhere to escape, or some way of escaping' (14F35).

These changes in the way people choose to live are unlikely to be reversed. Changing ways of living, including living alone, are facts to which we have to respond. One answer to the questions posed in *Housing Growth: Where Shall We Live?* is that greater flexibility is needed. However, the impact of larger numbers of people living alone will not solely be in terms of their impact in physical planning terms, or in housing, but will have repercussions also for localities, local services, lifestyles, and communities.

NOTES

1. Most of the discussion in this chapter is confined to England and Wales, with only occasional reference to Britain as a whole. One of the major data sets used is the ONS Longitudinal Study, which is restricted to England and Wales.
2. The population base used in 1991 was different from the one used in 1981. In 1981 the usually resident population included residents 'enumerated in households and communal establishments and also absent residents from households with at least one person present in the household. It excluded wholly absent households'. The 1991 Census base for the 'usually resident population' included the estimated (imputed) numbers of usually resident members of wholly absent households where no form was returned or no contact was made and so is not directly comparable to the 1981 base. OPCS has defined another population base for 1991, in order to make more direct comparisons with 1981, which includes only those residents of households where someone was present on census night and excludes any imputed households. Even these comparisons are affected by the different proportions of people missing from each census as well as other small variations, and very few 1991 tables use the 1981 base. One-person households are more likely to be absent on census night and therefore to have their values imputed. Around a half of all imputed households are one-person households. In addition, a higher proportion of all one-person households are imputed compared to all households (3.9 per cent and 2.1 per cent respectively).
3. The interview references begin with a numerical identifier, followed by an M or F indicating sex and a number indicating age.

12

Families of choice: autonomy and mutuality in non-heterosexual relationships

Jeffrey Weeks, Brian Heaphy, and Catherine Donovan

INTRODUCTION

The contemporary debate about the family is often presented in terms of a polarity. On the one hand there is an image of mutuality, interdependence, and resilience, represented by an ideal type of the family. Although it is widely acknowledged that the family may have changed radically over the years, at its most evocative this ideal type represents a haven of trust, mutual involvement, and shared responsibilities that many argue offers the best hope for a communitarian culture (Etzioni 1995). On the other hand, set against this is a vivid picture of the search for autonomy, for an individual fulfilment that often eschews commitment, and is the product of an individualistic and hedonistic culture (see, for example, Davies 1993; Dennis and Erdo 1993; Dench 1996*b*). Inevitably, the triumph of the latter ethos is seen as corroding and ultimately undermining the former. The quest for autonomy apparently undermines mutuality, and the well-advertised ills of contemporary society are the inevitable result.

In this stark scenario, non-heterosexual (lesbian, gay, bisexual) lifestyles are often presented as the exemplars of the striving for autonomy over the obligations of family, precisely because in the familiar stereotypes, homosexuality is lived outside, and in contradiction to, the ordinary exigencies of domestic life. Historically, of course, there might appear to be an element of truth in this. Non-heterosexuals, as is widely acknowledged, have often had to struggle for a sense of self against the norms of

This paper is based on research conducted for a project funded by the ESRC entitled 'Families of Choice: The Structure and Meanings of Non-heterosexual Relationships', Grant No. L315253030. The director of the project was Jeffrey Weeks, with Catherine Donovan and Brian Heaphy as research fellows. We are grateful to everyone who took part in the research process, to whom we have guaranteed confidentiality and anonymity. The interpretations of the interview data are, of course, our own.

heterosexual family life, and recent changes in social attitudes have accentuated in many ways a sharp sense of difference. The growing public presence of lesbians and gays since the late 1960s has, indeed, led to a strong assertion of individual rights and identity, encouraged and sustained by the emergence of a social movement asserting and affirming positive lesbian and gay ways of life (see Weeks 1996).

The contention of this paper, however, is that alongside this quest for autonomy, non-heterosexual people are also establishing complex patterns of relationships, often using the term 'family' in a broad sense, which reveal the development of new forms of mutual involvement and support. We call these 'families of choice'. As one sign of this, political campaigns around homosexuality have extended beyond traditional preoccupations with equal rights and legal protection to embrace questions about relationships: about the legal recognition of partnership rights, same-sex marriage, equal rights to adoption, and wider issues about non-heterosexual parenting. On one level, this can be seen as an inevitable consequence of the cultural acceptance, and social embeddedness, of the lesbian and gay community as part of a growing pluralization of society. On another level, however, these changing preoccupations can be seen as an aspect of a broadening debate about the meaning of 'family life', as part of a growing awareness of a wider transformation of relationships (Giddens 1992; Beck and Beck-Gernsheim 1995) which cut across the heterosexual–homosexual division. Despite the particularism of the homosexual experience, one of the most remarkable features of domestic change over recent years is, we would argue, the emergence of common patterns in both homosexual and heterosexual ways of life as a result of long-term shifts in relationship patterns (cf. Bech 1997). In both, it can be argued, the central drive is the search for satisfactory relationships as a key element in personal affirmation. In line with this analysis, we would argue that non-heterosexual patterns, far from representing a triumph of an individualistic ethos, reflect a search for forms of life which allow for both individual fulfilment and mutual involvement.

Yet, while there is an increasing recognition and acceptance of the existence of 'alternative families', differentiated by class, 'race' and ethnicity, life-cycle, single parenthood, chosen lifestyles, and the like (Weeks 1991), there is a continuing stigma attached to non-heterosexual forms. Throughout the Western world, the legitimacy of non-heterosexual relationships has become a major topic of political controversy, despite, or perhaps because of, the growing evidence that non-heterosexual women and men are establishing sophisticated social forms with that sense of involvement, security, and continuity over time which is traditionally associated with the orthodox family.

Until very recently there has been little empirical research that explores these 'families of choice', especially with reference to the British experience (Weeks, Donovan, and Heaphy 1996). This lack of sustained empirical research has been matched by uncertainty in the theorization of elective families (but see Weston 1991), and their relationship to wider social trends. In this paper, we attempt to address both these deficiencies, by analysing new empirical data on non-heterosexual forms of relationships[1] in the context of theoretical debates about the wider 'transformation of intimacy' (Giddens 1992). Put briefly, our argument is that new narratives about non-heterosexual ways of being have emerged and are in ever-growing circulation. These both reflect, and help realize, new possibilities—of friendship, chosen kin, egalitarian relationships, and commitment. Any attempt to understand the contemporary family must necessarily come to terms with the existence of chosen families, of which the non-heterosexual form is the clearest example.

NEW FAMILY STORIES

We are witnessing, we would argue, the emergence of new ways of conceiving of family and intimate life, which emphasize simultaneously the realization of individual needs and the mutuality involved in patterns of intimacy and trust. Plummer, among others, has conceptualized these developments in terms of the circulation of new narrative forms, or 'stories', that are significantly reshaping the ways in which we conceive of intimate life. He argues that

> Society itself may be seen as a textured but seamless web of stories emerging everywhere through interaction: holding people together, pulling people apart, making societies work . . . the metaphor of the story . . . has become recognised as one of the central roots we have into the continuing quest for understanding human meaning. Indeed culture itself has been defined as 'an ensemble of stories we tell about ourselves'. (Plummer 1995: 5)

If this is the case, then the emergence of new ways of expressing basic needs and desires ('new stories') may be seen as highly important, and deserving of serious sociological investigation. They are indicative both of changing perceptions and of changing possibilities. New stories about sexual and intimate life emerge, it may be argued, when there is a new audience ready to hear them in communities of meaning and understanding, and when newly vocal groups can have their experiences validated in and through them. This in turn gives rise to new demands for recognition and validation as the new narratives circulate. These demands may be the expressions of a minority, but they resonate with broader changes in intimate life.

In the case of the non-heterosexual world, there is both a growing audience, in the burgeoning lesbian and gay communities themselves, and an emergence of many individuals willing to vocalize new experiences. This has led to a conscious presentation of the viability of non-heterosexual ways of life. Consider, for example, this comment from a gay man in response to a question about why he was willing to be interviewed:

> because I think it's a really interesting project, and I think that one of the things that socially always happens is that lesbians and gay men are made into individuals with sad lives who are lonely . . . and I'm really looking forward to there being something that says, 'There are all these lesbian and gay men, and they're living completely connected lives, and they have got support, they have got community, and they're doing things, better than the heterosexual world, because they created this thing for themselves'. (M11)

Clearly, such a response raises important methodological issues, in terms of a subject's expectations, the kind of story that might be told, and the assumptions about the researchers' sympathies (Heaphy, Donovan, and Weeks 1998). Yet the fact that the subject wants to tell a happy story about relationships also gives us important insights into the new narratives that are emerging about families of choice, and the ways in which these stories are becoming part of a collective identity. We can see here two major themes that recur constantly in the stories of non-heterosexual women and men: an emphasis on self-creation, and therefore choice, in the development of alternative life patterns; and a stress on the importance of affirming positive identities and 'connected lives'—both set against a belief that, in spite of significant changes, the culture still fails to validate non-heterosexual lives.

CREATING CONNECTED LIVES

A family, a young lesbian comments, 'should provide support, acceptance of who you are and what you want to do' (F13). If the family of origin fails you, or even when it does not, alternatives must 'always be there to help you . . . my friends provide that . . . that's what I think a family should be and that's what these friends are for me' (F13). Many non-heterosexuals, therefore, stress the importance of creative choice in shaping their friendship patterns: 'I take my family [of origin] for granted, whereas my friendships are, to a degree, chosen and therefore they're created. And I feel a greater responsibility to nourish them' (M21). The narrative of self-invention is a very powerful one among our respondents, particularly in relation to self-identity and lifestyle. As a gay man in his late thirties put it: 'speaking from my generation . . . discovering that I was homosexual meant having to invent myself because there was nothing there . . . there weren't any role models. It may well be different for gay men coming out now . . . But there's still that element of self-invention' (M17–18). This story of creating your own life is widely echoed in the theoretical literature (for example, Foucault 1979; Giddens 1992; Weeks 1995) and reflects a perceived reality in the contemporary world of fluid identities. It particularly relates, however, to the narratives of many non-heterosexual women and men who see themselves as breaking away from the constraints of traditional institutional patterns which deny their sexuality and identity.

The recognition of the importance of such narratives of the self shaped our research, underlining in particular the importance of identity as itself a choice. Though same-sex desires may or may not be seen as inherent rather than socially formed, the identities organized around such desires are very much culturally contingent, as is well recognized by many non-heterosexuals. Here, for example, are a male couple responding to a question about whether they identify as gay:

A: I don't know what to call myself.
S: . . . nowadays it's hip to be queer . . . being gay . . . only exists through homophobia. I mean if homophobia didn't exist then being gay wouldn't exist . . . It's kind of like a reaction . . . But I suppose just generally for the sake of everyday use, I'd probably say, yeah, gay . . .
A: I don't know what I call myself.
S [to A]: You know, people have different names, different places at different times . . . from being homosexual to being . . . poofs or queers or gay or whatever . . .
A: But I'll tag along with gay, that's all. OK? (M37–8)

Similarly, a female couple when asked had doubts about the appropriate self-description:

S: I think I would call myself a lesbian definitely.
J: I can't answer it.
S: J isn't . . . you know. (F04–05)

Such reflexive accounts can be insightful in terms of the stories of identity that people can and cannot tell. They allow researchers to observe the extent to which cultural and even political motivations may influence the kind of story about self-identity that can be told. They also, of course, show the ways in which the researcher's own desire to categorize can force a subject to fit himself or herself into available identifications and categories (for a fuller discussion see Heaphy, Donovan, and Weeks 1998). It is because of the multiple forms of identity that potentially exist that we opted for the generic term 'non-heterosexual' rather than the more familiar 'homosexual', 'lesbian', or 'gay'—while recognizing its somewhat clinical nature.

Although the researcher has the inevitable urge to classify, the reality is of a more fluid, complex co-existence of various personal (and collective) identities. In our analysis, therefore, we have attempted to be honest to self-descriptions. By emphasizing these, the researcher is faced by the challenge, and possibilities, of accounting for the messy realities of people's lives and self-narratives. But whatever the fluidity and contingency of identity, it is apparent that a sense of self is confirmed through involvement with others, so that narratives of the self and narratives of chosen families are often inextricably interconnected: 'because I can't think of myself as being anything other than a gay man, having those friendships and support networks, I suppose, is extremely important. I think I'd be a very sad and pathetic person without them' (M05).

For many non-heterosexuals, the idea of a *chosen* family is a powerful affirmation of a new sense of belonging, and an essential part of asserting the validity of homosexual identities and ways of life. This does not mean that non-heterosexuals deny parallels with heterosexual life, just that the achievement of alternative forms has a different significance: 'I get a hell of a lot of support and understanding [from friends]; I mean, they know everything about me and they still accept me' (F13). In other words, the assertion of the positive value of non-heterosexual relationships has a political and cultural meaning for our subjects which transcends their mundane reality. Positive narratives have both individual and cultural effects.

Our emphasis on the importance of these narratives of intimate life and identity has profound implications for the nature of research into personal life. As Duncombe and Marsden (1996) note, until relatively recently sociologists have viewed problems of researching the private sphere as primarily a tactical one of 'interview method'. The aim, put simplistically, is to develop techniques which will provide access to the truths of experience held by the subject. That assumes, however, that the truth is readily available, and that the researcher is merely a conduit for the revelation of that truth. But if our aim is to understand the significance of the narrative being shaped for us, and to be reflexively aware that the interviewer is him/herself a participant in that shaping, then we must recognize that the interview, or group discussion, is being constructed within the interaction itself (see Steier 1991). What we are hearing are not only data about lives but ways of talking about experience, talking which includes aspiration, self-confirmation, politics, and values as well as empirical truth (although, inevitably, talking itself conveys its own form of truth).

We cannot claim, therefore, that our findings reveal the sole, essential, or comprehensive truth about non-heterosexual life today, in the sense that everyone's life is like this. That was not our intention, nor do we believe that it is possible in the way in which the issue is often posed. Our claim is both more modest, and perhaps more theoretically and methodologically interesting: that the new stories about families of choice tell us something important about ways in which social actors see the development of both the non-heterosexual world and the heterosexual world, and how they shape their lives accordingly. They reveal the *processes* by which our subjects give meaning to their daily lives and relationships. Plummer (1995: 171) distinguishes between three ways of testing the validity of accounts. The first, the correspondence theory, assumes a matching of the story with things that can be documented. The second, the aesthetic theory, is concerned with the grace and elegance, the literary effectiveness of a narrative and with new ways of telling them. But, Plummer argues, there is a third and more effective way of analysing accounts, which partly builds on the last point, but goes further—to take them seriously in their own right, not as historical truth (though historical truths do become apparent through them) but as narrative truth. And here the research objective is not so much to demonstrate final truths but rather to understand the consequences of telling a particular story under specific circumstances: what can be said, why it is said now and not at other times, and the effects of telling a particular story in a particular way. This is what Plummer calls the 'pragmatic connection', by which '*stories can now be examined for the roles they play in lives, in contexts, in social order*' (Plummer 1995: 172). Our argument is that stories about families of choice are opening new ways of thinking and living friendships and partnerships which are transforming the meaning of family.

FRIENDS AS FAMILY

The most common non-heterosexual relationship story is about friendships. As Nardi (1992: 115) puts it, in the gay community 'at the core of the concept of friendship is the idea of "being oneself" in a cultural context that may not approve of that self'. In the accounts of non-heterosexuals, friends provide emotional and material support, but also affirm identity and belonging, leading to a wide acceptance of the idea of 'friends as family': 'I think the friendships I have are family' (F02); 'we call each other family—you know, "they're family" . . . I have a blood family, but I have an extended family . . . my friends' (M04); 'it's like family really—very much so. Just to know we're going to stick together, no matter what . . . not everyone has got that in their lives' (F32).

It is important to note that the term 'family' is being used here in the broadest sense. It might embrace domestic patterns which include care for children or other dependants, but that is not the exclusive meaning. More generally, it is used to include friends and partners as well as blood relatives. Friendship circles are often perceived as being akin to the idealized family, offering 'companionship, love, respect' (M04); 'a feeling of belonging to a group of people who like me' (M05); 'pleasure in someone's company, new ideas, laughter, continuity' (F21). Friendships provide the 'lifeline' that the biological family, it is believed, should provide, but often cannot or will not for its homosexual offspring.

Because of the perceived problems with traditional families, the term 'family' is sometimes vigorously avoided, especially by older respondents: 'I think I'm just a bit outdated with feeling there's a difference with blood relatives, who often aren't actually as reliable, in fact' (F30). Yet many of our respondents believe that friendship circles can provide what the family of origin lacks:

> I think the way that I think about those people is the way that, you know, generally, people would regard family. Because they're people that I trust; people that I share things with—whether they be good or bad. I share my thoughts, I share my feelings with them. I share lots of the aspects of my life with them and they are the people I would go to if I was in trouble or if I was sick or if I needed money, or whatever. And I know that . . . that they would be there for me . . . with an element of caring that my actual family, I don't think, would have . . . (F01)

Recent studies have suggested that most people still make a basic distinction between friends and kin in terms of obligation and commitment (see, for example, Roberts and McGlone 1997), and this is also apparent among some of our respondents. But friendship has a meaning and depth that goes beyond its conventional implications: 'for my part I don't have friendships on the level that I think heterosexuals have friendships. I think my friendships are more intense' (F43). On the surface, at least, this lends credence to the idea that for many people friendships offer surrogate or 'pretend' families: substitutes for the real thing. But this is not how a large number of our respondents see the significance of their relationships. Weston (1991), analysing data from a study conducted in California, has concluded that in creating 'families we choose', lesbians and gays are involved neither in imitating heterosexual families nor in necessarily replacing or substituting a family of choice for a family of origin. Like Weston's research, our own suggests strongly that for many of our subjects the family of choice, embracing a variety of selected relationships that might include lovers, ex-lovers, and intimate friends, as well as selected members of the family of origin, is just like kin.

Weston (1991) herself has explored the value of the anthropological concept of 'fictive kin' in understanding these forms. The idea of fictive kin or 'continuous family' (Rapp 1987: 178) has been used to describe the way in which African-American, Native American, and white working-class families in the USA expand their kinship networks by absorbing friends and neighbours into them. There are obvious parallels with the non-heterosexual world, where the idea of a sexual community (Weeks 1996) provides some of the same elements of support as a working-class or ethnic neighbourhood, though not necessarily through geographical propinquity:

> in a general sense you could say that [town]'s lesbian and gay community is family in a funny way too . . . they can be family. There are times when, you know, you feel very, this is where you want to be, and those are the people you want to talk to and be around . . . when you first think that . . . you're the only one out there and there's not many others, and then you suddenly discover there's loads—that's a great feeling, and you want to encompass that in some way. (F22)

However, the fictive-kin concept still assumes the blood family as the starting point, whereas for many lesbians and gay men it is precisely the ambiguous relationship with family of origin that is the problem. A more useful starting point may be to conceive of elective families as a new social form, an index of changing social possibilities and demands. They build on historical experience. They are in many ways like changing patterns of friendship, having much in common with the extended networks of support created by other marginalized groups. But they can also be understood as examples of what Giddens (1992) conceptualizes as the 'everyday experiments in living' that people are required to undertake in an ever more complex world (for a discussion of this see Weeks, Donovan, and Heaphy 1998). This is certainly how a number of respondents describe the situation: 'we're constantly experimenting with just how far we want to go, and sometimes feel that we have some degree of mobility in a given situation . . . It's not so much political flag-waving, it's just doing what we want to do and trying to push the boundaries a bit, to see how people cope with it' (M21). As Weston has argued, what is new for homosexuals is less the necessity of building supportive networks than the historical possibility of realizing them: 'Only after coming out to blood relatives emerged as a historical possibility could the element of selection in kinship become isolated in gay experience and subsequently elevated to a constitutive feature of gay families' (Weston 1991: 110–11).

These life experiments, in the context of a major transformation of the possibility of living non-heterosexual lives, give rise to fluid and adaptable networks, at the core of which are selected friends. These relationships are sometimes created across class and ethnic barriers, and are frequently intergenerational. They are also generally non-hierarchical, in the sense that, given the frequent absence of children, there is no perceived ordering along lines of age, precedence, or role division. This is not to say that there are no disparities of income or personal or social power, or any absence of potential conflict. Such divisions are not, however, intrinsic to the relationships.

Like many friendship networks, there appears to be a tendency towards social homogeneity. Often they are single-sex: a number of male respondents claimed not to know many lesbians, and vice versa. In the nature of things, friendships often stretch across the homosexual–heterosexual binarism, though the inner core tend to be both homosocial and homosexual: 'I actually think I spend time with lesbians, I live around communities with lesbians, and I don't socialize generally in straight places. Or if I go, I go with lesbians' (F28).

Within such networks a distinctive ethos prevails (Blasius 1995), based around common experiences and self-knowledge, which shapes ongoing involvements: 'I suppose a lot of it comes down to choices—lesbian women have thought so much about where they are and what they're doing and hetero people avoid thinking [laughter] half the time, or seem to' (F33).

NEGOTIATING COMMITMENT

As same-sex relationships are constructed and maintained outside conventional institutional and legal support systems and structures, they are less likely than traditional patterns to be characterized by predetermined obligations, duties, and commitments. On the other hand, this should not be taken to indicate any lack of concern with such concepts. The overwhelming consensus among our subjects was that such issues were vitally important but were necessarily a matter of free and conscious choice that made for stronger bonds: 'I would like to think that people in gay relationships stay together because they actually want to stay together to a greater extent than people in heterosexual relationships do' (M15). This implies an active process through which commitments are constantly negotiated and renegotiated between equals, with the intention of recognizing both individual autonomy and shared responsibilities. This, we would suggest, is an aspect of wider developments which are shaping conventional kin involvements. Finch and Mason (1993), for example, have demonstrated the intricate processes by which responsibilities between kin are negotiated in the contemporary world, rather than seen as necessary obligations. They suggest that although ties to family of origin remain highly significant, they cannot be presumed, and are as much a product of 'working out' as of blood. The authors use the concepts of 'developing commitments' and of a sense of responsibility that is worked out over time to explain these processes, so that while kin relationships remain distinctive, the extent to which they differ from other relationships, particularly friendships, is blurred. Commitments, they suggest, are likely to feel particularly strong precisely because they are developed in negotiation with specific others. This is clearly of great significance in relationship to non-traditional commitments.

It is striking in this context that many of our respondents avoid the language of obligation, which they see as being about duty, something imposed from outside. Duty is 'Like some kind of moral code that people use to put on you . . . I don't think I need that kind of external thing put on me' (F04). Obligation and duty are compared unfavourably with the concepts of responsibility, mutual care, and commitment:

> Responsibility is something I decide to do and I keep to; obligation is when I feel I have to . . . (F01)

> duty is something that is imposed on you . . . if you feel responsible for someone . . . then you do that because you feel you want to, not because somebody else feels you ought to . . . (M44)

> the more I'm involved with someone, the greater the sense of responsibility, but it's always sort of commensurate on the degree of closeness, not dependent on whether they're family or not. (F29)

Ideas of care and responsibility appear to be situational, dependent on the needs of parent and blood relatives, as well as of friends, but the values themselves are potent, organized around notions of 'the right thing to do', especially with regard to parents and children: 'If my friends were ill I wouldn't feel obliged to care for them, I'd want to. But my mum and dad don't have that [that is, friends] . . . they did it for me when I was a bairn so, you know' (M11).

In the same way, in situations involving care for children, there is a strong sense of absolute obligation—that children's needs must come first, even if that endangers adult relationships: 'I would actually care for my daughter and my son. And my granddaughter . . . It's actually something I would want to do' (F28). Chosen relationships, however, have the potential to be free of imposed obligations, and therefore, are likely to be more intense:

> you have to find out who you are as a gay man. Because nobody ever tells you or teaches you . . . you have to be as hard as nails to be out there and survive, and . . . you build very intense relationships by peeling those layers of hard lacquer off yourself, very selectively, and with certain people. So I think they are much deeper and more intense relationships, perhaps . . . (M03)

For many gay men particularly, the experience of the AIDS crisis has confirmed the importance of a commitment to care and mutual responsibility: 'It makes some relationships more intense because they are inevitably going to be foreshortened' (M03). The AIDS epidemic has focused attention on the need for mutuality in an unprecedented way in the lesbian and gay community, but many other aspects of contemporary life, from the 'fateful moment' (Giddens 1992) of identity affirmation or 'coming out' to the complexities involved in childrearing, pose a similar challenge. It is not surprising, therefore, that the dominating element in the narratives of families of choice is the recognition of the need for 'some kind of connection with each other . . . [which] isn't quite about obligation . . . it's when the commitment or the connection goes somewhere beyond just social things or somewhere beyond—I almost want to say somewhere beyond choice' (F21).

FRIENDS AS PARTNERS

If friendship circles provide the wider context for the working-out of commitments, it is in one-to-one partnerships that the challenges are frequently most acutely experienced. Overwhelmingly, our subjects believe that non-heterosexual ways of life offer opportunities for more equal and fulfilling relationships than are available to most heterosexuals: 'I'd like to think that lesbians and gays tend to have a much more equal relationship. Much more understanding, too, because of similar gender and similar experiences' (F40–1; for a fuller discussion see Heaphy, Donovan, and Weeks 1998). There are also significant sociological accounts, of course, which indicate that the search for the 'pure relationship', with its concomitant notion of 'confluent love', is increasingly true for relations between men and women, largely as a result of the changing role of women and the 'transformation of intimacy' (Giddens 1992; Beck and Beck-Gernsheim 1995; Weeks 1995). The pure relationship suggests a constant striving for intimacy between equals, a social relation entered into for its own sake, for what can be derived by each person from a sustained association with another; and which is continued only as long as it is thought by both partners to deliver enough satisfaction for each individual to stay within it. Confluent love as an aspect of this presumes equality in emotional give-and-take, the more so the more any particular love tie approximates closely to the prototype of the pure relationship. Love here only develops to the degree that intimacy does, to the degree to which each partner is prepared to reveal cares and needs to the other and to be vulnerable to that other (Giddens 1992: 61–2).

While this thesis has been widely challenged on the grounds that it ignores the continuing ingrained difficulties of attaining real equality in male and female relationships, our research strongly suggests that many non-heterosexual men and women have consciously shaped their relationships in the light of this ideal, and in opposition to traditional marriage:

as far as I'm concerned, marriage or partnership rights, or whatever you want to call it, is about ownership—and I do not want to own another person. I don't want that at all. I'll be responsible for my own relationship but I will not own someone. And I think it's very strange that there are women who think that this is a good thing. Because marriage has never been in women's interests—ever. And I don't quite see how doing it with another woman or two men doing it with each other is going to make anything any different. (F02)

The assumption, among men as well as women, is that 'it's much easier to have equal relations if you're the same sex' (M31) because this equalizes the terms of the intimate involvement. As one of our lesbian subjects says, 'The understanding between two women is bound to be on a completely different wavelength' (F33). A male subject put it in this way: 'I think there is . . . less a kind of sense of possession, or property, in same-sex relationships, and more emphasis on . . . emotional bonding . . . that's not quite what I mean, but they're less ritualized really . . . I think that kind of creates a necessity for . . . same-sex relationships to kind of find their own identity' (M39). Or in the words of a lesbian respondent: 'I think there is a kind of empathy that I can't ever imagine having with a man' (F06). Equal standing means that issues around, for example, the division of labour in the household are seen to be a matter for discussion and agreement, not a priori assumption, because of 'being able to negotiate, being on an equal level to be able to negotiate in the first place' (M04); 'Everything has to be discussed, everything is negotiable' (F29) (cf. Tanner 1978; Blumstein and Schwartz 1983; McWhirter and Mattison 1984; Dunne 1997; Heaphy, Donovan, and Weeks 1998). There is, of course, plentiful evidence as well that egalitarian relations do not automatically develop. They have to be constantly struggled for against inequalities of income, day-to-day commitment, emotional labour, ethnic difference, and the like. Inequality of income is perhaps the most frequently divisive factor, especially as for some couples, sharing income or even ownership of a home was not only practically but emotionally difficult. Whatever the practical difficulties, however, there is a strong emphasis among our respondents on the importance of building intimate-couple involvement: 'being in a relationship helps to affirm one as a person and we all need that' (M44); 'I love the continuity . . . I like the sex. I like doing some things jointly . . . A sense that you are loveable' (F06). The underlying assumption is that this intimacy is achievable because of the possibility of egalitarian relationships that same-sex relationships offer. Dunne, in her study of lesbian relationships (1997: 200 ff.), makes a useful distinction between the 'intimate strangers' of heterosexual marriage and the 'intimate friendships' that characterize many lesbian relationships. This is the ideal of many of our subjects, male as well as female.

THE NATURAL CAREERS OF NON-HETEROSEXUAL COUPLES

Several American studies have attempted to investigate what might be called the 'natural careers' of lesbian and gay couples. Harry and DeVall (1978) suggest the absence of predictable patterns because of the lack of institutional expectations. Others, however, have attempted typologies. Laner (1977) divides homosexual couples into 'parallel' and 'interactional' types, the former suggesting independent lives, while the latter share a single world. Bell and Weinberg (1978) divide their male partnerships into 'closed couples' and 'open couples', while Silverstein (1981) offers 'excitement seekers' and 'home builders'. Tanner's (1978) study of lesbian couples suggested three prototypes: the 'traditional-complementary', the 'caretaking', and the 'negotiated-egalitarian'. McWhirter and Mattison (1984), in their study of 156 male couples, present the most extensive typology, with a six-stage model of relationship careers, from 'blending' and 'nesting' to 'releasing' and 'renewing'.

While each of these models no doubt exists, we would argue both that no single model can capture the complexity and fluidity of non-heterosexual patterns, and that the norm is the democratic-egalitarian model, which in fact suggests diversity of life choices within a common framework. The critical point is that each of these forms of commitment has to be negotiated, and although these negotiations may follow relatively well-defined pathways, the end result is not predetermined. The will and wish to go on is the most vital component:

> It's very fluid—and like we were saying about being monogamous or not—we're neither. There's no point in making a commitment to something that you don't know you can be committed to. And there's a lot of changes in the boundaries of our relationship and I'd much rather keep it as something fluid than commit to one thing and not be able to keep that commitment. (F14–15)

Inevitably, given the absence of an institutional framework, there is a recognition of a certain contingency in lesbian and gay relationships, but many see this as a positive rather than negative factor:

> I think it's an advantage for lesbian relationships that there isn't a kind of whole structure built around them, like marriage or whatever, because it allows you to be freer within the relationship to build the relationship that you want. And that's why I don't want public recognition in the way of any kind of ceremony or anything like that for lesbian relationships. (F06–07)

Yet a recognition that relationships do not last for ever does not mean they cannot be worked at 'as if' they will last: 'we've never, ever said that, you know, till death us do part. But we do plan . . . while the relationship is going well, we will be planning long-term. Because you can't keep planning short-term and expect long-term things to sort themselves out' (F06–07).

Commitment based on mutual trust is seen as the key to sustaining a relationship (cf. Weeks 1995), and this is not dependent on any institutional backing: 'Why do I need a licence to commit myself to somebody? The very idea is really quite abhorrent' (F43); 'we were very insistent when we had our meeting of thankfulness, that this was not a form of marriage and it was not creating a relationship or commitment because the commitment had been there for nine years' (M44). The commitment takes many forms, from sexual to domestic involvement, and there appears to be no common pattern. Sexual attraction may be the first step towards mutual involvement, but it is not necessarily the decisive factor. When asked if his relationship was primarily sexual, one gay man replied: 'No. I would say it's very much more a friendship . . . we don't have a tempestuous relationship at all. I think we have a very stable relationship. Sex is obviously part of it, but . . . I wouldn't say our relationship was based on sex' (M12). A lesbian similarly put sex in its place: intimacy 'is about closeness really. And there's different degrees of it. It's about trust . . . friendship, right through to sexuality. It's about being close and trusting' (F40–1).

Living together may be an essential for many partners, but something to be avoided by others. Commitment for our respondents broadly means two basic things: a willingness to work at difficulties, which implies a constant process of mutual negotiation; and a responsibility to care and to invest 'emotional labour' (cf. Johnson 1990; Marcus 1992). In this way, non-heterosexuals strive to achieve both personal autonomy and mutuality.

EQUALITY AND RIGHTS

Given the stress on freely chosen commitment, it is not surprising there is an ambivalence among many non-heterosexuals about the idea of legal partnerships or marriage:

> I don't necessarily think we should be wanting to mimic everything, kind of anything that heterosexual couples or heterosexual relationships have. I don't see that we need to be mimicking them. I think it's about having choice and about being able to be creative and decide what we want for ourselves, but to have these things validated. (F03)

Many, like this gay male subject, want:

minimal interference by the state in the way people live their lives . . . I think that people should be able to make a contract between them saying exactly what their relationship is . . . I also think that it is no good trying to apply laws that apply to heterosexual couples to homosexual couples. (M44)

On the other hand, there is strong hostility to what is widely seen as a discriminatory and homophobic legal system, and it is in this context that some sort of framework of partnership rights is seen (often reluctantly) as desirable:

I think we should be equal in the eyes of the law. I think we should have . . . well, equal age of consent and also equal rights around tax and the sort of benefits that straight people get for being married and having children. And I think if people want to get married they should be allowed to—but I wouldn't. (F36)

Two issues particularly appear to be the focus of the wish for equal partnership rights: parenting and property, especially when facing the ultimate disaster of illness and death. It is noticeable, for example, that most of the existing European legislation on lesbian and gay partnerships explicitly excludes rights to adoption (see, for instance, Bech 1997): non-heterosexual parenting rights remain a taboo. Not surprisingly, many lesbians and gays are particularly concerned with legal access to parenting rights, and questions of parenting rights remain the most delicate and fraught questions facing non-heterosexual parents (Martin 1993; Saffron 1994; Tasker and Golombok 1997). In this extract, a man involved in caring for his (biological) daughter with his male partner remarks that when he first heard arguments for partnership registration and marriage,

I just thought there were so many more important things that we ought to be addressing and dealing with, that it irritated the shit out of [me] . . . [But] if our relationship could be registered, and the fact that we are co-parents could be registered, then . . . when B [his daughter] was younger it would have made me feel more secure. As it was I had a certain amount of paranoia . . . about social workers barging into your life and deciding that this is not proper, and taking the child away . . . there was a fair amount of paranoia on my part. So I suppose if those rights existed, then it would remove some of the paranoia, but part of me is just suspicious that it's trying to be normal and trying to be 'Look, we're as good as heterosexuals'. And I don't actually care. It's got to the point in my life where I don't give a stuff. (M17)

With property issues, there were recurrent problems about access to pensions, mortgages, spousal rights, and so on. But the most emotive issues were around illness and bereavement:

You should have a right to have a say in each other's health care. If your partner was hospitalized, you should have the same rights as any other partner would have

. . . we should all be able to have a say in what happens, say with funeral things. I mean, S's funeral was horrific. His parents completely took it over; his boyfriend was hardly mentioned or . . . spoken to, and it was a very Christian burial. It was hideous. Absolutely nothing to do with his life—the preacher didn't know a thing about him and just stood reading from a piece of paper. And because his parents preferred his female friends, they had a bigger say in what happened than his partner did. And you just think, 'No way'. (F14–15)

For many respondents, then, the question of partnership recognition or lesbian and gay marriage was essentially a pragmatic question: ensuring legal rights and protection, without surrendering what was seen as the real core of non-heterosexual partnerships—the possibilities of more democratic relationships and of creating something different.

STIGMA

In creating spaces for life experiments, however, there is a constant awareness of the outside world. Stigma in various forms, despite all the changes that have taken place, is always a potential experience of lesbians and gays, however 'respectable' the relationship:

because it's monogamous, because we live together in a stable unit with a child, it sometimes feels in that sense that it's like [a marriage]. But I only have to walk out into the street to know that it's not . . . there's one neighbour next door that just won't speak to us. She spoke to us before we had the baby, and now she won't speak to us. So, you know, when it, when it feels like that, I only have to walk out the door, and I know it's not [like a marriage]. (F36)

The presence of children tends to accentuate the social pressure, sometimes dictating careful strategies of avoidance. As the male co-parents of the young girl B mentioned above observed, it is possible to come out as parents in small circles; coming out as gay parents at her school is quite another matter, not least because of the likely embarrassment to their daughter: 'it's like the difference between being out personally and the fact that you're out as a family. I think we're out as individuals, but the family isn't' (M17–18). Similarly, two lesbian parents, when asked what they most feared about being openly homosexual, replied it was 'the crap' their daughter would get:

S: I think with adolescence she's going to have a lot of problems of her own without . . . It's more a concern, you know, for her than for ourselves really, isn't it?
J: Mm. We're already aware that she has to be secretive. (F04–05)

Recognition and respect, therefore, are crucial goals for our subjects. Attitudes of friends are particularly important, and it is here that the wider family of choice can be vital, especially if relations with the family of origin are difficult or non-existent. They provide the meaningful context in which it becomes possible to confront an often hostile or discriminatory external world, and to work through the making of the egalitarian relationship, combining personal autonomy with mutual support.

CONCLUSION

We have argued that our data show two apparently contradictory tendencies. On the one hand, there is plentiful evidence for the emergence of what we have described as experiments in living, creative attempts on the part of many non-heterosexual women and men to construct patterns of relationships that are based on ideals of equality. Friendship circles and a wider sense of community provide the context in which partnerships develop, based on a sense of mutual commitment and trust. Friendships frequently provide the support which makes a non-heterosexual way of life possible: 'since I've come out as a lesbian and also I live on my own (that's generally speaking) I think I need that support, really, from friends' (F28). These fluid, but quite complex, arrangements are what we describe as 'families of choice'.

On the other hand, we also argue that these emergent relationship patterns reflect tendencies which are also reshaping heterosexual ways of life. In many ways, the emphasis on negotiated commitment in non-heterosexual friendship networks echoes changing patterns of kinship and friendship in heterosexual relationships, while the ideal of the egalitarian 'pure relationship' is common across the sexual binary divide. To put it another way, the development of non-heterosexual families of choice, and changes in traditional family life, are both aspects of significant social and cultural changes that are working to transform intimate life. New stories of family life are being told which affirm both the significance of individual choice and the importance of responsible commitment and trust. The family of choice is one significant result.

NOTE

1. The research involved in-depth interviews with 48 men and 48 women who broadly identified themselves as non-heterosexual. All first-person quotations in the chapter come from these interviews. All female interviewees are denoted

by 'F' and male interviewees by 'M', followed by a number reflecting the order in which the interviews took place. As explained later in the text, we chose the term 'non-heterosexual' as a neutral descriptor to cover the range of possible self-descriptions that our subjects use.

PART V
Young Motherhood

13

Family influences on teenage fertility

Kaye Wellings and Jane Wadsworth

INTRODUCTION

This analysis of data from the National Survey of Sexual Attitudes and Lifestyles seeks to contribute to a general understanding of the factors associated with early sexual expression and fertility. A review of the literature shows teenage sexual activity and parenthood to be strongly associated with characteristics of the family of origin. The prevalence of early sexual activity and parenthood are closely related to the structure and size of families, to patterns of relationships, and to the extent of disruption within them. Women from larger than average families, who lived with only one parent as a child, and who have parents who have been divorced, separated, or bereaved, have been shown to be more likely than other groups of women to give birth early (Hogan and Kitagawa 1985; Simms and Smith 1986; Miller and Jorgensen 1988). Teenage sexual activity and parenthood have also been shown to be influenced by family environment, by the ease and extent of discussion about sex, by parental attitudes towards teenage sexuality, and by the degree of discipline and constraint exerted over young people in the family.

Our data enabled teenage birth to be analysed by several relevant variables in this context, including size of the family of origin, whether the respondent had lived with both parents or only one, and, in the case of those living with only one parent, the reason for this and whether that parent was the respondent's mother, father, or an adoptive parent. It was also possible to analyse teenage birth by variables relating to family environment: the ease with which communication about sexual matters took place in the family, perceived parental strictness, and attitudes towards sex before marriage. Onset of sexual activity, measured by age at first sexual intercourse, was also analysed by these variables, because of its strong relationship to teenage birth.

METHODS

The National Survey of Sexual Attitudes and Lifestyles was based on a sample of 18,876 respondents aged 16 to 59, randomly selected from the Post Office's small-user postcode address file. Data were collected between May 1990 and November 1991 by means of personal interviews using a format combining a self-administered questionnaire with a face-to-face interview. The survey methodology has been fully described elsewhere (Wadsworth *et al.* 1993; Johnson *et al.* 1994). Attention is drawn here only to those aspects bearing specifically on the relationship between family of origin and teenage sexuality and fertility. Variations in bases in different analyses reported are explained by the fact that two versions of the questionnaire were used. The longer version—containing a full module of attitudinal questions and more detailed questions on family background and influences, first intercourse, and sex education—was given to a quarter of the sample (a fully representative random subset of the total selected) and a reduced module to the remaining three-quarters. This procedure resulted in some data being available for the total sample and other data being available only for the sub-sample who received the longer version of the questionnaire.

The key questions relating to reproductive experience were asked in the face-to-face section of the questionnaire. Respondents were asked 'Do you have, or have you had any children of your own, that you are the natural [MEN] father of? [WOMEN] mother of? Please include any who don't now, or never did live with you as part of your household.' Only natural live and still births were included in prevalence estimates of teenage births. Respondents were then asked 'How old were you when your first child was born (include stillbirth, died)?' Analysis by the age of the respondent at first birth yields a subgroup whose first child was born before age 20.

The key variable relating to teenage birth was analysed as a dependent and an independent variable by other variables considered likely to influence teenage fertility, or to be influenced by it, or both. The approach adopted here has been to demonstrate associations with other key variables by means of bivariate analysis and then to carry out multivariate analysis, by means of logistic regression models, to explore the extent to which they are independent of associations with related variables. Logistic regression models have been constructed only for women; the numbers of teenage fathers in the sample did not permit such analysis to be carried out for men, hence only the findings from bivariate analysis are presented for men.

RESULTS

Size of family of origin[1] *and teenage birth*

Respondents were asked in the long questionnaire, 'Do you have, or did you have any brothers or sisters, including adopted, half- or step-brothers or sisters?' They were then asked how many siblings they had and whether any of these, natural or otherwise, had lived with them at age 14. They were also asked whether they were the oldest or youngest child or in between. Responses were analysed to provide data on size of family and position within it. Information about this, and other analyses throughout the paper, are presented in summary form in Table 13.1.

Bivariate analysis shows teenage birth to vary consistently with the size of family of origin. Women with three or more siblings are three times as likely to be mothers before age 20 as those with none and nearly twice as likely as women with only one sibling. For men, the gradient is less clear but those with three or more siblings are more likely to have become teenage fathers than those with fewer or none.

Table 13.2 shows the marked association for all age groups between the number of siblings a women had and whether she herself had a child before the age of 20. Teenage motherhood is more common among women born between siblings, that is, 'middle' children. For men there was a marked difference in prevalence according to seniority. Eldest sons in families were more than twice as likely as youngest sons to father a child in their teens (Table 13.1). Multivariate analysis carried out to assess the strength of these associations shows them to be sustained but attenuated by including in the model current age, education, and age at first intercourse (Figure 13.1).

Structure of family of origin and teenage birth

Respondents were asked, 'Did you live more or less continuously with both of your natural parents at home until you were 16?' If the answer was no, they were asked whether that had been because of divorce, separation, or a death, or because the respondent was adopted; other reasons were also recorded. These responses formed the basis for analysis of the experience of teenage birth by that of having lived with only one parent, and the reasons for this. Bivariate analysis showed the prevalence of teenage parenthood to be higher for those who lived with only one parent than for those who had lived with two (Table 13.1). Nearly twice as many women who lived with one parent up to the age of 16 (21 per cent) had had a child in their teens compared with those from a two-parent family (12 per cent).

TABLE 13.1. *Characteristics of men and women aged 20 to 59 who had a teenage birth compared with those who did not*

	Women		Men	
Number of siblings in family of origin	Teenaged mothers (%)	N	Teenaged fathers (%)	N
0	6	242	2	197
1	10	578	3	519
2	12	549	2	417
3+	19	928	5	702
Position in family of origin				
Oldest child	12	660	4	576
Youngest child	13	612	2	509
In between	18	776	4	556
Only child	6	242	2	197
Family structure up to 16				
Lived with both parents	12	1,957	3	1,569
Parents separated or divorced	23	177	4	141
Death of one parent	19	107	5	84
Adopted parents	31	80	6	62
Lived with mother	18	218	6	171
Lived with father	28	47	3	44
Other	34	97	4	72
Family environment				
More strict	14	1,221	4	690
About the same	11	585	3	579
Less strict	13	371	3	472
Discussion easy	7	445	4	230
Discussion difficult	17	300	3	168
No discussion	15	1,347	3	1,297
Parents views on pre-marital sex				
Parental approval	15	125	4	166
Parental disapproval	12	1,706	4	1,113
Parental views balanced	12	164	2	197
Other	12	96	11	67

Among men, the increased likelihood was less marked (4 per cent vs. 3 per cent).

Bivariate analysis showed that those who lived with only one parent because of divorce or separation were more likely to have been teenage parents than those who had suffered the death of a parent (Table 13.1). Women who lived only with their father were more likely to become teenage mothers than were those who lived only with their mothers, and for men the reverse was true. At greatest risk were those men and women in the 'other' category, which aggregated those who had been adopted, fostered, or taken into the care of social services (the numbers here are small).

TABLE 13.2. *Prevalence of teenage birth, by size of family of origin*

	Number of siblings	% having teenage birth	N
Women aged 20–29	0	7	49
	1	9	184
	2	12	182
	3+	19	242
Women aged 30–39	0	8	61
	1	11	166
	2	11	149
	3+	25	297
Women aged 40–49	0	8	73
	1	4	136
	2	16	135
	3+	17	215
Women aged 50–59	0	3	58
	1	7	91
	2	8	83
	3+	9	173

Other studies have shown that adolescents—daughters in particular—from single-parent families begin sexual intercourse earlier (Rodgers, 1983; Hofferth 1987; Newcomer and Udry 1987; Forste and Heaton 1988; Miller and Bingham 1989). They have also shown that men and women who have separated parents are more likely to be parents themselves early in life (Hogan and Kitagawa 1985; Simms and Smith 1986; Miller and Jorgensen 1988). Those who lived with only one parent seem more likely to begin both sexual activity and reproduction early in their lives.

A logistic regression model was constructed to explore the association between disruption of the family of origin and the likelihood of teenage motherhood, adjusting for the variables of current age, age at first intercourse, educational level, and living with both parents up to age 16 (Figure 13.2). The odds ratios for these variables show that, in contrast to our bivariate analysis, women who had experienced the divorce of their parents and so lived with only one of them were *less* likely to have been teenage mothers than those who had lived with only one parent because of the death of the other. After adjusting for these other variables, the likelihood of teenage birth, compared with those who had lived with two parents, was nearly twice as high among women who lived with a divorced parent before the age of 16, and more than twice as high among those who had suffered the death of one of their parents before this age. The significance of the death of a parent on the likelihood of teenage fertility thus becomes apparent only after controlling for the effect of other

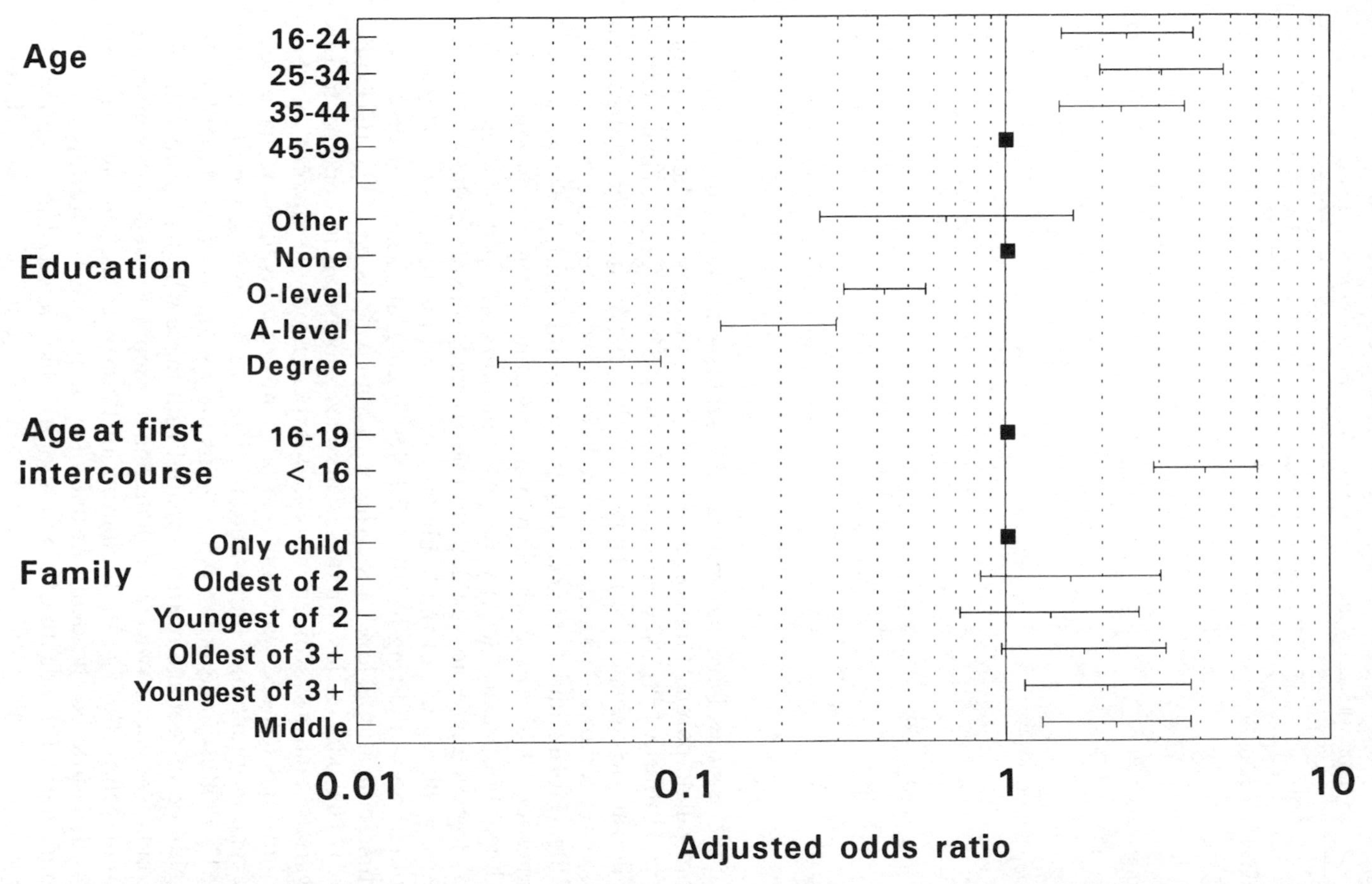

FIG. 13.1 Odds ratios for teenage motherhood, adjusted for size and position within family of origin

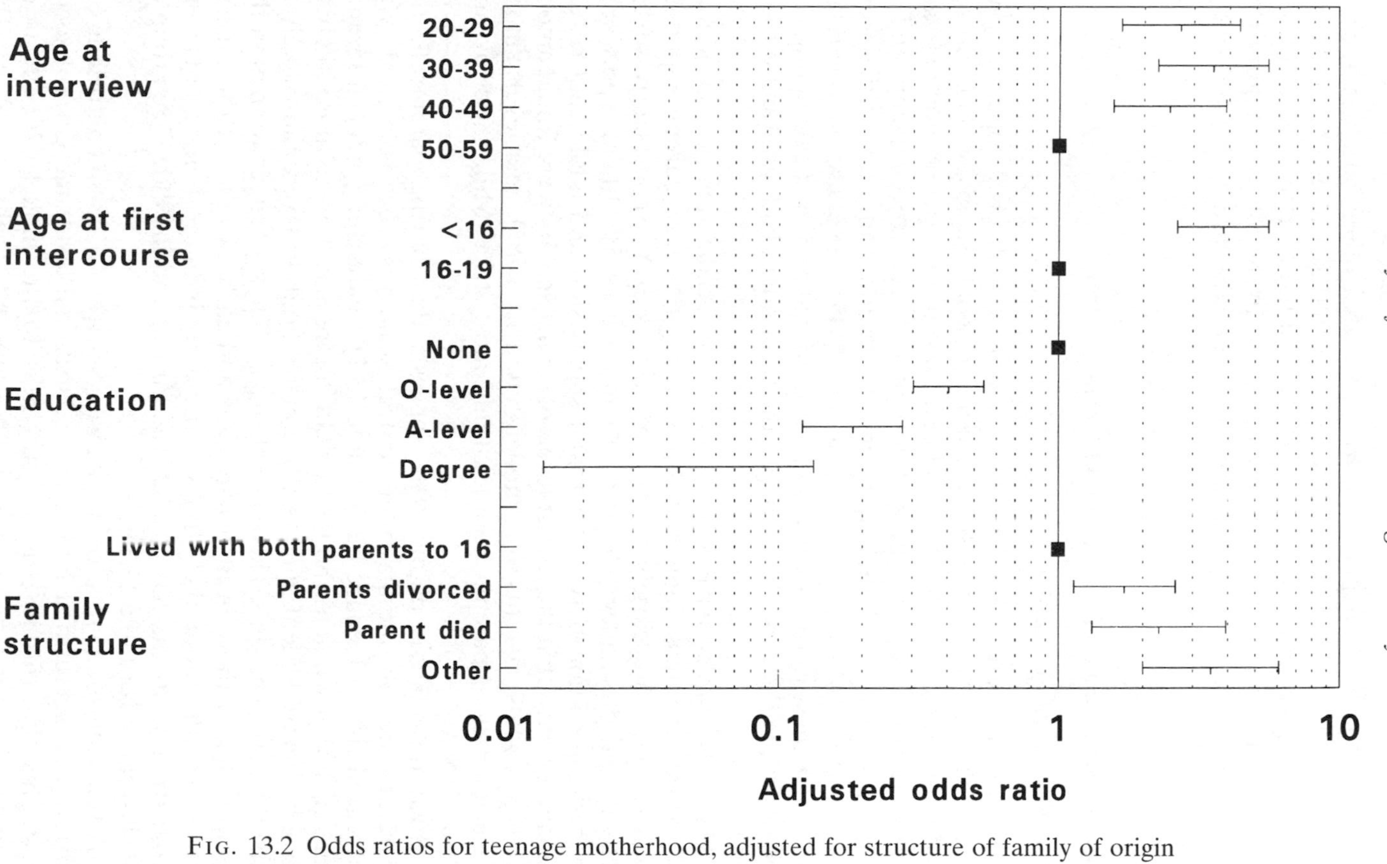

FIG. 13.2 Odds ratios for teenage motherhood, adjusted for structure of family of origin

variables. The likely explanation for this is that other variables, such as social class, confound the relationship between parental divorce and early childbearing. When the simultaneous effect of these on teenage fertility is examined, their influence is attributed. Those in the 'other' category, that is those who were adopted, fostered, or taken into care by social services, remained at greatest risk.

Environment of family of origin and teenage birth

Discipline in family of origin

Respondents were asked, 'When you were about 14, comparing your (parents/mother/father) with the parents of your friends, would you say that your (parents/mother/father) (were/was) more strict or more easygoing about allowing you to go out at night, to parties, social events, and so on?' Those who said they were more easygoing or more strict were asked further: 'Much more or a little more?' Five response options relating to strictness were provided and an additional option of saying that this did not apply (because, for example, the respondent had not wanted to go out).

US studies which have focused on family socialization have produced inconsistent findings. Some have shown that girls whose parents supervise their dating more closely tend to be less likely to report early sexual activity and pregnancy (Hogan and Kitagawa 1985). Others report a U-shaped association between parental supervision and adolescent sexual behaviour, such that the lowest levels of sexual activity were found among teenagers whose parents were moderately strict, with higher levels among teenagers whose parents were least and most strict (Miller, McCoy, and Olson 1986).

Bivariate analysis of our data suggests that having parents at the extreme ends of the parental control scale may be associated with increased risk of teenage birth (Table 13.1). There is a gender difference here such that women who had a child before age 20 were more likely to have had more lenient parents, while men who did so were more likely to have had strict parents. There are also age effects: younger women in the sample, that is, those in their late teens and early twenties at the time of interview, were more likely to give birth early in life if their parents were more strict, while the reverse was true for those in the older age group of 40–49-year-olds (Table 13.3).

A third logistic regression model was constructed, again controlling for current age, age at first intercourse, educational level, and current social class, this time fitting parental strictness to the model. No effects of parental discipline on teenage birth were statistically significant. This tends to suggest that any effect of parental strictness on teenage pregnancy

TABLE 13.3. *Prevalence of teenage birth, by family discipline*

	Strictness of parents	% having teenage birth	N
Women aged 20–29	More strict	16	299
	About the same	9	161
	Less strict	11	185
Women aged 30–39	More strict	18	386
	About the same	13	153
	Less strict	15	104
Women aged 40–49	More strict	12	310
	About the same	14	152
	Less strict	22	59
Women aged 50–59	More strict	8	226
	About the same	6	118
	Less strict	6	23

TABLE 13.4. *Prevalence of teenage birth, by ease of communication with parents*

	Ease of communication	% having teenage birth	N
Women aged 20–29	Easy	8	169
	Difficult	15	452
Women aged 30–39	Easy	7	128
	Difficult	18	513
Women aged 40–49	Easy	8	98
	Difficult	16	413
Women aged 50–59	Easy	3	49
	Difficult	8	329

operates through its effect on other variables, for example, age of onset of sexual activity.

Communication about sex within the family of origin

Respondents were asked, 'Also when you were about 14, did you find it easy or difficult to talk to your (parents/mother/father) about sexual matters, or didn't you discuss sexual matters with them at that age?' The response options provided were 'easy', 'difficult', 'didn't discuss', 'it varied', and 'can't remember'. Bivariate analysis showed the apparent effect of communication about sex to be stronger for women than men (Table 13.1). Women who found it easy to discuss sexual matters with parents were less likely to have had a child before age 20. Discussion about sexual matters is easier today than was formerly the case; nevertheless, as Table 13.4

shows, in every age group the prevalence of teenage birth is higher among those for whom discussion was difficult than among those for whom it was easy.

After controlling for the same, possibly confounding variables—current age, age at first intercourse, and educational level—likelihood of teenage pregnancy was more than twice as high among women who found discussion about sex difficult, or who did not discuss sex with parents, as among those who found discussion easy with parents, and these differences were statistically significant (Figure 13.3).

Attitudes towards sex before marriage

The role of the family in influencing contraceptive use may extend to being a source of information about birth control, to helping the process of obtaining contraception by providing informational, financial, or practical support, or to expressing approval or disapproval. US studies have found greater communication within the family to be associated with a lower probability of early sexual activity and an increased likelihood of use of birth control (Inazu and Fox 1980; Furstenberg *et al.* 1985; Newcomer and Udry 1985). Adolescents whose parents accept teenage sexuality have been shown to be more likely to use contraception (Baker, Thalberg, and Morrison 1988). However, the relationship between parental approval and teenage birth was not marked in these data (Table 13.1).

Interaction between structure and environment of family of origin

The effects on children of family characteristics such as size, structure, and environment are clearly not independent of one another. How many children there are in the family, for example, can be expected to significantly affect both the level of discipline and the extent of communication. Whether there is one parent or two will help determine the pattern of role modelling.

The interaction between family size, structure, and environment has been demonstrated in other studies. Parents whose marriages ended or who never married have been found to be more likely to discuss sex, pregnancy, and birth control than parents in intact marriages (Moore and Peterson 1989). Adolescents who experienced the divorce of their parents have been shown to hold more permissive attitudes about sex outside of marriage (Thornton and Camburn 1987). Moore *et al.* (1986) found parent–teenage communication to have no overall association with whether young people had sex, but analysis by parental values found daughters of traditional parents who communicated about sex to be less likely to have had sex than daughters of more liberal parents or daughters

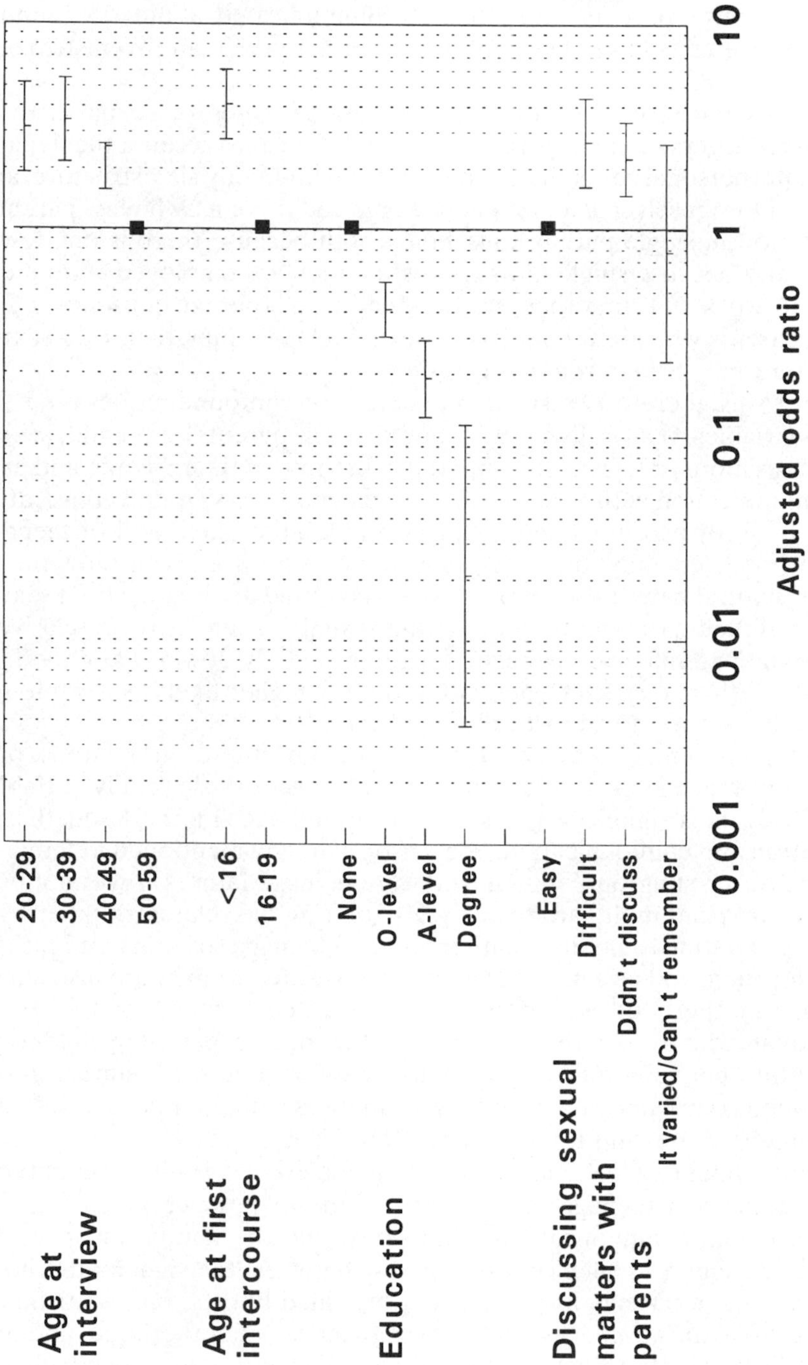

FIG. 13.3 Odds ratios for teenage motherhood, adjusted for discussion about sex in family of origin

of conservative parents who had not communicated about sex. Similar interaction effects have been reported by Fisher (1989) and Weinstein and Thornton (1989).

Reasons advanced by others for the higher rates of sexual activity among teenagers in single-parent households take into account the dynamics of interpersonal relationships associated with family size, structure, and climate. Dornbusch *et al.* (1985) have suggested there may be less parental supervision in single-parent households, both because there is one fewer parent and because single mothers—when they are employed—are more likely to work full-time than are mothers in two-parent households. For single parents who are themselves in sexual relationships, their own sexual behaviour may have a role-model effect.

There was, therefore, a strong possibility of confounding between the three variables, that is, living with one or both parents as a child, seeing parents as more or less strict compared with those of their friends, and ease of communication with parents about sexual matters. As noted above, after controlling for possibly confounding variables, the likelihood of teenage motherhood remained higher among women who lived with only one or neither natural parent and among those who found discussion about sexual matters difficult, or who did not discuss sexual matters. Having relatively easygoing parents was associated with a slightly lower likelihood of teenage birth, and stricter ones with a slightly higher likelihood, although these effects were not statistically significant.

As a preliminary step towards understanding these interactions, prevalence of teenage birth was examined in terms of those family variables apparently most significantly associated with teenage motherhood, that is, disruption and communication. For reasons already mentioned, relating to the size of the subgroup of men who were teenage fathers, it was not possible to carry out multivariate analysis exploring the relationship between variables relating to family environment and teenage sexuality and fatherhood for men, and as can be seen, the cell sizes for women are also small. Teenage motherhood is more likely to have been experienced by those individuals who lived with only one or neither natural parent in childhood, but within that subgroup it is more likely to have occurred among those who found communication about sexual matters with their parents difficult than among those who found it easy (Table 13.5).

A final model in this context was constructed to examine the simultaneous effects on teenage motherhood of the experience of having had a lone parent, communication about sex within the family, and parental discipline (Figure 13.4). The association between teenage motherhood and number of parents lived with was sustained but the only statistically significant association was that between teenage motherhood and not having lived with both natural parents for 'other' reasons (which included

TABLE 13.5. *Prevalence of teenage birth, by ease of communication and family disruption*

	Lived with both parents to age 16		Lived with one parent to age 16	
	% having teenage birth	N	% having teenage birth	N
Communication easy				
Women	7	403	12	42
Men	4	200	3	31
Communication difficult				
Women	16	261	25	39
Men	3	151	6	17
No discussion				
Women	14	1,175	22	172
Men	3	1,142	5	155

having been taken into the care of social services or having been fostered or adopted). Women in this category were nearly five times as likely to have been mothers before age 20 as those who lived with both their natural parents to age 16. There is clearly a strong association between having lived with adults other than natural parents and teenage motherhood. The association between parental discipline and teenage birth remained weak in multivariate analysis and was not statistically significant.

When all three variables are included in the model the only one for which all adjusted odds ratios are statistically significant is ease of discussion with parents. Women who found this difficult, and those from families in which there was no discussion about sexual matters, were more than twice as likely to have become mothers in their teens as those for whom it was easy, after controlling for the effects of current age, age at first intercourse, family structure, and parental strictness.

CONCLUSION

It is a somewhat unexpected finding that of all the characteristics of the family of origin, ease of family discussion about sexual matters appears to have the strongest effect on the likelihood of teenage motherhood. This is no doubt an important indicator of a more general climate relating to communication within the family. Nevertheless, the policy implications are clear. Where parents and children are able to talk freely about sexual matters, there appear to be definite gains for the prevention of teenage motherhood. The strong link between communication about sex in the

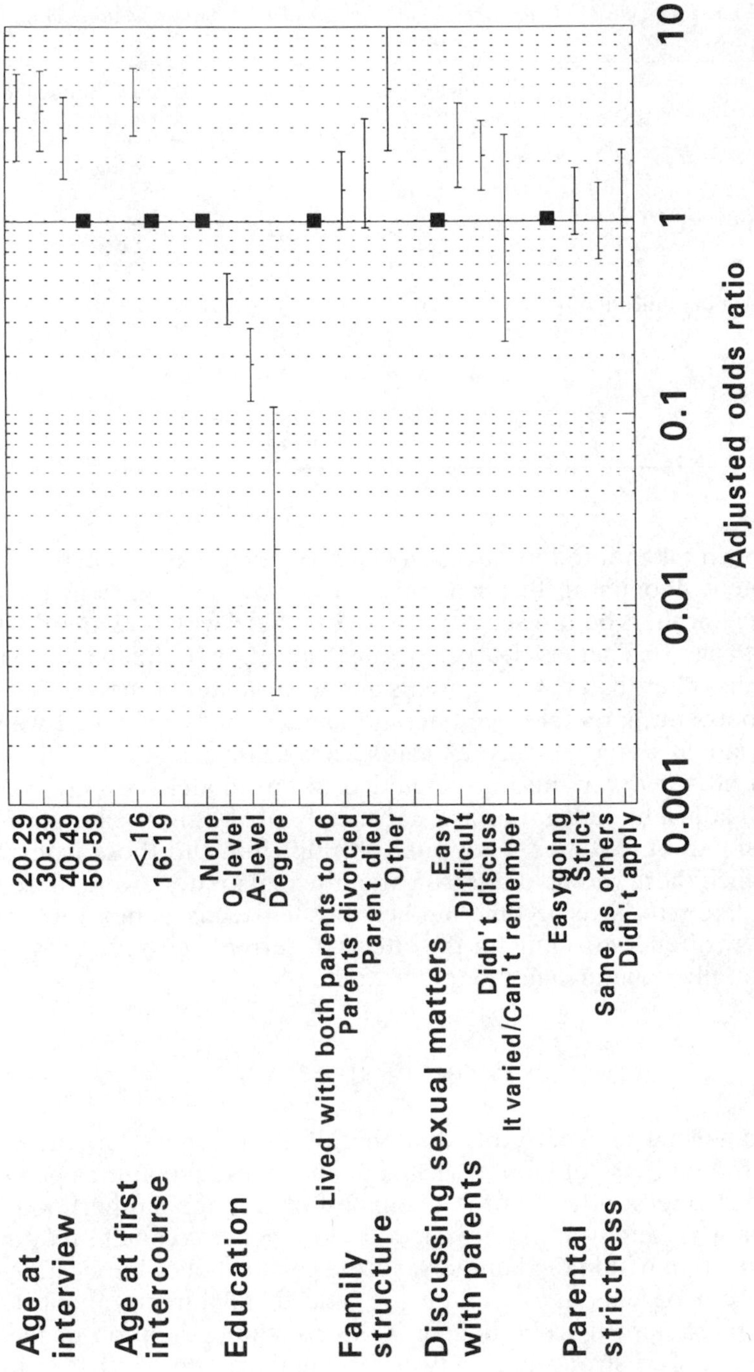

Age at interview
20-29
30-39
40-49
50-59

Age at first intercourse
<16
16-19

Education
None
O-level
A-level
Degree

Family structure
Lived with both parents to 16
Parents divorced
Parent died
Other

Discussing sexual matters with parents
Easy
Difficult
Didn't discuss
It varied/Can't remember

Parental strictness
Easygoing
Strict
Same as others
Didn't apply

0.001 0.01 0.1 1 10

Adjusted odds ratio

FIG. 13.4 Odds ratios for teenage motherhood, adjusted for family disruption, discipline, and discussion about sex

family and teenage birth underlines the importance of an environment in which sex can be easily discussed. The importance of discussion needs to be impressed upon parents, and the means by which such discussion might be facilitated be made available to them via educational materials and the media, and health professionals.

NOTE

1. The terms 'family of origin' and 'family of procreation' are used to describe, respectively, the family in which respondents grew up and the family subsequently produced by them.

14

Teenage mothers: decisions and outcomes

Isobel Allen and Shirley Bourke Dowling

INTRODUCTION

The study described in this chapter set out to examine the ways in which teenage mothers make decisions about their pregnancies and housing and living arrangements, both during pregnancy and after the birth of their babies. Almost 42,000 babies were born to teenage women in England and Wales in 1995, the year when the women in this study became mothers. Increasingly, public discussion has focused on teenage mothers as burdens on the state, who become so by choosing to have babies while single, by living on benefits in local authority housing, and by receiving housing priority over married couples with children. This widely held view of teenage mothers is not supported by research, which shows that most young women do not make a positive choice to become pregnant (Bury 1984; Hudson and Ineichen 1991), and do not become pregnant to receive benefits or to get priority in housing over other families (Hopkinson 1976; Clark 1989). Teenagers know very little about housing and benefits before they become pregnant (Clark 1989) and do not receive housing priority when they become pregnant (Institute of Housing 1993). Moreover, mothers under 18 are not usually allowed to put their names on local authority housing lists (Burghes and Brown 1995). Although early motherhood substantially increases the chances that a young woman's first major tenure will be social housing, such housing is usually entered with a partner (Ermisch 1996).

According to previous research, half of teenage mothers experience a number of different housing arrangements in their first year of motherhood (Simms and Smith 1986; Clark and Coleman 1991). They also tend to stay in poor-quality accommodation for many months before receiving more appropriate accommodation (Institute of Housing 1993). Although

The authors would like to acknowledge the valuable contribution made by Heather Rolfe throughout this research.

local authorities are required to house mothers with children who are homeless or fleeing from violence, they do not offer priority to single parents in this respect (Institute of Housing 1993).

The objectives of the study were to examine the factors surrounding teenagers' decisions to continue with a pregnancy; to identify the women's individual housing careers and examine their reasons for staying put or moving; to explore women's perceptions of their housing options during pregnancy and after the birth, and their perceptions of the role of the father of the baby, their own parents, and others in their decisions about the pregnancy and their housing and living arrangements; and to examine the women's awareness and utilization of benefits before and during pregnancy and after the birth. The study was conducted in three areas: Hackney, Leeds, and Solihull, which were selected to represent three different types of area, with high, medium, and relatively low teenage pregnancy rates.[1] The sample of women was drawn from hospital records of all women having a first baby when aged 16–19 during specific periods in 1995. Fathers and grandparents were approached through the teenage mothers interviewed. Details of the methods of sampling and approach are given below and in the full report (Allen and Bourke Dowling 1998).

Teenage mothers and household change

Few studies have examined young mothers' decisions about household change or the factors affecting these decisions, although some have identified patterns of household composition and the support available to young mothers (Hopkinson 1976; Clark and Coleman 1991; Hudson and Ineichen 1991). The amount of support available from parents, partners, friends, relations, and professionals varies widely, and is often related to the living arrangements of the young women. Family support has been noted as of paramount importance to young mothers leaving the parental home; Speak *et al.* (1995) found that some young mothers in their study spent a considerable amount of time at their parents' home in their first year of independence, using their own homes simply to sleep.

Many teenage mothers move during their pregnancy or in the first year after the birth of their babies (Hopkinson 1976; Clark 1989), but the relationship between pregnancy and moving has not been explored in much detail. Simms and Smith (1986) reported that 45 per cent of the teenage mothers in their sample were still living with their parents fifteen months after the birth of their babies, mainly in overcrowded conditions. Those who had moved were in better accommodation but financially less well off. The main reasons for young mothers moving include insecurity, overcrowding, lack of privacy, and family tension (Simms and Smith 1986; Clark 1989). Little has been written about teenage mothers who do not move.

There also has been surprisingly little research on the fathers of babies born to teenage mothers. It is clear that the role of the father of the baby is important both in the decision to continue with the pregnancy and in household formation and change, although there are indications that it has become relatively less important in recent years with the steady change in attitudes towards single mothers, the increase in the number of births outside marriage, and the decline in 'shotgun marriages'. Simms and Smith (1986) explored in some depth the relationships between teenage mothers and their partners. Hudson and Ineichen (1991) noted that any initial enthusiasm about the pregnancy and birth noticeably tailed off with the realization of the hard work and commitment required by a growing baby. There is a high rate of breakdown in teenage marriages and cohabiting relationships (McRae 1993).

We were particularly interested in this research to explore the role of the fathers in the decisions made by teenage mothers, and to examine the processes through which relationships change after a teenage woman becomes pregnant. The implications of the breakdown of relationships for changes in housing and living arrangements, as well as for increasing dependence on benefits, are clearly of vital importance in the debate about the future of welfare.

Research Methods

The main evidence collected in this study came from interviews conducted in 1996 with 84 women who had had a baby in 1995 when aged between 16 and 19 years. We interviewed 27 women in Hackney, 34 in Leeds, and 23 in Solihull. Our aim had been to interview one hundred women, but we experienced difficulty in achieving sufficient responses within a reasonable time from the available sampling frames in Solihull and Hackney. It was clear that there was considerable movement after the birth in both areas, but especially in Hackney, and we were unable to make contact with the numbers we had hoped for. We also interviewed 24 fathers of the babies and 41 grandparents (both maternal grandparents were interviewed in two cases). Access to fathers and grandparents was achieved through asking the women interviewed whether we could approach them. Only half of the women were still in a relationship with the father of the baby, and a relatively high proportion of the remainder had no contact at all with him. In other cases, women were reluctant for us to approach the fathers, or the fathers were reluctant to be approached; in some instances, we suspected, because of our interest in housing and benefits. Women did not always have close relationships with the grandparents of the baby, and, in addition, we were unable to interview those who lived some distance away.

Interviewing took place between June and November 1996, when the babies were on average 13 months old, using questionnaires which were fully structured, in that the exact wording of each question was specified and the questions were in a predetermined sequence. A fairly high proportion of questions allowed for an open-ended response and interviewers were expected to record these answers verbatim. The interviews were carried out by a team of experienced interviewers and Policy Studies Institute staff.

THE GENERAL PICTURE

Perhaps the most important feature of the women's experiences was that, by the time of interviews about one year after the birth, almost half (41) of the 84 women were no longer in a relationship with the father of the baby, while nearly one-fifth (16) had no contact at all with him.[2] Indeed, one of the main findings of our study of teenage mothers' lives was the constantly changing pattern of their relationships. All but six of the women had had what they described as a steady relationship with the father of their baby at the time they became pregnant. Thirty-five had been married or cohabiting at the time they became pregnant (compared with 38 at the time of the interview). But these simple figures conceal considerable movements in relationships, and, apart from the married women, all of whom remained married, we found a changing series of relationship patterns during pregnancy and after the birth, even among those who were still in a relationship with the baby's father at the time of the interview. The large majority (85 per cent) of the women who were no longer in a relationship with the baby's father were single and without a steady partner. The implications of this widespread breakdown in relationships among young women with small babies are far-reaching, and we traced the patterns of decisions which resulted in increasing dependence on benefits and social housing, in spite of the hopes with which many of those interviewed had embarked upon their pregnancies.

The large majority of the women we interviewed were born in the United Kingdom, of white ethnic origin, and nearly half said they had no religion. Nearly half also reported that her own mother had been a teenager at the birth of her first child, reflecting the pattern found in other studies; a quarter had siblings who were teenage parents. These young mothers came from larger than average families, and only just over half reported that their parents were still married to each other; most of those whose parents had separated had been under 5 at the time of the separation. This pattern reflects that found by Wellings and her colleagues in their analysis of teenage pregnancy (Wellings *et al.* 1996). Although most had contact with one or both parents, and over a quarter (22) were living with parents at the time of the interview, the vast majority had lived away from home at some point, with as many as 10 (12 per cent) having left home by the time they were 16, often because of discord within the family.

The teenage mothers we interviewed were early school-leavers: about one-fifth (16) had left school when aged 15 or younger, and a further 46 per cent had left at age 16. Two-thirds had educational qualifications, mainly at GCSE level, but not surprisingly, the younger they were when they left school the less likely they were to have any educational qualifications. Over a third had vocational qualifications. Pregnancy, however, had caused two-thirds to change their education, training, or work plans. But motherhood had affected more than educational achievement. Table 14.1 compares various characteristics of teenage mothers' lives before pregnancy and at the time of interview, about one year after the birth. In all instances shown, the opportunities open to these young women narrowed as a result of motherhood, while financial dependency increased. For example, although 38 per cent were in paid work when they became pregnant, this had fallen to 15 per cent by one year after the birth, while the proportion unemployed had risen to 71 per cent. Over this same period, the proportion in education more than halved. The diminished economic activity of these teenage mothers was reflected in their dependence on state benefits and social housing: at the time of interviews, one-third were in social housing, with another third waiting for such accommodation; over half (57 per cent) were totally dependent upon benefits as their sole source of income.

TABLE 14.1. *The impact of teenage pregnancy (%)*

Proportion of women	Before pregnancy	After the birth
Received any benefit (excluding Child Benefit and maternity pay)	36	93
On Income Support	25	81
Received Housing Benefit	11	49
In social housing[a]	5	33
(waiting for social housing)[a]		(33)
In paid work[a]	38	15
In education[a]	29	13
Unemployed[a]	31	71
N	84	84

[a] At the time of interviews.

DECIDING TO CONTINUE WITH A PREGNANCY

The most important factor in the histories of these young women was their decision to continue with their pregnancies—only one in four of which were planned. Their reasons for continuing with the pregnancy are explored below.

Although 40 per cent of the women were pleased or delighted to find that they were pregnant, a quarter were shocked and surprised, and a further quarter were scared or horrified. It must be a matter of concern that so many reacted like this when they must have known that they were running the risk of getting pregnant. Their reactions mirror those of women who seek a termination of pregnancy (Allen 1985), and underline the complex thinking among women who are fully aware of the risks of sexual intercourse without contraception and yet take chances or assume, for no valid reason, that 'it won't happen to me'.

Pinpointing the differences between the women who decide to have a termination and those who continue with a pregnancy is difficult. Some women were devastated when they found they were pregnant: 'I was gutted. I didn't want to be pregnant'—but continued with the pregnancy after considering termination. However, continuing with the pregnancy was often not so much a decision as an acceptance of what had happened, reflecting a rather fatalistic attitude which characterized much of the subsequent behaviour of many of these young women. It could be argued that those who opt for termination of pregnancy have to make a definite decision, while for an important minority of the women interviewed in the present study, the decision to have a termination was one which they felt they could not make, even though they did not want to be pregnant and knew that their relationship might founder.

Among those who had planned to become pregnant, little or no discussion took place with other people on what to do about it, mainly, it appeared, because the pregnancy was wanted. Among the others, however, there was often extensive discussion with a variety of people about the options. Women were often selective about the people with whom they discussed the pregnancy, and even more selective about what they discussed with whom. Although mothers were found to be the most helpful and supportive, only just over half the women had talked to their mother at all about their pregnancy. Those who had planned their pregnancy clearly saw little point in doing so, but others, especially those who might have expected a frosty reception, may well have avoided a conversation in which pressure might have been brought on them to terminate the pregnancy. The parents with whom women discussed their pregnancy were often shocked and disappointed, but most were said to have given total support to their daughter's decision and to have rarely tried to influence them one way or the other. In our interviews with grandparents, however, it became clear that not all mothers were quite as sanguine as described by their daughters, and, it should be stressed, the grandparents we interviewed were usually in close contact with their daughters and their babies.

Most women discussed their pregnancy with their partner, a high proportion of whom were shocked or surprised to learn of the pregnancy. Termination of pregnancy was discussed with over a third of the partners with whom any discussion had taken place. Some partners disappeared before the pregnancy was confirmed, making discussion impossible, while others were overjoyed about the pregnancy, making discussion unnecessary. Few partners suggested terminations, although those who did were often reported as reacting very brutally. However, by the time of the interview, many of the partners with whom discussions took place were no longer in a relationship with the woman, in spite of the fact that some of them were described as having been a key influence in the decision to continue with the pregnancy. Delight and joy at the thought of becoming a father was very short-lived among some of these young men.

Friends and relations were often hand-picked for discussions, and those who suggested termination of pregnancy or pointed out the potential disadvantages of teenage motherhood were not popular among the women interviewed. Professionals were mainly reported as supportive of the woman's decision to continue with the pregnancy, and few were said to have discussed the option of a termination of pregnancy. There were clear indications that many professionals followed the preferences of the women to continue with the pregnancy, and offered support in that decision. Those who did not were often reported as being unnecessarily unsympathetic. Professionals who disagree or try to put another point of view to women who want confirmation of their own decision are often thought to be unhelpful or unsympathetic, whatever the situation. It is perhaps significant that women seeking termination of pregnancy also often report lack of sympathy from professionals who do not agree with their decision.

When women were asked to assess the support offered by the people to whom they spoke, parents, particularly mothers, received a much higher rating than partners in terms of helpfulness, sympathy, practical assistance, and financial support. Partners received a low rating on most counts, apart from some financial support. Although a small proportion of women had not discussed the future of the pregnancy with their husbands or partners, most other partners and husbands were only rarely seen as playing a major role in the decision to continue with the pregnancy or in supporting the women throughout the pregnancy. It is perhaps ironic that many of those who clearly did play an important role in dissuading women from termination of pregnancy by promising devoted support were no longer around by the time of the interview.

Our analysis of the ways in which women made their decision to continue with the pregnancy suggests that most of them sought confirmation of their own decision to have the baby through their discussions with other people. If confirmation was not forthcoming, as it certainly was not from some of their partners, the women may have been shocked or upset, but they then sought support elsewhere, notably among their parents. Many of them heard from their parents what they wanted to hear. Some mothers were clearly delighted, but many were not. However, the interviews suggest that their daughters interpreted their parents' unwillingness to be too directive and their offers of support as a sanction for their decision to continue with the pregnancy. Sadly, many of the fears expressed by their parents, particularly their concern that the relationship with the baby's father would founder, had materialized by the time of the interviews.

In reaction to their pregnancies, few women expressed any doubts about their ability to cope with pregnancy or motherhood. Concerns were more likely to be related to fears about what their parents would say, rather than to practical considerations such as how and where and with whom they were going to live and what they were going to live on. It appeared that few of them had given much thought to the future, and that planning for life as a mother was as remote a concept as planning for pregnancy had been.

The reluctance to consider termination of pregnancy was striking, especially among young women whose relationship with the father of the baby was clearly shaky or, in some cases, violent. Many of these women had realized at a early stage, often before the pregnancy had been confirmed, that there was no future in their relationship and that they would not be able to rely on the father for any kind of support. We found, like Burghes and Brown in their study of single teenage mothers (Burghes and Brown 1995), a clear anti-abortion feeling among these young women, rarely based on religious grounds, although it was by no means universal.

Women who continued with the pregnancy in the knowledge that their relationship was unlikely to survive were not only those with low educational achievement or few potential alternatives to motherhood. Some women had plans for further education or careers which they knew would have to be put on hold, if not abandoned, and yet they continued with a pregnancy with little or no potential support from the father of the baby. Again, there was plenty of evidence that planning for the future was relatively unusual and that few of the women reacted to the pregnancy by attempting to take control of the situation. There was a strong sense in many of the interviews of young women being swept along by events over which they were neither willing nor, in many cases, able to exert any influence.

HOUSING AND HOUSEHOLD CHANGE

One of the aims of the study was to examine how decisions about housing and household change are made by teenage mothers during their pregnancies and after the birth of their babies. We were particularly interested in the role of other people in these decisions, and the extent and nature of their influence on whether the women moved or stayed put. We explored in detail the extent to which women moved during pregnancy and after the birth, documented the moves made, and attempted to establish a pattern of housing careers among these women in the relatively short period of 21 months between becoming pregnant and the time of the interview. We found that 73 per cent of the women had moved at least once in this period: 35 per cent only once, 21 per cent twice, and 17 per cent three or more times, with a small proportion of the last group moving up to 11 times over the period.

Our study may under-represent the extent to which teenage mothers move during pregnancy and after the birth, in that we were unable to make contact with many of those in our sampling frame simply because they had moved. It is therefore possible that we interviewed a higher proportion of women who had not moved at all than might be found in the general population of teenage mothers, although Simms and Smith (1986) found that as many as 45 per cent of teenage mothers were still living in their parents' homes 15 months after the birth of their baby, compared with the 26 per cent found in the present study. Among those who had not moved were two distinct groups: those living with husbands or partners throughout the period and those living with their parents, most of whom were no longer in a relationship with the baby's father by the time of the interview. However, we found that living at home with parents did not necessarily mean that women had not moved. For example, only half of those who were living with their parents at the time of the interview had never moved. We also found that a higher proportion had moved twice or more than was found in the Simms and Smith study, although a similar proportion in both studies had moved only once.

The broad changes in household formation and housing among these teenage mothers were as follows. From the time they became pregnant to the time of the interview, the proportion living with their parents (sometimes with partners as well) dropped sharply, from nearly one-half to one-quarter. The proportion cohabiting (sometimes while living with parents or in-laws) remained constant at just under one-third, concealing considerable household and relationship change, since nearly half of the original cohabiting relationships had broken down. The proportion living with a husband increased, from 11 per cent at the time they became pregnant to 18 per cent at the time of the interview (again sometimes living with parents or in-laws). A small number of women were living with friends or relatives at the time they became pregnant or at the time of the interview.

The most striking change, however, was the sharp increase in the proportion of those living alone, which rose from 7 per cent when they became pregnant to 29 per cent at the time of the interview. Very few of the young women we interviewed had intended to end up as lone mothers, but around half of them had done so, and well over half of these were living alone with their baby.

Decisions about housing and living arrangements

We have already commented upon the wide variety of advice and support given to the women in their decision to continue with the pregnancy, and the extent to which it appeared that most of them arrived at the decision to continue with the pregnancy *before* embarking on discussions about it. Discussions were therefore often related to seeking agreement with their decision or assurances of continuing support and help. The process of decision-making about where and with whom to live during pregnancy and after the birth was rather more complicated. First, the range of housing options or future living arrangements was, perhaps not surprisingly, closely related to the status and stability of a woman's relationship with the baby's father and also, in many cases, to her relationship with her parents. Secondly, when they became pregnant the women were living in a variety of places with a variety of people. Thus, not only did they have to decide where to live, but also with whom. Thirdly, whereas the decision to continue with the pregnancy was the result of consideration of two main options—to have the baby or to have an abortion—decisions about housing and living arrangements were considerably more complex, with many more factors to be taken into account. Perhaps the most important of these was often unknown to the women at the beginning of their pregnancy: whether their relationship with the baby's father would survive.

Among the women living alone with their parents, there had often been little or no discussion about housing since they usually had no option but to stay at home, mainly because their relationship had broken down and they were unable to support themselves away from their parents' home. Discussions here were described by both the women and the grandparents interviewed as brief and to the point. These young women were usually very satisfied both with their accommodation and the practical and emotional support received from parents. The desire for security was often uppermost in their minds.

Most of the women who had never moved had thought of moving, either to be alone with their partner, or to find more satisfactory accommodation, or to establish their independence from their parents. There was evidence of some tension within the parental home, particularly if there was overcrowding or the demands of a growing baby were beginning to cause strain within the household. However, some women, particularly a small group living only with their mothers, clearly had comfortable and happy households which nobody saw much point in disturbing, including one grandmother who told her daughter she could stay with her until she was 50 if she wished.

Among the women who had moved, there were often reports of conflicting advice from parents and partners about possible living arrangements, with parents often urging caution and partners suggesting plans which often foundered along with the relationship. Parents were reported as being much more helpful although there were difficult discussions with some parents. Most of the more helpful discussions were with parents who wanted their daughters to stay at home, but mothers also often played an important role in helping to find accommodation, set up home, or deal with housing officers. Discussions with friends and other relatives about housing and living arrangements were often very specific in terms of offers of accommodation or advice on how to get on the housing list. Few women reported discussions with professionals of any kind about housing or living arrangements, although, interestingly, most of those who had spoken to a midwife had received advice. The few housing officers who had been consulted were not found helpful; indeed, some were regarded as the most unhelpful people with whom housing had been discussed.

It was clear that decisions on housing and living arrangements were often not the subject of rational discussion, particularly those which involved a move. Moves were often precipitated by relationship breakdown, which was perhaps not the most comfortable situation in which to have reasoned discussions about where and with whom to live, particularly late in pregnancy or with a tiny baby. There were many indications in the housing histories of the women that they often felt that the moves were out of their control, not only in relation to deciding where to go but also when they would move. It was clear that many of them had expected to stay in accommodation longer than they had, but that other events, including relationship breakdown, had dictated otherwise. Again, there was a strong impression that many of these young women were often following rather than controlling what was happening to them, and that they felt powerless to influence the course their lives were taking. This was compounded by the fact that they had small babies, and that many of them had little money and few opportunities to earn more. If they had no partner or had an unemployed partner as well, it was perhaps not surprising that they found themselves sucked into a dependency culture which many of them had never contemplated.

It should, however, be remembered that a substantial minority of these teenage mothers had stable married or cohabiting relationships, had planned their pregnancies and any moves they had made. Their comments reflected the greater stability of their lives, and our interviews with fathers, most of whom were married or cohabiting, also reflected this pattern of behaviour and attitudes which differed markedly from the majority of the women in the study. It is important not to assume that teenage motherhood is necessarily accompanied by relationship breakdown, instability in living arrangements, and financial dependency, even if there is ample evidence to suggest that these are frequent consequences.

Local authority housing

One-third of the women were in local authority housing by the time of the interview and a further third were on local authority waiting lists. Half of those in local authority housing, and over half of those waiting for such housing, were lone mothers living alone with their babies. There was a definite move towards social housing among these teenage mothers, although there was little evidence that they had 'played the system' by trying the non-statutory homeless route or even that they knew of its existence. There was, instead, evidence of lack of knowledge, long waits on local authority housing lists, and an inability to understand the system, let alone manipulate it. We found many examples of lonely and isolated women in unsatisfactory and unsuitable local authority and privately rented accommodation.

The teenage mothers we interviewed had rarely known anything about local authority housing before they became pregnant and the few who thought they had known something were usually misinformed, particularly about whether they would get priority if they had a baby. There was no evidence to suggest that the women had become pregnant in order to get council housing, although when they were asked whether they thought that teenage mothers had babies in order to get housing, over half of them thought that this was true, at least of some teenagers. There was, however, general agreement among this group that although it might be true of others, it was not true of themselves.

But women were often sceptical about the idea that the possibility of council housing might induce teenagers to become pregnant—'To be honest, I think they're a bit crazy—all that aggravation just for a flat'—

and some were sure that housing was not the main reason for teenagers becoming pregnant: 'They make it sound like the council put you in palaces but they don't . . . Who'd want to get pregnant for the sake of being put in a council flat?'

The fathers we interviewed, most of whom were married or cohabiting, were more likely than the women to think that teenagers became pregnant to get council housing. There were views that it was an 'easy option', and that some teenagers might think it would be a good way of getting away from their parents: 'People who are unhappy at home go out and get pregnant and they get a house.' Grandparents were less likely to think that housing was an important motivation in teenage pregnancy, and were more likely than their daughters or the fathers to comment on the multiplicity of factors involved in teenage pregnancy, including lack of planning and judgement, as well as unrealistic expectations and lack of understanding of the responsibilities of having a baby. As one grandmother commented: 'Ignorance and carelessness possibly but not housing!' And others agreed that teenage pregnancies were often due to mistakes and lack of information: 'They need to use reliable contraception and know where to get it.'

There were mixed views among the women on whether single teenage mothers were more likely than young married couples to get council housing. Some married women thought that single women 'got the pick' of council housing, a view which was not supported by many of the single women: 'Where's my house then? I'm single. I'm a mother.'

It is unlikely that teenage mothers remain single in order to get council housing. Most of the women interviewed had thought that they would remain in a relationship with the baby's father when they had decided to continue with the pregnancy, whether or not they were cohabiting at that time. We have seen that both cohabiting and non-cohabiting relationships broke down, but there can be little doubt that few, if any, of the women we interviewed became pregnant with the idea that they would end up as single mothers, let alone that they were motivated by the thought of being a single mother in council accommodation. However, the (mostly married or cohabiting) fathers we interviewed were overwhelmingly of the opinion that single mothers did find it easier to be housed than married couples, and most cited examples among friends and acquaintances. Grandparents, on the other hand, were much less likely to agree. There were comments that single mothers had to know '*the ins and outs*' or '*fight tooth and nail*' and that their own daughters had not found it easy.

Nevertheless, by the time we conducted our interviews many of the women had turned to social housing, often as a key means in their attempts to become independent, whether they were still in a relationship with the baby's father or not. But it could be argued that few of the women living in local authority accommodation were really independent at all, and that increasing dependency on the state was a marked feature of the experiences of many of these teenage women over the period since they had become pregnant.

BENEFITS AND THE DEPENDENCY CULTURE

From the time these young women found themselves pregnant to the time of our interviews with them, the proportion receiving benefits (excluding the universal child benefit) increased from one-third to over 90 per cent. At interviews, over 80 per cent were on Income Support and 57 per cent were dependent on benefits as their sole source of income. Only 15 per cent were in employment of any kind.

Few of the women spoke of plans to enter or re-enter employment and it was rare for them to envisage a time when they might not be dependent on benefits, even if they were not happy about their present dependency. Again, there seemed to be an acceptance of a fate over which they saw themselves as having little control. They often bemoaned the fact that their previous work or study plans had changed as a result of the baby, but few appeared to have any idea of how they might change the pattern of their lives by laying the foundations for a return to work or study. These women were by no means all unqualified or without employment histories, and yet there appeared to be a marked reluctance to reduce their dependence on benefits.

One of the key factors with some was the expense of child care and the disincentive to work when most or all of their earnings would be taken by payment for child care. This was a subject which we could not explore in these interviews, but it is clearly an important issue for further investigation. A number of women made it clear that they would rather be working than dependent on social security benefits, a point reinforced in some of the interviews with grandparents, but they felt themselves caught in situations where they would be working for nothing after they had paid for child care. Few of the women interviewed thought that teenagers became pregnant to get extra social security benefits. The comments of one woman were echoed by many: 'The extra social security benefits never cover what a baby will cost you. I would say that is definitely untrue unless you're mental.'

However, just over a third of the women thought that some teenagers had babies because they knew that they would receive extra social security benefits. Married or cohabiting women were again more likely to think this than the single women, but most of them thought it was only true of some teenagers, who raised strong emotions among a few women: 'They shouldn't be allowed to have kids if they think like that.' Nearly half the fathers interviewed thought that some teenagers became pregnant to get extra social security benefits and we heard their views of women choosing the 'easy option' of having a baby, 'raking in so much from the social', and 'not having done a day's work in their life'.

But many of the fathers and the grandparents interviewed agreed with most women that the amount received in benefits would hardly cover the costs of having a baby. As one grandmother said: 'Those extra benefits are going to be gone before you can blink your eyes.' Grandparents often thought that any teenager embarking on pregnancy in order to get extra benefits would soon be disabused when she realized the costs involved, and were more likely to share the views of the women that the prospect of extra social security benefits was not an incentive to become pregnant.

GRANDPARENTS

The perspective of the grandparents we interviewed on the decisions made by the women added an important dimension to the research. We were able to achieve interviews with more grandparents than fathers of the babies, resulting in an interview with a parent or mother-in-law of nearly half the women in the study. Most of the interviews were with the babies maternal grandmothers, over half of whom had been teenage mothers themselves. We were more likely to interview grandparents with whom the mother and baby were living or in daily contact, so that we are not able to represent the views of grandparents who had little to do with the women we interviewed.

The main theme running through the interviews with grandparents was one of support and acceptance. They may well have had their doubts about the desirability of the pregnancy or the viability of the relationship, but the majority of them had stated time and again that they would support their daughters in whatever they decided to do. It was interesting that some of them stressed that the decision to continue with the pregnancy had to be their daughter's decision and expressed their reluctance to interfere in any way in case it was held against them in the future: 'It had to be her decision, her choice. We didn't want her to blame us later.' As we have seen, the anxieties which some of them had felt had proved correct, since nearly half of the daughters were no longer in a relationship with the baby's father. The support promised by the women's parents when the future of the pregnancy was discussed had been heavily called upon by the time of the interview in a substantial minority of cases, particularly by the women who had never moved from the parental home.

Grandparents, like the women themselves and the fathers, were often shocked and surprised by the news of the pregnancy, although it could be argued that they had more reason for surprise. But one-third of them were disappointed or upset or angry, and it was clear that they often felt that their daughters were too immature or not ready to have a baby and that they had expectations for their daughters which would not now be realized: 'I wanted more for her out of life.' But a quarter of the grandparents were pleased or even delighted by the news. Over half of them said that they had wanted their daughters to have the baby, a quarter said that it must be their own decision, and only around one in ten wanted them to terminate the pregnancy, even though others had considered it.

There were strong indications that the grandparents interviewed often felt themselves presented with a *fait accompli* by their daughters and recognized that any attempt to dissuade them from having the baby would be unwelcome. This confirmed the finding from our interviews with women that they tended to discuss the future of the pregnancy only with people who would agree with their decision to continue with the pregnancy and offer support in that decision.

Support was certainly forthcoming from the vast majority of grandparents interviewed and took many forms, including financial help, babysitting, and child care. This was not without its toll on the grandparents, and indeed some had changed their work plans, while one-third expressed concern at the pressures they were experiencing, especially if the mother and her baby were living with them. A small baby might have been acceptable, but by the time of the interviews babies were becoming toddlers and bringing additional pressures, particularly if there were other members of the family in the household.

Around half of the grandparents interviewed thought that things had worked out well, but their views were often tempered by their fears of how things might have worked out. There was evidence of considerable relief that their daughters were no longer in relationships they thought were unsuitable or even dangerous. 'Working out well' often meant 'working out better than expected'.

The support and help of their parents was often of crucial importance to the women, particularly if their relationship with the baby's father had broken down. But this underlined the isolation and loneliness of many of the women who were living alone with their babies at the time of the interview. As we have seen, we were rarely able to interview their parents, and indeed some of them stressed their poor relationship with their mothers and the fact that their fathers had never been part of their lives.

PLANNING, OUTCOMES, AND POLICY IMPLICATIONS

The lack of planning and foresight among the teenage mothers we interviewed has been a constant theme throughout the chapter. Only a quarter of the pregnancies were said to have been planned, and even among these planners there may well have been a certain amount of *post hoc* rationalization by the time of the interview. Two-thirds of the women said their work or study plans had been changed by their pregnancies, but there was little evidence that many of them had had firm long-term plans when they became pregnant. Even when they decided to continue with their pregnancies, many had unrealistic ideas of what was going to happen in their relationship with the baby's father, where and with whom they were going to live, and how they were going to support themselves and their babies. Our findings suggest that teenage mothers rarely had developed plans for their future or any strategy for realizing their expectations. In this respect, they were probably not unlike most teenagers, but they differed in that they found themselves with the responsibility for a baby.

One of the aims of the study was to examine the common perceptions that teenagers become pregnant to gain access to council housing and to gain extra social security benefits. It was abundantly clear in the interviews that such intentions had not even entered the heads of most of those we interviewed. They had not only been ill-informed about housing and benefits before they became pregnant but many of them had never thought that they would be in a position where they would need to know: 'It wasn't something I ever thought about before I was pregnant, or even when I was expecting the baby.'

An underlying theme which ran through the research was the fact that the vast majority of the teenage mothers in this study were not using contraception at the time that they became pregnant. We did not ask specifically about the use of contraception, as the interviews were very long and designed to explore decision-making about the continuation of the pregnancy and housing and living arrangements. Nevertheless, it was clear that few of the women had been actively taking steps to prevent pregnancy. But they were not the only participants, and not only were they taking risks but so were the young men.

Three-quarters of these young people may not have been planning to become pregnant, but they also were not planning to avoid pregnancy. The extent to which women risk pregnancy has always been apparent, even if the reasons are complex. It has been demonstrated time and again that ignorance of contraception is not an important factor among most women who have unplanned pregnancies (Allen 1985, 1991), even though perceptions that family planning services are inaccessible or lack guarantees of confidentiality may be a deterrent to teenagers (Allen 1991).

It has been demonstrated that teenage motherhood is beset with problems for a substantial proportion of women. This study, among others, has shown the risk that it will often result in negative short-term outcomes for women in terms of relationship breakdown, financial hardship, dependence on social security benefits, lack of a social life, unexpected responsibilities, and unsatisfactory housing, not to mention difficulties in forming new relationships if they are no longer in a relationship with the baby's father. Longer-term negative outcomes have been reported as including poor employment prospects, a high divorce rate, larger than average families, higher than average smoking rates, and poorer health status in later life (Wellings *et al.* 1996).

However, the same cannot necessarily be said of the fathers of babies born to teenage women. It appears from this and other research that for the fathers, the short-term consequences of the birth are largely determined by whether they remain in a relationship with the mother. It appears that few of the fathers were supporting the women or their babies if they were no longer in a relationship with them. Although there was ample evidence that many of those who were still in a relationship with the women were not contributing much to the support of their partners and babies, there appeared to be a greater commitment on their part to shoulder at least some of the responsibilities for bringing up the baby. It was impossible to gauge how long this would last, and there were disturbing signs of some rocky relationships even among those who were still together.

But teenagers are unlikely to be much influenced by the possibility of adverse longer-term outcomes to teenage motherhood. Young people simply do not look forward to what might be awaiting them in the future and there is little evidence that they modify their behaviour according to what might or might not happen to them, as can be seen by the high levels of teenage smoking, drinking, and drug-taking. There is a common belief, as demonstrated so often among women who become pregnant, that they are somehow immune from the possible or probable consequences of their behaviour or actions.

However, short-term consequences may be a different matter, and the result shown in this research of the breakdown of half the relationships with the baby's father by the time the baby was a year old could well be used in an educative way. Virtually none of these young women would have predicted this outcome, and few thought that they would end up as single lone mothers living in local authority accommodation on benefits within two years of getting pregnant. And yet many of them did, and they were by no means happy with their circumstances. The 'rosy' romantic view of love and motherhood had evaporated for many of these young women, who had continued with their pregnancies feeling assured of the lasting support of their partners.

Sex education programmes at school can have an impact on reducing teenage pregnancies, but research has shown that boys receive less adequate sex education than girls (Allen 1987). Further, sex education programmes which concentrate only on the 'mechanics' of reproduction and contraception are not as successful in preventing teenage pregnancies as those which explore personal relationships and allow time for discussion of feelings and emotions. It is also apparent that myths about happiness engendered by early motherhood need to be dispelled among teenagers of both sexes. We found that the young men were often more keen on the continuation of the pregnancy than the women, but many of them then abandoned the responsibility when it became real.

One of the main messages to be drawn from this analysis is that men should share the responsibility for teenage pregnancy and motherhood. However, it is obviously not enough to issue exhortations to young men that they must acknowledge their role and provide support if their partner has a baby. This would often fall on deaf ears, even if the women concerned were willing or able to pursue claims against them.

There is clearly a need for better and more co-ordinated programmes of education in sex and personal relationships, which are geared much more to exploring emotions and feelings as well as the roles and responsibilities of both men and women. But these should be laced with robust information about the likely short-term outcomes of teenage pregnancies and of the reduced opportunities available to teenage parents, particularly teenage mothers, to lead independent lives and to have fun. Educational programmes must be related to the lives teenagers lead and want to lead. The comments of one single non-working mother who was living alone with her baby summarized the views of an important minority and could be the starting point of any educational programme: 'If I could live my life over again, I'd be working now and I wouldn't have a kid.'

But there are many factors, apart from the romantic view of love and motherhood, to be overcome if educational programmes are to be successful. The belief that some teenagers become pregnant to get away from home and live on social security benefits because they cannot get a job was still prevalent, even among the women interviewed. It is well demonstrated that the longer a woman remains in education and the more qualifications she has, the less likely she is to be a teenage mother. But cause and effect should not be confused and a woman is clearly likely to stay longer in education and acquire more qualifications if she does not have a baby at an early age. There is a need not only to help lone parents return to work, but also to help all teenage mothers to improve their educational and vocational qualifications so that they are more able to become independent. As one of the grandmothers interviewed pointed out: 'If the mothers are blamed or victimized, then the children suffer and become our damaged adults of the future.'

CONCLUSION

A positive approach to reducing the adverse effects of teenage motherhood, while at the same time concentrating resources on reducing teenage pregnancy rates, is clearly essential. But there must be a change in the culture that accepts that young men can abandon all responsibility for their babies in spite of having taken no steps to prevent pregnancies and having encouraged their partners to continue with their pregnancies because they think abortion is wrong. Perhaps it is not surprising that men feel increasingly marginalized in our society today when they put themselves so deliberately outside the frame. But there are many dangers in sustaining a culture in which an important minority of young men have no role or responsibility in either work or family. This has been a recurrent theme in this research.

In this chapter, we have examined less than two years in the lives of a variety of teenage mothers and presented a complex picture of their characteristics and the factors affecting their decisions about pregnancy and their living and housing arrangements. In conclusion, it is important to note that half of the relationships had not broken down, and that among these teenage mothers were many who were happy with their babies, in stable relationships with young men who shared their responsibilities and maintained the delight so many of them had shown when their partners became pregnant. Not everyone was on social security benefits; some of the young women were working or studying for further qualifications and some were living in their own homes. The future was undoubtedly not all gloomy for many of the others, some of whom were redesigning their lives with the help and support of their parents or new partners while others were determined to make a new life for themselves and their babies.

NOTES

1. The conception rate (conceptions per 1,000 women) is a measure of pregnancies rather than births. In 1995, the conception rate for women of all ages in England and Wales was 73.7 per 1,000, while for teenage women it was 58.7. In Leeds, the conception rate was 59.0, almost the same as the national average. In East London and City (including Hackney) it was 100.5, a very high rate, and in Solihull it was 48.8, among the lowest in the country (ONS 1997*b*).
2. Those who had planned the pregnancy and those from ethnic minority groups were more likely than others still to be in a relationship with the baby's father, while those with educational qualifications were slightly more likely still to be with the baby's father.

15

Becoming a single mother

Richard Berthoud, Stephen McKay, and Karen Rowlingson

INTRODUCTION

During the last three decades in Britain there has been a rapid growth in the number of lone-parent families (Haskey 1994*a*). In 1971, there were about 570,000 lone parents; ten years later, this number had grown steadily to about 900,000. The rate of growth slowed slightly over the next few years, only to pass the one million mark by 1986. The rate of growth then picked up again to reach more than 1.5 million by 1995 (Haskey 1998*b*). Such families are often discussed as though they are all identical. There are, in fact, several different types of lone-parent family, although most are headed by the children's mother, with only about one in ten headed by a lone father. Until the early 1990s, the largest group of lone-parent families included women who had children while married and subsequently separated or divorced. A small, and shrinking, percentage of lone-parent families are headed by widows. The most rapidly increasing group includes women who had never married prior to motherhood, who are estimated to have outnumbered divorced lone mothers for the first time in 1991. By 1994, one in twelve of all families with dependent children were headed by never-married mothers (Haskey 1996*a*: 9–10). About half of these women, however, had previously lived with the father of their child(ren) in a cohabiting relationship.

The rapid growth of lone motherhood has raised a number of concerns, which focus most sharply on never-married lone mothers. These include the poverty and hardship experienced by women and children in such families, the cost to the public purse of paying benefits to lone parents, and the possible adverse effects on the development of children. Most recently, the Labour government has responded with policy changes designed to help lone mothers into the labour force. There has been extensive public discussion about the implications of rapidly growing rates of lone parenthood, but such debate has, for the most part, taken place in the absence of a fundamental understanding of the nature of that growth. The research reported in this chapter forms part of a study which sought to fill that gap by investigating the causes and consequences of the increase in lone parents in Britain over the past thirty years. The aims of this study were twofold: (1) to examine the dynamics of lone parenthood and the factors influencing the beginning and end of periods as a one-parent family, considering both never-married or cohabiting mothers and formerly married or cohabiting mothers; and (2) to gain insights into women's motivations at both ends of the period, through in-depth interviews with recent and former lone mothers. The study represents one of the few attempts to examine the experiences of never-married *single* lone mothers as opposed to never-married *formerly cohabiting* lone mothers. We think it likely that the latter have more in common with formerly married women than with women who became mothers without living with the fathers of their children, although this, of course, remains an open question empirically (see Rowlingson and McKay 1998 for full results of the study).

RESEARCH METHODS

The study combined quantitative and qualitative approaches.

Quantitative research

Quantitative analyses were based on data from the ESRC's Social Change and Economic Life Initiative (SCELI). Those data were derived from around 6,000 interviews carried out in six British towns among respondents who were aged between 16 and 60 at the time. The questionnaire covered a range of employment and personal areas, including movements in and out of paid work, dates of marriage and having children, and changes of living arrangements. Complete life and work histories were collected—to the nearest month for most questions—for the period from age 14 to the date of interview. As a result, we are able to use event-history analysis to investigate flows into and out of different family types, including lone parenthood (see Rowlingson and McKay 1998 for further information).

One of the main advantages of using SCELI is that information was collected on cohabitation and separation, rather than just marriage and divorce as was the case with data used previously to analyse lone parenthood (cf. Ermisch 1991), thus allowing more extensive analyses of the experiences of lone mothers. The main disadvantage of the survey is its age. Data were collected in 1986, and this is a serious limitation on what can be said about the most recent increase in single women having children. Nonetheless, the survey includes enough single lone parents to enable meaningful analyses of their characteristics and circumstances. Lone fathers were excluded from the quantitative analyses as they comprise a relatively small group who differ from lone mothers in systematic ways; for example, they are much more likely than women to have become lone parents through the death of a spouse and are more likely to be employed.

Qualitative research

The qualitative research involved in-depth interviews with 44 women who were, or had recently been, lone parents. Like the quantitative analysis, lone fathers were excluded, as were widows for similar reasons. The main method of locating respondents was to re-contact lone parents who had been interviewed as part of a large survey at the end of 1994. That sample did not include any recent lone parents, however, and to find them, we employed a combination of methods. If a respondent from the 1994 survey knew a recent lone parent, the interviewer would get in touch with that woman. Interviewers also wrote to child care groups and put up posters in community centres and other venues where lone parents might be found.

The 44 interviews broke down into three subgroups. The first comprised *recent* lone mothers—mothers who had been lone parents for less than two years, who were included in the study because their recall of the events leading to lone parenthood would be fresh in their minds. Some *long-term* lone parents were also interviewed: women who had been lone parents for more than two years. This group were interesting because they could tell us about how they became lone parents and also why they remained lone parents. The final group was *former lone parents*: women who had been lone parents but had found a partner in the last two years and were now living in a couple. These women could tell us about becoming a lone parent as well as about the process of leaving lone motherhood.

It should be pointed out that we interviewed only women—their former boyfriends or partners might have given a different picture of the events of interest. Other research reported in this volume involved talking to non-resident fathers (Bradshaw *et al.*, Chapter 17). Furthermore, we interviewed only lone parents. Thus, the qualitative analysis (unlike the quantitative) does not compare lone parents with the majority of women who had neither had a pre-marital child nor separated from their husbands.

DEFINING SINGLE MOTHERHOOD

We noted above the rapid growth in never-married lone parents. According to official statistics, about a third of all lone mothers in the early 1990s had never married. However, about half of these mothers entered lone parenthood through separation from a cohabiting relationship (McKay and Marsh 1994; Haskey 1998*b*) and thus may have more in common with formerly married lone mothers than with women who had their first babies while single (cf. Ermisch 1995). Because of this, both our quantitative and our qualitative analyses define single mothers in a different way from that used in official statistics—as women who had a first baby while not living with a partner. Thus, in selecting lone mothers for interviews, we chose two groups of women according to their circumstances at the time of the birth of their first baby: single or separated. Half (22) were chosen for interviews because they had become lone parents through marriage or cohabitation breakdown—we refer to these women as *separated lone mothers*; the other half (22) were chosen because they had become lone parents through having a baby while living without a partner—we call these women *single mothers*.

This distinction between separated and single mothers may seem fairly clear but in some cases it was not easy to decide into which category a particular lone mother should be placed. The boundaries around lone parenthood are vague and there are several different types of lone-parent family (Crow and Hardey 1992). The SCELI survey obscured any ambiguities in people's relationships, as the interviewers could only code whether a respondent said that they were living with someone or that they were not. Where there was doubt, the respondent had to make a choice about which side of the cohabitation line they were on. That survey therefore gives the impression that the boundaries around cohabitation, and single parenthood, are clear.

Our qualitative research tells a different story. For example, among the 22 *single* mothers, eight had never lived with men but had had regular boyfriends, including a 19-year-old woman who had been going out with her boyfriend for two years before she got pregnant. She was still living at home with her mother and her boyfriend stayed over occasionally. They continued seeing each other for some time after the birth but then separated. She was classified as *single* even though she had had a regular partner. Should she have been classified as a *separated* lone parent? We decided not to, because she had not actually lived with her boyfriend at the time she had her baby. A further six of the 22 single lone parents had previously lived with partners: three of whom had lived with someone in the past but not at the time they had conceived; and three of whom had been living with the father of their child at the time they conceived, but split up before the child was born. Table 15.1 summarizes the marital histories of the single lone mothers we interviewed up to the time of their first baby's birth.

TABLE 15.1. *Partnership histories of single mothers*

Number	Partnership history
16	Never cohabited
of whom 8	had casual or no boyfriends
8	had regular boyfriends
6	Cohabited prior to motherhood
of whom 3	stopped cohabiting before conception
3	separated while pregnant

THE GROWTH OF SINGLE MOTHERHOOD

Pre-marital conceptions and their outcomes

The growth in single motherhood since the early 1970s could be due to one or both of the following: more single women becoming pregnant, or more pregnant single women having a first child while still single. Having a baby when single is the beginning of lone parenthood, but it can also be seen as the end of a process which involves a number of stages: having sex while single; not using contraception or using it unsuccessfully; getting pregnant; not having an abortion; not getting together with the baby's father (or another partner); and not giving up the baby for adoption. At each of these stages, women face choices and constraints which affect their decisions and therefore the eventual outcome. Over time, the nature of that outcome has changed as, according to our research evidence, lone parenthood has come to be seen by some women as less problematic than the available alternative outcomes.

Between 1975 and 1993, the number of conceptions outside marriage more than doubled from 161,000 to 364,000 (Figure 15.1). Although this was accompanied by a substantial increase in the overall number of abortions, the proportion of all pre-marital conceptions which were terminated dropped slightly from 40 per cent to 33 per cent. There was no increase at all in the number of births to couples who married less than nine months before the birth of their baby; as a *proportion* of all pre-marital pregnancies, however, this outcome fell from 27 per cent to 8 per cent. There was an enormous increase in the number of births outside marriage jointly registered by the mother and the father, the majority of whom were

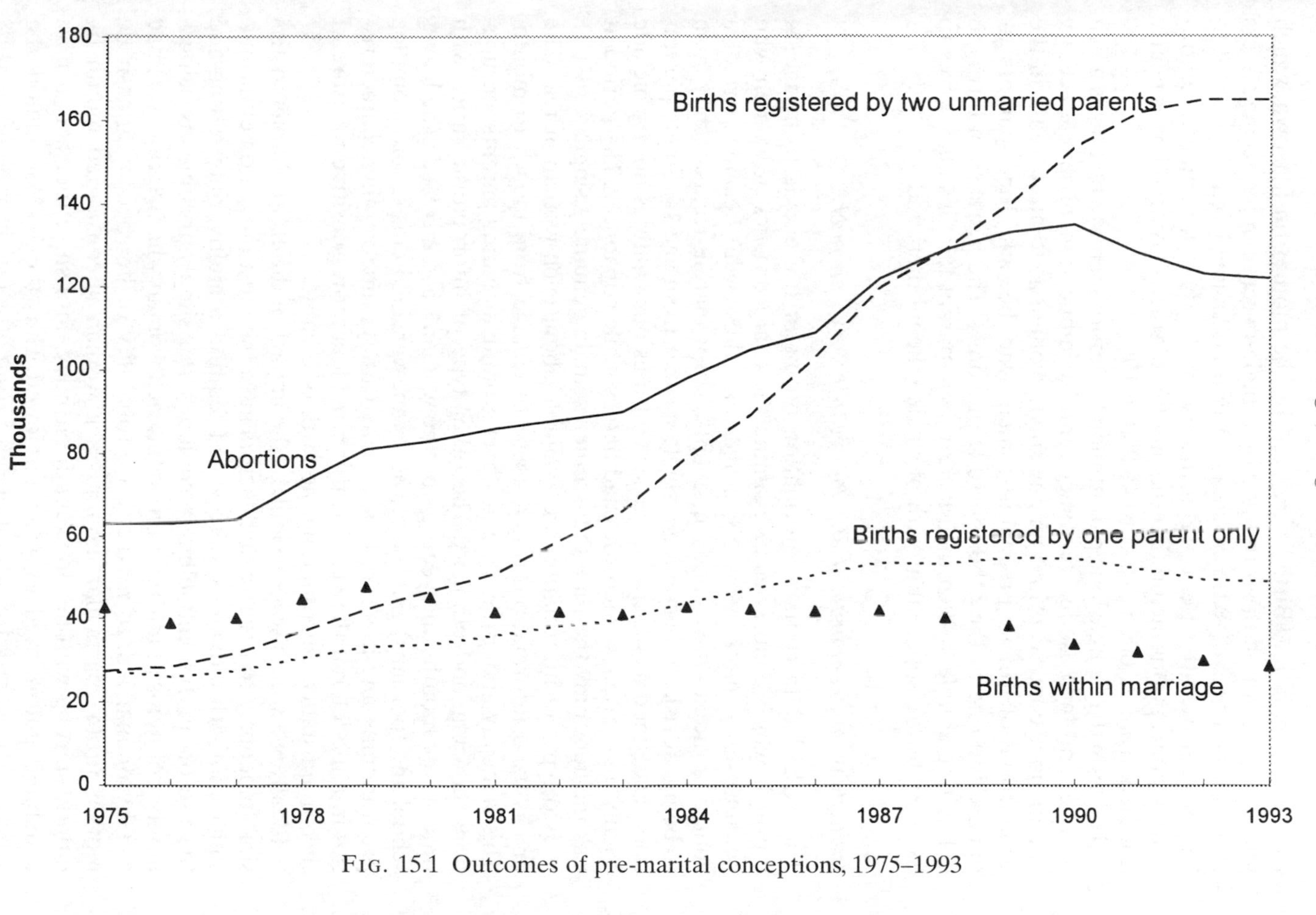

Fig. 15.1 Outcomes of pre-marital conceptions, 1975–1993

probably cohabiting. Births registered by the mother on her own, which give an indication of the formation of a single-parent family, became a less common outcome of extra-marital conceptions, falling from 17 per cent to 13 per cent over this period. But the rise in the overall number of extra-marital conceptions meant that the number of sole-registered births nearly doubled, from 27,000 in 1975 to 49,000 in 1993.

The growth of single lone parenthood therefore seems to be due as much to a general increase in pregnancy (and by implication, in sexual activity and/or poor contraception) among single women as to an increase in the proportion of single pregnant women who become lone parents as opposed to one of the other possible outcomes. The increase in births to cohabiting couples which then lead to lone-parent families also serves to exaggerate the apparent growth of single lone motherhood.

Influences on pre-marital births: an event-history approach

The SCELI data contain information on major life events from age 14 onwards which enables us to examine the characteristics of women who became single mothers by given ages and those who became part of a couple or did not have children. Event-history analysis treats each woman as being 'at risk' of becoming a single mother from age 14. Single parenthood is defined as described earlier and thus our analyses do *not* include legally unmarried women who had babies while cohabiting. The period at risk includes only the time that women remain genuinely single.

Two types of information are available about each woman at risk. The first is fixed information, which does not change from month to month. This is mostly about the woman's background, including parents' occupations, housing, and ethnicity. The other type of information varies with time: as the months and years go by, the woman's age increases; she leaves school and (perhaps) gets a job. These time-varying items require complex programming and it is rare to see many (if any) time-varying characteristics in a model, but they can clearly provide a more sensitive measure of the circumstances surrounding the birth of a baby.

Ideally, we would want to look at the impact of different characteristics simultaneously, to assess which factors have the most impact on entry into single motherhood; an exercise which requires a multivariate setting and the use of survival modelling techniques. Put simply, this means using a number of items of information about each woman who had not (yet) had a baby or married, to predict the probability of her becoming a single mother in any particular month. Each woman is considered month by month, starting with her fourteenth birthday, until she either had a baby, cohabited, got married, or was interviewed. Thus, the 3,379 women in the sample were at risk for a total of 276,537 months (an average of nearly 8 years per woman). The event in question—a pre-marital birth—occurred on 225 occasions, yielding a hazard rate of 8.1 births per 10,000 months (or about 1 per cent per year).

Table 15.2, and Table 15.3 later in the chapter, show the results of our analyses. The first column of each table is based on a straightforward comparison of the hazard rate—the chances of becoming a single mother—between categories, using only one variable at a time. The second column provides the results of a multivariate model in which logistic regression techniques were used to estimate probabilities, taking account of all the variables at once. This is designed to show the independent effect of each variable, holding all others constant. In each group, one item has been

TABLE 15.2. *Hazard rates for the birth of a child before marriage, by background factors*

	Simple analysis[a]	Multivariate model[a]	Sample size (woman-months)
Overall average	8.3 per 10,000		
Father's occupation	*R* = 0.060	Not significant	
Professional	0.37		49,825
Other non-manual	1.09		13,233
Self-employed	0.65		31,065
Technical/skilled manual	0.78		75,067
Semi-unskilled manual	1.00 (= 10.4)		67,511
Not known	1.23		28,969
Mother's occupation	*R* = 0.014	Not significant	
Professional	0.48		15,433
Non-manual	0.66		61,092
Self-employed	0.34		3,155
Technical/skilled	0.89		37,187
Semi-unskilled	1.00 (= 9.4)		75,546
Not known	1.09		73,257
Tenure at age 14	*R* = 0.094	*R* = 0.091	
Owner-occupier	1.00 (= 9.4)	1.00	108,816
Public rented	2.29	2.46	102,772
Private rented	0.90	1.33	33,790
Others	1.14	1.39	20,292
Ethnic group	*R* = 0.034	*R* = 0.043	
White	1.00 (= 8.3)	1.00	258,322
Asian	0.91	1.14	5,262
West Indian	4.83	5.91	995
Not known	0.00	0.04	1,091

[a] In each group, one element has been chosen as the reference category and assigned a relative risk of 1.0; the hazards in other categories are expressed as a ratio to that one. The actual risk (per 10,000) in the reference category is given in brackets. In the first panel of the table, for example, the risk of single motherhood is 10.4 per 10,000 for the daughter of a semi- or unskilled manual father. for women whose fathers had been in professional occupations, it was just over one-third of that.

chosen as the reference category and assigned a relative risk of 1.0. The hazards in the other categories are expressed as a ratio to the reference category. The figure for *R* associated with each heading is a measure of the power of each variable in distinguishing between women with high and low risks. None of the *R*s is very large (the theoretical maximum is 1.00), reflecting the fact that even high-risk women could go many months or years before they actually became single mothers, and no analysis can expect to explain much of this variance. The sample sizes look very large because the data have been converted from a sample of people to a sample of 'person-months'.

Social background

Studies have suggested that women from disadvantaged backgrounds are more likely than others to have children while unmarried and/or teenagers than others (Garfinkel and McLanahan 1986; Ermisch 1991). Analysis of the SCELI data using a measure of social class based on the woman's father's occupation is consistent with this (Table 15.2, first panel): the risk of single motherhood was lowest among women whose father was in a professional occupation, and high for those from a semi- or unskilled manual background. The high rate of single parenthood among women whose father's occupation was not known might be a further indicator of social disadvantage, as a number of these fathers may have been long-term unemployed; or alternatively, members of this category may have been lone-parent families (that is, no father in the household). Using the woman's mother's occupation produced a similar, though rather weaker, range of variation between professional and semi-unskilled workers' families (Table 15.2, second panel).

Housing tenure is another indicator of socio-economic position. Indeed, it has been argued (Marsh and McKay 1993) that the cleavage between owner-occupiers and council tenants is now more important than occupational class as a measure of the divisions in British society. That contention is supported by the results of this analysis, at least in relation to becoming a single mother. Women whose families had been social tenants when they were age 14 were more than twice as likely to become a single parent as those from other housing backgrounds (Table 15.2, third panel). Not only was this variable more powerful than either mother's or father's occupation; once all three were included in the analysis, tenure at age 14 captured all the effects of having a disadvantaged background, and the occupational variables no longer had any significant influence on the risk of single parenthood.

Another characteristic which women inherit from their family of origin is ethnic group. There is strong evidence from cross-sectional surveys that the main minorities in Britain adopt different family formation patterns, not only from the white population, but also from each other. The fourth national survey of ethnic minorities (Modood *et al.* 1997), for example, showed that Caribbean men and women have comparatively low rates of marriage: more than five times as many women of Caribbean origin as white women were bringing up children on their own, having never been (formally) married. In contrast, Asians place a high priority on marriage, and very few Asian single parents were identified by that survey.

Ethnic minorities in the UK are highly concentrated in certain large cities (Ratcliffe 1996) and a survey of six towns, such as SCELI, is unlikely to provide the best vehicle for studying ethnic variations in any depth. Our analysis based on SCELI data suggests that the risk of single motherhood was five times as high for West Indian women as for whites (Table 15.2, fourth panel). Although this is based on only five births to West Indian mothers in the sample, the result is nevertheless highly significant statistically; and it stood up to multivariate analysis. Because of the nature of the SCELI design, however, we would not place much weight on this finding on its own, were it not consistent with the results of other research (Modood *et al.* 1997).

The woman's situation at the time of the birth

Factors such as family background remain constant throughout an adult's life, but other potential influences on single parenthood vary over time. Our analysis now turns to these varying factors in order to assess the changing risk of single parenthood as women grow older, complete their education, look for work, and leave the parental home. It is important to think through the implications of any variations likely to be identified here. Some aspects of a woman's situation at any particular time can be considered to be the outcome of external influences upon her. This is undoubtedly the case for her age; it may also be partly the case for more personal aspects of a woman's situation. The time at which she leaves home, for example, could be a consequence of her family background or the availability of independent accommodation or some combination of these two. Decisions about leaving school or getting a job might be affected by the quality of local educational services and the availability of suitable employment. Thus, such factors might be considered independent influences on the probability of becoming a single mother. On the other hand, leaving home and/or school might be influenced by factors more directly associated with a woman's risk of single parenthood—and, indeed, her attitudes to parental authority or social convention might influence all three of these decisions. To that extent, associations between a woman's situation at the time of a birth and her chances of entering

TABLE 15.3. *Hazard rates for the birth of a child before marriage, by circumstances at the time*

	Simple analysis[a]	Multivariate model[a,b]	Sample size (woman-months)
Overall average	8.3 per 10,000		
Age at time			
Log of age	$R = 0.059$	$R = 0.060$	
(Log of age)^2	$R = 0.057$	$R = 0.058$	
Current housing	$R = 0.123$	$R = 0.097$	
Lives with parents	1.00 (= 7.6)	1.00	227,205
Current owner	0.43	2.06	6,168
Current social tenant	6.13	8.50	4,311
Current private tenant	1.07	2.40	11,062
Others/not known	1.56	3.89	16,924
Current activity	$R = 0.155$	$R = 0.136$	
Working	1.00 (= 9.4)	1.00	148,783
Unemployed	4.45	3.49	4,776
Sick or disabled	1.43	1.24	744
Full-time education	0.50	0.56	87,780
Full-time housewife	4.86	7.28	2,403
Not known	0.50	0.51	21,184

[a] See Table 15.2, note *a*.
[b] All 14- and 15-year-olds remained in full-time education and the overwhelming majority were living with their own parents. The multivariate model including current housing and current activity was therefore confined to women aged 16 or over.

single motherhood (or her hazard rate) would not necessarily indicate causal influences.

For these measures of a young woman's situation, we do not want to know her circumstances *after* having a baby, nor even those prevailing at the same time as the birth. Instead, analyses should be made in relation to her situation at the time she was taking steps or decisions which would determine whether she would have a baby—that is, between six and nine months beforehand (on the assumption that decisions about abortion would mostly be made during that period). Our analytical definition of 'current situation' is based, therefore, on a woman's circumstances nine months prior to the month being analysed as at risk.

An important first step is to understand how the risk of single parenthood varies as women grow older. The data assume that no woman had a baby before age 14, and that from 14 onwards, she was 'at risk'. The dashed line in Figure 15.2 shows how many members of the SCELI survey sample had babies while single at ages 14, 15, 16, and so on, in absolute terms. Most of the unwed mothers were teenagers at the time, and the rate of single

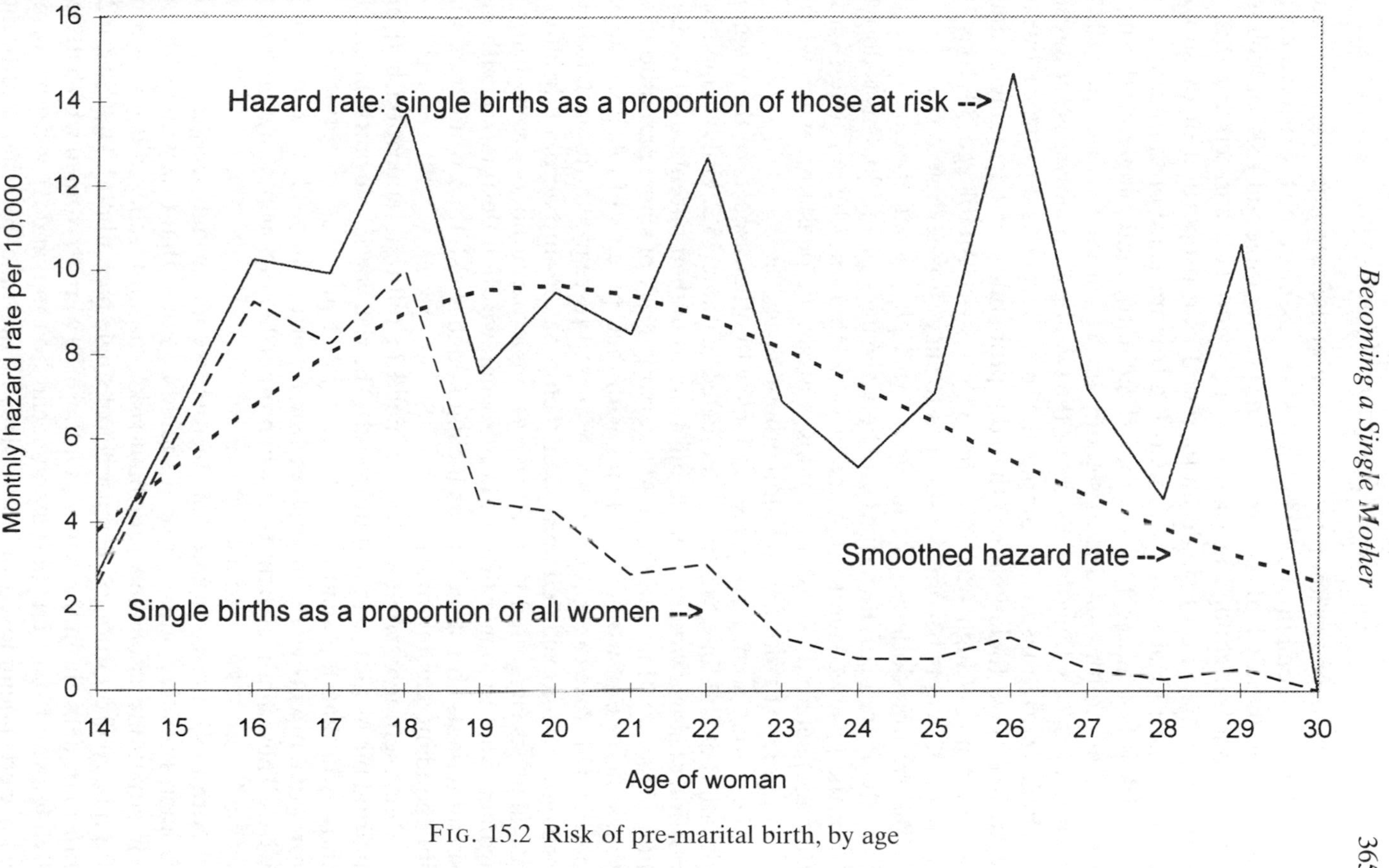

FIG. 15.2 Risk of pre-marital birth, by age

motherhood becomes low once women enter their twenties. This is because fewer women remain at risk by that stage, as more of them have either married or already had a baby and thus are no longer 'at risk' of having a *first* pre-marital child. The solid line in Figure 15.2 corrects for this, by expressing the rate of single motherhood as a proportion of those who were still at risk at each age. This is the true measure of the hazard rate. The risk is low at age 14—less than three entries into single motherhood per 10,000 months—and rises steadily up to fourteen entries per 10,000 months at age 18. Fluctuations across the twenties probably arise as a result of chance variations in the sample; the overall trend is downward, but the solid line nevertheless shows that the probability of becoming a single parent remains high well into the twenties—not until age 30 does the number of events become so small as to suggest a negligible risk.

The smooth dotted curve in Figure 15.2 plots what appears to be the underlying trend of the hazard rate between ages 14 and 30. This is derived from the positive sign for log age in Table 15.3, and the negative sign for (log age) squared. According to this analysis, the peak time when women are at greatest risk of single motherhood is age 19.

There were some strong associations with other aspects of the women's situation at the time, which are indicated in Table 15.3. Only a small proportion of single women were living away from their parents and in council housing at any time, but they had a very high risk of single parenthood: six times the rate of women still living with their parents (Table 15.3, second panel). This rose to eight times when 14- and 15-year-olds (almost all living at home) were excluded and other factors taken into account. Multivariate analysis suggested that the risk of single parenthood was high for all women who no longer lived at home, whatever their destination, although social tenants still stood out as having a higher risk than women in other independent accommodation.

Relatively few women who remained in full-time education had premarital births (Table 15.3, third panel). The risk was significantly higher for those who had left school and taken a job. But it was exceptionally high for women who were unemployed or reported themselves to be housewives. These findings held true when other factors such as age and background were taken into account.

Although these situational factors were strongly associated with women's relative rates of risk, it should be noted that few women were in the situations associated with high risks; therefore, they did not account for a large proportion of all episodes of single parenthood. There were 225 pre-marital births in the sample. Of these, 20 were to women who had been living away from their parents in social housing, and 31 were to women who were unemployed or housewives at the time: in other words, most babies were not born into high-risk situations.

Trends over time

So far, our analyses have assumed that women's chances of becoming single mothers (their hazard rates) were fixed over the whole period under consideration, from 1945 to 1984. In fact, these changed substantially over that period and one of the key objectives of this research was to describe, analyse and, if possible, explain these changes over time.

When the births to single mothers in the SCELI sample were plotted as hazard rates for each year between 1945 and 1984, the upward trend was not as steady as might have been expected (Figure 15.3). There was a period of rapid growth in the 'swinging sixties', but a clear fall in the 1970s, probably associated with the legalization of abortion. Nonetheless, the hazard rate was higher in the second half of the period under review than in the first. Between 1945 and 1966, the overall average was 4.8 pre-marital births per 10,000 months at risk; from 1967 to 1984, it was more than twice as high at 12.4 births per 10,000 months. Other analyses show that the increase was especially marked among very young mothers aged 14 and 15—the risk for them was four times as great after 1967 as it had been before, although they remained less likely to have a pre-marital child than older women.[1]

One of the main objectives of the analysis was to test whether the rising trend in entry to lone parenthood could be explained in terms of factors known to influence pre-marital births, such as council housing tenure and personal unemployment (see Tables 15.2 and 15.3). If there had been an increase over the years in the number of out-of-work women from council house backgrounds, that might have caused a rise in the number of births to single mothers. If so, the actual increase in the number would not have been so striking. However, the dashed line in Figure 15.3 plots the rate at which women would have been 'predicted' to have had children outside marriage over the period under study, on the basis of changes in the background factors identified in Tables 15.2 and 15.3. The predicted trend is almost flat, so the rise in the actual hazard remains strong, even after other factors have been taken into account.

Leaving lone parenthood

Although the primary focus of this chapter is on the process of *becoming* a single mother, it is relevant to refer to some findings from our analyses of the rate at which single mothers *left* that state by forming partnerships. In the 1960s, at the beginning of the period of growth of single motherhood, single women with a baby married or found a partner quite quickly—about half of single mothers left single parenthood within three years. This was much faster than the exits of separated and divorced

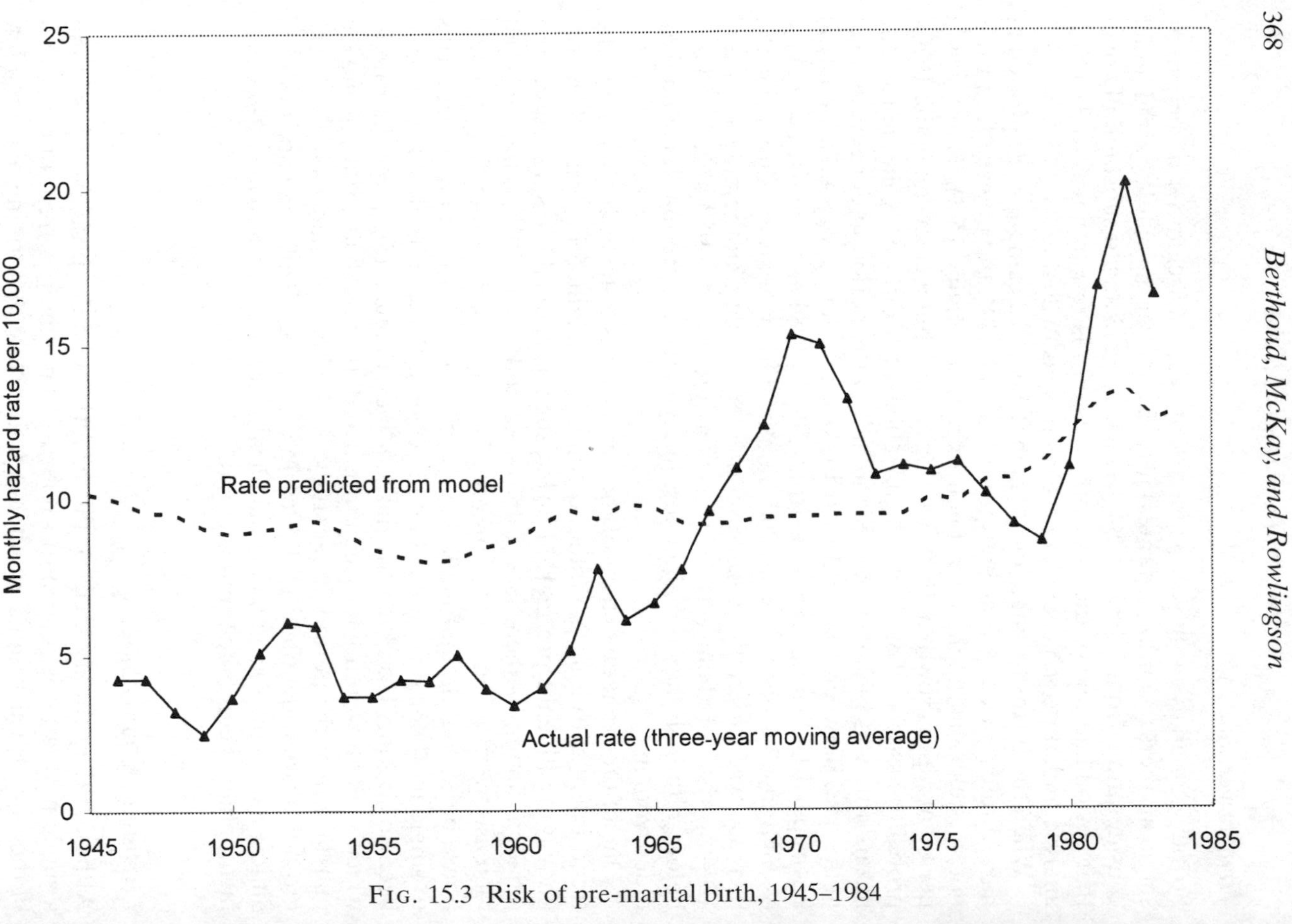

FIG. 15.3 Risk of pre-marital birth, 1945–1984

mothers, whose median duration was about eight years. But whereas the marriage or repartnering rate of previously married mothers has held steady over time, for single mothers the marriage or partnering rate has decreased, and at the end of the period they were remaining lone parents for as long as their formerly married counterparts. This means that the rise in the 'stock' of *separated and divorced* mothers is entirely due to an increase in the inflow into lone motherhood, but that the rise in the number of *single* parents is caused by a combination of more women having babies before marriage and more of them remaining single for longer periods.

THE EXPERIENCE OF SINGLE MOTHERHOOD: EVIDENCE FROM IN-DEPTH INTERVIEWS

As mentioned earlier in this chapter, the qualitative research highlighted great diversity within the category of single lone mother. This was true even of the relationships they were having at the time of conception: some had got pregnant after fairly casual sex; others had regular boyfriends with whom they were not cohabiting; while others had been cohabiting but had separated from their partners before the baby was either conceived or born. Only one woman we interviewed had deliberately planned to become a single mother. In common with previous research (Renvoize 1985), she was older and more middle-class than the other single mothers. The questions for our research were, therefore, why the remaining women became pregnant and why they had continued with the pregnancy to become single mothers (cf. Allen and Bourke Dowling, Chapter 14 of this volume).

Some single mothers got pregnant because they did not use contraception, even though they did not want to conceive. This was mostly due to trusting in a partner, taking risks, or a reluctance to feel, or be seen as, promiscuous:

> I didn't think I was capable [of getting pregnant]—does that sound silly? But when you're 16, you just . . . it was very much a trust thing with me.

Most women felt that the risk of getting pregnant was low and, although pregnancy was not considered a desirable outcome, neither was it seen as particularly disastrous. Some women were using unreliable contraception methods. Others fell pregnant because their contraception was unsuccessful; they missed one or more pills, for example, or were taking antibiotics which reduced the pill's effectiveness:

> I was on the pill . . . but the pills were at home . . . and I wasn't going home [every day]. It sounds stupid now, but I just missed them out and then next day, took two, and it just happened.

Becoming pregnant is only one step on the road to lone parenthood. Some women considered having abortions; others objected to abortion as a matter of principle. Some had had previous experiences of abortion they did not wish to repeat:

> When I was 17 I got pregnant . . . and he was black and mum and dad went crazy because . . . they're very racist . . . when mum and dad found out I was pregnant: 'You will get rid of it!' So I had an abortion . . . when I first had it done, I locked myself in my room every night for months and months and, I don't know—sometimes I look back and think: 'Oh, what would it be like?'

Others, however, after the initial shock had worn off, simply became accustomed to the idea of having a baby while single and did not see it as a problem which needed a solution such as abortion. This resonates with our quantitative results: women from poor socio-economic backgrounds saw motherhood as an acceptable, and in some cases desirable, alternative to life in low-paid, low-status work.

Motherhood in general may have had its attractions but this does not necessarily mean that *lone* motherhood would be attractive and these women might, in theory, have cohabited with the father of their child. However, some of the men involved would not consider living with the woman, while some of the women did not consider their boyfriends suitable for marriage or partnership, mostly because they were not seen as particularly industrious or trustworthy. Men without jobs, or in poorly paid jobs, were not considered useful as breadwinners, partners, or full-time fathers:

> He was just really young and immature and . . . not the marrying sort of material . . . he was completely irresponsible—never around, going off for days on end . . . oh, he also slept with my best friend . . . that was before I got pregnant . . . I wouldn't get married to him, yeah, because he was totally untrustworthy.

The final choice open to single women wanting to avoid lone parenthood is adoption. This was rarely considered, however, as it was incompatible with their identities as women and carers and regarded as more highly stigmatized than lone parenthood.

The reactions of the young woman's own mother and father were important in shaping the eventual outcome. Parents were usually shocked on first hearing the news of their daughter's pregnancy, but most ultimately were supportive and said that they would respect whatever choices their daughters made. None of the women interviewed seemed to have been threatened with a shotgun wedding:

> At first [my mother] was, I suppose, a bit angry. But she soon got used to the idea and she was all excited and, you know, she loved [my daughter] and spoilt her.

[My father] was quite mad about the situation . . . I was his little girl and, you know, shattered all his dreams . . . I had their full support, what I wanted. If I wanted to carry on through the pregnancy, it was perfectly fine. If I wanted to terminate the pregnancy, they'd go with me either way. I was under no pressure at all.

Thus, there is some evidence that single motherhood is not considered to be as much of a problem by the families of potential lone parents as it was in the past (cf. Marsden 1969). In any case, shotgun weddings in the past may only have served to postpone the creation of lone-parent families, as these marriages had a higher than average chance of ending in separation (Ermisch 1991; Rowlingson and McKay 1998). Today, a woman is more likely to move directly to becoming a *single* mother instead of having a rather short spell as a wife before becoming a *separated* lone mother.

Most women expected to receive social security in their own right once they became single parents. They did not expect this to be generous, but in some cases it was seen as preferable to the available alternatives, such as living on benefit as a couple. Moreover, living on benefits did not always entail a drastic drop in living standards compared with their previous situation:

[My boyfriend] was on Income Support to start with, it was all just put in his name, so like the cheque every week was just given straight to him and I had to ask him for money, that was part of why we finished and that . . . because I had to go to him for money and he's such a tight bastard.

When I was in the YTS, you only get paid for the day you went so I was probably on about £13 a week most weeks so, yeah, [I was] better off [on Income Support] as a lone parent. It was a secure, stable income of money.

In the past, the stigma against lone parenthood may have been enough to discourage single women from having or keeping babies. Our evidence suggests that this stigma is still a factor, but that single mothers did not identify themselves as being among those who deliberately get pregnant for social security and council housing reasons—a group most lone parents confidently asserted did exist. They could therefore dissociate themselves from much of the general stigma which exists.

CONCLUSIONS

Official statistics show that the number of never-married mothers increased fivefold between 1971 and 1992, and that never-married mothers represent about a third of all lone mothers. However, these statistics mask the fact that about half of the recent group of never-married mothers were in cohabiting relationships before becoming lone mothers. The number of *genuinely* single women who have babies is thus smaller than that suggested by official figures. In past decades, single women on becoming pregnant would most likely marry the father of their baby, but these unplanned marriages often ended in separation and lone parenthood. Today's single woman may bypass the shotgun wedding and head straight for lone parenthood. So concern about the growth of single motherhood should be tempered by the knowledge that official figures exaggerate its prevalence.

Nevertheless, research has shown that there has been a substantial increase in both the number of single women who have babies while not living with a partner, and the length of time that they remain in that state. This is in spite of technological and legal changes—contraception and abortion—which greatly reduce the risk that pre-marital sex will lead to the birth of a child. Few single women deliberately plan to get pregnant; but once they do so, many decide to have and keep the baby and remain single, rather than to undergo an abortion, marry the father, or follow the course which would have been enjoined upon them in the past, to give the baby up for adoption. They see lone motherhood as an option to be preferred to the alternatives available to them. Those from poor socio-economic backgrounds may see motherhood as providing better status and identity along with more meaningful work than that offered by low-paid jobs.

Our research suggests that people's views of these moral and social issues have been changing. Two generations ago, a single woman, her family, and her neighbours would have been appalled at the news that she was pregnant. The fact that many more single women have become pregnant over the past decades, in spite of the increased availability and effectiveness of contraception, and the fact that they remain single mothers for longer, are both consistent with the view that single motherhood is becoming an acceptable (if not a desirable) condition. Our quantitative analyses offered little support for the suggestion that these trends have been caused by other changes in economic and social structures. This leaves a change in social norms as the most likely explanation for the rise in numbers. Moreover, our qualitative interviews with the women concerned support the view that single parenthood is no longer seen, by them or by others, as the deep shame it once was. It may not be a single woman's objective, but it may nonetheless be preferred to some other outcomes.

That is not to say, to echo the phrase of one of our colleagues (Scott, Chapter 3 of this volume), that 'anything goes' nowadays. Single parent-hood may have become more acceptable, but young mothers still feel, or are made to feel, uneasy about their position. Moreover, there were signs in the qualitative research that behaviour is still influenced by strong moral values. Although many more pre-marital pregnancies are terminated by abortion than lead to single parenthood, many of those who had rejected that route quoted reasons of principle for their decisions. And it was striking how vehemently some women objected—on moral grounds—to adoption, which had so often been expected of them in the past. Social and moral considerations have not been abandoned. They have changed.

NOTE

1. The monthly hazard rate for the period 1945–66 (per 10,000 months at risk) for women aged 14 or 15 was 2.0, rising to 7.9 for the period 1967–84. The comparable figures for women aged 16–18 were 6.7 and 16.4 respectively.

PART IV
Divorce and After

16

Who divorces?

Kathleen Kiernan and Ganka Mueller

INTRODUCTION

The rise of divorce is one of the most important social developments of recent decades, and brings to the fore fundamental questions about the relations between men and women and the rearing of children in modern societies. Britain has one of the highest divorce rates in Europe. Yet, there are surprisingly few recent British studies on the characteristics of the divorced population or about which men, women, and couples are more prone to divorce. Some well-known features of the divorced population have been revealed by previous research in Britain and other countries. One of the most robust and consistent findings is that the earlier a partnership is formed, the more likely it is to break down, a tendency which persists after many years of marriage (Murphy 1985; Hoem 1991). Other demographic factors implicated in marital breakdown include having a pre-marital birth (Kravdal 1988; Bracher *et al.* 1993), cohabiting prior to marriage (Bennett, Blanc, and Bloom 1988; Haskey 1992; Ermisch 1995), and having a spouse who has been previously married (Martin and Bumpass 1989; Haskey 1983). Two of these tendencies—having a pre-marital child and cohabiting prior to marriage—may reflect a weaker adherence to traditional norms about marriage, particularly its permanence. The greater fragility of marriages where one partner has been married before may also be due to the greater willingness of those with prior experience of divorce to dissolve an unsatisfactory marriage. Some also argue (e.g. Martin and Bumpass 1989) that the attributes that may have increased the chances of a first marriage terminating are also carried into a second marriage, while others (e.g. White and Booth 1985) suggest

The support of the Economic and Social Research Council is gratefully acknowledged (Grant No. L315253015). The data used in this study—the Family Resources Survey, the British Household Panel Study, and the National Child Development Study—were supplied by the ESRC Data Archive at Essex University.

that second marriages are more complicated, especially if there are children from a previous marriage. There is evidence also that divorce begets divorce, in that individuals who experienced divorce in childhood are more likely to experience it in adulthood (Mueller and Pope 1977; Kiernan 1986; McLanahan and Bumpass 1988).

Economic factors have also been found to be related to divorce; namely, wives' participation in the labour market (Ermisch 1989) and husbands' unemployment (Haskey 1984), both of which have a positive effect on the risk of separation. There are a number of explanations for the link between women's employment and marital disruption. For example, working outside the home increases the chances of meeting alternative partners; having one's own earnings may lower economic barriers to dissolution; and combining work and family life may bring stress to a marriage. Such strains, both financial and emotional, may also be implicated in the higher probability of divorce found among couples where the husband is unemployed.

There are various positive and negative consequences of divorce, although the negative ones tend to get more attention (see Kitson 1990 for a review). Marital breakdown, for example, can adversely affect the economic, social, and psychological well-being and health status of those who experience it. For many, this may only be a temporary situation while others may spend a considerable part of their lives dealing with the repercussions of divorce.

In this chapter, we pose two broad questions: what are the characteristics of the currently divorced and who divorces? We use 'divorce' as an inclusive term to include separations from both marriage and cohabiting unions. In the first part of the chapter, we use data from a large national cross-sectional survey, the Family Resources Survey; in the second part, we use two longitudinal studies, the British Household Panel Survey (BHPS) and the National Child Development Study (NCDS). The BHPS covers men and women of all ages and has information on both partners prior to separation; this permits the examination of partnerships prior and subsequent to their breaking up. The NCDS, a longitudinal study of a birth cohort followed from birth into adulthood, allows us to examine childhood and adolescent factors that may be associated with partnership breakdown in adulthood.

DATA SOURCES

The Family Resources Survey

The Family Resources Survey (FRS) is a large annual survey, with interviews running from April in one year to March in the following year carried out by the Department of Social Security (for further information see DSS 1995). For our analysis, we have used the first FRS, carried out in 1993–4. Unfortunately, the FRS records only basic information on marital status and includes no information on marriage and family histories. Thus, it is impossible to determine how long people have been divorced or identify those who have experienced divorce or separation in the past—as even the basic identifier of remarriage is not included as a marital status category. This inevitably limits our analysis. However, on the plus side the large sample size (over 26,000 households and 47,000 adults) makes the survey a good source for investigating the characteristics of a relatively small population such as the currently divorced. In addition, the survey has a special interest in the financial circumstances of the respondents, an important domain with respect to divorce.

The British Household Panel Study

For our examination of who divorces and the dynamics of marital disruption, we use data from the British Household Panel Study (BHPS). The BHPS has been conducted annually since 1991 and collects a wide range of information from a sample of about 5,000 British households (see Buck *et al.* 1994 for further information). In 1992, in the second wave of the study, marriage and cohabitation histories were collected for all persons aged over 16. We take this year as the baseline and examine partnership dynamics over the following three years. By the time we carried out this study, there were five waves of data available to the research community and we make use of waves 2 through 5. Again, the scope of our analysis is inevitably limited, permitting the analysis of partnership dynamics only over a relatively short time-span. Despite this limitation, the BHPS is at present the best British source for the prospective study of marital disruption among men and women of different ages and is one of the few studies with more than minimal information on both partners in a relationship.

The National Child Development Study

In our analysis of the antecedents of divorce, we use the National Child Development Study (NCDS), a longitudinal study of children born in 1958 who have been followed from birth to age 33. Respondents have been contacted on five occasions after birth at ages 7, 11, 16, 23, and 33, and over the years a wealth of information has been collected on the cohort members and their families (Fogelman 1983; Shepherd 1985; Ferri 1993). At age 33, complete partnership histories were collected which included starting and ending dates of all marriages and of any co-residential cohabiting unions lasting longer than a month. Here, we confine our analysis to first partnerships and whether that partnership had ended, focusing on cohort members who had entered a first partnership and provided a union history at age 33. This encompassed 91 per cent of the cohort members (10,344), of whom 60 per cent began their first relationship in marriage, and 40 per cent began in cohabitation.

THE CURRENTLY DIVORCED

The composition of the divorced population at any given time is unlikely to be random. For example, different social groups may vary in their propensity to divorce and the likelihood of repartnering may not be evenly distributed among the divorced population. Moreover, some characteristics or experiences may enhance or reduce the chances of divorce or remarriage, while others may emanate directly or indirectly from the marital breakdown itself. In other words, who is found among the divorced population at any given moment is the result of a complex weave of factors: the propensity to divorce, the 'turnover rate'—or how long members of various social groups tend to stay divorced—as well as the impact that marital breakdown may have on them. In the following, while we sometimes speculate about the factors that may be operating, we do not attempt to disentangle their effects. We focus instead on the cross-sectional description of the pool of divorced individuals in Britain in the early 1990s and, in particular, draw out differences between divorced and married men and women. We use the term 'divorce' inclusively to encompass those who are separated but not legally divorced.

A range of research has shown that married people tend to enjoy higher material well-being, better health, and lower mortality rates than the unmarried (Waite 1995). However, when divorce occurs, major differences in the position of men and women within both the labour market and the domestic domain are brought sharply into focus. Women's economic situation worsens dramatically after divorce, while that of men is affected to a much lesser extent (Hoffman and Duncan 1988; Taylor *et al.* 1994). In terms of health, however, divorced men seemingly do less well than divorced women, with men tending to have higher morbidity and mortality rates (Lillard and Waite 1995). Furthermore, men have higher rates of remarriage than women. Given these findings, one might expect differences between the sexes in the divorced population.

Evidence from the Family Resources Survey

To what extent do currently divorced men and women differ from or resemble each other? Since the probabilities of divorce and remarriage, as well as their impact, vary across the life-span we conducted our comparisons within four groups, differentiated by age and presence of dependent children. We chose two age groups, 25 to 39 years and 40 to 59 years; although somewhat arbitrary, this division differentiates between two broad stages in the family life-cycle—formation and building, and rearing and shrinking—and provides sample sizes that are sufficiently large.

Parenthood was difficult to establish with certainty as the FRS does not include fertility histories. As a proxy, we used information about the presence of a dependent child in the family or about the payment of maintenance for children in order to identify individuals who have current parental responsibilities. As in the majority of the cases custody of the children is awarded to women after divorce, we are likely to have identified most mothers with dependent children. But this is less likely to be the case in relation to men: not all non-resident fathers pay maintenance. Those who do, however, are more likely to have continuing parental responsibilities.

The sample sizes and the percentage distribution in these four life-span categories are shown in Table 16.1. In this FRS sample, the share of the currently divorced among those aged between 25 and 59 years is about 9 per cent, or 2,638 persons. Divorced women within this age range outnumber men by a ratio of 2:1. However, as can be seen in Table 16.1, this imbalance exists primarily among groups with children. Whereas divorced women and men under 40 without dependent children are roughly equal in absolute numbers and as a share of their respective groups, the rest of the divorced population is around 60 per cent female. This difference is probably due in large part to men being more likely than women to remarry after divorce and to do so more quickly.

In the following, we examine the employment, economic, and health

TABLE 16.1. *Sample sizes and percentage distribution by marital status and sex for four life-span categories: FRS, 1993–1994*

	No children				With children			
	25–39		40–59		25–39		40–59	
	Men	Women	Men	Women	Men	Women	Men	Women
Married	32	43	73	77	85	74	91	84
Cohabiting	14	16	3	3	10	6	4	2
Never married	49	35	13	6	1	7	0	1
Divorced	5	6	10	13	4	13	5	13
N	2,831	2,098	4,173	4,772	3,850	5,239	2,983	2,391

circumstances of different groups of divorced men and women, and provide comparisons with married people.

Employment

Table 16.2 provides summary information on school-leaving age, employment, hours of work, and earnings. The only information on educational attainment included in the FRS is age at leaving continuous full-time education. Divorced respondents included in that survey were generally less likely than the married population to have left school above the minimum age, suggesting that they might also be more disadvantaged in the labour market. Marital status and parenthood are particularly likely to affect the labour force participation of women; thus we were not surprised to find major differences between women in employment status according to their family situations, as well as between men and women. Table 16.2 indicates that in all of the life-span categories, married women tended to have higher rates of employment than divorced women. Younger divorced women, in particular, were significantly less likely to be employed than were married women. The proportion of women in employment was much lower among those with dependent children than among those without such children. Among those without children, older women were less likely to be in work.

Divorced men were also less likely to be in employment than married men. Childless male divorcees, however, were in addition less likely to be employed than their female counterparts: 24 per cent of these men were unemployed as compared with 9 per cent of divorced childless women. Caring for children appears to constrain the labour force participation of divorced men. Divorced men who lived with dependent children were more likely than men in partnerships, with or without children, to be outside the labour force. The majority of these fathers (70 per cent) reported looking after children as their reason for not being in the labour force. In contrast, illness or disability was the most common reason given by other men for not being in employment or seeking work.

The relationship between unemployment and divorce may operate through selection or consequence. Previous research shows unemployment to be among the factors that precipitate divorce (for a review see Lampard 1994). In addition, unemployment may be a precursor to divorce, as we show below in our analysis of the BHPS. It may be that the deterioration of a marital relationship that precedes divorce affects performance at work and thereby increases the risk of unemployment. On the other hand, this may be a spurious association if there are other characteristics associated with people becoming both divorced and unemployed, such as alcoholism, violent behaviour, and mental or physical ill-health.

TABLE 16.2. *Education and occupational attributes by family status: FRS, 1993–1994*

	No children				With children			
	25–39		40–59		25–39		40–59	
	Men	Women	Men	Women	Men	Women	Men	Women
In full-time education above minimum age (%)								
Married	53	62	40	43	44	48	58	64
Divorced	44	56	36	48	37	32	57	56
In employment (%)								
Married	92	84	74	61	85	56	85	69
Divorced	68	81	50	59	65	37	67	59
Unemployed (%)								
Married	4	3	8	3	9	6	7	3
Divorced	24	9	18	12	12	12	14	9
Mean hours of work per week								
Married	44	37	45	30	46	25	46	27
Divorced	42	37	47	36	44	26	43	30
Mean hourly earnings (£)								
Married	7.68	6.74	7.62	5.24	7.71	5.42	9.12	5.96
Female–male ratio	88		69		70		65	
Divorced	7.05	6.77	7.33	5.8	6.74	4.97	8.37	5.79
Female–male ratio	96		79		74		69	
In professional and managerial occupations (%)								
Married	31	26	34	19	29	16	42	24
Divorced	23	22	30	26	24	12	38	26

In terms of number of hours worked (Table 16.2), men invariably work longer hours on average than women and this was as true for the childless divorcees as for other family categories. Thus to compare earnings of men and women, it is necessary to control for differences in the number of hours worked, which we did by comparing the hourly earnings of men and women. On average, women earned about 74 per cent of men's earnings but as can be seen in Table 16.2, there was substantial variation according to family situation and age band. Gender differences were greatest among the married, but this was mainly due to married men being among the highest earners. Older divorced men and divorced fathers have an earnings advantage over divorced women, but this was not the case among the younger childless divorced women, who mirrored childless divorced men in the extent to which they were employed in high-status occupations (which may account for the smaller difference in the earnings ratio observed in Table 16.2). A major reason for gender differences in earnings is that women tend to be clustered in female-dominated, low-paid occupations. In our analyses, the gender gap in occupational attainment increased among women with responsibilities for dependent children.

Living standards

We now consider the economic circumstances of all respondents, using information available on income, housing tenure, and receipt of benefits. As the distribution of personal incomes is related to employment patterns, one would expect differences between men and women, and between parents and non-parents; we show these in Table 16.3. Among the divorced, the pay differentials observed earlier between employed men and women are largely replicated. However, there is one noteworthy difference. Among divorced people with children, there is relatively little difference in the male–female income ratio. It may be that alternative sources of income, such as state support, help divorced women with dependent children to maintain their financial position relative to men in similar situations. Certainly, divorced mothers are the most likely to be receiving Income Support, a means-tested benefit paid to people without employment based on the concept of need and not related to a person's previous employment record (Roll 1991). Table 16.3 indicates that divorced mothers

TABLE 16.3. *Income, receipt of benefits, and housing tenure, by family status: FRS, 1993–1994*

	No children				With children			
	25–39		40–59		25–39		40–59	
	Men	Women	Men	Women	Men	Women	Men	Women
Mean weekly gross personal income (£)								
Married	313	227	299	120	319	113	376	146
Female–male ratio	73		40		35		37	
Divorced	232	218	219	176	264	174	304	215
Female–male ratio	94		80		66		71	
In receipt of income support (%)								
Married	3	1	6	1	13	2	8	1
Divorced	25	17	28	27	32	69	23	44
Home owners (%)								
Married	83	89	85	88	78	83	86	91
Divorced	64	59	52	55	39	33	64	57
In receipt of Housing Benefit (%)								
Married	13	17	32	37	36	45	40	42
Divorced	50	40	61	63	49	86	44	83

with children are twice as likely as divorced men with children to receive Income Support, while divorced men themselves are much more likely to be in receipt of Income Support than married men. Divorced men and women appear more economically disadvantaged than married couples even when they do not support dependent children, and this is reflected further in their housing tenure. Table 16.3 also indicates that divorced men and women are less likely to be homeowners than married couples. Whether this was the case prior to divorce or was a consequence of it cannot be determined from these data, although other research suggests that both selection and post-divorce factors are relevant (Grundy 1989; Symon 1990). With respect to receipt of Housing Benefit, divorced mothers, and both men and women among the childless divorced, were more likely to be in receipt of Housing Benefit in comparison with, respectively, divorced fathers or married mothers, and childless married couples.

Health

There is evidence that divorce has a negative impact on health and that this effect has been found to be stronger for men than for women (Dominian *et al.* 1991). The FRS provides three types of information for examining this issue: first, data about the presence of a long-standing illness which limits usual activities; secondly, data on whether such illness restricts the type or amount of work one can perform; and thirdly, information about the receipt of disability benefits. All three involve stringent assessment criteria and relate to conditions which can be classified as disabilities.

Table 16.4 shows some strong sex differences in health status among the divorced. Male divorcees under age 40 are more likely than female divorcees to have long-standing illnesses or illnesses that restrict employment, while male divorcees in general, but particularly those in the older age group, are more likely to be in receipt of disability benefits. All three indices reveal a common pattern, namely, that people in partnerships are less likely to be affected by disability than the divorced. This accords with research claiming that marriage has 'protective' and/or 'selective' effects on health (Lillard and Waite 1995). It also suggests that such claims might be extended to cohabiting unions. In the following analysis of the BHPS, we also show that people with disabilities are more prone to divorce.

The Family Resources Survey has provided valuable information on the current status and situation of the divorced population. We now change focus and enquire whether there are particular background factors that increase the chances of partnership breakdown.

TABLE 16.4. *Health status, by family status (%): FRS, 1993–1994*

	No children				With children			
	25–39		40–59		25–39		40–59	
	Men	Women	Men	Women	Men	Women	Men	Women
Suffering long-standing illness, disability, or infirmity								
Married	9	9	29	26	11	9	18	15
Cohabiting	8	8	27	27	13	9	18	15
Divorced	17	12	39	40	21	16	24	24
Restricted by health in amount or type of work								
Married	4	8	21	20	6	8	11	9
Cohabiting	6	4	16	16	9	8	13	13
Divorced	11	6	36	32	17	13	17	16
Receiving disability benefit								
Married	1	1	12	8	2	3	5	4
Cohabiting	1	1	10	9	3	2	6	2
Divorced	5	2	22	14	6	5	7	4

DETERMINANTS OF DIVORCE

Evidence from the BHPS

The research literature on divorce suggests that there are three broad groups of factors associated with marital dissolution (South and Lloyd 1995): first, factors relating to the characteristics of individuals, including various demographic and socio-economic characteristics; secondly, ones relating to family structure and the internal dynamics of relationships; and thirdly, contextual factors that shape the structure of constraints, incentives, and opportunities that affect decisions to end a partnership. We are concerned here with the first two of these groups.

We start our analysis with wave 2 of the BHPS survey, which took place in 1992, as this was the first instance when union histories were included, and examine which partnerships ended in divorce or separation in the following three years and the factors associated with these events. The background information included in our analyses also comes from the 1992 interview and thus pre-dates the break-up of the partnership. Information about outcomes comes from the three subsequent annual interviews. Some of the respondents in the original sample were lost after wave 2 and we include them as a separate category in our analysis. For the statistical analysis, we use a multinomial logit model which compares the odds of four possible outcomes in the case of cohabitation (remained in the same partnership, left partner, married partner, and not known due to attrition) and in the case of marriage (remained married, divorced, separated, and unknown). The focus in each case is on the comparison between the first two possible outcomes, that is, on the likelihood of a partnership breaking up versus its continuing.

Our analyses of the BHPS were conducted on two levels: that of the individual respondent and that of the couple. The samples of individuals and couples were not necessarily equivalent. To be included in the couple sample both partners had to be aged under 60 and to have provided information at the interview. There were also differences according to marital status between the individual and couple samples. As shown in Table 16.5, we selected two types of sample, each of which included individuals and couples who were at risk of partnership dissolution at wave 2 of the BHPS, that is, persons who were married or cohabiting, and the marriages and cohabiting unions that existed, at the time of the second interview. To simplify the analysis, we confined our attention to men and women in their first marriage and to cohabitants who had never been married. After excluding respondents with no usable information on marital status in subsequent waves, we were left with 1,977 women and 1,731 men who were in their first marriage, and 242 never-married women and 237 never-married men who were cohabiting. The couples available for analysis included 1,577 married couples and 187 cohabiting couples. Three per cent of the married couples (N = 48) and 20 per cent of cohabiting couples (N = 38) had experienced a separation over the three-year period being examined. Such small numbers are not ideal, as they place constraints on the analysis and raise questions about the generalizability of the findings.

TABLE 16.5. *Sample sizes by type of outcome: BHPS, 1992–1995*

	Individuals		
	Men	Women	Couples
Marriage			
Continuing	1,379	1,589	1,259
Broken	52	84	48
Unknown (widowed)	293 (7)	285 (19)	265 (5)
All	1,731	1,977	1,577
Cohabitation			
Continuing	77	77	59
Broken	45	40	38
Converted into marriage	68	73	57
Unknown	47	52	33
All	237	242	187

For our examination of partnership stability, we considered the following individual characteristics: age at time of interview, age at time of entry into the union, education level, employment status, income, housing tenure, receipt of benefits, perceived economic well-being, health, psychological well-being, and family-oriented values and attitudes. In all our analyses, an assessment was made of the simple bivariate association between these factors and partnership stability (model 1) as well as their effect net of, first, the age of the respondent (model 2) and secondly, the respondent's age at time of interview and at the start of the partnership (model 3). Age at start of partnership is an important control given the largely undisputed finding in divorce research that marital instability varies by age at marriage. Additionally, we wanted to assess the extent to which other factors operated independently and to what extent they operated through the timing of marriage.

Demographic and socio-economic factors

The results of our analysis (Table 16.6) were consistent with numerous other studies in showing that marriage instability is inversely related to current age; and that the younger the age at which people marry, the more likely they are to experience divorce or separation. We also found that cohabiting unions were more likely to be continuing the older the partners (Table 16.7). However, unlike marriages, the stability of these non-marital partnerships does not seem to be linearly related to the age at which they were formed, suggesting that cohabiting unions may be intrinsically more fragile than marriage regardless of the age at the beginning of the partnership.

Our evidence suggests that there are relatively few socio-economic factors associated with partnership dissolution (Tables 16.6 and 16.7). Level of educational attainment, type of housing tenure, and amount of personal income did not appear to be associated with the propensity to experience partnership breakdown. However, there was some evidence that married men and women who thought their financial situation was comfortable (27 per cent of married men and women) were less likely to separate over the next few years. Among men, this finding survived the introduction of controls for age at time of interview and age at marriage. There was also some evidence that married women who said that their financial situation was very difficult (4 per cent of married women) were more likely to separate.

The higher probabilities of partnership breakdown among the socio-economically disadvantaged was more clearly visible when we looked at couples rather than individuals. There is evidence that married couples where the family was in receipt of benefits or unemployed were more

TABLE 16.6. *Odds ratios from multinomial logistic regressions of partnership dissolution on selected demographic and socio-economic variables, men and women in first marriages: BHPS, 1992–1995*

Independent variable	Men			Women		
	Model 1	Model 2	Model 3	Model 1	Model 2	Model 3
Age at time of interview	0.89***	—	—	0.90***	—	—
Age at marriage	0.90***	0.93	—	0.91***	0.91*	—
Housing tenure						
Owner-occupier	1.00	1.00	1.00	1.00	1.00	1.00
Public rented	2.00†	1.48	1.36	1.89*	1.46	1.28
Private rented	1.38	0.82	0.78	0.73	0.48	0.48
Educational qualifications						
Degree or higher	0.47	0.32†	0.39	1.02	0.50	0.71
Intermediate	1.15	0.92	0.98	1.06	0.58	0.71
A-level	1.54	0.94	1.03	1.14	0.41†	0.48
O-level	0.98	0.59	0.62	1.29	0.58	0.66
Below O-level	1.07	0.67	0.71	1.64	0.80	0.88
None	1.00	1.00	1.00	1.00	1.00	1.00
Personal income						
Last month	0.89	0.98	1.01	0.82	0.79	0.92
Last year	0.98	0.99	0.99	0.99	0.99	1.00
Current financial situation						
Living comfortably	0.30*	0.35*	0.36*	0.42*	0.52†	0.58
Doing all right	0.92	0.80	0.81	0.99	0.96	0.98
Just about getting by	1.00	1.00	1.00	1.00	1.00	1.00
Finding it difficult	0.79	0.76	0.75	1.37	1.18	1.13
Finding it very difficult	0.98	0.80	0.75	2.76*	2.43*	2.43*

† $p < 0.10$.
* $p < 0.05$.
*** $p < 0.001$ (two-tailed tests).

likely to separate, and that cohabiting couples in receipt of benefits also had a higher rate of breakdown (Table 16.8). This suggests that the higher unemployment rates and reliance on state benefits observed among the currently divorced from the analysis of the Family Resources Survey may in part arise from these groups being more prone to divorce.

Health and well-being

The strongest divorce differentials with respect to health in our analyses were found among men in their first marriages (Table 16.9). Men, particularly those under age 40, who were registered as disabled at the time of the interview in 1992 had significantly higher rates of divorce in the

TABLE 16.7. *Odds ratios from multinomial logistic regressions of partnership dissolution on selected demographic and socio-economic variables, never-married cohabiting men and women: BHPS, 1992–1995*

Independent variable	Men			Women		
	Model 1	Model 2	Model 3	Model 1	Model 2	Model 3
Age at time of interview	0.92*	—	—	0.91**	—	—
Age at current union	0.99	1.17*	—	0.94	1.11	—
Housing tenure						
Owner-occupier	1.00	1.00	1.00	1.00	1.00	1.00
Public rented	0.78	0.61	0.71	0.84	0.60	0.63
Private rented	1.79	1.36	1.29	2.04	1.53	1.38
Educational qualifications						
Degree or higher	0.83	0.77	0.56	1.83	2.69	2.14
Intermediate	2.48	2.24	1.63	1.96	2.18	1.94
A-level	1.78	1.35	1.29	2.04	1.79	1.48
O-level	1.72	1.34	1.04	2.98	2.89	2.45
Below O-level	2.00	1.58	1.47	1.67	1.66	1.49
None	1.00	1.00	1.00	1.00	1.00	1.00
Personal income						
Last month	1.01	1.17	1.05	0.98	1.23	1.17
Last year	1.00	1.02	1.01	0.98	1.00	1.00
Current financial situation						
Living comfortably	0.69	0.73	0.74	0.71	0.81	0.84
Doing all right	0.95	0.94	0.98	1.43	1.35	1.29
Just about getting by	1.00	1.00	1.00	1.00	1.00	1.00
Finding it difficult	1.12	1.02	0.95	0.91	1.02	1.04
Finding it very difficult	0.60	0.67	1.03	1.50	1.45	1.50

* $p < 0.05$.
** $p < 0.01$.

ensuing few years. The proportion of men with disabilities is small (3 per cent of the sample) but the higher observed risk of divorce suggests that the stresses associated with being disabled may place additional strains on a marital relationship. Women who are registered as disabled also had higher odds of marital breakdown but this difference was not statistically significant, which may be due to the very small sample size.

One of the most clear-cut, and not unexpected, findings from this analysis was that people whose relationships were about to end (at some point over the next three years) were more likely to feel generally unhappy and to have higher scores on the 12-item version of the General Health Questionnaire (GHQ). The GHQ was originally developed to screen for psychiatric illness and is used in the BHPS as a general indicator of

TABLE 16.8 *Odds ratios from multinomial logistic regressions of partnership dissolution on selected socio-economic variables, couples: BHPS, 1992–1995*

Independent variable	Model 1	Model 2	Model 3
First marriage			
Either partner receives benefits	2.72**	2.04†	1.95†
Either partner unemployed	3.02**	2.28*	2.19*
Both partners working	0.70	0.74	0.77
Pre-marital cohabitation			
Either partner receives benefits	3.18*	2.78*	3.13*
Either partner unemployed	1.75	1.48	1.98
Both partners working	0.35*	0.43	0.32*

† $p < 0.10$.
* $p < 0.05$.
** $p < 0.01$.

TABLE 16.9. *Odds ratios from multinomial logistic regressions of partnership dissolution on health status and subjective well-being, married and cohabiting men and women: BHPS, 1992–1995*

Independent variable	Model 1	Model 2	Model 3
Men			
Married			
Registered disabled under age 40	1.45 5.06†	2.68 5.94*	2.48 5.63*
Subjective well-being index	1.08**	1.10***	1.10***
Cohabiting			
Registered disabled under age 40	—	—	—
Subjective well-being index	1.09*	1.10*	1.12*
Women			
Married			
Registered disabled under age 40	1.59 3.75	2.18 3.81	2.02 3.58
Subjective well-being index	1.07***	1.08***	1.07***
Cohabiting			
Registered disabled	—	—	—
Subjective well-being index	1.04	1.05	1.05

— Sample size too small for reliable analysis.
† $p < 0.10$.
* $p < 0.05$.
** $p < 0.01$.
*** $p < 0.001$ (two-tailed tests).

psychological well-being (Corti 1994). Respondents were asked how they had been feeling over the last few weeks. The items included in the inventory related to concentration, lost sleep, usefulness, decisiveness, strain, overcoming difficulties, enjoyment, problems, depression, confidence, worthlessness, and happiness. It is apparent from Table 16.9 that married men and women whose marriages subsequently break up had lower psychological well-being than their contemporaries who did not break up. This was particularly pronounced among the married but present also among cohabiting men. Lower emotional resiliency may be one of the reasons why partnerships fail, but lower emotional well-being may also represent a deterioration that occurs on the way to separation. As we will see in our subsequent analysis of the NCDS, there is evidence that lower emotional well-being in adolescence is associated with partnership breakdown in adulthood.

Family-oriented values

If one was to argue that divorce is an expression of the decreased importance of the family in the pursuit of personal happiness at the individual level, then one might also expect to find that holding traditional attitudes towards family life reduces the chances of divorce. If, on the other hand, the general situation of lower social support and lower expectations associated with the family, as well as the increased acceptance of divorce, are important, then such individual differences would matter less.

The BHPS asked respondents about the extent to which they supported four statements describing family life: 'It is better to divorce than to continue an unhappy marriage'; 'Living together outside marriage is always wrong'; 'Adult children have an obligation to look after their elderly parents'; 'The man should be the head of the household'. On all items, the dominant view tended towards the liberal. The greatest agreement among respondents related to divorce: 72 per cent of men and 78 per cent of women agreed with the statement that divorce was better than an unhappy marriage. The nature of the relationship between adult children and their parents was the issue on which opinions were the most divided, particularly between men and women, but also between married and cohabiting respondents. In both cases, women were more likely than men to disagree with the statement, while married men and women were more likely than their cohabiting counterparts to indicate disagreement. Cohabiting men and women both disagreed with the view that men should be the household head; in the case of cohabiting women, this reached 75 per cent disagreement (compared with 56 per cent of married women).

Tables 16.10 and 16.11 show how some of these family-related attitudes are associated with partnership dissolution. Attitudes to cohabitation are

TABLE 16.10. *Odds ratios from multinomial logistic regressions of partnership dissolution on family attitudes, men and women in first marriages: BHPS, 1992–1995*

Independent variable	Model 1	Model 2	Model 3
Men			
Divorce is better than unhappy marriage			
Disagree/strongly disagree	0.73	0.64	0.64
Neither	0.68	0.66	0.66
Agree	1.00	1.00	1.00
Strongly agree	1.78†	1.54	1.55
Adult children should care for parents			
Agree/strongly agree	1.21	1.44	1.53
Neither	1.00	1.00	1.00
Disagree/strongly disagree	1.46	1.54	1.58
Man should be head of household			
Agree/strongly agree	0.72	0.78	0.78
Neither	1.00	1.00	1.00
Disagree	1.15	0.99	0.98
Strongly disagree	1.98	1.33	1.36
Women			
Divorce is better than unhappy marriage			
Disagree/strongly disagree	0.71	0.70	0.68
Neither	0.82	0.74	0.72
Agree	1.00	1.00	1.00
Strongly agree	2.16**	1.79*	1.75*
Adult children should care for parents			
Agree/strongly agree	0.72	0.77	0.76
Neither	1.00	1.00	1.00
Disagree/strongly disagree	1.45	1.68†	1.70†
Man should be head of household			
Agree/strongly agree	0.90	1.02	0.98
Neither	1.00	1.00	1.00
Disagree	1.41	1.16	1.18
Strongly disagree	3.30***	2.08*	2.25*

† $p < 0.10$.
* $p < 0.05$.
** $p < 0.01$.
*** $p < 0.001$ (two-tailed tests).

not included, as they were not associated with partnership breakdown for either sex or type of partnership. Despite the broad consensus on attitudes towards divorce, such attitudes still differentiate between people with respect to their risk of marital disruption. Married men and women who expressed strong support for the proposition that divorce is preferable to an unhappy marriage were more likely to experience divorce in the next three years compared with those who did not (Table 16.10). Among

TABLE 16.11. *Odds ratios from multinomial logistic regressions of partnership dissolution on family attitudes, cohabiting never-married men and women: BHPS, 1992–1995*

Independent variable	Model 1	Model 2	Model 3
Men			
Divorce is better than unhappy marriage			
Disagree/strongly disagree	0.72	0.68	0.68
Neither	1.00	1.00	1.00
Agree/strongly agree	1.43	1.56	1.52
Adult children should care for parents			
Agree/strongly agree	1.22	1.26	1.20
Neither	1.00	1.00	1.00
Disagree/strongly disagree	0.89	0.90	1.03
Man should be head of household			
Agree/strongly agree	0.83	0.81	1.06
Neither	1.00	1.00	1.00
Disagree/strongly disagree	1.29	1.20	1.22
Women			
Divorce is better than unhappy marriage			
Disagree/strongly disagree	—	—	—
Neither	1.00	1.00	1.00
Agree/strongly agree	0.59	0.57	0.56
Adult children should care for parents			
Agree/strongly agree	1.79	1.76	1.73
Neither	1.00	1.00	1.00
Disagree/strongly disagree	1.58	1.44	1.39
Man should be head of household			
Agree/strongly agree	3.75	4.16	3.98
Neither	1.00	1.00	1.00
Disagree/strongly disagree	3.09†	2.97	2.69

— Sample size too small for reliable analysis.
† $p < 0.10$.

married men, this was the only attitude among the set asked of the BHPS respondents that was associated with a propensity to divorce, although the association was not statistically significant once age at time of interview and age at first partnership were taken into account. Among married women, marital stability also varied with their views on the role of adult children in the care of parents and on gender roles within the family (Table 16.11). Those who rejected the traditional division of gender roles encapsulated in the view that 'The man should be the head of the household' were more likely to divorce, as were women who believed that adult children had no obligation to care for their parents. Cohabitation, unlike marriage, is a less traditional family form and as a consequence, it might be expected that the association between the stability of such unions and values and attitudes that support the family would be weaker. Not surprisingly, this is what we broadly find (Table 16.11).

In sum, we find some limited evidence, especially among women, that traditional family-oriented values and attitudes are related to marital stability. The attitudinal data used in this analysis were collected prior to separation. However, marital separation can be viewed as a process that develops over time and culminates in the act of separation. Thus, it is difficult to say whether these attitudes precede or facilitate the decision to end the marriage or have developed in parallel.

The domestic domain

In the BHPS, there is little direct information on the quality of the partnership, the internal dynamics of the partnership, or the degree of interaction between partners. However, it does contain some information on the ways in which household finances and tasks are organized, the division of child care between the partners, and respondents' views on the fairness of their domestic arrangements. We used this information to examine how the structure of everyday life within the family might be related to marital disruption. The upshot of our analysis was that these factors were neither consistently nor robustly associated with either a reduced or a heightened propensity to dissolve either a marital or a cohabiting union. There were indications that married men who reported that child care arrangements were 'fair' rather than 'very fair', or who saw themselves as responsible for organizing household finances rather than as sharing this responsibility with their wives, had a higher risk of divorce over the next three years. Similarly, cohabiting never-married women who thought that their partners had 'the last word in financial decisions' were more likely to separate. These findings are similar to those reported for a US sample by Kurdek (1993), who found that couples who did not pool their finances were more likely to separate subsequently, and suggest that less egalitarian partnerships are more unstable. However, there were also results that pointed in the opposite direction. In the BHPS, for example, the risk of divorce was greater among couples where married women reported that housework was shared rather than being their sole responsibility, and where a third party was responsible for child care when the mother was working.

Overall, our analysis of BHPS data uncovered considerably fewer factors associated with the dissolution of cohabiting unions than with the dissolution of marital unions. In some cases, such as family-related attitudes, this was to be expected. However, the substantially smaller number of cohabiting unions as compared with marital unions and the even smaller number of dissolutions in the survey makes it difficult to know whether the differences between the findings with respect to de jure or de facto unions are genuine or a statistical artefact.

Evidence from the NCDS

The National Child Development Study (NCDS) provides information on childhood and family-of-origin factors that may be associated with partnership breakdown in adulthood. By age 33, 91 per cent of the total NCDS cohort contacted at that age (11,405) had entered a first partnership, 30 per cent of which had ended by this age. For our analysis, we used hazard models to estimate the duration of first partnerships. These models are the appropriate ones to use when the outcome variable is the duration of time until an event occurs, in this case the dissolution of a marriage or cohabiting union, and when there is censoring at the time of interview. In the NCDS sample, although 30 per cent of first partnerships had ended by age 33, the other 70 per cent remained at risk of dissolving at a later stage. Hazard models used two pieces of information to construct the outcome variable: first, the duration of the partnership at the last time the person was observed to be still in a partnership; and secondly, whether at the last observation the partnership had been dissolved or had remained intact. Our results are given in terms of relative risk ratios, namely, the excess risk for a particular group compared with a reference group.

Demographic factors

The first factor examined was whether there were different risks of dissolution according to type of first union. We divided the sample into three groups: (1) those whose first union was a marriage not preceded by a period of cohabitation (that is, those who married directly): 60 per cent of the cohort members who had a partnership fell into this category; (2) those who had cohabited before marrying their first partner (that is, their first union was a marriage preceded by cohabitation): 25 per cent of first partnerships; and (3) those whose first union was a cohabitation that was either still continuing or had dissolved by the time of the interview: 15 per cent of first partnerships.

Table 16.12 shows that similar proportions of first unions that were direct marriages or were preceded by a period of cohabitation had dissolved by age 33, and that the relative risk of pre-marital cohabitations dissolving was similar to that of the reference group, those who married directly. The group with a high and significantly different risk of dissolution was the third group, those who did not marry, or had not married, their first partner. Thus, at least for this British cohort, there is little evidence that those in their first union who cohabited prior to converting it into a

TABLE 16.12. *Type of first union and partnership dissolution: NCDS*

	Dissolved (%)	Relative risk of dissolution
Married directly (reference group)	23	1.00
Cohabited, then married	23	0.95
Cohabiting union continues or dissolved	72	4.9***
N	10,324	

*** $p < 0.001$.

TABLE 16.13. *Partnership dissolution by age at first partnership: NCDS*

Age at first partnership	Dissolved (%)	Relative risk
19 or younger	48	4.60***
20–21 years	34	2.66***
22–23 years	27	1.96***
24–26 years	21	1.47***
27 or older (reference group)	15	1.00

*** $p < 0.001$.

marriage had a higher risk of dissolution than those whose first union was a marriage. This was the case for both men and women in the sample.

In Table 16.13, we show the relative risks of partnership breakdown according to age at first partnership. The reference group includes those who formed their first partnership at ages 27 to 33. It is apparent that, compared with the reference group, those who formed partnerships at younger ages were more likely to have experienced partnership breakdown. For example, nearly one in two first partnerships entered into as teenagers had broken up by age 33 as compared with one in five of those formed in the mid-twenties (24–26 years). Obviously, partnerships formed at late ages had less time to dissolve by the time of interview, which is a problem intrinsic to longitudinal surveys. However, a more stringent test, limiting the analysis to those who had entered a partnership under age 25 (80 per cent of the cohort) so that they all had a minimum exposure time of eight years, showed the same highly significant pattern, as portrayed in Table 16.13.

Childhood and adolescent factors

Beyond the examination of these demographic parameters, our main interest in carrying out this research was to determine if there were factors or experiences in childhood and adolescence that enhanced or reduced the risk of partnership dissolution in adulthood. Here we examine educational attainment, financial circumstances, emotional well-being, and whether the child's parents had separated before s/he was age 16.

Educational attainment

Educational attainment is undoubtedly a major influence on future lives. We examined this factor in two ways: first, using children's scores on mathematics and reading tests at ages 7 and 16, and secondly, using their level of highest qualification as reported in the interview at age 23. In Table 16.14, we present the relative risks of experiencing partnership dissolution for people in different educational attainment groups at age 7 and age 16, and for level of qualifications attained and recorded at age 23. Model 1 shows the simple relative risk for the individual factors and subsequent partnership breakdown, while model 2 shows the relative risk when age at first partnership is taken into account. Educational performance at age 7 appears not to be associated with partnership breakdown in adulthood, whereas educational performance at age 16 and subsequent level of qualifications are so associated. With respect to level of highest qualification, it is clear in model 1 that the relative risk of partnership dissolution is highest among those with qualifications below A-level, in that compared to the reference group, namely those with degrees, cohort members with no qualifications were 1.6 times as likely to have experienced a partnership dissolution, while those with only O-levels were 1.4 times as likely to have had such an experience. In model 2, which includes a control for age at first partnership, the relative risks across all educational groups become very similar. This suggests that the risk of partnership dissolution among the less well educated is in large measure due to the fact that they form partnerships at an early age, and that if they do not form youthful partnerships, their chances of experiencing partnership dissolution do not differ markedly from those with higher educational attainment. However, this also suggests, from a policy perspective, that young people who experience partnership dissolution are, other things being equal, disproportionately drawn from the more educationally disadvantaged and as a consequence, they may be more economically disadvantaged in adulthood.

Emotional well-being, parental divorce, and financial circumstances

The association between educational attainment and partnership breakdown in adulthood is largely indirect, operating in the main through age at first partnership. However, this was not the case for some of the other background factors we went on to examine. The first of these was whether the parents of the cohort member had experienced marital dissolution before the cohort member was age 16. Among those who had experienced parental divorce, 43 per cent had themselves experienced a partnership

TABLE 16.14. *Educational attainment and partnership dissolution, relative risk ratios: NCDS*

	Model 1	Model 2
Age 7 test scores		
Lowest quartile	1.06	—
Second quartile	1.08	—
Third quartile	1.00	—
Upper quartile[a]	1.00	—
Age 16 test scores		
Lowest quartile	1.32***	0.96
Second quartile	1.25***	1.01
Third quartile	1.12*	0.99
Upper quartile[a]	1.00	1.00
Educational qualifications		
None	1.61***	0.97
Sub O-level	1.32***	0.85
O-level or equivalent	1.38***	0.98
A-level or equivalent	1.13	0.97
Higher level	0.99	0.85
Degree[a]	1.00	1.00

[a] Reference groups.

* $p < 0.05$.
*** $p < 0.001$.

dissolution by age 33 compared with 29 per cent who had lived with both their parents to age 16. The second background influence was a measure of emotional well-being at age 16, derived from a factor analysis incorporating various measures of behaviour as assessed by parents and teachers, as well as the Rutter Home Behaviour Scale. High scores on this index indicate lower emotional well-being. In our analysis, we compared those with scores in the top two deciles with the rest. Thirty-eight per cent of the high-scoring group had had a partnership dissolution compared with 29 per cent of those with lower scores. The third factor was whether the cohort member's family had had financial difficulties at the time of the interviews at ages 7 and 16. Among those with financial difficulties, 37 per cent had experienced partnership dissolution compared with 28 per cent without reported financial problems.

We present three models in Table 16.15. Model 1 gives the relative risk ratios of partnership dissolution for the individual attributes. Given that the three factors—emotional well-being, parental divorce, and financial difficulties—are likely to be interrelated, model 2 includes all the individual factors together. Model 3 includes all three factors, as in model 2, together with a control for age at first partnership. Let us consider

TABLE 16.15. *Background factors and partnership dissolution, relative risk ratios: NCDS*

Variables[a]	Model 1	Model 2	Model 3
Lower emotional well-being at age 16 (score in top 20% of index)	1.41***	1.42***	1.2**
Parental divorce, 0–16 years	1.68***	1.56***	1.35**
Financial problems at either age 7 or 16	1.4***	1.11	1.01
Parental divorce and lower emotional well-being	1.8***	1.02	1.09

[a] All variables are dichotomous.

** $p < 0.01$.
*** $p < 0.001$.

behavioural scores at age 16. Here we compare cohort members in the upper two deciles of the distribution with their peers with lower scores. Among those with high scores, the relative risk of partnership breakdown was 1.41, or 41 per cent greater than for those in the lower part of the behavioural index. However, when age at first partnership was taken into account (as shown in model 3), the excess risk was reduced to 20 per cent. This suggests that some of the effect of emotional well-being operates through age at first partnership, but that some of the effect may be more direct. There may be a greater tendency for young people with emotional problems at age 16 to form partnerships at a young age, which places them at greater risk of experiencing a partnership breakdown in later life, and that young people with emotional problems may be more likely to separate regardless of when they form partnerships.

Turning to consider the effect on cohort members of parental divorce during childhood, we see a similar pattern. For example, those who had experienced parental divorce during childhood were nearly 1.7 times as likely as those brought up with both parents to experience partnership breakdown in adulthood, but again there was a reduction in their excess risk (to 1.35) when age at first partnership was taken into account.

Children who had experienced financial difficulties while growing up also had a higher risk of partnership dissolution in adulthood. However, as is clear from model 2, this effect operated through other factors. In this example, we see that the excess risk associated with financial difficulties is significantly reduced when parental divorce and emotional well-being are included in the model. It is also clear that once age at first partnership is taken into account, there is no excess risk associated with financial deprivation in childhood and later partnership dissolution.

Children who have experienced parental divorce are more likely to have emotional problems and, not surprisingly, children who experienced parental divorce had higher scores on the emotional index at age 16 than their peers without such an experience. In the NCDS sample, men and women who had experienced parental divorce were twice as likely to be in the top two deciles of the emotional index as their peers who had not experienced parental divorce: 40 per cent of those who had experienced parental divorce were in the top 20 per cent of the distribution as compared with 20 per cent who had not had such an experience. Thus, we examined to what extent emotional well-being and divorce in combination were associated with subsequent partnership breakdown. As we see at the bottom of Table 16.5, for those with high emotional scores who had also experienced parental divorce, the relative risk of experiencing partnership disruption in adulthood was 1.8 times that of the rest of the sample. The next question is whether it is the lower emotional well-being or the parental divorce or the interaction between these two that lies behind this heightened propensity to partnership dissolution in adulthood. The results in model 2, which includes the separate factors of parental divorce and emotional scores at age 16 as well as an interaction term for parental divorce and emotional scores, clearly point to both emotional well-being and parental divorce being independently associated with partnership breakdown in adulthood.

Our analysis of the NCDS data identified only two factors from childhood and adolescence directly associated with the risk of partnership breakdown in adulthood: namely, a parental divorce and whether the young people had high scores on an index of emotional well-being. In an earlier study which addressed a similar question (Kiernan 1986), using data from the National Survey of Health and Development, a longitudinal study of a cohort of children born in 1946, we again found only two factors that were directly related to the probability of marriage breakdown in adulthood—whether the cohort member had experienced parental divorce during childhood and their psychological well-being assessed at age 15—and again both factors made an independent contribution to the risk of later marriage breakdown. The similarity of the findings across these two different generations suggest that emotional well-being in childhood and growing up with both parents are robust protective factors against marital breakdown in adulthood.

DISCUSSION

In this study, we have used the two main national longitudinal studies available to the research community that permit the investigation of the question of who divorces. The BHPS allowed us to examine this issue for individuals and couples of all ages, whereas the birth cohort data from the NCDS permitted examination of background factors from childhood and adolescence associated with partnership dissolution in adulthood. A number of insights emerged from our longitudinal analyses as well as from the cross-sectional analysis of the Family Resources Survey.

Unemployment, reliance on state benefits, and disability featured as characteristics of the currently divorced in the FRS sample and these factors, along with financial difficulties, were also important precursors of divorce, as shown in our analysis of the BHPS. This suggests that poor economic and somatic well-being may be important stresses in a relationship, and that the selection of vulnerable groups into divorce may be an important aspect of the poverty observed among the formerly married, in addition to the deprivation that may be a by-product of the divorce itself. This suggests that the deprived are more at risk of divorce and that divorce may well compound their deprivation.

There was also evidence from both the BHPS and the NCDS of an association between psychic factors and subsequent partnership breakdown. The analysis of the BHPS showed that men and women with lower psychological well-being were more likely to divorce in the ensuing few years, while analysis of the NCDS data suggested that pre-existing emotional problems were important signposts for subsequent partnership breakdown. Again, these two findings speak to the possibility of selection effects and emotional problems, emerging post-partnership but preceding separation, being implicated in the lower emotional well-being of the divorced. These, together with the lowered mental well-being associated with the event and its aftermath, add to the potential of further lowering the psychic well-being of the divorced. The legacy of pre-partnership and post-partnership emotional problems may also differ and affect the extent to which the mental health of the divorced improves or deteriorates.

Previous demographic research led us to expect that type of first partnership and age at first partnership would be associated with the risk of divorce. This was confirmed explicitly in the NCDS sample. However, for our analysis of type of first union we differentiated between cohabiting first unions that led to marriage and cohabiting unions that did not. When such a distinction is made, we find that those who cohabited prior to their first marriage did not have a higher rate of marital dissolution. This suggests that in considering the role of pre-marital cohabitation in subsequent divorce, it is important to make a clear distinction between individuals who had more than one partnership prior to marriage and those who did not. The heightened propensity to divorce of those who cohabit before marriage may arise from the subset who have experienced partnership turnover prior to marrying.

The other demographic factor implicated in partnership breakdown was whether men and women in the NCDS sample had experienced parental divorce during childhood. Subsequent analyses (Kiernan and Cherlin

1999) that have looked at this issue in more detail have also shown that children whose parents divorce when they are grown up are also more likely to experience partnership dissolution. If divorce begets divorce in the sense of partnership dissolution, then we would expect it to increase still further for later generations of children, who were reared during a period of more divorce than when the NCDS sample born in 1958 were growing up.

In sum, from these relatively rich data sets we were able to identify only a few important and direct factors associated with partnership dissolution. People who embark on partnerships at an early age, cohabitants, those who have experienced parental divorce, and those who are economically, somatically, and emotionally vulnerable have higher risks, but beyond these factors, which in several instances pertain only to small subsets of the population, there was little else that clearly distinguished those who divorce from those who do not. It may be that there are other factors that are not measured in these wide-ranging surveys which would enlighten us further. White, in her review of research in the 1980s on the determinants of divorce, remarked, 'Although we have made substantial progress in the last decade, we still know comparatively little about how divorce is related to relationship quality, family structure or socio-psychological factors' (White 1990: 907). To date, the relationship between demographic and economic variables and divorce has been extensively examined but this needs to be matched by empirical research in other domains. The prominence of demographic and economic correlates in divorce research probably reflects the absence of surveys of representative samples of the population appropriate for studying family processes. Much of what we know comes from secondary analysis of more general-purpose surveys rather than surveys designed to examine family dynamics, relationships, and processes, and if we are to enhance our understanding of the process of divorce this situation needs to be rectified.

17

Non-resident fathers in Britain

Jonathan Bradshaw, Carol Stimson, Christine Skinner, and Julie Williams

INTRODUCTION

One of the consequences of the changes taking place in families today is an increase in non-resident fatherhood.[1] Non-resident fathers emerge in one (or more) of three ways: a single man has sexual relations with a woman, which results in her becoming pregnant and carrying the baby to term; a married couple separate after the wife becomes pregnant or after becoming parents; and a cohabiting couple separate, either following pregnancy or the birth of a child. Non-marital births and relationship breakdowns are still on the increase. The latest estimate by Haskey (1998*a*) is that the number of lone-parent families reached 1.6 million in 1996 from 0.57 million in 1971. These lone-parent families contain 2.8 million children; about 8 per cent are headed by men and about 4 per cent by widows. The rest all have non-resident biological fathers of their children. The prevalence of non-resident fathers is much higher, however, than the number of lone-mother families. Most lone mothers repartner and are no longer lone mothers,[2] but the fathers of their children remain non-resident fathers as long as their children are children.[3]

Despite their prevalence, despite the plethora of research that is now available on lone-parent families, despite the hugely expanding literature on fathering and fatherhood (for a recent review see Burghes, Clarke, and Cronin 1997), little has been known to date about the circumstances of non-resident fathers. Unlike lone mothers, they are not, as a group, particularly likely to be dependent on public services (at least, not as non-resident fathers). Partly for that reason, they are difficult to identify. There is no register of non-resident fathers. Birth registration records provide details of fathers only for births to married couples and for jointly registered births outside marriage. Thus, little basic information about the fertility history of men has ever been collected and there is practically no basic demographic information about non-resident fathers.

Non-resident fathers have been depicted in the past in mainly negative ways. Indeed, it was this firm anti-'absent father' ideology that was responsible to some extent for the way that the Child Support Act 1991 was launched, with extraordinarily little known about the circumstances of non-resident fathers. In the United States, non-resident fathers are known as 'deadbeat dads' while in the UK, they have been presented as 'feckless ne'er-do-wells' passing on their responsibilities to the taxpayer. Margaret Thatcher set the tone of child support policy-making in talking about fathers 'walking away from marriage . . . neither maintains nor shows any interest in the child . . . No father should be able to escape his responsibility' (Thatcher 1990).

Yet non-resident fathers have increasingly become the focus of policy concerns in the 1990s, particularly in relation to family law and child support. The objectives of this research were to contribute to knowledge about the circumstances of non-resident fathers in Britain. We hoped as well to contribute to the understanding of the nature of fathering in modern Britain and to inform policy-making on maintenance, conciliation, and social security and thereby produce a companion baseline survey to that provided by *Lone Parent Families in the UK* (Bradshaw and Millar 1991).

RESEARCH METHODS

In this context, we sought to interview a representative sample of non-resident fathers.[4] Non-resident mothers were excluded from consideration on the grounds that they are much less prevalent than non-resident fathers, as were lone-parent fathers who lived with their children. Over 90 per cent of lone parents are women and about a quarter of lone fathers are widowers (Haskey 1998*a*). We also chose to exclude fathers who did not live with their children because the children were away at boarding school or living in care, a residential home, or a hostel.

The sample was identified using a screening question in the omnibus surveys operated by two survey agencies, National Opinion Polls (NOP) and the Office of Population and Census Surveys (OPCS). Included in these surveys (between questions on voting behaviour and washing powder) was the following question: 'Are you the father of any child under 16 or under 18 and in full-time education who normally lives with their mother in another household?' Between April 1995 and April 1996, 33,958 men aged 16–65 were screened. Just less than 5 per cent acknowledged that they were the father of a dependent child living in another household, and 45 per cent of these agreed to be interviewed. OPCS achieved interviews with almost all the non-resident fathers they identified. NOP, unfortunately, only achieved interviews with three-quarters of the fathers who had agreed to be interviewed. As the NOP omnibus is three times the size of that of OPCS, this meant that we only achieved interviews with 38 per cent of the men who identified themselves as non-resident fathers. We had originally envisaged a sample size of 1,000, and because of the response rate we extended the data collection period from the original six months to ten months, and then by a further four months. Even then, we did not achieve our aim but nevertheless obtained interviews with over 600 non-resident fathers (Table 17.1).

Prior to the start of the research, there had only been one other British source of information on non-resident fathers. At the request of the Department of Social Security, Marsh (1993) undertook a secondary analysis of non-resident parents in the 1991 sweep of the National Child Development Survey (the 1958 birth cohort) when they were 33 years old. He found that nearly 6 per cent of parents and 8 per cent of men admitted to having a child living in another household. The sweep covered only 70 per cent of the original sample of 16,500 children and Marsh took the view that about a third of non-resident fathers were missed by the survey, in part because of bias in attrition.

Since this project began, some useful additional sources of information on non-resident fathers have become available. Simpson, McCarthy, and Walker (1995) have published their study of the experiences of 91 fathers who were in the process of divorce, having followed them for five years. Maclean and Eekelaar (1997*b*) published their investigation into the views of 250 parents identified by methods similar to those used here. Only 55 individuals in their sample were non-resident parents, including only 49 men. Clarke, Condy, and Downing (1998) undertook an analysis of the British Household Panel Survey 1992 and found that 16 per cent of all fathers had children living in another household; they estimate that this is about 6 per cent of men in the sample. Finally, McKay (1997), who has been using the Family and Working Lives Survey to trace family change,

TABLE 17.1. *Response to omnibus screen*

	NOP	OPCS	Total
Number of men screened	25,824	8,134	33,958
Non-resident fathers identified	1,186	464	1,650
(% of men screened)	(4.6)	(5.7)	(4.9)
Fathers agreeing to an interview	477	258	735
(% of non-resident fathers identified)	(40)	(56)	(45)
Interviews achieved	361	258	619
(% of non-resident fathers identified)	(30)	(56)	(38)

agreed to do some special analyses to provide information for this study. McKay found that 268 or 6 per cent of the men aged 16 to 69 had non-resident children, while 3 per cent of women could be described as non-resident mothers.

Our proportion of 5 per cent of men aged 16–65 who are non-resident fathers is similar to the proportions found by Clarke *et al.* (1998) and McKay (1997) but lower than that of Marsh (1993). Numerically, 5 per cent translates into just less than one million non-resident fathers in Britain. This estimate is too low, however, and given the number of lone mothers in Britain, we believe that there are at least two million non-resident fathers.

Non-response bias

We always knew that this was going to be a difficult sample to obtain. There are undoubtably fathers who do not know they are fathers of a child, fathers who think they are fathers of a child but who are not, and mothers who think that a certain man is the father of their child when he is not.[5] Given these problems and the high level of non-response, we have been at pains to investigate the representativeness of the sample we obtained. It is only possible to speculate about the characteristics of those men who did not know or who failed to admit that they were non-resident fathers. One can suggest that they were probably more likely to have been the fathers of children born outside marriage or cohabitation, where the relationship with the mother was fleeting or at least where there was no common residence. It is also possible that they were more likely to be men who would have had to be interviewed in the presence of new wives or partners or other new relations, and who therefore did not feel able to be as frank as they might otherwise have been.

A great deal more can be discovered about the characteristics of those men who identified themselves as non-resident fathers but with whom an interview was not obtained because they either refused or the survey agency failed to achieve one. All omnibus surveys collect standard data on the characteristics of their samples. The data collected by NOP and OPCS are not identical but with a modest amount of manipulation it was possible to combine the two data sets for most relevant variables.

There were no significant differences between fathers who were interviewed and those who were not in respect of the gender of the household head, current marital status, age at which full-time education ended, tenure, number of people in the household, children in the household, cars available in the household, or gross income. However, those who were interviewed were statistically *less likely* than those who were not interviewed to be single, unskilled manual workers, unemployed, and under 30. Thus, not surprisingly perhaps, non-respondents tended to be young, unemployed, working-class, single men.

These factors are likely to interact and therefore to establish the nature of these interactions a logistic regression was undertaken of the odds of being interviewed. In the best-fitting model, after controlling for other characteristics, the sample who were interviewed was significantly different from those who were not only in respect of marital status and social class. The data were therefore weighted by these variables, using as weights the proportion in each family composition/social class cell for the whole sample identified as non-resident fathers. This weighting procedure resulted in adjusting the characteristics of the respondents so that there were no longer any significant differences between respondents and non-respondents.

There remains reason to be anxious about the representativeness of this sample. Weighting compensates for known response bias, but not for unknown response bias or for any bias in the sample of men who identified themselves as non-resident fathers. As we have described, non-resident fathers have been subject to a considerable degree of vilification in recent years. They have also been pursued for child support (albeit incompetently) by a new government agency. There is also a good deal of sadness, anger, and ambivalence among non-resident fathers about their role and status. It is not surprising, therefore, that men who are approached by a survey agency, even if they know that they are non-resident fathers, might decide to hide the fact. This needs to be borne in mind in considering the results in the rest of this chapter.

RESULTS

The survey covered a range of topics, including the past partnerships and present circumstances of the fathers, contact with their children, child support, income, housing, employment, and family relations as well as attitudes, beliefs, feelings, and sense of well-being. In this chapter, we focus on some of the results pertaining to three topics: the processes and transitions involved in becoming a non-resident father; contact between the father and the children living with their mother in another household; and child support.[6]

Becoming a non-resident father

We found that 10 per cent of the fathers had never lived with the mother of their non-resident child, while 23 per cent had cohabited with her and 67 per cent had been married to her. This classification of marital status is based, however, on the most recent or only relationship which involved non-resident children. Looking more widely reveals that 61 (10 per cent) of the fathers had had more than one such relationship, 54 had had two, four had had three, and three had had four—and this only counts relationships which produced children who were still dependent. Furthermore, the fertility histories of these men were not yet over, in the sense that many were now or would be in new relationships which might involve the birth of children and which might also founder. So the sample is really a truncated portion of the full lives of non-resident fathers.

The relationship status of the non-resident fathers at the time of their interviews was 58 per cent single, 24 per cent married, and 18 per cent cohabiting. Again, this simple accounting hides the real complexity of the fathers' lives. For example, the large 'single' group includes the previously single, the formerly married (some of whom are now separated and some divorced), and the formerly cohabiting. Table 17.2 provides a detailed summary of the relationship status of the fathers, both in the past with the mothers of their non-resident child and currently. The largest single group is those who are divorced from a previous marriage (25 per cent). It is important to remember that between these points, many of the men will have passed through other relationships, of which a few will have involved the birth of a child now absent from the father's home.

About 10 per cent of the fathers were single and had never lived with the mother of their non-resident child. Many of them were young when they first became a father, with over a third (36 per cent) under 20 at the time. Many of the mothers of the children were also young—52 per cent

TABLE 17.2. *Relationship status at becoming a non-resident father and relationship status now (%)*

Relationship with the mother at the point of becoming a non-resident father		Relationship status now	
Single	10	Married	1
		Cohabiting	1
		Single	8
Married	67	Separated	10
		Divorced	25
		Cohabiting	14
		Remarried	19
Cohabiting	23	Single	16
		Re-cohabiting	3
		Married	4
N	590		590

were under 20. The majority (74 per cent) of these single men had only one absent child. Of those with more than one child, two-thirds had had more than one past partnership involving the birth of a child.

Cohabitation breakdown is now the fastest-growing source of new lone-parent families and nearly a quarter of the men were in cohabiting relationships before they became non-resident fathers (McKay and Marsh 1994). These fathers tended to be slightly older than the single men; nevertheless, 19 per cent were under 20 when they first became fathers, as were 34 per cent of their partners. The majority (68 per cent) of these men had only one absent child.

Formerly married fathers were still the largest group of non-resident fathers, and had the largest number of non-resident children. The average age of the child at separation was 4 years and the average length of time that fathers had lived with the mother before the birth of the child was four years and two months; in other words, their relationships had lasted, on average, over nine years. Formerly married fathers had lived with their children for the longest period of time and, as we shall see below, they were also more likely to remain in contact with them. They tended to be older than the other two groups when they had their first child—only 11 per cent of the fathers and 23 per cent of their wives had been under 20 at that time. Some of their marriages, however, had been of fairly short duration: 16 per cent of the formerly married fathers had lived with their wives for less than a year before the birth of the child, while 17 per cent had separated within a year after the birth of the child.

Fathers who had ever lived with the mother of their non-resident child (whether married or cohabiting) were asked about the circumstances that led to the decision to separate. For the formerly married, it was most commonly the mother who made the decision to separate (42 per cent). In only a third of the cases was it the father and in the rest (26 per cent) it was both. For the formerly cohabiting, more fathers than mothers made the decision (35 per cent against 26 per cent) and more joint decisions to separate were taken (39 per cent). Fathers were also asked to give the reasons why separation had been decided upon. Obviously, the reasons why relationships end are complex, vary over time, interact, and are difficult to summarize in response to a structured questionnaire. The reason most commonly given by fathers was that *their partner* had found someone else, committed adultery, or been unfaithful. This was the only reason given by a quarter of the sample and mentioned as one reason by a third. Another common reason was that the couples had been rowing a lot, followed by 'lack of communication/did not talk'. Money problems were mentioned in 16 per cent of cases. Their own adultery was only admitted as a reason by 11 per cent of men. Most strikingly, violence was mentioned as a reason by only 2 per cent. In the Bradshaw and Millar (1991) study, lone parents mentioned violence as a reason for the break-up in 20 per cent of cases and as the main reason in 13 per cent of cases. There appears to have been a clear reluctance on the part of these fathers to acknowledge or admit violent behaviour.

Fathers were asked about their present feelings about the break-up of their relationships through a question similar to that used by Bradshaw and Millar (1991); the results and comparative data are summarized in Table 17.3. Few fathers regretted the break-up of their relationships: 5 per cent wished that they had stayed with their partner and 5 per cent wished that their partner had stayed with them. In contrast, 58 per cent were glad that they had not stayed with their partner and 10 per cent that their partner had not stayed with them. The main difference between this study and that of Bradshaw and Millar is that in our study a much higher proportion of non-resident fathers than lone mothers said that they had no say in the break-up of their relationship. This suggests that non-residential fatherhood may have been thrust upon these fathers, an outcome which may well have implications for their attitudes to contact and child support issues.

Contact with children

One of the most important issues to be investigated in this study was the extent and quality of the contact between the non-resident fathers and

TABLE 17.3. *Feelings about the breakdown of the relationship (%)*

	Ex-married	Ex-cohabiting	All	Lone mothers (Bradshaw and Millar 1991)
I'm glad I did not stay with my partner	57	61	58	51
I am glad my partner left	10	9	10	17
I did not have a say in the break-up from my partner	16	15	16	8
I wish my partner had stayed with me	6	4	5	5
I wish I had stayed with my partner	5	5	5	4
Not applicable (N)	(5)	(2)	(7)	(10)
Don't know	4	5	4	5
N	409	145	554	885

their children. A major grievance of fathers in this study, certainly more important than concerns over child support, was the difficulties that they experienced in seeing their children. Nevertheless, contact with their non-resident children was higher than expected. Only 21 per cent of our sample had not seen their children in the last year and 47 per cent saw their child at least every week. This is a much higher rate of contact than that derived from studies of lone parents. The lone mothers studied by Bradshaw and Millar (1991), for example, reported that only 25 per cent of non-resident fathers had contact at least once a week and that 47 per cent had had no contact with their child for over a year. Bradshaw and Millar found that 40 per cent of the fathers had lost contact with their children within two years of separation or childbirth. These findings have been much quoted in discussions about the consequences of family breakdown. The findings of our study that only 3 per cent had no contact at all suggests that there might be something wrong with the reliability of the results in this study or Bradshaw and Millar's or both.

However, it is important to remember that the samples are not matched. Bradshaw and Millar's study contained both lone mothers and lone fathers, and lone mothers reported lower rates of child contact with their past partners than did lone fathers. Furthermore, the former partners of non-resident fathers are not necessarily lone mothers. Thus, the sample of fathers is not matched by a sample of lone mothers. In our study, 86 per cent of the fathers knew the present circumstances of their former partner, 57 per cent of whom reported that their former partners had repartnered. So we would expect to find some differences in the contact rates reported by fathers in our study and the lone mothers in the Bradshaw and Millar study.

Further, and more profoundly, the emphasis on seeing the child in the questions about contact used in these surveys may be, with hindsight, too imprecise a definition of contact and therefore fail to pick up the essence of the relationship between fathers and their children. 'Seeing' did not perhaps tap alternative ways of maintaining fairly close and perhaps

TABLE 17.4. *Frequency of father's contact with non-resident children from all past partnerships (%)*

At least once a week	47
At least once a fortnight	14
At least once a month	7
Once or twice a year	10
Once every 1–3 years	8
Less than once every 3 years	10
Not at all	3
N	620

valued relationships between fathers and their children, including regular phoning, correspondence, and even e-mail.

These points notwithstanding, we need to attempt to reconcile the disparity between the findings of Bradshaw and Millar and those reported here. In an attempt to do so, we reanalysed the Bradshaw and Millar survey in order to produce estimates of contact for only the fathers of the children of lone mothers and to match these to the classification of contact used in the present study. However, even after controlling for marital status and length of lone parenthood/non-resident fathering, fairly substantial differences remained between the surveys. Comparing, for example, the formerly married in each survey who had been separated for at least three years, we found that 60 per cent of lone mothers in the Bradshaw and Millar study reported that their children had not seen their fathers in the last month, compared with 33 per cent of fathers in the present study who had not seen their children.

There are three possible explanations for the differences observed. First, as discussed above, the two samples are not matched. Secondly, it is possible that our study was biased in favour of men with contact—those without contact could well have been reluctant to acknowledge that they were the father of a child in another household at the screening survey. Thirdly, lone mothers and non-resident fathers may perceive and report contact differently—lone mothers may not welcome, and be reluctant to acknowledge, the continuing involvement of a non-resident father; they may feel, alternatively, that the nature of that contact is too trivial to recognize. In contrast, non-resident fathers may want to assert their parental role and perhaps claim greater involvement than they have in reality.

Table 17.5 presents an analysis of some socio-demographic factors that we speculated would influence contact. The bivariate analysis (column (1)) takes each variable in turn and shows how the proportion having regular contact (defined as at least monthly) varies—for example, fathers living alone ('Family now' panel) are 2.82 times as likely to have regular contact as a father living in a household with children; fathers who have (re)married ('Marital status now' panel) are two-thirds less likely to see children regularly. In addition, older fathers, employed fathers, and fathers with higher incomes, with younger children, who have lived together with the child, who have recently separated, or who live close to the child are all much more likely to have regular contact with their absent child.

However, a number of these factors interact and so columns (2) and (3) present the results of a multivariate logistic regression. The best-fitting model selected four variables which contribute to the odds of a father having regular contact—being in employment, living close, having only one child, and living in a household without children. Thus, for example, if the

TABLE 17.5. *Relative chances of a father seeing his child regularly (at least monthly): bivariate and multivariate analysis*

Variable	Bivariate (1)	Simultaneous (2)	Best-fitting (3)
Income quintile			
1	1.00	1.00	
2	0.96	1.92	
3	1.93*	1.71	
4	1.57	1.27	
5	2.73**	2.38	
Time lived with child			
Never lived together/separated before child born	1.00	1.00	
Separated within 1 year	1.00	1.41	
1–3 years	1.02	1.02	
3–6 years	2.59*	1.48	
Over 6 years	3.89***	4.20	
Marital status at child's birth			
Cohabiting	1.00	1.00	
Married	1.06*	2.69*	
Single	0.95	2.44	
Age when first became father			
Under 20	1.00	1.00	
20–24	2.03**	0.40	
25–30	3.06***	0.72	
31+	3.16***	0.58	
Employment status			
Employed	1.00	1.00	1.00
Self-employed	0.80	0.43	0.40
Inactive	0.54***	0.55	0.39**
Age of youngest child			
0–4	1.00	1.00	
5–10	0.60*	0.48	
11–18	0.50**	0.13*	
Time to travel to child			
Under 10 minutes	1.00	1.00	1.00
10 minutes–half an hour	0.61	0.54	0.52
Half an hour–1 hour	0.43	0.40	0.34*
1–2 hours	0.16***	0.13**	0.12***
2 hours+	0.04***	0.04***	0.06***
Length of absent fatherhood			
1–2 years	1.00	1.00	
3–5 years	0.47*	2.01	
6–9 years	0.26***	1.14	
10+ years	0.16***	2.24	
Parents live within 10 miles			
No	1.00	1.00	
Yes	1.35	0.94	

TABLE 17.5. (cont.)

Variable	Bivariate (1)	Simultaneous (2)	Best-fitting (3)
Number of children			
1	1.00	1.00	1.00
2	1.18	0.27**	0.43**
3 or more	1.74	0.41	0.91
Family now			
With children	1.00	1.00	1.00
No children	2.09***	2	2.34*
Lives alone	2.82***	2.28	2.56**
Sex of children			
Only boys	1.00	1.00	
Only girls	1.43	1.41	
Boys and girls	1.76*	1.57	
Marital status now			
Single	1.00	1.00	
Married	0.39***	1.09	
Cohabiting	0.63	1.25	

* $p < 0.05$
** $p < 0.01$
*** $p < 0.001$

other variables are held constant, the chances of a father who lives more than two hours' travelling time from his child having regular contact is 94 per cent less than if he lives only ten minutes away.

Relationship with the mother

We also found that the father's relationship with the mother was a critical determinant of contact. Fathers who had an amicable relationship with the mother were much more likely to have regular contact with their child than those whose relationship with the mother was hostile. About half (47 per cent) of those with contact described their relationship with their former partner as amicable and another quarter as amicable but distant. In contrast, only 14 per cent of the fathers who did not have regular contact with their child described their relationship with the mother as amicable and 9 per cent as amicable but distant. We also found that fathers who are now living in households with children have less amicable relations with their former partner than those who live alone or with a new partner but without children. It appears from this that new children and new stepchildren may be associated with poorer relationships with former partners and perhaps be competing for time and attention with the non-resident children.

Child support

Policy background

The issue of child support has become probably the most salient policy affecting non-resident parents since Margaret Thatcher declared:

> No father should be able to escape his responsibility and that is why the Government is looking for ways of strengthening the system for tracing an absent father and making arrangements for recovering maintenance more effective. (Thatcher 1990)

Until then, child support had been a neglected policy issue. Existing maintenance rewards through the courts were low, irregularly paid, and often not reviewed over time. The 'liable relative' procedures had also become a relatively neglected part of the work of the Department of Social Security. The new interest arose partly as a result of the sharp increase in the numbers of lone parents and their increased dependence on Income Support—the aim was to reduce benefit expenditure and encourage more lone parents into employment. But there was also a fundamentally moral view being reasserted, that biological parents should be responsible for their children throughout their lives. Indeed, at the second reading of the Child Support Bill, the hope expressed by some MPs on the government benches was that enforcing the obligation to pay child support might persuade fathers to maintain their marital and paternal duties and be less inclined to conceive children outside marriage.

This is not the place to review the debacle of child support since the Child Support Agency (CSA) began operations in April 1993, but it must rank as one of the worst policy-making disasters in modern British history—on a par with the Poll Tax. It is widely agreed that the Act contained some fundamental flaws, including its retrospective nature, the absence of a disregard for those on Income Support, and a formula which was too complicated to understand but at the same time allowed no scope for taking account of exceptional circumstances or special needs. The Bill was poorly scrutinized by Parliament. There was general support for the principle of the Act, but not enough attention paid to the detail. The implementation of the Act by the Child Support Agency was a fiasco, with inadequate computer systems, poor management, and ill-prepared staff. The consequence was huge delays and backlogs, inaccurate assessments, and incompetent or non-existent enforcement, resulting in confusion, misery (including some suicides), and a general loss of confidence in the Agency by both lone parents and non-resident fathers. After five years of operation, an amending Act, endless changes in regulations, the departure of two Chief Executives, six parliamentary select committee inquiries, and repeated critical reports from the National Audit Office, the child support system is still failing to deliver on all its objectives. Non-compliance and collusion are thought to be epidemic; arrears in 1998 amounted to over £2 billion. Instead of the single child-support regime envisaged, a dual system has been re-established, one for lone parents on means-tested benefits, and arrangements through lawyers and the courts for others. The proportion of lone parents receiving regular child support is little different from what it was under the old system and the level of payments, which has fallen due to changes in the original formula, is not much greater (taking into account inflation since 1989). It is arguable that, if account is taken of the costs of administering the Child Support Agency, then the savings to the public purse have been minuscule or non-existent compared to the system it replaced. At the time of writing, the Labour Government is reviewing the Child Support Act. There is a strong body of political opinion in support of abandoning the Act and returning to a court-based, or at least judicial, system that allows more flexible, individualized justice than the current formula-driven scheme.

The Child Support Agency began operating in 1993. As the research for this study was undertaken between April 1995 and April 1996, we expected to contribute to a preliminary evaluation of how it was operating and what it was achieving. But because, as a result of the changes in policy and operations, so few of the fathers we interviewed had had any involvement with the Agency, this study proved not to be a particularly good vehicle for exploring the operation of the Act. Nonetheless, we are able to provide new information relevant to the operation of the Agency about the attitudes and behaviour of non-resident fathers in relation to their child support obligations.

Paying maintenance

We found that 77 per cent of the fathers had ever paid maintenance, and that 57 per cent were doing so currently. As with contact with children, this is a much higher proportion than the 30 per cent of lone mothers who reported receiving regular maintenance in Bradshaw and Millar (1991), a figure subsequently confirmed in the series of studies of lone parents from the Policy Studies Institute (PSI) (Marsh and McKay 1993; McKay and Marsh 1994; Ford, Marsh, and McKay 1995; Ford, Marsh, and Finlayson 1998). As with the disparity in the findings in relation to contact, we found that some—but by no means all—of the gap could be closed if we controlled for the differences between non-resident fathers in this sample and the non-resident fathers of the children of lone mothers in Bradshaw and Millar (1991). Again, there are three possible explanations for the discrepancy: the current sample is not representative and is biased in favour of non-resident fathers who pay maintenance (it is possible that the

Bradshaw and Millar sample is also biased, although this is unlikely given that the PSI studies have identical findings); secondly, non-resident fathers are exaggerating the extent to which they pay maintenance; or thirdly, lone mothers are denying that they receive maintenance. There is, in fact, no incentive for lone mothers in receipt of Income Support (the majority) to declare that they receive maintenance: since there is no disregard, to do so is to risk losing benefit. Non-resident fathers, on the other hand, stand to gain by claiming maintenance payments, in that making such payments enhances their reputation as responsible fathers.

Table 17.6 presents the results of an analysis of the factors which have a bearing on whether child support is currently being paid. The table follows the same pattern used in Table 17.5. The best-fitting model shows that maintenance is much less likely to be paid if the father was not in employment, if he was under 20 when he first became a father, if he did not provide informal support, if he had never made a formal arrangement for paying maintenance, if the mother received Income Support, and if he had no contact with the mother. Thus, the best-fitting model shows that contact with the mother overrides contact with children when it comes to paying maintenance. Further, where the mothers were not receiving Income Support, the odds of their receiving maintenance were increased more than fivefold. Among those paying maintenance, the average amount paid was £25 per child per week but there was a good deal of variation in the amounts being paid. Fathers who were economically inactive, for example, paid only £17 per week. Overall, fathers paid an average of 14 per cent of their net equivalent income in maintenance.

Paying potential

We have seen that non-payment of maintenance is related to whether the father is in employment. The question arises as to what scope there is for increasing the proportion of fathers who are paying maintenance. If there is to be an effective child support regime, what should its target be? What evidence is there that non-payers are financially able to pay but nevertheless deliberately avoid their obligations? In an attempt to tackle these questions, non-payers were divided into four groups:

- *No paying potential*: Accounting for 63 per cent of non-payers, this group included the unemployed, the non-active, those on Income Support or with an equivalent net disposable income in the bottom quintile of the income distribution, and those with shared care[7] of their children.
- *Possible paying potential*: These included those not in the first group but who had new family commitments and equivalent net disposable income in the second and third quintile range, which means that there would be

TABLE 17.6. *Factors associated with the chances of currently paying child support: bivariate and multivariate analysis*

Variable	Bivariate	Simultaneous	Best-fitting
Net income quintile			
1	1.00	1.00	
2	1.38	0.34	
3	4.24***	0.54	
4	15.26***	1.60	
5	19.75***	1.80	
Don't know income	3.61***	0.48	
Employment status			
Employed	1.00	1.00	1.00
Self-employed	0.67	0.79	0.77
Inactive	0.06***	0.04***	0.05***
Current marital status			
Single	1.00	1.00	
Married	1.50*	0.60	
Cohabiting	1.58*	1.31	
Current family circumstances			
Lives with children	1.00	1.00	
No children	2.08***	0.55	
Lives alone	1.29	0.28	
Age when first became a father			
Under 20	1.00	1.00	1.00
20–24	3.29***	3.65**	3.49**
25–30	4.78***	5.61**	4.00**
31+	3.76***	6.40**	3.84*
Relationship to mother			
Married, now divorced	1.00	1.00	1.00
Married, now separated	0.80	0.90	1.13
Cohabited, never married	0.33***	0.43	0.45*
Never lived with mother	0.52*	5.66	2.08
Time lived with mother			
Less than one year	1.00	1.00	
1–4 years	1.27	5.91	
5–9 years	2.51***	3.99	
10 years or more	2.44***	1.30	
Time since separation			
Less than 2 years	1.00	1.00	
2–5 years	1.05	0.84	
5–9 years	1.19	0.56	
10 years or more	0.85	0.55	
Distance lived from child			
0–9 miles	1.00	1.00	
10–25 miles	1.27	1.37	
26+ miles	0.77	0.45	

TABLE 17.6. *(cont.)*

Variable	Bivariate	Simultaneous	Best-fitting
Age of youngest child			
0–4	1.00	1.00	
5–10	1.95**	1.74	
11–18	1.90**	2.36	
Number of non-resident children			
1	1.00	1.00	
2	1.62**	1.49	
3 or more	1.77	6.21*	
Contact with child			
No	1.00	1.00	
Yes	3.29***	1.21	
Mother's employment status			
Working	1.00	1.00	
Not working	0.27***	0.58	
Don't know	0.28***	0.71	
Mother lives with a new partner			
Yes	1.00	1.00	
No	1.10	2.78*	
Don't know	0.33***	0.55	
Mother receives Income Support			
Yes	1.00	1.00	1.00
No	3.16***	6.69***	5.30***
Don't know	0.76	1.48	1.33
Contact with mother			
Yes	1.00	1.00	1.00
No	0.29***	0.45	0.36**
Relations with mother			
Amicable	1.00	1.00	
Amicable/distant	1.29	2.35	
Not amicable	0.72	1.77	
No relationship	0.26**	1.34	
Gives informal support			
No	1.00	1.00	1.00
Yes	4.27***	2.35	3.17**
Maintenance arrangement			
Court/DSS/CSA at some time	1.00	1.00	1.00
No formal arrangement	0.33***	0.07***	0.11***
Assessed by the CSA			
Yes	1.00	1.00	
No	0.75*	1.11	

Notes: Total number of cases in regression = 360.

* $p < 0.05$
** $p < 0.01$
*** $p < 0.001$

competition for whatever resources were available in the household. They constituted 13 per cent of non-payers.

- *Probable paying potential*: These men had incomes in the second and third quintile of the income distribution but no new family commitments, which meant that there was no competition for household resources; 15 per cent of non-payers.
- *Certain paying potential*: Individuals not in the previous three groups, with incomes in the top two quintiles; 9 per cent of non-payers.

These results suggest that there is rather little scope for increasing the proportion of non-resident fathers who pay maintenance.

Informal support

Although fathers who paid maintenance were also more likely to provide informal support, two-thirds of fathers who were not paying maintenance nonetheless provided informal support. The most common forms of provision were children's presents, clothes and shoes, children's pocket money, and money for holidays and outings. Few fathers offered help with general household expenses, housing costs, or car expenses. Not surprisingly, as some support items would be given directly to children, patterns of provision reflected the amount of contact fathers had with their children.

The fathers estimated that over one year, they spent about £16 per week on informal support. There is evidence of some substitution between formal and informal support. While there was no difference in the mean amounts of informal support between fathers who were paying maintenance and those who were not, the informal support provided by non-payers was a much higher proportion of their net disposable incomes. Those fathers with a certain paying potential (fourth group) who were not paying maintenance paid much larger absolute amounts in informal support than the other groups. Only 15 per cent of fathers were paying neither maintenance nor informal support. A third of these were classified as having some paying potential but 83 per cent of these saw their children less than yearly or never.

Attitudes to child support

When they were interviewed, only 43 per cent of the sample had had any contact with the Child Support Agency and of those, only just over half (55 per cent) had received an interim or final assessment. Although this means that the study is of limited usefulness as a vehicle for evaluating the CSA, a number of points are worth making on the basis of the findings on non-resident fathers' attitudes to child support.

Much has been made of the increases in maintenance amounts brought about by the formula (at least until the revisions). Of those with a final assessment, the mean amount of maintenance was £49 or 19 per cent of equivalent average income. However, this represented an increase in the amount due in only 41 per cent of cases—for 29 per cent, the final assessment was actually less than they had already been paying. Only two-thirds of those who had a final assessment said that they were paying the amount assessed at the time of the interview. The majority (77 per cent) of fathers who had had an increase in their assessment thought that the assessment was unfair. The most popular reason for this was that the assessment did not take account of living expenses (81 per cent), followed by: the amount was too high (72 per cent), it did not take account of housing costs (61 per cent), and it did not take account of the costs of seeing children (53 per cent).

There is some evidence in the study of the possible behavioural consequences of the CSA assessments. Of those assessed, 61 per cent thought that the assessments would have an impact on their present living standards. Just over half the fathers expected that the assessment would worsen their relations with their former partner (64 per cent), their current partner (39 per cent), or their absent child (27 per cent). Some fathers felt that the assessment would lead to a breakdown in the relationship with their new partners (18 per cent). A third said that it would lead to a reduction in informal payments or gifts for their children, while substantial minorities thought that it would have an impact on their labour supply and/or on their willingness to repartner and have another family.

These possible behavioural responses to CSA assessments have been much neglected in discussions about the policy and deserve more detailed investigation. There is evidence from other work that CSA assessment affects the labour supply behaviour of unemployed men by increasing their reservation wage (Lowerson 1997), and evidence from our qualitative work and that of others (Clarke, Glendinning, and Craig 1996) that the impact on relationships may be quite profound. The following case study from our qualitative interviews illustrates some of the complexities involved.

Peter is a social care worker aged 40. His CSA assessment increased the amount he was required to pay in maintenance for his three children, who live with his former wife. As a result, he can no longer afford to provide the same level of informal support to his children as he had in the past. This reduction in Peter's financial help affected everyone. His former wife resorted to emotional blackmail to persuade Peter to buy shoes for his children. Peter described the situation as follows:

> That's why I got a bit annoyed at the beginning; 'cause you pay £120 to the CSA and then a few days later you'd get a call [from mother] . . . '[Oldest daughter] hasn't got any shoes and if you don't get her any shoes then I'll send her to school

in her slippers, and you can't send kids to school in slippers so I'd go out and buy them a pair of shoes. But I weren't happy about it 'cause I'd just spent £120, and now I were having to spend another £20.

However, Peter's financial difficulties were compounded because of his rule of treating all his children equally:

But once I'd bought one of them a pair of shoes, so I had to buy another pair of shoes and another pair of shoes for the third one. So your £20 soon became £60 and it got silly, I were skint all the time and I hadn't any money spare to do what I wanted to do. So I weren't too happy at that point. I blame the CSA more than I do [ex-wife's name], because we had it settled before the CSA got involved, we were fine before the CSA got involved.

Peter said 'everybody suffered' as a result of CSA involvement. His children did not receive informal support; they could no longer go on holiday with their father or be treated to days out, or have new clothes and shoes. Peter despaired because he was unable to provide in this way and he felt his emotional relationship with his children had deteriorated. Indeed, the very core of Peter's fathering was made manifest through the provision of informal support, as this was how he expressed his love for, and commitment to, his children. Following the involvement of the CSA, with no maintenance disregard, the mother received less income. From Peter's perspective, his maintenance money was now being used for household expenses to support his ex-wife, her husband, and their new child. He began to object to paying maintenance because he felt it was not going specifically to his children. He felt he was taking on part of the responsibility of breadwinner for his ex-wife's new family and he was adamant that that responsibility belonged to the mother's new husband.

Peter concluded that the CSA's involvement made 'everybody unhappy'. On the surface, this unhappiness was directly related to the financial and emotional consequences of paying more in maintenance and less in informal support. But at a deeper level, it appeared to refer to behavioural changes. According to Peter, his children had become resentful of their mother because she could not make up the loss of his informal support and could not provide adequate clothing or take them swimming or for days out. This resentment expressed itself in the children's behaviour, presenting both parents with difficulties in disciplining the children across two households. In particular, Peter felt torn between supporting the mother in disciplining the children (something he had always done) or sympathizing with the children in their resentment against the mother. Peter's commitment to providing financial support for his children was not in doubt. However, the effect of CSA involvement made him much more ambivalent about his legal obligation to pay maintenance. Peter felt that he was being turned into the breadwinner of another man's family, and at one point stopped paying his previously reliable maintenance.

The Child Support Act 1991 is based on the principle that biological fathers have an absolute and unreserved responsibility to provide financial support for their children throughout their lives. Not all the fathers accepted this principle. The maintenance obligation is one that was negotiated. Fathers arrived at a commitment to pay maintenance by weighing up the strength of the financial obligation in the context of their own personal, financial, and family circumstances and those of the mother and children. In practice, the obligation to pay was never unconditional, but always depended on circumstances: the father's ability to pay, the children's material need for maintenance, and the mother's ability (and her partner's if she had one) to provide financially. But most importantly, it depended upon the history of the relationship with the mother. From the father's perspective, it is the mother who claims maintenance (albeit on behalf of children), not the children. This claim had to be *legitimized* before fathers would pay. Primarily, the mother's right to claim maintenance on behalf of children was accepted if she at least recognized, if not actively supported, the father's independent relationship with his child(ren). If the mothers failed to accept the father–child relationship or failed to sustain it through granting contact, then the fathers found this extremely difficult to comprehend. This incomprehension induced an overwhelming sense of victimization and powerlessness among men who wanted a relationship with their children but were unable to achieve it in the face of what they saw as selfish and callous mothers. The resultant attitudes tended to be that there was no point in paying maintenance as the children would not know their fathers were supporting them; that there was no guarantee that the money would be spent for the children's benefit; and that the fathers were 'paying for a child they were not seeing'. Thus, not only would fathers get 'nothing back' in return for maintenance (contact with their children) but payment was meaningless, as the father's act of giving was rendered invisible to the children themselves. Children would be unaware of the symbolic expression of love and care embedded within the act of giving maintenance money, particularly when, in the absence of contact, there was no other means through which fathers could demonstrate their affection to children directly. Therefore, the obligation to pay maintenance was intimately linked with contact through the relationship with the mother, and the different outcomes of the process of negotiation (payment or non-payment) primarily hinged upon this relationship.

CONCLUSION

This chapter has presented some of the results from a recent study of non-resident fathers. Non-resident fathers are a common new family form arising from the increase in births outside marriage and the breakdown of marriages and cohabiting relationships. The popular prejudice about the fecklessness of non-resident fathers—that typically such a father 'walks away from marriage', 'neither maintains nor shows any interest in the child'—is not the picture that has emerged from this research. The great majority of the fathers are maintaining relationships with their children, albeit with considerable difficulty. The majority are also making financial contributions to their upbringing, either formally through child support or informally, although this is often difficult given their obligations to new children and their low income and high levels of unemployment. The evidence suggests that non-payment of child maintenance is due primarily to incapacity to pay. Moreover, those who do not pay maintenance or informal support seem to be particularly estranged from their children. Our research also suggests that mothers on Income Support are much less likely to receive child maintenance. It is probable that fathers who have limited financial resources do not see the point of paying maintenance where the mother and the child reap no benefit, and that they believe it is better for all concerned to support the children informally. The entry of the Child Support Act into this emotionally charged area has made relationships between fathers and their old and new partners, and between fathers and their children, more difficult without any apparent benefit to the vast majority of lone mothers or indeed the general taxpayer. Non-resident fathers do not accept that they have an unreserved obligation to pay maintenance. The Child Support Act was bound to fail because it did not understand or seek to understand the complex dynamics in the relationships between a sense of obligation and the emotional bond between the father, his child, and his former partner. We hope that this study will contribute to a greater understanding of the dynamics of non-resident fathers and enable policy-makers to make rather better policy in the future than they have in the past.

NOTES

1. This research project originally had the title 'Fathers Apart in Britain'. We preferred it to the tendentious use of 'absent father' in the child support legislation. However, in the course of the project we became increasingly dissatisfied with the words 'fathers apart', mainly because they implied a physical and emotional distance between fathers and their children which was not reflected in the research. We therefore started using 'non-resident fathers', despite the fact that many of these fathers are sometimes resident with the children who normally live with their mother in another household, as well as commonly being a resident social and/or biological father of other children.

2. Haskey (1989) and Haskey and Kiernan (1989) estimate that two and a half years after divorce a third of women had remarried and a third were cohabiting.
3. Another reason for not basing estimates of the prevalence of non-resident fathers on the prevalence of lone mothers is the fact that Bradshaw and Millar (1991) found that their sample of lone mothers contained a proportion of children derived from more than one partnership. About 7% of lone parents in that study had had at least one child by a second childbearing relationship; 1% had had a child from a third childbearing relationship; and 5 lone parents had had at least one child from a fourth childbearing relationship (no one in the sample had had more than four childbearing relationships). As we note later in the text, 11% of fathers in this study had (dependent) children with more than one past partner and 3% had fathered children with up to three past partners.

   More or less all fathers eventually become non-resident as their children leave home. We chose the age cut-off in our survey which is traditionally used to define a lone parent (child under 16 or under 18 and in full-time education). It is also employed in social policy and child benefit is payable on that basis. Also, under the Child Support Act parents are no longer required to pay child support after the youngest child is 18. But it is arguable that in the context of older and later transitions from the parental home, 18 is far too early a cut-off. Certainly, there are dependent children living with their (lone) mothers long after the age of 18 and they also have non-resident fathers (who have not been covered in this study).
4. The survey of fathers was complemented by two qualitative studies: one, by Carol Stimson, exploring contact between the fathers and their children; and the other, by Christine Skinner, exploring financial relationships and maintenance.
5. Some insight into this is found in the experience of the Child Support Agency: 16% of non-resident fathers approached by the CSA disputed paternity; in 7% of cases, DNA tests proved that the alleged father of the child could not have been the biological father. Coleman (1996*c*) reports that a review of false paternity data for the US gives a range of 2.1% to 11.8%, but figures based on cystic fibrosis cases found only 1.4% of false paternity cases for the UK. Clarke *et al.* (1998) suggest from their analysis of the BHPS that the under-reporting of male fertility runs between 10% and 15% of all births and up to 30% to 50% of non-marital births.
6. 'Child maintenance' and 'child support' are used interchangeably in this chapter.
7. That is, children spend roughly equal amounts of time living in their mother's and father's households.

18

The residential mobility of divorced people

Robin Flowerdew, Alaa Al-Hamad, and Lynn Hayes

INTRODUCTION

Household structure in Britain has been undergoing considerable change over the last few decades, with the life courses of individual people becoming more complex (Bonvalet and Lelièvre 1997). In particular, the increasing numbers of people living alone (Hall *et al.* 1997, Chapter 11 of this volume) and of movements in and out of marriage and cohabiting relationships have implications for demographic structure and for residential mobility. The divorce rate in Britain increased substantially throughout the 1970s with some slowing down in the 1980s (Haskey 1996*b*). If divorce continues at the present rate, around a quarter of couples presently entering marriage are likely to divorce within ten years and around a third will have divorced within twenty years (Grundy 1992*b*: 173). Divorce statistics underestimate the incidence of marital breakdown since they exclude those who are separated but not legally divorced. Nor do they include couples who have cohabited and then separated.

In general, the breakdown of a marriage implies that residential movement will take place for at least one partner (Grundy 1992*b*). Such moves may be only temporary and may be followed by further movement as the divorced partners readjust their family and housing circumstances. The number of second and subsequent marriages has also increased, and in some cases provides the reason for the preceding divorce of one or both partners (Murphy 1990). As with first marriage, remarriage is likely to involve residential movement for at least one partner, although

This chapter was produced as part of an ESRC-funded project conducted under the Population and Household Change Programme. We acknowledge use of Crown Copyright data from the 1991 Census, purchased for the academic community by ESRC, JISC, and DENI. We are indebted to our colleagues, Richard Davies and Jennifer Mason, for their assistance in the project.

cohabitation frequently precedes second marriages and mobility will take place at that time rather than at the time of the marriage itself.

This chapter discusses evidence about migration in relation to divorce from the limited perspective available from census data. Because of data limitations, most of the discussion is about the migration of divorced people (that is, those who identified themselves as divorced on census night), which may include moves that have nothing to do with the occurrence of divorce, and may occur years or decades later. Likewise, it may exclude moves related to the breakdown of the relationship, which are likely to be made some time before divorces are finalized.

However, use of the Household Sample of Anonymised Records (SARs) does allow figures and tables to be constructed from census data in a way which has not previously been possible. In particular, it is now possible to work out who divorced migrants moved with, and who they met and joined at their new destination. This allows more information to be gained (for a large sample) about the household changes accompanying migration for divorced people, as well as comparison of the circumstances of divorced and other migrants.

Review of the literature

Previous British studies of migration in relation to marital status (for example, Devis 1983) have shown that divorced people have higher levels of migration than married people. Moves by those who are separated, widowed, or divorced are much more likely to be intra-urban than interregional (Halfacree *et al.* 1991). Although there may be cases where marital breakdown coincides with labour migration, most people are likely to prefer moving locally, to remain in touch with local support networks, and in many cases with jobs, friends, and children. Grundy (1992*b*: 173) reports that divorced women have lower rates of interregional mobility than other women of similar ages, although they have higher levels of shorter-distance mobility than do married women.

McCarthy and Simpson (1991) examine the post-divorce housing moves of those occupying different tenure groups during marriage. They conclude that owner-occupiers have more options available to them on separating than those who have rented during marriage. Owner-occupiers often change tenure on separating (also noted by Buck 1994 from British Household Panel Survey data), but this change may be temporary. However, there is evidence that even those who manage to remain in owner-occupation often end up in worse property than that which they occupied during the marriage. The longer a couple had been married, the more likely it is that they were in owner-occupation during the marriage and the more likely they were to stay in owner-occupation after divorce.

McCarthy and Simpson (1991) argue that long-married couples will have paid off more of their mortgage and thus be able to release a larger amount of capital on separation, which then enables both partners to consider the purchase of property, albeit often smaller or of lower quality than the marital home. Alternatively, one partner may choose to remain in the marital home, perhaps taking out a further mortgage to buy out the other partner. Those who had been married for shorter periods were more likely to move in with family or friends on separation than people who had been married longer. Geographical location, and the differing availability of housing associated with it, can also affect the options open to separating couples.

Murphy (1990: 30) summarizes the housing options open to divorcing women as follows:

> certain combinations of housing 'packages' are more obviously available: sharing in the owner-occupied sector (for those whose parents are in that sector); obtaining local authority accommodation of their own (likely to be of high standard with respect to amenities, but quite likely to be a flat)—however, this option is much more feasible for those with larger family sizes; and the privately-rented sector for the childless which, although it permits independent living, is likely to have the well-documented drawbacks of this sector, including poor amenities, high cost, insecurity, and small size.

He goes on to suggest that women with large families are more likely to have difficulty in finding privately rented accommodation because of opposition from landlords. However, a large family is also likely to put a greater additional strain on any household it joins, making it difficult, for example, for a divorced woman to return to, or remain for any length of time in, her parents' home (Murphy 1990: 34).

McCarthy and Simpson (1991: 74) found that moving into the home of family or friends is a frequent initial option for both men and women and all tenure groups, although one which tended to be temporary. Sullivan (1986: 43) found remarkably high numbers of men living in the parental home after separation, especially for those aged under 30. Most of these young men had manual occupations. Brailey (1986) argues that divorced women were unwilling to impose on relatives and felt the need for their own independence; additionally, some felt they might lose the opportunity of local authority housing if they were known to have a home with relatives. Indeed, in all age groups, the proportion of divorced and separated men who were living with parents outnumbers the proportion of similarly aged women doing so (Sullivan 1986).

Adequate accommodation for children is the main housing-related concern of custodial parents, but children's needs are also important for those granted access but not custody (McCarthy and Simpson 1991: 78).

They want a place which can accommodate visits and occasional stays by their children. The need for accommodation suitable not only for the separated parents themselves but also for visiting children may contribute to frequent moving as parents attempt to establish themselves in housing which satisfies both sets of needs. A fifth of McCarthy and Simpson's sample had made two or more moves, with non-custodial fathers having made the greatest number of moves (McCarthy and Simpson 1991: 72).

Sullivan (1986: 37), using the Family Formation Survey, found that 46 per cent of wives moved out of the family home at the time of breakdown; younger women were more likely to move out than women in their forties, three-quarters of whom stayed in the marital home. Women with children were also less likely to move out of the marital home than childless women. In another study, a volunteer sample of 92 divorced men included 40 cases where the husband left, 38 where the wife left, 12 where both left, and one where the divorced couple still occupied the marital home (Ambrose *et al.* 1983: 54). Generally, the person who had petitioned for divorce was more likely to stay put. Custody of children was also highly relevant: in six out of eight cases where a man was awarded custody, he remained in the marital home. McCarthy and Simpson (1991: 20) found in their study that 61 per cent of custodial fathers and 41 per cent of custodial mothers stayed in the family home. Symon (1990: 116) points out that not all divorced women who get the family home are able to keep it. They may be forced to move subsequently if they are unable to meet mortgage repayment costs.

DATA SOURCES

Data released for the 1991 Census included for the first time a sample of individual-level records allowing users to create their own tables by combining any census variables they wish. The records are anonymised so that individual people and households cannot be identified. This process makes it difficult to distinguish between the experiences of people in different small geographical areas but where this is not an important consideration, it allows many types of analysis that were not possible previously. In this project, we use the 1 per cent Household Sample of Anonymised Records (there is also a 2 per cent sample of individual records) to investigate relationships between household composition, migration, and other variables. For each household, the Household SARs give the relationship of each member to the head of household (the first person mentioned on the census form), allowing more to be said about the relationships of people within households than has been possible previously.

Inferences may be made about changes in household composition within the previous year, given certain assumptions. This can be done by exploiting the information about individuals' residence one year before census night. For each member of a household, the SARs indicate whether they are at the same address or not, and if they have moved, the distance of their move (calculated by assigning grid references to their original and current postcodes). It is also possible to compare different members of the same household, to see who was at the same address one year before or at different addresses. The distance of move is recorded in one of fifteen distance bands (including 'outside Britain' and 'not stated'). If two household members moved different distances to the home they now share, it is clear that they were not part of the same household one year before. The previous regions of residence are also given for all household members, and if these are different it can again be inferred that they were in different households. If they moved the same distance, from the same region, it is not necessarily the case that they were part of the same household one year before, but it is fairly likely that they were.

Whether or not they were cannot always be ascertained, but the SARs contain further relevant evidence: wholly moving households are distinguished—that is, households where all members were at the same place one year before (though other members of the household one year before may not have moved). However, there are some households which are not wholly moving where some members may nevertheless have moved together, perhaps to join somebody at a new destination (for example, a woman and her children may have moved to join a new partner). In households which were not wholly moving, we have examined the relationships of the household members who had moved the same distance from the same region, assuming they moved together if they are closely related (for example, parent and child, cohabiting partners) and otherwise they did not. There is still some ambiguity, therefore, in deciding whether household members who have travelled the same distance as a migrant are (1) people he or she moved with or (2) people who were met at the destination. There were relatively few cases, however, where an arbitrary decision had to be made and our experience with the data suggests that the margin of error is small.

It should be emphasized that the Census does not tell us the structure of a migrant's household one year before, any more than it tells us his or her marital status, occupation, housing tenure, or anything else one year before (except address). We can only observe the household structure at the time of the Census, and make inferences as described about which household members accompanied the migrant in the move. Even then, it is possible that some people may have accompanied the migrant but since have moved on, or that people who have moved from the same address may have done so at different times and independently of one another.

The data used in this chapter require certain assumptions about the links between household composition, marital status, and migration. The most important assumption is probably the one discussed above, that household members living in the same distance band away from their current address one year ago were living together, as modified by the considerations mentioned. Multiple moves within the previous year cannot be identified, and so are ignored. It is also assumed that movers' marital status did not change between the move and the Census—for example, that divorced people who were movers did not move with their spouse and divorce subsequent to the move.

TYPES OF DIVORCED MIGRANT

The SARs allow construction of a typology of movers, according to three criteria. First, it is possible to distinguish between those who *moved alone* and those who *moved with others*. The former category refers to individuals who do not share the same distance of move with anybody else in their current household; they may, of course, have moved with somebody who has subsequently died or moved on. The latter category refers to individuals who are thought to have moved from the same place as others in their household; in some instances they may have lived at different addresses which happened to be the same distance away. It is also possible that people may have moved from the same old address to the same new address at different times during the year prior to the Census; although in this case they did not strictly move together, the chapter discusses them as if they did.

Secondly, individuals may have moved to *join* others. In other words, a mover has joined a household which includes one or more persons who were at the address one year before. If the mover did not join others, this implies that no household member was at the address one year before. Again, it is possible that one household member may have moved in the eleven months before the Census and been joined by another a few months later; however, we have no information from the Census about the dates of the moves concerned, and so this situation would be regarded as falling in the next category.

Thirdly, individuals may have moved to *meet* others. This occurs where a mover is in a household which also contains one or more person not at their current address one year before and who had moved from a different place from the individual we are concerned with. Alternatively, there may be no such household members. In some cases, if the other household members moved earlier than the one we are concerned with, this may be better classified as a move to join, rather than to meet, but we have no way of knowing if this is so, and so this possibility is ignored. It is also possible that some moves to meet others, involving distances of move classified in the same distance band, may have been misclassified as moves with others, rather than moves to meet others.

Of course, moves may include any combination of the above criteria. Whether or not they move alone or with others, migrants may or may not join other people, and they may or may not meet other migrants. The typology therefore includes eight possible situations, all of which are represented in the Household SARs, although people who moved with others to meet some household members and to join others are few in number. The typology can be developed further by considering the relationship of these household members to the migrant; subcategories are identifiable according to who the migrant moved with, who they joined, and who they met. It could be applied to all migrants or to any subset of them, but in this chapter it is applied to divorced migrants, the composition of whose household is of particular interest to this project.

DIVORCED MIGRANTS IN THE SARS

The Household SARs includes records of 531,170 people, of whom 269,494 are male and 261,676 are female. Of these, 25,546 (5 per cent of the total and 6 per cent of people aged 18 and over) are divorced; 10,678 (42 per cent) are male and 14,868 (58 per cent) female. The category 'divorced' in the SARs does not include people who are separated but not legally divorced. Part of this substantial sex differential is because of females' higher life expectancy, but most is probably due to the greater propensity of males to remarry after divorce.

There are 49,133 movers in the SARs, of whom 3,203 (6.5 per cent) are divorced; considering only the 38,424 movers aged 18 and over, 8 per cent are divorced. The migration rate for the whole Household SARs is 9 per cent, with only minor differences by gender or age. The migration rate for *divorced* people is considerably higher at 12.5 per cent, and higher for males (14 per cent) than for females (11 per cent).

The age distribution of divorced migrants differs from that of other migrants. Only 15 per cent of male divorced migrants and 23 per cent of female divorced migrants are under 30, compared with 54 per cent of adult male migrants and 59 per cent of adult female migrants in other marital status categories. In contrast, 67 per cent of male divorced migrants and 61 per cent of female divorced migrants are between 30 and 49, compared with 33 per cent and 27 per cent respectively of migrants with other marital statuses. This reflects the overall age distribution of divorced people, only 9 per cent of whom are under 30, and 56 per cent between 30 and 49. Thus, the migration rate for divorced people under 30 is 26 per cent, 14 per cent for people aged 30 to 49, and 6 per cent for people aged 50 and over, being slightly higher for males than females at all ages. The equivalent figures for non-divorced people are clearly lower at 21 per cent, 8 per cent, and 3 per cent.

The typology outlined in the previous section allows us to divide divorced migrants into eight categories, although for most purposes we concentrate on the distinction between people who moved alone and people who moved with others. Table 18.1 shows the relative numbers in each category. The sample includes 1,628 who moved alone and 1,575 who moved with other people. Although the majority of moves (67 per cent) do not result in additions to the divorced mover's household, a substantial minority do, especially the 503 cases where a divorced person moved alone to join others and the 248 cases where he or she met other migrants at a new address. The clearest gender difference is between those people moving alone and those moving with others. Only 36 per cent of male divorced migrants moved with others, compared with 61 per cent of female divorced migrants.

Of divorced migrants under 30, 59 per cent moved with other people, while in the 30–49 age group, this proportion was only 52 per cent. The oldest divorced migrants (50 and over) are more likely than the others to move alone: 72 per cent of them did so. There are big differences between male and female divorced migrants in this respect. In the under-30 age group, 46 per cent of divorced migrants who moved alone were female, but 74 per cent of those who moved with others. In the 30–49 age group, 65 per cent of those moving alone were male, but 65 per cent of those moving with others were female. Only for those aged 50 and over was there little difference in type of move between the sexes.

The group of divorced migrants who moved alone included 967 men and 661 women. Of these, 517 men (53 per cent) moved to meet or join some-

TABLE 18.1. *Type of move, divorced movers*

	Male	%	Female	%	Total	%
Moved and stayed alone	450	30	388	23	838	26
Moved and stayed with others	465	31	852	50	1,317	41
Moved alone to meet others	158	11	90	5	248	8
Moved with others to meet others	33	2	74	4	107	3
Moved alone to join others	326	22	177	10	503	16
Moved with others to join others	38	3	99	6	137	4
Moved alone to meet and join others	33	2	6	—	39	1
Moved with others to meet and join others	3	—	11	1	14	—

— Less than 0.5%.

body else, while only 273 women (41 per cent) did so. Older people are more likely to stay alone, 289 of 394 (73 per cent) doing so, compared to 49 per cent of people aged 30 to 49 and only 29 per cent of divorced movers aged under 30. At all ages, divorced women moving alone are more likely than divorced men to remain alone. Combining divorced migrants who moved alone and those who moved with others, the most likely group to meet or join others were males under 30, but even in this group, 52 per cent did not do so. Among divorced male migrants aged 30 to 49, 61 per cent did not meet or join anybody, compared with 68 per cent of those aged 50 and over. Divorced female migrants were even less likely to meet or join others after the move: this applies to 67 per cent of the under-30 group, 73 per cent of those aged 30 to 49, and 84 per cent of those aged 50 and over. There was no major difference in the proportions meeting others and joining others, the latter being more common for all age and sex groups, especially among those over 50.

This analysis suggests that it is harder for divorced females than for divorced males to join or start a new household, and that it gets increasingly difficult with age. However, the gender difference hides a much wider difference between those moving alone and those moving with other people. Only 26 per cent of migrant divorced males under 30 who moved alone remained in a single-person household, compared with 91 per cent of those who moved with other people. Among migrant divorced females under 30, the equivalent figures were 32 per cent and 81 per cent. Some of this difference occurs because some of these divorced migrants had a partner before the move and so perhaps had no need to join or start a new household, but much of it seems likely to relate to the presence of children, which appear to have a strong deterrent effect on moving to meet or join others.

Isolating those divorced migrants moving with children and no partner showed that 76 per cent did not meet or join anybody else compared with 51 per cent of those moving alone. There is still a gender effect, however; 78 per cent of women moving with children only did not meet or join anybody compared with 64 per cent of men in analogous circumstances.

Divorced migrants moving with other people

The 1,575 divorced people who moved with others included 539 men and 1,036 women. These people were much less likely to meet or join somebody else. Only 14 per cent of men and 18 per cent of women did so. The most common situation was for divorced people to move with children—945 did so—while 698 people moved with a partner (261 of these moving with both partner and children). Of the remaining people in this group, 112 moved with unrelated individuals, while 25 moved with a parent or parents and 26 with other relatives. There is a big difference between male and female divorcees in the people they move with; just 59 men moved with children only whereas 625 women did. Men were more likely to move with partners: 384 of 539 did so, compared to only 314 of 1,036 women. Men were more likely than women to move with unrelated individuals, with 68 men and 44 women making moves of this type. Only 25 people moved with parents and 26 with other relatives.

Moves to join other people

The majority of divorced people who moved alone to join an established household were in three categories: 182 (36 per cent) joined a partner, 127 (25 per cent) joined unrelated individuals, and 127 (25 per cent) joined parents, while only 20 (4 per cent) joined children and 25 (5 per cent) joined other relatives. Moves of this type were made more often by men (326 cases) than by women (177 cases). Men were slightly more likely than women to join non-relatives or parents, and women were slightly more likely to move to join a partner.

Of the 137 divorced people moving with others to join an existing household, the majority (72 per cent) were female, almost all of whom (87 per cent) moved with children. In contrast to those moving alone, the largest proportion (35 per cent) moved to join parents, with 29 per cent joining a partner and 26 per cent joining unrelated individuals. Men in this category were more likely than females to be moving to join non-relatives and less likely to be moving to join partners.

Moves to meet other people

This category involved 408 divorced people moving to establish a new household with others, 227 men and 181 women. The majority of these (191 men and 96 women) moved alone; in the other cases, especially among women, the divorced person was likely to move with children (11 men and 58 women) or with non-relatives (29 cases) and in a few cases (16) with partners. The people they met in the new household were most likely to be unrelated individuals (49 cases); 30 divorced women, but only 5 divorced men, moved to meet partners, and 23 people (8 men and 15 women) moved to meet children.

Housing tenure and divorced migrants

There are important differences in tenure between divorced and non-divorced migrants after the move (the Census does not provide any information about migrants' tenure before the move). Divorced migrants are less likely to be owner-occupiers or private renters and more likely to be renters from local authorities or Housing Associations. The latter is particularly true for women, 34 per cent of divorced women migrants being in these tenures compared with 22 per cent of non-divorced women migrants. Male migrants are more likely to be private renters and female migrants to rent from local authorities or Housing Associations, this difference being considerably greater for divorced migrants than for others. Table 18.2 shows the tenure of divorced movers.

In comparison with divorced non-migrants, members of the divorced migrant sample were more likely to be in private rented accommodation (23 per cent compared to 10 per cent of all divorced people and 8 per cent of non-divorced), with fewer in both owner-occupation and renting from local authorities or Housing Associations. As with all divorced people, female divorced migrants were better represented in local authority housing than males. Males moving with others were particularly likely to be owner-occupiers, whereas women moving with others were particularly likely to rent from local authorities or Housing Associations.

Housing type and divorced migrants

Migrants are less likely to be in detached and semi-detached houses and more likely to be in flats, bedsitters, and non-permanent accommodation than the population as a whole. Divorced migrants show the same trends to a greater degree. While 23 per cent of the non-divorced population aged 18 and over live in detached housing and 32 per cent in semi-detached housing, the corresponding proportions for non-divorced migrants aged 18 and over are 18 per cent and 23 per cent, and for divorced migrants 12 per cent and 23 per cent. In contrast, 30 per cent of divorced migrants live in flats compared to 26 per cent of non-divorced migrants and 15 per cent of non-divorced non-migrants.

Male divorced migrants are particularly unlikely to be in detached or semi-detached housing, although rather more likely than females to be in flats, bedsitters, and non-permanent accommodation. Divorced migrants moving alone are particularly unlikely to be in detached (9 per cent) or semi-detached (20 per cent) housing, and particularly likely to be in flats (36 per cent), bedsitters (5 per cent), or non-permanent accommodation

TABLE 18.2. *Tenure of divorced movers*

	Male	%	Female	%	Total	%
Owner-occupier	708	47	767	45	1,475	46
Private renter	388	26	346	20	734	23
Renter (local authority/ Housing Association)	410	27	584	34	994	31

(2 per cent). Those moving and staying alone are much more likely to move to flats or smaller dwellings than those moving to join another household and, to a lesser extent, those moving to meet others. Of those staying alone after the move, only 44 per cent were in houses, compared to 79 per cent of those moving to join others and 69 per cent of those moving to meet others.

Distances moved by different categories of divorced migrant

The distances moved by all migrants in the Household SARs tend to be longer than those for divorced migrants. In particular, 14 per cent of moves made by non-divorced migrants were 80 kilometres or more, while only 9 per cent of those by divorced migrants were of this length. Over half the moves made by divorced movers were under 5 kilometres, female divorced migrants tending to move shorter distances than males. Divorced migrants moving with others were particularly likely to move short distances—57 per cent of this group moved under 5 kilometres, compared with 44 per cent of divorced migrants moving alone. This is true for both males and females, with females in both categories being more likely to have made moves of this distance.

Relatively longer moves were made by people moving alone to meet others (only 30 per cent were under 5 kilometres and 11 per cent were 80 kilometres or more). Of those moving and staying alone, 52 per cent were under 5 kilometres, as were 59 per cent of those moving and staying with others. Those moving alone to join others were less likely to move under 5 kilometres than those staying alone but more likely than those moving to meet others.

This analysis excludes migrants with origin not stated, who were only slightly more numerous among divorced migrants (6 per cent) than non-divorced migrants (5 per cent). Among divorced migrants, those moving alone were particularly likely not to state their origin (8 per cent). The category '80 kilometres or more' used above excludes migrants from outside Britain, although the latter group has been used in calculating percentage figures. There is a difference in the percentage of divorced (3 per cent) and non-divorced (7 per cent) migrants who have moved from outside Britain. A higher proportion of female divorced migrants moving alone (5 per cent) have moved from outside Britain than is the case for other groups.

CONCLUSION

The main methodological conclusion is that the Household SARs have great potential for telling us more about the relationship between migration, marital status, and household composition. The large sample makes it possible to pick out differences in trends between different groups; and although the analysis has contained few surprises, it does allow us to quantify some effects which have previously been the source of speculation or the results of rather smaller sample analyses. Some of the work requires considerable time and care; our typology of migration according to whether migrants moved alone or with others and whether they met or joined others at their new address required painstaking analysis of household records. There is however considerable potential to extend this analysis beyond what is presented here. For example, we have concentrated on divorced movers, and similar kinds of findings could be reached for other marital status groups. We have only looked at a few of the many variables which could have interesting relationships to migration and marital status; other variables which could also be fruitfully explored include social class, education, and ethnic group.

There are many empirical conclusions. We think it is a useful addition to our knowledge of migration behaviour to get a clearer idea of who moves. Most of the literature either treats migrants as totally autonomous individuals or as heads of coherent and indissoluble household groups. Our approach has focused on people who through divorce have split from their existing households, and it has shown a large number of moves resulting in additions to households, through meeting or joining others. We have also been able to show who moves with divorced migrants, who they move to meet or to join, and how far they move.

Summarizing some of the principal findings, it is clear that divorced people are more migratory than others and that divorced migrants tend to be rather older than other migrants. About half of the divorced migrants have moved with others, in most cases with a new partner or children or both; women are far more likely to move with children than are men. A high proportion of divorced migrants are now cohabiting, in many cases with other divorced people. Divorced migrants tend to be more likely to be renters than either divorced non-migrants or non-divorced migrants, with males more likely to be in privately rented accommodation, and females, especially if they move with children, more likely to be in local authority or Housing Association accommodation. Divorced migrants are more likely to move short distances than other migrants, especially those moving with children. The shorter distances moved by female compared to male divorced migrants is accounted for by the effect of moving with children.

It is clear that many divorced migrants have entered new relationships, and a reasonable number appear from their tenure and house type to be doing well. Others, however, especially older females, remain alone, or alone with their children, in smaller rented accommodation. This analysis can only present the results of general tendencies; qualitative research is necessary to supplement it by illuminating the processes which led to these moves and the diverse situations which divorced migrants find themselves in.

BIBLIOGRAPHY

ABRAMS, M. (1978), *Beyond Three Score Years and Ten*, London: Age Concern.

ALLAN, G. (1989), *Friendship: Developing a Sociological Perspective*, Hemel Hempstead: Harvester Wheatsheaf.

ALLEN, I. (1985), *Counselling Services for Sterilisation, Vasectomy and Termination of Pregnancy*, London: Policy Studies Institute.

——(1987), *Education in Sex and Personal Relationships*, London: Policy Studies Institute.

——(1991), *Family Planning and Pregnancy Counselling Projects for Young People*, London: Policy Studies Institute.

——(1997), *Teenage Mothers: Housing and Household Change*, ESRC End of Award Report No. L31525301, Swindon: ESRC.

——and BOURKE DOWLING, S. (1998), *Teenage Mothers: Decisions and Outcomes*, London: Policy Studies Institute.

——HOGG, D., and PEACE, S. (1992), *Elderly People: Choice, Participation and Satisfaction*, London: Policy Studies Institute.

——and PERKINS, E. (eds.) (1995), *The Future of Family Care for Older People*, London: HMSO.

ALTERGOTT, K. (1988), *Daily Life in Later Life*, Newbury Park, Calif.: Sage Publications Inc.

ALWIN, D., BRAUN, M., and SCOTT, J. (1992), 'The Separation of Work and Family: Attitudes towards Women's Labour Force Participation in Germany, Great Britain and the United States', *European Sociological Review*, 8: 13–37.

——and SCOTT, J. (1996), 'Attitude Change—Its Measurement and Interpretation Using Longitudinal Surveys', in B. Taylor and B Thomson (eds.), *A Decade of Change in Social Values*, Aldershot: Dartmouth, 75–106.

————and BRAUN, M. (1997), *Sex-role Attitudes Change in the United States: National Trends and Cross-national Comparisons*, Ann Arbor, Mich.: Institute of Social Research, University of Michigan.

AMATO, P. R. (1994), 'The Implications of Research Findings on Children in Stepfamilies', in A. Booth and J. Dunn (eds.), *Stepfamilies: Who Benefits? Who Does Not?*, Hillsdale, NJ: Lawrence Erlbaum.

AMBROSE, P., HARPER, J., and PEMBERTON, R. (1983), *Surviving Divorce: Men beyond Marriage*, London: Wheatsheaf.

ANDERSON, M. (1971), *Family Structure in Nineteenth Century Lancashire*, Cambridge: Cambridge University Press.

ANGEL, R. J., ANGEL, J. L., and HIMES, C. L. (1992), 'Minority Group Status, Health Transitions, and Community Living Arrangements among the Elderly', *Research on Aging*, 14: 496–521.

ANTONUCCI, T. (1985), 'Personal Characteristics, Social Support, and Social Behaviour', in R. Binstock and E. Shanas (eds.), *Handbook of Aging and the Social Sciences*, New York: Van Nostrand Reinhold and Company, 95–128.

ANTONUCCI, T. (1995), 'Convoys and Social Relations: Family and Friendships within a Life Span Context', in R. Blieszner and V. H. Bedford (eds.), *Handbook of Aging and the Family*, New York: Greenwood Press, 355–71.

—— and AKIYAMA, H. (1987), 'Social Networks in Adult Life: A Preliminary Examination of the Convoy Model', *Journal of Gerontology*, 4: 519–27.

ARBER, R. J., GILBERT, G. N., and EVANDROU, M. (1988), 'Gender, Household Composition and Receipt of Domiciliary Services by Elderly Disabled People', *Journal of Social Policy*, 17: 153–75.

ARBER, S., and GINN, J. (1991), *Gender and Later Life*, London: Sage.

ARMITAGE, R., and BABB, P. (1996), 'Population Review (4): Trends in Fertility', *Population Trends*, 84: 7–13.

ATKINSON, A. B., RAINWATER, L., and SMEEDING, T. (1995), *Income Distribution in OECD Countries: Evidence from the Luxembourg Income Study*, Paris: OECD.

AXINN, W., and THORNTON, A. (1992), 'The Relationship between Cohabitation and Divorce: Selective or Causal Influence?', *Demography*, 29: 357–75.

BABB, P. (1993), 'Teenage Conceptions and Fertility in England and Wales, 1971–91', *Population Trends*, 74: 12–17.

BAKER, S. A., THALBERG, S. P., and MORRISON, D. M. (1988), 'Parents' Behavioural Norms as Predictors of Adolescent Sexual Activity and Contraceptive Use', *Adolescence*, 23: 265–82.

BAMFORD, C. (1994), *Grandparents' Lives: Men and Women in Later Life*, Edinburgh: Age Concern Scotland.

BARNARTT, S., and HARRIS, R. (1982), 'Recent Changes in Predictors of Abortion Attitudes', *Sociology and Social Research*, 66: 320–34.

BARNES, J. A. (1954), 'Class and Committees in a Norwegian Island Parish', *Human Relations*, 7: 39–58.

BARRETT, M., and MCINTOSH, M. (1982), *The Anti-social Family*, London: Verso.

BARROW, C. (ed.) (1996), *Family in the Caribbean: Themes and Perspectives*, Kingston: Ian Randle Publishers.

BARROW, J. (1982), 'West Indian Families: An Insider's Perspective', in R. N. Rapoport, M. P. Fogarty, and R. Rapoport (eds.), *Families in Britain*, London: Routledge and Kegan Paul, 220–32.

BARTIAUX, F. (1991), 'La Composition des ménages des personnes agées en Italie', *European Journal of Population*, 7: 59–98.

BATCHELOR, J., DIMMOCK, B., and SMITH, D. (1994), *Understanding Stepfamilies: What Can Be Learned from Callers to the Stepfamily Telephone Counselling Service?*, London: Stepfamily Publications.

BECH, H. (1997), *When Men Meet: Homosexuality and Modernity*, Cambridge: Polity Press.

BECK, U. (1992), *Risk Society: Towards a New Modernity*, London: Sage.

—— and BECK-GERNSHEIM, E. (1995), *The Normal Chaos of Love*, Cambridge: Polity Press.

BECKER, G. S. (1981), *A Treatise on the Family*, Cambridge, Mass.: Harvard University Press.

BELAND, F. (1987), 'Multigenerational Households in a Contemporary Perspective', *International Journal of Aging and Human Development*, 25: 147–66.

BELL, A. P., and WEINBERG, M. S. (1978), *Homosexualities: A Study of Diversity among Men and Women*, London: Mitchell Beazley.

BELL, C. (1968), *Middle Class Families*, London: Routledge and Kegan Paul.

BENGTSON, V. L., and ACHENBAUM, W. A. (1993), *The Changing Contract across the Generations*, New York: Aldine de Gruyter.

——and Kuypers, J. A. (1971), 'Generational Difference and the Developmental Stake', *Aging and Human Development*, 2: 249–60.

——WARNER SCHAIE, K., and BURTON, L. M. (eds.) (1995), *Adult Intergenerational Relations*, New York: Springer.

BENNETT, N., BLANC, A. K., and BLOOM, D. E. (1988), 'Commitment and the Modern Union: Assessing the Link Between Premarital Cohabitation and Subsequent Marital Stability', *American Sociological Review*, 53: 127–38.

——JARVIS, L., ROWLANDS, O., SINGLETON, N., and HASELDEN, L. (1996), *Living in Britain Results from the General Household Survey Report 1994*, London: ONS.

BERLIN, I. (1976), *Vico and Herder: Two Studies in the History of Ideas*, London: Hogarth Press.

BERRINGTON, A. (1996), 'Marriage Patterns and Inter-ethnic Unions', in D. Coleman and J. Salt (eds.), *Ethnicity in the 1991 Census*, vol. 1, London: OPCS/HMSO, 178–212.

——and DIAMOND, I. (1997), 'Marital Dissolution among the 1958 British Birth Cohort: The Role of Cohabitation', paper presented at the Population Association of America meetings, Washington, DC 29.

BERTHOUD, R., ROWLINGSON, K., and MCKAY, S. (1997), *Explaining the Growth of Lone Parenthood in Great Britain*, ESRC End of Award Report No. L31593002, Swindon: ESRC.

BETTIO, F., and VILLA, P. (1996), *A Mediterranean Perspective on the Breakdown of the Relationship between Participation and Fertility*, Discussion Paper 5, Trento: Dipartimento de Economia, Universita degli Studi di Trento.

BIEN, W., MARBACH, J., and TEMPLETON, R. (1992), 'Social Networks of Single-person Households', in C. Marsh and S. Arber (eds.), *Families and Households*, London: Macmillan, 157–73.

BLACK, J. (1994), *Convergence or Divergence? Britain and the Continent*, London: Macmillan.

BLAKE, J. (1961), *Family Structure in Jamaica: The Social Context of Reproduction*, New York: Free Press.

BLASIUS, M. (1994), *Gay and Lesbian Politics: Sexuality and the Emergence of a New Ethic*, Philadelphia: Temple University Press.

BLUMSTEIN, P., and SCHWARTZ, P. (1983), *American Couples*, New York: William Morrow.

BLUNDELL, R., and PRESTON, I. (1995), 'Income, Expenditure, and the Living Standards of UK Households', *Fiscal Studies*, 16: 40–54.

BOGUE, D., ARRIAGA, E., and ANDERTON, D. (eds.) (1993), *Readings in Population Research Methodology*, Chicago: Social Development Center for the United Nations Fund for Population Activities.

BONVALET, C., and LELIÈVRE, E. (1989), 'Mobilité en France et Paris depuis 1945: Bilan Résidentiel d'une Génération', *Population*, 44: 531–60.

BONVALET, C., and LELIÈVRE, E. (1997), 'The Transformation of Housing and Household Structures in France and Great Britain', *International Journal of Population Geography*, 3: 183–201.

BOOTH, A., and JOHNSON, D. (1988), 'Pre-marital Cohabitation and Marital Success', *Journal of Family Issues*, 9: 255–72.

BORNAT, J., DIMMOCK, B., JONES, D., and PEACE, S. (1999), 'Generational Ties in the "New" Family: Changing Contexts for Traditional Obligations', in E.B. Silva and C. Smart (eds.), *The New Family?*, London: Sage, 115–28.

BORNAT, J., PEACE, S., and DIMMOCK, B. (1997), *The Impact of Family Change on Older People: The Case of Stepfamilies*, ESRC End of Award Report No. L315253003, Swindon: ESRC.

——DIMMOCK, B., JONES, D., and PEACE, S. (1997), 'The Impact on Family Change on the Lives of Older People', paper presented at the World Congress of Gerontology, Adelaide.

————————(1996), 'Finding People to Interview: Issues in Sampling in a Study of The Impact of Family Change on Older People', paper presented at the IV International Conference on Social Science Methodology, University of Essex.

BORSCH-SUPAN, A. H. (1990), 'A Dynamic Analysis of Household Dissolution and Living Arrangement Transitions by Elderly Americans', in D. A. Wise (ed.), *Issues in the Economics of Aging*, Chicago: National Bureau of Economic Research, 89–114.

BOSHUIZEN, H. C., and VAN DE WATER, H. P. A. (1994), *An International Comparison of Health Expectancies*, Leiden: TNO Health Research.

BOSVELD, W. (1966), *The Ageing of Fertility in Europe: A Comparative Demographic-Analytic Study*, Amsterdam: Thesis Publishers.

BOTT, E. (1957), *Family and Social Networks*, London: Tavistock.

BOWLING, A., FARQUHAR, M., and BROWNE, P. (1991), 'Life Satisfaction and Associations with Social Network and Support Variables in Three Samples of Elderly People'. *International Journal of Geriatric Psychiatry*, 6: 549–66.

BRACHER, M., and SANTOW, G. (1990), 'The Family Histories of Australian Women', *European Journal of Population*, 6: 227–56.

————MORGAN, S. P., and TRUSSELL, J. (1993), 'Marriage Dissolution in Australia: Models and Explanations', *Population Studies*, 47: 403–25.

BRADSHAW, J., and MILLAR, J. (1991), *Lone Parent Families in the UK*, Department of Social Security Research Report No. 6, London: HMSO.

BRAILEY, M. (1986), 'Splitting Up and Finding Somewhere to Live', *Critical Social Policy*, 17: 61–9.

BRAMLEY, G., MUNRO, M., and LANCASTER, S. (1997), *The Economic Determinants of Household Formation: A Literature Review*, London: Department of the Environment , Transport and the Regions.

BRASS, W. (1983), *The Formal Demography of the Family: An Overview of Proximate Determinants*, OPCS Occasional Paper No. 31, London: OPCS.

BRATHWAITE, E. (1978), *The Development of Creole Society in Jamaica 1770–1820*, Oxford: Clarendon Press.

BRAUN, M., SCOTT, J., and ALWIN, D. (1994), 'Economic Necessity or Self-actualization? Attitudes toward Women's Labour Force Participation in East and West Germany', *European Sociological Review*, 10: 29–47.

Brock, C. (1996), *The Caribbean in Europe*, London: Frank Cass.

Brubaker, T. H. (1985), *Later Life Families*, Beverly Hills, Calif.: Sage.

Bryson, A., Ford, R., and White, M. (1997), *Making Work Pay: Lone Mothers, Employment and Well-being*, York: Joseph Rowntree Foundation.

Buck, N. (1994), 'Housing and Residential Mobility', in Buck *et al.* (1994), 130–53.

——and Ermisch, J. (1995), 'Cohabitation in Britain', *Changing Britain*, 3: 3–5.

——and Scott, J. (1994), 'Household and Family Change', in Buck *et al.* (1994), 61–82.

——Gershuny, J., Rose, D., and Scott, J. (eds.) (1994), *Changing Households: The British Household Panel Survey, 1990–1992*, Colchester: ESRC Centre on Micro-social Change, University of Essex.

Bulmer, A. (1987), *The Social Basis of Community Care*, London: Allen and Unwin.

Bumpass, L. (1990), 'What's Happening to the Family? Interactions between Demographic and Institutional Change', *Demography*, 27: 483–98.

Burch, T. K., and Matthews, B. J. (1987), 'Household Formations in Developed Societies'. *Population and Development Review*, 13: 495–511.

Burchardt, N. (1990), 'Stepchildren's Memories: Myth, Understanding and Forgiveness', in R. Samuel and P. Thompson (eds.), *The Myths We Live By*, London: Routledge.

Burghes, L. (1993), *One Parent Families: Policy Options for the 1990s*, York: Joseph Rowntree Foundation.

——and Brown, M. (1995), *Single Lone Mothers: Problems, Prospects and Policies*, London: Family Policy Studies Centre.

——Clarke, L., and Cronin, N. (1997), *Fathers and Fatherhood in Britain*, London: Family Policy Studies Centre.

Burgoyne, C., and Morrison, V. (1997), 'Money in Remarriage: Keeping Things Simple and Separate', *Sociological Review*, 45: 363–95.

Burgoyne, J., and Clark, D. (1984), *Making a Go of it: A Study of Stepfamilies in Sheffield*, London: Routledge and Kegan Paul.

Burr, J. A. (1990), 'Race/Sex Comparisons of Elderly Living Arrangements', *Research on Aging*, 12: 507–30.

Burt, M. R. (1986), 'Estimating the Public Costs of Teenage Childbearing', *Family Planning Perspectives*, 18: 221–6.

Bury, J. (1984), *Teenage Pregnancy in Britain*, London: Birth Control Trust.

Cafferata, G. L. (1987), 'Marital Status, Living Arrangements and the Use of Health Services by Elderly Persons', *Journal of Gerontology*, 42: 613–18.

Capron, D., and Corner, I. (1990), 'Sub-national population and household projections by central government', in *Population Projections: trends, methods and uses. OPCS Occasional Paper 38*, London: OPCS, 55–63.

Carpenter, J., Chauvire, Y., and White, P. (1994), 'Marginalisation, Polarisation and Planning in Paris', *Built Environment*, 20: 218–30.

——and Lees, L. (1995), 'Gentrification in New York, London and Paris: An International Comparison', *International Journal of Urban and Regional Research*, 19: 286–303.

CARTER, T. (1986), *Shattering Illusions: West Indians in British Politics*, London: Lawrence and Wishart.

CASTELLS, M. (1996), *The Rise of the Network Society*, Oxford: Blackwell Publishers Ltd.

CASTLES, F. G. (ed.) (1993), *Families of Nations: Patterns of Public Choice in Western Democracies*, Aldershot: Dartmouth.

—— and FLOOD, M. (1993), 'Why Divorce Rates Differ: Law, Religious Belief and Modernity', in Castles (1993), 293–326.

CHAFETZ, J. (1995), 'Chicken or Egg? A Theory of the Relationship between Feminist Movements and Family Change', in K. Mason and A. M. Jenson (eds.), *Gender and Family in Industrialized Countries*, Oxford: Clarendon Press, 63–81.

CHAMBERLAIN, M. (1977), *Narratives of Exile and Return*, London: Macmillan.

—— and GOULBOURNE, H. (1998), *Living Arrangements, Family Structure, and Social Change of Caribbeans in Britain*, ESRC End of Award Report No. L315253009, Swindon: ESRC.

CHAMBERLAYNE, P. (1994), 'Women and Social Policy', in J. Clasen and R. Freeman (eds.), *Social Policy in Germany*, Hemel Hempstead: Harvester, 173–90.

CHANDOLA, T., COLEMAN, D. A., and HIORNS, R. W. (in press), '*Patterns of Recent European Fertility Data: Fitting Curves to Distorted Distributions*', to be published in 'Population Studies'.

Chartered Institute of Housing (1993), *One Parent Families: Are They Jumping the Housing Queue*?, briefing paper, Coventry: Institute of Housing.

CHERLIN, A., and FURSTENBERG, F. (1986), *The New Grandparents*, New York: Basic Books.

CLARK, E. (1989), *Young Single Mothers Today: A Qualitative Study of Housing and Support Needs*, London: National Council for One Parent Families.

—— and COLEMAN, J. (1991), *Growing Up Fast: A Follow-up Study of Teenage Mothers in Adult Life*, London: Trust for the Study of Adolescence.

CLARK, R. L., and WOLF, D. A. (1992), 'Proximity of Children and Elderly Migration', in A. Rogers (ed.), *Elderly Migration and Population Redistribution*, London: Belhaven Press, 77–96.

CLARKE, C. J., and NEIDERT, L. (1992), 'Living Arrangements of the Elderly: An Examination of Differences According to Ancestry and Generation', *The Gerontologist*, 32: 796–804.

CLARKE, E. (1957), *My Mother who Fathered Me*, London: Allen and Unwin.

CLARKE, K., CRAIG, G., and GLENDINNING, C. (1996), *Small Change: The Impact of the Child Support Act on Lone Mothers and Children*, London: Family Policy Studies Centre.

CLARKE, L., CONDY, A., and DOWNING, A. (1998), *Fathers: A Socio-demographic Profile*, London: Family Policy Studies Centre.

COALE, A. J., and WATKINS, S. C. (1986), *The Decline of Fertility in Europe*, Princeton, NJ: Princeton University Press.

COCHRAN, M., LARNER, M., and RILEY, D. (1990), *Extending Families*, Cambridge: Cambridge University Press.

COLEMAN, D. A. (1991), 'European Demographic Systems of the Future: Convergence or Diversification?', in Eurostat (ed.), *Human Resources at the Dawn of*

the twenty-first Century, Luxemburg: Publishing Office of the European Communities, 137–79.
——(1993), 'Britain in Europe: International and Regional Comparisons of Fertility Levels and Trends', in M. Ní Bhrolcháin (ed.), *New Perspectives on Fertility in Britain*, London: HMSO, 67–93.
——(ed.) (1996*a*), *Europe's Population in the 1990s*, Oxford: Oxford University Press.
——(1996*b*), 'New Patterns and Trends in European Fertility: International and Sub-national Comparisons', in Coleman (1996*a*), 1–61.
——(1996*c*), 'Male Fertility Trends in Industrial Countries: Theories in Search of some Evidence', paper presented at the Conference on Fertility and the Male Life Cycle in the Era of Fertility Decline, Mexico City.
——(1997), *Britain's Place in Europe's Population*, ESRC End of Award Report No. L315253006, Swindon: ESRC.
Collins, S. (1995), 'Ideological Assumptions in the Lives of Stepchildren', in J. Brannen and M. O'Brien (eds.), *Childhood and Parenthood*, London: University of East London/Institute of Education, 79–92.
Connidis, I. A. (1989), *Family Ties and Aging*, Toronto: Butterworths.
Coontz, S. (1992), *The Way We Never Were: American Families and the Nostalgia Trap*, New York: Basic Books.
Cooper, J. (1991), 'The Divergence between Period and Cohort Measures of Fertility', *Population Trends*, 63: 19–21.
Coppée, I. (1990), *La Taille des Ménages dans les Grandes Villes et les Départements*, Paris: INSEE.
Corner, I. (1985), *BREHEP Headship Program for Household Projections: User's Guide and Program Listings*, Watford: Building Research Establishment.
——(1989), 'Developing Centralised Household Projections for National and Sub-national areas', in P. Congdon and P. Batey (eds.), *Advances in Regional Demography: Information, Forecasts, Models*, London: Belhaven, 91–106.
Corti, L. (1994), 'For Better or Worse? Annual Change in Smoking, Self-assessed Health and Subjective Well-being', in Buck *et al.* (1994), 199–219.
Cotterill, P. (1994), *Friendly Relations? Mothers and their Daughters-in-Law*, London: Taylor and Francis.
Council of Europe (1990), *Household Structures in Europe: Report of the Select Committee of Experts on Household Structures*, Population Studies 22, Strasburg: Council of Europe.
——(1997), *Recent Demographic Developments in Europe 1997*, Strasburg: Council of Europe.
Craig, J. (1997), 'Population Review', *Population Trends*, 88: 5–12.
Crimmins, E. N., and Ingegneri, D. G. (1990), 'Interaction and Living Arrangements of Older Parents and their Children', *Research on Aging*, 12: 3–35.
Crosbie-Burnett, M., and Lewis, E. A. (1993), 'Use of African-American Family Structures and Functioning to Address the Challenges of European-American Post-divorce Families', *Family Relations*, 42: 243–8.
Cross, M., and Entzinger, H. (eds.) (1988), *Lost Illusions: Caribbean Minorities in Britain and the Netherlands*, London: Routledge.

CROW, G., and ALLEN, G. (1994), *Community Life*, Hemel Hempstead: Harvester Wheatsheaf.

——and HARDEY, M. (1992), 'Diversity and Ambiguity among Lone Parent Households in Modern Britain', in C. Marsh and S. Arber (eds.), *Families and Households: Divisions and Change*, London: British Sociological Association, 142–56.

DALLEY, G. (1996), *Ideologies of Caring: Rethinking Community and Collectivism*, London: Macmillan.

DAVIES, J. (ed.) (1993), *The Family: Is it Just Another Lifestyle Choice?*, London: Institute of Economic Affairs.

DAVIS, J., and JOWELL, R. (1989), 'Measuring National Differences: An Introduction to the International Social Survey Programme (ISSP)', in R. Jowell, S. Witherspoon and L. Brook (eds.), *British Social Attitudes: Special International Report*, Aldershot: Gower, 1–13.

DAVIS, J., and SMITH, T. (1994), *General Social Surveys: Cumulative Codebook, 1972–1994*, Chicago: National Opinion Research Centre.

DAVIS, K., BERNSTAM, M. S., and RICARDO-CAMPBELL, R. (eds.) (1986), *Below-Replacement Fertility in Industrial Societies*, New York: Population Council.

DAYKIN, C. D. (1997), *A Crisis of Longer Life: Problems Facing Social Security Systems Worldwide and Options for Reform*, London: Government Actuary's Department.

DECROLY, J. M., and GRASLAND, C. (1992), 'Frontières, systèmes politiques et fécondité en Europe', *Espace, populations, Sociétés*, 2: 135–52.

——and VANLAER, J. (1991), *Atlas de la population Européenne*, Brussels: Éditions de l'Université de Bruxelles.

DE GRAFF, N. D., and EVANS, G. (1996), 'Why are the Young More Post-materialist? A Cross-national Analysis of Individual and Contextual Influences on Post-material Values', *Comparative Political Studies*, 28: 608–35.

DENCH, G. (1992), *From Extended Family to State Dependency*, London: Institute of Community Studies.

——(1996*a*), *The Place of Men in Changing Family Cultures*, London: Institute of Community Studies.

——(1996*b*), *Transforming Men: Changing Patterns of Dependency and Dominance in Gender Relations*, New Brunswick, NJ and London: Transaction Publishers.

DENNIS, N., and ERDOS, G. (1993), *Families without Fatherhood*, London: Institute of Economic Affairs.

DENZIN, N. K. (1986), 'Interpretive Interactionism and the Use of Life Stories', *Revista Internacional de Sociologia*, 44: 321–37.

DEVIS, T. (1983), 'People Changing Address: 1971 and 1981', *Population Trends*, 32: 15–20.

DIMMOCK, B. (1997/8), 'The Contemporary Stepfamily: Making Links with Fostering and Adoption', *Adoption and Fostering*, 21: 49–56.

DoE (Department of the Environment) (1995*b*), *Projections of Households in England to 2016: 1992 Estimates of the Numbers of Households for Regions, Counties, Metropolitan Districts and London Boroughs*, London: HMSO.

——(1996), *Household Growth: Where Shall We Live?*, London: HMSO.

DOLINSKY, A. L., and ROSENWAIKE, I. (1988), 'The Role of Demographic Factors in the Institutionalization of the Elderly', *Research on Aging*, 10: 235–57.

DOMINIAN, J., MANSFIELD, P., DORMOR, D., and MCALLISTER, F. (1991), *Marital Breakdown and the Health of the Nation*, London: One Plus One.

DORNBUSCH, S. M. (1985), 'Single Parents, Extended Households, and the Control of Adolescents', *Child Development*, 56: 326–41.

DOUGLAS, G., and LOWE, N. (1990), 'Grandparents and the Legal Process', *Journal of Social Welfare Law*, 2: 89–106.

DOWRICK, S., and NGUYEN, D. T. (1989), 'OECD Comparative Economic Growth in the Post-war Period: Evidence from Models of Convergence'. *American Economic Review*, 79: 1010–30.

DRIVER, G. (1982), 'West Indian Families: An Anthropological Perspective', in R. Rapaport and M. Fogarty (eds.), *Families in Britain*, London: Routledge and Kegan Paul, 205–19.

DSS (Department of Social Security) (1994), *Social Security Statistics 1993/4*, London: HMSO.

——(1995), *Family Resources Survey: Great Britain 93/94*, London: HMSO.

——(1997), *Social Security Statistics 1997*, London: HMSO.

DUMON, W. (1992), 'General Conceptualizations and Perspectives', Paper presented at the International Workshop on *Reconstituted Families in Europe*, The Catholic University, Leuven, Belgium.

DUNCOMBE, J., and MARSDEN, D. (1996), 'Can We Research the Private Sphere? Methodological and Ethical Problems in the Study of the Role of Emotions in Personal Relationships', in L. Morris and S. Lyon (eds.), *Gender Relations in Public and Private: New Research Perspectives*, Basingstoke and London: Macmillan, 144–55.

DUNNE, G. (1997), *Lesbian Lifestyles: Women's Work and the Politics of Sexuality*, Basingstoke and London: Macmillan.

DURKHEIM, E. (1933), *The Division of Labour in Society*, New York: Free Press.

DURR, J. M. (1992), 'Six Millions de Personnes Seules: Recensement de la Population de 1990', *INSEE première*, 200, (Moy): not paginated.

DWORKIN, R. (1993), *Life's Dominion: An Argument about Abortion and Euthanasia*, London: HarperCollins.

EADE, J., VAMPLEW, T., and PEACH, C. (1996), 'The Bangladeshis: The Encapsulated Community', in J. Eade, T.Vamplew, and C. Peach (eds.), *Ethnicity in the 1991 Census: The Ethnic Minority Populations of Britain*, London: HMSO, 150–60.

EASTERLIN, R., MACDONALD, C., and MACUNOVICH, D. (1990), 'How have American Baby Boomers Fared? Earnings and Economic Well-being of Young Adults', *Journal of Population Economics*, 3: 277–90.

ECONOMIST (1997), '*Election Briefing*', special issue.

ERMISCH, J. (1985), *Economic Implications of Demographic Change*, London: Centre for Economic Policy Research.

——(1989), 'Divorce: Economic Antecedents and Aftermath', in H. Joshi (ed.), *The Changing Population of Britain*, Oxford: Blackwell, 42–55.

ERMISCH, J. (1991), *The Economics of Lone Parenthood*, London: National Institute for Economic and Social Research.

——(1995), *Pre-marital Cohabitation, Childbearing and the Creation of One Parent Families*, 95-17, ESRC Research Centre on Micro-social Change Working Paper 95-17, Colchester: ESRC Research Centre on Micro-social Change, University of Essex.

——(1996), 'The Economic Environment for Family Formation', in Coleman (1996*a*), 144–62.

——DI SALVO, P., and JOSHI, H. (1995), *Household Formation and Housing Tenure Decisions of Young People*, Occasional Paper 95-1, Colchester: ESRC Research Centre on Micro-social Change, University of Essex.

ERMISCH, J. F., and FRANCESCONI, M. (1996), *The Increasing Complexity of Family Relationships: Lifetime Experiences of Single Motherhood and Stepfamilies in Great Britain*, Working Paper No. 96-11, Colchester: ESRC Research Centre on Micro-social Change, University of Essex.

——and OVERTON, E. (1985), 'Minimal Household Units: A New Approach to the Analysis of Household Formation', *Population Studies*, 39: 33–54.

ETZIONI, A. (1995), *The Spirit of Community: Rights, Responsibilities and the Communitarian Agenda*, London: Fontana Press.

European Commission (1995), *The Demographic Situation in the European Union, 1994*, Luxemburg: Office for Official Publications of the European Communities.

EUROSTAT (1996), *Under the Same Roof: Living Arrangements in the European Union*, Statistics in Focus: Population and Social Conditions 1996/5, Luxemburg: Office for Official Publications of the European Communities.

——(1997) Demographic Statistics 1997. Luxemburg, Office for Official Publications of the European Communities.

Family Policy Studies Centre (1997), *A Guide to Family Issues*, Family Briefing Paper No. 2, London: Family Policy Studies Centre.

——(1998), *Welfare to Work and the Family*, Family Briefing Paper No. 5., London: Family Policy Studies Centre.

FANON, F. (1968), *Black Skin, White Masks*, London: Macgibbon and Kee.

FAVELL, A. (1998), *Philosophies of integration*, London: Macmillan.

FEINSTEIN, S. S. (1994), *The City Builders: Property, Politics and Planning in London and New York*, Oxford: Blackwell.

FERRI, E. (1984), *Stepchildren: A National Study*, Slough: NFER Nelson.

——(ed.) (1993), *Life at 33: The Fifth Follow-up of the National Child Development Study*, London: National Children's Bureau.

FIELDING, A. J. (1993), 'Migration and the Metropolis: An Empirical and Theoretical Analysis of Inter-regional Migration to and from South-east England', *Progress in Planning*, 39: 71–166.

FIELDING, T., and HALFORD, S. (1993), 'Geographies of Opportunity: A Regional Analysis of Gender-specific Social and Spatial Mobilities in England and Wales 1971–81', *Environment and Planning A*, 25: 1421–40.

FINCH, J. (1989*a*), *Family Obligations and Social Change*, Cambridge: Polity Press.

——(1989*b*), 'Kinship and Friendship', in R. Jowell, S. Witherspoon, and L. Brook (eds.), *British Social Attitudes: Special International Report*, Aldershot: Gower, 53–72.

——(1995), 'Responsibilities, Obligations and Commitments', in I. Allen and E. Perkins (eds.), *The Future of Family Care for Older People*. London: HMSO, 51–64.

——and GROVES, D. (eds.) (1983), *A Labour of Love: Women, Work and Caring*, London: Routledge and Kegan Paul.

——and MASON, J. (1993), *Negotiating Family Responsibilities*, London: Routledge.

——and WALLIS, L. (1994), 'Inheritance, Care Bargains, and Elderly People's Relationships with their Children', in D. Challis, B. Davies, and K. Traske (eds.), *Community Care: New Agendas and Challenges*, Aldershot: Ashgate/British Society of Gerontology, 110–19.

——MASON, J., MASSON, J., WALLIS, L., and HAYES, L. (1996), *Wills, Inheritance, and Families*, Oxford: Clarendon Press.

FINLAY, B. (1981), 'Sex Differences in Correlates of Abortion Attitudes among College Students', *Journal of Marriage and the Family*, 43: 571–82.

FIREBAUGH, G. (1989), 'Methods of Estimating Cohort Replacement Effects', in C. C. Clogg (ed.), *Sociological Methodology*, Cambridge, Mass.: Basil Blackwell, 243–62.

FIRTH, R. (1956), *Two Studies of Kinship in Britain*, London: Athlone Press.

FISCHER, C. S. (1982), *To Dwell amongst Friends*, Chicago: University of Chicago Press.

FISHER, T. D. (1989), 'An Extension of the Findings of Moore, Peterson, and Furstenberg (1986) regarding Family Sexual Communication and Adolescent Sexual Behavior', *Journal of Marriage and the Family*, 51: 637–9.

FITZGERALD, M. (1988), 'Afro-Caribbean Involvement in British politics', in Cross and Entzinger (1988), 250–66.

——(1990), 'The Emergence of Black Councillors and MPs in Britain', in H. Goulbourne (ed.), *Black Politics in Britain*, Aldershot: Avebury, 17–32.

FLINN, M. W. (1981), *The European Demographic System 1500–1820*, Baltimore: Johns Hopkins University Press.

FOGELMAN, K. (ed.) (1983), *Growing Up in Great Britain: Papers from the National Child Development Study*, London: Macmillan Press.

FONER, N. (1979), *Farewell Jamaica: Jamaican Migrants in London*, London: Routledge and Kegan Paul.

——(1987), 'The Jamaicans: Race and Ethnicity among Migrants in New York City', in N. Foner (ed.), *New Immigrants in New York*, London: Columbia University Press, 195–217.

FORD, R., MARSH, A., and FINLAYSON, L. (1998), *What Happens to Lone Parents*, Research Report No. 77, London: DSS.

————and MCKAY, S. (1995), *Changes in Lone Parenthood 1989–93*, London: HMSO.

FORSTE, R. T., and HEATON, T. B. (1988), 'Initiation of Sexual Activity among Female Adolescents', *Youth and Society*, 19: 250–68.

FOUCAULT, M. (1979), *The History of Sexuality*, London: Allen Lane.

FRANKENBURG, R. (1966), *Communities in Britain*, Harmondsworth: Penguin.

FRIEDLANDER, D. (1961), 'A Technique for Estimating a Contingency Table given the Marginal Totals and some Supplementary Data', *Journal of the Royal Statistical Society*, Series A, 124: 412–20.

FURSTENBERG, F. (1987), 'The New Extended Family: The Experience of Parents and Children after Remarriage', in K. Pasky and M. Ihinger-Tallman (eds.), *Remarriage and Stepparenting. Current Research and Theory*, New York: Guilford Press, 42–61.

——BROOKS-GUNN, J., and MORGAN, S. P. (1987), *Adolescent Mothers in Later Life*, Cambridge: Cambridge University Press.

——MOORE, K. A., and PETERSON, J. L. (1985), 'Sex Education and Sexual Experience among Adolescents', *American Journal of Public Health*, 75: 1331–2.

GARFINKEL, I., and MCLANAHAN, S. (1986), *Single Mothers and their Children: A New American Dilemma*, Washington, DC: Urban Institute Press.

GAUTHIER, A. H. (1996), *The State and the Family: A Comparative Analysis of Family Policies in Industrialized Countries*, Oxford: Oxford University Press.

GERSHUNY, J. (1997), 'Sexual Divisions and the Distribution of Work in the Household', in G. Dench (ed.), *Rewriting the Sexual Contract*, London: Institute of Community Studies, 141–52.

GIARUSSO, R., STALLINGS, M., and BENGTSON, V. L. (1995), 'The Intergenerational Stake Hypothesis Revisited: Parent-Child Differences in Perceptions of Relationships 20 Years Later', in V. L. Bengtson, K. W. Schaie and L. M. Burton (eds.), *Adult Intergenerational Relations: Effects of Social Change*, New York: Springer, 227–88.

GIDDENS, A. (1991), *Modernity and Self-Identity*, Cambridge: Polity Press.

——(1992), *The Transformation of Intimacy*, Cambridge: Polity Press.

——(1996), 'Living in a Post-traditional Society', in A. Giddens (ed.), *In Defence of Sociology*, Cambridge: Polity Press, 8–64.

GIERVELD, DE JONG, J., LIEFBROER, A. C., and BEEKINK, E. (1991), 'The Effect of Parental Resources on Patterns of Leaving Home among Young Adults in the Netherlands', *European Sociological Review*, 7: 55–71.

GILGUN, J. F. (1992), 'Definitions, Methodologies, and Methods in Qualitative Family Research', in J. F. Gilgun, D. Daly, and G. Handel (eds.), *Qualitative Methods in Family Research*, London: Sage, 22–39.

GILJE, E. (1972), *Analytic Graduation of Age-specific Fertility Rates*, Oslo: Statistik Sentralbyrå.

GILLIS, J. R. (1985), *For Better, for Worse: British Marriages, 1600 to the Present*, Oxford: Oxford University Press.

——(1997), *A World of their Own Making: A History of Myth and Ritual in Family Life*, Oxford: Oxford University Press.

GLASER, B. G., and STRAUSS, A. L. (1967), *The Discovery of Grounded Theory: Strategies for Qualitative Research*, New York: Aldine de Gruyter.

GLASER, K., MURPHY, M., and GRUNDY, E. (1997), 'Limiting Long-term Illness and Household Structure among People aged 45 and Over, Great Britain 1991', *Aging and Society*, 17: 3–19.

GLASER, R. (1997), 'The Living Arrangements of Elderly People', *Reviews in Clinical Gerontology*, 7: 63–72.

GLASS, R., and FRENKEL, M. (1948), 'How they Live at Bethnal Green', in A. Weidenfeld and H. Hastings (eds.), *Britain between East and West*, London: Contact Books, 36–43.

GOLDSCHEIDER, F. K., and WAITE, L. J. (1991), *New Families, No Families?*, Berkeley and Oxford: University of California Press.

GOLDTHORPE, J. (1984), 'The End of Convergence: Corporatist and Dualist Tendencies in Modern Western Societies', in J. Goldthorpe (ed.), *Order and Conflict in Contemporary Capitalism: Studies in the Political Economy of Western European Nations*, Oxford: Clarendon Press, 315–43.

GOODMAN, A., and WEBB, S. (1994), *For Richer, for Poorer: The Changing Distribution of Income in the United Kingdom, 1961–1991*, IFS Commentary No. 42, London: Institute for Fiscal Studies.

GORDON, S. (1996), 'I Go To Tanties: The Economic Significance of Child-shifting in Antigua, West Indies', in Barrow (1996), 106–19.

GORRELL BARNES, G. (1992), 'Growing Up in Stepfamilies: Some Preliminary Observations', in E. De'ath (ed.), *Stepfamilies: What Do We Know, What Do We Need to Know?*, London: Significant Publications, 39–48.

——THOMPSON, P., DANIEL, G., and BURCHARDT, N. (1998), *Growing Up in Stepfamilies*, Oxford: Oxford University Press.

GOSLING, A., MACHIN, S., and MEGHIR, C. (1994), *The UK Male Wage Distribution 1966–92*, Social Policy Research No. 52, York: Joseph Rowntree Foundation.

GOULBOURNE, H. (1980), 'Oral History and Black Labour: An Overview', *Oral History Journal*, 8: 24–34.

——(1991*a*), *Ethnicity and Nationalism in Post-imperial Britain*, Cambridge: Cambridge University Press.

——(1991*b*), 'Varieties of Pluralism: The Notion of a Pluralist Post-imperial Britain', *New Community*, 17: 211–27.

——(1998*a*), 'The Participation of New Minority Ethnic Groups in British Politics', in T. Blackstone, B. Parekh, and P. Sanders (eds.), *Race Relations in Britain: A Developing Agenda*, London: Routledge, 181–203.

——(1998*b*), *Race Relations in Britain since 1945*, London: Macmillan.

——and CHAMBERLAIN, M. (1998), *Living Arrangements*, Family Structure and Social Change of Caribbeans in Britain, ESRC End of Award Report No. L315253009, Swindon: ESRC.

GOVERNMENT ACTUARY (1995), *1992-based National Population Projections*, London: HMSO.

GRANBERG, D., and GRANBERG, B. (1980), 'Abortion Attitudes, 1965–1980: Trends and Determinants', *Family Planning Perspectives*, 12: 250–61.

GRASLAND, C. (1990), 'Systèmes démographiques et systèmes supranationaux: la fécondité européenne de 1952 à 1982', *European Journal of Population*, 6: 163–92.

GREEN, A. E. (1997), 'A Guestion of Compromise? Case Study Evidence on the Location and Mobility Strategies of Dual Career Households', *Regional Studies*, 31: 641–57.

GREGG, P., and WADSWORTH, J. (1995), 'Gender, Households, and Access to Employment', in J. Humphries and J. Rubery (eds.), *The Economics of Equal Oppor-*

tunities, Manchester: Equal Opportunities Commission, 345–64.

GRUNDY, E. (1987), 'Household Change and Migration among the Elderly in England and Wales', *Espace, Populations, Sociétés*, 1: 109–23.

——(1989), *Women's Migration: Marriage, Fertility and Divorce*, London: HMSO.

——(1992*a*), 'Household Circumstances and Transitions', in T. Warnes (ed.), *Homes and Travel: Local Life in the Third Age, Carnegie UK Trust* Research Paper No. 5. Fife: Carnegie United Kingdom Trust, 20–34.

——(1992*b*), 'The Household Dimension in Migration Research', in T. Champion and T. Fielding (eds.), *Migration Processes and Patterns. Volume 1: Research Progress and Prospects*, London: Belhaven, 165–74.

——(1992*c*), 'Socio-demographic Variations in Rates of Movement into Institutions among Elderly People in England and Wales: An Analysis of Linked Census and Mortality Data 1971–1985'. *Population Studies*, 46: 65–84.

——(1993), 'Moves into Supported Private Households among Elderly People in England and Wales', *Environment and Planning A*, 25: 1467–79.

——(1996*a*), 'Population Ageing in Europe', in D. Coleman (1996*a*), 267–96.

——(1996*b*), 'Population Review (5): The Population aged 60 and Over', *Population Trends*, 84: 14–20.

——(1997), 'The Health of Older Adults 1841–1991', in J. C. Charlton and M. Murphy (eds.), *The Health of Adult Britain*, London: HMSO, 182–203.

——and GLASER, K. (1997), 'Trends in, and Transitions to, Institutional Residence among Older People in England and Wales 1971–91', *Journal of Epidemiology and Community Health*, 51: 531–40.

——and HARROP, A. (1992), 'Co-residence between Adult Children and their Elderly Parents in England and Wales', *Journal of Social Policy*, 21: 325–48.

——and MURPHY, M. (1997), *Intergenerational Relationships and Household Change*, ESRC End of Award Report No. L315253010, Swindon: ESRC.

HAGESTAD, G. O. (1991), 'The Aging Society as a Context for Family Life', in N. S. Jecker (ed.), *Aging and Ethics: Philosophical Problems in Gerontology*, New York: Humana, 123–46.

HAKIM, C. (1996), 'The Sexual Division of Labour and Women's Heterogeneity', *British Journal of Sociology*, 47: 178–88.

——(1997), 'Diversity and Choice in the Sexual Contract: Models for the twenty-first Century', in G. Dench (ed.), *Rewriting the Sexual Contract*, London: Institute of Community Studies, 165–79.

HALFACREE, K., FLOWERDEW, R., and JOHNSON, J. H. (1991), 'The Characteristics of British Migrants in the 1990s: Evidence from a New Survey', *Geographical Journal*, 158: 157–69.

HALL. D., and ZHAO, J. (1995), 'Cohabitation and Divorce in Canada: Testing the Selectivity Hypothesis', *Journal of Marriage and the Family*, 57: 421–7.

HALL, R., and OGDEN, P. E. (1992), 'The Social Structure of New Migrants to London Docklands: Recent Evidence from Wapping', *London Journal*, 17: 153–69.

————(1997), *Changes in Household Structures, Household Transitions, and Geographical Mobility*, ESRC End of Award Report No. L315253011, Swindon: ESRC.

——— and HILL, C. (1996), 'Household Changes in London and Paris 1981–91, with Particular Reference to Lone-person Households', paper presented at the Royal Geographical Society Annual Conference, University of Strathclyde.
——— ——— (1997), 'The Pattern and Structure of One-person Households in England and Wales and France', *International Journal of Population Geography*, 3: 161–81.
HAMNETT, C. (1994*a*), 'Social Polarization in Global Cities: Theory and Evidence', *Urban Studies*, 31: 401–24.
—— (1994*b*), 'Socio-economic Change in London: Professionalization not Polarisation', *Built Environment*, 20: 192–203.
—— (1995), 'Housing Equity Release and Inheritance', in I. Allen and E. Perkins (eds.), *The Future of Family Care for Older People*, London: HMSO, 163–79.
—— HARMER, M., and WILLIAMS, P. (1991), *Safe as Houses: Housing Inheritance in Britain*, London: Paul Chapman.
HARDING, S. (1988), 'Trends in Permissiveness', in R. Jowell, S. Witherspoon, and L. Brook (eds.), *British Social Attitudes: The fifth Report*, Aldershot: Gower, 35–52.
HAREVEN, T. K. (1992), 'Family and Generational Relations in the Later Years: A Historical Perspective', *Generations*, 17: 7–12.
HASKEY, J. (1983), 'Marital Status Before Marriage and Age at Marriage: Their Influence on the Chance of Divorce', *Population Trends*, 32: 4–14.
—— (1984), 'Social Class and Socio-economic Differentials in Divorce in England and Wales', *Population Studies*, 38: 419–38.
—— (1988*a*), 'A Demographic Profile of One-parent Families in Great Britain', *Population Trends*, 51: 18–26.
—— (1988*b*), 'Mid-1985 based Population Projections by Marital Status', *Population Trends*, 52: 30–2.
—— (1989), 'One-parent Families and their Children in Great Britain: Numbers and Characteristics', *Population Trends* 55: 27–33.
—— (1992), 'Pre-marital Cohabitation and the Probability of Subsequent Divorce: Analyses using Data from the General Household Survey', *Population Trends*, 68: 10–19.
—— (1994*a*), 'Estimated Numbers of One-parent Families and their Prevalence in Great Britain in 1991', *Population Trends*, 78: 5–19.
—— (1994*b*), 'Stepfamilies and Stepchildren in Great Britain', *Population Trends*, 76: 17–28.
—— (1996*a*), 'Population Review (6): Families and Households in Great Britain', *Population Trends*, 85: 7–24.
—— (1996*b*), 'The Proportion of Married Couples who Divorce: Past Patterns and Current Prospects', *Population Trends*, 83: 25–36
—— (1998*a*), 'One-parent Families and their Dependent Children', *Population Trends*, 91: 5–15.
—— (1998*b*), 'One-parent Families and their Dependent Children in Great Britain', in R. Ford and J. Millar (eds.), *Private Lives and Public Responses: Lone Parenthood and Future Policy in the UK*, London: Policy Studies Institute, 22–41.
—— and KIERNAN, K. (1989), 'Cohabitation in Great Britain—Characteristics and Estimated Numbers of Cohabiting Partners', *Population Trends*, 58: 23–32.

Hattersley, L., and Creeser, R. (1995), *Longitudinal Study 1971–1991: History, Organisation and Quality of Data*, LS No. 7, London: HMSO.

———— (forthcoming), 'Sex, Money and the Kitchen Sink: Power in Same Sex Couple Relationships', in J. Seymour and P. Bagguley (eds.), *Relating Intimacies: Power and Resistance*, Basingstoke and London: Macmillan.

Heaphy, B., Donovan, C., and Weeks, J. (1998:), 'That's Like My Life: Researching Stories of Non-heterosexual Relationships', *Sexualities*, 1: 453–70.

Heath, A., and Martin, J. (1996), 'Changing Attitudes towards Abortion: Life Cycle, Period and Cohorts Effects', in B. Taylor and K. Thomson (eds.), *A Decade of Change in Social Values*, Aldershot: Dartmouth, 55–74.

Henriques, F. (1953), *Family and Colour in Jamaica*, London: Eyre and Spottiswoode.

Hills, J. (1998), *Income and Wealth: The Latest Evidence*, York: Joseph Rowntree Foundation.

Hobcraft, J., and Kiernan, K. (1995), *Becoming a Parent in Europe*, Welfare State Programme Paper WSP/116, London: LSE/STICERD.

Hoem, B., and Hoem, J. M. (1997), *Fertility Trends in Sweden up to 1996*, Stockholm: Stockholm University Demography Unit.

Hoem, J. (1991), *Trends and Patterns in Swedish Divorce Risks 1971–1989*, Stockholm University Research Reports in Demography, Stockholm: Stockholm University.

Hofferth, S. L., and Hayes, C. D. (1987), *Risking the Future: Adolescent Sexuality, Pregnancy, and Childbearing*, Washington, DC: National Academy Press.

Hoffman, S. D., and Duncan, G. (1988), 'What are the Economic Consequences of Divorce?', *Demography*, 25: 302–6.

Hogan, D. P., and Kitagawa, E. M. (1985), 'The Impact of Social Status, Family Structure, and Neighborhood on the Fertility of Black Adolescents', *American Journal of Sociology*, 90: 825–55.

Holmans, A. (1981), 'Housing Careers of Newly Married Couples', *Population Trends*, 24: 10–14.

Home Office (1998), *Asylum Statistics, United Kingdom 1997*, Home Office Statistical Bulletin, Issue 14/98, London: Home Office.

Hopkinson, A. (1976), *Single Mothers: The First Year*, Edinburgh: Scottish Council for Single Parents.

House, J., and Kahn, R. (1985), 'Measures and Concepts of Social Support', in S. Cohen and L. Syme (eds.), *Social Support and Health*, New York: Academic Press, 83–108.

Hoyert, D. L. (1991), 'Financial and Household Exchanges between Generations', *Research on Aging*, 13: 205–25.

Hudson, F., and Ineichen, B. (1991), *Taking it Lying Down: Sexuality and Teenage Motherhood*, London: Macmillan.

Hylton, C. (1995), *Coping with Change: Family Transitions in Multi-cultural Communities*, London: Stepfamily Publications.

Inazu, J. K., and Fox, G. L. (1980), 'Mother–Daughter Communication about Sex', *Family Relations*, 29: 347–52.

Ingelhart, R. (1977), *The Silent Revolution: Changing Values and Political Styles among Western Publics*, Princeton, NJ: Princeton University Press.

——(1990), *Culture Shift in Advanced Industrial Society*, Princeton, NJ: Princeton University Press.

INKELES, A. (1997), *National Character: A Psycho-social Perspective*, New Brunswick, NJ: Transaction Publishers.

INSEE (Institut national de la statistique et des études économiques) (1995*a*), *Echantillon Démographique Permanent: manuel de l'utilisateur en statistiques et études*, Paris: INSEE.

——(1995*b*), *Les Femmes*, Paris: INSEE.

IRWIN, S. (1995), 'Social Reproduction and Change in the Transition from Youth to Adulthood', *Sociology*, 29: 293–315.

JENKINS, S. (1994), 'Income Inequality and Living Standards: Changes in the 1970s and 1980s', *Fiscal Studies*, 12: 1–28.

JERROME, D. (1996*a*), 'Continuity and Change in the Study of Family Relationships'. *Aging and Society*, 16: 93–104.

——(1996*b*), 'The Ties That Bind', in A. Walker (ed.), *The New Generational Context: Intergenerational Relations, Old Age, and Welfare*, London: UCL Press, 81–99.

JOHANSSON, S., and MOLLER, E. L. (1992), *Fertility in a Life-Perspective*, Stockholm: Statistiska Centralbyran.

JOHNSON, A. (1994), *Sexual Attitudes and Lifestyles*, Oxford: Blackwell Scientific.

JOHNSON, C. L. (1988), *Ex Familia: Grandparents, Parents and Children Adjust to Divorce*, Brunswick, NJ: Rutgers University Press.

——(1993), 'Divorced and Reconstituted Families: Effects on the Older Generation', in L. Burton (ed.), *Fomilies and Caring*, New York: Baywood, 33–42.

JOHNSON, S. E. (1990), *Staying Power: Long Term Lesbian Couples*, Tallahassee, Fla.: Naiad Press.

JONES, G. (1987), 'Leaving the Parental Home: An Analysis of Early Housing Careers'. *Journal of Social Policy*, 16: 49–74.

——(1993), 'Is Demographic Uniformity Inevitable?', *Journal of the Australian Population Association*, 10: 1–16.

Joseph Rowntree Foundation (1995), *Inquiry into Income and Wealth*, Vol. 1, York: Joseph Rowntree Foundation.

JOSHI, H. (1985), *Motherhood and Employment: Change and Continuity in Post-war Britain*, OPCS Occasional Paper No. 34, London: OPCS.

——(1989), 'The Changing Form of Women's Economic Dependency', in H. Joshi (ed.), *The Changing Population of Britain*. Oxford: Basil Blackwell, 157–76.

——(1990), 'The Cash Opportunity Costs of Childbearing—An Approach to Estimation using British Data', *Population Studies*, 44: 41–60.

JOWELL, R., BROOK, L., and DOWDS, L. (1993), 'Technical Details of Surveys (Appendix 1)', in R. Jowell, L. Brook, and L. Dowds (eds.), *International Social Attitudes: The tenth BSA Report*, Aldershot: Gower, 143–62.

KAHN, J. R., and ANDERSON, K. E. (1992), 'Intergenerational Patterns of Teenage Fertility', *Demography*, 29: 39–55.

KAHN, R., and ANTONUCCI, T. (1980), 'Convoys over the Life Course: Attachment, Roles and Social Support', in P. B. Baltes and O. Brim (eds.), *Life-span*

Development and Behaviour, New York: Academic Press, 253–86.

KAMO, Y., and ZHOU, M. (1994), 'Living Arrangements of Elderly Chinese and Japanese in the United States', *Journal of Marriage and the Family*, 56: 544–58.

KAUFMAN, F.-X., KUIJSTEN, A., SCHULZE, H.-J., and STROHMEIER, K. P. (eds.) (1997), *Family Life and Family Policies in Europe. Volume 1: Structures and Trends in the 1980s,* Oxford: Clarendon Press.

KAUFMANN, J. C. (1993), *EC Single People, Single Person Households, Isolation, loneliness: A Status Report*, Brussels: European Communities.

——(1994), 'Les Ménages d'une personne en Europe', *Population*, 49: 935–58.

KEDOURIE, E. (1985), *Nationalism*, London: Hutchinson, First pub. 1960.

KEILMAN, N. (1987), 'Recent Trends in Family and Household Composition in Europe', *European Journal of Population*, 3: 297–325.

KERR, C. (ed.) (1962), *Industrialism and Industrial Man*, London: Heinemann.

——(1983), *The Future of Industrial Societies: Convergence or Continuing Diversity*?, Cambridge, Mass.: Harvard University Press.

KEYFITZ, N. (1985), *Applied Mathematical Demography, 2nd edn.*, Berlin: Springer-Verlag.

KIERNAN, K. (1986), 'Teenage Marriage and Marital Breakdown: A Longitudinal Study', *Population Studies*, 40: 35–54.

——(1992), 'The Impact of Family Disruption in Childhood on Transitions in Young Adult Life'. *Population Studies*, 46: 213–34.

KIERNAN, K. (1995), *Transition to Parenthood: Young Mothers, Young Fathers—Associated Factors and Life Experiences*, STICERD Discussion Paper No. WSP/113, London: London School of Economics.

——(1996), 'Partnership Behaviour in Europe: Recent Trends and Issues', in Coleman (1996*a*), 62–91.

——(1997), 'Becoming a Young Parent: A Longitudinal Study of Associated Factors', *British Journal of Sociology*, 48: 406–28.

——and CHERLIN, A. J. (1999), 'Parental Divorce and Partnership Dissolution: Evidence from a British Cohort Study', *Population Studies*, 53: 39–48.

——and ESTAUGH, V. (1993), *Cohabitation, Extramarital Childbearing and Social Policy*, London: Family Policy Studies Centre.

——Land, H., and LEWIS, J. (1998), *Lone Motherhood in Twentieth-Century Britain*, Oxford: Clarendon Press.

KITSON, G. (1990), 'The Multiple Consequences of Divorce: A Decade Review', *Journal of Marriage and the Family*, 52: 913–24.

KNIGHT, F. (1997), 'Pluralism, Creolisation and Culture', in F. Knight (ed.), *Slave Societies of the Caribbean,* UNESCO General History of the Caribbean, Vol. 3, London: Macmillan Caribbean, 271–86.

KNIPSCHEER, K., DE JONG GIERVELD, J., VAN TILBURG, T. G., and DYKSTRA, P. A. (eds.) (1995), *Living Arrangements and Social Networks of Older Adults*, Amsterdam: VU University Press.

KNOX, P., and TAYLOR, P. J. (eds.) (1995), *World Cities in a World System*, Cambridge: Cambridge University Press.

KOBRIN, F. E. (1976*a*), 'The Fall in Household Size and the Rise of the Primary Individual in the United States', *Demography*, 13: 127–38.

——(1976*b*), 'The Primary Individual and the Family: Changes in Living Arrangements in the United States since 1940', *Journal of Marriage and the Family*, 38: 233–8.

KONO, S. (1987), 'The Headship Rate Method for Projecting Households', in J. Bongaarts, T. Burch, and K. Wachter (eds.), *Family Demography: Methods and their Applications*, Oxford: Clarendon Press, 287–308.

KRAMAROW, E. A. (1995), 'The Elderly who Live Alone in the United States: Historical Perspectives on Household Change', *Demography*, 32: 335–52.

KRAVDAL, Ø. (1988), 'The Impact of First-birth Timing on Divorce: New Evidence from Longitudinal Analysis based on the Central Population Register of Norway', *European Journal of Population*, 4: 247–69.

KUIJSTEN, A. C. (1996), 'Changing Family Patterns in Europe: A Case of Divergence?', *European Journal of Population*, 12: 115–43.

KURDEK, L. A. (1993), 'Predicting Marital Dissolution: A 5-year Prospective Longitudinal Study of Newlywed Couples', *Journal of Personality and Social Psychology*, 64: 221–42.

LAFANCHEUR, N. (1989), 'Personnes Seules à Paris: Nouveaux Célibataires ou Veuves Solitaires', *Données Sociales, Île-de-France*, Paris: INSEE.

LAING, W. (1993), *Financing Long-term Care: The Crucial Debate*, London: Age Concern.

LAMPARD, R. (1994), 'An Examination of the Relationship between Marital Dissolution and Unemployment', in D. Gallie, C. Marsh, and C. Vogler (eds.), *Social Change and the Experience of Unemployment*, Oxford: Oxford University Press, 264–98.

LAND, K., and ROGERS, A. (eds.) (1992), *Multidimensional Mathematical Demography*, New York: Academic Press.

LANER, M. R. (1977), 'Permanent Partner Priorities: Gay and Straight', *Journal of Homosexuality*, 3: 21–39.

LANG, F., and CARTENSEN, L. (1994), 'Close Emotional Relationships in Later Life: Further Support for Proactive Aging in the Social Domain', *Psychology and Aging*, 9: 315–24.

LASLETT, P. (1972), 'Introduction', in P. Laslett and R. Wall (eds.), *Household and Family in Past Time*, Cambridge: Cambridge University Press, 1–89.

——(1983), *The World We Have Lost Further Explored*, London: Routledge.

——(1984), 'The Significance of the Past in the Study of Aging', *Aging and Society*, 4: 379–89.

LAUMANN, E., GAGNON, J., MICHAEL, R., and MICHAEL, S. (1994), *The Social Organisation of Sexuality*, Chicago: University of Chicago Press.

LAYARD, R., PIACHAUD, D., and STEWART, M. (1978), *The Causes of Poverty*, Royal Commission on the Distribution of Income and Wealth, Background Paper No. 5, London: HMSO.

LERIDON, H., and VILLENEUVE-GOKALP, C. (1988), 'Les Nouveaux Couples: nombres, caractéristiques et attitudes', *Population*, 43: 331–74.

LESTAEGHE, R. (1991), *The Second Demographic Transition in Western Countries*, IPD Working Paper, Brussels: Centrum Sociologie, University of Brussels.

——(1995), 'The Second Demographic Transition in Western Countries: An Interpretation', in K. O. Mason and A.-M. Jensen (eds.), *Gender and Family Change in Industrialized Countries*, Oxford: Clarendon Press, 17–62.

LESTAEGHE, R., and MEEKERS, D. (1986), 'Value Changes and the Dimensions of Familism in the European Community', *European Journal of Population*, 2: 225–68.

——and MOORS, G. (1996), 'Living Arrangements, Socio-economic Position and Values among Young Adults: A Pattern Description of France, West Germany, Belgium, and the Netherlands', in Coleman (1996*a*), 163–221.

——and SURKYN, J. (1988), 'Cultural Dynamics and Economic Theories of Fertility Change', *Population and Development Review*, 14: 1–45.

——and WILSON, C. (1986), 'Modes of Production, Secularization, and the Pace of the Fertility Decline in Western Europe, 1870–1930', in Coale and Watkins (1986), 261–92.

LEWIS, J., and KIERNAN, K. (1996), 'The Boundaries between Marriage, Nonmarriage, and Parenthood: Changes in Behaviour and Policy in Postwar Britain', *Journal of Family History*, 21: 372–87.

LILLARD, L. A., and WAITE, L. J. (1995), 'Till Death Us Do Part: Marital Disruption and Mortality', *American Journal of Sociology*, 100: 1131–56.

LIN, G., and ROGERSON, P. A. (1995), 'Elderly Parents and the Geographic Availability of their Adult Children', *Research on Aging*, 17: 303–33.

LOUVOT, C. (1994), *Projection du Nombre de Ménages à l'Horizon 2020*, Résultats, No. 315, Paris: INSEE.

LOWERSON, R. (1997) *Cutting Both Ways?*, Dissertation for the M.A. in Social Security Management, University of York.

MACFARLANE, A. (1978), *The Origins of English Individualism*, Oxford: Basil Blackwell.

MACLEAN, M., and EEKELAAR, J. (1997*a*), *Families and the Law: Regulating the Economic Obligation of Parenthood*, ESRC End of Award Report No. R000234433, Swindon: ESRC.

————(1997*b*), *The Parental Obligation: A Study of Parenthood across Households*, Oxford: Hart.

MAGAZINER, K., CADIGAN, D. A., HEBEL, J. R., and PARRY, R. (1988), 'Health and Living Arrangements among Older Women: Does Living Alone Increase the Risk of Illness?', *Journal of Gerontology*, 43: M127–33.

MALINOWSKI, B. (1963), *The Family among the Australian Aborigines: A Sociological Study*, New York: Schocken.

MANLOVE, J. (1997), 'Early Motherhood in an International Perspective: The Experiences of a British cohort', *Journal of Marriage and the Family*, 59: 263–79.

MANTON, K., and STALLARD, E. (1996), 'Changes in Health, Mortality, and Disability and their Impact on Long-term Care Needs', *Journal of Aging and Social Policy*, 7: 25–52.

——and VAUPEL, J. W. (1995), 'Survival after the Age of 80 in the United States, Sweden, France, England and Japan', *New England Journal of Medicine*, 333: 1232–5.

MARCUS, E. (1992), *The Male Couple's Guide: Finding a Man, Making a Home, Building a Life*, New York: Harper Perennial.

MARSDEN, D. (1969), *Mothers Alone: Poverty and the Fatherless Family*, Harmondsworth: Penguin.

Marsh, A. (1993), 'Absent Parenthood', Policy Studies Institute Mimeo.

——Ford, R., and Finlayson, L. (1997), *Lone Parents, Work and Benefits*, London: HMSO.

——and McKay, S. (1993), *Families, Work and Benefits*, London: Policy Studies Institute.

————(1994), *Poor Smokers*, London: Policy Studies Institute.

Marsh, C. (1993), 'The Sample of Anonymised Records', in A. Dale and C. Marsh (eds.), *The 1991 Census User's Guide*, London: HMSO, 395–411.

Martin, A. (1993), *The Guide to Lesbian and Gay Parenting*, London: Pandora.

Martin, J. (1996), 'Structuring the Sexual Revolution', *Theory and Society*, 25: 105–51.

——and Roberts, C. (1984), *Women and Employment: A Lifetime Perspective*, London: OPCS/HMSO.

Martin, T. C., and Bumpass, L. L. (1989), 'Recent Trends in Marital Disruption', *Demography*, 26: 37–51.

Marx, K. (1974), *Capital: A Critique of Capitalist Production*, Moscow: Progress Publishers, First pub. 1867,

Maslow, A. (1954), *Motivations and Personality*, New York: Harper and Row.

Mason, K., and Lu, Y. H. (1988), 'Attitudes towards Women's Familial Roles: Changes in the United States, 1977–1985', *Gender and Society*, 2: 39–57.

Mason, M. (1994), *The Making of Victorian Sexuality*, Oxford: Oxford University Press.

Mason, W., and Fienberg, S. (1985), *Cohort Analysis in Social Research: Beyond the Identification Problem*, New York: Springer-Verlag.

McAllister, F., and Clarke, L. (1998), *Childless by Choice: A Study of Childlessness in Britain*, London: Family Policy Studies Centre.

McCallister, L., and Fischer, C. (1978), 'A Procedure for Surveying Personal Networks', *Sociological Methods and Research*, 7: 131–47.

McCarthy, P., and Simpson, B. (1991), *Issues in Post-divorce Housing*, Aldershot: Avebury.

McGlone, F., and Cronin, N. (1994), *A Crisis in Care? The Future of Family and State Care for Older People in the European Union*, London: Family Policy Studies Centre.

——Park, A., and Roberts, R. (1996), 'Relative Values: Kinship and Friendship', in R. Jowell, J. Curtice, A. Park, L. Brook, and K. Thomson (eds.), *British Social Attitudes: The 13th Report*, Aldershot: Dartmouth, 87–104.

————and Smith, K. (1998), *Families and Kinship*, London: Family Policy Studies Centre in partnership with the Joseph Rowntree Foundation.

McGoldrick, M., and Carter, B. (1989), *The Changing Family Life Cycle: A Framework for Family Therapy*, Boston, Mass.: Allyn and Bacon.

McGuire, A., and Hughes, D. (1995), *The Economics of Family Planning Services*, London: Family Planning Association.

McKay, S., and Marsh, A. (1994), *Lone Parents and Work: The Effects of Benefits and Maintenance*, London: HMSO.

McKibbin, R. (1998), *Classes and Cultures: England 1918–1951*, Oxford: Oxford University Press.

McLanahan, S., and Bumpass, L. (1988), 'Intergenerational Consequences of Marital Disruption', *American Journal of Sociology*, 94: 130–52.

McLeod, M. (1991), *Trading with the Inner City: Ethnic Minorities and the Development of Caribbean Trade*, Coventry: Centre for Research in Ethnic Relations, University of Warwick.

McRae, S. (1991), *Maternity Rights in Britain: The Experience of Women and Employers*, London: Policy Studies Institute.

——(1993), *Cohabiting Mothers: Changing Marriage and Motherhood*?, London: Policy Studies Institute.

——(1996), *Women at the Top: Progress after Five Years*, King-Hall Paper No. 2, London: Hansard Society for Parliamentary Government.

——(1997), 'Cohabitation: A Trial Run for Marriage?', *Sexual and Marital Therapy*, 12: 259–74.

McWhirter, D., and Mattison, A. M. (1984), *The Male Couple: How Relationships Develop*, Englewood Cliffs, NJ: Prentice Hall.

Meadows, P. (1996), *The Future of Work: Contributions to the Debate*, Social Policy Summary No. 7, York: Joseph Rowntree Foundation.

Meltzer, H. (1994), *Day Care Services for Children*, London: OPCS/HMSO.

Meulders-Klein, M. T., and Thery, I. (1993), *Les Recompositions familiales aujourd'hui*, Parks: Nathan.

Michael, R. T., Fuchs, V., and Scott, S. (1980), 'Changes in the Propensity to Live Alone 1950–1976', *Demography*, 17: 39–56.

Miller, B. C., and Bingham, C. R. (1989), 'Family Configuration in Relation to the Sexual Behavior of Female Adolescents', *Journal of Marriage and the Family*, 51: 499–506.

Miller, B. C., McCoy, J. K., Olson, T. D., and Wallace, C. M. (1986), 'Parental Discipline and Control Attempts in relation to Adolescent Sexual Attitudes and Behavior', *Journal of Marriage and the Family*, 48: 503–12.

Mintz, S. (1993), *Goodbye, Columbus: Second Thoughts on the Caribbean Region at Mid-millenium*, Coventry: University of Warwick Press.

——and Price, R. (1992), *The Birth of African-American Culture: An Anthropological Perspective*, Boston: Beacon Press.

Mishan, E. J. (1988), What Future for a Multi-cultural Britain?' *Salisbury Review*, 6: 4–12, 18–27.

Mitchell, J. C. (1969), *Social Networks in Urban Communities*, Manchester: Manchester University Press.

Modood, T., Berthoud, R., Lakey, J., Nazroo, J., Smith, P., Virdee, S., and Beishon, S. (1997), *Ethnic Minorities in Britain: Diversity and Disadvantage*, London: Policy Studies Institute.

Mohammed, P. (1988), 'The Caribbean Family Revisited', in P. Mohammed and C. Shepherd (eds.), *Gender in Caribbean Development*, Cave Hill Barbados: University of the West Indies Press, 170–82.

Moore, K., and Petersen, J. (1989), *The Consequences of Teenage Pregnancy*, Washington, DC: Child Trends Inc.

——Simms, C., and Betsey, C. L. (1986), *Choice and Circumstances*, New Brunswick, NJ: Transaction Books.

Mueller, C. W., and Pope, H. (1977), 'Marital Instability: A Study of its Transmission between Generations', *Journal of Marriage and the Family*, 39: 83–93.

Munro, M. (1988), 'Housing, Health and Inheritance', *Journal of Social Policy*, 17: 417–36.

Murphy, M. (1985), 'Demographic and Socio-economic Influences on Recent British Marital Breakdown Patterns', *Population Studies*, 39: 441–60.

——(1990), 'Housing Consequences of Marital Breakdown and Remarriage', in P. Symon (ed.), *Housing and Divorce*, Glasgow: University of Glasgow Centre for Housing Research, 1–51.

——(1991), 'Modelling Households: A Synthesis', in M. Murphy and J. Hobcraft (eds.), *Population Research in Britain*, supplement to *Population Studies*, 45: 157–76.

——(1992), 'Economic Models of Fertility in Post-war Britain: A Conceptual and Statistical Re-interpretation', *Population Studies*, 46: 235–58.

——(1993*a*), 'The Contraceptive Pill and Women's Employment as Factors in Fertility Change in Britain 1963–1980: A Challenge to the Conventional View', *Population Studies*, 47: 221–43.

——(ed.) (1993*b*), 'Time Series Approaches to the Analysis of Fertility Change,' in M. NT Bhrolchaín (ed.) *New Perspectives on Fertility*, London: HMSO, 51–66.

——(1996*a*), 'The Dynamic Household as a Logical Concept and its Use in Demography', *European Journal of Population*, 12: 363–81.

——(1996*b*), 'Family and Household Issues', in A. Dale (ed.), *Looking towards the 2001 Census*, papers presented at a joint conference of the British Society for Population Studies and the Royal Statistical Society, City University, 6 Apr. 1995, OPCS Occasional Paper No. 46, London: OPCS, 29–38.

——(1997), 'Changes in the Living Arrangements in Britain in the Last Quarter-century: Insights from the General Household Survey', in O. Rowlands, N. Singleton, J. Maher, and V. Higgins (eds.), *Living in Britain: Results from the 1995 General Household Survey*, London: The Stationery Office, 178–89.

——and Grundy, E. (1993), 'Co-residence of Generations and Household Structure in Britain: Aspects of Change in the 1980s', in H. A. Becker and P. L. J. Hermkens (eds.), *Solidarity of Generations: Demographic, Economic and Social Change and its Consequences*, II, Amsterdam: Thesis Publishers, 551–73.

————(1996), 'Changes in Intergenerational Support Transfers in the 1980s: The Case of Living Arrangements', in EAPS and IUSSP (eds.), *European Population Conference Proceedings: Evolution or Revolution*, vol. 2, Milan: Franco Angeli, 249–64.

——and Wang, D. (1996), 'A Dynamic Multi-state Projection Model for Making Marital Status Population Projections in England and Wales', in A. Dale (ed.), *Exploiting National Census and Survey Data: Longitudinal and Partnership Analyses*, Manchester: CCSR, 103–26.

————(1997*a*), *Evaluation of DSS Risk Group Model of Family Change*, London: DSS.

————(1997*b*), 'Uncertainty in Family Forecasting', paper presented at the IUSSP General Congress, Session 39, Beijing.

MURRAY, C. (1990), *The Emerging British Underclass*, London: Institute of Economic Affairs.
MUTCHLER, J. E., and BURR, J. A. (1991), 'A Longitudinal Analysis of Household and Non-household Living Arrangements in Later Life', *Demography*, 28: 375–90.
MYRDAL, G. (1944), *An American Dilemma: The Negro Problem and Modern Democracy*, London and New York: Harper and Brothers Publishers.
——(1969), *Objectivity in Social Research*, London: Duckworth.
NARDI, P. (1992), 'That's What Friends Are For: Friends as Family in the Lesbian and Gay Community', in K. Plummer (ed.), *Modern Homosexualities: Fragments of Lesbian and Gay Experience*, London: Routledge, 108–20.
NEWCOMER, S. F., and UDRY, J. R. (1987), 'Parental Marital Status Effects on Adolescent Sexual Behavior', *Journal of Marriage and the Family*, 49: 235–40.
NEWMAN, P., and SMITH, A. (1997), *Social Focus on Families*, London: The Stationery Office.
NHS Centre For Reviews and Dissemination (1997), 'Preventing and Reducing the Adverse Effects of Unintended Teenage Pregnancies', *Effective Health Care*, 3: 1–12.
OAKLEY, A. (1997), 'A Brief History of Gender', in Oakley and Mitchell (1997), 29–55.
——and MITCHELL, J. (eds.) (1997), *Who's Afraid of Feminism? Seeing Through the Backlash*, London: Hamish Hamilton.
O'CONNOR, P. (1992), *Friendships between Women*, Hemel Hempstead: Harvester Wheatsheaf.
OECD (Organisation for Economic Co-operation and Development) (1997), *Trends in International Migration*, SOPEMI Annual Report 1996, Paris: OECD.
OGDEN, P. E., and HALL, R. (1998), 'Personnes Seules et Migration en France et en Grande-Bretagne: Analyse Comparative des Recensements et des Études Longitudinales', *Economie et Statistique*, 6/7: 77–95.
OLWIG, K. (1996), 'The Migration Experience: Nevisian Women at Home and Abroad', in Barrow (1996), 135–49.
ONS (Office for National Statistics) (1992–3), *Labour Force Survey*, Winter 1992–3, London: ONS.
——(1997*a*), *Birth Statistics for England and Wales 1995*, London: HMSO.
——(1997*b*), *Conceptions in England and Wales 1995*, London: HMSO.
——(1997*c*), *International Migration 1995*, London: HMSO.
——(1997*d*), *Population Trends 89*, London: The Stationery Office.
——(1998*a*), *Labour Force Survey*, Mar. 1998, London: ONS.
——(1998*b*), *Labour Market Trends*, Feb. 1998, London: ONS.
——(1998*c*), *Results for Autumn 1997*, LFS Quarterly Bulletin No. 23 (Mar. 1998), London: ONS.
OPCS (Office of Population and Census Surveys) (1984), *Demographic Review*, London: HMSO.
——(1986), *Birth Statistics for England and Wales*, London: HMSO.
——(1987), *Birth Statistics: Historical Series 1837–1983*, London: HMSO.
——(1988), *Birth Statistics for England and Wales*, London: HMSO.

——(1993), *1991 Census, Historical Tables: GB*, London: HMSO.
——(1996*a*), *Living in Britain: Results from the 1994 General Household Survey*, London: HMSO.
——(1996*b*), *1994-based National Population Projections*, OPCS Monitor PP2 96/1, London: OPCS.
——(1998), *Living in Britain: Results from the 1996 General Household Survey*, London: The Stationery Office.
OPPENHEIMER, V. K., and LEW, V. (1995), 'American Marriage Formation in the 1980s: How Important was Women's Economic Independence?', in V. K. Oppenheim, K. Mason, and A.-M. Jensen (eds.), *Gender and Family Change in Industrialized Countries*, Oxford: Clarendon Press, 105–38.
OPPENHEIM MASON, K., and JENSEN, A. M. (eds.) (1995), *Gender and Family Change in Industrialized Countries*, Oxford: Clarendon Press.
OWEN, D. (1993), *Ethnic Minorities in Great Britain: Housing and Family Characteristics*, Coventry: National Ethnic Data Archive, University of Warwick.
——(1996), 'Size, Structure and the Growth of the Ethnic Minority Populations', in D. Coleman and J. Salt (eds.), *Ethnicity in the 1991 Census*, vol. 1, London: HMSO, 80–123.
PACIONE, M. (1997), *Britain's Cities: Geographies of Division in Urban Britain*, London: Routledge.
PAMPEL, F. C. (1983), 'Changes in the Propensity to Live Alone: Evidence from Consecutive Cross-sectional Surveys, 1960–1976', *Demography*, 20: 433–47.
——(1992), 'Trends in Living Alone among the Elderly in Europe', in A. Rogers (ed.), *Elderly Migration and Population Redistribution*. London: Belhaven, 97–117.
PAPERNOW, P. (1993), *Becoming a Stepfamily: Patterns of Development in Remarried Families*, San Francisco: Jossey-Bass.
PASLEY, K., and IHINGER-TALLMAN, M. (1987), *Remarriage and Stepparenting: Current Research and Theory*, New York: Guilford Press.
PATTERSON, O. (1967), *The Sociology of Slavery*, London: Macgibbon and Kee.
PATTERSON, S. (1965), *Dark Strangers: A Study of West Indians in London*, Harmondsworth: Penguin.
PEACH, C. (1968), *West Indian Migration to Britain: A Social Geography*, London: Oxford University Press.
PEARLIN, L. (1985), 'Social Structure and Processes of Social Support', in S. Cohen and L. Syme (eds.), *Social Support and Health*, New York: Academic Press, 43–60.
PHILLIPSON, C., BERNARD, M., and PHILLIPS, J. (1998), *Patterns of Kinship in the Urban Environment: The Experiences and Responses of Older People*, ESRC End of Award Report No. L315253021, Swindon: ESRC.
————— and OGG, J. (1996), *Social Networks and Social Support in Old Age*, Keele: Centre for Social Gerontology, University of Keele.
————————(1998), 'The Family and Community Life of Older People: Household Composition and Social Networks in Three Urban Areas', *Ageing and Society*, 18: 259–90.
PHOENIX, A. (1991), *Young Mothers?*, Cambridge: Polity Press.

PLUMMER, K. (1995), *Telling Sexual Stories: Power, Change, and Social Worlds*, London: Routledge.

PORTELLI, A. (1981), 'The Peculiarities of Oral History', *History Workshop*, 12: 96–107.

PORTER, E. (1996), 'Culture, Community and Responsibilities: Abortion in Ireland'. *Sociology*, 30: 279–98.

PORTER, R. (1994), *London: A Social History*, London: Hamish Hamilton.

PROHASKA, T., MERMELSTEIN, R., MILLER, B., and JACK, S. (1993), 'Functional Status and Living Arrangements', in J. F. Van Nostrand, S. E. Furner, and R. Suzman (eds.), *Health Data on Older Americans: United States, 1992 Series 3*, Hyattsville, Md.: National Centre for Health Statistics, 23–39.

PRYCE, K. (1979), *Endless Pressure: A Study of West Indian Lifestyles in Bristol*, Harmondsworth: Penguin.

PULLINGER, J. (ed.), *Social Trends 28* (1998), London: ONS.

—— and SUMMERFIELD, C. (eds.) (1997), *Social Focus on Families*, London: ONS.

QURESHI, H., and WALKER, A. (1989), *The Caring Relationship*, London: Tavistock.

RAMPRAKASH, D. (ed.), *Social Trends 11* (1981), London: HMSO.

RAMPTON, A. (1981), *West Indian Children in our Schools: Interim Report of the Committee of Inquiry into Education of Children of Ethnic Groups*, London: HMSO.

RANDOLPH, B. (1989), 'Housing Markets, Labour Markets and Discontinuity Theory', in J. Allen and C. Hamnett (eds.), *Housing and Labour Markets: Building the Connections*, London: Unwin Hyman, 16–51.

RAPP, R. (1987), 'Towards a Nuclear Freeze? The Gender Politics of Euro-American Kinship Analysis', in J. F. Collier and S. Yanagasiko (eds.), *Gender and Kinship: Essays towards a Unified Analysis*, New York: Stanford University Press, 119–31.

RATCLIFFE, P. (ed.) (1996), *Ethnicity in the Census: Social Geography and Ethnicity in Britain*, London: HMSO.

REISS, I. (1990), *An End to Shame: Shaping our Next Sexual Revolution*, Buffalo, NY: Prometheus Books.

RENVOIZE, J. (1985), *Going Solo: Single Mothers by Choice*, London: Routledge and Kegan Paul.

REX, J., and TOMLINSON, S. (1979), *Colonial Immigrants in a British City: A Class Analysis*, London: Routledge and Kegan Paul.

RIBBENS, J., EDWARDS, R., and GILLIES, V. (1996), 'Parenting and Step-parenting after Divorce/Separation: Issues and Negotiations', *Changing Britain*, 5: 4–6.

RIX, V. (1996), 'Social and Demographic Change in East London', in T. Butler and M. Rustin (eds.), *Rising in the East: The Regeneration of East London*, 20–56.

ROBERTS, C. (1996), *The Place of Marriage in a Changing Society*, Family Policy Studies Centre Working Paper 2, London: Family Policy Studies Centre.

—— and MCGLONE, F. (1996), *Kinship Networks and Friendship: Attitudes and Behaviour in Britain 1986–1995*, ESRC End of Award Report No. L315253023, Swindon: ESRC.

ROBERTS, G., and MILLS, D. (1958), *Study of External Migration affecting Jamaica, 1953–55*, Kingston: Institute of Social and Economic Studies, University of the West Indies.

ROBINSON, M. (1980), 'Step-families: A Reconstituted Family System', *Journal of Family Therapy 2*, 1: 45–69.

——and SMITH, D. (1993), *Step by Step: Focus on Stepfamilies*, Hemel Hempstead: Harvester Wheatsheaf.

RODGERS, B., and PRYOU, J. (1998), *Divorce and Separation: The Outcomes for Children*, York: Joseph Rowntree Foundation.

RODGERS, J. L. (1983), 'Family Configuration and Adolescent Sexual Behavior', *Population and Environment: Behavioral and Social Issues*, 6: 73–83.

ROLL, J. (1992), *Lone Parent Families in the European Community: A Report to the European Commission*, London: Family Policy Studies Centre.

ROSEMAYER, L., and KOCKEIS, E. (1963), 'Propositions for a Sociological Theory of Aging and the Family', *International Social Service Journal*, 15: 410–26.

ROSENTHAL, G. (ed.) (1993), 'Reconstruction of Life Stories', in R. Josselson and A. Lieblich (eds.), *The Narrative Study of Lives*, London: Sage, 59–91.

ROSSER, C., and HARRIS, C. C. (1965), *The Family and Social Change*, London: Routledge and Kegan Paul.

————(1983), *The Family and Social Change: A Study of Family and Kinship in a South Wales Town*, London: Routledge and Kegan Paul (abridged edn. of Rosser and Harris 1965).

ROUAULT, D. (1994), 'The *Echantillon Démographique Permanent*: A French Equivalent to the Longitudinal Study', *LS Newsletter*, May, 3–6.

ROUSSEL, L. (1983), 'Les Ménages d'une Personne: l'Évolution Récente', *Population*, 38: 995–1015.

——(1993), 'Fertility and Family', in UN ECE/Council of Europe/UNFPA (eds.), *European Population Conference 1993*, vol. 1. Strasburg: United Nations, Council of Europe, 35–118.

ROWLANDS, O., SINGLETON, N., MAHER, J., and HIGGINS, V. (1997), *Living in Britain: Results from the 1995 General Household Survey*, London: HMSO.

ROWLINGSON, K., and MCKAY, S. (1998), *The Growth of Lone Parenthood: Diversity and Dynamics*, London: Policy Studies Institute.

Royal Commission On Population (1949), Report Cmd 7695 London: HMSO.

RUSSELL, J. K. (1988), 'Early Teenage Pregnancy', *Maternal and Child Health*, 13: 43–6.

RYAN, J. (1997), 'Homophobia and Hegemony: A Case of Psychoanalysis', in Oakley and Mitchell (1997), 129–43.

RYDER, N. (1964), 'The Process of Demographic Translation', *Demography*, 1: 74–82.

——(1965), 'The Cohort as a Concept in the Study of Social Change', *American Sociological Review*, 30: 843–61.

SAFFRON, L. (1994), *Alternative Beginnings*, London: Cassell.

SANTI, L. L. (1988), 'The Demographic Context of Recent Change in the Structure of American Households', *Demography*, 25: 509–19.

SASSEN, S. (1991), *The Global City*, Princeton, NJ: Princeton University Press.

SAUNDERS, P. (1990), *A Nation of Home Owners*, London: Unwin Hyman.

SCHMIDT, M. G. (1993), 'Gendered Labour Force Participation', in Castle (1993), 179–237.

SCHUMAN, H. (1992), 'Context Effects: State of the Past/State of the Art', in, N.

Schwarz and S. Sudman (eds.), *Context Effects in Social and Psychological Research*, New York: Springer-Verlag, 5–20.

SCOTT, A. M. (ed.) (1994), *Gender Segregation and Social Change*, Oxford: Oxford University Press.

SCOTT, J. (1987), *Conflicting Values and Compromise Belief about Abortion*, Ann Arbor: University of Michigan.

——(1997*a*), 'Changing Households in Britain: Do Families Still Matter?', *Sociological Review*, 45: 591–620.

——(1997*b*), 'Patterns of Change in Gender-Role Attitudes', in G. Dench (ed.), *Rewriting the Sexual Contract*, London: Institute of Community Studies, 126–40.

——(1998*a*), 'Changing Attitudes to Sexual Morality: A Cross-national Comparison', *Sociology*, 32: 815–45.

——(1998*b*), 'Generational Changes in Attitudes to Abortion: A Cross-national Comparison', *European Sociological Review*, 14: 177–90.

——and BROOK, L. (1996), *Family Change: Demographic and Attitudinal Trends across Nations and Time*, ESRC End of Award Report No. L3152533024, Swindon: ESRC.

——ALWIN, D., and BRAUN, M. (1996), 'Generational Changes in Gender-role Attitudes: Britain in a Cross-National Perspective', *Sociology*, 30: 471–92.

——BRAUN, M., and ALWIN, D. (1993), 'The Family Way', in R. Jowell (ed.), *British Social Attitudes, Tenth Report*, Dartmouth: Gower, 23–47.

SEIDMAN, S. (1992), *Embattled Eros: Sexual Politics and Ethics in Contemporary America*, New York: Routledge.

SEWELL, T. (1993), *Black Tribunes: Black Political Participation in Britain*, London: Lawrence and Wishart.

SHAW, C. (1998), '1996-based National Population Projections for the United Kingdom and Constituent Countries', *Population Trends*, 91: 43–9.

SHELDON, S. (1948), *The Social Medicine of Old Age*, Oxford: Oxford University Press.

SHEPHARD, P. (1985), *The National Child Development Study: An Introduction to the Background to the Study and Methods of Data Collection*, London: City University.

SHRYOCK, H. S., SIEGEL, J. S., and STOCKWELL, E. G. (1976), *The Methods and Materials of Demography*, New York: Academic Press.

SILVERSTEIN, C. (1981), *Man to Man: Gay Couples in America*, New York: Morrow.

SIMEY, T. S. (1946), *Welfare and Planning in the West Indies*, Oxford: Clarendon Press.

SIMMS, M., and SMITH, C. (1986), *Teenage Mothers and their Partners*, London: HMSO.

SIMONS, J. (1986), 'Culture, Economy and Reproduction in Contemporary Europe', in D. A. Coleman and R. S. Schofield (eds.), *The State of Population Theory: Forward from Malthus*, Oxford: Basil Blackwell, 256–78.

SIMPSON, B., MCCARTHY, P., and WALKER, J. (1995), *Being There: Fathers after Divorce*, Newcastle-upon-Tyne: Relate Centre for Family Studies.

SMART, C., and NEALE, B. (1999), *Family Fragments*, Cambridge: Polity Press.

SMITH, D. (1990), *Stepmothering*, Hemel Hempstead: Harvester Wheatsheaf.

SMITH, M. G. (1962), *Kinship and Community in Carriacou*, New Haven: Yale University Press.

——(1974), *Corporations and Society*, London: Duckworth.

——(1988), 'Pluralism, Race and Ethnicity in Selected African Countries', in J. Rex and D. Mason (eds.), *Theories of Race and Ethnic Relations*, Cambridge: Cambridge University Press, 187–225.

SMITH, R. M. (1981), 'Fertility, Economy, and Household Formation in England over three Centuries', *Population and Development Review*, 7: 595–623.

——(ed.) (1986), *Land, Kinship and Life-cycle*. Cambridge: Cambridge University Press.

——(1989), 'Monogamy, Landed Property and Demographic Regimes in Pre-industrial Europe: Regional Contrasts and Temporal Stabilities', in J. Landers and V. Reynolds (eds.), *Fertility and Resources*, Cambridge: Cambridge University Press, 164–88.

SMITH, R. T. (1988), *Kinship and Class in the West Indies: A Genealogical Study of Jamaica and Guyana*, Cambridge: Cambridge University Press.

——(1996), *The Matrifocal Family: Power, Pluralism and Politics*, London: Routledge.

SMITH, T. (1990), 'Report: The Sexual Revolution?', *Public Opinion Quarterly*, 54: 415–35.

——(1993), 'Influence of Socioeconomic Factors on Attaining Targets for Reducing Teenage Pregnancies', *British Medical Journal*, 306: 1232–5.

SMOCK, P., and MANNING, W. (1997), 'Cohabiting Partners' Economic Circumstances and Marriage', *Demography*, 34: 331–41.

SOLDO, B. (1996), 'Cross Pressures on Middle-Aged Adults: A Broader View', *Journal of Gerontology*, 51: 271–3.

——WOLF, D. A., and AGREE, E. M. (1990), 'Family, Households, and Care Arrangements of Frail Older Women: A Structural Analysis', *Journal of Gerontology*, 45, Suppl., 238–49.

SONDEREN, E., GUNNARSON, L., and HENDERSON, C. (1990), 'Personal Network Delineation: A Comparison of the Exchange, Affective and Role-relation Approaches', in K. Knipscheer and T. Antonucci (eds.), *Social Network Research: Substantive Issues and Methodological Questions*, Amsterdam: Swets and Zeitlinger, 101–20.

SOUTH, S. J., and LLOYD, K. M. (1995), 'Spousal Alternatives and Marital Dissolution', *American Sociological Review*, 60: 21–35.

SPEAK, S., CAMERON, S., WOODS, R., and GILROY, R. (1995), *Young Single Mothers: Barriers to Independent Living*, London: Family Policy Studies Centre.

SPEARE, A., AVERY, R., and LAWTON, L. (1991), 'Disability, Residential Mobility, and Changes in Living Arrangements', *Journal of Gerontology*, 46, Suppl., 133–42.

SPITZE, G., and LOGAN, J. R. (1992), 'Helping as a Component of Parent-Adult child relations', *Research on Aging*, 14: 291–312.

STEIER, F. (1991), *Research and Reflexivity*, London: Sage.

STEIN, G. (1997), *Mounting Debts: The Coming European Pension Crisis*, London: Politeia.

STEINER, G. (1981), *The Futility of Family Policy*, Washington: The Brookings Institution.
STINNER, W. F., BYUN, Y., and PAITA, L. (1990), 'Disability and Living Arrangements among Elderly American Men', *Research on Aging*, 12: 339–63.
STONE, L. (1995), *Road to Divorce*, Oxford: Oxford University Press.
STROHMEIER, K. P., and KUIJSTEN, A. (1997), *Family Life and Family Policies in Europe: An Introduction*, Oxford: Oxford University Press.
SULLIVAN, O. (1986), 'Housing Movements of the Divorced and Separated', *Housing Studies*, 1: 35–48.
SUNDSTRÖM, G. (1994), 'Care by Families: An Overview of Trends', in OECD (ed.), *Caring for Frail Elderly People*, Paris: OECD, 15–55.
SUTTON, C., and CHANEY, E. (1987), *Caribbean Life in New York: Socio-cultural Dimensions*, New York: Centre for Migration Studies.
SWANN, M. (1985), *Education for All: Report of the Committee of Inquiry into the Education of Children from Ethnic Minority Groups*, London: HMSO.
SYMON, P. (1990), *Housing and Divorce*, Studies in Housing, Glasgow: University of Glasgow Centre for Housing Research.
SZRETER, S. (1996), *Falling Fertilities and Changing Sexualities in Europe Since c.1850: A Comparative Survey of National Demographic Pattterns*, Canberra: Australian National University Research School of Social Sciences.
TANNER, D. M. (1978), *The Lesbian Couple*, Cambridge, Mass.: Lexington Books.
TAPINOS, G. (1996), *Europe méditerranéenne et changements démographiques: existe-t-il une spécificité des pays du sud?*, Turin: Fondazione Giovanni Agnelli.
TASKER, F. L., and GOLOMBOK, S. (1997), *Growing Up in a Lesbian Family: Effects on Child Development*, New York and London: Guilford Press.
TAYLOR, M., KEEN, M., BUCK, N., and CORTI, L. (1994), 'Income, Welfare and Consumption', in Buck *et al.* (1994), 83–113.
TEBBITT, N. (1990), 'Fanfare of being British', *The Field*, May, 78–9.
THATCHER, M. (1990), George Thomes Society Lecture, National Children's Home, London, 17 Jan.
THOMAS, K., and WISTER, A. (1984), 'Living Arrangements of Older Women: The Ethnic Dimension', *Journal of Marriage and the Family*, 46: 235–50.
THOMAS, M., WALKER, A., WILMOT, A., and BENNETT, N. (1998), *Results from the 1996 General Household Survey*, London: HMSO.
THOMAS-HOPE, E. (1980), 'Hopes and Reality in West Indian Migration to Britain', *Oral History Journal*, 8: 35–42.
——(1992), *Explanation in Caribbean Migration*, London: Macmillan.
THOMPSON, P. (1978), *The Voice of the Past: Oral History*, Oxford: Oxford University Press.
——ITZIN, C., and ABENDSTERN, M. (1990), *I Don't Feel Old: The Experience of Later Life*, Oxford: Oxford University Press.
THORNS, D. C. (1994), 'The Role of Housing Inheritance in Selected Owner-occupied Societies', *Housing Studies*, 9: 473–510.
THORNTON, A., and CAMBURN, D. (1987), 'The Influence of the Family on Premarital Sexual Attitudes and Behavior', *Demography*, 24: 323–40.
TOULEMON, L. (1995), 'Très peu de couples restent volontairement sans enfant', *Population*, 50: 1079–110.

Townsend, P. (1957), *The Family Life of Old People*, London: Routledge and Kegan Paul.

——(1979), *Poverty in the United Kingdom*, Harmondsworth: Penguin.

Tribalat, M., Garson, J. P., Moulier-Boutang, Y., and Silberman, R. (1991), *Cent ans d'immigration: étrangers d'hier, Français d'aujourd'hui*, Paris: Presses Universitaires de France.

Twigg, J. (1998), 'Informal Care of Older People', in M. Bernard and J. Phillips (ed.), *The Social Policy of Old Age: Moving into the Twentieth Century*, London: Centre for Policy on Ageing, 128–41.

Ungerson, C. (1987), *Policy is Personal*, London: Tavistock.

van da Kaa, D. J. (1987), 'Europe's Second Demographic Transition', *Population Bulletin*, 45: 1.

——(1994), 'The Second Demographic Transition Revisited: Theories and Expectations', in G. C. N. Beet (ed.), *Population and Family Life in the Low Countries 1993: Late Fertility and other Current Issues*, Amsterdam: Swets and Zeitlinger, 81–126.

van Groenou, M. B., and Van Tilburg, T. (1996), 'Network Analysis', in J. Birren (ed.), *Encyclopedia of Gerontology*, New York: Academic Press, 197–210.

Van Hoorn, W. (1994), *Living Alone: Choice, Coincidence or Fate*, Working Paper 37, ECE/Eurostat Joint Work Session on Demographic Projections, Luxembourg: ECE/Eurostat.

van Imhoff, E. (1994), *LIPRO 3.0 User's Guide and Tutorial*, NIDI Working Papers 1994/1a and 1994/1b, The Hague: NIDI.

——and Keilman, N. W. (1991), *LIPRO 2.0: An Application of a Dynamic Demographic Projection Model to Household Structure in the Netherlands*, Amsterdam: Swets and Zeitlinger.

Vansina, J. (1965), *Oral Tradition: A Study in Historical Methodology*, Harmondsworth: Penguin.

Van Solinge, H. (1994), 'Living Arrangements of Non-married Elderly People in the Netherlands in 1990', *Aging and Society*, 14: 219–36.

Visher, E. B., and Visher, J. S. (1996), *Therapy with Stepfamilies*, New York: Bruner Mazel.

Wadsworth, J. (1993), 'Methodology of the National Survey of Sexual Attitudes and Lifestyles', *Journal of the Royal Statistical Society*, 156: 407–21.

——Taylor, B., Osborn, A., and Butler, N. (1984), 'Teenage Mothering: Child Development at Five Years', *Journal of Child Psychology and Psychiatry*, 25: 305–13.

Waite, L. J. (1995), 'Does Marriage Matter?', *Demography*, 32: 483–507.

Wall, R. (ed.) (1983), *Family Forms in Historic Europe*, Cambridge: Cambridge University Press.

——(1984), 'Residential Isolation of the Elderly: A Comparison over Time', *Aging and Society*, 4: 483–503.

——(1989), 'The Residence Patterns of the Elderly in Europe in the 1980s', in E. Grebenik, C. Hohn, and R. Mackensen (eds.), *Later Phases of the Family Cycle: Demographic Aspects*, Oxford: Clarendon Press, 222–44.

——(1990), 'Inter-generational Relations in the European past', paper presented at the British Sociological Association Annual Conference, Guildford.

WALL, R. (ed.) (1991), 'English and French Households in Historical Perspective', in *Actes du colloque 'Beyond National Statistics: Household and Family Patterns in Comparative Perspective'*, INSEE méthodes 8, Paris: INSEE, 17–27.
——(1995), 'Elderly Persons and Members of their Households in England and Wales from Preindustrial Times to the Present', in D. I. Kertzer and P. Laslett (eds.), *Aging in the Past*, Berkeley: University of California Press, 81–106.
WANG, D., and MURPHY, M. (1997), 'Birth Interval and Infant Survival: a Bayesian Averaging Approach', paper presented at the Population Association of America meetings, Washington, DC.
WARNES, A. M. (1995), 'The Residential Histories of Parents and Children and Relationships to Present Proximity and Social Integration', *Environment and Planning A*, 16: 1581–91.
WEBER, M. (1995), *Max Weber: Selections in Translation*, Cambridge: Cambridge University Press.
WEEKS, J. (1991), *Against Nature: Essays on History, Sexuality and Identity*, London: Rivers Oram Press.
——(1995), *Invented Moralities: Sexual Values in an Age of Uncertainty*, Cambridge: Polity Press.
——(1996), 'The Idea of a Sexual Community', *Soundings*, 2: 71–84.
——(1997), *Families of Choice: The Structure and Meaning of Non-heterosexual Relationships*, ESRC End of Award Report No. L315253030, Swindon: ESRC.
——DONOVAN, C., and HEAPHY, B. (1996), *Families of Choice: Patterns of Non-heterosexual Relationships, a Literature Review*, Social Science Research Papers 2, London: South Bank University.
————(1998), 'Everyday Experiments: Narratives of Non-heterosexual Relationships', in E. Silva and C. Smart (eds.), *The New Family*?, London: Sage, 83–99.
WEINICK, R. E. (1995), 'Sharing a Home: The Experiences of American Women and their Parents over the Twentieth Century', *Demography*, 32: 281–97.
WEINSTEIN, M., and THORNTON, A. (1989), 'Mother–Child Relations and Adolescent Sexual Attitudes and Behavior', *Demography*, 26: 563–77.
WELLINGS, K., and WADSWORTH, J. (1990), 'AIDS and the Moral Climate'. in R. Jowell, S. Witherspoon, and L. Brook (eds.), *British Social Attitudes: The 7th Report*, Aldershot: Gower, 109–26.
——FIELD, J., JOHNSON, A., and WADSWORTH, J. (eds.) (1994), *Sexual Behaviour in Britain*, Harmondsworth: Penguin.
——WADSWORTH, J., JOHNSON, A., and FIELD, J. (1996), *The National Survey of Sexual Attitudes and Lifestyles: Relevance to Family Formation*, ESRC End of Award Report No. 315253030, Swindon: ESRC.
————FIELD, B., and PETRUCKEVICK, A. (1996), *Teenage Sexuality, Fertility and Life Chances*, London: London School of Hygiene and Tropical Medicine.
WELLMAN, B. (1990), 'The Place of Kinfolk in Personal Community Settings', *Marriage and Family Review*, 15: 195–228.
WENGER, C. C. (1995), 'A Comparison of Urban with Rural Networks in North Wales', *Aging and Society*, 15: 59–82.

Wenger, G. C. (1984), *The Supportive Network: Coping with Old Age*, London: George Allen and Unwin.
——(1992), *Help in Old Age. Facing Up to Change: A Longitudinal Network Study*, Liverpool: Liverpool University Press.
Western, J. (1992), *A Passage to England: Barbadian Londoners Speak of Home*, London: UCL Press.
Weston, K. (1991), *Families We Choose*, New York: Columbia University Press.
White, L. K. (1990), 'Determinants of Divorce: A Review of Research in the Eighties', *Journal of Marriage and the Family*, 52: 904–12.
——and Booth, A. (1985), 'The Quality and Stability of Remarriages: The Role of Stepchildren', *American Sociological Review*, 50: 689–98.
Wilkinson, F. (1996), *Unhealthy Societies: The Afflictions of Inequality*, London: Routledge.
Willmott, P. (1986), *Social Networks, Informal Care and Public Policy*, London: Policy Studies Institute.
——and Young, M. (1960), *Family and Class in a London Suburb*, London: Routledge and Kegan Paul.
Wilson, C. (1984), 'Natural Fertility in Pre-industrialised England 1600–1799', *Population Studies*, 38: 225–40.
——and Airey, P. (1997), 'What can Transition Theory Learn from the Diversity of Low-growth Demographic Regimes?', paper presented to the IUSSP 23rd General Population Conference, Beijing.
Wilson, F. (1980), 'Antecedents of Adolescent Pregnancy', *Journal of Biosocial Science*, 12: 141–52.
Wilson, S. H., Brown, T. P., and Richards, R. G. (1992), 'Teenage Conception and Contraception in English Regions', *Journal of Public Health Medicine*, 14: 17–25.
Wolf, D. A. (1984), 'Kin Availability and the Living Arrangements of Older Unmarried Women', *Social Science Research*, 13: 72–89.
——(1988), 'The Multistate Life Table with Duration-dependence', *Mathematical Population Studies*, 1: 217–45.
——(1990), 'Household Patterns of Older Unmarried Women: Some International Comparisons', *Research on Aging*, 12: 463–506.
——(1994), 'The Elderly and their Kin: Patterns of Availability and Access', in L. G. Martin and S. H. Preston (eds.), *Demography of Aging*, Washington, DC: National Academy Press, 1259–76.
——(1995), 'Changes in the Living Arrangements of Older Women: An International Study', *The Gerontologist*, 35: 724–31.
——and Soldo, B. J. (1988), 'Household Composition Choices of Older Women', *Demography*, 25: 387–403.
Wood, B., Botting, B., and Dunnell, K. (1997), 'Trends in Conceptions Before and After the 1995 Pill Scare', *Population Trends*, 89: 5–12.
Young, M., and Willmott, P. (1957), *Family and Kinship in East London*, London: Routledge and Kegan Paul.

INDEX